CW01418461

WAR,
CITIZENSHIP,
TERRITORY

List of Contributors

Nadia Abu-Zahra
Davina Bhandar
Stephen J. Collier
Deborah Cowen
Stuart Elden
Matthew Farish
Melissa L. Finn
Colin Flint
Emily Gilbert
Stephen Graham
Matthew G. Hannah
Maureen Hays-Mitchell
Jennifer Hyndman
Engin F. Isin
Andrew Lakoff
Tamar Mayer
Marcus Power
Alan Smart
Neil Smith
Rachel Woodward

WAR,
CITIZENSHIP,
TERRITORY

EDITED BY

DEBORAH COWEN
AND EMILY GILBERT

Routledge
Taylor & Francis Group
New York   London

Routledge
Taylor & Francis Group
270 Madison Avenue
New York, NY 10016

Routledge
Taylor & Francis Group
2 Park Square
Milton Park, Abingdon
Oxon OX14 4RN

© 2008 by Taylor & Francis Group, LLC
Routledge is an imprint of Taylor & Francis Group, an Informa business

Printed in the United States of America on acid-free paper
10 9 8 7 6 5 4 3 2 1

International Standard Book Number-13: 978-0-415-95513-3 (Softcover) 978-0-415-95693-2 (Hardcover)

No part of this book may be reprinted, reproduced, transmitted, or utilized in any form by any electronic, mechanical, or other means, now known or hereafter invented, including photocopying, microfilming, and recording, or in any information storage or retrieval system, without written permission from the publishers.

Trademark Notice: Product or corporate names may be trademarks or registered trademarks, and are used only for identification and explanation without intent to infringe.

Library of Congress Cataloging-in-Publication Data

War, citizenship, territory / edited by Deborah Cowen and Emily Gilbert.
    p. cm.
  Includes bibliographical references and index.
    ISBN 978-0-415-95513-3 (pbk.) -- ISBN 978-0-415-95693-2 (cloth)
    1. War and society. 2. Social conflict. 3. Citizenship. 4. Human territoriality--Political aspects. I. Cowen, Deborah. II. Gilbert, Emily, 1969-

HM554.W37 2007
303.6'6--dc22
                                                          2007000912

Visit the Taylor & Francis Web site at
http://www.taylorandfrancis.com

and the Routledge Web site at
http://www.routledge.com

Contents

Acknowledgments

The idea for this book began with a lively set of sessions at the 2005 annual meeting of the Association of American Geographers (AAG) in Denver—"Governing War, Citizenship and Territory." A number of people participated in this series and helped shape this collection in important ways, even if their work does not appear in its pages. We thank Susannah Bunce, Ipsita Chatterjee, Martín Félix, Richard C. Powell, and Gerry Kearns for their insight and energy. Authors had the opportunity to workshop their contributions in two organized sessions that followed.

We organized a series of sessions for the 2005 Canadian Association of Geographers' meeting in London, Ontario with Nadia Abu-Zahra, "Sites and Scales of Citizenship at the Border," and then another at the 2006 AAG meeting in Chicago. Several more scholars participated in these sessions and shared exciting research and ideas. We would like to thank Irus Braverman, Deirdre Conlon, Karine Côté-Boucher, Ghazi Falah, Elizabeth A. Gagen, Carolyn Gallagher, Nupur Gogia, Merje Kuus, Anna Lawrence, Lydia Mason, Geraldine Pratt, Robert Ramsay, Jennifer Ridgley, Samah Sabra, Jana Sladkova, Janet C. Sturgeon, Janine Wiles, Madeleine Wong, and filmmaker Beth Bird. Thanks too to the many colleagues at the University of Toronto, York University, and New York University who have joined us in animated discussions on these issues over the past several years. Grants from the Social Sciences and Humanities Research Council have helped to defray some of the costs associated with our research.

For tremendous support through the early stages of organizing the collection we thank Dave McBride. Cheryl Adams, Russ Heaps, Anne Horowitz, Joon Won Moon, and Stephen Rutter at Routledge have provided exemplary care with guiding the manuscript through the production process. We thank Celia Braves who produced the thorough index. We thank all the contributors for producing such quality work (and largely on time!), and we are especially grateful to Heidi Nast, Jamie Scott, Neil Smith, and Leah Vosko for comments and support through the long process of bringing this collection together. Nicholas and Joshua Scott created distractions at every turn, but they also made us laugh, and for that we are thankful.

Deborah Cowen and Emily Gilbert

1

The Politics of War, Citizenship, Territory

DEBORAH COWEN AND EMILY GILBERT

Who is a friend?
Who is an enemy?
Who is a target?
Who is a terrorist?
Who is a combatant?
Who is innocent?
Who is "high risk"?
Who is "illegal"?
Who is free?
Who serves?
Who belongs?
Who decides?
Who's next?

These simple questions emerge forcefully out of contemporary political crises. They constitute some of the most basic and pressing challenges of citizenship in the context of war. They prompt us to think about how organized human violence shapes our spaces, practices, and identities. They are questions about territory, for political belonging in the modern world has meant formal belonging to a spatially bounded state. More broadly, as the "spatial turn" in the social sciences and humanities has illustrated, being political is always a matter of being, becoming, *in place* and *through space*. Being political does not necessarily entail engagement in formal or electoral politics but occurs in a broad range of relations between people and groups wherein norms, practices, ideas, and ways of organizing material life are challenged, questioned, and potentially reconstituted. The above questions ask us to think war and territory through social and political subjects—or, in other words, through the lens of citizenship. In this sense, these questions prompt the provocative investigations that constitute the seventeen chapters of this book.

For millennia, conflicts over the control of people and places have reshaped the organization of collective human life. War kills, starves, displaces, and destroys. War can be deeply rupturing—an exceptional event—that shat-

1

ters the institutions and norms of citizenship while it ravages human bodies, and natural and social worlds. War fractures the habits and common sense of everyday life, sometimes unexpectedly and instantaneously. A destructive frenzy of war can erupt quickly and destroy rights and relations that have taken generations to cultivate. Civil rights, political freedoms, cosmopolitanism, and multiculturalism are all repeat casualties of war. But this violence also entails *creative* destruction; war has repeatedly fostered the invention of new political forms. War has been a watershed for citizenship. It has helped cultivate expanded social entitlements, strengthened collective identities, and broadened suffrage and other citizenship rights to new groups. War has generated countless new political forms and social technologies throughout recorded history.

In the modern era, a geography of absolute national spaces has been mapped and regularly reconfigured through organized human violence. For more than two hundred years, political territory was assembled along national lines. At the same time, wars were typically fought between nation-states or by factions within them seeking national sovereignty. In this international state system, formal citizenship became interchangeable with nationality. Despite their relatively brief history as the scalar metrics of global political geography, nation-states and national citizenship were invested with a sense of primordial being. Both nations and nation-states have been naturalized, such that they became the assumed territorial unit of political community across space and time. It is not uncommon to find citizenship defined as the equivalent of formal belonging within a nation-state, even by scholars who would otherwise extol a more nuanced historical and geographical sensibility. Nation-states became the common sense of politics, assumed and uninterrogated, and yet, this normalized and nationalized political geography was constituted and reproduced through tremendous expenditure of labor and extreme and coordinated violence. The state system that emerged out of eighteenth-century Europe heralding the birth of industrial capitalism was the product of violent bourgeois revolutions, and the European-centered nationalization of the state, politics, and war at this time was premised upon a globalizing political economy of imperial rule. The birth of national citizenship in Europe therefore presupposed new forms of colonial violence abroad that contradicted these very premises of European nation-state building. This collection focuses primarily, though not exclusively, on the amalgam of state, politics, and war as it took shape in Europe, an experience that came forcefully to shape politics in colonial and postcolonial states, even in the systematic breach.

It is perhaps only as the national geography of war, citizenship, and territory is recast that its former contours have become so crisp and visible. Roland Barthes famously described "mythologies" as collectively generated ways of knowing the world that allow people to make sense of their daily lives and through which they orient their practice. Mythologies are not false or untrue;

they are knowledges and narratives that govern our relationships to the world and to ourselves. Mythologies do not hide the "true" world, but organize our relationship to it in particular ways. When they operate successfully they appear natural rather than historical and geographical in their constitution. Most importantly, Barthes suggests that mythologies become visible as such only when they become outmoded. It is when they can no longer usefully govern our relationship to a changing world, when they are not able to maintain a practical ordering, that we are confronted by the contours of mythologies as particular rather than universal ways of knowing and acting. The contributions to this volume question the resilient mythologies around war, citizenship, and territory, to problematize their historical salience and the presumed universality of their applicability, as well as to understand their contemporary resonance.

Across the wide-ranging interpretations of contemporary politics and violence, there is broad consensus that things have changed. Although emergent since World War II, the end of the Cold War has given way to a heightened period of conflict between nonstate bodies, supranational bodies, coalitions of nation-states, subnational groups, and private military companies hired by states and corporations, working around the world, unregulated, and on violent and uncharted paths. National militaries hold no monopoly on the "human resources" of war, nor do they maintain close ties to the obligations of citizenship in many nation-states. Long-standing obligations to military service through conscription have been severed in a growing list of countries, where the benefits of education, health care, housing, and pensions that come from service life are distributed according to a voluntary market logic, in good neoliberal form. Cities have emerged at the center of both violence and belonging, and this urban geography operates in complicated ways within a world still carved up into absolute spaces of national territory. A wide range of questions regarding belonging has been prompted by our changing political and cultural geographies, by increased human migration and the related complexities of mobility and identity. The reliance of many nations on temporary migrant work pushes communities to ask whether working and living in a place should constitute entitlements to the rights of citizenship. Dual citizenship and diaspora push national governments to question their ethical obligations to protect citizens who live abroad. Official policies of multiculturalism push courts and politicians to consider whether religious or ethnic communities within the nation should be entitled to govern themselves differently. Genocide prompts international agencies to question national sovereignty in light of debates regarding the ethical "obligation to protect" other peoples (Hyndman, this volume). Mythologies of primordial nation-states fighting other states for sovereign power over sovereign territory cannot account for the complex forms, agents, and spaces of war we see today. So too, popular mythologies of peaceful politics, if they ever made any practical sense, are now entirely obsolete.

This collection takes up the challenge of thinking politics in their wake. The chapters that follow, in different ways, suggest that it is at the nexus of war, citizenship, and territory that the monumental and mundane of political life are reproduced. The authors explore both the constitution of national forms through these forces, as well as instances where alternative political geographies are in evidence. They all insist that a deliberate focus on these themes yields new ways of understanding not only our present, but also our past and possibly our future. The contributions offer a historical and geographical diversity that suggests that the nexus of war, citizenship, and territory is rich terrain for investigating the political. Before delving into the specific questions addressed in the chapters that follow, we explore the distinct and entwined nature of our central concepts. How might war, citizenship, and territory combine in changing and lasting assemblages? How does scholarly work on each theme help and hinder an entwined analysis? What is the power of looking at war, citizenship, and territory, together, today?

War

> Social science gives us precious few tools for answering these fundamental questions of modern society. Most disciplines . . . write war out of the analysis. . . . But if war is a regular, recurring, indeed structural feature of modernity, it remains a profoundly troubling one, which retains its capacity to unsettle the assumptions of social and political analysis.
>
> **Shaw (2000, 112)**

War has long been a central feature of political life. War is pervasive and recurrent. It shapes the everyday lives of millions of people. When we take a global perspective and consider the perpetual nature of warfare over the last century, it becomes clear that war is a regular, rather than exceptional, event. As Shaw suggests, war is a defining feature of modernity, its presence uninterrupted for nearly one hundred years. "The world as a whole has not been at peace since 1914, and is not at peace now," asserts the eminent historian Eric Hobsbawm (2002), who has also called the twentieth century "the most murderous in recorded history." And yet, beyond the confines of the discipline of international relations (IR), which focuses almost exclusively on the state as political actor and holds national war as perhaps axiomatic, there is a dearth of scholarship devoted to this vital topic. Traditional social science, with its concern for typical phenomena and norms of social life, has tended to bracket war as an anomaly. "Peace is seen as a shorthand for a complex set of relations," Kirby (1994, 301) argues, "whereas war is a thing in and of itself; moreover, peace is normal, whereas war is an aberration that interrupts and punctuates normalcy." We might qualify these claims by limiting their historical and geographical breadth. The specific traditions of scholarship to which they apply are those which developed, in their modern incarnations, within the context of the national state. War was a central topic of academic and political inquiry prior to and during the consolidation of national territory, but since then became increasingly specialized and contained. War was simultaneously assigned to specialists in fields like strategic studies and IR, and at the same time was consigned to interstate relations making peace the norm of analysis within national society.

In the context of more recent scholarship, Kirby (1994, 301) suggests that a reason for the neglect of war in so many fields of study relates to the geography of academic production, which stands in stark contrast to the geography of conflict itself. "Anglo social science has been cocooned by nearly fifty years of peace," he argues. Concentrated in the advanced capitalist nations that frequently fight wars, but rarely on their own soil, Anglo social science is "punctuated only infrequently and partially by territorial struggles in distant places such as Korea, Aden, Algeria, Vietnam, Nicaragua, and Kuwait." Since 1945, war has increasingly been waged outside Europe and North America, creating an uneven geography of war. The shift in the geography of conflict to the poorer regions of the world is, according to Kirby, part of what allows academics in the wealthiest regions to neglect the central importance of war to the politics of everyday life.

From the perspective of Anglo social science and advanced capitalist regions of the world, warfare is a cutting example of John Berger's prescient claim that today it is space that "hides consequences from us" (Berger 1974). Kirby (1994, 301) echoes this observation when he writes, "In reality of course, there is perpetual warfare around the globe, but these wars appear as the struggles of others, even when fought on our behalf and probably with our tax dollars." In places outside the Western hegemon, war has been less of an unusual rupturing event and instead a more constant feature of politics. Struggles against imperial and colonial rule, and militarized conflicts in the aftermath of colonialism, have been a definitive aspect of political life for perhaps the majority of the world's peoples.

Given its perpetual and powerful presence on the planet, war has indeed been underinvestigated in many disciplines. However, there are important exceptions to any rule. Many scholars and schools of thought have written extensively on the topic of war in relation to politics, and some even directly address questions of citizenship and territory. But even if it were possible to outline all of the important scholarly work that addresses the topic of war, it is certainly not our goal here. Large bodies of highly insightful scholarship have described war as central to the reproduction of the global capitalist political economy (Luxemburg [1913] 2003; Klare 1974; Blaut 1970; Cohen 1973; Melman 1974; Shiva 2002); to its specifically racist and colonial powers (Fanon 1965; Davis 1971; Amin 1976; Barkawi 2005); to the American Empire's particular brand of "military Keynesian," "permanent war economy," and "military industrial complex" (Cliff 1957; Kidron 1970; O'Connor 1973); and to patriarchal and masculinist relations of rule (Enloe 1988, 2000; Theweleit 1993; Mies 1988). These critical interventions and others have helped to map the contours and effects of armed conflict and resistance in different times and places as features of broader political struggles.

However, it is only recently that widespread critical attention has focused on the normalcy of war and placed it at the center of theoretical scrutiny. War is typically understood as the shape political struggles take when they get out of civil hands and beyond the everyday avenues of conflict resolution. This has become the common sense of war—it is defined as the violent acts that happen when politics are taken to the extreme. Whether contemporary scholars mobilize this conception of war deliberately or unknowingly, the notion that war is an intense form of political conflict has a history. It was almost 200 years ago that the then controversial thinker Karl von Clausewitz insisted on the political nature of war. What were then provocative and radical claims— that war was a political act—helped propel him to iconic status in military and strategic thought. For Clausewitz, war begins when politics ends, when bullets "take the place of diplomatic notes" (Huntington 1957, 57; Clausewitz 1976, 87). Samuel P. Huntington, leading Anglo theorist of civil-military relations in the post–World War II period, insists that Clausewitz's role in military thought is "roughly comparable to that of Marx in the history of socialist theory." He explains how "most of the writing which came before him was preliminary, fragmentary, and subsequently embodied in his work," while "that which came after him was exegetic and interpretive of the meaning of the master" (Huntington, 1957, 56).

As an aside, Karl Marx was himself a reader of Clausewitz, and in a letter to Friedrich Engels, he exclaimed that "the rascal has a common sense bordering on wit" (quoted in Howard 1976, 44). War metaphors are furthermore in evidence in Marx's own descriptions of the operation of power. These are clearly operative when Marx draws parallels between military organization and the emerging division of labor in the context of early industrial capitalism. Marx writes,

> Just as the offensive power of the squadron of a cavalry, or the defensive power of a regiment of infantry, is essentially different from the sum of the offensive or defensive powers of the individual cavalry or infantry soldiers taken separately, so the sum total of the mechanical forces exerted by isolated workmen differs from the social force that is developed, when many hands take part simultaneously in one and the same divided operation. (Marx [1867] 1976, 308; see also Foucault 1979, 163–64)

This use of military metaphors, and the connections that this comparison draws between social organization in military and industrial forms, hints at a different relationship between politics and war than that set out by Clausewitz. Indeed, a number of scholars have begun tracing a productive role for war in everyday political life (Klausen 1999; De Landa 1991; Cowen 2005; Drake 2002; Dijkink 2005; Segal 1989; Skolpol 1992; Van Doorn 1975).

The notion that war has given us crucial elements of our peace has gained a following. One of the best-known theorists of war of the postwar period, Paul Virilio, has theorized war as the engine of human social and spatial order. In his *Speed and Politics* (Virilio 1986), he develops a "war model" of social change wherein he focuses on the development of new technologies of war-fare over time, and in particular the ways in which they have transformed the politics of speed, or what he terms "dromology." For Virilio, war explains the broad shifts in human society and specifically the growth of modern urban forms. Other scholars working on a wide range of topical and spatiotempo-ral domains have made arguments that parallel Virilio's with regard to the productive nature of war in propelling transformations in human social and spatial practice. In an influential piece, Charles Tilly (1985) has argued that war making is at the center of state making, and that both activities are best understood as organized but legitimated forms of crime. For Tilly, "state makers" warred in order to protect their power within a secure or expand-ing territory, and it was to finance war that the logic of capital accumulation became so implanted into modern national politics (1985, 172). Richard Tit-muss (1958) traces how policies developed for soldiers in the United Kingdom and United States in the context of major twentieth-century wars were sub-sequently extended to civilian populations. He concludes that war has been a primary driving force in the development of civilian social policy. This reso-nates with Jacques Donzelot's assessment of the operative logic of state welfare in his work on the history of social politics. He argues that social insurance was a crucial invention of the late nineteenth century as part of the birth of "solidarity." Based upon Otto von Bismarck's experiments with social insur-ance in the 1880s, a "new school" of social economists was able to promote the practical value of solidarity over rival liberals, traditionalists, and socialists, by mediating the individualist thrust of liberalism and giving the working classes a stake in the capitalist and national social order (Donzelot 1988, 399). Importantly, Bismarck's experiments emerged out of efforts to raise a national military, and so solidarity and social insurance must also be understood as military innovations (Kirwin 1996; Cowen 2008). Mitchell (1988) offers a cru-cial reminder of the importance of the political geography of wartime innova-tions in citizenship. He argues that it is not any random battlefield, but very often *colonial* ones, that have been the context for the genesis of technolo-gies that subsequently reshaped the political order. He considers the emer-gence of disciplinary power, which in Michel Foucault's account was central to the birth of modern political rule. Mitchell asserts that the panopticon, the "model institution whose geometric order and generalized surveillance serve as motif for this kind of power, was a colonial invention . . . devised on

Europe's colonial frontier with the Ottoman Empire, and examples of the panopticon were built for the most part not in northern Europe, but in places like colonial India" (Mitchell 1988, 35).

Clausewitz's argument that war is an extension of politics has been entirely and explicitly reframed by a number of thinkers in recent decades. Hannah Arendt may have been the first to speak directly of reversing Clausewitz's maxim to make politics something of an extended form of war. Arendt suggests that in the post–World War II period, war became the "basic social system," and argues that peace "is the continuation of war by other means—is the actual development in the techniques of warfare" (Arendt 1970, 9). Michel Foucault's recently translated lectures, collectively entitled "Society Must Be Defended," have helped to reframe critical investigation of war. Foucault follows the same tack as Arendt in that he questions whether *politics can be understood as war by other means*; however, he does not just address the post-war period, but also extends his analysis to the formation of the modern state system. Foucault asks, "Are military and warlike institutions, and more generally the processes that are implemented to wage war, the nucleus of political institutions in either an immediate or remote sense, in either a direct or an indirect sense?" (Foucault 1997, 267). Indeed, Foucault offers some hypotheses in response to his own questions. He suggests that modern politics "sanctions and reproduces" the inequalities that are operative in war. War is posited as "the motor behind institutions and order."

Clausewitz's work contributed to bringing into being a historically and geographically specific set of practices. Perhaps most importantly, his arguments offered a contribution to the nation building of his time. Clausewitz's analysis of war and politics must be understood in relation to the articulation of modern theories of state sovereignty. These were contingent on investing the budding nation-state with a monopoly on legitimate violence so as to bring an end to rampant civil war. In this sense Clausewitz's arguments were a contribution to the constitution of nation-state building, and so were not simply descriptive but also *performative*. Hardt and Negri have recently made this point. They argue that in distinguishing war from politics in a context where war was constituted as an international and not domestic relation, Clausewitz in fact exteriorizes war to the sovereign nation-state. War was effectively "expelled from the internal national social field and reserved only for the external conflicts between states" (Hardt and Negri 2004, 6). In this sense, landmark *theories* of war and representations of armed conflict are placed firmly *within* the "terrain" of political struggle.

Clausewitz may well retain a following in strategic studies and within social and political thought; however, the power of his work is deeply in question given both the recent theoretical work on war, as well as the empirical shifts in the practice of warfare. Nation-states are not in any sense disappearing, and yet the calibration of war and national political space has transformed dramatically. Hobsbawm (2002) offers an account of some of the most significant shifts in war since the legal rules of war were codified in the Hague Conventions one hundred years ago:

> Conflicts were supposed to take place primarily between sovereign states or, if they occurred within the territory of one particular state, between parties sufficiently organised to be accorded belligerent status by other sovereign states. War was supposed to be sharply distinguished from peace, by a declaration of war at one end and a treaty of peace at the other. Military operations were supposed to distinguish clearly between combatants—marked as such by the uniforms they wore, or by other signs of belonging to an organised armed force—and non-combatant civilians. War was supposed to be between combatants. Non-combatants should, as far as possible, be protected in wartime.

Each of these assumptions about war has been regularly trespassed since World War II, and few if any can still be said to define the norms of armed conflict. Intrastate war has surpassed interstate war in both frequency and scale of violence; it is often regional, supranational, or transnational forces rather than nation-states that are engaged in armed struggle. War is also fought perpetually, although rarely officially declared as such; and violent conflict persists after the formal declaration of peace in the rare cases where war was officially declared, and there is no better example than the current war in Iraq. Writing in 1968, Robert S. McNamara affirms how exceptions to the laws of war were becoming the norm. He reports that

> in the eight years through late 1966 alone there were no less than 164 internationally significant outbreaks of violence, each of them specifically designed as a serious challenge to the authority of the very governments in question. Eighty-two different governments were directly involved, and what is striking is that only 15 of these 164 significant resorts to violence were military conflicts between two states, and not a single one of the 164 conflicts was a formally declared war. Indeed, there has not been a single declaration of war anywhere in the world since World War II. (1968, 62)

As a part of these shifts, the status of combatants is today complex and highly charged. Combatants are frequently civilians, sometimes mercenaries, and often children. They can work for private transnational corporations, or private transnational insurgent groups. Combatants now routinely take their own lives as they take others in increasingly regular suicide bombings (Isin and Finn, this volume). Machines have entirely replaced combatants for high-budget militaries in high-risk conflict zones, where drones now do the work of surveillance and sometimes slaughter. Uniformed "public" soldiers are certainly not obsolete, but they are often drawn from foreign lands in exchange for political and social citizenship rights, rather than from a citizenry from whom patriotic responsibility to the polis is expected. Many countries have abandoned conscription and instead offer extensive welfare and education benefits or even the formal status of citizenship to "aliens" in exchange for voluntary service. Women are increasingly serving and dying in uniform, with policies implemented in many countries, as well as supranational bodies, to promote their participation.[1] Sexual violence is not new in the context of war, nor is its use as a deliberate strategy of warfare; nevertheless, the scale and frequency of sexual violence as military strategy are prompting growing outrage and response.[2] This is tied to the civilianization of "collateral damage"; casualties of war are today most concentrated among civilians rather than official combatants. The increasing urbanization of warfare over the course of the twentieth century compounds this trend (Graham, this volume; Graham 2004). This leaves established theories of war that assume a national geography deeply in question. Through the following discussions, we suggest that the contemporary politics of war are best understood through an examination of the shifting nexus of citizenship and territory.

Citizenship

Why think of war and territory through the lens of citizenship? Citizenship is a powerful way into these themes as it is oriented toward both the singular actors who constitute a political community and the collective body politic, simultaneously. Citizenship exists in the *relationships* between members of a polis, and between those members and the groups, authorities, and institutions that govern. Citizenship is thus a dynamic concept that prioritizes *process* and *emergence* in the constitution of both lasting and fleeting political forms. The focus on relations within and between groups means that an investigation of citizenship calls on us to examine how struggle between groups in the form of armed conflict, and the politics of and within a territorialized collectivity, actually bring one another into being. Political practice is also spatial practice, and relations of force and violence are central in constituting relations of rule. War, citizenship, and territory became powerfully calibrated over the last several hundred years with the nation-state as a driving logic in all three domains. Investigating war and territory through the practice of citizenship allows us to ask how that logic was constituted and challenged, and what political and geographic forms are emergent today.

But what exactly do we mean by "citizenship"? Citizenship is generally thought to comprise several characteristics: identity, belonging, status, rights, and responsibilities. In Bryan Turner's words, citizenship is a "set of practices (juridical, political, economic and cultural) which define a person as a competent member of society and which, as a consequence, shape the flow of resources to persons and social groups" (Turner 1993, 2). Formal citizenship status is derived through official membership in the nation-state, achieved by either birth or "naturalization." Yet as transnational pathways and allegiances are reshaped by global and neoliberal forces, with the devolution of powers to the local and to the private sector, the nation-state no longer retains the autonomy that it was presumed to have at the beginning of the twentieth century. Just as the future of the nation-state is at the core of academic and public debates, so too are questions around citizenship, whether with respect to national belonging or of how to conceive of a socially and politically active and engaged public (Kymilicka 1995). These are hence important questions regarding new ways of understanding politics and the political, including contradictory emphases on "active" citizens, from right-wing approaches that focus on individual responsibility over social rights, to left-wing approaches that privilege social activism against corporate and state oppression (Rose 1999). There is broad-based concern for the future of the "social in citizenship" in the wake of the Keynesian welfare state and its commitments to "universal," rights-based citizenship (cf. Isin 2008). To understand the full implications of these transformations and questions for the politics of war and territory, it is helpful to consider a genealogy of citizenship, which we sketch out here in abbreviated fashion with a focus on the constitution of national citizenship.[3]

The history of citizenship is long and is often traced back to the Greek era, when it denoted political membership in a city-state or polis. This history was called upon by Enlightenment thinkers of the seventeenth and eighteenth centuries who saw themselves as the inheritors of "Western civilization" as they aspired to build principles of national belonging. Writers such as John Locke and Jean-Jacques Rousseau were particularly foundational, and drew upon a longer tradition of citizenship of the Greek and Roman eras.[4] For the ancients, citizens were married men, land and slave owners, who because of their citizenship were entitled to deliberate and make decisions about the forms of governance and security under which they were ruled. Citizens, however, were also subject to duties, for example participation in military service, so that political membership was understood as both enabling and demanding participation in formal politics. Locke's emphasis was on individual rights, which has been formative to contemporary discourses of citizenship. Locke's notion of individual rights was organized through property in particular, and the central purpose of the state was to protect property from theft. Security was thus a core rationale for the existence of the state, wherein police and military forces were rationalized so as to protect property and freedom locally and internationally. A central problematic in the emergent discussions of citizenship was how to reconcile the place of the individual within society. The idea of the social contract was proposed to rationalize the limits and possibilities of individual freedoms within the constraints of social life. Implicit to the social contract is a sense of citizenship, that is, *formal* membership in the political community. However, there were strict conditions for achieving membership. In practice, citizenship was an exclusive status and "freedom" and individual liberty were limited to male property owners, much as it had been in Greek and Roman times when marriage was also a prerequisite to citizenship, while the rest of the population was governed by a wholly different set of norms, laws, and expectations. This is nowhere more evident than with regard to military conscription. Locke could never reconcile the priority of individual freedom with a model of national service in his theorizing, but he found a resolution to this conflict in practice. It was the unpropertied classes who were expected to sacrifice and serve, and protect the freedom of the propertied liberal citizen (Cohen 1985, 135; Carter 1998, 74; Cowen 2006, 174).

Notions of freedom and individual liberty were to prove foundational to the revolutions in the United States and France, and their declarations of independence (1776 and 1789, respectively). In each of these documents, albeit with different emphases, liberty is central, but so too is a certain dedication to the state, so that both the state and the individuals within the state are presumed to be sovereign and autonomous to make their own decisions and to decide their own futures. In the United States, the emphasis was on removing limits to individual freedom imposed by religion and the imperial state, while still affirming the unity of the American colonies in a united federation. Freedom was also conceived in terms of security, with a statement in the U.S. Bill of Rights on the liberty to bear arms: "A well regulated militia, being necessary to the security of a free State, the right of the people to keep and bear arms, shall not be infringed." In France, independence was promoted through the figure of the *citoyen*, but it was always alongside the notion of *fraternité*, or solidarity. Since the French Revolution, the figure of the national citizen has been tied to the raising of a mass army to defend the polity. "Fraternity" was the bond of citizens in struggle, defending the new nation. The *levée en masse* following the French Revolution set a highly influential precedent of national conscription, which came to define not only modern militaries but also expectations around citizenship. Hence in each of these liberatory movements, military defense and territory were each affirmed alongside bourgeoning ideas of citizenship.

By the nineteenth century, both war and citizenship became increasingly organized and linked through the nation-state. The duty of defense became a core feature of citizenship in Western states, and conscription was introduced domestically and in the colonies of the European states (Cohen 1985; Mann 1988; Mitchell 1988). Even within the imperial context, citizenship was firmly linked to the national community, through which belonging, rights, and responsibilities were all channeled. Moreover, with the rising forms of nationalism in this period, citizenship became grafted onto an ideal of cultural and ethnic homogeneity rooted in a particular territory. Citizenship became less associated with the civic state than with a nationalist state whereby entitlement and belonging were determined on the basis of cultural and ethnic attributes. The ways that citizenship was forged through ethnic divisions associated with national borders became especially noticeable in the aftermath of the first two world wars, when displaced and stateless peoples, who were bereft of political status after purges and ethnic cleansing, garnered international attention (Arendt 1951; see also Agamben 2005).

If war was a central mechanism in ushering in the independence and liberty conceived by the revolutions in the United States and France, it was also central to the emergence of new social visions after the world wars. The geopolitical climate of World War II and the militarism of the Cold War encouraged a new strain of citizenship in the twentieth century and a new form of collective security—social security. In 1949 T. H. Marshall identified the rise of social citizenship, with its promise to provide "the whole range [of social rights] from the right to a modicum of economic welfare and security to the right to share to the full in the social heritage and to live the life of a civilised being according to the standards prevailing in society" (Marshall 1950, 78). Keynesian macroeconomics offered an economic rationale for the provision of social services and welfare, while an ideology of resource redistribution was designed to bring the socially and economically dispossessed within the folds of the nation-state so as to entrench national solidarity in the face of polarized Cold War geopolitics (Gilbert forthcoming; Guest 1985).

Marshall's analysis was particularly concerned with the contradictory logics of democratic citizenship and capitalism. On one hand, democratic citizenship is premised on the participation of the population, or at least this potential, and so relies upon a degree of equality among citizens. Capitalism, on the other hand, generates extraordinary inequalities of wealth and power and thus undermines democratic citizenship. For Marshall, social citizenship promised to mediate the extreme inequalities of the capitalist economy and thus had the potential to make citizenship and capitalism more workable, and durable. With social citizenship the state also invested more closely in the lives of its citizens, such as their health and well-being, an intensification of the modern state's biopolitical forms of rule (Foucault 1990). Citizenship thus also became a tool for managing the population, and not simply within the nation-state (Cruickshank 1999). As Daiva Stasiulis and Abigail Bakan forcefully insist, national citizenship needs to be understood in terms of capitalism's uneven global power relations, whereby the rights and responsibilities afforded to some under the emancipatory rubric of citizenship are predicated on the labor and subjugation of the Global South (Stasiulis and Bakan 2003; see also Sales 2002). The only very recent acquisition of citizenship by indigenous peoples affirms accusations of persistent state racism.

Other criticisms of citizenship arise from the conflation of citizenship within the nation-state. As Marshall proclaimed, "The citizenship whose history I wish to trace is, by definition, national" (Marshall 1950, 95; see McEwen and Moreno 2005). For him, a nationalized social citizenship was the apotheosis of social development, but there have been numerous challenges to this evolutionary framework from civil, to political, to social citizenship. Postcolonial critics have taken umbrage with this formula that presents the Western historicization of citizenship as normative, with no possibility for the formerly colonized to develop and adopt their own models of development (Chakrabarty 2000; see Smart, this volume). There are also emerging forms of supranational citizenship, from partial citizenship status amongst members of the European Union, to the demands for the recognition of global human rights at the United Nations and the International Criminal Court, or even through new forms of cyberdemocracy and netizens. Recently, other questions have emerged regarding the status of noncitizens, particularly as migration and immigration increase. We can think here of temporary workers, permanent or landed residents, illegal immigrants, and undocumented workers who have neither formal nor substantive claims to citizenship (Soysal 1994; Stasiulis and Bakan 2003). At the other extreme are those elite "flexible citizens," to use Aihwa Ong's words, who are able to capitalize upon their mobility and access citizenship rights in multiple global sites (Ong 1999).

These contemporary questions also point to long-standing concerns regarding the presumed universality of citizenship. As feminist scholars have cautioned, social citizenship rights may have been described as "universal"; however, this universalism was exclusive and particular (Lister 1997; Mayer 2000). From the ancient era until today, citizenship has been constituted vis-à-vis privileged and idealized social subjects, usually delineated in terms of divisive identity formations along class, gender, racial, and sexual lines. With respect to social citizenship, for example, entitlement to social provisions at first hinged upon participation in the workforce, which meant that women were largely excluded, or included only as family dependents (Fraser and Gordon 1992; Christie 2000). The normative nuclear family was thus upheld as a foundational social structure (Cowen and Gilbert, this volume), while the long-standing separation of public and private spheres in which men were aligned with the former and women with the latter was reinforced. In most liberal state societies, women are no longer as explicitly excluded from individual citizenship claims, but that is not to say that citizenship doesn't remain intensely gendered. With the retrenchment of social citizenship rights and the privatization of services that were once publicly available, neoliberalism places the labor of social reproduction heavily into the hands of women. There has been a responsibilization for both individuals and families that has undermined the social and public realm, under a rubric of individual freedoms. These tendencies have also undermined attempts to recognize and affirm forms of subnational group citizenship, for example among indigenous peoples, that have been used to try to address historical inequities through contemporary redistribution (Fraser 1997; Taylor 1994).

In the contemporary context, then, already marginalized groups bear the brunt of ongoing restructuring, particularly with respect to discrepancies between formal rights and substantive rights. The uneven distribution of resources intensifies, and social divisions along the lines of race and class reinforce social inequities. With the decline of social rights and notions of entitlements that characterized postwar citizenship, the distinction between a "deserving" and "undeserving" poor has resurfaced, and this newfound emphasis on the obligations of citizenship is clearly evident in the shift from welfarism to workfarist citizenship. But also particular questions have been raised around children whose human rights have been affirmed in a series of international conventions, but who lack formal political and even legal rights (Chen 2003). The ability to participate and be included in political structures are formidable concerns, and the lack of citizenship participation has been sounded as the death knell of liberal democracy.

Yet the new forms of ideal citizens that are being brought into being are reconstituting the citizen subject. Here, too, there are tensions between universal claims to citizenship and exclusion and inequality based on ideal types of citizens. The concept of the ideal citizen has been a crucial fulcrum, from the virtuous citizen of the Roman era to the nuclear family of the Cold War era. Scholars today write of a new kind of citizen ideal, *homo economicus*, who is a flexible, mobile, entrepreneurial, professionalized, self-disciplining, risk-bearing, and self-governing individual (Ong 1999; Rose 1999). Ong remarks that globalizing and neoliberalizing pressures have disarticulated aspects of citizenship (rights, responsibilities, etc.) in ways that reinforce differentiated hierarchies of claims linked to market principles of performance (Ong 2006). However, whilst the image of the ideal citizen retains a certain amount of influence, Engin Isin identifies counternarratives at work (Isin 2004). He introduces the figure of the neurotic citizen to draw attention to the ways that people are governed, by others and themselves, with respect to neuroses, affect, and emotion. The moral regulation of *homo economicus* and the gatekeeping surrounding ideal and neurotic citizen forms have perhaps become most explicit at the border (Ong 1999; Bhandar, this volume; Gilbert 2007). Security has itself been radically reconfigured from the social forms that were dominant in the middle part of the twentieth century (Collier and Lakoff, this volume), and the meaning of "security" is itself hotly contested. Crucial for citizenship, the distinction between different forms of security inside and outside the national state, embodied in the different laws and labor forces of the police and military, is itself showing signs of blurring (Kraska 2001; Wilson 2002).

This potted history of citizenship gestures toward its interconnections with both war and territory. It also identifies some of the key principles associated with citizenship today: a sense of belonging, formal and substantive legal and political rights, and responsibilities. How these manifest themselves differ across space. Crucial are questions of who is included. As noted above, contemporary formal citizenship still largely denotes a national subject, and it is through the nation-state that the rights and responsibilities associated with citizenship are distributed. As questions around the future of nation-states loom large, so too do questions about citizenship, both of which entail resonant concerns about the future and viability of democracy and political representation and engagement. The shifting *geographies* of war and citizenship, however, are a linchpin to understanding our political future, and so we turn our attention now to the question of territory.

Territory

A focus on territory reveals the past and present entanglements of war and citizenship. But what exactly is "territory," and why does it have such a lasting relationship to both war and citizenship? "Territory" is a term that is often used interchangeably with land or space, but it connotes something more precise. Territory is land or space that has had something *done to it*—it has been acted upon. Territory is land that has been identified and claimed by a person or people. Muir (1997, 12) defines territoriality as the "attempt by an individual or group to affect, influence, or control people, phenomena, and relationships by delimiting and asserting control over a geographic area." Territory is thus a spatial expression of power, while also crucial in constituting power relations. It is a bounded space to which there is a compulsion to defend and secure—to claim a particular kind of sovereignty—against infringements by others who are perceived to not belong. Borderlines are often contested not only because they are the sites where the regulation of belonging is most clearly in evidence, but also because of claims to territorial expansion and resistance to such claims.

Over the last several hundred years, the sine qua non of territorialization has been the formation of the nation-state, which by the twentieth century had become the principal framework through which much of the world was organized. State sovereignty became axiomatic, and was protected and legitimated through international law and treaties. The clear and sharp delineation of nation-states on a world map belies the overt struggles both between states and against states that have been exerted in the achievement of these modern spaces of political community. Whether we think of the political revolutions that gave way to the bourgeois nation-states of Europe in the eighteenth and nineteenth centuries, the violence of colonialism and the struggles against colonial rule, or the secessionist movements that have created new nations in more recent history, the nation-state has been made and remade through war. And yet, it is not simply that the material spaces of modern politics have been constituted through war, but also that the modern Western political imaginary is itself governed by its logic. As Susan Buck-Morss has argued in the context of the Cold War, capitalism has been defined by a national imaginary of solidarity in contrast to the class- and party-based solidarity of the communist political imaginary (Buck-Morss 2000; see also Flint, this volume).

Historically, biological or natural theories of territorial organization have dominated social science scholarship, with social and cultural attributes mapped onto particular national formations. The influential works of classic geopoliticians from the late nineteenth and early twentieth centuries were premised on the nation-state as the natural unit of political conflict and strategic and scholarly analysis. It would not be unfair to say that classical geopolitics became in effect a "science" of the warring nation-state. For Friedrich Ratzel, one of the founders of geopolitical thought, the nation-state was an organic entity with an inbuilt drive for expansion. Territorial expansion was rationalized as the acquisition of enhanced *Lebensraum* or "living space," understood to be essential for the growth of the nation. Imperial expansion was thus legitimated as a national right. The national state was so central to the work of the classic geopoliticians that war was in fact *defined as conflict between national states*. Within this model, other forms and scales of armed conflict were simply unintelligible as war, and their problematic existence was managed through an alternative classification. "Revolution," for example, came to signify forms of struggle that were not nationally organized (cf. O'Sullivan 1983). In this sense, despite the later entrée of classic geopolitics onto the political and intellectual scene, there are important parallels between the work of Clausewitz and the work of geopoliticians like Ratzel. Both articulated theories that simultaneously asserted the political nature of their respective fields, war and geography, while restricting politics to the activities of the sovereign state (Farinelli 2000; Cowen and Smith 2006).

Indeed, the academic discipline of geography is deeply implicated in the history of drawing borders and in the wars waged that have defined their contours. Historiographers of the discipline have traced the rise of geography's professionalization alongside the "civilizing mission" of colonialism, and have identified geography's complicity with imperialism (Clayton 2004, 453; Driver 2000). Geography's responsibility has historically been as "handmaiden to the state" (Godlewska and Smith 1994) in the development and mobilization of spatial strategies such as exploration, mapping, surveying, and planning. Geographers such as Sir Halford Mackinder and Isaiah Bowman, for example, played crucial roles in negotiating the new state system that emerged after World War I with the Treaty of Versailles (Dodds and Sidaway 2004; Smith 2003). As this example suggests, war is endemic to these practices, for it has been through war that the modern political borders and boundaries of the state have been constituted, and the territory of the nation-state mapped and divided (Tilly 1985; Hobsbawm 1990).

More recently, a strand of critical scholarship has emerged within the discipline of geography, which shuns naturalized and nationalized conceptions of territory. Approaches developed over the past three decades out of engagements with feminist, Marxist, postcolonial, critical race, queer, and other poststructuralist theory do not deny the ontological power of territory, but emphasize its variable historical and geographical constitution. Territoriality is no longer interpreted as a natural drive, as with Ratzel's *Lebensraum*; both the struggles for territory and the theories that naturalize them are understood as a form of and stake in power relations between groups (Lefebvre 1991). Even classic geopolitical analysis has been revived and reworked by scholars and popular critics for a variety of political and scholarly projects. To this end John Agnew provides a review of the international relations literature and classical political geography, with their tendencies toward realism and idealism, to reveal the territorial assumptions of these traditions and the ways that they are fixed on static notions of state sovereignty and national territorial absolutism (Agnew 1995). "Critical geopolitics" explicitly sheds these national and strategic assumptions, and the singular concern with the national state as political actor (Dalby 1991, 1994; Ó Tuathail 1996; Slater 1997; Ó Tuathail and Dalby 1998). Rather, critical geopolitics uncovers the ways that territories are socially produced, and reveals the practices and discourses through which territorial formations and associated identity politics are constituted and reproduced (Paasi 2000; Gilbert forthcoming). This destabilizes the naturalized relationship between territory and power, and points toward ways of understanding ongoing reterritorializations, and the nuanced forms of belonging and inclusion that persist alongside increasing mobility and migration. Moreover, critical geopolitics not only examines the ways that power is wielded at the scale of the nation-state, but also provides a more complex articulation of power that operates not only at the substate level (the home, the city) but also at the suprastate scale (regional, global), and in this sense connects with the dynamic body of literature on the role of power in the constitution of scale itself (Marston and Smith 2001; Swyngedouw 1997).

Geopolitics in its critical incarnation is tied to the classic tradition only insofar as it offers deconstructive analyses of the scripting of international politics and war. Critical geopolitics is also joined by what Jennifer Hyndman (2004) terms "feminist geopolitics," which comes as an extension of the long-standing and powerful work of feminist political geography and focuses explicitly on the gendered discourses, organization, and effects of politics, security, and violence. Feminist geopolitics is deliberately situated, embodied, and partial, and attends to asymmetrical power dynamics, particularly those of gender (Staeheli and Kofman 2004). A focus on the lives and experiences of women has helped to reveal the masculinist traditions of geopolitics, but at the same time, the very construction of the category of women is also interrogated. Drawing upon the critical theory of authors such as Gayatri Spivak, feminist geopolitics reveals the ways that difference is constituted and reified. At the same time, the emphasis is not solely on the deconstruction of political processes, but also the move toward "a potentially reconstructive political dimension" for political analysis (Hyndman 2004, 309). This includes writing on the politics of resistance, and drawing attention to collectives above and beyond those formalized through the state. Moreover, feminist geopolitics examines the constitution of political subjects and the question of agency. The processes and practices of citizenship, and its inclusionary and exclusionary dimensions, have been central to this analysis. In particular, feminists have interrogated the delineation of public and private spaces, and the differential and inequitable constitution of women through discourses and practices (Young 1990; Mouffe 1995).

These traditions of political geographical thought are highly relevant to discussions about citizenship, territory, and war. And yet, academic geography holds no monopoly on understanding or describing spatial practice. Interdisciplinary academic and popular debates on topics like globalization, cosmopolitanism, transnationalism, empire, urbanization, and spatial scale capture aspects of contemporary spatiality. We have seen a simultaneous explosion of interest in the construction of nationalism and in its questioning over the past two or three decades. A vital body of work investigates the constitution of national political geographies, political identities, and forms of citizenship, as well as ways in which fixed forms have come undone (Soysal 1994; Ong 2006; Holston and Appadurai 1999; Isin 2002; Varsanyi 2006; Bhabha 1999; Brysk and Shafir 2004; Cairns 1999; Shapiro 1997). The end of the Cold War was a crucial moment for the emergence of new global political geographies and geographical imaginaries (Luke 1996). Hardt and Negri provocatively term the post–Cold War era the "new war," refusing the sacred binary of peace and war, or at least its assumed sequential ordering. They suggest this "new war" is characterized by the breakdown of the national contours and mythologies of war and politics. The "modern strategy of isolating war to interstate conflict," they argue, "is less and less viable today given the emergence of innumerable global civil wars, in armed conflicts from Central Africa to Latin America and from Indonesia to Iraq and Afghanistan" (2004, 7). They argue that war is now "permanent and general; the exception has become the rule, pervading both foreign relations and the homeland" (Hardt and Negri 2004, 7). Yet these arguments have provoked criticism from those who demand closer scrutiny of the territorialization of both politics and war, for Hardt and Negri assert that this new form of war has no spatial limits, even as they use geographical concepts, such as "foreign" and "homeland" (14).

Others prefer to *locate* power more explicitly by describing the present as a new moment of *American* imperialism (Smith 2003; Harvey 2003; Mann 2003; Johnson 2004; Sparke 2000; Roy 2006). In these accounts, the forms and logics of power and violence may change, but a geographic center still holds. Here it is not just a global and unbounded "Empire" but an American-centered imperialism that is called upon to make sense of the world, even if, as Neil Smith argues, a geopolitical logic of national state power has largely given way to a "geoeconomic" one. Theories of primitive accumulation have recirculated and are once again theorized as a core logic of warfare wherein "accumulation by dispossession" organizes disparate forms and geographies of violence (Luxembourg 1913; Perelman 2000; Harvey 2003). These transformations create immense challenges for those who are trying to uphold the status quo of power relations and social order, as well as for those who aim to extinguish it. Citizens, noncitizens, workers, activists, insurgents, military managers, soldiers, immigration officials, and state lawyers all face new hurdles. But alongside new challenges, new opportunities also emerge for actors to further their ends, hence the transformations in strategies and tactics of struggle and not only of rule. In this light, there has been growing focus in policy and academic debates on the lived spaces through which citizenship is mobilized, such as at the urban, and the counterpolitics of place (Isin 2002; Young 1990).

Most profoundly, we see unfolding the proliferation of diverse political geographic assemblages. Crises of military recruitment across countries with voluntary enlistment, the crisis of "homegrown terrorism," and the crisis of large-scale civilian slaughter are just a few of the symptoms and signposts of tectonic political shifts. However, in none of this would we suggest that the national state is withering away or becoming unimportant. Indeed, since the initiation of the War on Terror, national securitization is at the center of the reconfiguration of global political geographies. Rather than ask if the national state is dissolving or strengthening, whether it is powerful (or not), or whether it is a meaningful category of analysis for contemporary political analysis (or not), this collection urges us to consider what kind of roles and forms it assumes in contemporary citizenship and violence, and the nature of its effects. If the territorial form of the modern state was assembled at the nexus of citizenship and war, what new role and form does it take on today, and what new geographies of politics and violence are calling?

Chapter Overview

The chapters in this volume address issues arising from the intersections of war, territory, and citizenship from a variety of perspectives. The papers in the first section, "At War: Struggle, 'Strategy,' and Spatiality," pay particular attention to the changing dimensions of warfare over the last several decades, many of which deemphasize the central role of the nation-state while also attending to questions relating to the logistical implications of these transformations. But while several of the papers resonate with some of the international political economy literature in this area, here we find a much more spatially attuned analysis that addresses the implications of the shifting nature of war for citizens and citizenship. Stephen Graham's paper on the rise of urban warfare evokes questions regarding the unknowability of urban spaces. These issues are particularly relevant, he suggests, under the United States' ongoing "Revolution in Military Affairs" and the shifting military policy and planning which increasingly target cities of the Global South. The implications for the populations of these cities portend to be enormous, as new kinds of computerized military technologies are being employed that dehumanize those in the Global South, reducing their cities to battle spaces, in an attempt to protect Western soldiers and remove Western citizens ever further from the theater of war. In his examination of the struggles between the Red Army Fraction (RAF, or Baader-Meinhof Gang) and the West German state in the late 1970s, Matthew G. Hannah draws attention to the spatial tactics of the RAF as they eluded state surveillance, and thus, like Graham, raises questions of power-knowledge and urban space. In so doing, he supplements Giorgio Agamben's theorization of the "state of exception" (2005) with the caveat that to exert sovereignty requires being able to know and to spatially contain the "terrorist" threat. He thus argues that there are geographical limits to the population's vulnerability as virtual *homines sacri* precisely because of the complexity of the landscapes in which contemporary conflicts unfold. Questions regarding vulnerability and responsibility provoked by changing acts and actors of war are also central to the discussion of suicide bombing and its contemporary "banalization" by Engin Isin and Melissa Finn. Investigating new tactics of armed conflict through the figure of the soldier-martyr, who is both warrior and weapon, the authors also offer an ethical framework for understanding their actions that neither dismisses suicide bombers as fully evil nor celebrates their holy martyrdom. Rather, Isin and Finn seek to understand whether suicide bombing can be considered a meaningful act of citizenship, but they also argue that the suicide bomber must be answerable for his or her actions even as he or she is annihilated.

In quite different ways, the banality of war also figures in the chapters by Matthew Farish and by Stephen J. Collier and Andrew Lakoff, which address the implications of the Cold War on the U.S. public. Farish writes of the militarization of everyday life through civil defense initiatives that sought to both perpetuate and manage collective panic around "national security"—discourses that are evocative of U.S. homeland security in the contemporary moment. He describes the ways that programs geared to educating and preparing the population for potential nuclear war seeped into mundane practices around the home, in the community, and on the road alongside appeals to homogeneous patriotism by U.S. citizens. Collier and Lakoff ask a different set of questions about security of this same era while refuting the notion of the militarization of U.S. society and the central role of the military that this argument presumes. They suggest that civil defense introduced a form of collective security, which was defined and managed through a distinctive political logic they call "distributed preparedness," and which mediated between concerns over intrusive federalism and public and private local capabilities to respond to and plan for security threats. Rather than enter into the conventional debates about whether there is *too much* or *not enough* security, they instead insist that we question the form of security and type of threat being described, as we consider the changing nexus of war, citizenship, and territory.

Recent developments in our understanding of warfare, as well as in its practice, provide a more nuanced account of engagement, and in particular the risks faced by both combatants and civilians as the lines between them become increasingly blurred. War can be productive for citizenship, and the papers in the following section, "Re/constituting Territory," are a testament to that. These chapters consider a wide range of examples where attempts to reconcile struggles over territory with the demands of the population in the aftermath of conflict have resulted in both intentional and inadvertent expansion of formal and/or substantive citizenship rights. These questions are certainly being considered in Iraq, where the United States has led the initiative to draft a constitution that would manage territorial settlement and fragmented political identities to be implemented after U.S. military withdrawal. As Stuart Elden describes, however, although the foundations of the Iraq Constitution have passed in a referendum, the U.S. military presence persists, compromising Iraq's independence. Elden's analysis also points to underlying political and territorial frictions not addressed by the constitution, and the problem of extraterritorial intervention. National and extraterritorial interests are also difficult to reconcile in Angola and Mozambique, where a quite different scenario is underway. Here, new forms of expanded citizenship rights and social welfare have been made possible through the demands of disabled war veterans. Marcus Power argues, however, that the role of foreign aid and nongovernmental organizations (NGOs) in the process and their relationship with local governments reveal a lingering differentiation and segregation of the colonial "citizen" and indigenous "subject" in the postcolonial state apparatus. Yet another scenario is unfolding in Peru, where a formal Truth and Reconciliation Commission was initiated in 2001 to provide a forum for discussing the human rights violations of the previous two decades. Maureen Hays-Mitchell offers hope that awareness of the ways that civil violence reinforced cleavages along the lines of class, "race," indigeneity, and gender, as well as between rural and urban dwellers, might help galvanize initiatives that will attend to these structural inequities. She suggests that truth and reconciliation processes may well be limited in terms of their power and authority, but carry the potential to deepen citizenship in a postconflict context. Hays-Mitchell, however, insists that this does not abdicate the international responsibility to promote such transformations.

The expansion of citizenship through war is not always benevolent or direct. Alan Smart's chapter on Hong Kong in the 1950s examines how insecurities over the indigenous Chinese population, fueled by broader Cold War geopolitical anxieties, resulted in a Squatter Resettlement Programme that in the 1970s evolved into a public-housing scheme. The provision of social welfare reform was used in China as a mechanism for securing the loyalty of the colonized population—and hence to mitigate security threats—but did not eliminate political and social divisions. Even where there are ambitions to move toward a more global application of human rights or global citizenship, such social and political divisions persist. Jennifer Hyndman warns that the aspirations to global citizenship claimed by the UN-endorsed policy of human security and its framework policy, "Responsibility to Protect," are thwarted in practice by claims to state sovereignty and a selective and uneven political will to assist those in conflict. Interventions in the name of human security are conditional and selective, and adjudicated in terms of asymmetrical geo-political relations rather than a binding legal framework. Paradoxically, then, this humanitarian mandate reinforces the differentials of the international state system that are at the very root of the breaches of human security that it claims to thwart. As the papers in this section reveal, war and conflict have resulted in the expansion of citizenship rights, but largely in ways that do not transcend domestic structural inequities, yet also reveal tensions in the international state system.

The papers in the final section of this volume, "Citizens and the Body Politic," look explicitly at the ways that the bodies of citizens are governed within an ethos of war, militarization, and securitization. The chapter by Deborah Cowen and Emily Gilbert examines the ways that with the War on Terror, the family has reemerged as a central model of political relations. We argue that the affective politics associated with the idea of "family," and in particular the nuclear family, have been mobilized to offset the anxieties and insecurities that have been generated by increased securitization, but in turn have been used to rationalize greater state interventions in domestic life as well as reinforce normative moral politics organized around the nuclear family. Questions around securitization and militarization have also been particularly evident at the border, where border crossers undergo questioning regarding their status as members of the political community. Davina Bhandar examines the racial ontologies of immigrant and migrant communities at moments of heightened border tensions in Canadian-U.S. border practices, from the anti-Asiatic riots of the 1900s to the War on Terror. Each of these moments reveals the racialization of border practices, and so the implicit racial politics of citizenship within these nation-states. In a different context, Nadia Abu-Zahra writes of contemporary forms of identity documents in Israel that are being used to control the Palestinian population through registration, and the limits that are imposed on their mobility, labor potential, and ability to make decisions about their personal lives. The Wall that is being built to sever the West Bank is but a more tangible and visible example of this demographic engineering, but effectively these strategies all have a colonial effect through depopulation and deterritorialization.

Tamar Mayer addresses questions of Israeli borders and citizenship from yet another angle. Here it is the masculinized constructions of Israeli national identity, and the ways that this connection has persisted, although gradually recast, alongside a transformed understanding of Israeli territory and homeland in the twentieth century. Border skirmishes in the years after statehood encouraged particularly virulent forms of hypermasculinity that were demeaning of immigrating Arab Jews. In the intervening years, the ongoing wartime politics of the Jewish state have produced militarized citizen-subjects, with compulsory military service just one dimension of this. An increasingly militarized society is also the backdrop to Colin Flint's chapter, which looks at the ways that narratives of "failure" and collaboration falsely attached to U.S. prisoners of war in Korea were mobilized by conservatives to buttress mythical U.S. values and institutions. Flint suggests that in the context of an imperial war where territorial sovereignty was not in jeopardy, the defense of U.S. institutions and values supplanted a territorially based notion of sovereignty. Imperial war, and the rationalization that the American capitalist way of life needed protection, supported a militarization of society such that domestic space became a "battleground" for the moral geopolitics of the Cold War. The soldier is also at the heart of Rachel Woodward's chapter, which examines soldiers' autobiographies to see how they make sense of their military participation. Woodward provides a cautionary supplement to those accounts that emphasize the role of national pride and national service in the motivations of soldiers, and, rather, traces the importance of personal incentives and "mateship" or comradery with other soldiers as crucial to understanding their participation and solidarity. Each of the papers in this section, therefore, looks to understanding the ways that citizen bodies are governed and mobilized in particular ways vis-à-vis ongoing or looming violence.

These chapters, in all their diversity, insist that citizenship is a crucial lens on questions of war, and that a geographic inquiry is essential to developing nuanced understandings of its persistence and transformation. The contributors to this volume offer profound insights on historical and contemporary problems. There are also clearly many questions, conflicts, and geographical regions that are not addressed at all or adequately here, but that are crucial to understanding the central themes of the collection. For instance, war and armed conflict in entire regions of the world including South Asia and Central Africa, or "hot spots" like Chechnya and Bosnia, for starters, are not addressed in any way. Questions of "race" and racialization, the political economy of warfare, the gendering of contemporary military violence, and imperialism and postcolonialism are crucial ones that are taken up in a few chapters, but certainly not in proportion to their role in armed conflict today. The fact that the scholars presented in this volume all live and work in a handful of advanced capitalist Anglophone countries is an obvious and important limitation to the inclusiveness and breadth of the work showcased. But it is in the face of all these limitations and strengths that we suggest that the most important contribution of this collection may be vital new ways of asking questions. With this dynamic group of contributions, we hope to help foster further research and debate on topics that demand more critical attention than multiple volumes of this size could ever address adequately. With the devastating awareness that questions of war, citizenship, and territory constitute so much of everyday life for so many people today and will be with us for some time, we offer some ways of answering pressing questions, but most importantly we offer more questions for future inquiry.

Notes

1. For example, in 2000 the United Nations Department of Peacekeeping Operations (DPKO) organized a workshop entitled "Mainstreaming a Gender Perspective in Multidimensional Peace Support Operations" hosted by the government of Namibia, which generated the Namibia Plan of Action. Following its release, the DPKO has implemented policy to promote the recruitment of women into peacekeeping missions and encourage more recruitment of women into the national military forces from which UN personnel are drawn. See the UN secretary-general's report on women, peace, and security (S/2004/814; United Nations 2004), and the report of the NGO Working Group on Women, Peace, and Security (2005).

2. The use of rape as a strategy of warfare has been a feature of many recent conflicts. During the 1994 genocide in Rwanda, at least 250,000 and as many as 500,000 women were raped by soldiers (Human Rights Watch 1996). Jefferson (2004) reports that during the 1990s, more than 20,000 Muslim women were raped as part of an ethnic cleansing campaign in Bosnia. The United Nations Development Fund for Women (UNIFEM; 2006) reports the rape of thousands of women and girls during fighting in the Democratic Republic of Congo. Gang rape was so widespread and brutal that doctors began classifying vaginal destruction as a combat-related crime (Jefferson 2004).

3. For some more comprehensive overviews of citizenship, see Isin and Wood (1999) and Heater (2004).

4. Citizenship wasn't so crucial to political identity in the medieval period, although aspects of citizenship (duties, belonging) remained in ecclesiastical dioceses (or political regions). The other worldliness of Christian religion, however, and its emphasis on Church conformity (rather than freedom) diminished the quotidian importance of citizenship to the population.

References

Agamben, G. 2005. *State of exception*, trans. K. Attel. Chicago: University of Chicago Press.

Agnew, John. 1995. The territorial trap. In *Mastering space: Hegemony, territory and international political economy*, ed. John Agnew and Stuart Corbridge. London: Routledge.

Amin, S. 1976. *L'impérialisme et le Développement Inégal*. Paris: Edition de Minuit.

Arendt, Hannah. 1951. *The origins of totalitarianism*. New York: Harcourt Brace.

———. 1970. *On violence*. New York: Harcourt Brace.

Barkawi, T. 2005. *Globalization and war*. Boulder, CO: Rowman & Littlefield.

Berger, John. 1974. *Ways of Seeing*. London Penguin.

Bhabha, J. 1999. Belonging in Europe: citizenship and post-national rights. *International Social Science Journal* 51:11–23.

Blaut, J. 1970. Geographic models of imperialism. *Antipode* 2 (1): 65–85.

Brysk, A., and G. Shafir, eds. 2004. *People out of place: Globalization, human rights and the citizenship gap.* New York: Routledge.

Buck-Morss, S. 2000. *Dreamworld and Utopia: The passing of mass Utopia in East and West.* Cambridge, MA: MIT Press.

Carter, A. 1998. Liberalism and the obligation to military service. *Political Studies* 46:68–81.

Cairns, A. ed. 1999. *Citizenship, deversity, and pluralism: Canadian and comparative perspectives.* Montreal: McGill-Queen's University Press.

Chakrabarty, D. 2000. *Provincializing Europe: Postcolonial thought and historical difference.* Princeton, NJ: Princeton University Press.

Chen, Xiaobei. 2003. The birth of the child-victim citizen. In *Reinventing Canada: politics of the 21st century,* ed. Janine Brodie and Linda Trimble, 189–202. Toronto: Prentice Hall.

Christie, N. 2000. *Engendering the state: Family, work and welfare in Canada.* Toronto: University of Toronto Press.

Clausewitz, C. von. 1976. *On war,* ed. M. Howard and P. Paret. Princeton, NJ: Princeton University Press.

Clayton, Daniel. 2004. Imperial geographies. In *A companion to cultural geography,* ed. James S. Duncan, Nuala C. Johnson, and Richard H. Schein, 449–68. Oxford: Blackwell.

Cliff, T. 1957. Perspectives for the permanent war economy. *Socialist Review* (March): http://www.marxists.org/archive/cliff/works/1957/05/permwar.htm (accessed March 12, 2007).

Cohen, B. 1973. *The question of imperialism: The political economy of dominance and dependence.* New York: Basic Books.

Cohen, Eliot. 1985. *Citizens and soldiers: The dilemmas of military service.* Ithaca, NY: Cornell University Press.

Cowen, D. 2005. Welfare warriors: Towards a genealogy of the soldier citizen in Canada. *Antipode* 37 (4): 654–78.

———. 2006. Fighting for "freedom": The end of conscription and the project of citizenship in the United States. *Citizenship Studies* 10 (2): 167–83.

———. 2008. *Military workfare: The soldier and social citizenship in Canada.* Toronto: University of Toronto Press.

Cowen, D., and N. Smith. 2006. After geopolitics? Geoeconomics and the territorial politics of security. Paper presented at the Militarization, Society and Space Symposium, Edinburgh University, November 23.

Dalby, S. 1991. Critical geopolitics: Difference, discourse and dissent. *Environment and Planning D: Society and Space* 9 (3): 261–83.

———. 1994. Gender and critical geopolitics: Reading security discourse in the new world disorder. *Environment and Planning D: Society and Space* 12 (5): 595–612.

Davis, A. 1971. *If they come in the morning: Voices of resistance.* London: Orbach and Chambers.

De Landa, M. 1991. *War in the age of intelligent machines.* New York: Zone Books.

Dijkink, G. 2005. Soldiers and nationalism: The glory and transience of a hard-won territorial identity. In *The geography of war and peace: From death camps to diplomats*, ed. C. Flint. Oxford: Oxford University Press.

Dodds, Claus, and James S. Sidaway. 2004. Halford Mackinder and the "geographical pivot of history": A centennial retrospective. *Geographical Journal* 170 (4): 292–98.

Donzelot, J. 1988. The promotion of the social. *Economy and Society* 17: 395–427.

Drake, Michael. 2002. *Problematics of military power: Government, discipline and the subject of violence*. London: Routledge.

Driver, Felix. 2000. *Geography militant: Cultures of exploration and empire*. Oxford: Blackwell.

Enloe, C. 1988. *Does khaki become you? The militarization of women's lives*. London and San Francisco: Pandora Press and Harper/Collins.

———. 2000. *Maneuvers: The international politics of militarizing women's lives*. University of California Press: Berkeley.

Fanon, F. 1965. *A dying colonialism*. New York: Grove Weidenfeld.

Farinelli, F. 2000. Friedrich Ratzel and the nature of (political) geography. *Political Geography* 19: 943–55.

Foucault, M. 1990. *The history of sexuality: An introduction*. London: Verso.

———. 1997. *Society must be defended: Lectures at the College de France, 1975–6*. New York: Picador.

———. 1977. *Discipline and punish: The birth of the prison*. ed, Alan Sheridan. New York: Vintage Books.

Fraser, N. 1997. *Justice interruptus: Critical reflections on the postsocialist condition*. New York: Routledge.

Fraser, N., and L. Gordon. 1992. Contract vs. charity: Why is there no social citizenship in the United States. *Socialist Review* 22 (3): 45–67.

Gilbert, Emily. 2007. Leaky borders and solid citizens: Governing security, prosperity and quality of life in a North American partnership. *Antipode* 39 (1): 77–98.

———. 2007. "Money, Citizenship, Territoriality and the Proposals for North American Monetary Union" *Political Geography* 26 (2): 141–158.

Godlewska, A., and N. Smith, eds. 1994. *Geography and empire*. Oxford: Blackwell.

Graham, S., ed. 2004. *Cities, war, and terrorism*. London: Blackwell.

Guest, D. 1985. *The emergence of social security in Canada*. Vancouver: University of British Columbia Press.

Gupta, A., and J. Ferguson. 1997. Beyond "culture": Space, identity and the politics of difference. In *Culture, Power, Place*, ed. A. Gupta and J. Ferguson, 33–51. Durham, NC: Duke University Press.

Hardt, M., and M. Negri. 2004. *Multitude: War and democracy in the age of empire*. New York: Penguin.

Harvey, D. 2003. *The new imperialism*. New York: Oxford University Press.

Heater, D. 2004. *A brief history of citizenship*. New York: New York University Press.

Hobsbawm, E. 1990. *Nations and nationalism since 1780: Programme, myth, reality*. Cambridge: Cambridge University Press.

———. 2002. The future of war and peace. *CounterPunch*, February 27, http://www.counterpunch.org/hobsbawm1.html.

Holston, J., and A. Appadurai. 1999. Cities and citizenship. In *Cities and citizenship*, ed. J. Holston. Durham, NC: Duke University Press.

Howard, M. 1976. The influence of Clausewitz. In Karl von Clausewitz, *On war*, ed. M. Howard and P. Paret. Princeton, NJ: Princeton University Press.

Human Rights Watch. 1996. Shattered lives: Sexual violence during the Rwandan genocide and its aftermath. http://www.hrw.org/reports/1996/Rwanda.htm (accessed November 8, 2006).

Huntington, S. P. 1957. *The soldier and the state: The theory and politics of civil-military relations.* Cambridge: Harvard University Press.

Hyndman, J. 2004. Mind the gap: Bridging feminist and political geography through geopolitics. *Political Geography* 23:307–22.

Isin, E. F. 2002. *Being political: Genealogies of citizenship.* Minneapolis: University of Minnesota Press.

———. 2004. The neurotic citizen. *Citizenship Studies* 8 (3): 217–35.

———, ed. 2007. *Recasting the social in citizenship.* Toronto: University of Toronto Press.

Isin, E., and P. Wood. 1999. *Citizenship and identity.* Thousand Oaks, CA: Sage.

Isin, E. ed. 2008. *Recasting the social in citizenship.* Toronto: University of Toronto Press.

Jefferson, L. R. 2004. Human Rights Watch world report 2004, in war as in peace: Sexual violence and women's status. January. http://www.hrw.org/wr2k4/15.htm (accessed April 3, 2005).

Johnson, C. 2004. *Blowback: The costs and consequences of American empire.* New York: Henry Holt.

Kidron, M. 1970. *Western capitalism since the war.* Harmondsworth, UK: Penguin.

Kirby, A. 1994. What did you do in the war, daddy? In *Geography and empire*, ed. A. Godleska and N. Smith, 300–15. Oxford: Blackwell.

Kirwin, W. 1996. The future of the welfare state during the decline of the nation state. In *Ideology, development and social welfare: Canadian perspectives*, ed. W. Kirwin, 205–14. Toronto: Canadian Scholars' Press.

Klare, M. 1974. The political economy of arms sales to the Persian Gulf. *Society*, September–October, 41–49.

Klausen, J. 1999. *War and welfare: Europe and the United States, 1945 to the present.* New York: St. Martin's.

Kraska, P. 2001. *Militarizing the American criminal justice system: The changing roles of the armed forces and the police.* Boston: Northeastern University Press.

Kymlicka, W. 1995. *Multicultural citizenship: A liberal theory of minority rights.* Oxford: Oxford University Press.

Lefebvre, H. 1991. *The production of space.* Oxford: Blackwell.

Lister, R. 1997. *Citizenship: Feminist perspectives.* New York: New York University Press.

Low, A. M. 1943. *Benefits of war.* London: J. Gifford.

Luke, T. 1996. Governmentality and contragovernmentality: Rethinking sovereignty and territoriality after the Cold War. *Political Geography* 15 (6–7): 491–507.

Luxemburg, R. [1913] 2003. *The accumulation of capital.* New York: Routledge.

Mann, M. 1988. *States, war and capitalism: Studies in political sociology.* Oxford: Basil Blackwell.

———. 2003. *Incoherent empire.* London: Verso.

Marshall, T. H. 1950. *Citizenship and social class.* Cambridge: Cambridge University Press.

Marston, S. A., and N. Smith. 2001. States, scales and households: limits to scale thinking? A response to Brenner. *Progress in Human Geography* 25:615–19.

Marx, Karl. [1867] 1976. *Capital*, vol. 1. London: Penguin.

Mayer, T. 2000. *Gender ironies of nationalism: Sexing the nation.* New York: Routledge.

McEwen, N., and L. Moreno, eds. 2005. *The territorial politics of welfare.* London: Routledge.

McNamara, R. S. 1968. *The essence of security: Reflection in office.* New York: Harper & Row.

Melman, S. 1974. *The permanent war economy: American capitalism in decline.* New York: Simon & Schuster.

Mies, M. 1988. *Woman: The last colony.* London: Zed.

Mitchell, T. 1991. *Colonizing Egypt.* Berkeley: University of California Press.

Moskos, C. 1996. *All that we can be: Black leadership and racial integration the army way.* New York: Basic Books.

Mouffe, C. 1995. Feminism, citizenship and radical democratic politics. *Social postmodernism: Beyond identity politics.* ed. L. Nicholson, S. Seidman. Cambridge: Cambridge University Press.

Muir, R. 1997. *Political geography: A new introduction.* Basingstoke: MacMillian Press.

NGO Working Group on Women, Peace and Security. 2005. Recommendations for the Special Committee on Peacekeeping Operations. January 28. http://www.peacewomen.org/un/ngo/ngopub/C34recommendations05.pdf (accessed March 12, 2007).

O'Connor, James. 1973. *The fiscal crisis of the welfare state.* New York: St. Martin's.

Ong, A. 1999. *Flexible citizenship: The cultural logics of transnationality.* Durham, NC: Duke University Press.

———. 2006. *Neoliberalism as exception: Mutations in citizenship and sovereignty.* Durham, NC: Duke University Press.

Ong, A. 2006. *Neoliberalism as exception: Mutations in sovereignty and citizenship.* Durham: Duke University Press.

O'Sullivan, P. M. 1983. *The geography of warfare.* New York: St. Martin's.

Ó Tuathail, G. 1996. *Critical geopolitics: The political of writing global political space.* London: Routledge.

Ó Tuathail, G., and S. Dalby, eds. 1998. *Rethinking geopolitics.* London: Routledge.

Paasi, A. 2000. Territorial identities as social constructs. *Hagar* 1:91–113.

Perelman, M. 2000. *The invention of capitalism: Classical political economy and the secret history of accumulation.* Durham, NC: Duke University Press.

Rose, N. 1999. *Governing the soul: The shaping of the private self.* London: Free Association of Books.

Roy, A. 2006. Praxis in the time of empire. *Planning Theory* 1 (5): 7–29.

Sales, R. 2002. The deserving and the undeserving? Refugees, asylum seekers and welfare in Britain. *Critical Social Policy* 22 (3): 456–78.

Segal, D. 1989. *Recruiting for Uncle Sam: Citizenship and military manpower policy.* Lawrence: University Press of Kansas.

Shapiro, M. 1997. *Violent cartographies: Mapping cultures of war.* Minneapolis: University of Minnesota Press.

Shaw, M. 2000. Has war a future? *New Political Economy* 5: 112–16.

Shiva, V. 2002. *Water wars.* Cambridge, MA: South End Press.

Skocpol, T. 1992. *Protecting soldiers and mothers: The political origins of social policy in the United States.* Cambridge, MA: Belknap Press of Harvard University Press.

Slater, D. 1997. Spatialities of power and postmodern ethics: Rethinking geopolitical encounters. *Environment and Planning D: Society and Space* 15:55–72.

Smith, N. 2003. *American empire: Roosevelt's geographer and the prelude to globalization.* Berkeley: University of California Press.

Soysal, Y. 1994. *Limits of citizenship: Migrants and post-national membership in Europe.* Chicago: University of Chicago Press.

Sparke, M. 2000. Graphing the geo in geopolitical: Critical geopolitics and the re-visioning of responsibility. *Political Geography* 19:373–80.

Staeheli, L., and E. Kofman. 2004. Mapping gender, making politics: toward feminist political geographies. In *Mapping women, mapping politics: Feminist perspectives on political geography*, ed. Lynn A. Staeheli, Eleonore Kofman and Linda Peake, 1–13. New York: Routledge.

Stasiulis, D., and A. Bakan. 2003. *Negotiating citizenship: Migrant women in Canada and the global system.* London and Toronto: Palgrave and University of Toronto Press.

Swyngedouw, E. 1997. Excluding the Other: The production of scale and scaled politics. In *Geographies of economies*, ed. R. Lee and J. Wills. London: Arnold.

Taylor, C. 1994. The politics of recognition. In *Multiculturalism: Examining the politics of recognition*, ed. Amy Gutmann, 25–73. Princeton, NJ: Princeton University Press.

Theweleit, K. 1993. The bomb's womb and the genders of war (war goes on preventing women from becoming the mothers of invention. In *Gendering war talk*, ed. M. Cooke and A. Woollacott, 283–316. Princeton, NJ: Princeton University Press.

Tilly, C. 1985. War making and state making as organized crime. In *Bringing the state back in*, ed. P. Evans, D. Rueschmeyer, and T. Skocpol, 169–86. London: University of Cambridge Press.

Titmuss, R. 1958. War and social policy. In *Essays on "the welfare state."* London: George Allen and Unwin.

Turner, B. 1993. *Citizenship and Social Theory.* London: London Sage Publications.

UNIFEM. 2006. Women, war, peace and violence against women—fact sheet. http://www.womenwarpeace.org/issues/violence/violence.htm (accessed August 11, 2006).

United Nations. 2004. UN secretary-general's report on women, peace, and security. S/2004/814. New York: United Nations.

Van Doorn, J. 1975. *The Soldier and social change: Comparative studies in the history and sociology of the military.* Beverley Hills, CA: Sage.

Varsanyi, M. 2006. Interrogating "urban citizenship" vis-à-vis undocumented migration. *Citizenship Studies* 10(2): 224–44.

Virilio, Paul 1986. *Speed and politics: An essay on dromology.* New York: Semiotext(e).

Weber, M. 1981. *General economic history.* New Brunswick, NJ: Transaction.

Wilson, L. 2002. The law of posse comitatus: Police and military powers once statutorily divided are swiftly merging. *CovertAction Quarterly*, http://www.thirdworldtraveler.com/Civil_Liberties/Posse_Comitatus_Law.html.

Young, I. M. 1990. *Justice and the politics of difference.* Princeton, NJ: Princeton University Press.

Part I
At War: Struggle, "Strategy," and Spatiality

2

Imagining Urban Warfare
Urbanization and U.S. Military Technoscience

STEPHEN GRAHAM

Introduction

> For Western military forces, asymmetric warfare in urban areas will
> be the greatest challenge of this century.... The city will be the strate-
> gic high ground—whoever controls it will dictate the course of future
> events in the world.
>
> **Dickson (2002a, 10)**

Western military theorists and researchers are increasingly preoccupied with
how the geographies of Global South cities, and processes of Global South
urbanization, are beginning to influence both the geopolitics and the technoscience of post–Cold War political violence. Indeed, almost unnoticed within
"civil" urban geography and social science, a large "shadow" system of military urban research is quickly being established. Funded by Western military
research budgets, this is quickly elaborating how such effects are allegedly
already becoming manifest, and how the global intensification of processes of
urbanization will deepen them in the future (Graham 2004a). Such research is
important in directly constituting the imagination of future Western military
operations in so-called urban terrain across the Global South.

Fueled by the growing realization that the scale and significance of contemporary processes of urbanization across the world might significantly reshape
the geopolitics, doctrine, and realities of post–Cold War Western military
strategy, such research fuels a set of technomilitary discourses. Within and
through these, attempts are currently being made to reconstitute the structure, orientation, and technoscience of Western military power to directly
reflect the alleged implications of such urbanization.

The central consensus amongst the wide variety of Western military theorists pushing for such shifts is that "modern urban combat operations will
become one of the primary challenges of the 21st century" (Defense Intelligence Reference Document [DIRC] 1997, 11). Major Kelly Houlgate (2004),
a U.S. Marine Corps commentator, notes already that "of 26 conflicts fought

over [by U.S. forces]" between 1984 and 2004, "21 have involved urban areas, and 10 have been exclusively urban."

The widening adoption of "urban warfare" doctrine follows centuries when Western military planners preached Sun Tzu's mantra from 1500 B.C. that the "worst policy is to attack cities." It follows a post–World War II Cold War period marked by an obsession with mass, superpower-led, "air-land" engagements centered on the North European plain within and above the spaces between *bypassed* European city regions. Whilst numerous wars were fought by Western forces in developing world cities during the Cold War, as part of wider struggles against independence and terrorist movements and "hot" proxy wars, such conflicts were very much seen by Western military theorists as unusual sideshows to the imagined superpower "air-land" and tactical and global nuclear engagements (Davis 2004a). Consequently, the doctrine of urban warfare, already neglected, received very little attention during the Cold War and became even more marginalized within Western military rhetoric (Hills 2004). On the rare occasions when urban warfare was specifically addressed in Cold War military doctrine, the United States' forces, in the euphemistic language so typical of military forces, tended to "approach the urban area by rubbling or isolating the city," using tactics unchanged since World War II (Grubs 2003, iii). That is, they either ignored, or sought to systematically annihilate, urban places (as at Hue during the Vietnam War).

In the place of such neglect of Western military doctrine, which specifically addresses the challenges of counterinsurgency warfare within cities, a highly contested, diverse, and complex set of institutional and technoscientific battles are now emerging through which attempts are being made to try to reimagine and reshape Western military forces so that counterinsurgency operations within large urban areas become their de facto operations (Hills 2004). Prevailing conceptions of Western military engagement are thus being widely challenged to address the perceived perils of engaging in "military operations on urban terrain" (or MOUT).

The textual and visual discourses that both result from and sustain this "urban turn" in Western military doctrine comprise an important area of concern for critical social scientists keen to understand intersections of war, territory, technology, and citizenship within the post–Cold War world. From the perspective of this book, they raise at least two key questions, which will be our concern here. First, how are Global South cities being imagined and represented within Western militaries' discourses about the putative effects of urbanization on Western military doctrine, technology, and tactics? Second, what does such imaginative and representational work imply for the urban citizenship of the residents of those cities, and the wider citizenship of Western militaries intervening in them?

As the world's preeminent military power, the military forces of the United States provide the most interesting and important example of how discursive constructions of "urban terrain" are being used to justify attempts at the "transformation" of the technologies, tactics, and strategies of national military intervention more broadly (see Ek 2000). U.S. military forces will be our central concern here because U.S. military research on "urban operations" dwarfs that of all other nations combined (Hills 2004). The bloody experience of the Iraq urban insurgency is already looming large in these debates. A major review of the imperative of urban warfare "doctrine" for U.S. forces, prepared by Major Lee Grubbs in 2003, for example, stated baldly that

> as the Iraq plan evolves, it is clear that the enemies of the United States' military have learned a method to mitigate the Joint [U.S.] Force's dominance in long range surveillance and engagement. The enemy will seek the city and the advantages of mixing with non-combatants. (2003, 56)

One particularly important feature of U.S. military discourses on urbanization looms large in such debates. This is the way in which the sheer three-dimensional complexity and scale of Global South cities allegedly undermine the United States' expensively assembled and hegemonic advantages in surveillance, targeting, and killing through "precise" air- and space-based weapons systems (Graham 2003; Davis 2004b).

The discussion which follows falls into three parts. In the first, the discursive problematization of Global South cities produced by U.S. military urban researchers and commentators is reviewed. Emphasis is placed on how developing world cities are depicted as intrinsically labyrinthine, chaotic, structureless, and deceptive physical environments which substantially frustrate the wider U.S. geopolitical strategy based on the U.S. military's advantages in air- and space-based surveillance, digital processing, and "network-centric" warfare—transformations which, together, are sometimes labeled the "Revolution in Military Affairs" (or RMA; Gregory 2004).

The second part of the chapter goes on to analyze the way in which key actors within the U.S. military-industrial complex are suggesting deeply technophiliac "solutions" to this purported erosion of U.S. geostrategic power through Global South urbanization. Here, what I call the "urban turn" of the RMA—the shift in technophiliac discourses from discussions of planet-straddling weapons systems to technological innovations designed to allow the microspaces of developing world "megacities" to be controlled—is analyzed in detail. Centered on the concept of "persistent area dominance," such strategies entail the saturation of "adversary" cities with large numbers of miniature surveillance and targeting systems. These are being designed to support continuous targeting, and destruction, of detected "targets." The final part of the chapter draws brief theoretical and research conclusions for the intersections of war, territory, and citizenship that are the concern of this book.

Dreams Frustrated? Urbanization and the
"Revolution in Military Affairs" (RMA)

> Urban operations represent a black hole in the current Revolution in Military Affairs pantheon of technological advantage. . . . The technologies traditionally ascribed to the current Revolution in Military Affairs phenomenon will have negligible impact on Military Operations in Urban Terrain.

> **Harris(2003, 38–41)**

The military strategies to project, sustain, and deepen U.S. geopolitical power in the post–Cold War period (see Roberts, Secor, and Sparke 2003; Kirsch 2003; Barnett 2004) rest on the exploitation of a "transformation" of U.S. military power through what has been termed a "Revolution in Military Affairs" (see Ek 2000; Pieterse 2004). Centering on the technologies of "stealth," "precision" targeting, and satellite geopositioning, the RMA has widely been hailed amongst U.S. military planners as the means to sustain U.S. dominance in the post–Cold War world (Stone 2004).

Central to the RMA is the notion that "military operations are now aimed at defined effects rather than attrition of enemy forces or occupation of ground" (Cohen 2004, 395). Through the interlinkage of the "system of systems" of U.S. military technologies, RMA theorists argue that a truly "network-centric warfare" is now possible through which U.S. forces can continually dominate societies deemed to be their adversaries through their increasingly omnipotent surveillance and "situational awareness," devastating and precisely targeted aerial firepower, and suppression and degradation of the communications and fighting ability of any opposing forces (Arquilla and Ronfeldt 2001; Graham 2005). Thus, RMA theorists imagine U.S. military operations to be a giant, integrated, "network enterprise"—a "just-in-time" system of posthuman, cyborganized warriors which utilizes many of the principles of logistics chain management and new-technology-based tracking that are so dominant within contemporary management models (Gray 2003).

Crucial here is the argument that this reduced risk (to U.S. forces) of undertaking military operations is making such interventions much more common, aggressive, and preemptive, as the central basis for U.S. strategy (Barocas 2002). Such perceptions were central to the Bush administration's launching the "preemptive war" as part of an ongoing and unbounded "War on Terror" after the 9/11 attacks. They were also central to the influential pronouncements of the neoconservative Project for the New American Century in 2000 that U.S. forces needed to be redesigned in the post–Cold War era so that they could "fight and decisively win multiple, simultaneous major theatre wars" (2000; see Harris 2003; Roberts, Secor, and Sparke 2003). Typical of such arguments, O'Mara argues,

It is now possible to use America's military might with a greatly reduced chance of suffering friendly casualties or equipment loss. The reduction of American casualties afforded by the marriage between stealthy aircraft and precision guided munitions has had a profound effect on America's willingness to intervene militarily . . . the military must also adapt to its new role as a tool of choice, rather than a tool of last resort. (2003, 4)

Importantly, however, such technophiliac discourses depicting an RMA ushering in a new, relatively reduced-risk, "clean," and painless strategy of U.S. military dominance assumed that the vast networks of sensors and weapons that needed to be integrated and connected to project U.S. power would work *uninterruptedly*. Global scales of flow and connection have thus dominated RMA discourses; technological mastery, omnipotent surveillance, real-time "situational awareness," and speed-of-light digital interactions have been widely portrayed as processes which, intrinsically, would usher in U.S. military "full-spectrum dominance" on a planetary scale, irrespective of the geographical terrain that was to be dominated.

RMA discourses have, in this sense, been notably ageographical. Crucially, from the point of view of the current chapter, little account was taken of the geographical specificities of the spaces or geographical terrains inhabited by the purported adversaries of the United States in the post–Cold War period (or how they are changing through processes of urbanization and globalization). A key axiom of RMA rhetoric has been the idea that the United States was now able to prosecute its global strategies for geopolitical dominance through a "radical non-territoriality" (Duffield 2002, 158).

In response to this neglect of global urbanization within RMA discourses, and spurred on by the catastrophic and ongoing urban insurgency since the U.S.-U.K. invasion of Iraq in 2003, an increasingly powerful range of counterdiscourses has emerged within the U.S. military. Through these, a second group of U.S. military theorists has asserted that the technophiliac dreams of RMA will either fail, or be substantially undermined, by global processes of urbanization, especially in the Global South cities where they imagine U.S. forces being most often engaged. The pronouncements of those advocating an "urban turn" in the RMA have had two main features.

Signal Failures: Urban Environments as Physical
Interrupters to "Network-Centric Warfare"

In simple terms walls tend to get in the way of today's battlefield communications and sensor technologies.

Hewish and Pengelley (2001)

Their first major feature has been the strong suggestion that the urban terrain in poor, Global South countries is a great leveler between high-tech U.S. forces and their low-tech and usually informally organized and poorly equipped adversaries (Gregory 2004; Graham 2004b). The complex and congested terrain below, within, and above cities is seen here as a set of physical spaces that limit the effectiveness of high-tech space-targeted bombs, surveillance systems, and automated, "network-centric," and "precision" weapons. The U.S. defense research agency, DIRC, for example, argues that "the urban environment negates the abilities of present U.S. military communications equipment," resulting in dead spots, noise, signal absorption, and propagation problems that severely undermine the principles and technologies of "network-centric warfare" (DIRC 1997).

The architects Misselwitz and Weizman are amongst the very small number of critical urban researchers who have addressed the ways in which urbanization undermines the technologies produced by the RMA. They conclude that, within contemporary cities,

> high-tech military equipment is easily incapacitated. Buildings mask targets and create urban canyons, which diminish the capabilities of the air force. It is hard to see into the urban battlespace; it is very difficult to communicate in it, because radio waves are often disturbed. It is hard to use precision weapons because it is difficult to obtain accurate GPS satellite locations. And it becomes more and more difficult (but not impossible) for the military to shoot indiscriminately into the city. For all these reasons, cities continue to reduce the advantages of a technologically superior force. (Misselwitz and Weizman 2003, 8)

The "urbanization of battlespace" is therefore seen by U.S. urban warfare commentators to reduce the ability of U.S. forces to fight and kill at a distance (always the preferred way because of their "casualty dread" and technological supremacy). Cities are therefore seen to produce rapidly escalated risks for U.S. forces fighting preemptive, expeditionary wars. "From refugee flows to dense urban geography, cities create environments that increase uncertainty exponentially" (DIRC 1997). Military operations in cities are therefore seen as treacherous, Trojan horse–style events which might allow weak and poorly equipped insurgents to gain victory over the world's remaining military superpower (Glenn, Steed, and Matsumara 2001).

The critical technology of Global Positioning Systems (GPS), for example—the basis for "precision" targeting, and detailed navigation and communication in the RMA—"does not work well in the urban landscape" (Dickson 2002b, 6). This "leaves soldiers blinded and their commanders ignorant of their location and situation. Communications are also severely limited in cities, isolating units from commanders, whilst slowing information flows and preventing leaders from making timely decisions" (6). In the Iraq insurgency, moreover, radios, developed for line-of-sight communications in the open areas of imagined Cold War conflicts, often failed completely within Iraq's cities, forcing the soldiers of the world's most powerful and high-tech armed forces to improvise through screaming to each other across city streets (Erwin 2004).

The "Urbanization of Insurgency": Global South Cities, U.S. Vertical Power, and the Obliteration of Urban Citizenship

> Opposition forces will camouflage themselves in the background noise of the urban environment. Within the urban environment, it is not the weapon itself rather the city which maximises or mutes an arm's effectiveness. In claustrophobic alleys and urban canyons, civilians are impossible to control or characterize as friendly or not. Weapons hidden beneath a cloak, in a child's carriage, or rolled in a carpet, can get past security personnel undetected.
>
> **DIRC (1997, 11)**

A second main feature of U.S. urban warfare discourses is that the breaking down of high-technology sensors and weapons, because of the physical morphology of cities, will directly and causally lead to an increasing tendency amongst the United States' political adversaries to take refuge within cities. "The long term trend in open-area combat," writes the leading U.S. "urban warfare" commentator, Ralph Peters (1996, 6), "is toward overhead dominance by US forces." As a result, he predicts,

> Battlefield awareness [for U.S. forces] may prove so complete, and 'precision' weapons so widely available and effective, that enemy ground-based combat systems will not be able to survive in the deserts, plains, and fields that have seen so many of history's main battles. (6)

As a result, Peters argues that the United States' "enemies will be forced into cities and other complex terrain, such as industrial developments and inter-city sprawl" (1996, 4). Grau and Kipp (1999, 4) concur, suggesting that

> urban combat is increasingly likely, since high-precision weapons threaten operational and tactical manoeuvre in open terrain. Commanders who lack sufficient high-precision weapons will find cities appealing terrain ... provided they know the city better than their opponent does and can mobilize the city's resources and population to their purposes.

Central to this perception of the incentives underlying what RAND theorists Jennifer Taw and Bruce Hoffman (2000) have termed the "urbanization of insurgency" is the notion that insurgents exploiting the physical geographies of Global South cities can force U.S. military personnel to come into very close physical proximity and so expose U.S. politicians to much higher casualty rates than stipulated within RMA doctrine. DIRC argues,

> The weapons [such insurgents] use may be 30 to 40 years old or built from hardware supplies, but at close range many of their inefficiencies are negated. The most effective weapon only needs to exploit the vulnerabilities that the urban environment creates. Each new city will create a different pool of resources and thereby create different urban threats. (DIRC 1997, 8)

Here, the obvious limits of attempting to understand the complex geographies of cities through the verticalized surveillance systems emphasized by the RMA, and the hypermilitarized paradigms of the U.S. military, are a major bone of contention amongst those promulgating the counterdiscourses emphasizing the urbanization of insurgency. A common tendency here is to naturalize and essentialize the complex physical and social geographies of Global South cities as "jungle"-like environments, in which small insurgent groups gain political and financial support from the wider population, that necessitate new techniques to ensure the "cleansing" of the city (Glenn 2002). As is very common in U.S. military and political literature on the threats of future urban insurgencies (see Norton 2003), the DIRC report emphasizes that informal and favela districts in Global South cities add great power to the strategies of insurgent and criminal groups utilizing the classic techniques of guerrilla and "asymmetric" warfare against potential U.S. or Western incursion. Civilian urban populations, where visible at all, are rendered not as bodies of urban citizens with human and political rights requiring protection. Rather, they emerge as little but physical and technical noise within an all-encompassing "battlespace"—as a set of targets to themselves be coerced, rendered passive, or manipulated through strategies ranging from "psychological operations" to military action. The DIRC report argues that

> the shanty sprawl of the developing city frequently allows insurgents to adapt their rural strategy more effectively to an urban environment. Asymmetric forces have the same benefits and advantages that have traditionally been enjoyed in the jungle of forest base: control over territory, allegiance (whether voluntary or coerced) of much of a country's population, inaccessibility to security forces. The urban environment adds reasonably secure bases for operations around the heart of government and its administrative and commercial infrastructure. . . . The urban geography of slums favors the tactics of an unconventional force. . . . Guerilla campaigns need not be overall military urban success, but rather need only to make the opposition's campaigns appear unpalatable to its domestic support. Urban warfare favors the media age. (DIRC 1997, 6)

Dreams Reclaimed? From Preemptive War to "Persistent Area Dominance"?

The time has come to change the perception that the high-tech US war machine fights at a disadvantage in urban areas.

Houlgate (2004)

Urban areas should become our preferred medium for fighting. We should optimize our force structure for it, rather than relegating it to Appendix Q in our fighting doctrine, treating it as the exception rather than the norm. . . . It is time to tell Sun Tzu to sit down. . . . Instead of fearing it, we must own the city [*sic*].

Lt. Col. Leonhard, U.S. Army (2003)

With the widespread perception that the intensifying urbanization of the parts of the Global South that the U.S. military envisage being their dominant areas of operation is radically undermining their broader efforts at technoscientific transformation, a wide range of projects and initiatives are emerging aimed at specifically tailoring the RMA to the specific geographies of urban areas in the Global South. With the urban insurgency in Iraq as an ongoing fulcrum war, a "transformation" based on the technophiliac celebrations of the death of geography through new technologies is, ironically, being transformed into a major technoscientific effort to develop and experiment with surveillance, communications, and targeting systems that are specifically tailored to the fine-grain physical and human geographies of Global South cities.

Troublingly, however, the promulgation of dreams of automation by certain key actors within the U.S. military-industrial-entertainment complex (Der Derian 2001) means that the citizenship of both urban civilians and the U.S. military personnel themselves is denied and rendered invisible. Instead, fantasies of cyborganized warfare are common. Within these, machinic agency increasingly usurps the role of U.S. military personnel (who become physically removed and insulated from the horrors of street warfare). Urban citizens, meanwhile, are usually invisible bystanders as their city is transmuted into a "battlespace" that is represented purely as a physical, three-dimensional space.

This denial of the politics of urban citizenship is replicated through the widespread use, design, and production of urban warfare video games for the training and the entertainment of U.S. forces. Within these, urban civilians are never represented; every Arab person appearing is a "terrorist" target to be attacked by U.S. forces. Thus, local, urban populations are equated with demonized, monster-like, and dehumanized "terrorists" against which only lethal military force is an option.

The inevitable presence of urban civilians is sometimes recognized in U.S. military MOUT discourses. However, they are often rendered in computerized simulations as mere software avatars—passive bystanders within wider, simulated military struggles between U.S. forces and armed insurgents. At worst, urban civilians are present only as real or potential "collateral damage"—the direct results of hypermilitarized and technologized dreams of reasserting U.S. military control through which, in Leonhard's words (above), U.S. forces learn to "own" the colonialized, Global South city through technological and military mastery.

It is now widely argued within U.S. military strategic organizations and think tanks that the RMA needs to be reconfigured to address the challenges of tightly built Global South cities; that new bodies of "urban" research need to be built up to understand how to use military violence to deliver precise "effects" in such cities; and that the doctrine, weaponry, training, and equipment of U.S. forces need to be comprehensively redesigned so that urban military operations are their de facto function. A large output of conceptual, technoscientific, and research and development material has been created by the "urban turn" of the RMA, especially since the Iraq invasion (see Grubbs 2003; Houlgate 2004). The overwhelming rhetoric in such efforts emphasizes that new military technoscience, specifically developed to address cities, will turn Global South urban environments into areas that U.S. forces can completely dominate, using their technological advantages, with minimum casualties to themselves.

The "urban" turn in the RMA is also backed up by a wide range of projects that develop physical and electronic simulations of Global South urban environments through which war games and simulated urban conflicts can be rehearsed and new doctrine, weapons, and technologies tested. A wide range of geospatial urban simulation models have been developed. These imitate the allegedly "geotypical" built environments of many of the Global South megacities that are anticipated to be the most likely environments for U.S. urban warfare interventions. Urban terrain zone models, for example, are widely created not just for the typical built form and materials of individual megacities, but also for the geographic contrasts in these between the older cores and sprawling peripheries of the cities involved (Luft 2005; see figures 2.1a and 2.1b). Such templates are then superimposed on the actual urban geographies of real Global South cities that are imagined as most likely future "battlespaces" for U.S. forces (see figure 2.2). Such simulations even model the "rubbling" and "cratering" effects of different U.S. bullets and weapons on the various building materials that are allegedly "typical" of each city and city district. (These are drawn from global construction practices databases; Tyson 2004.) Finally, a wide range of training exercises based on physical and virtual "cities"—and "hybrids" fusing both—has been undertaken to hone training, tactics, and weapons for fighting in megacity environments. These come complete with electronically simulated populations, building interiors, and vehicles, all of which can be "entered" and exploited by simulated friendly and enemy forces fighting protracted urban wars.

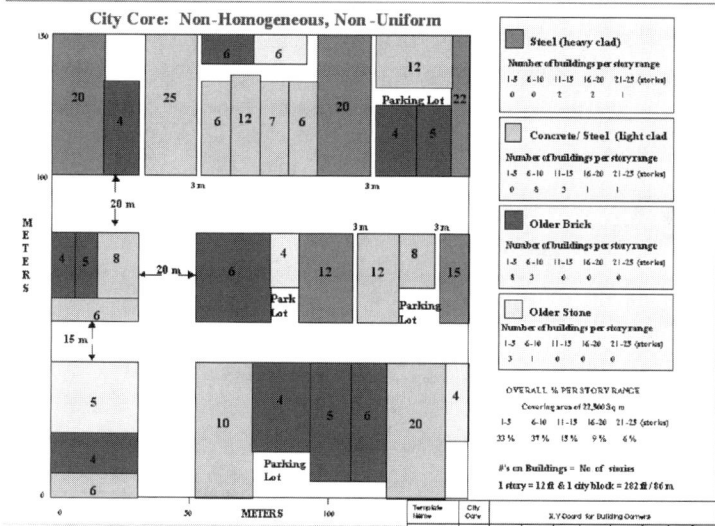

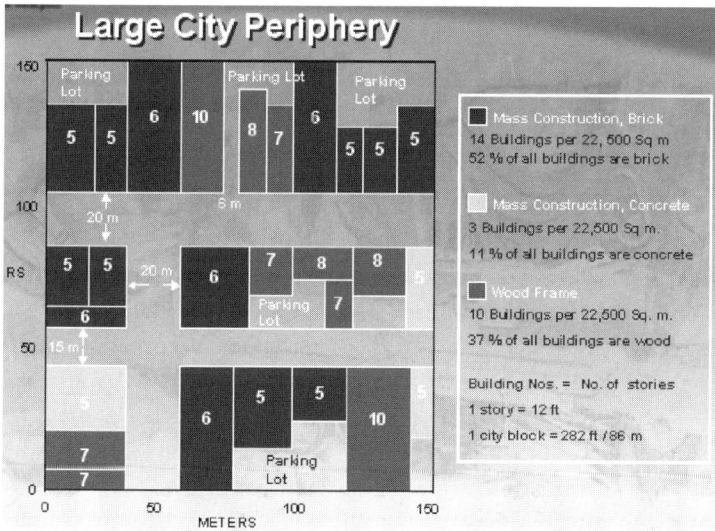

Figure 2.1 Generic "Urban Terrain Templates" for the urban form and building materials in the city core and suburbs of a generalized Global South city, which are used to predict the effectiveness of U.S. weapons systems and urban warfare tactics in Global South cities. (Luft 2005).

Figure 2.2 Urban Terrain Zone Mapping Techniques Applied to an Area of Kuwait City. (Luft 2005).

In the most important electronically simulated urban war game—named Urban Resolve—a huge swathe of eight square miles of Jakarta, the capital of Indonesia, has been carefully digitized and "geospecifically" simulated in three dimensions. This has been done down to the interior of the (1.6 million) buildings, and also involves 109,000 mobile "vehicles" and "civilians," as well as the subterranean infrastructures. The initiative is being used as the basis for a series of massive military simulations, between 2003 and 2008 (see figure 2.3). These project the city as the site of a massive urban war involving U.S. forces in 2015, complete with a range of imagined new U.S. sensors and weapons geared toward warfare in such a massive megacity (figure 2.4). The only recognition of urban citizens within this imaginative geography, however, is through their transmutation into millions of dumb software avatars within a landscape of targets. Thus, the time-space rhythms of the virtualized "Jakarta" have even been simulated, but only to add realism to the urban battlespace: "roads are quiet at night, but during weekday rush hours they become clogged with traffic. People go to work, take lunch breaks and visit restaurants, banks and churches." (Walker 2004).

In a rejoinder to those stressing the hazards to U.S. forces of being drawn into close urban warfare, Vickers and Martinage (2001, 22–23), evaluating a major series of earlier U.S. "urban war games" in the late 1990s, project a future where technophiliac dreams of vertical and electromagnetic omnipo-

Figure 2.3 Example of a Digitized "Neighborhood" in Jakarta that is animated with moving "people" and "vehicles" to provide an environment for warfare between hostile and friendly forces in 2015, as part of the ten-year "Urban Resolve" Exercises. (Budge 2005).

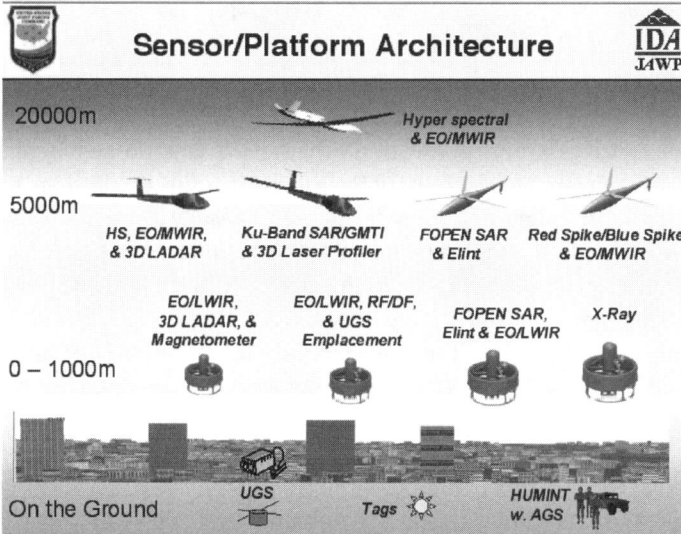

Figure 2.4 "Sensor/Platform Architecture" the as-yet undeveloped sensor platforms envisaged in Urban Resolve exercises to equip U.S. urban warfare forces in 2015. These center on a simulated war within an eight-square-mile stretch of Jakarta (note the digitized cityscape below). ELINT = electronic intelligence teams; GMTI = ground moving target indicator; HUMINT = human intelligence; LADAR = laser radar; MWIR = mid-wave infrared detectors; and UGS = unmanned ground sensors. (Budge 2005).

tence are reclaimed, even within Global South megacities. In their scenario, they excitedly predict that

> the combination of theater and local precision-strike capabilities and heightened situational awareness could potentially transform the urban battlespace from a sanctuary, in which enemy forces can easily hide, into a 'glass prison', in which they can be cut off from external support and then precisely targeted and destroyed in detail. For example, see-through-the-wall radars, micro air vehicles, and micro robots could substantially increase local-area transparency within future urban environments. . . . This is not to suggest, however, that evicting enemy units from the sprawling urban megacities of tomorrow will ever be either undemanding or swift.

New weapons and sensor programs, specifically designed to enhance the ability of future U.S. forces to control and dominate Global South cities through network-centric means, are already emerging from the wider efforts at physical and electronic simulation, war gaming, and the evaluation of the experience of the Iraq insurgency. These center, first, on unveiling Global South cities through new sensor technologies, and, second, on developing automated and robotic weapon systems linked to such sensors.

Technophiliac Unveilings of Global South Cities: Dreams
of "Real-Time Situational Awareness"

The first key effort to redirect the RMA to the purported challenges of U.S. forces attempting to dominate and control Global South cities involves programs designed to saturate such cities with myriads of networked surveillance systems. The dream of U.S. military theorists is that this can be done to such an extent that any identified target can be automatically identified at any time and so exposed to the high-technology tracking and killing powers of "network-centric" weapons. Such visions imagine pervasive and interlined arrays of "loitering" and "embedded" sensors as overcoming all the limits and interruptions that megacity environments place in the way of successfully implementing network-centric warfare. Ackerman (2002), for example, suggests that such sensor suites will be designed to automatically trace dynamic change rather than constantly soaking up data from unchanging environments: observing "change" rather than observing "scenery," as he puts it. In other words, algorithms will be designed to only function when definable changes occur. They will thus identify purported notions of "normality" against the "abnormal" behaviors and patterns that can then be assessed as targets.

One major example of such a development is the tellingly titled Combat Zones That See (CTS) project led by the U.S. Defense Advanced Research Projects Agency (DARPA). Launched at the start of the Iraq insurgency in 2003, CTS "explores concepts, develops algorithms, and delivers systems for utilising large numbers (1000s) of algorithmic video cameras to provide the close-in sensing demanded for military operations in urban terrain." Through installing computerized closed-circuit TV across whole occupied cities, the project organizers envisage that, when deployed, CTS will sustain "motion-pattern analysis across whole city scales," linked to the tracking of massive populations of individualized cars and people through intelligent computer algorithms linked to the recognition of number plates and scanned-in human facial photos. Combat Zones That See, the launch report suggests,

> will produce video understanding algorithms embedded in surveillance systems for automatically monitoring video feeds to generate, for the first time, the reconnaissance, surveillance, and targeting information needed to provide close-in, continuous, always-on support for military operations in urban terrain. (DARPA 2003, 6)

A direct response to the interruptive effects of city environments on older notions of air- and space-based network-centric warfare, it is envisaged that, once it has been developed beyond experimental technology, and deployed operationally in urban war zones, CTS will be able to specifically address the "inherently three-dimensional nature of urban centres, with large buildings, extensive underground [passageways, and concealment from above]" (DARPA 2003, 7).

The central challenge of CTS, according to DARPA, will be to build up fully representative data profiles on the "normal" time-space movement patterns of entire subject cities so that algorithms could then use statistical modeling to "determine what is normal and what is not" (quoted in Sniffen 2003). This will be a purported aid to identifying insurgents' activities and real or potential attacks, as well as warning of the presence or movement of target or suspect vehicles or individuals. The report states that the CTS project will

> include . . . analysis of changes in normalcy modes; detection of variances in activity; anomaly detection based on statistical analyses; discovery of links between places, subjects and times of activities; and direct comparison and correlation of track data to other information available to operators. Predictive modelling, plan recognition, and behavior modeling should alert operators to potential force protection risks and hostile situations. Forensic information (where did a vehicle come from, how did it get here?) should be combined and contrasted to more powerful 'forward-tracking' capabilities (where could the vehicle go? where is the vehicle going?) to allow operators to provide real-time capabilities to assess potential force threats. (DARPA 2003, 13)

After a stream of protests from U.S. civil liberties groups, DARPA stressed that, whilst the initial test of mass, urban tracking will take place at a U.S. Army

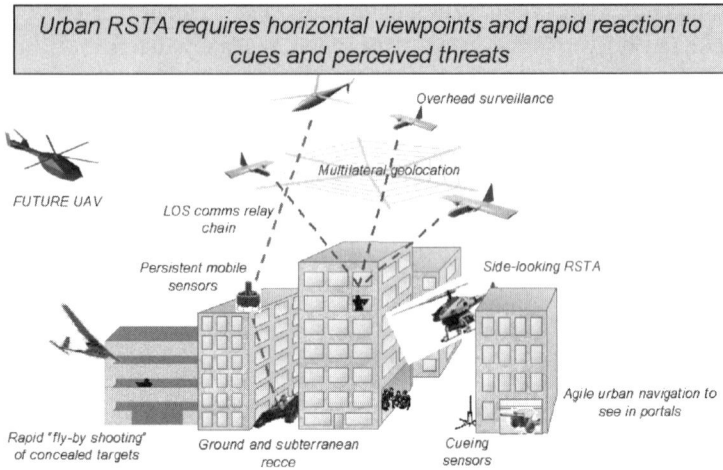

Figure 2.5 DARPA Urban Reconnaissance, Surveillance, and Target Acquisition (RSTA) Platforms as Envisaged by Its HURT Programme. (DARPA 2004). (LOS = line of sight).

base within the United States (Fort Belvoir, Virginia), the deployment of CTS will only take place in "Foreign urban battlefields" ("Combat Zones" 2004).

Saturating occupied or target cities with microscale and even nanoscale sensors and cameras is also being investigated by the CTS Program and an associated program labeled HURT (Heterogeneous Urban RSTA Team; RTSA stands for reconnaissance, surveillance, and target acquisition). Table 2.1 and Figure 2.5 show the range of "persistent" and unmanned surveillance platforms currently being considered by DARPA through its CTS and HURT Programs. General Andrew Davis already boasts that in certain urban warfare training complexes, "what you see looks like normal garbage you might see on the street—bricks, pieces of concrete, dented oil cans. What they actually are, are different types of sensors" (quoted in Book 2002).

"Persistent Area Dominance": Toward Robotic Killing Systems in Urban Warfare?

The second main area of defense research and development to help assert the dominance of U.S. forces over Global South cities focuses on a shift toward robotic air and ground weapons which, when linked to the persistent surveillance and target identification systems just discussed, will be deployed to continually and automatically destroy purported targets in potentially endless streams of automated killing. The dreams of linking sentient, automated, and omnipotent surveillance—which bring Godlike levels of "situational awareness" to U.S. forces attempting to control intrinsically devious Global South megacities—to automated machines of killing pervade the discourses of the urban turn in the RMA (see, for example, Huber and Mills 2002). A

Table 2.1 DARPA's Table of Urban Surveillance and Weapons Platforms under Development by Its Heterogeneous Urban RTSA (Reconnaissance, Surveillance and Target Acquisition) Team (HURT) Program

Platform	Payload	Range	Endurance	Sensors	Control
Raven MOUT UAV	0.4 lb	10 km	75 min	One IR or combo of down- and side-looking daylight camera.	GPS autopilot.
PUMA "urbanized" Pointer UAV	2 lb	8 km	120 min	Daylight camera housing; side-look capable.	GPS autopilot.
Matilda ground robot	125 lb	1.5 km	N/A	Modular payload	Teleoperated only.
Dragon Eye UAV	1 lb	4.0 km	60 min	Downward-looking EO/IR.	GPS autopilot.
Maverick UAV	300 lb	200 km	7 hours	Modular payload	SEC asset, variable autonomy
Silver Fox UAV	4 lb	2400 km	24 hours	Downward-looking EO/IR.	GPS autopilot.
OAV (29" version)	20 lb	50 km	90 min	EO/IR downward and slant-angle.	GPS + ?
Yamaha RMAX Autonomous	60 lb	200 km	90 min	Modular payload, inc. new stabilized sensor ball	GPS autopilot.
Predator	450 lb	5500 km	40 hr	EO/IR sensor ball plus SAR, ESM, comms, SIGINT/ELINT	Piloted or GPS waypoints
Fire Scout	200 lb	320 km	6 hrs	EO/IR sensor ball plus SAR, ESM, comms, SIGINT/ELINT	TCS

23

Source: DARPA (2004).

Note: GPS = Global Positioning System; IR = infrared; OAV = organic air vehicle; and UAV = unmanned aerial vehicle.

telling example comes from the discussion of a model near-future U.S. "urban operation," described by *Defense Watch* magazine during its discussions of DARPA's CTS Program just discussed ("Combat Zones" 2004).

In their scenario, swarms of microscale and nanoscale networked sensors pervade the target city, providing continuous streams of target information to arrays of automated weaponry. Together, these systems produce continuous killing and "target" destruction: a kind of robotized counterinsurgency operation with U.S. commanders and soldiers doing little but overseeing the cyborganized, interlinked, and increasingly automated killing systems from a safe distance. *Defense Watch* ("Combat Zones" 2004) thus speculates about "a battlefield in the near future" that is wired up with the systems which result from the CTS program and its followers. Here unbound technophiliac dreams of omnipotent urban control blur into long-standing fantasies of cyborganized and robotized warfare. "Several large fans are stationed outside the city limits of an urban target that our [*sic*] guys need to take," they begin:

Upon appropriate signal, what appears like a dust cloud emanates from each fan. The cloud is blown into town where it quickly dissipates. After a few minutes of processing by laptop-size processors, a squadron of small, disposable aircraft ascends over the city. The little drones dive into selected areas determined by the initial analysis of data transmitted by the fan-propelled swarm. Where they disperse their nano-payloads.

"After this, the processors get even more busy," continues the scenario:

Within minutes the mobile tactical center have a detailed visual and audio picture of every street and building in the entire city. Every hostile [person] has been identified and located. From this point on, nobody in the city moves without the full and complete knowledge of the mobile tactical center. As blind spots are discovered, they can quickly be covered by additional dispersal of more nano-devices. Unmanned air and ground vehicles can now be vectored directly to selected targets to take them out, one by one. Those enemy combatants clever enough to evade actually being taken out by the unmanned units can then be captured or killed by human elements who are guided directly to their locations, with full and complete knowledge of their individual fortifications and defenses.... When the dust settles on competitive bidding for BAA 03-15 [the code number for the Combat Zones That See program], and after the first prototypes are delivered several years from now, our guys are in for a mind-boggling treat at the expense of the bad guys [*sic*]. (2004)

Such omnipotence fantasies extend even further to the automated surveillance, through emerging brain-scanning techniques, of people's inner mental attitudes to any U.S. invasion. This allows "targets" deemed to be resistant to be automatically identified and destroyed:

Robotic systems push deeper into the urban area.... Behind the fighters, military police and intelligence personnel process the inhabitants, electronically reading their attitudes toward the intervention and cataloguing them into a database immediately recoverable by every fire team in the city (even individual weapons might be able to read personal signatures, firing immediately upon cueing).... Smart munitions track enemy systems and profiled individuals.... Satellites monitor the city for any air defense fires, curing immediate responses from near-space orbiting "guns." Drones track inhabitants who have been "read" as potentially hostile and "tagged." ("Combat Zones" 2004)

Such dreams of continuous, automated, and robotized urban targeting and killing are far from being limited to the realms of such futuristic speculation, however. Rather, as with the CTS program, they are fueling very real multimillion-dollar research and weapons development programs aimed at developing ground and aerial vehicles which not only navigate and move robotically, but also select and destroy targets without "humans in the loop" based on algorithmically driven "decisions."

Lawlor (2004), for example, discusses the development of "autonomous mechanized combatant" air and ground vehicles or "tactical autonomous combatants" for the U.S. Air Force. These are being designed, he notes, to use "pattern recognition" software for what he calls "time-critical targeting," that is, linking sensors very quickly to automated weapons so that fleeting "targets" both within and outside cities can be continually destroyed. Such doctrine is widely termed "compressing the kill chain" or "sensor to shooter warfare" in U.S. military parlance (Hebert 2003). The "swarming of unmanned systems" project team at U.S. Forces Joint Command Experimentation Directorate, based in Suffolk, Virginia, he states, is so advanced in such experimentation that "autonomous, networked and integrated robots may be the norm rather than the exception by 2025."

By that date, Lawlor predicts that "technologies could be developed . . . that would allow machines to sense a report of gunfire in an urban environment to within one meter, triangulating the position of the shooter and return[ing] fire within a fraction of a second," providing a completely automated weapon system devoid of human involvement. He quotes Gordon Johnson, the Unmanned Effects team leader for the U.S. Army's Project Alpha, as saying of such a system that

> if it can get within one meter, it's killed the person who's firing. So, essentially, what we're saying is that anyone who would shoot at our forces would die. Before he can drop that weapon and run, he's probably already dead. Well now, these cowards in Baghdad would have to play with blood and guts every time they shoot at one of our folks. The costs of poker went up significantly. . . . The enemy, are they going to give up blood and guts to kill machines? I'm guessing not. (Hebert 2003, 3)

Lawlor (2004, 2) predicts that such robo-war systems will "help save lives by taking humans out of harm's way." Here, tellingly, only U S forces are considered to fall within the category "human."

In addition, unmanned aerial vehicles armed with "intelligent munitions" are already being designed which will, eventually, be programmed to fire on, and kill, "targets" detected by U.S. Force's real-time surveillance grids, in a completely autonomous way. Such munitions will loiter over targets for days at a time, linked into the data links, until "targets" are detected for destruction (Kenyon 2004). A program called the Total Urban Dominance Layered System (TUDLS), for example, is currently underway to provide what Plenge (2004) describes as "long hover and loiter propulsion systems, multidiscriminant sensors and seekers, mini- and micro-air vehicles, mini-lethal and non-lethal warheads, autonomous and man-in-the loop control algorithms, and a strong interface with the [urban] battlespace in formation network."

Crucially, such munitions will be equipped with algorithms designed to separate "targets" from "nontargets" automatically. The ultimate goals, according to C. Pinney, an engineer at Raytheon, is a "kill chain solution" based on "1st look, 1st feed, 1st kill," where each armed unmanned vehicle continuously "seeks out targets on its own" (2003, 16). J. Tirpak (2001), a U.S. Air Force specialist, envisages that humans will be required to make the decisions to launch weapons at targets only "until UCAVs establish a track record of reliability in finding the right targets and employing weapons properly." Then the "machines will be trusted to do even that."

Conclusions: War, Citizenship, and Territory on an Urbanizing Planet

> The ultimate expression of sovereignty resides . . . in the power and capacity to dictate who may live and who must die.
>
> **Mbembe (2003, 11)**

The above analysis of what I call the "urban turn" in the U.S. military's Revolution in Military Affairs raises key questions about the intersections of war, territory, and citizenship in the post–Cold War world. With the catastrophic counterinsurgency war on the streets of Iraq's cities continuing as I write (March 2007), this chapter has shown that technophiliac and hypermilitarized approaches to dealing with future "urban operations" are emerging within the U.S. military complex, which seem likely to strongly shape the culture, doctrine, and technologies through which U.S. forces perceive, plan, and undertake military intervention in Global South cities in the future. These discourses, imaginations, and representations tend overwhelmingly to render whole cities as mere physical battlespaces to be controlled and dominated through high-technology means. They offer the seductive hope of removing U.S. citizens from the bloody, face-to-face struggle seen in Iraq's cities. They render urban civilians, and urban citizenship, invisible, as urban civilians are constructed as mere "bare life" (Agamben 1998) inhabiting wider urban landscape constituted entirely as collections of physical and military targets. Finally, these discourses are replete with racist and colonial omnipotence fantasies featuring automated, cyborganized warfare. In these, increasingly machinic and distanciated systems of surveillance, targeting, and killing emerge to gain complete and continuous mastery over the complex and three-dimensional landscapes of Global South megacities in the future.

We should remember, of course, that the "technological fanaticism" so palpable here has deep roots within U.S. political, popular, and military culture (Sherry 1987; Franklin 1988; Gannon 2003). As Jeremy Black (2001, 97) suggests, we therefore need to be careful to interpret the RMA, and its "urban turn," not as some quasi-rational response amongst U.S. military and political elites to changing geopolitical conditions, but, rather, as "symptomatic of a set of cultural and political assumptions that tell us more about modern western society than they do about any objective assessment of military options."

The discourses sustaining this particular imagination of future U.S. military "urban operations" must be analyzed with caution. Many in the U.S. military themselves, especially the U.S. Army, are deeply skeptical as to whether such technophiliac dreams of omnipotence, through some urbanized "RMA" or "network-centric warfare," are realistic, even in narrow, military terms. The relatively high casualty rates of U.S. forces—forced to come down from forty thousand feet, or withdraw from ceramic armor, to attempt to control and "pacify" violent insurgencies within sprawling Iraqi cities after the initial U.S. "victory"—are a testament to the dangerous wishful thinking that pervades all military fantasies of "clean," "automated" "battlespace" replete with "posthuman" cyborg warriors and their unfortunate victims (Graham 2004b; Gray 2003).

Nevertheless, while bearing such caveats in mind, the sheer research and development resources currently being devoted to pursuing dreams of automated urban war mean that military strategies and systems are being developed which might offer U.S. commanders the fantasy of undertaking continuous, robotized, counterinsurgency warfare in Global South cities in the medium-term future. The clear risk here is that discourses purporting to emphasize the biopolitical rights of U.S. soldiers to be withdrawn from the streets of urban war zones might add justification to the deployment of automated killing systems, which bring urban civilians in the Global South into the crosshairs of an aggressive colonial hegemon seduced by fantasies of cyborganized war. More troubling still, such dreams of automated urban war might combine with a political desire amongst U.S. political elites to try to project continuous power across wide swathes of our urbanizing planet whilst simultaneously exploiting U.S. dominance in high technology to be seen to be moving U.S. military personnel out of harm's way. With continuous, colonial aggression still being legitimized by influential neoconservative geopolitical and military commentators, as a means of using forced neoliberal globalization to try to violently transform purportedly recalcitrant Middle Eastern and Global South societies, activism and critical social science must work urgently to expose and contest the urban turn in the RMA (see Barnett 2004, 2005). A basic starting point is to deny the reduction of Global South cities to physical, uninhabited spaces whose very geographies are essentialized as a geopolitical risk to the verticalized power of the U.S. military, for these discourses directly lead to the dehumanization of the citizens of these cities within the hyper-militarized rhetoric that dominates the U.S. military, a process which, in turn, renders their lives, deaths, and citizenship of no account.

Acknowledgments

Thanks to the British Academy for the support which made this research possible. *Note*: Some of the arguments in this chapter draw from material in a chapter published in Lyon, D. (2006), *Theorizing Surveillance*.

References

Ackerman, R. 2002. Persistent surveillance comes into view. *Signal*. http://www.afcea. org/signal/ (accessed February 2005).

Agamben, G. 1998. *Homo sacer: Sovereign power and bare life*. Stanford, CA: Stanford University Press.

Arquilla, J., and D. Ronfeldt, eds. 2001. *Networks and netwars*. Santa Monica, CA: RAND.

Barnett, T. 2004. *The Pentagon's new map: War and peace in the 21st century*. New York: Putnam.

———. 2005. *Blueprint for action*. New York: G.P. Putnam.

Barocas, S. 2002. 9-11: A strategic ontology: Pre-emptive strike and the production of (in)security. *InfoTechWarPeace*, August 6. http://www.watsoninstitute.org/info-peace/ (accessed March 2005).

Black, J. 2001. *War*. London: Continuum.

Book, E. 2002. Project metropolis brings urban wars to US Cities. *National Defense*, April. http://www.findarticles.com/p/articles/mi_go2148/is_200204/ai_n6918069 (accessed February 2005).

Budge, F. 2005. Urban Resolve experiment update: Joint Urban operations human-in-the-loop experiment. Phase 1 report. Washington, DC: U.S. Joint Forces Command.

Cohen, E. 2004. Change and transformation in military affairs. *Journal of Strategic Studies* 27 (3): 395–407.

Combat zones that "see" everything. 2004. *Defense Watch*. http://www.argee. net/DefenseWatch/Combat%20Zones%20that%20'See'%20Everything.htm (accessed March 2005).

DARPA. 2003. *Combat Zones That See program: Proper information*. http://www. darpa.mil/baa/baa03-15.htm (accessed February 2005).

———. 2004. *HURT: Heterogeneous Urban RSTA Team, briefing to industry*. Washington, DC: DARPA.

Davis, M. 2004a. The urbanization of empire: Megacities and the laws of chaos. *Social Text* 22 (4): 9–15.

———. 2004b. The Pentagon as global slum lord. *TomDispatch*, April 19. http://www. tomdispatch.com (accessed June 10, 2004).

Defense Intelligence Reference Document (DIRC). 1997. *The urban century: Developing world urban trends and possible factors affecting military operations*. Quantico, VA: Marine Corps Intelligence Agency.

Der Derian, J. 2001. *Virtuous war: Mapping the military-industrial-media-entertainment complex*. Boulder, CO: Westview.

Dickson, K. 2002a. The war on terror: Cities as the strategic high ground. Mimeo. Joint Forces Staff College, Norfolk, Virginia.

———. 2002b. Future war as urban war: How asymmetric strategies will affects cities. Mimeo. Joint Forces Staff College, Norfolk, Virginia.

Duffield, Mark. 2002. War as a network enterprise: The new security terrain and its implications. *Cultural Values* 6:153–165.

Ek, R. 2000. A revolution in military geopolitics? *Political Geography* 19:841–874.

Erwin, S. 2004. Urban battles highlight shortfalls in soldier communication. *National Defense*, September. http://www.nationaldefensemagazine.org/issues/2004/Sep/Urban_Battles.htm (accessed March 2005).

Franklin, H. B. 1988. *War stars: The superweapon and the American imagination.* Oxford: Oxford University Press.

Gannon, C. 2003. *Rumors of war and infernal machines: Technomilitary agenda-setting in American and British speculative fiction.* Liverpool, UK: Liverpool University Press.

Glenn, R. 2002. Cleanse the polluted urban seas, Rand, Summer. http://www.rand.org/publications/randreview/issues/rr.08.02/urbanseas.html.

Glenn, R., R. Steed, and J. Matsumara, eds. 2001. *Corralling the Trojan Horse: A proposal for improving U.S. urban operations preparedness in the period, 2000–2025.* Santa Monica, CA. RAND.

Graham, S. 2003. Lessons in urbicide. *New Left Review* 19 (January–February): 63–78.

———. 2004a. Vertical geopolitics: Baghdad and after. *Antipode* 36 (1): 12–19.

———. 2004b. Cities and the "war on terror." *International Journal of Urban and Regional Research* 30 (2): 255–76.

———. 2005. Switching cities off: Urban infrastructure and US air power. *City* 9 (2): 170–92.

Grau, L., and J. Kipp. 1999. Urban combat: Confronting the spectre. *Military Review* 89 (4): 9–17.

Gray, C. 2003. Posthuman soldiers and postmodern war. *Body and Society* 9 (4): 215–26.

Gregory, D. 2004. *The colonial present.* Oxford: Blackwell.

Grubbs, L. 2003. *In search of a joint urban operational concept.* Fort Leavenworth, KS: Advanced Military Studies.

Harris, David. 2003. Support to the Warfighter: Fort Lewis gets major urban warfare site. http://www.hq.usace.army.mil/cepa/pubs/jan03/story16.htm.

Hebert, Adam. 2003. Compressing the kill chain. *Air Force Magazine*, March, 34–42.

Hewish, M., and R. Pengelley. 2001. Facing urban inevitabilities: Military operations in urban terrain. *Jane's International Defence Review*, August, 13–18.

Hills, A. 2004. *Future wars in cities.* London: Frank Cass.

Houlgate, K. 2004. Urban warfare transforms the corps. *Naval Institute Proceedings*, November. http://www.military.com/NewContent/0,13190,NI_1104_Urban-P1,00.html (accessed February 2005).

Huber, Peter, and Mark Mills. 2002. How technology will defeat terrorism. *City Journal* 12:24–34.

Kenyon, H. 2004. Connectivity, persistent surveillance model future combat. *Signal*, February. http://www.afcea.org/signal/ (accessed February 2005).

Kirsch, S. 2003. Empire and the Bush doctrine. *Environment and Planning D: Society and Space* 21:1–6.

Lawlor, M. 2004. Robotic concepts take shape. *Signal*, February. http://www.afcea.org/signal/ (accessed February 2005).

Leonhard, R. 2003. Sun Tzu's bad advice: Urban warfare in the information age. *Army Magazine*, April. http://www.ausa.org/www/armymag.nsf/0/AA1C74DA9302525585256CEF005EED3D?OpenDocument (accessed February 2005).

Luft, K. 2005. Urban terrain zone co-ordination project. Washington, DC: U.S. Army Combat Support Team.

Lyon, D., ed. 2006. *Theorizing surveillance. The Panopticon and beyond.* Cullompton, UK: Willan.

Mbembe, A. 2003. Necropolitics. *Public Culture* 15 (1): 11–40.

Misselwitz, P., and E. Weizman. 2003. Military operations as urban planning. In *Territories*, ed. A. Franke, 272–75. Berlin: KW Institute for Contemporary Art.

Norton, R. 2003. Feral cities. *Naval War College Review* 56 (4): 97–106.

O'Mara, R. 2003. Stealth, precision, and the making of American foreign policy. *Air and Space Power Chronicles*, June. http://www.airpower.maxwell.af.mil/airchronicles/cc/omara.html (accessed February 2005).

Peters, R. 1996. Our soldiers, their cities. *Parameters* (Spring): 1–7.

Pieterse, J. 2004. Neoliberal empire. *Theory, Culture and Society* 21 (3): 118–40.

Pinney, C. 2003. *UAV weaponization.* Washington, DC: Raytheon.

Plenge, B. 2004. Area dominance: Area dominance with air-delivered loitering munitions aids the warfighter. http://www.afrlhorizons.com/briefs/apr04/mn0308.html.

Project for the New American Century. 2000. *Rebuilding America's defenses.* Washington, DC: Project for the New American Century.

Roberts, M., A. Secor, and M. Sparke. 2004. Neoliberal geopolitics. *Antipode* 35 (5): 886–97.

Sherry, M. 1987. *The rise of American air power: The creation of Armageddon.* New Haven, CT: Yale University Press.

Sniffen, M. 2003. Pentagon project could keep a close eye on cities. *Philly.com.* http://www.philly.com (accessed February 2005).

Stone, J. 2004. Politics, technology and the revolution in military affairs. *Journal of Strategic Studies* 27 (3): 408–27.

Taw, J., and B. Hoffman. 2000. *The urbanization of insurgency.* Santa Monica, CA: RAND.

Tirpak, J. 2001. Heavyweight contender. *Air Force Magazine* 85 (7): http://www.afa.org/magazine/July2002/ (accessed August 15, 2005).

Tyson, A. 2004. US tests new tactics in urban warfare. *Christian Science Monitor.* http://www.csmonitor.com (accessed February 2005).

Vickers, M., and R. Martinage. 2001. *Future warfare 20XX Wargame series: Lessons learned report.* Washington, DC: U.S. Government Center for Strategic and Budgetary Assessment.

Walker, R. 2004. Urban resolve. *Small Wars Journal.* http://www.smallwarsjournal.com/blog.htm/UrbanResolve (accessed August 14, 2005).

3

Spaces of Exception and Unexceptionability

MATTHEW G. HANNAH

The writings of the Italian philosopher Giorgio Agamben have become, rather suddenly, one of the obligatory references for critical academic interpretations of U.S.-dominated geopolitics since September 11, 2001. The reason is not difficult to discern. Agamben's analyses of politics focus on fundamental philosophical questions and unfold chiefly by way of close commentary on ancient and modern legal and constitutional doctrines. Nevertheless, his account of the primordial basis of state sovereignty seems to have found perfect illustrations in the blinkered, bound, and orange-clad "enemy combatants" held at Guantánamo Bay; the hooded victims of the torture filmed at Abu Ghraib prison in Iraq; and the mysterious unidentified captives moved by "extraordinary rendition" to CIA-run "black sites" for interrogation. These prisoners are examples of what Agamben, drawing on ancient Roman jurisprudence, calls *homo sacer*, or, following Walter Benjamin, "bare life," that is, people who have been subjected to the sovereign "ban," individuals "set outside human jurisdiction without being brought into the realm of divine law" (Agamben 1998, 82). As such they not only represent violations of international law, as has often been remarked since 9/11, but also, much more fundamentally, *embody and reveal what Agamben, writing before the attacks, had theorized as an absolutely fundamental keystone of modern political life.*

For all its allusiveness and abstraction, Agamben's account of the structure of sovereignty does indeed offer useful insights into the current geopolitical situation. But I argue that the explanation he gives for how and why there can be places like the war prison at Guantánamo Bay needs to be situated in a more complete geographical context. Once this is done, the "origins" of political sovereignty turn out themselves to have very specific geographical prerequisites, which may or may not be fulfilled in any particular case. While the argument here does not refute Agamben's theorization, it does complicate the genealogy of sovereignty by linking it more explicitly with the problematic of territorial control. I start with a gloss of Agamben's account of sovereignty,[1] explaining such terms as *homo sacer* and "state of exception" in more detail, and point to the geographical questions left unanswered by his narrative. The importance of these questions is then highlighted with reference to the struggle between the left-wing extremist Red Army Fraction (RAF, also known as the Baader-Meinhof Gang) and the West German state in the late 1970s. The final section systematizes the insights turned up along the way, with a view to supplementing Agamben's argument, and explores some of the possible implications for the concepts of "citizenship" and "war."

Agamben: Sovereign Power and Bare Life

Agamben begins his most important study, *Homo Sacer: Sovereign Power and Bare Life*, by taking up threads of Michel Foucault's arguments regarding the centrality of biological life in modern politics (Agamben 1998, 3–12). Agamben credits Foucault with having recognized that "a society's 'threshold of biological modernity' is situated at the point at which the species and the individual as a simple living body become what is at stake in a society's political strategies" (Agamben 1998, 3). But in his consistent practice of preferring not to think about power in the juridical and institutional categories common to traditional theories of sovereignty, Foucault had (according to Agamben) hesitated to extend his analysis of the politics of life to encompass such phenomena as the Holocaust. In his last years, Foucault began to recognize the need to bring issues of sovereignty back into his account of modern power relations. But his death in 1984 cut short his pursuit of the promising insight that techniques of subjective individualization and procedures of objective totalization have been integrated to an unprecedented degree by modern Western states. Agamben homes in on precisely this "vanishing point" of the "different perspectival lines of Foucault's inquiry," and asks, "What is the point at which the voluntary servitude of individuals comes into contact with objective power?" (Agamben 1998, 6). His conclusions, as previewed at the beginning of the book, bear extended quotation because in this form they also help explain how Agamben's writings can seem both timeless and contemporary:

> What this work has to record among its likely conclusions is precisely that the two analyses [which Foucault had held apart, namely, of biopolitics and of sovereignty] cannot be separated, and that the inclusion of bare life in the political realm constitutes the original—if concealed—nucleus of sovereign power. *It can even be said that the production of a biopolitical body is the original activity of sovereign power....* Placing biological life at the center of its calculations, the modern State therefore does nothing other than bring to light the secret tie uniting power and bare life, thereby reaffirming the bond (derived from a tenacious correspondence between the modern and the archaic which one encounters in the most diverse spheres) between modern power and the most immemorial of *arcana imperii*. (Agamben 1998, 6, emphasis in original)[2]

State of Exception

In what sense is the politicization of "bare life" constitutive of sovereign power? Drawing on Carl Schmitt, Hannah Arendt, Walter Benjamin, Alain Badiou, and a range of classical sources, Agamben argues that sovereignty is a paradoxical concept because the sovereign "is, at the same time, outside and inside the juridical order.... [T]he sovereign, having the legal power to suspend the validity of the law, legally places himself outside the law" (Agamben 1998, 15). Agamben explains this suspension by means of the term "state of exception" taken from the German political philosopher Carl Schmitt. A passage from Schmitt's ([1922] 1990) *Politische Theologie* already clearly suggests what Agamben means when he says that biopower and sovereignty are inextricable:

> The exception appears in its absolute form when it is a question of creating a situation in which juridical rules can be valid. Every general rule demands a regular, everyday frame of life to which it can be factually applied and which is submitted to its regulations. The rule requires a homogeneous medium. This factual regularity is not merely an "external presupposition" that the jurist can ignore; it belongs, rather, to the rule's immanent validity. There is no rule that is applicable to chaos. Order must be established for juridical order to make sense. A regular situation must be created, and sovereign is he who definitely decides if this situation is actually effective. All law is "situational law." The sovereign creates and guarantees the situation as a whole in its totality. (Schmitt [1922] 1990, quoted in Agamben 1998, 16)

If we read "regular, everyday frame of life" as the realm of biopolitics, and Schmitt's distinction between "order" and "juridical order" as distinguishing biopolitics from legality, Schmitt can be taken to argue here that sovereignty is the ability of the sovereign to step outside the law in order to (re)establish the biopolitical regularity or normalcy of life necessary for law itself, the juridical order, to function. In *Homo Sacer* Agamben is keen to draw attention to what he calls the "topology" of this relation of exception.

> [T]he most proper characteristic of the exception is that what is excluded in it is not, on account of being excluded, absolutely without relation to the rule.... *The rule applies to the exception in no longer applying, in withdrawing from it.* The state of exception is thus not the chaos that precedes order but rather the situation that results from its suspension. In this sense, the exception is truly, according to its etymological root, *taken outside (ex capere)*, and not simply excluded.... Here what is outside is included not simply by means of an interdiction or an internment, but rather by means of the suspension of the juridical order's validity— by letting the juridical order, that is, withdraw from the exception and abandon it. The exception does not subtract itself from the rule; rather,

the rule, suspending itself, gives rise to the exception and, maintaining itself in relation to the exception, first constitutes itself as a rule. (Agamben 1998, 17–18, emphasis in original)

This peculiar enfolding of what is outside the rule thus "traces a threshold" between inside and outside, and makes the relation of exception "unlocalizable" (Agamben 1998, 19–20). The state of exception is

thus not so much a spatiotemporal suspension as a complex topological figure in which not only the exception and the rule but also the state of nature and law, outside and inside, pass through one another. It is precisely this topological zone of indistinction, which had to remain hidden from the eyes of justice, that we must try to fix under our gaze. (Agamben 1998, 37)

It is already possible to see why such a reading of sovereignty would seem intensely relevant to post-9/11 geopolitics. In a follow-up volume published in 2005, Agamben makes the connection explicit:

The immediately biopolitical significance of the state of exception as the original structure in which law encompasses living beings by means of its own suspension emerges clearly in the "military order" issued by the President of the United States on November 13, 2001, which authorized the "indefinite detention" and trial by "military commissions" (not to be confused with the military tribunals provided for by the law of war) of noncitizens suspected of involvement in terrorist activities. (Agamben 2005, 3)

Homo Sacer

These "enemy combatants" are a modern illustration of the other side of Agamben's account of sovereignty. They embody with unprecedented clarity the fact that the sovereign's ability to decide on the state of exception and to act exceptionally presupposes the existence of a sort of "equal and opposite" figure, the person *subject to and vulnerable to the sovereign's extralegal, exceptional actions*. If the sovereign's actions are to be effective in creating or restoring biopolitical order, there must be embodied people vulnerable to becoming objects of these actions. And embodiment is crucial: their fundamental exposure to sovereign actions outside the law is of a direct, biological character. For Agamben, this biological vulnerability is crystallized in the ability to be killed. The sovereign's ability to move outside the law in deciding on the state of exception is inherently and at the same time the rendering biologically vulnerable of human life. Human life understood in its basic biological vulnerability to sovereign power is traced by Agamben to the Roman juridical concept of *homo sacer*, or "sacred life":

The political sphere of sovereignty . . . takes the form of a zone of indistinction between sacrifice and homicide. *The sovereign sphere is the sphere in which it is permitted to kill without committing homicide and without celebrating a sacrifice, and sacred life—that is, life that may be killed but not sacrificed—is the life that has been captured in this sphere.* (Agamben 1998, 83, emphasis in original)

This sphere marked by the possibility of an unnatural death that is neither a punishable crime nor a religious sacrifice is the sphere of the political. "The sovereign is the one with respect to whom all men are potentially *homines sacri*, and *homo sacer* is the one with respect to whom all men act as sovereigns" (Agamben 1998, 84). Juridical order, the "rule of law," can obtain only in a society whose members could be killed extralegally by the sovereign if their deaths were necessary to reestablish the basis for the rule of law. As Agamben put it in a 1994 essay, absolute sovereign power is founded on "naked life, which is kept safe and protected only to the degree to which it submits itself to the sovereign's (or the law's) right of life and death" (Agamben [1994] 2000, 5).

History and Geography of Sovereignty

Agamben's historical argument about what distinguishes modern sovereignty from earlier forms is quite complex, but it can be summarized without too much simplification in a series of propositions:

1. The peculiar relation of exception has been at the root of political order throughout human history (Agamben 1998, 36).
2. Only in the modern age, however, does it come "more and more to the foreground as the fundamental political structure and ultimately begins to become the rule" (Agamben 1998, 20; cf. 148).
3. As the locus of sovereignty has devolved from the body of the king to the nation, and in democratic societies, to every individual, so, too, has the condition of bare life been "shattered" and "disseminated" into every individual. Thus, every modern citizen is invested both with a part of sovereignty and with a basic vulnerability to state power (Agamben 1998, 124). "Bare life is no longer confined to a particular place or a definite category. It now dwells in the biological body of every living being" (140).
4. Yet the very politicization of life that this complex of changes has brought about requires repeated decisions "concerning the threshold beyond which life ceases to be politically relevant, becomes only 'sacred life,' and can as such be eliminated without punishment" (Agamben 1998, 139). Euthanasia movements of the early twentieth century were but a particularly obvious expression of this ongoing compulsion to draw a line of exclusion. In other words, while

everyone is now potentially *homo sacer*, every social order only "activates" this potentiality for some specific groups or individuals.

Crucially for the argument of this chapter, Agamben's historical account has a geographical dimension. As his remarks on the topology of the exception suggest, the zone of abandonment into which *homo sacer* is thrown is "unlocalizable," that is, it cannot be equated in any simple way with a concrete location. However, an important watershed in the genealogy of sovereignty was reached most infamously by the Nazis:

> When our age tried to grant the unlocalizable a permanent and visible location, the result was the concentration camp. The camp—and not the prison—is the space that corresponds to this originary structure of the *nomos*. (Agamben 1998, 20)

> [T]he camp—as the pure, absolute, and impassable biopolitical space (insofar as it is founded solely on the state of exception)—will appear as the hidden paradigm of the political space of modernity, whose metamorphoses and disguises we will have to learn to recognize. (Agamben 1998, 123)

In a key passage toward the end of his book, Agamben draws conclusions from the camps of the Holocaust that are directly relevant to the current geopolitical conjuncture:

> Insofar as its inhabitants were stripped of every political status and wholly reduced to bare life, the camp was also the most absolute biopolitical space ever to have been realized, in which power confronts nothing but pure life, without any mediation. This is why the camp is the very paradigm of political space at the point at which politics becomes biopolitics and *homo sacer* is virtually confused with the citizen. The correct question to pose concerning the horrors committed in the camps is, therefore, not the hypocritical one of how crimes of such atrocity could be committed against human beings. It would be more honest, and above all, more useful to investigate carefully the juridical procedures and deployments of power by which human beings could be so completely deprived of their rights and prerogatives that no act committed against them could appear any longer as a crime. (Agamben 1998, 171)

A lingering geographical question and a case study

To anticipate the argument below, these "procedures and deployments of power by which human beings could be so completely deprived of their rights and prerogatives" are not merely "juridical" in character; to an important extent, they are a matter of concrete territorial control. Here I attempt to move from abstract formulations to issues of empirical application by specifying these geographical procedures and deployments as carefully as possible. In particular, I focus on Agamben's claim that in the modern age we have all become, virtually, *homines sacri*. To put the question as bluntly as possible, what are the geographical presuppositions of our purported vulnerability, and how universally can they be said to apply? Guantánamo Bay may represent a space of exception into which captives are placed, but before they can be placed there, they must be captured. This requires not only that sovereign power be able to dominate life *within* the walls of the camp but also, if it is to be able to find bodies to put there in the first place, that it have a very basic level of access to and control over the territory *outside* the walls of the camp. Insofar as biological vulnerability to sovereign power has become a general condition we all share, whole populations must be geographically within effective reach of sovereign force. What makes this accessibility possible?

To illustrate the importance of this question, and to link Agamben's theorization of sovereignty more concretely with issues of territorial control, it is helpful to consider a specific case in which the sovereign ability to capture individuals, taken for granted by Agamben, was not immediately established. The struggle between the Red Army Fraction (RAF) and the West German security forces during the late 1970s has many parallels with the geopolitics of the post-9/11 world and the Bush administration's "War on Terror." There are also many differences, of course, such as the transnational scale of the twenty-first-century conflict, and the fact that prisoners taken by the West German government in the mid-1970s had actually taken part in violent attacks against the state order, whereas most of those held indefinitely by the U.S. government have no known connection to violent attacks. But the similarities are very suggestive. In both instances there are notorious spaces of exception, legal "black holes" in which captives are denied the basic rights granted to normal citizens and to other prisoners. The West German counterpart to Guantánamo Bay was Stammheim prison, a purpose-built maximum security tract near Stuttgart into which most of the RAF members held by the government were eventually put. In Stammheim, normal regulations regarding maximum time in isolation, rules of socializing, and other basic bodily and psychological needs were suspended or at least rendered situational (Schiller 2001, 164). The legal proceedings brought against the RAF captives likewise stripped them of most of the normal protections afforded accused persons, for example, the right to be present to face charges and the confidentiality of consultations with attorneys (the latter because it was widely believed that the prisoners used their attorneys to communicate with RAF cells still at large; Aust 1998, 337–482). A key parallel between the West German conflict and the current "War on Terror" is that the state was not immediately able to capture its quarry, and key figures remained at large for years. One danger of viewing the Bush administration's "War on Terror" through Agambenian lenses is that the compelling logical symmetry between the sovereign decision on the state of exception and the figure of captive *homo sacer* tends to obscure the continuing failure to capture Osama bin Laden and other important al Qaeda operatives. And this is not merely a product of the international scale of the al Qaeda network. The value of the West German case is that it shows how such a failure could also be registered *within* the boundaries of the modern Western nation-state. In the 1970s, as in the 2000s, the plight of those who were captured tended to distract attention from the fact that many remained at large.

The RAF was formed out of the splintering of the West German antiauthoritarian movements of the late 1960s, and eventually became the most notorious among a range of leftist groups willing to use deadly violence. The membership of these groups was numerically tiny compared with the numbers active in the nonviolent peace, antinuclear, environmental, and women's movements that also evolved during the 1970s. But their headline-making attacks, and widespread outrage at the way RAF members were treated by the government once captured, ensured that they would continue to occupy a prominent place in public awareness. According to its public statements and the testimony of surviving members, the RAF understood itself originally as an "urban guerrilla" organization dedicated to bringing the fight against West German involvement in U.S.-led imperialism "back home" to the metropolitan core. As Irmgard Möller put it in an interview, "We wanted to make it clear that there is no calm hinterland anywhere in the world for these crimes" (Möller and Tolmein 1999, 65). Although making use of Marxist concepts, the primary ideological inspiration for the RAF came from Third World liberation movements and their theorists (the Vietnamese National Liberation Front, Frantz Fanon, Che Guevara, and the Uruguayan Tupamaros; Aust 1998, 96). RAF attacks were focused chiefly on symbols and representatives of globalizing capitalism and U.S.-led Cold War militarism, such as U.S. military bases in West Germany. After the "first-generation" RAF leaders were apprehended and had begun to serve time through the mid-1970s, these goals came to take a back seat to the plight of the imprisoned leaders. (See Aust [1998] for an exhaustive chronicle of the RAF.)

Of central importance here is the fact that, as with the U.S. failure to locate bin Laden, the West German government was not able immediately to seize its foes. Almost two and a half years elapsed between the founding illegal action of the RAF's first generation in January 1970 and the capture of Andreas Baader, Gudrun Ensslin, Ulrike Meinhof, Holger Meins, Jan-Carl Raspe, and Gerhard Müller in the summer of 1972. Over the subsequent five years, while these RAF leaders battled constantly with the legal system and the appalling conditions under which they were imprisoned, a "second generation" of RAF carried out a series of bombings and killings. In the early autumn of 1977, this campaign of violence culminated in the assassination of Chief Federal Prosecutor Siegfried Buback; the killing, during an aborted kidnap attempt, of Jürgen Ponto, head of the Dresdner Bank; and finally, the coordinated kidnapping of Hans-Martin Schleyer, head of the West German Industrial Council, and hijacking (in cooperation with the Palestinian Liberation Organization) of a Lufthansa flight. These actions of what came to be known as the "German Autumn" were directed at forcing the government of Chancellor Helmut Schmidt to release Baader, Ensslin, and the other surviving RAF leaders (Ulrike Meinhof and Holger Meins were already dead, Meinhof by an apparent suicide, and Meins as the result of a hunger strike). The morning after the hijacking failed, Baader, Ensslin, and Raspe were found dead in their cells at Stammheim, and Irmgard Möller gravely injured, all apparently successful or attempted suicides. Shortly thereafter, Hans-Martin Schleyer was killed. During this whole five-year period, and in some cases for a further three years, RAF operatives as well as members of a number of other left extremist groups remained at large despite continuous efforts by security agencies to hunt them down.

In terms of Agamben's analysis, although spaces of exception stood ready to receive them, these RAF members were able to avoid the status of *homo sacer*. They were able to remain *unexceptionable* for quite some time. The price they had to pay to remain physically free was high, especially for Ulrike Meinhof, who gave up both a celebrated career as a critical journalist and her two children, whom she tried (unsuccessfully) to have sent to the Middle East to be brought up by Palestinian militants (Aust 1998, 104, 110, 134–36). RAF militants were unable to lead anything approaching "normal" lives, which tends rather to confirm than to deny Agamben's claim that our physical vulnerability is basic to modern sovereignty. But the arrangements the RAF operatives made that enabled them to elude the state for a time can help give more concrete geographical contours to this vulnerability.

The unexceptionable spaces of the RAF

The West German state would only be successful in its attempts to stop the RAF if it possessed *knowledge* about where RAF members were and *physical access* to those locations. Within the borders of the Federal Republic, access was rarely an issue: the security services could and did use force to enter whatever public or private spaces they believed harbored militants. Insofar as pursuit of the RAF crossed national boundaries, access became a more complicated matter, as it has more recently in the case of the U.S. "War on Terror." The focus here, however, is on domestic territory. The meaning of sovereignty on the international stage is of course complex, but highlighting this fact is less useful if the point is (as it is here) to show that Agamben's theorization of sovereignty *must* take into account concrete geographical conditions. Demonstrating that this is true at the international scale is easy enough, but such a demonstration would fail to establish the *inescapability* of geographical questions for Agamben. My argument will be stronger if it can be shown that, even in the domestic territorial context of the classic nation-state, there are geographical limits to the population's vulnerability as virtual *homines sacri*.

In the domestic West German context, then, the key issue was not physical access but knowledge, and the unexceptionable spaces the RAF was able to link together were beyond the reach of the state chiefly because their locations were unknown: they were spaces of anonymity. Together these spaces, described below, formed an articulated system composed of elements of both private and public spheres.

"Conspiratorial Apartments" (Konspirative Wohnungen)

These were the core of the system of unexceptionable spaces, the hideouts in which underground RAF members planned actions and laid low once actions were carried out. Irmgard Möller recalls the paramount value of these hideouts:

> The most dangerous thing was not movement in everyday life but that they [the security services] would happen upon an apartment by chance, by betrayal, or via a dragnet search and then sit there and wait until someone returned. That was always our nightmare. The capture of Tommy Weisbecker, Manfred Grashof and Rolf Heißler happened that way, the killing of Elisabeth von Dyck. (Möller and Tolmein 1999, 45)

In the early 1970s, before Baader, Meinhof, and the other first-generation RAF members were apprehended, these apartments were usually acquired or borrowed through friends and acquaintances from pre-RAF days rather than through political comrades. Ulrike Meinhof, through her many connections, was able to provide housing on numerous occasions (Aust 1998, 160, 195). Margrit Schiller describes one of these early hideouts in her memoirs:

> The apartment looked like all RAF apartments: a couple of foam mattresses and covers, a telephone, two radios, a few suitcases and bags, tools, weapons, ammunition, explosives. The windows were hung with fabrics and had viewing slits through which one could see the street in front of the apartment house. (Schiller 2001, 12)

Experience would later lead the kidnappers of Hans-Martin Schleyer to improve on this layout by making sure the front room of the apartment they had rented was furnished in typical bourgeois style, so that any neighbors or delivery workers who happened to glance through the open door would see nothing unusual (Aust 1998, 490).

The acquisition and the geographical situation of conspiratorial apartments followed a pattern not missed by the Bundeskriminalamt (BKA, the West German equivalent of the FBI in the United States): security deposits, rent, and electricity were all paid in cash; and the apartments were always in high-rise buildings with underground garages, located near autobahn access ramps (Aust 1998, 488). The cash payments of course maintained anonymity, as did the microcultures of the high-rise buildings themselves (Schiller 2001, 46). The underground garages made it easier to switch and hide automobiles used to escape from the scene of bombings and of the robberies through which the RAF funded some of its activities.

Transportation and Communication

As the need for automobiles indicates, the RAF could not avoid making use of public spaces and infrastructures such as roads, railways, and telephone lines. With the ubiquitous wanted posters and the sustained manhunt of the security services, militants could not count on the ability to make use of these systems unobserved. Thus a range of additional precautions was necessary, many of them familiar from espionage and organized crime literature and cinema: use of public phones in crowded spaces, bank robberies to fund operations, car theft and the falsification of license plates and serial numbers, travel by train whenever possible, and a preference for leaving hideouts only at night to make recognition more difficult. These actions needed to be carried out with meticulous attention to geographical detail. Margrit Schiller describes the conditions necessary for a successful auto theft: the autos

> had to be parked in semi-darkness. There could not be apartment buildings in the vicinity from which the theft could be observed, and also no police stations from which the police could reach the scene of the crime quickly in the event of an alarm. In addition, one had to observe at which times in the night the patrol cars normally made their rounds through the area. (Schiller 2001, 60)

As with the decoration of apartments, the method of auto theft became more sophisticated over time. The RAF developed an approach that would later impress investigators. Members would watch parking lots until an auto of the desired type was driven away, then follow it to the owner's house. A few days later, they would appear with documents identifying them as working for a public opinion research institute, and collect all the data on the auto, including its serial number. With this information they would prepare a false registration, and go in search of another auto with the identical technical specifications, color, and so on. This second auto would be stolen, and the registration number ground off to be replaced with that of the first auto. Thus, if they were pulled over and the police officer radioed in to see if the auto was stolen, records would show that it was not (Aust 1998, 148).

The basic considerations for bank robberies were similar to those for auto theft, but with a focus on escape routes and car changes. Schiller recalls an enumeration of the ground rules for robberies by Jan-Carl Raspe:

> No matter what you decide you must always work with a city map. Where is the closest police station, how long do they need to get there if

the alarm sounds. The most important thing is the escape route, where can the escape auto park during the action, how do you immediately disappear from view, where can you change vehicles inconspicuously, and where do you stay with the cash. (Quoted in Schiller 2001, 63)

Geography of the "Sympathizer Scene"

The most complicated, extensive, and politically sensitive element of the RAF's system of unexceptionable spaces reached out into the whole "archipelago" of West German extraparliamentary oppositional culture. By the end of the 1970s, the RAF had become quite isolated from wider progressive social movements. But while Baader, Meinhof, and the other first-generation leaders were still at large, public sympathy for the RAF was substantial. A 1971 survey found one in twenty West Germans willing to harbor an RAF member for a night (Aust 1998, 189). Even in later years, although the magnitude of support had diminished, the alternative scene continued to provide the RAF and other groups with recruits, and Red Aid (*Rote Hilfe*) chapters, set up at the end of the 1960s to support and publicize the plight of "political prisoners," continued their activities (Aust 1998, 280).

The groups and individuals who made up this loosely connected scene were animated by a wide range of political causes, from environmental protection to advocacy for guest workers to antiwar agitation to radical labor organization. But they all tended to be antiauthoritarian, which helps explain the lingering sympathy for the plight of RAF prisoners despite rejection of RAF methods. More importantly for my purposes, the residential geographies of alternative groups shared some basic characteristics. First, oppositional West Germans, especially younger progressives, tended to live in "residential collectives" (*Wohngemeinschaften*, or WGs), group apartments founded expressly as alternatives to mainstream bourgeois nuclear family arrangements. Many WGs were primarily about alternative lifestyles, but many others were also organized around very specific public issues. The degree of political militancy varied dramatically, from strict adherence to nonviolence at one end of the spectrum to groups such as some West Berlin anarchists who clashed regularly with police at the other. The squatter (*Hausbesetzer*) movement that emerged in the 1970s was an important development: hundreds of abandoned buildings in the largest cities were taken over and defended against all attempts at eviction. Irmgard Möller recalls that the struggle over abandoned housing was very important for the RAF (Möller and Tolmein 1999, 152). This makes sense: as general left support for the RAF eroded through the 1970s, new recruits tended less and less to be individuals convinced by RAF propaganda. In the place of ideas, direct experience of police violence became the more common motivation, and squatter communities, regularly faced with police raids, were most likely to gain that experience. One particular squatter block, on the Eckhoffstrasse in Hamburg, was a key source of recruits for later RAF generations (Aust 1998, 286; Schiller 2001, 116). Stefan Wisniewski, who moved from Eckhoffstrasse into the RAF, gives a telling glimpse into this complex, loosely connected scene:

> [D]ecisive for me was the antiauthoritarian movement, the new lifestyles, *Wohngemeinschaften*, Stones music, long hair, all of that had an enormous attraction for me. Added to that was socialism and other revolutionary theories, above all the sense for justice borne of revolt. I went to Red Aid, was involved in a squat, the Eckhoffstrasse, a house of the New Homeland. (Wisniewski 1997, 17)

Margrit Schiller entered the RAF by way of the Socialist Patient Collective (SPK) in Heidelberg, an antipsychiatry group whose actions sometimes crossed the borders of legality (Schiller 2001, 30ff.).

Horst Herold and the exceptional hunt for knowledge

Illuminating this dark, complicated geography was the primary goal of Horst Herold, controversial director of the BKA from 1971 until 1981. Herold was a modernizer, and soon came to embody Orwell's "Big Brother" for many West Germans. He was a champion of what he called the "sunshine state" (*Sonnenstaat*), a system of policing and social regulation that would render West German society completely transparent and allow law enforcement agencies to move from their traditional reactive role to more sophisticated preventive social engineering (Aust 1998, 211–18). Herold was a devotee of the computer, and invested his main energies in developing comprehensive databases in which the whole alternative scene was registered. A 1979 inventory of the BKA's files and databases revealed that Herold had collected some 4.7 million names and information on thirty-one hundred organizations, and had amassed a fingerprint collection of 2.1 million persons, a photo collection covering 1.9 million, as well as more extensive files on 3,500 people thought particularly militant. In addition, Herold had assembled a "commune file" of WGs, in which some one thousand "objects" (addresses) and 4,000 persons were registered. The "organization file" contained information on protest groups and citizens' initiatives concerned with a wide range of issues. Another file recorded information on every person who had visited anyone incarcerated for connections to terrorist organizations (Aust 1998, 216–17). Among many others, Margrit Schiller would later learn that she was already in Herold's files as a member of the Heidelberg SPK before going underground to join the RAF (Schiller 2001, 66).

Herold defended his system of computerized surveillance before the Interior Committee of the West German Bundestag in September 1977, with explicit reference to the terrorism:

> It is a matter not of a problem concerning individual people but, unfortunately of a mass problem. Nobody in the *Bundesrepublik* can keep 1200 very dangerous people under observation. . . . Everyone knows that complete observational coverage requires around 20 officials per person. 1200 times 20—the entire German criminal police does not have that many personnel. That shows the special and outstanding significance of a permanent, routine, dragnet-like observation of this circle of people in the form of computerized surveillance. (Horst Herold, quoted in Aust 1998, 475)

In the German Autumn of 1977, especially after Schleyer was kidnapped, Herold would oversee the largest dragnet search in the country's history. Among the more spectacularly strenuous attempts to find the RAF operatives was an autobahn action ordered by Herold, in which groups of police officers would fly along highways in a helicopter, drop down to exit and entrance ramps, erect temporary roadblocks, and question or search all vehicles stuck in the resulting jam, then fly off to select another ramp (Aust 1998, 250). When it became clear that Schleyer was being held somewhere in the Köln (Cologne) area, Herold's staff was able to draw on his computer files to compile a list of eight apartments that fit all the suspicious criteria. The fourth on the list, it would later turn out, was indeed where Schleyer was held. It was described thus in an all-points bulletin of September 9, 1977:

> erfstadt-liblar, zum renngraben 4th floor, apartment 104, reportedly a mrs. annerose lottmann-bueckler took the apartment on 7-21-77. . . . [A] security deposit of 800 dm was paid immediately in cash. Mrs. l.-b. took the money from her handbag, in which there was reportedly a whole bundle of notes. (Quoted in Aust 1998, 516)

Primarily because the decision making was centralized under Bonn control rather than left to local police, who had already noticed this apartment, a number of opportunities to search it were passed up. Schleyer was later taken from the apartment and killed on the way to a border crossing.

The longer-term effects of this whole saga were, on the one hand, a definitive turning away from violence by many on the left, and, on the other, a decade of repeated clashes between the state and the left over issues of surveillance, data protection, privacy, and anonymity (Cobler 1976, 52–71). These clashes culminated in widespread boycott movements against planned federal censuses in 1983 and again in 1987. The transparency sought by Horst Herold and, more broadly, the knowledge needed to ensure that every West German was indeed a virtual *homo sacer* remained very contentious issues.

The other side of "bare life": "territory laid bare"

What I have attempted to show in this chapter is that Agamben's innovative philosophical analysis of the foundations of sovereignty in the state of exception and bare life needs to be supplemented with a geographical analysis of actual possibilities for rendering normal citizens into bare life. The intent is not to refute Agamben but to show that there is more to the story than what he has proposed. Approaching this issue through the exceptional case study of the struggle between the West German government and the RAF in the 1970s made it possible to see more clearly which aspects of "normal" daily lives make us physically vulnerable to sovereign power. In modern Western countries like West Germany, the main obstacle facing the organs of the state, and hence the main qualification to the assumption of sovereignty, is the lack of knowledge about the people who threaten social order and where they are to be found. As this empirical example has also made clear, the search for knowledge must itself be seen as a distinct element of sovereignty and an inherently geographical exercise. The obstacles to epistemological sovereignty include the general anonymity of movement in public space and the use of other public infrastructures, collective living arrangements, and the commandeering of spaces beyond the limits of the registered world. It is against this background that such things as the USA PATRIOT Act, domestic electronic surveillance by the National Security Agency (NSA), and other controversial domestic elements of the "War on Terror" must be seen. They illustrate that sovereignty is a matter of ongoing struggle, often about the *knowledge* necessary to make populations physically vulnerable to state force. As both the West German example and the current "War on Terror" illustrate, the salient issue in a state of exception is not the fact that the vast majority of citizens already are virtual *homines sacri* but rather the fact that a tiny, organized group may remain unexceptionable.

Davina Bhandar argues that a state of exception like the one we have entered in the aftermath of September 11, 2001, will tend to produce a new and more differentiated regime of citizenship (Bhandar 2004). In this regime, which she terms the "new normal," economic and personal privileges such as easy cross-border mobility can be obtained in exchange for submitting oneself to a heightened level of preemptive transparency through background checks and so on. Those unable to afford such privileges see their relative economic disadvantages increase, and in addition become the focus of more intense surveillance. Citizenship comes to be understood more prominently in terms of policing and self-policing in the interest of "security," and "freedom" comes to be understood as a privilege contingent to a significant extent on the individual delivery of security. The "new normal," and the different forms and ranks of citizenship it produces, do not fundamentally alter the link between the privileges of citizenship and the vulnerability of bare life, or the basic set of geographical preconditions on which this link rests. But the current state of exception does make it clearer that the political terrain between everyday exercises of freedom and the sort of deadly struggle that took place in the German Autumn of 1977 is best understood as a continuum rather than a qualitative break. Insofar as citizens are able to wriggle out of the geographical and epistemological preconditions for their sovereign subjection, administration and policing shade into domestic warfare.

Acknowledgments

I would like to thank Deb Cowen and Emily Gilbert for helpful suggestions on the chapter, and Rema Hammami for pointing me to useful sources. I am grateful also to Matthew Coleman, Derek Gregory, Gerry Kearns, Stephen Legg, Claudio Minca, John Morrissey, Ulf Strohmayer, and two other audience members for their insightful commentary on a version of the paper presented in Amsterdam in March 2006.

Notes

1. The summary of Agamben's account of sovereignty offered here is based chiefly on the book *Homo Sacer* (Agamben 1998). Although some of his emphases changed as he developed the argument further in *States of Exception* (2005), and although additional insights appear in other works, I take the basic logic of his theorization of sovereign power to be best laid out in the 1998 book.
2. Mika Ojakangas disputes Agamben's reading of Foucault, asserting that sovereignty and biopower share no secret underlying unity, however inextricably they might be entangled in concrete political conjunctures (Ojakangas 2005). I find Ojakangas's argument unconvincing for two reasons. It is based on a too strictly policed distinction between the death orientation of sovereignty and a purely life-affirming understanding of Foucault's concept of biopower. The latter is too simplistic and leads to the absurd implication that the life affirmed by the principles of biopolitics cannot be internally contradictory or involve competing claims to life on the part of different beings, groups, or species. On this point, see Mbembe (2003). Secondly, from the other side of the distinction, if one reads sovereignty fundamentally as a matter of unilateral *intervention*, with fatal violence being only the most extreme form of intervention, it is clear that biopolitical practices, too, involve sovereignty.

References

Agamben, Giorgio. [1994] 2000. Form of life. In *Means without end*, trans. Vincenzo Binetti and Cesare Casarino, 3–15. Minneapolis: University of Minnesota Press.

———. 1998. Homo sacer *sovereign power and bare life*, trans. Daniel Heller-Roazen. Palo Alto, CA: Stanford University Press.

———. 2005. *State of exception*, trans. Kevin Attell. Chicago: University of Chicago Press.

Aust, Stefan. 1998. *Der Baader-Meinhof Komplex*. Hamburg: Hoffman und Campe Verlag.

Bhandar, D. 2004. Renormalizing citizenship and life in Fortress North America. *Citizenship Studies* 8 (3): 261–78.

Cobler, Sebastian. 1976. *Law, order and politics in West Germany*, trans. Francis McDonagh. New York: Penguin.

Mbembe, Achille. 2003. Necropolitics, *Public Culture* 15 (1): 11–40.

Möller, Irmgard, and Oliver Tolmein. 1999. *"RAF—das war für uns Befreiung"*: *Ein Gespräch mit Irmgard Möller über bewaffneten Kampf, Knast und die Linke*. Hamburg: Konkret Literatur Verlag.

Ojakangas, Mika. 2005. Impossible dialogue on bio-power: Agamben and Foucault, *Foucault Studies* 2:5–28.

Schiller, Margrit. 2001. *Es war ein harter Kampf um meine Erinnerung: Ein Lebensbericht aus der RAF.* Munich: Piper Verlag.

Schmitt, Carl. [1922] 1990. *Politische Theologie: Vier Kapitel zur Lehre von der Souveraenitaet.* Berlin: Duncker und Humblot.

Wisniewski, Stefan. 1997. *Wir waren so unheimlich konsequent: Ein Gespräch zur Geschichte der RAF mit Stefan Wisniewski.* Berlin: ID Verlag.

Bombs, Bodies, Acts
The Banalization of Suicide

ENGIN F. ISIN AND MELISSA L. FINN

We try retrospectively to impose some kind of meaning on it, to find some kind of interpretation. But there is none. And it is the radicality of the spectacle, which alone is original and irreducible.

Jean Baudrillard[1]

Two and a half decades ago, it would have been fanciful to imagine; men and women ramming into targets and blowing themselves and all else around them into bits with bombs strapped to their bodies or vehicles. It would have been even more difficult to imagine that such acts would become everyday occurrences in places as geographically separated and culturally diverse as Algiers, Baghdad, Beirut, Buenos Aires, Cairo, Colombo, Grozny, Islamabad, Istanbul, Jerusalem, Kabul, Karachi, London, Madrid, Moscow, New York, and St. Petersburg. Then, the radicality of these acts of suicide violence was their original and irreducible character, as Baudrillard saw, which gave life and death new meanings.[2] Now, the acts are no longer unexpected, unpredictable, or original, but rather routinized, ritualized, and mimetic practices. If Albert Camus thought suicide was the only serious philosophical problem, what would he have thought of banalized suicide violence?[2]

The literature on suicide violence appears clustered around two diametrically opposed positions. On the one hand suicide violence appears as an absolute evil, and on the other as an absolute good. What theoretical resources are available to us to interpret suicide violence as acts without condemning them as absolute evil (thus refusing to recognize the grounds on which suicide violence became possible, even justifiable) or as absolute good (thus participating in their senselessness)? It is obvious to us that it is irresponsible to refuse to see the conditions under which suicide bombings are justified and then condemn them as evil acts. Yet, it becomes complicity to recognize the conditions and say the acts, in their succession, are justifiable self-defense when the self-defense itself enacts the very oppression it laments. While remaining sensitively aware of the grounds that make acts of suicide violence possible, we wish to explore how the once radical act of authenticity and originality has been reduced to an act of imitation, and how it has been transformed into a routinized, ritualized, and mimetic practice. It is troubling that suicide bombings have become habitus (as Bourdieu understood that concept as a relatively enduring and socially produced disposition through instituted and repetitive practices in specific fields such as war, media, politics, and art).[3] That suicide violence has become habitus increasingly renders it both unquestioned and unquestionable while it is also both imagined and unimaginable. This mimetic logic continually produces a compulsion for repetition, which, in turn, creates a neurosis of the body politic and of the citizen through which the fear of repetition creates more repetition.[4] We suggest that the "War on Terror" and suicide violence may have become two aspects of the same cycle of repetition that produces the neurotic citizen and suicide violence as both its cause and effect.

To an extent, things were easier for Camus than for us: he thought that suicide was a confession by those for whom life either was too much or was beyond understanding.[5] Camus could not see suicide as revolt. For Camus, living was revolt. While revolt gives life its value, suicide escapes it. Can we follow Camus to refuse suicide violence as revolt? Things were indeed much easier for Camus. From Émile Durkheim to Camus, Western thought has always individualized suicide, seeing it as the act of a singular individual.[6] In fact, as Slavoj Žižek observed, for both Durkheim and Camus "suicide becomes an *existential* act, the outcome of a pure decision, irreducible to objective suffering or psychic pathology."[7] While suicide violence always involves the act of an individual, it is much more complicated by the fact that by being resolutely directed toward and involving the other, it produces a new figure—the soldier-martyr—as the actor. This new figure is simultaneously a warrior against oppression, injustice, and abjection *and* a weapon.

While suicide violence has been justified as the weapon of the weak and the only means available to actors who lack advanced tactical weaponry to resist domination, oppression, injustice, and abjection, the banalization of such acts is revealed in the transformation of means into ends and in the transformation from the act to an everyday practice. The banal effects of this violence can be seen not only in its systematization, routinization, rationalization, and ritualization among potential new actors, but also in the modern-day soldier-martyr who remains (or who seems to remain) calmly detached when carrying out these acts—acts that seem to target combatant and noncombatant populations with the same kind of virulence and indifference and in fact erase the difference between the two. The banalization of suicide is tied to the normalization of violence and the senseless destruction of life. The ultimate act of sacrifice is no longer only for the brave, but also for people who, by way of heedless or reactionary or disciplined acts, snuff out themselves and others.

We use the term "banalization" here as an adjective to describe the effects and affects of suicide violence; the terms "banalization" or "banality" are employed not to trivialize the grounds of the act, the suffering of those who are caught in the act (which includes both victims and the perpetrators), or the act itself (or, worse, to reify suicide violence along Orientalist lines). The social and political conditions that produce suicide violence are real to those who experience its effects on the ground. We draw our inspiration from Hannah Arendt's brave use of the term.[8] Arendt treated banality as the complete lack of imagination of an actor who followed evil orders. The actor is a cog in the war machine built by the Nazis. What we wish to discuss in this chapter is not "banality of evil" but "banalization of acts." We use "banalization" to refer to the increasing predictability, cliché, and prosaicism of suicide violence in the world. While we wish to recognize the grounds on which acts of suicide violence against life may become justifiable (domination, oppression, injustice, and abjection), we also insist that their transformation from acts into ongoing practices that produces habitus erodes their legitimacy.[9]

The long-running debate over violence and politics in social and political thought involved illustrious scholars.[10] Frantz Fanon, Jean-Paul Sartre, Carl Schmitt, Georges Sorel, and Max Weber, despite their differences, tended to recognize violence as both justifiable and legitimate foundation of a body politic.[11] By contrast, Hannah Arendt, Walter Benjamin, and Jacques Derrida were much more ambivalent about the equivalence between justification and legitimization of violence.[12] Arendt expressed this crucial distinction well. She insisted that while those who have been subjected to abject conditions and injustice may well be justified in using violence against their oppressors, violence itself could not be considered a legitimate foundation of a body politic. She was aware that "under certain circumstances violence—acting without argument or speech and without counting the consequences—is the only way to set the scales of justice right again."[13] Moreover, while Arendt insisted on seeing violence as antipolitical she rejected interpreting acts of violence as emotional or rational.[14] Yet, for Arendt, violence against injustice, however justifiable, when it is rationalized becomes irrational.[15] It has been recognized that much of modern-day suicide violence is not generated by irrational or emotional yearnings that are intrinsic to the cultures or religions from which they spring. But that does not mean that suicide violence is inherently rational either. Rather, suicide violence that *becomes* rationalized and banalized becomes irrational. The banalization of suicide is the repetition that reveals rationalizations, especially with regard to noncombatant life. While we do not aim to engage with this literature on violence, we draw upon it to conclude that in understanding suicide violence as political acts, there must be a necessary differentiation between justification and legitimacy.

Understanding Acts of Suicide Violence

Much—we feel perhaps too much—has already been said about suicide violence. Nonetheless, there have been useful (and necessary) classifications, histories, documents, ethnographies, and accounts of both acts and actors.[16] But do we *understand* suicide violence? Arendt makes a useful distinction between knowledge and understanding. She says knowledge makes words into weapons. Knowledge becomes less interested in understanding than in having correct information and classification.[17] Knowledge aims to develop unequivocal results, judges with certainty, and aims to intervene with effectiveness. By contrast, understanding "is an unending activity by which, in constant change and variation, we come to terms with and reconcile ourselves to reality, that is, try to be at home in the world."[18] We aim to understand suicide violence as acts that become practices and then habitus.[19]

We appreciate the ambiguous, open-ended, and nonessential nature of act and being to avoid reproducing dominant representations of acts of suicide violence.[20] The fundamental difficulty about discussing suicide violence is that we are attempting to make sense of its senselessness. To recognize its senselessness is not to condemn the grounds (domination, oppression, injustice, and abjection) on which violent acts can become possible and justifiable. Any interpretation of the meaning of acts of suicide violence risks closing off alternative understandings of the actor and the act; the choice of silence becomes implicated in problems of ethics, fairness, and integrity.[21] The starting point, then, is to recognize, as Esslin eloquently puts it, the "illusoriness and absurdity of ready-made solutions and prefabricated meanings."[22]

With regard to the aporia of understanding phenomena such as suicide violence, we can now mention several caveats. While we recognize the insightful and ethical approach taken by Mikhail Bakhtin and others on representation, we also recognize that even the subtitle of this chapter, "banalization of suicide," already begins to represent suicide violence as banalized, thus moving us away from the pure Bakhtinian ethics. Representation is unavoidable. Bakhtin moreover argues that aestheticizing, historicizing, and abstracting acts force a split between the substance of the act, the individual experience of it, and the event as it unfolds.[23] In anticipation of concerns that may be raised with regard to historicizing, abstracting, and ethics, we would suggest the following.

First, there is an important difference between representing an act as an object of knowledge and understanding it. It is indeed clear that suicide violence should not be immediately categorized, reified, and represented because in doing so we try to contain it and seal off what the act (and the actor) can and cannot be (according to our own arbitrary specifications). The experience of those who are caught in the act is incalculably more profound than any observer's understanding or witnessing of it. Second, in order to understand the act of suicide violence, we must recognize its historical and political grounds. Suicide violence must be contextualized within the system of power relations and domination, oppression, injustice, and abjection that compel actors to enact acts of death. Third, regarding the problem of abstraction, while it may seem that we abstract suicide violence by saying that it is banalized, we are not referring to the acts of suicide violence, but rather to the way in which the succession and series of acts are transformed into everyday practices. *It is the succession and repetition that banalize the act, thereby transforming it from an act into a practice, routine, and eventually habitus.* Fourth, regarding the problem of capturing an event as it is unfolding and possibly diminishing the interplay that occurs between an actor's processes of development and self-understanding, and his or her capacity to change, we would say that Bakhtin's analysis confronts a challenge when suicide violence is analyzed because, if successful, the actor actually commits to death and dies.[24] The act of suicide violence is like no other act. It is not like the act of commanding because when people command, they are still alive and are evolving and changing.[25] With suicide violence, however, there is the problem of the suicide at which point the actor ceases to be, ceases to be in flux, and ceases to exist as a body. We are dealing with an act that not only effaces itself but also is aimed at the effacement of the other. Arendt would say that the originality of acts of suicide violence is horrible, not because they are new but because they constitute a rupture with our understanding; these acts explode the categories of political thought and standards of judgment.[26]

Freedom and Responsibility

We shall emphasize the three elements of the act: actor, freedom, and responsibility. Although state occupation creates the conditions for suicide violence (domination, oppression, injustice, and abjection), actors are still radically responsible for rendering acts of suicide violence. Yet, there are problems related to the contingencies of *facticity* and the problem of the *alibi*, the former referring to the nature of the constraints on the actor and the latter referring to the kinds of excuses used by actors to abdicate responsibility. So the questions of freedom and responsibility of actors get entangled with questions of facticity and alibi.

The Question of Facticity

Jean-Paul Sartre argues that acts shape the world, which suggests an orientation of means and ends, and a fundamental and inextricable linkage to the Other. Sartre always insisted that no contingency or fact could be a cause over or determine action; the being orients itself freely from a state of existence to one that has yet to unfold. There is a cause for all acts, and yet, the act is still oriented intentionally toward a future as-not-yet-realized. The nature of the act is not already determined or constituted, but is rather commanded by the life of the being which is constantly oriented toward its potentiality. The project of being-in-the-world always involves choice. The being is constrained by contingencies that develop out of the choices it has made; the potentiality of some future path is made concrete as it unfolds. *Since beings can refer to no one as having already constituted the future path, they are radically responsible for the act and that which springs from the act.* In every instance, the subject must fashion his criterion for action because, according to Sartre, there is no universal code for action or categorical imperative that can render such acts justifiable. To say that a categorical imperative exists is to fall back on a false projection (to project oneself in the name of a universal law of conduct).[27]

The implications for acts of suicide violence are as follows: the soldier-martyr is a free actor, to the extent that he or she may make choices, and may establish a particular motive and an end goal for which radical responsibility is established. The soldier-martyr makes himself and is constituted within each moment of enactment (which ultimately ends with death). The moment the soldier-martyr enacts himself, the moment the soldier-martyr has realized his goal of self-annihilation and -immolation as responsive action and political message, he is no longer able to stand accountable and responsible for his acts. This invariably creates a problem for the being who is responsible for the deaths of the victims but who can no longer stand to be judged for the act. There is, moreover, the problem of how each enactment of suicide violence increases the attractiveness of the act as a form of responsive action because of the impression and desire it leaves in the mind of another to do the same. Thus, as Emmanuel Lévinas points out, it is of irreducible significance that our responsibility for the death of the Other invariably puts an ethic upon us (and we are equally responsible for the host of other actors who see our original acts as precedent and inspiration to act similarly).[28] In other words, soldier-martyrs, like all actors, are implicated in the consequences of their acts and the way those consequences affect others.

Now, it is "radical" rather than "absolute" responsibility that is enjoined upon acting beings. The actor's responsibility is not absolute because all beings are constrained by various forms of facticity such as *place, past, environment, relational Other,* and *death* that cannot be changed by free will. According to Sartre, beings insert "action into the network of determinism."[29] The *place* consists of that which is manifested to the being (the location of birth, the place of relations); where someone is born constrains choice and opens up other opportunities. Thus, the soldier-martyr may face limited choices by being born in a violent society, but his birthplace does not *cause* the actor to decide to self-annihilate.[30] There are many people in similar conditions who do not choose this path in life. The *past* of the actor includes any previous choices made that cannot be undone, but the past does not determine the future, nor does it direct the actor *irrevocably* toward a future decision to self-annihilate. As for the *environment,* the field of action is always conducted through a configuration of objects (certain immovable or movable objects, buildings, sets of infrastructure, natural settings, etc.) that are placed and unplaced and that are wholly indifferent and undecided by the actor. The actor is, however, free and responsible in a situation despite the "unpredictability and the adversity of the environment."[31] The *relational Other* is a contingent fact that is existent and discovered in every choice in life. Beings are free (despite the givenness of the Other who has not come into the world through them) to apprehend the Other as subject or object, as real or abstracted. While the actor cannot necessarily decide what the Other will do or do to him, he is radically responsible for his action as it becomes implicated in the life of the Other. The last kind of facticity described by Sartre is *death*. The being, despite the inevitability and finitude of death, can direct his project toward or in spite of death, and he can realize and actualize his own freedom-to-die; the being enjoys a totality of "free choice of finitude."[32] But death does not necessarily mean finitude to the soldier-martyr. The soldier-martyr acts toward death, motivated not necessarily by its finality, but by the belief that such acts are worthy of reward in an afterlife. It is possible therefore that the soldier-martyr may actualize his own "freedom-to-die" as a free choice while denying the finality of death. The soldier-martyr ruptures death as facticity (as a constraint to his realm of choices).

There are contradictions of banality vis-à-vis the question of death in modern suicide violence. On the one hand, the soldier-martyr projects himself freely toward a "final possibility" in death and, in so doing, actualizes the authentic existence, one that is pried away from the banalization of the ordinary and attains "the irreplaceable uniqueness" of itself.[33] On the other hand, the increasingly common and increasingly ordinary character of these acts substantially undermines their "irreplaceable uniqueness," the legitimacy and honor of an authentic life and projected death. It has become the once ultimate act of authenticity degraded down to repetition and mimesis. It is an act of followers and no longer of leaders. The lamb is not unique, and its slaughter is like a thousand others. Moreover, the choice of death robs the life and situation of its meaning and sacrality, while the problems that the act was meant to address remain unresolved. The choice to escape the ineffability of one's facticity (the presence and imposition of place, past, environment, relational others, and future death) through death is weakness, for alternative solutions to the life were not acted upon. In Sartre's words,

> Suicide is an absurdity which causes my life to be submerged in the absurd. . . . Death [nihilation] is not only the project which destroys all projects and which destroys itself. . . . It is also the triumph of the point of view of the Other over the point of view which I am toward myself.[34]

The concept of radical responsibility is deflated by claims that actors are limited by ignorance and error. This reminds us of Max Weber and Talcott Parsons, both of whom emphasized that acts are rational despite the ignorance and error of the actors that arise from their inadequate or incorrect knowledge of the conditions or situations of their acts.[35] Moreover, they argue, so long as acts are rational, they involve responsibility. Such thinking tends to deflate the freedom and responsibility enjoined upon acting beings, including soldier-martyrs. Action can be, however, motivated by a real or perceived injustice that renders violence by annihilation a desirable response. Arendt writes that engagement is transformed into enragement not necessarily because of injustice, but rather hypocrisy. Here the suicide violence is understandable: the soldier-martyr desires

> [t]o tear the mask of hypocrisy from the face of the enemy, to unmask him and the devious machinations and manipulations that permit him to rule . . . to provoke action even at the risk of annihilation so that the truth may come out.[36]

It is for this reason that Arendt thinks violence can be justified.[37]

With regard to freedom, and the relations of the actor with outside collectivities, this much is possible: it is possible that some forms of indoctrination, community norms and expectations, and propaganda, wield considerable power and influence in creating conditions that foster or support suicide violence as a response (e.g., encouraging the soldier-martyr to act), or, on the flip side, that stymie debate or suppress legitimate political grievances.[38] It is possible that an individual, group, or people, when faced with premeditated mass murder, terrorization, or torture of the people they identify with, can become temporarily unreasonable by projecting their problems on substitute others. On the other hand, again, freedom and responsibility are undermined when excuses are made and action is blamed on the influence of collectivities; despite the facticity of the relations of a collectivity to an actor, the soldier-martyr still acts freely with tenacity, virulence, and indifference toward combatants and noncombatants. Violent or hostile reactions are not, moreover, *necessarily and simply* caused by oppression; instead, some violence is fueled by the ego, delusion, and a "sense of impotence."[39] Acts of suicide violence against human life are acts that attempt to overcome an enemy or an object. Writing along similar lines, Bakhtin argued that "[a]n indifferent and hostile reaction is always a reaction that impoverishes and decomposes its object: it seeks to pass over the object in all its manifoldness, to ignore it or to overcome it."[40]

The Problem of the Alibi

An act, if it is to be an act, must rupture facticity as a limit on action; an act must rupture the need to present an alibi. If one understands an actor (or, equally as important, if the actor understands himself) as operating as a secret representative for some cause, for religion, or for God, one turns the actor (or he turns himself) into an imposter or pretender. In principle, a claim to alibi is a claim to avoid responsibility, a claim to avoid an act of one's own choosing.

What we are *enacting* here is a refusal to think of the being as severed from his ontological roots in personal participation (the ongoing event of Being) because who the actor is is inextricably associated with the kinds of acts he enacts. The choice of the solider-martyr to participate in and carry out an act of suicide violence through death to self and others is ontologically grounded in the act, its consequences, and the being itself.

Actors often employ euphemisms regarding war and violence as alibis. Euphemisms give the impression that an act was carried out under the auspices of a more benign or legitimate purpose than is possible given the nature of such attacks. Euphemisms for war, violence, terrorism, extermination, liquidation, and killing such as "evacuations," "surgical strikes," and "martyrdom" operations are important linguistic choices, indications perhaps of either an evasion of responsibility through the invocation of an alibi, or an easing of the conscience.[41] The use of "war" as an excuse (an alibi about which) to commit violence against innocent people not only is inexcusable[42] but also calls the legitimacy of the act into question.

In this discussion of facticity, freedom, responsibility, and alibi, what we are driving toward is the answerability of the actor: the ability of the actor to answer for the content of the act and the being who enacts it in a succession of moments in the Being-as-event, to bring the act and the Being into communication.[43] The *answerable act* is the act that does not claim an alibi to evade responsibility;[44] it is an act that is answerably aware of itself.[45] Actors who invoke an alibi often invoke a universal ethic (a categorical imperative); they take shelter, so to speak, under a universal principle that is said to justify the act. Bakhtin writes, "The principle of formal [Kantian] ethics moreover is not the principle of an actually performed act at all, but is rather the principle of the possible generalization of already performed acts in a theoretical transcription of them."[46] Sartre concurs in a slightly different way by arguing that the Kantian ethical system substitutes doing (action) for being (actor) as the most important aspect of the act.[47] Sartre and Bakhtin are emphasizing an ethics of being: the unfolding event of Being and act cannot be predetermined, assumed into a generality, and therefore theorized upon from this perspective.

The answerable act is the fulfillment of a decision to act. The answerable act is accountable, other oriented, and answerably aware of itself. Thus the act of suicide violence, in its annihilation of the actor and its claims of justification vis-à-vis an ideology or movement, is not an answerably aware act. By its very nature, suicide violence annihilates the actor and its answerability. The actor cannot stand to account for the act, and the act ceases to be. The act is not answerable if the actor obeys orders because of indoctrination or if military discipline is used as an alibi. The actor—in our case, the soldier-martyr—knows what he is doing; he is responsible for the act. Being unable to answer for it, however, in the Bakhtinian sense (because of death) does not mean that the actor is released from the act and therefore need not account for the act.

The Prosaicism of Suicide

The concept of the act involves an effort to change some aspect of the world, a set of means orientated toward some kind of end, and an implicit serial connectedness of action such that changes effected by one act will affect a subsequent act, thereby producing a desired goal.[48] Arendt wrote in *On Violence* that violence is a form of instrumental means whose ends condition the thought and action of people and therefore require guidance and justification.[49] Acts of suicide violence aim to question and unsettle domination, oppression, injustice, and abjection. Violence is predicated on a mean-ends evaluation, and violent actors are always faced with the possibility that their means may overwhelm their ends.[50]

When means are evaluated in relation to ends or an end goal, it is often said that the end justified the means. In talk of means and ends, one can look at the ways, in current times, that suicide violence has been rendered fashionable. It ensures the continued glorification of the actor as hero and the act as a statement of authentic bravery. As acts of violence, suicide violence employs volunteerism, self-annihilation and -immolation, and killing as means to achieve an end that places value and importance on the desired end of emancipation. Taken from this, we want to examine the ways in which "war theaters" have ushered in a new kind of means-ends dichotomy that has transformed the means into the end in itself and thus made them routinized and habitual practices.

One can see the banalization of suicide violence unfolding through a means-turned-ends shift: the killing, the carnage, becomes an end in itself; and the method of delivering a violent message is the end in banalized violence. Acts of suicide violence may have originated on justified grounds of domination, oppression, injustice, and abjection. However, when the act of suicide violence became an everyday enactment, it appeared that perspectives changed (or perhaps many lost their perspective), that it was no longer horrible to kill human beings indiscriminately, and in fact that was often the goal. The original purposes of the goal, a struggle for emancipation or resistance, somehow get lost or clouded by a succession of violent acts that employ bloodshed as a tool of negotiation. We are reminded here of Friedrich Nietzsche's caution that just because a thing comes into being for a purpose does not means that it always serves that purpose.[51] When the means become ends in the context of a "war theater," that "theater" becomes absurd, robbed of its purpose, its originary goals, and its political roots; it becomes, as it were, a symbol of senseless life senselessly taking life. It is an irremediable exile from being human, a depravation of one's relation with the Other.[52]

A violent act has the capacity to make us aware of a grievance, but there is always the danger that violence will move unconsciously in ways that overwhelm the goals and in directions that reproduce and reinforce the conditions of its grievance.[53] The contemporary crisis, writes Bakhtin, is that there is often an abyss between the actual motivation for an act and its end; the end makes indeterminate (it is walled off from) the actual motivation for the act.[54] Thus, the means-turned-end shift signals two things: first, the original motivations of emancipation or martyrdom are severed, because of the killing that becomes the end, from any form of liberation that inevitably results. This is clearly the case because the end no longer exists when the banalized repetition of means (the act of killing as means) appears to replace the end as the goal. Second, the original motivations of emancipation and martyrdom are lost in the serially recurrent acts of bodies and bits that not only are prosaic and cliché-like, but also have been robbed of their uniqueness and their honor. Modern soldier-martyrs believe that they carry an impressive or legitimate message, but such fantasies are not revealed through their deaths.

In addition to the shift toward calculability, the banalization of suicide is revealed in the concurrent streams of attacks that are being perpetrated on a daily basis. Suicide violence has become everyday. Suicide violence acts have become practices. Such practices are unimaginative, predictable, and inane, though this in no way trivializes their effects or affects. One can experience firsthand, or read and hear about, an act of suicide violence in which large numbers of civilians are maimed or killed. Suicide violence is so routinized that bombers have been woven into the daily functioning of people in and outside of war or occupation; it is part of a global experiential montage. On the news, suicide violence no longer shocks the sensibilities of people. The day of suicide attacks, of yesterday or today or tomorrow, is "heavy and dangerous," and with each passing milestone, we, as a global collective, are weary because the "calamity of yesterday" has changed who we are.[55] And yet, as Esslin argues, "the more things change, the more they are the same"; the tears of the world are its terrible stability.[56] The repetitive sameness of moving time is what violence produces in its banalized succession. The banalization of suicide violence is also evidenced in the rising rates of volunteerism for martyrdom operations or missions. More and more people are not only becoming but also *choosing* to become part of the banalized repetition of day in and day out annihilating bodies. This certainly raises serious questions about the gloriousness of a mission when it is like a thousand others. There is, moreover, a degree of banality, cliché, and superficiality in the soldier-martyr's formulaic approach to entering heaven.[57]

It is the everydayness of mimetic murders, wanton vigilantism, and vengeance that is banalizing the acts of suicide violence and their effects. Justice is lost when a single human being, a single soldier-martyr, can arbitrarily render his verdict on the guilty-as-imagined as judge, jury, and executioner. The everydayness of suicide violence and their effects are robbing people of a sacred appreciation of the soul and twisting the divine purpose of martyrdom, which has always been to defend family and home, not strike a people because they attend a different religious center.

Actor and the Face of the Other

Acts of suicide violence are, unequivocally, acts of violence against the face or being of another. The soldier-martyr does not see the face of the Other. Rather, he sees the Other as a force or barbarity that must be overcome.[58] The face, however, "opposes violence with metaphysical resistance" and forces the subject to accept responsibility;[59] the existence of the metaphysical face of the Other is the existence of a covenant between human beings.[60] The soldier-martyr strikes instead with the calculation that he will no longer be alive to bear his own suffering or the suffering of his victims. It is a calculation that unsuccessfully attempts to physically, psychologically, and metaphysically erase the face of the Other from sympathy, empathy, consciousness, and memory. Of course, the inevitably futile attempt to erase the face of the Other is meant to ease existential angst about killing and deny the sacred connectedness shared by human beings. The sacred connectedness of human beings is described by Esslin as the ability to recognize and admit that we are the Other and the Other is us.[61]

Acts of suicide violence appear to treat Otherness as fixed and incapable of changing; the Other is portrayed as an inherent or inescapable enemy. It is therefore not only perfectly acceptable to terrorize and murder them, but also such acts close off who the Other is and how and if he can transform; it suggests that people can slip into Otherness but hardly ever slip out of it.[62] Using clichés such as "faceless enemy," moreover, is the feeble attempt of violent actors to render nontransformative the capacity of the Other to be other than expected. Agathangelou and Ling mention that the Other is often targeted as the cause of violence and destruction; the self often constructs itself as "innocent, victimized, moral, and rational," and the Other as "demonic, murderous, and radically barbaric." Militarization is therefore regarded as a moral imperative.[63]

For Lévinas, ethics is the ethics of the Other. An ethics with respect to the face of the Other is perhaps encapsulated in the phrase "human qua Other" (human in the capacity of the Other); it is an imaginary substitution: the ability of the self to substitute itself for the other (e.g., to know that we are the Other and the Other is us).[64] Here, it is important to point out that there is a difference between substitution and the substitute Other, however connected the concepts may be. Substitution is identification, to be in the capacity of the Other; the substitute is the person for whom anger is wrongly directed. The ethical act not only is the choice of the actor to substitute himself for the Other, but also ensures that anger is not directed against substitutes. Sigmund Freud spoke about the theme of wrongly directed anger when he said that sometimes people seek to exact punishment for a crime committed even if it does not fall on the guilty party.[65] Similarly, Arendt argued that rage and violence become irrational when they are directed against substitutes.[66] There is often a false sense of certainty attached to suicide violence such that the actor feels that the targets of his action are in some way guilty, but when innocent people are involved, his anger is usually directed at substitutes. Use of the term "self-defense" to justify attacks on substitute targets invariably becomes a tactic to impose limitless aggression, stymie questions about culpability and historical inquiry, and render retaliation as if it were always moral.

The banalization of suicide violence is further exposed through the judgments that are used to justify it. Many strict and literalistic forms of religious exotericism—and many soldier-martyrs are doctrinally exoteric—see order being maintained when people are coded, classified, and restrained.[67] The perceived crimes of a "lesser Other" are coded and classified such that it is a crime to be other than the soldier-martyr's group, to not pick up arms against the occupier, and to fail to pray as often as is required by God (many widely accepted judgments about the Other tend to legitimize repetitive acts of violence against the Other). The disciplining effects of group surveillance over a population are a form of intimidation that determines with arbitrary exclusivity who is a criminal body and who is worthy of death or punishment. In most cases, criminality is what the Other does that does not accord to the religious, political, or nationalist expectations of the soldier-martyr's group. We envisage social, political, and religious forms of surveillance, discipline, and correction between social groups as a kind of "panoptic judgment" (the panoptic overseeing of one group upon another produces arbitrary and wide-sweeping judgment, and the recipients of such judgment check their behavior when they feel they are being watched or when they feel they may be punished or harmed); this is not unlike Foucault's notions of surveillance and discipline vis-à-vis the Panopticon. In order to self-annihilate and destroy innocent life, the soldier-martyr must treat the targets of his attack as if they are all guilty for some perceived crime. The purpose of panoptic judgment, like the Panopticon, is power: "to induce in the [moral, religious, or political Other] a state of conscious and permanent visibility that assumes the automatic functioning of power."[68] In the panoptic view, the Other is abstracted and generalized, which renders this body an "easy target for contempt. Devoid of humanity, the abstract Other is outside of history, incapable of development, destined for servitude, and degraded to a valueless object."[69] Like the imperial colonizers, modern-day state oppressors and soldier-martyrs who target noncombatants strive to embolden the perpetrator mentality, which justifies the destructive machinery that robs humans of their humanness, their soul; it renders them "spiritless matter, raw material."[70]

Acts to Habitus: The Banalization of Violence

The banalization of suicide violence is complete when the act is rationalized, systematized, routinized, and glorified. These are the other effects and affects of suicide violence. The fog of war is as dense for the soldier-martyr as it is for any state. Clarity of mind (the ability of the actor and the masses to gaze upon the effects of violence in their midst) is substantially reduced as time passes. It is not easy for a collective to step back from itself, from the acts of its people, and from the conditions on the ground in order to question whether their own complacency has allowed for the normalization of violence. The rationalization is always there that because the "act" cut right into the heart of a state oppressor, it was also morally and religiously permissible. Suicide violence is now habitus for anyone seeking vengeance or restitution; never mind God, religion, morality, ethics, or the sacrality of the human being. Suicide violence not only has been normalized and banalized, but so also have its effects and affects. Modern suicide violence becomes systematic, calculative, orderly, and murderous. In a systematic and calculative sense, soldier-martyrs calculate the incalculable benefits of martyrdom, imagining that the deed will tip the divine scales in their favor; in this calculation, the martyr gets immediate access to heaven and can put in a word for his next of kin as well. The figure of the soldier-martyr reproduces the militarism of the state against which it originated.

Current forms of suicide violence are also routine and commonplace. With each instance of suicide violence, the act (and its effects vis-à-vis detonated bomb, shrapnel, and body bits) becomes part of the routine of one's day. Of course, the act is fueled by narratives of grandeur about the place of the martyr in heaven, which only serve to further glorify the act despite its most grievous effects vis-à-vis the carnage of human life. Actors who carry out acts of suicide violence peer over and attempt to control the masses through threats of punishment. Disloyalty is heavily punished. Suicide violence has therefore taken on its own actor; it is now the site of an apparatus of capture. The actor and the act are actually struggling for control over its effects and affect. At what point in this violent mechanism does the actor have to stop thinking, and the machine's "artificial" intelligence take over? At what point does the act of suicide violence become the means, the ends, and the only remaining actor in the event as it unfolds? The bombers are dead or are dying; the only thing keeping this violent mechanism going is the act itself. Thus the act is no longer an act but habitus.

The banalization and normalization of suicide violence can also be witnessed in the way the act is transformed into a gesture, a pantomime of the imagination that no longer indicates creation and a will to act (uniquely), but rather the endurance and continued support of a status quo (locked in "the sphere of a pure and endless" mediocrity).[71] The notion of gesture or pantomime suggests that the actor must divorce his humanity, on some level, from his act; the actor must step outside of himself to do the act. He must stage the action (the mime) by mimicking previous suicide attacks, all the while posing and presenting a lionhearted image to the world. Though few would doubt that it takes tenacity and bravery to plunge knowingly into death, the actors' act still contributes to the normalization of a violent status quo and the desensitization of the masses to violence. As spectator, victim, and perpetrator, it is intolerable and ineffable to us that human beings all over the world are being tortured, raped, hacked, macheted, and blown to bits, but we are desensitized to the ongoing event of violent being and we tolerate it; violence has reached its banalized end, we are rarely shocked, and when we are, the effects are temporary and, more worryingly, just as routinized.[72] Moreover, few can ignore the way the pantomime unfolds in a social and cultural ritual. When we suggest that suicide violence is ritualized, we not only mean the act itself (recruitment, planning, training, recording, executing, and claiming) but also how the act is represented and imagined through cultural and social symbols that normalize it. In some cases, the suicide bomber becomes the "living martyr," the new Achilles of the abject. In seeking a glorious death, the martyred is memorialized by his people. It is a habitus among the families of the martyred soldiers to name future children after their dead son or daughter. The notion of "replacement children," children regarded as replacing the soldier-martyr in life and mimicking in death, is a cultural and social and domestic practice of banalized suicide violence.

Is it any wonder that the "suicide bomber doll," as some commentators have called it, would make its appearance as a cultural symbol? In making and playing with this doll, a violent habitus is cultivated. It is a toy for the imagination emulating reality, and a toy for reality emulating the imagination, or imagined desires. However, the "suicide bomber doll" is not something conjured up in the imaginative boardrooms of America. Children do not play with the doll to escape their own harsh and abject conditions, but rather to face such conditions with defiance. In conditions of abjection, it reveals to young minds how transforming can bring emancipation and how the child can move from uncertainty to certainty about the world. The doll itself is a symbol of resistance, but what kind of resistance? To teach them that an honorable death is to die to kill the Other? It is a resistance banalized from its originary purposes. The unfortunate truth of the doll is that it no longer represents a glorious death, but now a banalized one.

Though his purpose was to disrupt a capitalist icon by fitting a bomb belt to her waist and equipping her with a detonator button, Simon Tyszko's agitprop artwork, *The Suicide Bomber Barbie*, reveals how banalized violence has seeped into the collective imaginaries. The artist has identified a cultural icon, a cultural toy, one that is mimicked and adored for her sharp fashion sense, and is saying through his art, "See how Barbie is eyeing and identifying new 'symbols of revolution'"? In his interview with a nine-year-old Palestinian girl,

Tyszko said that the girl once wished to be a doctor, but now that she could no longer study or sleep at night, she wanted to be a martyr. Tyszko, inspired by this conversational exchange, made banalized violence an art in the West. The young girl had "effectively bought the notion of suicide bombing as a lifestyle choice—it has become aspirational, an off the shelf peer led option." Tyszko's Barbie confronts the absurdity of the original suicide bomber doll by symbolizing violence that became habitus.[73] Tyszko also seems to have rekindled an earlier controversy about the photograph of a baby bomber found in Hebron. The child is shown in this photograph wearing the outfit of a Hamas suicide bomber, with belts holding bullets and bombs, and the red bandanna of the well-recognized soldier-martyr.[74]

As humans, the "pang of conscience" is that we may be human, we may be weak, and we may actually sin.[75] It is through our conscience that we become aware that we can sin; our conscience guides us, and it encourages us to reject the urge to punish and destroy. Nietzsche says that the conscience made humans responsible and that this is a late but significant fruit. In defense of the soldier-martyr, he actually ruptures the "pang of conscience" on many levels, but not without grievous effects. There is a measure of calm detachment, quiet arrogance, cool calculation, and total certainty attached to an act of suicide violence. The soldier-martyr calculates, but not in deference to the calculations of his conscience; his calculation instead benefits individual and group interests. The soldier-martyr shuts off the conscience by means of this overconfidence, so to speak (some would say by way of his religious certainty): of course, in his mind, the soldier-martyr who strikes innocent life is assured that he is committing a noble self-sacrifice and that his sacrifice is naturally to counteract the injustice perpetrated against those he identifies with; he walks the higher moral ground and is not the cause of a further injustice; and he sees lofty illusions of martyrdom as fulfilling a personal narrative to have lived a noble life and to have died an idealized death.[76] Confronting banalized violence is about tracking down how a succession of violent acts can destroy collective memory, conscience, and recognition of Otherness and destroy the capacity for answerability.

Conclusion

Arendt often argued that what makes men and women political beings is their capacity to act.[77] She ascribed particular importance to the ancient Greek conception of act, which meant both governing and beginning.[78] To act means to set something in motion, to begin not just something new but also oneself as that being that acts to begin itself.[79] The fact is that we are beings endowed with the capacity to act (or, as Sartre would say, "to be is to act") and that to act is to realize a rupture in the given; to act always means to enact the unexpected and unpredictable.[80] As Arendt would put it, "[T]he human heart is the only thing in the world that will take upon itself the burden that the divine gift of action, of being a beginning and therefore being able to make a beginning, has placed upon us."[81] We have elaborated an argument that suicide violence against domination, oppression, injustice, and abjection, however justifiable as original and radical, loses its character as an act when it becomes routine, or as Arendt would say about violence in general, it becomes most irrational when it becomes rationalized.[82] Two very important aspects of the banalization of suicide violence are the means-turned-ends shift, in which the goal of liberation is subordinated by the goal of bloodshed, and the everyday quality of the act, in which the daily practice of detonating bombs has become prosaic and mimetic. Thus, we concluded, suicide violence is no longer an act, a beginning, but habitus. We briefly addressed how indifference, panoptic judgments, and totalizing devaluations of the Other have banalized and normalized suicide violence, and how such effects and affects are also realized in their systematization, routinization, rationalization, and glorification.

It is an ethical impossibility for actors to evade the responsibility that is afforded to them as acting and choosing beings by arguing that constraining contingencies and the pressure from their groups, for example, gave them no other choice but to self-annihilate and take a few dozen people with them. This is an ethical impossibility despite the inherent complicity of the founding violence of states in creating the conditions for suicide violence to flourish in the first place. An aporia of freedom vis-à-vis suicide violence is that it is not created in a vacuum (e.g., the acts of Others often create the conditions for violence), and yet, in the end, it is the actor who is still radically responsible for choices he makes.

We ought not to consider soldier-martyrs as "dupes or mechanisms of an impersonal social force, but actors with responsibility."[83] Yet, when acts of suicide violence are transformed into habitus and become embodied in the body politic, it will be almost impossible to restore its qualities as an act. This mimetic logic that becomes embedded as habitus continually produces a compulsion for repetition. Robson spoke of "[t]his compulsion to repeat, to repeat acts of suicide, to replicate a suicidal state such that it becomes a global suicidal state."[84] The repercussions of this create a neurosis of the body politic and of the citizen through which the fear of repetition creates more repetition.[85] The "War on Terror" and suicide violence become two aspects of the same cycle of repetition that produces the neurotic citizen.[86]

Acknowledgments

We would like to thank Deborah Cowen, Emily Gilbert, and Greg Nielsen for their critical reading and insightful comments on an earlier draft.

Notes

1. Jean Baudrillard, *The Spirit of Terrorism and Other Essays*, trans. Chris Turner (London: Verso, 2003).

2. Albert Camus, *The Myth of Sisyphus* (New York: Penguin, 1975), 11.
3. Pierre Bourdieu, *Practical Reason: On the Theory of Action* (Stanford, Calif.: Stanford University Press, 1994); and Pierre Bourdieu, *The Logic of Practice* (Stanford, Calif.: Stanford University Press, 1980).
4. Engin Isin, "The Neurotic Citizen." *Citizenship Studies* 8, no. 3 (2004): 217–35.
5. Camus, *Myth of Sisyphus*, 13; Pierre Bourdieu, *Practical Reason* Pierre Bourdieu, *The Logic of Practice On the Theory of Action* (Stanford, CA: Stanford University Press, 1994), (Stanford, CA: Stanford University Press, 1980).
6. Émile Durkheim, *Suicide: A Study in Sociology*, ed. George Simpson, trans. John A. Spaulding and George Simpson (Glencoe, Ill.: Free Press, 1951).
7. Slavoj Žižek, *On Belief* (London: Routledge, 2001), 102.
8. Hannah Arendt, *Eichmann in Jerusalem: A Report on the Banality of Evil* (New York: Viking Press, 1963).
9. We use the concept of abjection as used by Julia Kristeva, *Powers of Horror: An Essay on Abjection, European Perspectives* (New York: Columbia University Press, 1982).
10. Two more recent and notable examples are David Campbell and Michael Dillon, eds., *The Political Subject of Violence* (Manchester, UK: Manchester University Press, 1993); and John Keane, *Violence and Democracy, Contemporary Political Theory* (Cambridge: Cambridge University Press, 2004). Both discuss the prominent figures and issues in the debate.
11. Frantz Fanon, *The Wretched of the Earth* (New York: Grove Press, 1963); C. Wright Mills, *The Power Elite* (London: Oxford University Press, 1956); Jean-Paul Sartre, "Preface," in Fanon, *The Wretched of the Earth*; Carl Schmitt, *The Concept of the Political* (Chicago: University of Chicago Press, 1932); Georges Sorel, *Reflections on Violence*, ed. Jeremy Jennings, Cambridge *Texts in the History of Political Thought* (Cambridge: Cambridge University Press, 1999); and Max Weber, "Politics as a Vocation," in From Max Weber: *Essays in Sociology*, ed. H. H. Gerth and C. Wright Mills (New York: Oxford University Press, 1919).
12. Hannah Arendt, "On Violence," in her *Crises of the Republic: Lying in Politics, Civil Disobedience, on Violence, Thoughts on Politics and Revolution* (New York: Harcourt Brace Jovanovich, 1969); Walter Benjamin, "Critique of Violence," in *Reflections: Essays, Aphorisms, Autobiographical Writings*, ed. Peter Demetz (New York: Harcourt Brace Jovanovich, 1978); and Jacques Derrida, "Force of Law: The 'Mystical Foundation of Authority,'" in his *Acts of Religion* (New York: Routledge, 2002).
13. Arendt, *"On Violence,"* 161.
14. Ibid., 161.
15. Ibid., 163.
16. Mia Bloom, *Dying to Kill: The Allure of Suicide Terror* (New York: Columbia University Press, 2005); Diego Gambetta, *Making Sense of Suicide Missions* (Oxford: Oxford University Press, 2005); Farhad Khosrokhavar, *Suicide Bombers: Allah's New Martyrs* (London: Pluto Press, 2005); A. M. Oliver and Paul F. Steinberg, *The Road to Martyrs' Square: A Journey into the World of the Suicide Bomber* (New York: Oxford University Press, 2005); Ami Pedahzur, Suicide Terrorism (Cambridge: Polity, 2005); Christoph Reuter, *My Life Is a Weapon: A Modern*

History of Suicide Violence (Princeton, N.J.: Princeton University Press, 2004); and Shaul Shay, *The Shahids: Islam and Suicide Attacks* (New Brunswick, N.J: Transaction Publishers, 2004).

17. Hannah Arendt, "Understanding and Politics," in her *Essays in Understanding, 1930–1954: Formation, Exile, and Totalitarianism* (New York: Schocken Books, 2005), 307–27.

18. Arendt, "Understanding and Politics," 307–8.

19. Mikhail M. Bakhtin, *Toward a Philosophy of the Act* (Austin: University of Texas Press, 1993), 2–13.

20. Roxanne Doty, "Aporia: A Critical Exploration of the Agent-Structure Problematique in International Relations Theory," *European Journal of International Relations* 3, no. 3 (1997): 365–92.

21. J-P. Sartre, "Being and Doing: Freedom," in his *Being and Nothingness: An Essay on Phenomenological Ontology* (New York: Philosophical Library, 1956), 433–85; see also Massimo Lollini, "Alterity and Transcendence: Notes on Ethics, Literature, and Testimony," and "Postscript," in *Who Exactly Is the Other? Western and Transcultural Perspectives*, ed. Steven Shankman and Massimo Lollini (Eugene: Oregon Humanities Center, 2002).

22. Martin Esslin, *The Theatre of the Absurd* (New York: Doubleday, 1969), 64.

23. Bakhtin, *Toward a Philosophy of the Act.*

24. Ibid.

25. Adolf Reinach, "The Apriori Foundations of Civil Law" (1913), reprinted in *Aletheia* 3 (1983): 1–142.

26. Arendt, "Understanding and Politics," 309–10; and Pierre Bourdieu, "Understanding," *Theory, Culture & Society* 13, no. 2 (1996): 17–37.

27. Sartre, "Being and Doing."

28. Emmanuel Lévinas, "Freedom and Command," in his *Collected Philosophical Papers* (Pittsburgh, Pa.: Duquesne University Press, 1998), 25.

29. Sartre, "Being and Doing," 482.

30. Soldier-martyrs do not create themselves; the blank-slate baby does not just become a bomber, although many mothers now dream that the child in their wombs will be a martyr and will therefore die a martyr's death.

31. Sartre, "Being and Doing," 482–509. We understand empathetically that many people live in terribly suffocating conditions, and have their land stolen and their homes destroyed, but we emphatically reject the claim that this gives them no other option than to engage in routinized suicide violence.

32. Ibid., 533.

33. Ibid., 534.

34. Ibid., 540.

35. T. Parsons, "The Theory of Action," in his *The Structure of Social Action* (New York: Free Press, 1968), 66; and Max Weber, "Basic Sociological Terms," in *Economy and Society*, ed. G. Roth (Berkeley: University of California Press, 1968), 6.

36. Hannah Arendt, *On Violence* (New York: Harcourt, Brace and World, 1969), 65–66.

37. Ibid., 52.

38. Max Weber, "Basis Sociological Terms," 14.

39. Hannah Arendt, *On Violence*, 54.

40. Bakhtin, *Toward a Philosophy of the Act*, 64.

41. Arendt, *Eichmann in Jerusalem*, 80, 102–3.
42. Ibid., 93.
43. Bakhtin, *Toward a Philosophy of the Act*, 2–3.
44. Ibid., 41–42.
45. Ibid., 31.
46. Ibid., 27.
47. Sartre, "Being and Doing," 431.
48. Ibid., 432.
49. Arendt, *On Violence*, 51.
50. Ibid., 4.
51. Friedrich Nietzsche, *On the Genealogy of Morality* (Cambridge: Cambridge University Press, 1994), 12.
52. Esslin, *The Theatre of the Absurd*, 4–5; see also Emmanuel Lévinas, *Alterity and Transcendence* (New York: Columbia University Press, 1999).
53. Arendt, *On Violence*, 79–81.
54. Bakhtin, *Toward a Philosophy of the Act*, 55.
55. Ibid., 31.
56. Esslin, *The Theatre of the Absurd*, 31.
57. The formula for many soldier-martyrs is the following: martyrdom is near guaranteed when one strikes the infidel with solid faith in the unity of God. Of course, who the "infidel" is is the subject of arbitrary specifications; the infidel can be a non-Muslim, an atheist, a combatant or occupying force, and even a member of another religious sect.
58. Lévinas, "Freedom and Command," 19.
59. Pierre Hayat, "Introduction," in Lévinas, *Alterity and Transcendence*, xiii.
60. Lévinas, "Freedom and Command," 33.
61. Esslin, *The Theatre of the Absurd*.
62. David McNally, *Another World Is Possible: Globalization and Anti-Capitalism* (Winnipeg, Canada: Arbeiter Ring, 2002), 11.
63. Anna M. Agathangelou and Lily Ling, "Power, Borders, Security, Wealth: Lessons of Violence and Desire from September 11," *International Studies Quarterly* 48, no. 3 (2004): 521.
64. Robert Bernasconi, "Forward," in Emmanuel Lévinas. *Existence and Existents*, trans. Alphonso Lingis (Pittsburgh, Pa.: Duquesne University Press, 2001), xiv.
65. Sigmund Freud, "Thoughts on War and Death," in *Civilization and Its Discontents*, ed. James Strachey (London: Hogarth Press and the Institute of Psycho-Analysis, 1963), 45.
66. Arendt, *On Violence*, 64.
67. Soldier-martyrs place profound emphasis on the exoteric aspects of religion, including religious doctrine and jurisprudence, though the majority are lacking in the formal education of these sciences.
68. Michel Foucault, *Discipline and Punish: The Birth of the Prison* (New York: Vintage Books, 1995), 201.
69. Maria Mies, "Reproductive Technologies," in Maria Mies and Vandana Shiva, *Ecofeminism* (London: Zed, 1993), 178; see also McNally, *Another World Is Possible*, 11.
70. Maria Mies, "Reproductive Technologies," 177.

71. Giorgio Agamben, *Means without Ends: Notes on Politics* (Minneapolis: University of Minnesota Press, 2000), 56–59.
72. Ibid., 122–25.
73. See Simon Tyzsko, "Suicide Bomber Barbie," http://www.theculture.net/barbie/.
74. See Mark Robson, "The Baby Bomber," *Journal of Visual Culture* 31, no. 1 (2004): 63–76.
75. Friedrich Nietzsche, "Second Essay: 'Guilt,' 'Bad Conscience' and Related Matters," in his *On the Genealogy of Morals* (Cambridge: Cambridge University Press, 1994).
76. Lévinas, *Alterity and Transcendence*, 29.
77. Arendt, "On Violence," 179.
78. Hannah Arendt, *The Human Condition* (Chicago: University of Chicago Press, 1958), 177; and Arendt, "Understanding and Politics," 321.
79. Arendt, Human Condition, 177.
80. Sartre, "Being and Doing," 613; and Arendt, *Human Condition*, 178.
81. Arendt, "Understanding and Politics," 322.
82. Arendt, "*On Violence,*" 163.
83. Judith Butler, *Precarious Life: The Power of Mourning and Violence* (London: Verso, 2004), 15.
84. Robson, "The Baby Bomber," 71.
85. Isin, "The Neurotic Citizen," 235.
86. Robson, "The Baby Bomber," 74.

.

5
Panic, Civility, and the Homeland

MATTHEW FARISH

Histories of the Homeland

As the American presidential race gathered momentum and vitriol in September 2004, the U.S. Department of Homeland Security (DHS) announced National Preparedness Month. In a "national address" on September 9, two days before the third anniversary of the event now known colloquially as 9/11, and hard on the heels of a combative Republican National Convention in New York City, Homeland Security Secretary Tom Ridge noted that each of the hundreds of planned activities for the month would contribute to the "mission and the mandate of an entire nation . . . a philosophy of shared responsibility, shared leadership, and shared accountability."[1]

These were familiar generalities, heralding the strength of American resilience, and the association of Ridge's voice with such platitudes was so strong that most major news organizations did not grant the event significant coverage. But a different story can be found in the list of organizations enlisted in the initiative (from the Red Cross to the Outdoor Advertising Association); the provision of "preparedness information and tools" at retailers such as Home Depot, Wal-Mart, Costco, and Starbucks; and the production of public service announcements for television and radio (U.S. Department of Homeland Security 2004a, 2004b). At a critical political moment, the American government, alongside corporate and nonprofit partners, was furthering the correlation between risk and citizenship, once again turning the nation itself into a jeopardized space, held together by communal character and the necessity of war.

Homeland security—or, as it is occasionally presented in campaign or press conference backdrops, "securing the homeland"—is a phrase, to the delight and chagrin of critics, that is both effortlessly certain and impossibly vague. It is a source of frequent satire, particularly in the form of parodies which twist the DHS's maddening, ambiguous, and yet cleverly nonspecific "color-coded" alert systems for different purposes (see Flynn 2005). In this respect it unsurprisingly resembles the civil defense initiatives of the early Cold War. The parallels are not exact; for instance, civil defense was linked, but only tangentially, to the notorious Cold War programs of domestic surveillance spear-headed by such legendary figures as J. Edgar Hoover and Joseph McCarthy, whereas the DHS rests at the heart of an archipelago of new "War on Terror" projects, including such little-known agencies as the Pentagon's Counterintelligence Field Activity (CIFA), said to employ over one thousand staff (although the number is not public), and the Air Force Office of Special Investigations' "Eagle Eyes" program (Pincus 2005, A06).

However, the official presentation of civil defense and homeland security suggests identical attempts to achieve what one historian of the former has appropriately dubbed the militarization of everyday life. Cold War fears of atomic devastation, concerns common to the point of sheer banality, frequently positioned the "nuclear" family and its members as partners in the military defense of the nation before, during, and after this hypothetical assault. Civil defense, moreover, perfectly captured and reconciled the strange state of life in the Cold War United States: neither combat nor peace, total mobilization nor demobilization, but "national security," a twilight condition requiring, among other sources of sustenance, routine propaganda exercises which would ideally perpetuate forms of personal and collective panic and simultaneously manage them. This is the language of security, but civil defense was additionally, explicitly phrased as a response to a *military* attack on the United States, an attack likely featuring the nuclear weapons that were also becoming increasingly important components of American foreign policy (McEnaney 2000, 4–5, 12; see also Grossman 2001).

Regardless of one's political sentiments, it is indisputable that this same mandate of managing panic and militarizing American society is an outcome, even a rationale, of recent Department of Homeland Security pronouncements and policies. Just as "terror" can represent both an action and a condition, to be an American citizen during an indefinite struggle against a shadowy foe is to be both a victim and a participant in this conflict. Encouraging remarks such as "Go about your lives normally" and "Get out and shop" are both negated and balanced by color-coded warnings that appear to hold equally little substance, perhaps because they cannot be explained fully due to security concerns, or because they are manufactured out of suspiciously flimsy evidence. It is possible to protest that this uncomfortable dualism of citizenship is a necessary one. Yet this is not the issue of concern; it is, rather, whether the contradictions of civility and panic are acknowledged or exploited by those responsible for their perpetuation—for the production and reproduction of the homeland as a space of war.

The ties between the Cold War and the War on Terror, whether as epochs or, perhaps more appropriately, less fixed signifiers of *conditions*, are of course not limited to demands for a homogeneous patriotism, ironically dependent on narrow and particular forms of expressive citizenship. A world divided into two camps, requiring the frequent demonization of an oppositional population and a global search for amorphous instigators, not to mention the invigoration, and investigation, of area studies programs on American campuses, are among the other startling manifestations of this comparison, which might be enough to prompt reflections on the basic premises of geopolitical knowledge. Such parallels are not just academic; in a May 2006 commencement address at the U.S. Military Academy, President Bush drew a direct comparison between his administration and the Cold War policies of Harry Truman. "Like the cold war," Bush proclaimed sweepingly, "we are fighting the followers of a murderous ideology that despises freedom, questions all dissent, has territorial ambitions and pursues totalitarian aims" (quoted in Bumiller 2006).

This chapter, then, is a more systematic examination of the idea, and the institutions, of homeland security, in the light of Cold War precedents.[2] The list of examples ripe for juxtaposition is long and includes educational efforts, desert construction sites, and urban simulations. As such, my aim is not to create a complete roster, but instead to scrutinize the presumptions fortifying these and other instances of militarism's geographies. Under conditions where militarism is understood as pervasive, Rachel Woodward writes, "its effects on spaces, places, environments, and landscapes" require attention from geographers, particularly those with a talent for historical analysis. War, the central subject for traditional "terrain and tactics" approaches to military geography, constitutes only "the endpoint of a range of processes, practices, ideas and arguments which make it possible" (Woodward 2005, 721, 722, 727).

"Homeland," a word which American presidents prior to George W. Bush were not in the habit of uttering, suggests a specific territory, a *domestic* space in all senses of the word. If the events of September 11 revealed, once again, the permeability of national borders, then homeland security, since that date, has been the key discursive and practical attempt to shore up lines of division between the United States and other spaces, and between American citizens and others. Like Cold War civil defense—which, owing to the precedent of the Second World War, did not require a term of such gravity to stir emotions—the edges of the homeland outlined by the Bush administration are not quite synchronous with the signs, fences, and guard posts delineating physical borders. As Tom Ridge's successor, Michael Chertoff, indicated in March 2005, his department would not be able to prevent every occurrence of terrorism on American soil, but would instead focus (in the words of the *New York Times*) on "more serious or catastrophic strikes," and concurrently offer a "more restrained and coordinated public message" (Lipton 2005). This is slippery categorization and terminology indeed, and suggests that we must begin by considering the *work* that "homeland" has done through pronouncements, publications, and policies. In an astute reflection on precisely these issues, Amy Kaplan argues that although the invocation of homeland security in one sense clearly strengthens a cordon between domestic and foreign spaces, in another sense it "depends on a radical insecurity," placing the "home in a constant state of emergency" and providing for the creation or strengthening of agencies whose mandate is to seek, limit, or negate, often very aggressively, the presence of dangerous foreign identities and objects within the supposedly sacred boundaries of the nation-state (Kaplan 2003, 90).

The popularization of "homeland security" followed the successful rendering of the terrorist attacks on the World Trade Center and the Pentagon as a national calamity. This was, as Neil Smith argued late in 2001, not necessarily an automatic outcome, however much it might have been presented as such, not instantly but rapidly, to the millions of people glued to their televisions on September 11 of that year. To return to the scale of the nation notwithstanding both shocking *local* events and the *global* networks responsible for them was to provide not only an odd sort of comfort, but also a justification for war, even though the perpetrators were rapidly identified as nonstate actors (Smith 2001). In a recent *New Yorker* essay, Louis Menand (2004) noted that "[by] nearly every statistical measure, and by common consent, Americans are the most patriotic people in the world." And the legitimization of a long, perhaps even perpetual war, as well as the broader condition of militarism fueling it, depended not only on rousing an outraged citizenry, but also on convincing every American that he or she was equally at risk. Only certain bodies would have to be sacrificed, but far more minds were required.

A National Target

In 1945, shortly after the existence of atomic weapons became public knowledge, the Social Science Research Council established a Committee on the Social Aspects of Atomic Energy. As the implications of atomic technology washed into every corner of intellectual inquiry, this committee was disbanded (in 1947), and its concerns taken up by a multitude of other panels, but not before studies on public opinion and urban vulnerability were generated. Unlike most of the other scientific achievements of the Second World War, after the destruction of huge swaths of the Japanese cities Hiroshima and Nagasaki the bomb was never perceived as just a technological device; its awesome capabilities were as much an incentive for studies in "social nature" as they were an indication that "physical nature" had been mastered. It was also acknowledged that the sheer destructiveness of the bomb, in addition to the unusual conditions of peace-as-war characterizing the Cold War, lent credence to alternative methods of combat, particularly those that struggled with the "inner landscape" of "national and international psyches" (Capshew 1999, 181; Herman 1995, 9, 124, 137).

Hiroshima and Nagasaki were central to the remarkable U.S. Strategic Bombing Survey (USSBS), an initiative that actually began in November 1944, and considered for a first case study German landscapes subject to an equally devastating level of destruction, if only of the "conventional" type. The work of the European Survey was designed to aid the efficiency of ongoing firebombing over Japan, and once two atomic bombs had been dropped on August 6 and August 9, 1945, President Harry Truman authorized the formation of the Pacific Survey, which moved in less than a month later to specifically assess the damage wrought by atomic weaponry. But the USSBS was much more than a vehicle for the analysis of city form. German and, later, Japanese spaces were turned into sites for the collection of evidence and the testing of previously vague theories, a place where the principles and methods of cutting-edge social science could be applied to a definite geography. Carried to familiar environs, the results were then modified by a dosage of American spatial and sociological character, and thus made suitable for domestic usage.

As the bomb's testing moved, in a neocolonial repatriation, from Japan, then the South Pacific (long a laboratory for military science), and back to the United States, it shaped at least one more American "boom town"—Las Vegas, located just south of the Atomic Energy Commission's (AEC) Nevada Test Site (Hill 1951). Drawing inspiration from Los Alamos, the center of the Manhattan Project, the dual frontiers of science and the geographic West were prolonged in America as deserts, "empty" spaces that were "never vacant enough" (Findlay 1995, 34). Cities were brought to these naturalized landscapes in a series of bombing exercises that began during World War II in Utah's Dugway Proving Ground and culminated a decade later in extraordinary rehearsals of atomic explosions near emblematic suburban housing, complete with mannequins, erected at the Nevada Test Site.

At Dugway, the German Jewish architect Eric Mendelsohn, a prominent modernist, created a miniature Berlin suburb with exacting detail. The complex, built with Utah prison labor, was "firebombed and completely reconstructed at least three times between May and September of 1943." An equivalent Japanese "village" was also erected and destroyed (Davis 1999, 94). "Among the points that had to be determined," according to the official history of the Chemical Warfare Service, "was the degree of penetration of bombs, and the time-temperature factor for igniting the typical Japanese target" (Brophy, Miles, and Cochrane 1959, 185). But the postwar incarnation of urban construction in the desert, a "survival city" west of Dugway in Nevada's Yucca Flats, received far more publicity. In the suitably titled Operation Doorstep, conducted on March 17, 1953, the AEC, U.S. Department of Defense, and Federal Civil Defense Administration (FCDA) collaborated to stage a small atomic blast in the vicinity of two "typical" American homes stuffed with mannequins. The residences were also equipped with basement shelters, while eight outdoor shelters and a "variety of typical passenger cars" dotted the Nevada moonscape. Doorstep was followed on May 5, 1955, by Operation Cue, which included a novel set of civil defense field exercises, from rescue to feeding services, in the wake of the explosion (FCDA 1953a, 1955a, 1956; see also Vanderbilt 2002, 69–95).

Both operations "defined who and what was endangered by the atomic age: families, homes, consumer commodities." But administrators in attendance at the deeply symbolic Nevada tests perceived a broader purpose—a contribution to the "general conclusions" for the public "which will apply in the majority of cases under the principle of the 'calculated risk' which is basic to all realistic civil defense planning" (McEnaney 2000, 54; FCDA 1953a, 3). A pamphlet issued to residents of the area near the Nevada Test Site assured them that they were in "a very real sense active participants in the Nation's atomic test program," that each test was only conducted due to "national need," and that proper safety concerns were being addressed (AEC 1957, 1, 2, 5). Whether in the terminology of cutting-edge social science practiced under the aegis of the USSBS, or in the lurid photographs of Nevada tests published in popular magazines, the role of civil defense as a national program of awareness and, hopefully, response was becoming solidified, perhaps even to the extent that it provided opportunities for humor or flippancy. The United States was the target of a Cold War enemy, and as such all of its citizens had a duty to enroll—or were simply enrolled—as citizens of the atomic age. Civil defense administrators, meanwhile, were determined to manage this process carefully.

Panic in the Streets?

The successes of civil defense campaigns may have ultimately been minimal, but the attention these programs have received from historians is testament to the fecundity of civil defense iconography, spectacle, and propaganda, and the nationalization and normalization of militarism during the early Cold War. These trends were strikingly apparent in the FCDA's plan for an "Alert America" convoy, developed in late 1951. A train of vehicles traveled across the United States, visiting selected "target cities" and offering attendees a view of "dramatic visualizations" sketching the extent of the atomic threat:

> Through photographs, movies, three-dimensional mock-ups, and scientific action-dioramas they depict the possible uses of atomic energy in both peace and war. Visitors to the exhibits see the damage that could be done to American communities by atomic bombs, nerve gas, and germ warfare. Visitors experience a vivid dramatization of a mock A-bomb attack on their own cities. They learn what they can do through civil defense to protect themselves and the freedoms they cherish. (FCDA 1952, 15)[3]

One of these freedoms was mobility, linked closely to automobile ownership, itself tied to broader concerns for privacy and social order. As several scholars of civil defense have noted, discussing the aftereffects of nuclear war with Americans required systems of psychological management designed to specifically stifle *panic*, which in turn could lead to traffic jams, violence, racial tension, and all-around chaos (Oakes 1994; Grossman 2001). In 1955, the FCDA published a small pamphlet titled *4 Wheels to Survival* (1955b). (See figure 5.1.) The family car, the pamphlet argued, could "help you move away from danger," and auto owners were encouraged to keep the gas tank full, the tires inflated, the trunk stocked with groceries and first aid supplies,

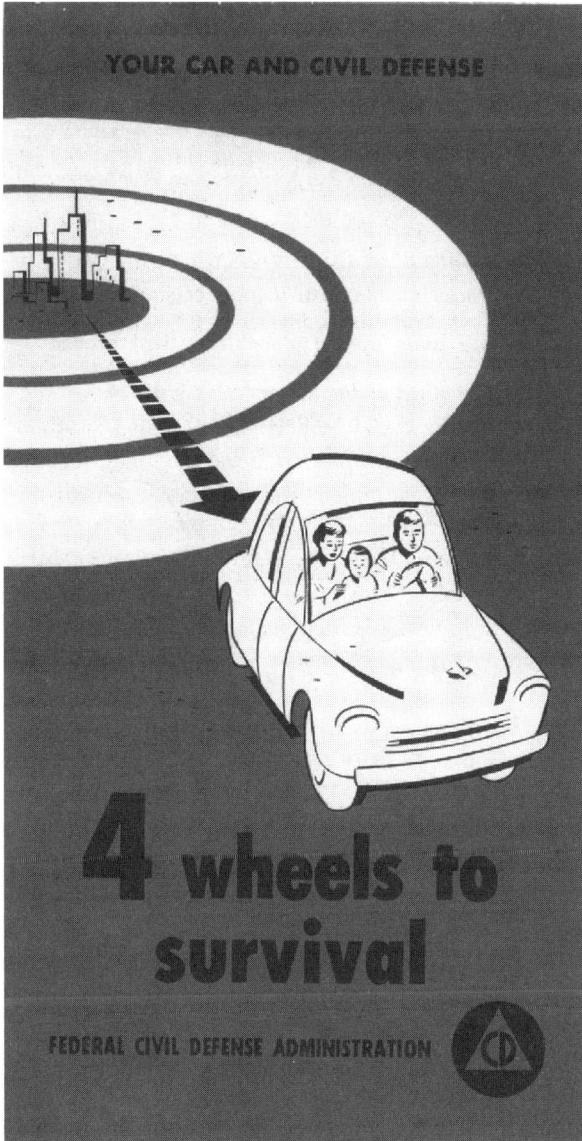

Figure 5.1 Civil Defense Driving: 4 Wheels to Survival.

and the rest of the vehicle in good shape. More interestingly, *4 Wheels to Survival* noted that tests in the Nevada desert could protect Americans from blast effects, and provided a fairly detailed explanation of what to do with vehicles before and after attack. Cars effectively provided a "small movable house" for the maintenance of the nuclear family in times of emergency, and a link to the authoritative civil defense radio broadcasts of CONELRAD (control of electromagnetic radiation) that would direct auto traffic in an orderly fashion out of cities. "Civil defense driving," the pamphlet concluded, depended on courtesy and patience: "If traffic gets stalled, don't lean on the horn. Your impatience may become someone else's panic. That could cost lives!" (FCDA 1955b, n.p.).

Like many similar civil defense publications of the period, *4 Wheels to Survival* is a decidedly mundane artifact, but it remains important for the ways in which American drivers and their passengers are clearly incorporated into a military geography of pre- and postconflict mobility. Much of the advice is applicable to any emergency, but this is precisely the point. Just as Cold War disaster scholars used models and theories derived from flood and tornado events to predict human behavior after a nuclear attack, the increasingly popular act of driving and moving along highway spaces was turned into a matter of national security by normalizing risk. Visit the Department of Homeland Security's public information website today, moreover, and you will find very similar instructions, as well as announcements of funding for programs such as the American Trucking Association's Highway Watch surveillance initiative.[4] Although the home, and the neighborhood, are obvious foci for historians of civil defense, as a space rich with symbolic meaning, the road—specifically the highway—is equally intriguing. After the Second World War, the new interstate highways, writes Steven Goddard (1994, 197), "were the cathedrals of the car culture, and their social implications were staggering," changing "how Americans lived, worked, played, shopped, and even loved." And the proposal to lace the nation with freeways in the mid-1950s faced no major challenges (Davies 1975, 4). At least part of the logic advanced by the Eisenhower administration and its supporters derived from the claim that the interstate system would serve the dual military purpose of aiding evacuation and facilitating the movement of troops and equipment during war. During the Second World War the application of strategic language to highways, as important defensive instruments, had begun in earnest, and the proposed highway network was frequently called the "military system" (Gutfreund 2004, 42).

Dwight Eisenhower traveled Germany's autobahn network after V-E Day—a trip that helped him "see the wisdom of broader ribbons across the land"—and during his first term as president he was determined to sort out the differences among competing interest groups and "fix" the nation's roads, finally securing support for and expanding the network proposed by the 1944

Highway Act but never completed (quoted in Weingroff 1996). Ike's appointment of General Lucius Clay to head an advisory committee on the interstate system, not to mention the nomination of General Motors CEO Charles Wilson as defense secretary, sealed the links between the automobile industry, highway construction, and defense—at least in a rhetorical sense. As Thomas Lewis notes in his history of the interstates, since nuclear fear had transfixed the nation, huge numbers of urban Americans believed their city or town would be on the list of Soviet targets. "The case for defense," in other words, "could help to sell highways to Congress" and the public, and so the initiative was renamed, with the momentous Federal-Aid Highway Act of 1956, to the National System of Interstate and Defense Highways. Given enough warning, citizens would theoretically "be able to pack the family car and head out of town on one of the new superhighways" (Lewis 1997, 107, 108).

The chief of transportation for the U.S. Army, however, estimated that a full-scale war would mandate the evacuation of some seventy million Americans. As this figure suggests, evacuation, particularly in the age of the hydrogen bomb, was considered by many to be impossible. In her 1970 critique *Superhighway-Superhoax*, Helen Leavitt revealed that the interstate builders had never actually consulted with the Pentagon on such matters as the proper height of bridges so as to allow the transit of Atlas missiles (Leavitt 1970, 187–88; see also Goddard 1994, 194). But it was ultimately American drivers who would have to support the massive expenditures of the interstate program, and whether highways would *actually* aid national defense was secondary. In his 1958 essay "The Highway and the City," Lewis Mumford captured this dynamic precisely, calling the linking of highway construction to defense "specious, indeed flagrantly dishonest." He went on to indict the "religion of the motorcar" that seemed to have saturated American life, and argued that the nascent "highway program will, eventually, wipe out the very area of freedom that the private motor car promised to retain." Predicting only additional congestion if motorists fled the metropolis en masse, Mumford suggested ironically that the construction of highways had already had the same impact upon "vegetation and human structures as the passage of a tornado or the blast of an atom bomb," leaving behind "a tomb of concrete roads and ramps covering the dead corpse of a city" (Mumford 1963, 237, 238).

Alongside evacuation schemes, planners, scientists, politicians, and civil defense officials put forward a variety of even more ambitious plans for urban decentralization in the late 1940s and 1950s, and all emerged from the assessment that American cities were "concentrated spatially," too dense and "geographically bound" (Borden 1946, 65; see also Zarlengo 1999, 936; Galison 2001; Farish 2003). The most grandiose proposals were quickly dismissed as economically and socially impossible, and support for dispersal initiatives faded by the end of the 1950s. There were several reasons for this, from alterations in Cold War strategy to the development of new weapons, but we should not ignore the fact that by 1960, civil defense organizations had essentially "written off the possibility of protecting urban populations" barring impossibly seamless evacuations, a conclusion that no doubt also reflected changes to the demographic profile of major American cities in the preceding two decades (Oakes 1994, 109).

The themes of urban chaos and evacuation were central to the 1950 film *Panic in the Streets*, which featured two cast members and a director, Elia Kazan, who later wound up on opposite sides of the Hollywood blacklist fostered by the infamous House Un-American Affairs Committee (HUAC). The movie is also notable for its setting—it was shot entirely on location in New Orleans, to a soundtrack of jazz and blues—and for its narrative premise: a health inspector's desperate attempt to prevent an immigrant-based plague from spreading beyond the boundaries of the city. The presentation of this pandemic is clearly part of what Andrew Ross (1989, 45) calls "the Cold War culture of germophobia," on display both inside and outside the pliable boundaries of the nation-state, and epitomized by the geopolitical concept of containment. But the "documentary noir" approach of *Panic in the Streets*, as well as the similarly structured and more famous New York drama *The Naked City* (1948), is also a celebration of urban *interdiction*, in the form of modern detection and other scientific approaches to society (McNamara 1996, 176). And yet by the end of the film, despite his successes in the seedy districts of New Orleans, Clinton Reed, the protagonist, decides that his suburban home is not far enough removed from the dangers of the city, and plans to move further into the "country."

The Social Science of Survival

American civil defense discourse of the 1950s is now associated, often satirically, with educational films such as the legendary *Duck and Cover* (1951) and its timid star, Bert the Turtle (see Brown 1988).[5] However, civil defense must still be treated as an important and *visible* component of Cold War culture, bringing together (in occasionally awkward fashion) geopolitics, technoscience, and social psychology to bombard American citizens with information concerning the survivability of a nuclear attack. The geographic locus of civil defense bulletins, videos, radio alerts, and other media forms was, of course, the suburban home, where nuclear families were removed from the dense diversity and confusion of inner cities, and were able to smoothly follow the suggestions in such publications as the FCDA's *Home Protection Exercises* (1953b).[6] But civil defense was also explicitly a national program, linking proper domestic behavior to the health of the national body, in a framework that Stephen Collier and Andrew Lakoff (Chapter 6, this volume), call "distributed preparedness." As such, although the FCDA and associated agencies suffered from a regular lack of interest in their programs, and although those responsible for civil defense planning never fully settled on a single method of protecting a wide range of American landscapes, the fascinating premises of civil defense, and its ubiquity, signal its importance to Cold War scholars (McEnaney 2000, 6).

In addition, despite its frequently caricatured representations of American bodies and behavior, civil defense was consistently bolstered by, and relied on, a substantial interdisciplinary literature of social scientific research in what might be called "disaster studies," although this does not suggest the extent to which such scholarship was premised on both the assumed condition of the Cold War and on various symbolic geographic markers, from the nation to the city to the home. Second World War innovations such as operations research had already indicated that joining scientific theory with new analytical techniques and empirical data could solve pressing military dilemmas within a centralized command and control setting. By the 1950s, it was increasingly believed that those same techniques could be used to tackle practical problems within civil society, such as those faced by the United States' burgeoning postwar urban centers and regions, problems increasingly overseen and managed by the state (Light 2003). In other words, because the Cold War—from its technological devices to its espionage narratives—turned every property, household, and individual into a prospective target, an urban concern such as population density or traffic was also a suitable topic for military study. This was exactly the premise behind the FCDA's various initiatives, particularly more abstract calculations of evacuation models and theories of mass unrest.

The marriage of cutting-edge social science with the geography of everyday life, of detached analytical techniques with strategic social intervention, was apparent in research conducted across the emergent military-industrial-academic complex (Leslie 1993). At the University of Washington (UW), for instance, geographers and like-minded associates were enlisted to participate in a high-profile 1954 evacuation test dubbed Operation Rideout, a dispersal of Bremerton, Washington's population by car and ferry. In a memo to a National Research Council (NRC) Disaster Studies Committee member, William Garrison, a UW faculty member and a leader of geography's "quantitative revolution," mentioned that his "observation team" had recommended the use of aerial photography and a "Time-Space Car Tracking Plan" to Washington State civil defense leaders. His suggestions were obviously impressive, because he and a team of graduate students were soon enlisted to conduct research for the state's 1956 "Survival Plan."[7]

The NRC and its partner organization, the National Academy of Sciences, made one of the most substantial bureaucratic investments in civil defense and disaster studies, bringing many prominent researchers together on advisory committees within its Division of Anthropology and Psychology to identify suitable approaches and marginalize those deemed inappropriate. As one Council-Academy report noted, social science could be brought to bear on all aspects of what was called "nonmilitary" or "passive" defense, from the management of facilities such as radar stations to sociological and economic recovery following an atomic attack. High-profile research topics included the "psychology of threat," from group and individual problem solving under conditions of "danger, confusion, isolation, and deprivation" to survival studies in "austere environments." Many of the fashionable tools and techniques of Cold War social science, from simulation exercises to systems analysis, were cited as applicable to these inquiries. The intention was to "study the American people in as many disaster situations as possible," extrapolating the impact of floods and tornadoes, for instance, to account for the unknown dimensions of sudden atomic attack.[8] The comparison and extension were sensible, but also hinted at the "natural" character of a profoundly human event and the arms race presumably perpetrating it.

That the same methods and themes were equally present in multiple types of strategic studies was no coincidence; they were common to the dilemmas of life in atomic America, behind an unstable shield of security whose breach would have devastating consequences. Similar sponsors were present as well. In the midst of its program in the behavioral sciences, the Ford Foundation also funded the NRC's Committee on Disaster Studies, after initial support from the Army, Navy, and Air Force medical services had expired. In a 1956 letter to a Ford Foundation representative, Glen Finch, the executive secretary of the NRC's Division of Anthropology and Psychology, outlined the major interests pursued by the committee. In particular, NRC researchers, he wrote, were interested in the "patterns of social interaction and communication before, during, and after disaster," from the dysfunction of panic to the functional development of a "therapeutic community" through citizen solidarity. If it was not already clear, Finch went on to describe the advantages of disaster study for broader knowledge and theory in the behavioral sciences: not only did the processes examined have a "starting point, a definite concrete event," but a disaster also provided a rationale for the infiltration of communities via participant observation and interviews. Finally, and most crucially, disasters were both unique and generalizable. They could not be "duplicated in the laboratory," and produced *abnormal* human activity, but were concurrently understood as aberrations from an understandable norm, and were thus relatable to that standard using the same vocabulary.[9]

The FCDA briefed the NRC's Committee on Disaster Studies at the National Civil Defense Training Center in January 1953. FCDA staff presented papers on psychological warfare, medical care, and other challenges, while committee members were shown a demonstration of an air raid warning system, shown a mock "Rescue Street," and participated in a map exercise on "City X." The following year, the committee produced a statement on the "problem of panic," which set out to delineate the term in order to grasp it objectively: "it is desirable to confine it to highly emotional behavior which is excited by the presence of an immediate severe threat, and *which results in increasing the danger for the self and for others rather than reducing it.*"[10] While hardly precise, this definition indicated that the central indicator of chaos was the viral spread of irrationality across a collective, often through technological networks. It is not surprising, then, that one of the committee's key members, Irving Janis, later coined the term "groupthink" (see Janis 1972). But civil defense, aided by social science, was a proactive concept; as Nikolas Rose (1999, vii) has noted, "[T]he psy disciplines and psy expertise have had a key role in constructing 'governable subjects.'"

Bolstered by the abstract rationality of social science—and, more generally, claims to authority, expertise, and even classified knowledge—Cold War civil defense and contemporary homeland security both aim to produce a particular type of American citizen. In the publications of the FCDA and the DHS, and the pronouncements of their representatives, exercising a certain type of behavior is a demonstration of thoughtful maturity, of the right to participate in political life (Isin 2002). The domestic contours of the War on Terror are still taking shape, but in the case of the early Cold War it is clear that appropriate citizenship was a geographic practice, suited to specific local landscapes and helping to maintain those spaces as secure and stable in the midst of national uncertainty. For this reason, the importance of such federal programs cannot entirely be downplayed by reference to the sluggish sales of backyard shelter kits or the ridiculousness of duct tape protection techniques. And yet *federal* is the key term; the power of civil defense or homeland security narratives is not all-encompassing, and what "counts" as citizenship during a national security crisis is a narrow range of expressions and positions. The example of Cold War antinuclear groups (or more recently formed solidarity and peace organizations) offers alternative typologies of citizenship, and alternative grounds for political behavior, particularly at local scales (see Wittner 1993–2003; Goldberg 2004). That such activism, and its geographic terrain, is frequently targeted by the apparatus of national security suggests precisely that challenging the militarization of everyday life threatens dominant definitions of citizenship in a time of war, however ambiguous that war might be in duration and direction. As with territorial boundaries, the very notion of a secure American identity is constantly disturbed by its constructed opposites—upon whom it relies for existence—"always slipping back across the porous . . . borders to disturb and subvert from the inside" (Hall 1996, 252).

Novelty and Normalcy

If you spend it, they will come: Since al-Qaeda hit the Pentagon, more people have moved to greater Washington than to any other non-Sunbelt region. Call it denial, call it playing the odds; having weighed the certainty of good jobs versus the threat of future catastrophe, people have voted with their moving vans. The threat is real. Last year, Rand Corp., the granddaddy of national security think tanks, proposed a complex formula for estimating the risk of major terrorist attacks in U.S. cities. The cities with the most dense urban cores, New York and Chicago, ranked first and second because of the prospect of many deaths in a relatively small area. Washington, despite much lower density, was third, because of its obvious strategic importance. (Von Drehle 2006, W10)

Some fifty years after *Duck and Cover* was shown and staged in classrooms across the United States, school exercises, urban simulations, propaganda-heavy pronouncements, and, most importantly, calls for the mobilization of minds in the service of militarism once again combined to constitute the character, and the boundaries, of a threatened American homeland. Bert the Turtle was replaced by the "Ready Deputy" Contest sent students into their neighborhoods as recruiters, directing families to assemble emergency preparedness kits. The school enlisting the most families received $10,000 and then Homeland Security Secretary Ridge as principal for a day. The deadline was October 29, 2004, four days before the presidential election (Ode 2004).[11] Entire neighborhoods, even towns, were co-opted or purchased by the Department of Homeland Security for antiterrorism training and other simulations, while the always useful "empty space" of the Nevada Test Site received $13 million in 2004 for the construction of "mock border stations, a simulated airline inspection terminal and a seaport" to stage the transmission of radiological materials into the country (Romero 2004; Tetreault 2004).

Moreover, as any recent visitor to a major American city can testify, homeland security implies a variety of visible and less visible forms of urban militarization which echo and update Cold War procedures. Washington, D.C.'s Joint Operations Command Center, set up after 9/11 and shared by the Secret Service, the FBI, and the Defense Intelligence Agency, among others, possesses a "three dimensional map of all downtown buildings," permitting "technicians to simulate bomb blasts and debris projections" (Brzezinski 2003, 43). A series of major exercises have simulated biological and other attacks in places such as Seattle and Chicago, where during 2003's Top Officials 2 (TOPOFF 2) conference the spread of plague was supplemented by a concurrent (staged) explosion and plane crash, so as to involve more response agencies (Johnson 2003). But the Bush administration has also been repeatedly charged with ignoring or underfunding certain aspects of homeland security—certainly compared to its widespread military operations in Iraq, Afghanistan, and beyond, but specifically in locations such as New York City—a policy that resembles the dismissal of certain urban areas as doomed (and dangerous, should their populations spill outward) during the 1950s (Chait 2003; Crowley 2004; Newfield 2004; Ripley 2004; Lipton 2006).

Homeland security activities, and the climate of fear and uncertainty which accompanies them, are, to borrow Joan Didion's phrasing, part of the "new normal," a contemporary condition of novelty said to have been brought about by 9/11. Laws and language change, but these alterations, many with far-reaching cultural, political, and social consequences, are treated by politicians and pundits as overwhelmingly understandable, even though care is taken to discuss them with the aim of reducing anxiety. The erosion of civil liberties, and the acceptance of state-sanctioned torture are not only couched in the terminology of necessity, but have also become amnesiac fantasies rife with the diversions of sophism and stereotypes (Didion 2004).

Even as the Bush administration and a Republican-controlled Congress pushed through substantial tax cuts and other measures of "compassionate conservatism," the institutions of governance with a hand in military and security matters were expanding at a frightening rate. When it began formal operations on March 1, 2003, the Department of Homeland Security represented a massive new bureaucratic presence, incorporating almost two dozen distinct federal agencies and nearly 200,000 employees (Brzezinski 2004). Despite an initial budget of some $36 billion (Brzezinski 2003, 40), it faced innumerable challenges, particularly given the even greater expenses and energy spent on the invasion and occupation of Iraq in the same year. Measures of domestic security deemed basic were given extremely poor "grades" by the prominent 9/11 Commission (see Kean et al. 2005). The failings and limitations of the DHS, however, have been overshadowed and obscured by continued pronouncements of progress and even victory in the War on Terror's various campaigns.

But as with Cold War civil defense, the determination of DHS setbacks and successes—whether expressed by political sponsors or opponents, employees, prominent independent critics, journalists, or others—is only part of the story. Its diverse arms, its controversial programs, and even its very existence and title all suggest crucial redefinitions of the relationship between citizenship and territory, and certainly a heightened sensitivity to this relationship. Through numerous well-documented (and no doubt other less-documented) forms of monitoring, from the FBI's "national security letters" to the National Security Agency's wiretapping efforts, the Bush administration has made the category of "American" *more refined and yet also more suspect* than ever before—even more so than during the Cold War, when surveillance was a comparatively rudimentary concept. The way in which such challenges to legal norms are justified through the contradictory rhetoric of safeguarding "liberties" while adjusting to a radically changed "security environment" is nothing short of astonishing (see, e.g., White House 2006).

"Homeland security" suffers not only from the impossible premise of its second word, but also from the vague spatial presumptions of the first. The perception, among those with the power to articulate such ideas, that some regions of the American homeland are worth securing more than others is far older than the Department of Homeland Security, but this variant of "heartland geopolitics" (Sparke 1998) was particularly resonant in late August and September 2005, when Hurricane Katrina swept across the coastlines of Alabama, Mississippi, and Louisiana. Not only were various politicians, including President Bush, and government agencies, including the DHS, unprepared for a storm of such magnitude, despite direct warnings from disaster officials, but also their response to Katrina's astounding impact was halfhearted at best. As an editorial in the April 2006 issue of *The Nation* indicated,

> [T]he record of the past six months is one of promises unkept, funding delayed and denied, and machinations of politicians and their corporate cronies to profit from the catastrophe. The net effect has been the disenfranchisement and continued displacement of the poor and minority population of New Orleans, which suffered disproportionately from the hurricane. ("Neglect in New Orleans" 2006)[12]

The failure to evacuate or provide comfort and shelter to more of this population is strikingly similar to the neglect of "poor and minority" groups in Cold War civil defense models and exercises, particularly those located in the South and in major cities (see Farish 2004).

"When the levees broke," the liberal rights theorist (and current Liberal member of the Canadian Parliament) Michael Ignatieff wrote several weeks later, "the contract of American citizenship failed"—although presumably not for the first time. Those critical of liberalism might note that such a contract has historically depended on exclusion, on the power to restrict citizenship as much as to grant it, but this is not to deny that even as an abstraction its range and force are significant. As Ignatieff (2005) noted, it was the individuals and groups most affected by the hurricane who most powerfully invoked and impugned this national contract through straightforward expressions such as "We are American." That those taking shelter in the New Orleans Convention Center were able to articulate, under conditions of dislocation and suffering, a more inclusive homeland, while damning a more vacuous version, should not be surprising. An awareness of a particular historical geography had prepared them for it, even as news anchors and pundits expressed shock that such "scenes" were possible in their own country.

Several weeks after Katrina made landfall on the Gulf Coast, the *New York Times* reported that city officials across the United States were reviewing their evacuation plans, and finding very little encouraging material: "in many places highways would clog quickly, confusion would reign and police resources would soon be overtaxed." These were conclusions reached though substantial mathematical calculation, to be sure, but they also hinted at assumptions concerning human behavior in the aftermath of a disaster or terrorist attack. Such behavior is a "significant factor," according to Washington, D.C.'s deputy mayor for public safety, who oversaw a 2005 Fourth of July drill that left crowds leaving the Mall "confused, but not panicked," and concluded that the event was "not exactly comparable to an emergency evacuation" (Broder

2005; Horowitz and Davenport 2005, A01). It was not necessarily that plans were lacking, then, or even that such plans reminded citizens of their status in a world of risks, but that a gap still existed between a plan and its operational "reality," or the cultural landscapes in which it would be implemented.

The paradox of this reality is that it is seen as triumphing over even the most clever and comprehensive plan, and yet it remains vague and elusive. The result is that the most ambitious of Department of Homeland Security initiatives, linked into the architecture of the War on Terror, are, like their Cold War counterparts, also governmental attempts to influence citizens in advance of an unknown event, and ideally to narrow the possible range of responses to this event. What is at once obvious and profoundly significant, then, is that the specific nature of this event—indeed, even its occurrence at all—is not of first-order importance. Producing a particular type of American, and thus a particular form of homeland, is.[13]

Meanwhile, in March 2006, city workers discovered a sealed stockpile of provisions and medical supplies inside the foundations of New York's Brooklyn Bridge. Many of the boxes were stamped "Office of Civil Defense" and labeled "1957" or "1962." The estimated 352,000 calorie-packed crackers were judged to be "still edible" (Chan 2006).

Notes

1. Department of Homeland Security (2004c). Ridge had already repeatedly linked his department's apparent successes with what he called "the president's leadership in the war against terror" (quoted in Bumiller 2004). Ridge announced his resignation on November 30, 2004, with a decidedly mixed record as secretary (Lichtblau and Drew 2004). President Bush's first choice for a successor, former New York Police Commissioner Bernard Kerik, was a spectacular failure, while the second, federal judge Michael Chertoff, oversaw many of the most controversial domestic aspects of the War on Terror while serving as assistant attorney general under John Ashcroft (VandeHei 2005). Chertoff subsequently came under heavy criticism for his department's poor response to Hurricane Katrina, and asserted before a subsequent congressional panel that he would "re-engineer" emergency management in his department (Hsu 2005).

2. As such, the chapter is a companion piece to my "Targeting the Inner Landscape" (Farish 2006), which examines the Cold War geography of psychological warfare and its contemporary resonance. Out of necessity, both chapters mention a few of the same programs and events, but are otherwise only parallel in orientation.

3. This is clearly the public face of the "vulnerability mapping" discussed by Stephen Collier and Andrew Lakoff in the next chapter. For more on both aspects of "target cities," see Farish (2003).

4. The website is http://www.dhs.gov/dhspublic/ (Department of Homeland Security n.d.).

5. The FCDA was very active in schools, urging a "greater emphasis . . . on teaching a keen awareness of national dangers and the necessary precautions against them." Elementary school students should understand, among other civil

defense-related subjects, "principal target areas and plans for their defense," as well as the "effects of nuclear attack or major natural disaster upon our large metropolitan areas" (U.S. Department of Health, Education, and Welfare, Office of Education 1956, 1, 42).

6. The gendered implications of such publications are detailed in Zarlengo (1999). Franke-Ruta (2003) describes a more recent "homeland security gender gap" and lampoons preparedness as "a high-stress equivalent of baby-proofing."

7. Memo, William Garrison et al. to Harry B. Williams, n.d., folder "Anthropology and Psychology: Disaster Research Group—Studies: Civil Defense Evacuation Test—Bremerton: Final Report, 1955," National Research Council-National Academy of Sciences Archives, Washington, D.C. (hereafter, NN).

8. National Academy of Sciences-National Research Council (1958, 21, 26); and "Proposal for Disaster Studies Program," attached to letter, John R. Wood to M. C. Winternitz, May 29, 1951, folder "Anthropology and Psychology: Committee on Disaster Studies—beginning of Program, 1951," NN, 1.

9. Glen Finch to Bernard Berelson, December 31, 1956, folder "Anthropology and Psychology: Committee on Disaster Studies—Sponsors: Ford Foundation," NN, 2.

10. Committee on Disaster Studies, National Research Council, "Report to the Surgeons General, Departments of the Army, Navy and Air Force," March 31, 1955, folder "Anthropology and Psychology: Committee on Disaster Studies—Reports to Sponsors: Department of Defense, 1955," NN; and "The Problem of Panic," June 1, 1954, folder "Anthropology and Psychology: Committee on Disaster Studies—Subcommittee on Panic: Problem of Panic, 1954," NN, original emphasis.

11. A copy of the Ready Deputy instructions can be found at http://www.norwichbulletin.com/legacy/customerservice/emergencypreparedness/emergency-prep_16.pdf (accessed May 2, 2007). The currecnt site for similar information and programs is www.ready.gov.

12. See Kean et al. (2005).

13. See, for instance, White House (2006).

14. After 2004's Hurricane Ivan, Mike Davis chillingly anticipated the southern divisions of class and race laid out even more clearly by Katrina; see Davis (2004).

15. And in doing so, as the journalist Steve Coll (2006) has noted, definitions of American enemies are yoked, through the bluster of homeland security pronouncements, to debates over illegal immigration, dangerously expanding an artificial division of identities.

References

AmericanPrepared.org. N.d. http://www.americaprepared.org/rd_rules.html (accessed March 12, 2007).

Atomic Energy Commission (AEC). 1957. *Atomic tests in Nevada*. Washington, DC: Government Printing Office.

Borden, William. 1946. *There will be no time: The revolution in strategy*. New York: MacMillan.

Broder, John M. 2005. In plans to evacuate US cities, chance for havoc. *New York Times*, September 25.

Brophy, Leo P., Wyndham D. Miles, and Rexmond C. Cochrane. 1959. *The Chemical Warfare Service: From laboratory to field*. Washington, DC: Office of the Chief of Military History, Department of the Army.

Brown, JoAnne. 1988. "*A* is for *atom*, *B* is for *bomb*": Civil defense in American public education, 1948–1963. *Journal of American History* 75:68–90.

Brzezinski, Matthew. 2003. Fortress America. *New York Times Magazine*, February 23, 38–45, 54, 70, 75–76.

———. 2004. Red alert. *Mother Jones*, September–October. http://www.motherjones.com/news/feature/2004/09/08_400.html.

Bumiller, Elisabeth. 2004. Intelligence chief without power? Support leaves questions. *New York Times*, August 3.

———. 2006. At West Point, Bush draws parallels with Truman. *New York Times*, May 28.

Capshew, James. 1999. *Psychologists on the march: Science, practice, and professional identity in America, 1929–1969*. Cambridge: Cambridge University Press.

Chait, Jonathan. 2003. The 9/10 president: Bush's abysmal failure on homeland security. *New Republic*, March 10.

Chan, Sewell. 2006. Inside the Brooklyn Bridge, a whiff of the Cold War. *New York Times*, March 21.

Coll, Steve. 2006. Citizens. *New Yorker*, June 5. http://www.newyorker.com/talk/content/articles/060605ta_talk_coll.

Crowley, Michael. 2004. Playing defense: Bush's disastrous Homeland Security Department. *New Republic*, March 15.

Davies, Richard. 1975. *The age of asphalt: The automobile, the freeway, and the condition of metropolitan America*. Philadelphia: J. B. Lippincott.

Davis, Mike. 1999. Berlin's skeleton in Utah's closet. *Grand Street* 69:93–100.

———. 2004. Poor, black and left behind. *TomDispatch*, September 23. http://www.tomdispatch.com/index.mhtml?pid=1849.

Didion, Joan. 2004. Politics in the "new normal" America. *New York Review of Books*, October 21. http://www.nybooks.com/articles/17489.

Farish, Matthew. 2003. Disaster and decentralization: American cities and the Cold War. *Cultural Geographies* 10 (3): 125–48.

———. 2004. Another anxious urbanism: Defence and disaster in Cold War America. In *Cities, war and terrorism: Towards an urban geopolitics*, ed. Steven Graham, 93–109. Oxford: Blackwell.

———. 2006. Targeting the inner landscape. In *Violent Geographies*, ed. Derek Gregory and Allan Pred, 255–71. New York: Routledge.

Federal Civil Defense Administration (FCDA). 1952. *Annual report for 1951*. Washington, DC: Government Printing Office).

———. 1953a. *Operation Doorstep*. Washington, DC: Government Printing Office.

———. 1953b. *Home protection exercises*. Washington, DC: Government Printing Office.

———. 1955a. *Operation Cue*. Washington, DC: Government Printing Office.

———. 1955b. *4 wheels to survival*. Washington, DC: Government Printing Office.

———. 1956. *Cue for survival*. Washington, DC: Government Printing Office.

Findlay, John M. 1995. Atomic frontier days: Richland, Washington, and the modern American West. *Journal of the West* 34 (3): 32–41.

Flynn, Stephen E. 2005. Color me scared. *New York Times*, May 25.

Franke-Ruta, Garance. 2003. Homeland security is for girls. *Washington Monthly*, April. http://www.washingtonmonthly.com/features/2003/0304.franke-ruta. html.

Galison, Peter. 2001. War against the center. *Grey Room* 4:6–33.

Goddard, Steven. 1994. *Getting there: The epic struggle between road and rail in the twentieth century.* New York: Basic Books.

Goldberg, Michelle. 2004. Outlawing dissent. *Salon*, February 11. http://dir.salon. com/story/news/feature/2004/02/11/cointelpro/.

Grossman, Andrew D. 2001. *Neither dead nor red: Civilian defense and American political development during the early Cold War.* New York: Routledge.

Gutfreund, Owen D. 2004. *Twentieth-century sprawl: Highways and the reshaping of the American landscape.* Oxford: Oxford University Press.

Hall, Stuart. 1996. When was "the post-colonial"? Thinking at the limit. In *The post-colonial question: Common skies, divided horizons*, ed. Iain Chambers and Linda Curti, 242–60. London: Routledge.

Herman, Ellen. 1995. *The romance of American psychology: Political culture in the age of experts.* Berkeley: University of California Press.

Hill, Gladwin. 1951. Atomic boom town in the desert. *New York Times Magazine*, February 11, 14.

Horowitz, Sari, and Christian Davenport. 2005. Terrorism could hurl D.C. area into turmoil. *Washington Post*, September 11, A01.

Hsu, Spencer. 2005. Chertoff vows to "re-engineer" preparedness. *Washington Post*, October 20, A02.

Ignatieff, Michael. 2005. The broken contract. *New York Times Magazine*, September 25. http://www.ksg.harvard.edu/ksgnews/Features/opeds/092505_ignatieff.htm.

Isin, Engin F. 2002. *Being political: Genealogies of citizenship.* Minneapolis: University of Minnesota Press.

Janis, Irving L. 1972. *Victims of groupthink: A psychological study of foreign-policy decisions and fiascoes.* Boston: Houghton, Mifflin.

Johnson, Gene. 2003. Mock explosion launches bioterror drill. *Washington Post*, May 13, A03.

Kaplan, Amy. 2003. Homeland insecurities: Reflections on language and space. *Radical History Review* 85: 82–93.

Kean, Thomas H., commission chair, et al. 2005. *Final report on 9/11 Commission recommendations*, December 5. http://www.9-11pdp.org/press/2005-12-05_report.pdf.

Leavitt, Helen. 1970. *Superhighway—superhoax.* Garden City, NY: Doubleday.

Leslie, Stuart W. 1993. *The Cold War and American science: The military-industrial-academic complex at MIT and Stanford.* New York: Columbia University Press.

Lewis, Thomas. 1997. *Divided highways: Building the interstate highways, transforming American life.* New York: Viking.

Lichtblau, Eric, and Christopher Drew. 2004. Ridge's record: Color alerts and mixed security reviews. *New York Times*, December 1.

Light, Jennifer. 2003. *From warfare to welfare: Defense intellectuals and urban problems in Cold War America.* Baltimore: Johns Hopkins University Press.

Lipton, Eric. 2005. Security chief signals a shift in approach to terror. *New York Times*, March 17.

———. 2006. Homeland security grants to New York slashed. *New York Times*, May 31.

McEnaney, Laura. 2000. *Civil defense begins at home: Militarization meets everyday life in the 1950s*. Princeton, NJ: Princeton University Press.

McNamara, Kevin. 1996. *Urban verbs: Arts and discourses of American cities*. Stanford, CA: Stanford University Press.

Menand, Louis. 2004. Patriot games: The new nativism of Samuel P. Huntington. *New Yorker*, May 17. http://www.newyorker.com/critics/books/?040517crbo_books.

Mumford, Lewis. 1963. *The highway and the city*. New York: Harcourt, Brace and World.

National Academy of Sciences-National Research Council. 1958. *The adequacy of government research programs in non-military defense: A report by the advisory committee on civil defense*. Washington, DC: National Academy of Sciences-National Research Council.

Neglect in New Orleans. 2006. *The Nation*, April 10. http://www.thenation.com/doc/20060410/lede.

Newfield, Jack. 2004 Bush to city: Drop dead. *The Nation*, April 19. http://www.the-nation.com/doc.mhtml?i=20040419&s=newfield.

Oakes, Guy. 1994. *The imaginary war: Civil defense and American cold war culture*. New York: Oxford University Press.

Ode, Kim. 2004. Prepared, or scared? Homeland security contest for students sidesteps families, plays on kids' fears. *Minneapolis Star-Tribune*, August 22. http://www.startribune.com/stories/389/4936890.html.

Pincus, Walter. 2005. Pentagon expanding its domestic surveillance activity. *Washington Post*, November 27, A06.

Ripley, Amanda. 2004. How we got homeland security wrong. *Time*, March 29. http://www.time.com/time/archive/preview/0,10987,1101040329-603192,00.html.

Romero, Simon. 2004. In desert town, training for "terror attacks." *New York Times*, September 26.

Rose, Nikolas. 1999. *Governing the soul: The shaping of the private self*. 2nd ed. London: Free Association Books.

Ross, Andrew. 1989. Containing culture in the Cold War. *No respect: Intellectuals and popular culture*, 42–64. New York: Routledge.

Smith, Neil. 2001. Scales of terror and the resort to geography: September 11, October 7. *Environment and Planning D: Society and Space* 19:631–37.

Sparke, Matthew. 1998. Outsides inside patriotism: The Oklahoma Bombing and the displacement of heartland geopolitics. In *Rethinking Geopolitics*, ed. Gearóid Ó Tuathail and Simon Dalby, 198–223. London: Routledge.

Tetreault, Steve. 2004. Test site gets new security mission. *Las Vegas Review-Journal*, June 9. http://www.reviewjournal.com/lvrj_home/2004/Jun-09-Wed-2004/news/24066101.html.

U.S. Department of Health, Education, and Welfare, Office of Education. 1956. *Education for national survival: A handbook on civil defense for schools*. Washington, DC: Government Printing Office.

U.S. Department of Homeland Security. 2004a. Hundreds of activities planned, millions reached during National Preparedness Month. September 1. http://www.dhs.gov/xnews/speeches/speech_0204.shtm (accessed May 2, 2007).

———. 2004b. National organizations partner to launch National Preparedness Month. August 10. http://www.dhs.gov/xnews/releases/press_release_0481.shtm (accessed May 2, 2007).

———. 2004c. Remarks by Secretary of Homeland Security Tom Ridge at the National Preparedness Month kickoff. Washington, DC, September 9. http://www.dhs.gov/dhspublic/interapp/speech/speech_0204.xml.

———. N.d. [Public information Web site]. http://www.dhs.gov/dhspublic/.

VandeHei, Jim. 2005. Bush names Homeland Security nominee. *Washington Post*, January 12, A01.

Vanderbilt, Tom. 2002. *Survival city: Adventures among the ruins of atomic America.* Princeton, NJ: Princeton Architectural Press.

Von Drehle, David. 2006. Rallying 'round the flag. *Washington Post*, April 9, W10.

Weingroff, Richard F. 1996. Federal-Aid Highway Act of 1956: Creating the interstate system. *Public Roads.* www.tfhrc.gov/pubrds/summer96/p96su10.htm.

White House. 2006. President discusses use and reauthorization of USA PATRIOT Act. January 3. http://www.whitehouse.gov/news/releases/2006/01/20060103.html.

Wittner, Lawrence. 1993–2003. *The struggle against the bomb.* 3 vols. Stanford, CA: Stanford University Press.

Woodward, Rachel. 2005. From military geography to militarism's geographies: Disciplinary engagements with the geographies of militarism and military activities. *Progress in Human Geography* 29 (6): 718–40.

Zarlengo, Kristina. 1999. Civilian threat, the suburban citadel, and atomic age American women. *Signs: Journal of Women in Culture and Society* 24 (4): 925–58.

6
Distributed Preparedness
Space, Security, and Citizenship in the United States

STEPHEN J. COLLIER AND ANDREW LAKOFF

Disaster response in the United States traditionally has been handled by state and local governments, with the federal government playing a supporting role. Limits on the federal government's role in disaster response are deeply rooted in American tradition. State and local governments—who know the unique requirements of their citizens and geography and are best positioned to respond to incidents in their own jurisdictions—will always play a large role in disaster response. The federal government's supporting role respects these practical points and the sovereignty of the states as well as the power of governors to direct activities and coordinate efforts within their states.

> *The Federal Response to Hurricane Katrina: Lessons Learned (White House 2006, 11)*

Recent events (White House 2006, 11) such as the attacks of 9/11 and Hurricane Katrina have raised basic questions concerning the spatial and political logic of government in the United States: how should the government respond to a complex field of threats—such as natural disasters, terrorism, and pandemic disease—across national space? And what are the obligations of the government to individuals and communities in anticipating and responding to potentially catastrophic events?[1]

In this chapter, we situate these questions within an "American tradition" for identifying and managing perceived threats to collective security. In fact, as we will show, this "tradition" rests on a relatively recent set of developments: the invention of an organizational framework and set of techniques that we call "distributed preparedness."

Distributed preparedness was initially articulated in civil defense programs in the early stages of the Cold War, when U.S. government planners began to conceptualize the nation as a possible target of nuclear attack. They assumed that the enemy would focus its attacks on urban and industrial centers that were essential to U.S. war-fighting capability. Distributed preparedness provided techniques for mapping national space as a field of potential targets, and grafted this map of vulnerabilities onto the structure of territorial administration in the United States. It presented a new model of coordinated planning for catastrophic threats, one that sought to limit federal intervention in local life and to preserve the characteristic features of American federalism.

The first section of the chapter places the emergence of distributed preparedness in the broader context of civil defense planning and post–World War II national security strategy. With the emergence of strategic bombing and total war, planners increasingly viewed the cities, industry, and population of the United States as possible targets of nuclear attack. Civil defense was organized to ensure that, if attacked, the nation could fight back. In this sense, distributed preparedness was one part of the continual mobilization for war that characterized the Cold War national security state.

The following sections take up two dimensions of distributed preparedness that were initially developed in the context of civil defense planning, but that have had enduring importance beyond this context. We call these "emergency federalism" and "vulnerability mapping." Emergency federalism is an organizational framework for coordinating autonomous sovereign entities through joint planning during normal times and unified command in the case of emergencies. As a model for how local, state, and federal governments can respond together to events that exceed local capacities, emergency federalism can be understood as a "state spatial form"—that is, in Brenner's description, a way to "integrate state institutions and policy regimes across geographical scales and among different locales within the state's territory" (Brenner 2004, 91). Vulnerability mapping, meanwhile, refers to a set of techniques and procedures for mapping urban areas as sites of potential catastrophe. Vulnerability mapping makes it possible to assess required response capacities, and the weaknesses in those capacities, so that planners can direct their efforts toward them. In combining these two elements, distributed preparedness grafts a spatial understanding of vulnerability onto the federal structure of the United States, creating a distinctive political logic for identifying and managing perceived threats to collective life.

Our discussion is based on an analysis of some of the key documents in which distributed preparedness was articulated. We focus in particular on two of these: first, the 1950 report *United States Civil Defense*, the so-called blue book that was the foundation for the 1951 Civil Defense Act; and, second, a 1953 manual entitled *Civil Defense Urban Analysis*, produced by the Federal Civil Defense Administration (FCDA). By focusing on these technical documents, our aim is not to assess the extent to which plans were reflected in a subsequent reality, a question that has been taken up in a number of studies on civil defense (Blanchard 1986; Fehr 1999; Grossman 2001; Lee 2001; Tyler 1967). Rather, our goal is to characterize distributed preparedness as a distinctive political logic, and to consider its implications for contemporary discussions of security.[2]

In the context of the Cold War, distributed preparedness was a response to the exigency of nuclear confrontation with the Soviet Union. But both the specific techniques developed in civil defense planning and the overall model of distributed preparedness have since migrated to other institutional contexts where they have been deployed to address threats other than nuclear attack: the Federal Emergency Management Agency (FEMA) and the rise of "all-hazards planning" for disaster response in the 1970s; planning for pandemic disease by local, state, and federal public health agencies; and, most recently, the U.S. Department of Homeland Security (DHS)—in which terrorist attacks have been added to the list of potential catastrophes that are to be managed through distributed preparedness.

The final section of the chapter reflects briefly on this diffusion of distributed preparedness, and on its significance for the critical analysis of contemporary security. Much critical scholarship has understood recent government security measures in terms of a process of "militarization." Through reference to examples such as the USA PATRIOT Act, extrajudicial handling of terror suspects, and urban security measures, this scholarship argues that the civilian sphere of autonomous rights is being curtailed, and that domestic space is being partitioned through limitations on access, movement, and legal protections. Its diagnosis is that we are faced with an encroaching and increasingly oppressive security apparatus. Meanwhile, the constant refrain in most public discussion of security threats is that we are not secure enough.

Our approach differs from both of these positions. It does not begin with the question of whether there is currently "too much" or "too little" security. Rather, it initially asks, What type of security is being discussed? And what are its political implications? As Nyers (2004) points out, "[A]n important means by which sovereign states have historically claimed legitimacy is through the provision of security and protection to their citizens." But the relationship between security and citizenship in a given context can only be understood by asking questions such as: how are threats defined within a given political logic of security? And how is responsibility for the provision of security defined and distributed among various levels of government?

The norms, techniques, and practices of distributed preparedness tend to fall below the radar of much critical scholarship on security. This is at least in part because these practices are ubiquitous and mostly taken for granted—they hold the status of an unexamined common sense. But this common sense is based on a historically situated logic of security, one that involves a distinctive way of imagining threats and vulnerabilities, and of preparing for and responding to a certain category of events. The task of this chapter, then, is to help understand how this logic has *become* common sense; how experts, politicians, pundits, and key figures in the media learned to think and speak in a certain way about "security" problems; and how a diverse range of possible events—natural disasters, pandemic diseases, and terrorist attacks—came to be seen as part of the same class of security threats, and as manageable through the same set of techniques.

Distributed Preparedness, Civil Defense, and National Security

The articulation of distributed preparedness in Cold War civil defense planning was closely linked to a series of political and technological developments that transformed strategic thinking about warfare in the United States and Europe over the first half of the twentieth century. The rise of total war meant that the entire industrial capacity of a country was regarded as critical to its war effort, thus blurring the lines between civilian and military facilities, and making civilian installations and populations into military targets. Meanwhile, the increasing centrality of airpower meant that this expanded range of military targets could be directly and suddenly attacked. And with the dawn of the nuclear age, the impact of a surprise air attack would be devastating.

One important aspect of this broader shift in military strategy was the emergence of "strategic bombing," an approach that was reflected in U.S. Air Force doctrine before World War II and put into practice by the United States and Britain in the air war in Germany and Japan.[3] Strategic bombing did not focus on "theater operations"—that is, attacks on enemy deployments. Rather, it targeted facilities that were crucial to an enemy's capacity to conduct industrial warfare. In particular, strategic bombing focused on the critical vulnerabilities of industrial production chains—the "vital links that if targeted would bring the system to a halt" (McMullen 2001, 8).

Post–World War II civil defense efforts were, in some sense, the defensive counterpart of strategic bombing doctrine. As Galison (2001) notes, U.S. strategists began to see national territory from the vantage of an enemy in a total war—as a space of potential targets.[4] The question was how, in an air-nuclear age, to organize the home front to prepare for nuclear attack.

The basic argument for establishing a comprehensive, national civil defense program was established in the U.S. Strategic Bombing Survey (USSBS; 1947), a massive effort to assess bomb damage in Japan, Germany, and Britain, conducted in the immediate aftermath of World War II.[5] In the course of investigating bomb damage, the USSBS also examined and assessed the civil defense efforts of these countries. It found that civil defense could be an important tool in mitigating the effects of urban bombing campaigns, and in maintaining an ongoing capacity to wage war in the face of attack.

Based on these findings, the USSBS concluded that a concerted national effort at civil defense planning was necessary. This conclusion was echoed in a series of subsequent reports, which more or less repeated the broad recommendations of the survey, and which began to elaborate a systematic approach to civil defense planning in the United States.[6] The planning process culminated in a 1950 report entitled *United States Civil Defense* (U.S. National Security Resources Board [NSRB] 1950). *United States Civil Defense* was a pivotal document that laid the groundwork for the 1951 Civil Defense Act—which in turn created the FCDA—and it remained a basic reference for civil defense planners in the years that followed.[7] More broadly, the document laid out a new model that would subsequently be adopted in a range of other contexts for managing "emergency" situations.

It is noteworthy that *United States Civil Defense* was produced by the NSRB, which had been created, along with the National Security Council, in the defense reorganization of 1947. The purpose of these organizations was to align the work of nonmilitary agencies in the government with the demands of an emerging concept of "national security." This concept of national security increasingly oriented both military and nonmilitary agencies in the government to ongoing war mobilization, in order to defend against what was perceived as a broad external threat to national existence.[8]

The approach articulated in *United States Civil Defense* was firmly situated in this emerging national security doctrine. Civil defense, it argued, was "a missing element in our system of national security" in an air-nuclear age in which the United States was vulnerable to "a sudden devastating attack" (NSRB 1950, 5). The document's justification for civil defense was primarily military. "The outcome of two world wars," it noted,

> has been decided by the weight of American industrial production in support of a determined fighting force. In any future war, it is probable that an enemy would attempt at the outset to destroy or cripple the production capacity of the United States and to carry direct attack against civilian communities to disrupt support of the war effort. (NSRB 1950, 8)

Following the assumptions of strategic bombing doctrine, the report assumed that an attack would manage to strike critical targets in the United States. The question, then, was whether such an attack "would succeed in destroying America's productive power" (NSRB 1950, 5). Success, in turn, "would depend in the main on the organization and functional efficiency of the country's civil defense" (NSRB 1950, 5). These general assumptions pointed to a series of practical questions: How should planners conceptualize the United States as a target space? What kinds of preparations would be appropriate for meeting this threat? And who should be responsible for organizing them?

The answer to this set of questions, as laid out in *United States Civil Defense* and a range of other planning documents, was the framework and set of techniques for coordinated planning and response that we call "distributed preparedness." By "distributed," we mean that responsibility was delegated to different levels of government, and to both public and private agencies, according to their competencies and capacities, and according to their spatial relationship to a critical target. By "preparedness," we indicate a form of planning for unpredictable but potentially catastrophic events—intended not to prevent these events from happening, but rather to manage their consequences (Lakoff 2007; Collier and Lakoff 2006).

In the context of civil defense, many of the details of distributed preparedness were specific to the exigencies of nuclear confrontation—such as the techniques for envisioning the impact of a nuclear strike on a city, which we describe below. But the broader model of distributed preparedness—and the practices and organizational forms it entailed—had longer term significance outside of the context of nuclear confrontation. The discussion that follows examines two of these: *emergency federalism* and *vulnerability mapping*. Emergency federalism was developed as an organizational framework for coordinated planning and response among autonomous local governments and private actors in the United States' system of distributed sovereignty. Vulnerability mapping involved a set of techniques for identifying likely targets of nuclear bombing, and assessing the impact of nuclear blasts that made it possible—by imaginatively enacting an attack—to pinpoint weaknesses in civil defense preparations and to direct the resources and efforts of civil defense planners.

Autonomy, Economy, and Coordination: Emergency Federalism

The question of who would take responsibility for civil defense planning in the post–World War II United States was initially a contentious one. The military, which had been involved in civil defense preparations during and immediately after the war, consistently opposed adding civil defense functions to its basic responsibilities. By the late 1940s there was a broad consensus that civil defense planning should be a civilian endeavor (see the discussion in Lee 2001, ch. 2). But the prospect of civilian administration raised a number of problems that reflected broader tensions in the postwar United States about the growth of the federal government.

The New Deal had dramatically expanded the scope of federal intervention into the social and economic life of the national population. The new federal prerogatives were opposed by conservatives committed to principles of self-reliance and local government as fundamental characteristics of the American political system. These tensions shaped debates about the U.S. state during and then after World War II. As Hogan (1998) has shown in a detailed political history of the period, Truman and many liberal Democrats assumed that declining military expenditures would allow increases in social welfare programs, including a national health service. Conservative Republicans, who opposed expanded social programs and a larger central government, agreed that military expenditures should decline, but thought that the peace dividend should pay for tax cuts.

The political divisions that formed around the conflicting priorities of social welfare and tax cuts were reframed by the international crises of the late 1940s, including the Soviet atomic bomb test and developments in Korea.

These events pushed political opinion toward an emerging consensus around a "national security state" and, consequently, around a dramatic expansion of military expenditures to maintain continual mobilization and war preparedness in the face of the Soviet threat (Hogan 1998; Yergin 1977).

This consensus required concessions on both sides, although within a framework that allowed each to hold to some core beliefs (see, e.g., Gold 1977; Hogan 1998; Waddell 1999). Conservatives made concessions to an enlarged federal government, in part on the condition that the basis of its growth would not be welfare programs or intervention in the economy, but rather military-related spending. Liberal Democrats, meanwhile, yielded in their aspirations for bold new social welfare programs, in part on the understanding that military spending would act as an economic stimulus and, thus, an instrument for positive government economic policy. What emerged was a model of "Cold War liberalism."[9] It was based on what Gold has called a "military-Keynesian consensus," realized by "pushing Keynesianism toward an emphasis on economic growth and making growth itself dependent upon the military and private production, not on social spending" (1977, 136–37).[10] As Hogan puts the point, the broad shift was decisively away from a "welfare" state toward a "warfare" state, though one that, through interventions in aggregate demand, did play a role in promoting economic growth.

In the context of this early Cold War liberal consensus, civil defense was in an awkward position. On the one hand, it was considered by many to be crucial to national security. On the other hand, in contrast to military buildup, civil defense moved back into the realm of domestic questions such as welfare, public health, and local police and fire services that conservatives wanted to defend against incursions by the federal government. Moreover, a national program of civil defense might limit the independence of state governments, local governments, community-level coordinators, and industrial plants— all of which had to be involved in civil defense planning. The prospect of a national civil defense program, therefore, raised questions about the basic terms of the Cold War liberal consensus: about the autonomy of local governments and individuals, about federal intrusion in the organization of collective life, and about the expansion of government budgets required to implement civil defense programs.[11] It also raised questions concerning the basic bargain of citizenship: what was the scope of government responsibility in providing security? And what limitations on individual and local autonomy would have to be accepted in the name of collective security?

These political questions were directly related to the organizational basis of civil defense. As the U.S. Strategic Bombing Survey had discovered, civil defense worked well in cases where there were both principles of local "self-protection" and clear hierarchical command and control. Thus, on the one hand, the survey noted that in German civil defense,

> The individual was trained to take care of himself, protect his property, and join with a few others in a small group under a warden to help others to do likewise when the task was too great for them to bear alone. This training of the individual in self-protection and the feeling of confidence he had that all would be done that could be done kept alive a strong spirit in civilian defense forces which, in no small measure, was responsible for the fact that the home front did not collapse. (USSBS 1947, 13)

At the same time, the survey noted, "The control exercised by the German regular police from the national level through the local level made for simplicity of control and command. The emergency created by war in civilian communities requires concentration of authority" (1947, 13). But what organization in the U.S. governmental structure could provide both self-protection and centralized control simultaneously? And how could this combination of self-protection and centralized control be reconciled with the distributed sovereignties of U.S. federalism? Or with concerns about the expansion of federal spending and federal bureaucracies?

United States Civil Defense (1950) explicitly acknowledged these problems at the outset. The report noted that with the expansion of the military that had accelerated in 1949, "the drain upon America's resources [would] necessarily be great" (NSRB 1950, 3). Therefore, plans for civil defense had to be made "with full recognition of the importance of maximum economy in the use of the available supply of men, money, and materials" (NSRB 1950, 3). Likewise, the report was self-conscious about the need to avoid infringing upon the sovereignties of states, localities, families, and individuals. And it repeatedly noted that local governments were in a better position than the federal government to respond to local problems:

> [T]he States are established with inherent powers and accompanying responsibility, and have clear qualifications to coordinate civil defense operations within their boundaries, and in emergency to direct them. Similarly, the cities, countries, and towns are best qualified to handle their own operating functions. (NSRB 1950, 5)

The solution to these tensions between centralization and decentralization, between the collective demand for organizing for civil defense and the presumptive priority given to local sovereignties, was the formulation of an organizational framework that we call "emergency federalism." Emergency federalism recognized that preparation for enemy attack on critical civilian targets was a problem of national security and, therefore, related to the core functions of the federal government. But it sought to minimize, to the extent possible, direct federal intervention—and to limit the financial impact of civil defense planning—by distributing civil defense functions among a range of public and private actors, and by devising systems for coordinated planning and response in the event of an emergency.[12]

In the framework of emergency federalism laid out in *United States Civil Defense*, the basic principle for the distribution of responsibility was self-protection. Civil defense, the report held, was first of all incumbent upon individuals and families, and upon the governmental institutions that were closest to the individual and the community (NSRB 1950, 4). The key actors in civil defense would not, thus, be members of a new bureaucracy of federal officials. Rather, they would be local fire and police services, local health agencies, and local government officials, who would incorporate civil defense planning into their routine activities. "Civil defense rests," the report argued,

> upon the principle of self-protection by the individual, extended to include mutual self-protection on the part of groups and communities. Manned largely by unpaid part-time volunteer workers, each service of civil defense will work in cooperation with the others for the common good. All men and women who make up these services will belong to a national team—The United States Civil Defense Corps. (NSRB 1950, 3)

The argument for emergency federalism in *United States Civil Defense* then proceeded in the classical style of liberal political thought. Having begun from the individual and local government as the basic bearers of rights and responsibilities, the report proceeded to ask in what cases it would be justified to qualify the right to self-government and the burden of self-protection through intervention by states and by the federal government. For example, the report argued that some situations would overwhelm the capacity of individuals or families to provide themselves with adequate sustenance (a function that was notably not considered a normal responsibility of the state):

> Under wartime disaster conditions, many self-sustaining families and individuals may suddenly find that they have to depend temporarily on others for even the simplest essentials of life. After a disaster, a family may be left on the street without housing or adequate clothing, with no place to eat, wash, or sleep, with no means of transportation and perhaps without money or the ability to care for immediate needs. (NSRB 1950, 69)

Consequently, emergency welfare services were required to assist families in such situations, and were a necessary part of civil defense plans.

Likewise, communities and local governments would be unable to deal with the overwhelming devastation of a nuclear attack. "No community," the report maintained, "could afford the establishment of complete self-sufficiency" (NSRB 1950, 45). Nor would such self-sufficiency be practical, since "surplus resources unnecessary in peacetime would be vulnerable to destruction in event of attack" (NSRB 1950, 45). For these reasons, the principle of local self-protection could be supplemented by a system of support from other governmental entities. Such a program would meet the demands of economy, "because it does not call for a tremendous procurement program, or an unusual drain on men, money, and materials. Instead, it provides for the organized use of existing equipment, following the principle that location is more important than quantity" (NSRB 1950, 4).

United States Civil Defense proposed two kinds of coordinated response that would bring aid to communities whose capacities were overwhelmed: "mutual aid" and "mobile response." (See figure 6.1.) Mutual aid was defined as "voluntary arrangements by which the protective services of organized communities assist each other in time of need, usually on the basis of prior planning and voluntary contractual agreements between communities" (NSRB 1950, 45). It was a form of "horizontal" coordination through which adjacent communities would be organized collectively in the event of an attack. The report noted that many informal mutual aid agreements already existed. The task was to formalize these agreements, and to develop mutual aid plans that could be "tested in practice" so that, in an emergency, "the mutual-aid forces [could] be established with precision and speed" (NSRB 1950, 47).

Mobile support, by contrast, was aid "directed by State authority into a stricken area" (NSRB 1950, 45). It expressed, in this sense, not an obligation established by agreement between equals but an obligation of the government to protect individual citizens and communities. Mobile support was envisioned as a vertically organized emergency standby capacity provided by "self-contained services or teams" that would provide specialized aid in areas such as rescue, first aid, emergency feeding, radiological and chemical defense, engineering, and police and fire services (NSRB 1950, 47). The primary responsibility for such mobile support was borne by state governments. But the report also postulated a role for the federal government.[13] State governments might request that the military provide "assistance where possible in the event of war-caused disasters" (NSRB 1950, 16).

The broad picture that emerges is a framework for coordination in a federal system—one with a distinctive temporal structure. During normal periods planning would be conducted through cooperation among different agencies within the U.S. federal system. In the case of events that overwhelmed local capacities, however, unified structures of command and coordination would be established. This model for dealing with emergency situations did not involve the suspension of legality or civilian rule (although the report noted that there might be circumstances in which martial law would be declared after a nuclear attack). Rather, it called for temporarily establishing a unified command to "meet the exigencies of a given situation (Lee 2001, 49)."[14]

But emergency federalism was only a formal administrative framework. The questions that then arose were: what kinds of mutual aid would be necessary in the event of attack? What kinds of mobile support should be orga-

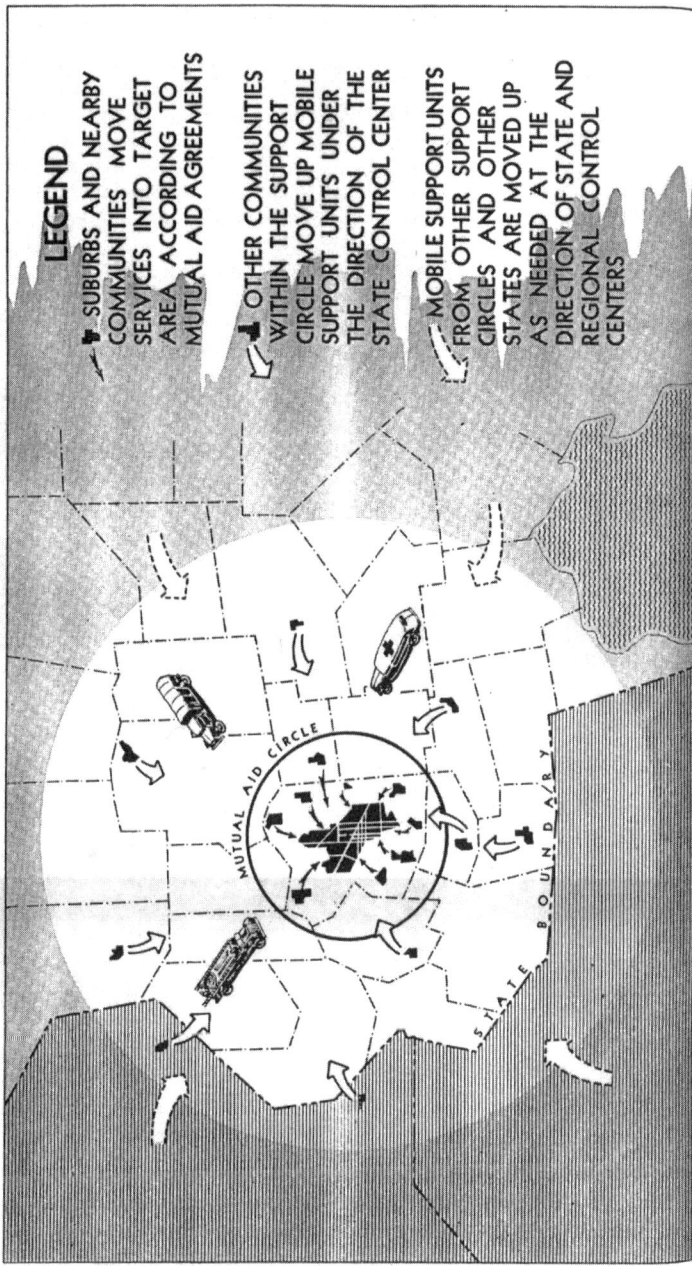

Figure 6.1 Mutual Aid and Mobile Support Pattern.

nized, and where? In other words, emergency federalism, with its distinctive organizational and temporal structure, had to be given spatial and substantive form.

Vulnerability Mapping

In order to apply the principles of emergency federalism to a given city, it was necessary to understand what response capacities would be required in the event of an attack. *United States Civil Defense* and subsequent planning documents proposed a set of techniques for doing so, which we refer to collectively as "vulnerability mapping." Vulnerability mapping produced a new form of spatial knowledge about cities—as sites of potential future disaster and as complex spaces of response. Civil defense planning documents gave technical instructions for producing maps that visually juxtaposed an attack's projected impact against the existing infrastructure of an urban area. Using these maps, planners could assess weaknesses in existing response capacities and determine where resources would have to be directed to improve civil defense preparedness.

Imaginative Enactment and Urban Analysis

Vulnerability mapping was based on a new understanding of urban life. As opposed to statistical knowledge about the condition of the population, such as epidemiology or demography, this form of knowledge was not archival—it did not track the regular occurrence of predictable events over time. Rather, vulnerability mapping generated knowledge about events—such as a surprise nuclear attack—whose probability could not be known, but whose consequences could be catastrophic. Such knowledge entailed not the calculation of probabilities but rather the imaginative enactment of events for which civil defense services would have to be prepared, and the detailed analysis of how urban features would be affected by such events.[15]

As described in *United States Civil Defense*, the starting point for this new form of knowledge was to envision enemy strategy in a nuclear attack. Imagining the enemy mind-set was not, of course, a new problem. But before the era of total war, anticipating the intentions of the enemy had been important mainly for planning theater operations—that is, force deployments and strategies of attack. In an era of strategic bombing, the question shifted: how did the enemy conceptualize the features of U.S. territory as a set of targets?

United States Civil Defense assumed that a potential attacker would plan an attack based on the same principles of strategic bombing that were at the center of U.S. Air Force doctrine. As the report put it,

> The considerations which determine profitable targets are understood by potential enemies as well as our own planners. Such considerations include total population, density of population, concentration of impor-

tant industries, location of communication and transportation centers, location of critical military facilities, and location of civil governments. (NSRB 1950, 8)

Once a likely target had been identified, an attack scenario could then be imaginatively enacted in order to analyze its likely impact and the capacities that would be required for response.[16] As an illustration, *United States Civil Defense* provided a "hypothetical attack problem." (See figure 6.2.)

The hypothetical attack problem was a scenario developed through an "attack narrative" (NSRB 1950, 117). This narrative described two atomic detonations over an imaginary city x: one an air burst at twenty-four hundred feet, and one an underwater burst. The narrative then laid out the immediate impact of the attack: the water surge and lethal cloud of radioactive mist from the underwater burst; the explosive impact of the air burst and the flash fires that spread out up to a mile from ground zero; the casualties, including 14,000–17,000 from "mechanical injury" (that is, from the blast itself), 7,000–8,000 burn cases, and 1,000–3,000 cases of radiation sickness from the air burst. The attack narrative also included a description of the immediate damage that would be inflicted on communications, transportation, utilities, and medical facilities.

Such information allowed planners in given civil defense–related services—such as transportation planning, medical response, and so on—to prepare for the specific challenges they might face in the event of an attack. "The hypothetical attack problem," *United States Civil Defense* instructed, "should be realistic in order to bring out planning requirements in all segments of civil defense operations. The planners should accept the assumed effects, and analyze their needs accordingly" (NSRB 1950, 114). The hypothetical attack problem, thus, provided a kind of test that allowed the groups involved in civil defense planning to assess "the details of their plans drawn thus far, in accordance with the conditions stated in the attack hypothesis, so that each segment of the plan can be modified as needed in the light of the problem" (NSRB 1950, 114).

The question then was, how would these techniques be applied in a specific urban setting? A series of technical manuals published by the Federal Civil Defense Authority gave local officials detailed instructions on how, concretely, to engage in vulnerability mapping in a given city. Here we consider a 1953 manual entitled *Civil Defense Urban Analysis* (*CDUA*) (FCDA 1953). This manual was intended to help local planners develop flexible mapping tools to be used in contingency planning. It allowed local planners to produce a spatialized assessment of the impact of a nuclear attack, one that could be used by civil defense services to plan their response.

The manual exemplifies a new understanding of urban existence as *under threat*. Civil defense authorities saw that in the era of total war, the very sys-

HYPOTHETICAL ATTACK
CITY "X"

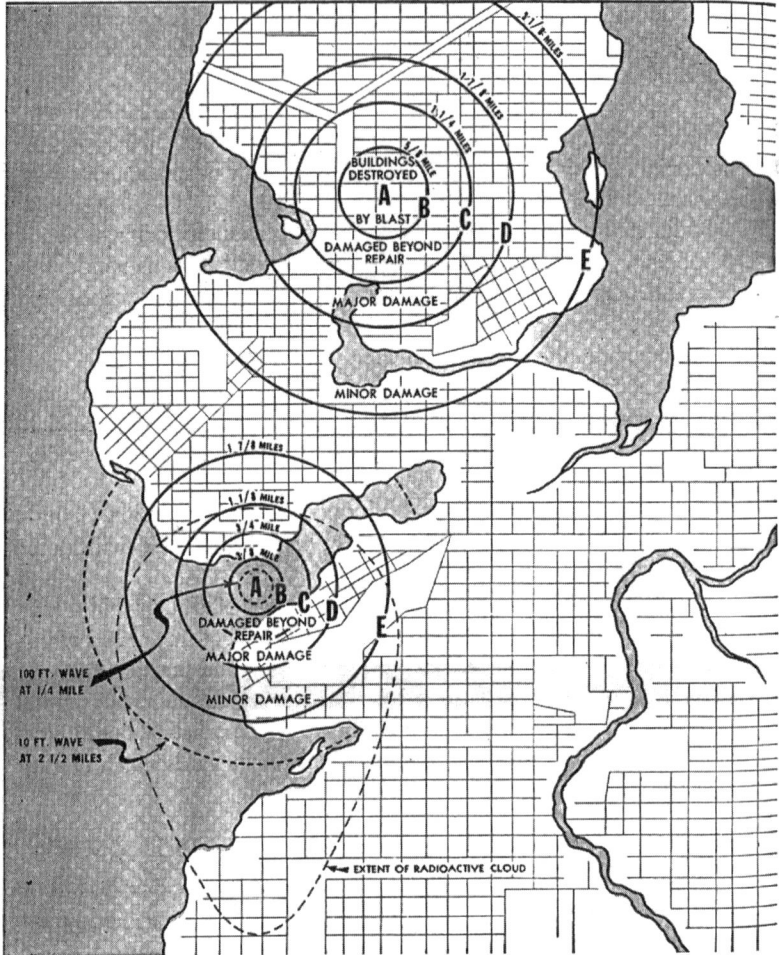

Figure 6.2 Hypothetical Attack City *X*.

tems that had been developed to support modern urban life were now sources of vulnerability and, as such, likely targets of enemy attack. Health facilities, systems of transportation and communication, and urban hygiene systems—whose construction had been essential to modern social welfare provision—were now understood in a new light, as possible targets and as necessary aspects of any emergency response.

In order to conduct an "urban analysis," it was initially necessary to cata-
logue the city's features. As the manual put it, "Since the primary purpose of
a civil defense urban analysis is to provide the tools for undertaking realistic
civil defense planning, all pertinent aspects of the city must be considered"
(FCDA 1953, 1).[17] The manual listed these "pertinent aspects" in a table of
forty-seven "urban features." These features included patterns of land use,
building density, industrial plants, population distribution, police stations,
the water distribution system, the electric power system, streets and highways,
streetcars, port facilities, the telephone system, hospitals, zoos, penal institutions, underground openings (caves and mines), topography, and prevailing
winds (FCDA 1953, 66–77).

The table indicated relevant sources of information about these features
and the specific details of each to be included in civil defense planning. It also
pointed to the "significance" of these features for specific areas of civil defense
planning. Thus, for example, information about land use could help both in
estimating possible damage to urban facilities and in mapping the distribution of population—which was crucial, as we will see below, to assessing likely
casualties from a blast. Industrial plants were significant as possible targets
of sabotage or bombing, and as important elements in police and fire control
planning. Many features had a "double" character: not only were they crucial
in understanding the impact of an attack, but they were also understood to
play a critical role in response. Water distribution systems were a potential
target of sabotage and might be destroyed or disabled by a nuclear blast; they
were also critical to fire control plans and were needed for emergency provision for attack victims and civil defense workers. Likewise, streets and sub-
ways were potential targets, particularly at vulnerable points such as bridges
and tunnels. At the same time, they served as routes for evacuation, mutual
aid, and support; and subway stations could be used as bomb shelters.

Producing Maps

After cataloguing these urban features, the next step for local civil defense
planners was to develop maps for use by specific urban services in developing
their own contingency plans. To make these maps, planners selected and spatially juxtaposed the features of the city that would be relevant to specific civil
defense services in the event of an attack. As the manual put it,

> All related features needed for general civil defense planning opera-
> tions or for use by one particular service (fire, police, etc.) should, if
> practicable, be assembled on one map. The various features represented
> are dissimilar but are significant because of their interrelationship. For
> example, one particular street may be important as an emergency route
> because bordering buildings are not sufficiently high to block the street
> with rubble in event of their destruction by bomb blast. (FCDA 1953, 8)

The production of these maps proceeded through three steps. First, local governments were to undertake a target analysis to determine the enemy's "assumed aiming point." Second, they were to use mapping techniques to estimate the impact of strikes on all features of a city related to the organization of response. Finally, on the basis of this assessment, local governments, state governments, and emergency response services would develop detailed contingency plans. These plans could then be tested through exercises to identify weakness in preparation, practice response, direct resources to the most serious vulnerabilities, and develop a plan for "emergency federalist" coordination with other localities and with state and federal governments.

The first step—the target analysis—sought to determine where a rational enemy would target an attack in order to cause the most possible damage. To find this "assumed aiming point," planners were instructed to place a transparent acetate overlay with regularly spaced concentric circles on top of a map of industrial facilities and population concentrations. Each circle marked a zone in which the impact of a blast would be felt with a common intensity. Damage from the blast in each zone could be estimated using information from a document that had been prepared by the Atomic Energy Commission and the U.S. Department of Defense, called *The Effects of Atomic Weapons* (U.S. Scientific Laboratory, 1950). This document, based on data gathered in Hiroshima and Nagasaki, provided tables indicating blast damage from a nuclear strike at various distances from ground zero. By positioning the acetate overlay on top of different possible targets on the map, the planner could test out different aiming points to determine which would cause maximum destruction.

The point of identifying an assumed aiming point was not to predict the exact location of an attack. As the manual notes, the target was not precisely known, and, in any case, the enemy might miss. Rather, the goal was to determine the maximum possible damage from an attack to ensure that response plans were "sufficiently broad and flexible to meet all possible conditions" (FCDA 1953, 8). Once the assumed aiming point was determined, it served as "a logical center for the pattern of civil defense ground organization of the community as a whole" (FCDA 1953, 10).

The second step in developing vulnerability maps was to estimate the damage a given sized bomb, hitting a certain point, would inflict on significant urban features. These included not only the potential targets of enemy attack, but also those features relevant to emergency response. *CDUA* divided significant urban features in two categories: facilities and population. In the case of facilities, the factors determining damage were the size of the blast itself and possible damage from an ensuing firestorm. Physical damage from the blast was estimated by using the acetate overlay method in combination with a table—provided in *CDUA*—that indicated the amount of damage to structures made from various materials in specific blast zones (FCDA 1953). (See

TABLE I.—Continued

Radii and areas of concentric zones of A-, B-, C-, and D-damage

Bomb size	Zone of A-damage		Zone of B-damage		Zone of C-damage		Zone of D-damage	
	Radii (miles)	Areas (square miles)	Radii (miles)	Areas (square miles)	Radii (miles)	Areas (square miles)	Radii (miles)	Areas (square miles)
1(X)	0.0 to 0.5	0.8	0.5 to 1.0	2.3	1.0 to 1.5	3.9	1.5 to 2.0	5.5
2(X)	0.0 to 0.6	1.3	0.6 to 1.3	3.8	1.3 to 2.0	6.2	2.0 to 2.5	8.7
2½(X)	0.0 to 0.7	1.5	0.7 to 1.4	4.2	1.4 to 2.0	7.1	2.0 to 2.7	10.1
3(X)	0.0 to 0.7	1.6	0.7 to 1.4	4.9	1.4 to 2.2	8.1	2.2 to 2.9	11.4
4(X)	0.0 to 0.8	2.0	0.8 to 1.6	6.0	1.6 to 2.4	10.0	2.4 to 3.2	14.0
5(X)	0.0 to 0.9	2.3	0.9 to 1.7	6.9	1.7 to 2.6	11.5	2.6 to 3.4	16.1
6(X)	0.0 to 0.9	2.6	0.9 to 1.8	7.8	1.8 to 2.7	13.0	2.7 to 3.6	18.2
7(X)	0.0 to 1.0	2.9	1.0 to 1.9	8.6	1.9 to 2.9	14.4	2.9 to 3.8	19.4
8(X)	0.0 to 1.0	3.1	1.0 to 2.0	9.4	2.0 to 3.0	15.7	3.0 to 4.0	22.0
50(X)	0.0 to 1.8	11.0	1.8 to 3.7	32.0	3.7 to 5.5	53.0	5.5 to 7.4	74.0

The radii of the zones of blast damage shown in the above table are based on the joint AEC-Department of Defense publication, *The Effects of Atomic Weapons*. For A-bombs between 1(X) and 10(X) sizes, this publication indicates that radii of the zones of blast damage vary with the cube root of the energy release of the bomb. The radii for damage from thermal radiation should approximate this same scale.

In speculating about the effects of atomic bombs of higher yields, this relationship between energy release and extent of damage can be used as a rough guide. Calculations made for such weapons cannot be considered authoritative. The figures for the 50(X) bomb are given merely as an example.

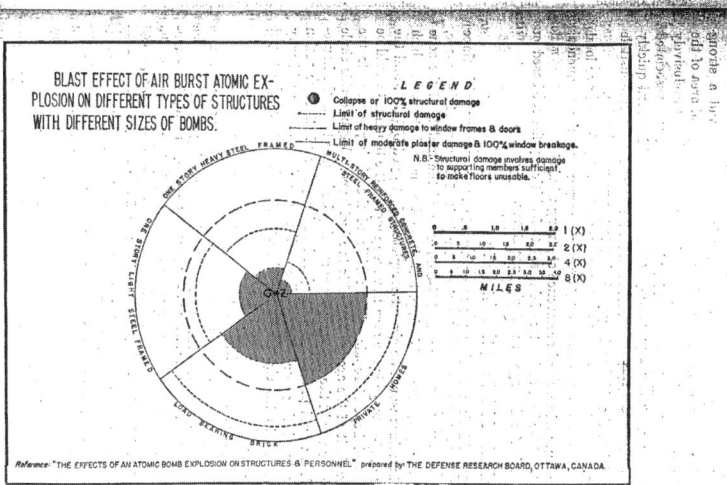

Figure 6.3 Blast Effect of Air Burst.

figure 6.3.) Fire damage depended on such factors as building density, construction materials, precipitation, and wind velocity.[18]

To map the city's probable number and distribution of casualties, planners were to represent the distribution of the population in the city at the time of attack on a map, based on estimates of daytime migration patterns. This preparatory map was then paired with a table (provided by the FCDA) of the estimated percentage of fatalities and nonfatal injuries in a zone. Using this table and the acetate overlay method, the planner would then "record the fatal casualties, nonfatal casualties and uninjured as calculated for each ring and for the various bomb sizes" (FCDA 1953, 36). With this information, the planner could generate "isorithmic maps": sets of lines on a city map indicating the number of fatalities in a given sector. These maps brought urban populations into view as a spatially distributed set of casualty figures, so that plans could be developed to provide relief in the wake of an attack, such as emergency medical and housing services.

The third and final step in the map-making process was to juxtapose selected features on maps to be used by the various services that would be engaged in response to an attack. *CDUA* noted,

> Each service should be given a map of the overall defense pattern of the city (web defense map or other) and an emergency street and highway map developed by the engineering services which shows the traffic control and evacuation assembly plan. In addition, each service should be furnished specific maps and information pertinent to their operations. (FCDA 1953, 50)

These maps not only estimated the physical damage of a likely blast and the casualties that would result from it. More importantly, they indicated the spatial distribution of physical damage and casualties over the existing structure of the city, providing information for civil defense services that would guide contingency planning. For example, information about damage to streets and highways, or general information about the spatial distribution of casualties, might be provided to engineering departments and "incorporated in the general civil defense transportation map" (FCDA 1953, 53). Evacuation routes would thus be planned on the basis of the likely volume of evacuees over certain routes. Planners could also carefully examine these routes to determine areas where fallen buildings or trees might block exit routes, and plan alternatives accordingly. Isorithmic maps of casualties, meanwhile, would show "at a glance where the people are in the city and [would be] especially valuable for estimating shelter needs and the probable distribution of casualties and uninjured-unhoused."[19] These maps would also identify critical vulnerabilities in systems of response. "For example," *CDUA* noted,

> one police station may house all of the police broadcasting equipment and one electric station may have the only available transformer which can change voltage from a distant source of electrical power to the voltage used for distribution through the city. (FCDA 1953,12)

Vulnerability mapping also enabled local planners to apply the framework of emergency federalism to the specific needs of a given community in a likely attack scenario, effectively bringing the process of civil defense planning full circle. Using vulnerability maps, civil defense services could assess their own capacities and determine requirements for mutual aid and mobile support. As *United States Civil Defense* summarized this logic of coordinated planning, "Civil Defense is conceived as a system which will depend largely on cooperation between critical target areas and the communities around them" (NSRB 1950, 4). (See figure 6.4.)

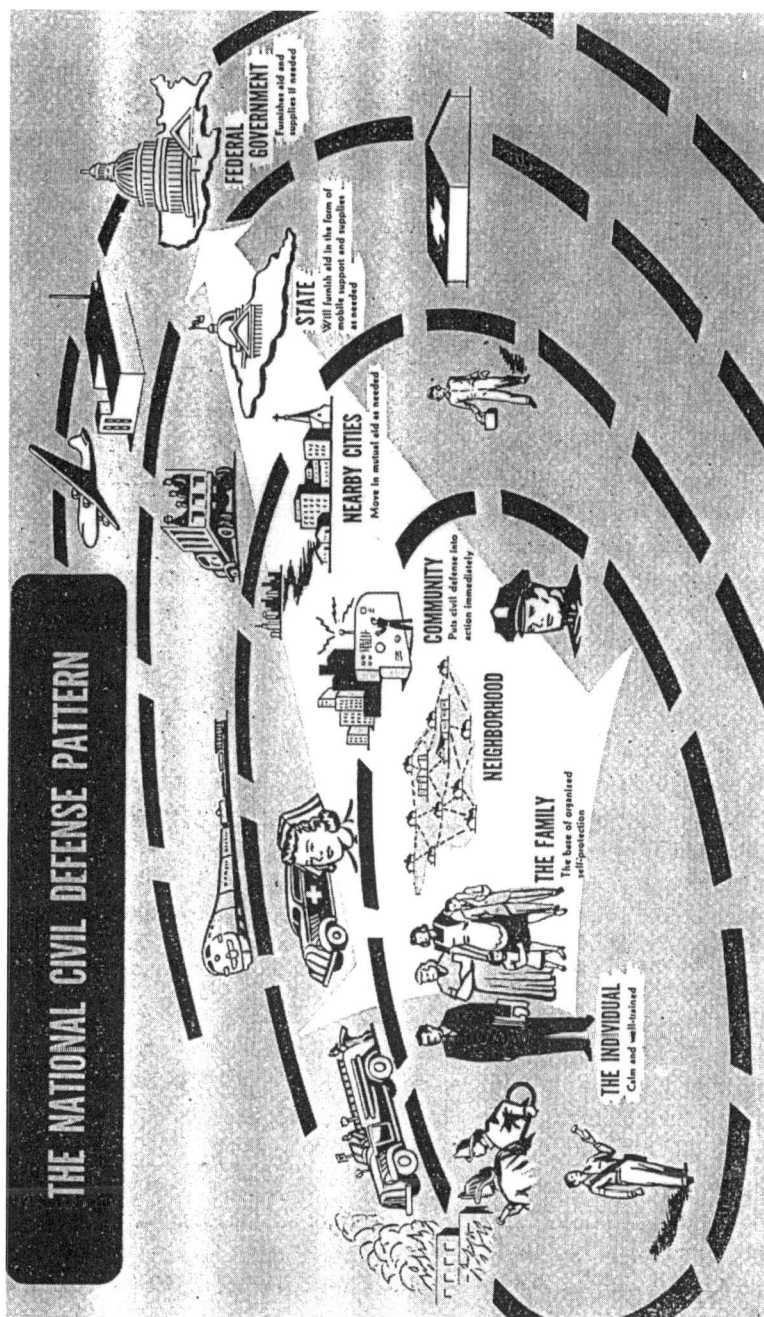

Figure 6.4 The National Civil Defense Pattern.

This overall vision was a distinctive adaptation of the needs of civil defense in an air-nuclear age to the territorial system of governmental administration in the United States. Distributed preparedness linked emergency federalism to vulnerability mapping, grafting spatial knowledge of likely targets onto the federal organization of the U.S. government.

Distributed Preparedness and the Politics of Contemporary Security

In this chapter, we have described distributed preparedness as a novel political logic of collective security that emerged in the context of superpower confrontation during the early Cold War. In conclusion, we briefly track the subsequent diffusion of distributed preparedness from civil defense to other domains over the course of the period after World War II. We then consider the significance of this process for critical understandings of security after the attacks of 9/11, as distributed preparedness moved to the center of security policy in the United States.

Beginning in the mid-1950s, some local civil defense officials—skeptical about the very possibility of preparing for a nuclear attack—recognized that elements of distributed preparedness could be used to approach other possible threats, such as hurricanes, earthquakes, and floods (FCDA 1957; Quarantelli n.d.). These officials applied the techniques of vulnerability mapping, and the emergency federalist model of coordination, to the challenges of domestic natural disaster response. In doing so, they defined a new field of expertise—"emergency management."[20]

During the 1970s, this field of expertise and the forms of response associated with it were institutionalized at the national level. A concern with environmental dangers such as nuclear accidents and toxic spills prompted state governments to request that governmental preparedness for various potential emergencies be centralized. In 1979, the Federal Emergency Management Agency was established to coordinate state and local response to major disasters. The new agency consolidated multiple federal emergency management and civil defense functions under the rubric of "all-hazards planning." It extended the techniques of vulnerability mapping to deal with various possible catastrophes, including earthquakes, floods, and major industrial accidents, in addition to enemy attacks. And FEMA adopted the emergency federalist model of response coordination as well, taking shape as a small coordinative agency rather than an extensive bureaucratic organization.

Over the following two decades, while distributed preparedness crystallized as a model for federal emergency management, its logic extended into a number of new settings, both inside and outside the government, to address diverse problems such as terrorism, public health, and humanitarian emergencies. In the United States, distributed preparedness is now most visible in the Department of Homeland Security, established after the attacks of 9/11. When

FEMA was incorporated into the department in 2002, DHS inherited the techniques and organizational framework that had been developed in emergency management and civil defense, as well as FEMA's orientation to all-hazards planning. Thus, the National Preparedness Guidance—the basic DHS strategy document released in the spring of 2005—is based on fifteen "scenarios," including a dirty bomb attack, a major hurricane, and an influenza epidemic (U.S. Department of Homeland Security 2005). Like the "hypothetical attack problem" from *United States Civil Defense*, these were imagined events that were to be enacted in order to determine needed response capacities, and to identify vulnerable nodes in critical response systems. The use of these scenarios would also allow U.S. territory to be mapped as a space of vulnerabilities, and so would serve as a tool for prioritizing the distribution of funds for preparedness activities among states. Thus, the novel formation of "homeland security" was at least in part a crystallization and new institutionalization of the logic of distributed preparedness.

Distributed preparedness is now central to U.S. government policy related to collective security. And it has become so during what might be considered the largest reorganization of the federal government since the 1947 National Security Act (White House 2006). As in the early Cold War, this reorganization has raised critical questions about the politics of security, and about its relationship to liberal-democratic institutions of citizenship and civilian administration.

As we noted in the introduction, a common tendency in critical scholarship has been to equate recent transformations in the organization of security with a "militarization" of the civilian sphere, and with the curtailment of civil liberties.[21] Our analysis suggests a different critical vantage, one that begins with the premise that there are multiple types of security. From this vantage, in order to diagnose the political stakes of a given security measure, it is initially necessary to specify which type of security is in question: what is its political logic? What kinds of threats does it seek to manage, and what are its implications for welfare or civil liberties?

Our analysis indicates that the extension of distributed preparedness to new domains should not be equated with a process of "militarization." The U.S. military has never wanted to engage in distributed preparedness—not in 1949 and not in 2006. And as we have seen, the explicit concern of those who initially developed distributed preparedness was with how preparation and response to certain kinds of security problems might take place *without* compromising the distributed sovereignties of American federalism and the liberal traditions of the American political system. If anything, the rise of distributed preparedness is best understood as a response to conservative apprehension about federal interference with free enterprise and local government, rather than as an erosion of the civilian sphere.[22]

What is needed, then, is not an overarching diagnosis of "militarization" or "securitization," but an analytics that allows us to distinguish among different processes underway in a complex field of contemporary security problems. With such an analytics, it becomes possible to distinguish among the political implications of various types of security measures. For example, some provisions in the Patriot Act and measures to allow for extrajudicial detentions increase the legal power of the federal government and curtail civil liberties and protections. An approach based on distributed preparedness, by contrast, would seek to maintain the decentralized power of the U.S. federal system, and would emphasize transparency and communication across public and private actors rather than secrecy and centralization. Or, to take another example, the pursuit of increased security through attacks on foreign enemies requires military expenditures that drain resources from health and social security measures. Measures based on distributed preparedness, meanwhile, might instead draw attention to vulnerabilities that are the products of decaying infrastructure, isolated areas of poverty, or weak public health services—and would thus lead to spending that would complement social welfare efforts. In this sense, a more differentiated analysis of current security measures may point not only to salient sites of critique but also to unexpected possibilities for intervention into the politics of contemporary security.

Notes

1. We are grateful for the suggestions of the editors of this volume, Deborah Cowen and Emily Gilbert, as well as for comments by Carlo Caduff, Kerstin Mikalbrown, Gregoire Mallard, Paul Rabinow, and Dale Rose on an earlier draft of this chapter.
2. Michel Foucault refers to this approach as a study of problematizations (see Rabinow 2003). For a discussion of this approach in relation to security problems, see Collier, Lakoff, and Rabinow (2004), and Collier and Lakoff (2006).
3. For a discussion, see McMullen (2001); for a broader analysis of military preparations for postwar mobilization during World War II, see Sherry (1977).
4. Civil defense was not the only response to this new awareness of the United States as a target. For example, policies to promote industrial dispersion were also implemented (see Galison 2001; Light 2003).
5. U.S. Strategic Bombing Survey (1947). McMullen (2001) discusses the relationship of the USSBS to the transformation in Air Force doctrine.
6. For a review of these studies, see Lee (2001) "Careful Studies and Indecision."
7. Lee (2001, 60) argues that *United States Civil Defense*—referred to as the "blue book"—served "as the blueprint for structuring the Federal Civil Defense administration."
8. Hogan (1998, 210) writes that NSRB was to provide "a peacetime agency to coordinate mobilization plans across the government, assess military readiness and the availability of essential commodities, and advise the president on strategic resources and the proper balance between civilian and military requirements."
9. The phrase is Hogan's.

10. This coalition also involved corporate actors who had been concerned with state incursions on free enterprise during World War II. Waddell (1999, 241) writes: "The experience of war mobilization convinced key corporate leaders to value the compensatory role played by the state and to appreciate a national state apparatus tamed by the wartime influx of corporate executives. They welcomed a new era of growth based on a business-oriented Keynesianism in preference to both a mythic laissez-faire and a social Keynesianism rooted in a redistributive welfare state."

11. These concerns were an explicit part of discussions about civil defense. Thus, Lee (2001, 37) notes, "Certainly, there were some who reacted with dismay over the prospect of an intrusive civil defense program. Not surprisingly, others objected for economic reasons."

12. This framework of emergency federalism was one among a number of efforts after World War II to reconcile a growing state sector with the institutions of U.S. federalism. One prime example is the fiscal federal theory of James Buchanan (1949). Similar "federalist" solutions to security problems were also being worked out in domains such as health surveillance (see Fearnley 2005).

13. Discussion of the federal role in the report was substantially broader than this question of mobile support. It focused on coordination, planning, and redistribution functions. First, the federal role was needed to ensure uniformity of equipment, and to ensure that roughly standard procedures and assumptions were used for planning in various U.S. target areas. Second, the federal role was necessitated by the concern to avoid burdening critical target areas. Thus, the federal government might have a redistributive role to play in aiding communities with a disproportionate civil defense burden. Finally, the federal role was determined by the allocative problem of ensuring that minimum standards for civil defense preparation were reached in critical target areas, since, by definition, reaching such minimum standards for critical targets was a concern not merely of localities but also of the national security of the country as a whole.

14. Hopley, quoted in Lee (2001, 49). "Unified" command is different from "unitary" command in that the latter implies command and control relationships within a hierarchically organized bureaucratic structure, while the former implies only temporary concentration of decision making among entities not related to each other through bureaucratic hierarchy. Although the point cannot be developed here, this structure for approaching "emergency situations" varies very substantially from what is theoretically assumed in much contemporary literature on sovereignty and the "state of emergency" in that it does not involve a sovereign exception to normal legality. The use of a Schmittian analytic of the "state of exception" (see, for example, Agamben 2005) thus misses much of what is important in current discussions of security in the United States.

15. Ulrich Beck (1999) has argued that the proliferation of incalculable but potentially catastrophic threats is a central characteristic of the "risk society." He notes that these threats outstrip the insurantial mechanisms developed to manage collective security problems under the aegis of welfare, and suggests that social consciousness of these new threats will lead to the mobilization of new antitechnocratic politics. However, Beck fails to note the emergence over the

period after World War II of new techniques—such as those we are describing here—for approaching these types of threats (for a discussion, see Collier and Lakoff 2006; Lakoff 2007).

16. These techniques of imaginative enactment and exercise were borrowed from military planners, who faced a similar challenge of anticipating—and preparing for—uncertain but potentially catastrophic events (Lee 2001).

17. The text also points to the need for ongoing revision of such plans in relation to new needs: "because of constant changes in the various factors, results of civil defense urban analyses must be subjected to constant review and revision with civil defense plans being altered accordingly" (FCDA 1953, 2).

18. The key question was whether a blast would become a firestorm by spreading among neighboring buildings, which would increase structural damage considerably.

19. The "uninjured-unhoused" were those whose housing had been destroyed and who therefore needed emergency shelter but were otherwise unharmed. Nonfatal casualty figures provided an estimation of the needs for hospital beds and other emergency medical services (FCDA 1953, 40).

20. As a leading figure in the field put it, "At the national level, a civil defense system developed earlier than any comparable disaster planning or emergency management system. However, at the local level, the prime concern after World War II became to prepare for and respond to disasters" (Quarantelli n.d., 10).

21. For examples of this impulse in the literature, see the special issue of *Theory, Culture, and Society* 19 (4) 2002; as well as Graham (2004) and Light (2002).

22. This conservative apprehension about distributed preparedness may be reflected in the Bush administration's lack of enthusiasm for homeland security.

References

Agamben, Giorgio. 2005. *States of exception*. Chicago: University of Chicago Press.

Beck, Ulrich. 1999. *World risk society*. Cambridge: Polity.

Blanchard, Wayne B. 1986. *American civil defense 1945–1984: The evolution of programs and policies*. Monograph Series. Washington, DC: Government Printing Office.

Brenner, Neil. 2004. *New state spaces: Urban governance and the rescaling of statehood*. Oxford: Oxford University Press.

Buchanan, James M. 1949. The pure theory of government finance: A suggested approach. *Journal of Political Economy* 57 (6): 496–505.

Collier, Stephen J., and Andrew Lakoff. 2006. Vital systems security. Berkeley, CA: Anthropology of the Contemporary Research Collaboratory. http://www.anthropos-lab.net (accessed March 12, 2007).

Collier, Stephen J., Andrew Lakoff, and Paul Rabinow. 2004. Biosecurity: Towards an anthropology of the contemporary. *Anthropology Today* 20 (5): 3–7.

Fearnley, Lyle. 2005. "From chaos to controlled disorder": Syndromic surveillance, bioweapons, and the pathological future. Berkeley, CA: Anthropology of the Contemporary Research Collaboratory. Working paper No. 10. http://www.anthropos-lab.net (accessed March 12, 2007).

Fehr, Kregg Michael. 1999. Sheltering society: Civil defense in the United States, 1945–1963. Ph.D. diss., Texas Tech University.

Galison, Peter. 2001. War against the center. *Grey Room* 4 (Summer): 6–33.

Gold, David. 1977. The rise and decline of the Keynesian coalition. *Kapitalstate* 6: 129.

Graham, Stephen. 2004. Cities as strategic sites: Place annihilation and urban geopolitics. *In Cities, war and terrorism*, edited by Stephen Graham, 31–53. Malden, MA: Blackwell.

Grossman, Andrew. 2001. *Neither dead nor red: Civil defense and American political development during the early Cold War*. London: Routledge.

Hogan, Michael J. 1998. *A cross of iron: Harry S. Truman and the origins of the National Security State, 1945–1954*. Cambridge: Cambridge University Press.

Lakoff, Andrew. 2007. Preparing for the next emergency. *Public Culture* 19 (2).

Lee's chapter "Careful Studies and Indecision."

Lee, C. 2001. An exercise in utility: Civil defense from Hiroshima to the Cuban Missile Crisis. Ph.D. diss., St. Louis University.

Light, Jennifer S. 2002. Urban Security from Warfare to Welfare. *International Journal of Urban and Regional Research* 26 (3).

———. 2003. *From warfare to welfare: Defense intellectuals and urban problems in Cold War America*. Baltimore: Johns Hopkins University Press.

McMullen, John K. 2001. The United States Strategic Bombing Survey and Air Force Doctrine. Maxwell Air Force Base, AL: School of Advanced Airpower Studies.

Nyers, Peter. 2004. Introduction: What's left of citizenship? Citizenship Studies 8 (3): 203–15.

Quarantelli, E. L. N.d. Disaster planning, emergency management and civil protection: The historical development of organized efforts to plan for and respond to disasters. Newark: Disaster Research Center, University of Delaware. http://www.udel.edu/DRC/preliminary/227.pdf (accessed March 12, 2007).

Rabinow, Paul. 2003. *Anthropos today: Reflections on modern equipment*. Princeton, NJ: Princeton University Press.

Sherry, Michael. 1977. *Preparing for the next war: American plans for postwar defense, 1941–1945*. New Haven, CT: Yale University Press.

Theory, Culture, and Society. 2002. 19 (4).

Tyler, Lyon G. 1967. *Civil defense: The impact of the planning years, 1945–1950*. Durham, NC: Duke University.

U.S. Department of Homeland Security. 2005. National preparedness guidance. *Homeland security presidential directive 8: National preparedness*. Washington: U.S. Department of Homeland Security.

U.S. Federal Civil Defense Administration. 1953. *Civil defense urban analysis*. Washington, DC: Government Printing Office.

———. 1957. *Annual report for 1956*. Washington, DC: Government Printing Office.

U.S. National Security Resources Board. 1950. *United States civil defense*. Washington, DC: Government Printing Office.

U.S. Scientific Laboratory, Los Alamos, New Mexico. 1950. *The effects of atomic weapons*. Washington, DC: Government Printing Office.

U.S. Strategic Bombing Survey. 1947. *Civilian defense division final report*. Washington, DC: Government Printing Office.

Waddell, Brian. 1999. Corporate influence and World War II: Resolving the New Deal political stalemate. *Journal of Policy History* 11 (3): 223–56.

White House. 2006. *The federal response to Hurricane Katrina: Lessons learned*. Washington, DC: Government Printing Office.

Yergin, Daniel. 1977. *Shattered peace: The origins of the Cold War and the national security state*. Boston: Houghton Mifflin.

Part II
Re/constituting Territory

7

Reconstituting Iraq

STUART ELDEN

When the full history of this bloody circus is written, people will look back slack-jawed at the scale and brazenness of the occupation's corruption and incompetence. History will record Halliburton's colossal greed; the Bush administration's reckless ideological delusions; Paul Bremer's capricious mismanagement; the venality and duplicity of Chalabi, Allawi and the other disobedient, incompetent puppets. And this criminal farce will be visually branded, linked to images of bombed mosques in Falluja, the burning Baghdad with idle US troops watching, sexual torture and humiliation in Abu Ghraib, and to the swollen skulls of children sick from radiation poisoning.

Christian Parenti (2004, 206–7)

Three Days

1 May 2003: Standing on the flight deck of the USS *Abraham Lincoln* aircraft carrier off the coast of San Diego, California, George W. Bush declared that "major combat operations in Iraq have ended." Bush had just landed in a Navy S-3B Viking aircraft of which he had briefly taken the controls, and dressed in full combat gear—an action figure toy was soon available, with extensive waiting lists (BBC News 2003)—he waved to the assembled forces and posed for pictures before changing into a business suit for the formal speech. With a banner proclaiming "mission accomplished" behind him, he suggested the program and position his administration has attempted to follow since:

> In the battle of Iraq, the United States and our allies have prevailed. And now our coalition is engaged in securing and reconstructing that country. . . .

> The transition from dictatorship to democracy will take time, but it is worth every effort. Our coalition will stay until our work is done. Then we will leave, and we will leave behind a free Iraq. (Bush 2003b)

28 June 2004: Paul Bremer, head of the Coalition Provisional Authority (CPA), conducts a brief ceremony in Baghdad, hands a two-paragraph letter to an

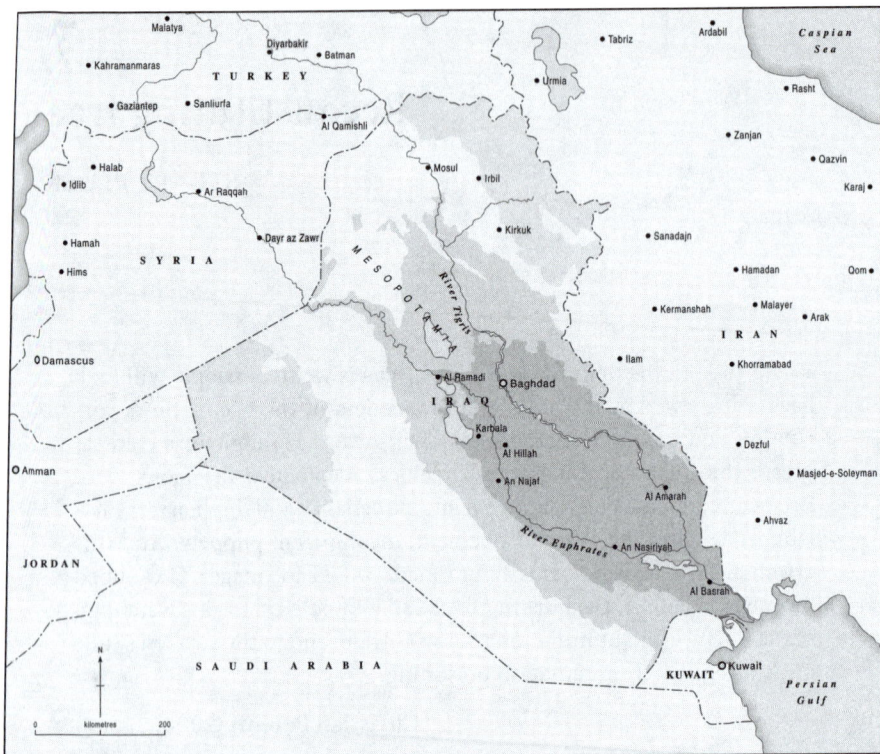

Figure 7.1 Map of Iraq. (Design and Imaging Unit, Durham University)

Iraqi judge, and promptly leaves by helicopter and C-130 (Meek 2004). Bush was informed of the handover of power to unelected Iraq officials, including Prime Minister Ayad Allawi, at a NATO summit in Turkey. He was passed a piece of paper by then National Security Advisor Condoleezza Rice on which was written, "Mr President, Iraq is sovereign. Letter was passed from Bremer at 10:26 a.m. Iraq time—Condi." Bush wrote, "Let Freedom Reign!" on the note,[1] and shook hands with British Prime Minister Tony Blair. The photo of this event shows Blair contorting his face into a gritted teeth smile which is presumably meant to demonstrate both resolve and satisfaction.[2]

In a speech in Istanbul later that day, Bush declared,

> Earlier today, 15 months after the liberation of Iraq, and two days ahead of schedule, the world witnessed the arrival of a free and sovereign Iraqi government. . . . After decades of brutal rule by a terror regime, the Iraqi people have their country back.

> This is a day of great hope for Iraqis, and a day that terrorist enemies hoped never to see. The terrorists are doing all they can to stop the rise of a free Iraq. But their bombs and attacks have not prevented Iraqi sov-

ereignty, and they will not prevent Iraqi democracy. Iraqi sovereignty is a tribute to the will of the Iraqi people and the courage of Iraqi leaders.

This day also marks a proud moral achievement for members of our coalition. We pledged to end a dangerous regime, to free the oppressed, and to restore sovereignty. We have kept our word. (Bush 2004)

18 November 2005: Two Shi'a mosques in the town of Khanaqin in the northeast of the country are attacked by suicide bombers, leaving eighty dead (BBC News 2005j). The UN calls for an inquiry after the discovery of mass torture of Sunni prisoners in a Baghdad detention center only two days before (*Guardian* 2005g; Muir 2005). Sharp exchanges between Republican officials, journalists, and critics of the Iraq policy continue in Washington, following the fallout from Vice President Dick Cheney's counterattack (Cheney 2005; see Froomkin 2005). Controversy over the use of white phosphorus in the operations in Falluja rages after the U.S. admission of its deployment (BBC News 2005i).

Three days. One of hubris; one of exception; one increasingly routine. The process of reconstruction and securitization Bush claimed was initiated by the end of combat operations continues four years later. Since that time, the trial of Saddam Hussein was begun, adjourned, restarted, and was completed, mired in controversy about its validity, operation, and remit, as well as the murders of those involved in the process and his execution at its end. The Iraq Constitution was finally agreed on and then put to popular vote on 15 October 2005, gaining both a majority and insufficient opposition to lead to full elections on 15 December. Debates about the presence of troops continue, with some suggesting that to withdraw now would abandon Iraq to chaos at best, or civil war at worst, and others claiming that the coalition forces, even with UN mandates, are a barrier to progress.

This chapter looks at the reconstitution of Iraq through the process and document of its constitution. Of course, writing about these topics so close to the events themselves raises a number of problems, including the lack of much primary information and the limitations of the journalism that has appeared. In addition, large elements of a comprehensive analysis have been excluded from this study. For example, it does not seek to discuss the justifications for the war in the first place, nor examine the wider issues about international law and the relation between territory and sovereignty that the invasion brought into sharp focus (see Elden 2005, 2006a, 2007, and the references in those pieces). Nor does it look at the conduct of the war itself (see Keegan 2004; Beck and Downing 2003). The focus on the reconstruction is situated within the wider political process since the assumption of coalition control, although it largely eschews analysis of the financial side, which is the largest U.S. program since the Marshall Plan, but with the crucial difference that while the former was funded by the United States, the reconstruction of Iraq is paid for by the

Iraqis themselves, from oil revenue (Harriman 2005, 3; see International Crisis Group [ICG] 2004; BBC News 2005h). Instead, it offers an analysis which concentrates on the territorial and identity issues. The transfer of authority from the CPA to the interim government illustrates the problematic rendering of state sovereignty, just as the refusal to engage with the territorial settlement and the problem of political identity masks some important political evasions.

The Political Process

General Jay Garner was appointed as head of the Office of Reconstruction and Humanitarian Assistance (ORHA), a division of the U.S. Department of Defense, in February 2003, with the brief of managing the civilian needs of Iraq after the invasion and expected quick victory. The remit of reconstruction and assistance demonstrated that the United States was not expecting to govern (Feldman 2004, 113). Yet very swiftly after that declared victory, with less than a month in Iraq, the CPA replaced the ORHA, and Paul Bremer took control on 12 May (Stansfield 2005; Phillips 2005). This was ostensibly due to the lack of political progress, the widespread looting of museums and ancient sites (see Schuster and Polk 2005), and appalling infrastructural issues, but other reports suggest that Garner was keen on early elections and against the privatization policies (Leigh 2004). Under U.S. plans, energy, heavy industry, and the media would be privatized, but as Barber notes, "[T]he choice between a public or a private economy is perhaps the most important democratic choice a people can make, and by making that choice for the Iraqis the Americans effectively stole from them a marker of their sovereignty" (2004, 25). The purpose of the CPA was to prepare Iraq for self-sovereignty, implying that it was clearly not ready to immediately take over, and that some sort of nation building was needed (Feldman 2004, 113). The United Kingdom's ambassador to the United States, Christopher Meyer, describes the attitude of the Pentagon, and particularly then U.S. Deputy Secretary of Defense Paul Wolfowitz, as not to bring "perfect democracy but start with a fairly rough and ready version that would be the basis from which you could move on to higher things" (Glover and MacAskill 2005).

Two key problems have undermined such an approach: the failures of the CPA and the challenge to U.S. and UK forces. The CPA was housed in Saddam's old Palace of the Republic, now called the Green Zone. This is a heavily fortified complex, removed both spatially and politically from the "outside" of Iraq (see Parenti 2004, 42).[3] This led, inevitably, to a certain detachment, with UK envoy Jeremy Greenstock suggesting that "the promise of the postwar period had been 'dissipated in poor policy analysis and narrow-minded execution'" (reported in Bright 2005). In a more naïve, or perhaps patently dishonest, assessment, the U.S. government listed one hundred ways, in ten categories, that the situation in Iraq, one hundred days after the end of major combat operations, had improved (White House 2003). The challenge has been described variously as resistance, insurgency, or terrorism. The most favorable way, from a U.S. perspective, was to label it as "pro-Saddam militias with support from Islamic organizations associated with Al-Qaeda" (Stansfield 2005, 151; see Parenti 2004, 88–89; Corera 2005), since this enabled a number of key moves: to delegitimate resistance by labeling it as pro-Saddam and therefore reactionary; to further suggest a link between Saddam and al Qaeda; and to enable a branding of Iraq as the central front in the War on Terror.[4] A certain bravado punctuated Bush's pronouncements. In July 2003, for example, he suggested that "there are some who feel like—that the conditions are such that they can attack us there. My answer is, bring them on" (Bush 2003c). As Daalder and Lindsay note in their analysis of Bush's foreign policy, "His taunt may have been unwise. The next day, two more American soldiers were killed in combat and nineteen wounded" (2003, 155). The linkage between these two problems is key: for Parenti, "The CPA, a policy wonk's Disneyland at the center of hell, rests on a base of brutal and difficult military labor" (2004, 48).

In reconstructing Iraq politically, the United States and United Kingdom were in an awkward position, as their occupation was bound by the Hague Convention, notably the clause that they must "take all the measures in [their] power to restore, and ensure, as far as possible, public order and safety, while respecting, unless absolutely prevented, the laws in force in the country" (1907, Article 43). On several occasions, CPA officials invoked a sovereign exception to this (see Feldman 2004, 54–55). British International Development Secretary Clare Short, a critic of the war in the first place, finally resigned on 12 May, explicitly around the limits to the powers of the occupying forces and their obligations under international law. Short argued that under the Hague and Geneva (1949) Conventions, humanitarian needs, the keeping of order, and the running of civil administration allowed the occupation to administer, but that it was "not entitled to make major political, economic and constitutional changes," and that only the UN Security Council (UNSC) was able to do this (Short 2003; see also Short 2005, 169; Benvenisti 2004).

On 22 May, UNSC Resolution 1483 recognized precisely this restriction on "all states concerned." On 13 July 2003, an Interim Governing Council (IGC) was established, which was welcomed by the UN as "broadly representative" and "as an important step towards the formation by the people of Iraq of an internationally recognized, representative government that will exercise the sovereignty of Iraq" (UNSC Resolution 1500, 15 August 2003). In the more critical assessment of Parenti, though, it was

a body of twenty-five notables, many of [them] former exiles. During its first year the IGC was known mostly for its duplicity, vacillation, inaction, timidity, and interminable deadlock over small and irrelevant decisions. . . . More concrete tasks—like writing a new constitution, creating government institutions and reviving the economy (or just privatising everything)—were left to the CPA and later the US Embassy. (2004, 48)

This construction of a viable political process was a key issue, as it was decided that a new constitution was needed for the building of the new polity. And yet, the question of who would frame the constitution was an instance of the problem of founding. On the one hand, the constitution was designed to allow for the election of a representative government, but it needed to be written by someone. Grand Ayatollah Ali al-Sistani was central to ensuring the framers were elected, rather than selected, issuing a fatwa in the summer of 2003, which in Feldman's words was "pure democratic theory, with nary a reference to Islamic legal texts . . . designed to appeal not only to religiously observant Shi'is but to all Iraqis" (2004, 40).[5] This view was shared by numerous international lawyers, and transitional arrangements were therefore put in place. Initially this was under the CPA with the Transitional Administration Law (TAL), eventually leading to Bremer's transfer in June 2004 to the interim government that would pave the way for elections to constitute Iraq. The tension was that Sistani did not want sovereignty transferred to an unelected government, but the United States was committed to transfer of sovereignty before a practical date for elections, in part due to the November 2004 U.S. presidential election (see Feldman 2004, 116–17).

The view from the official "Historic Review of CPA Accomplishments," a seemingly unselfconsciously congratulatory document, is that the CPA had provided Iraq with "four foundational pillars for their sovereignty: Security, Essential Services, Economy, Governance" (CPA 2004, 2). Iraq was now a "fully sovereign nation," and the CPA had "achieved its primary goal," now ceasing to exist. In the more forthright assessment of one provincial governor,

> The United States showed complacency, certainly, and perhaps arrogance too, about Iraqis and their reaction to occupation, and, in their frustration with existing security structures such as the United Nations, simply ignored the accumulation of practical experience gained by such organisations in similar ventures. If it cannot be proved that this atmosphere of miscalculation, rivalry and dissent exacerbated CPA's practical difficulties, the empirical evidence for the charge remains strong. (Etherington 2005, 238)

In part, of course, the CPA recognized its own unpopularity, and sought both the quasi-legitimacy of the IGC and their role in drafting the TAL.[6] A CPA poll, leaked in May 2004, suggested that "92 per cent of those surveyed saw the coalition forces as occupiers, and 55 per cent believed they would feel safer if those forces left immediately" (Short 2005, 5). As Etherington notes, "the consent of ordinary Iraqis" had made possible its operations, and this was not as stable as the CPA might have hoped (2005, 197). In Feldman's terms, the United States propping up an illegitimate government could lead to the "worst-case scenario for the American occupation of Iraq: Vietnam, but in Lebanon" (2004, 120). Hence the hurry for Bremer to symbolically hand over sovereignty and leave the scene.

> Drafted and agreed [on] by Iraqi leaders, the TAL is Supreme Law of Iraq during the transitional period. The TAL provides for Iraq's first ever democratic elections to be held no later than end January 2005, and for the drafting of a permanent constitution by December 2005. Under the TAL, the system of government in Iraq will be republican, federal, democratic, and pluralistic. Federalism will be based on geography, history and separation of powers, and not on ethnicity or sect. (CPA 2004, 44; see Diamond 2005)

The elections held on January 30, 2005, were largely boycotted by Sunni Arabs, with only two percent turnout in Anwar Province. Shi'as won just under fifty percent of the seats with four million votes, forty-eight percent of the total cast on an overall fifty-eight percent turnout. The Kurdish alliance came second with 2.2 million votes, 26 percent; and the coalition of Ayad Allawi, 1.2 million, 14 percent (Carroll 2005a). In total, then, the Shi'as and Kurds held 221 of 275 seats, and would therefore dominate the constitutional committee charged with producing a draft, and although fifteen Sunnis were co-opted onto the panel of seventy-one in order to strive for a constitution that could be truly representative, questions have been raised about whether these appointees represent their own community (Carroll 2005g). As Brown notes, the "Sunni committee members . . . preferred to be called the representatives of those boycotting the January elections" (2005b, 1).

It is important to note that these categories of Shi'a, Sunni, and Kurd are not unproblematic. Sunni, for instance, is not an uncontested category, given that they do not necessarily self-identify in that way. In addition, the majority of Kurds are adherents of Sunni Islam, but "Sunni" is often now used as shorthand for Sunni Arab (see ICG 2005b). The disbanding of the Ba'ath Party and the association of Sunnis with Saddam's regime have caused problems in asserting an identity (Allaf et al. 2004, 5). Indeed, they have problems with the suggestion of discrete Sunni, Shi'a, and Kurdish identities, particularly in the way this is presented. The secretary-general of the Arab League, Amr Moussa, for example, declared,

> I do not believe in this division between Shi'a and Sunni and Muslims and Christians and Arabs and Kurds. . . . I don't buy this and I find in this a true recipe for chaos and perhaps a catastrophe in Iraq and around it. (BBC News 2005d; see *New York Times* 2005)

There is certainly a danger of seeing ethnic and religious affiliation as relevant political categories, which has led Simon Jenkins to note that "voting is not political but religious and ethnic" (2005b), seeing this as a sign of political immaturity. Some Islamic groups have tried to minimize differences, with the slogan "Not Sunni, not Shi'i—Islamic unity!" but as Feldman notes, "[T]he implicit assumption of these messages was that Sunni and Shi'i were the default identities to which people would probably have recourse, and that universalising Islamic identity should be used to find common ground between them" (Feldman 2004, 78). Equally there is a danger of seeing these groups as a homogeneous unity, each seeking similar outcomes. The Kurds, for example, both under the de facto sovereignty before the invasion and subsequently, are divided into two main factions, the Kurdistan Democratic Party (KDP) of Sheikh Massoud Barzani and the Patriotic Union of Kurdistan (PUK) led by Jalal Talabani. Both have political differences (and indeed fought a civil war until 1998) and geopolitical strengths, as Turkey favors the former and Iran the latter as negotiating partners given their dominance in the northeast and southwest sectors of the region (see Marr 2003; Brewin 2005).

The Process of Constitution

Under the TAL Article 61, the National Assembly was charged with writing a draft of the permanent constitution by 15 August 2005, to be put to a referendum on 15 October that year. The constitution needed to pass two hurdles: an overall majority in Iraq, and not being rejected by three or more governorates by two-thirds majorities. Although in the final outcome, the rejectionist governorates were Sunni, this was originally a veto concession for the Kurds (Cole 2004). If accepted, the process would lead to 15 December elections, with a new full government to assume office by the end of the year; if rejected, those elections would be for a new National Assembly which would be asked to redraft a constitution, with the political process set back a year. The 15 August deadline for writing the constitution could be extended, but by request of the "president of the National Assembly, with the agreement of a majority of the members' votes . . . no later than 1 August 2005," and "for only six months . . . [and] may not be extended again." The article is quite clear that if they fail to meet this deadline without a request for extension, a new drafting assembly should be elected on 15 December. It was not at all certain that resolution would eventually be found, and at various stages a new assembly looked likely with some international organizations calling for more time to allow proper consultation (ICG 2005a). Various setbacks dogged the process, including boycotts in response to assassinations, the leaking of parts of the constitution, and complaints about the procedures (Beehner and Otterman 2005). And disinformation abounded, including rumors of changes to the position of foreign bases being stationed in Iraq, announced and later retracted by http://www.electroniciraq.net (Electronic Iraq n.d.).

Although I will focus on the territorial issues, there were a number of other concerns (see, generally, Brown 2005a). One of them was the name of the polity being constructed, including various combinations of "Federal," "Arab," or "Islamic" as qualifiers to "Republic." The issues are more than merely formality. The Kurds want to see it as federal to underline their status, but also to recognize that a federal state is a union of equals, rather than their status being that of autonomy granted by the larger polity. While the Kurdish people see themselves as part of a larger Kurdish homeland, the Arabs think Iraq is part of a larger Arab homeland, and the Shi'as part of a wider Islamic community (Assyrian International News Agency 2005). Amr Moussa raised concerns about the lack of recognition of Iraq's "Arab identity" (BBC News 2005d), and yet the constitution works cautiously round this, declaring that Iraq is "part of the Islamic world and its Arab people are part of the Arab nation" (Article 3). It thus recognizes the separation and lack of a wholesale identity of the country. The question of scale thus works both ways: down to subnational areas and up to supranational groupings. Although some elements of the Sunnis wanted "Arab" in the title, in the end the straightforward Republic of Iraq was chosen. Identity issues were also at play in the choice of official languages, of which Arabic and Kurdish were decided upon, including the use of Arabic as an official language in Kurdish areas. The role of religion also proved contentious, with extensive debate as to whether it should be *a* source of legislation, or *the* source of legislation. The solution, apparently brokered by U.S. Ambassador Zalmay Khalilzad, was for it to be "a primary source" (Carroll and Borger 2005): qualified but privileged.

In the event, the clauses of Article 61 of the TAL were ignored, with the process going through several delays, with initially seven extra days being added to the August 15 deadline at the last minute. This required a two-thirds majority, but unanimity was achieved just twenty minutes before midnight (BBC News 2005a; Carroll 2005c). As Carroll notes, the legality of amending the TAL was "dubious but with neither side wanting elections there were no objections" (2005c). Although some of the delegates wanted much more time, the United States kept up the pressure, eventually making their own proposals through Khalilzad (Carroll 2005b). Khalilzad later tried to put a positive spin on the delay, suggesting that

> notwithstanding their success in narrowing differences Iraqi leaders made an important decision not to rush the completion of such an historic document . . . Iraq's free will and its democratic process were on display for the world to see. (2005b)

The United States also tried to underplay its own involvement, stating on the White House website that:

> This was an Iraqi deal, brokered by brave and courageous Iraqi leaders.

The United States, working with our allies and the UN, served as a facilitator where necessary and supported the efforts of all sides to broker favorable compromises.

Nothing would have been done without sophisticated and mature Iraqi leadership. (2005b)

The deadline was again extended, by three days, with an incomplete draft being submitted on 22 August at eight minutes to midnight (Carroll 2005e). But the constitution was withdrawn and not voted upon (*Guardian* 2005a). The reason for this was that although the Shi'a and Kurds had largely agreed, the Sunni negotiators did not accept this as a consensus. Although it could have been pushed through, it was withheld with an attempt made to bring the Sunnis on board, or to marginalize them further (Carroll 2005e). Again, key U.S. figures saw this positively, with a White House statement on 22 August 2005 suggesting that democracy was "difficult and often slow, but leads to durable agreements" (2005a; see also Rice 2005). Donald Rumsfeld declared on 23 August that it was "delayed a bit, but democracy has never been described as speedy, efficient or perfect" (2005), an optimistic outlook he has been perfecting ever since his comments in the early days after the victory, when he accepted looting and rioting as inevitable, declaring that "stuff happens" and "freedom's untidy" (reported in Loughlin 2003).

Compromise was not found, although there was some confusion, as it was suggested that it did not need parliamentary approval on 25 August because this had been given on the 22nd. Eventually, shortly after the midnight deadline expired, another day was added to the deliberations (Carroll 2005f), although this did not offer any hope for the Sunnis to be brought in. The gamble of excluding the Sunnis was to upset the United States, who believed that it was essential to bring them into the process. For Khalilzad, "if the Sunnis do not buy into this draft then it would be a problem. It could assist the insurgency" (reported in Carroll 2005g). From elements within that community, there was immediate condemnation, with top negotiator Saleh al-Mutlaq saying the compromises were "far from what we need," while Sunni Vice President Ghazi al-Yawer suggested that the constitution was "somewhat remote from the aspirations of all segments of the Iraqi people" (reported in BBC News 2005b), and there were calls for the UN and Arab League to intervene (BBC News 2005c). Al-Mutlaq's suggestion that passing the constitution could cause "an insurgency amongst the Sunnis" was effectively dismissed by Bush:

And you talk about Sunnis rising up. I mean, the Sunnis have got to make a choice—do they want to live in a society that's free, or do they want to live in violence. And I suspect most mothers, no matter what their religion may be, will choose a free society, so that their children can grow up in a peaceful world. (Bush 2005a; see Bush 2005b)

In part, then, this tactic was deliberate, in that Sunnis would be forced to vote in the referendum in order to say no, drawing them into the political process (see Corera 2005). For Laith Kubba, spokesman of the government, "[I]f that is the price to pay, we lose six months and have to start [the constitution] again, then it is worth it" (reported in Carroll 2005g).

One concession that merely deferred problems was the eleventh-hour deal brokered by Zalmay Khalizad, which meant that the new parliament could propose changes to the constitution (Jeffery 2005; Carroll and al-Bashir 2005b; BBC News 2005e), reinforcing the sense that the constitution is a holding operation. Many contentious elements either were not worked through or were removed in part as a response to U.S. pressure on time because a constitution could be portrayed as one of the signs of success and allow a withdrawal, but also in order to instill a sense of compromise in some elements of the Sunni population. The committee could be set up, but no guarantee proposals would be accepted. As the *Guardian* noted, the constitution was therefore "probably unique," as "it became shorter and shorter in the process of being written." It is therefore described as a "colour-by-numbers book, with the shapes broadly outlined but the all-important colours left to be filled in later" (2005e). But for Williams and Spencer (2005), writing in the *Boston Globe*, such objections miss the point. What the Iraqis are working on, they claim, is a "political compact," setting out how they will resolve future problems. Thus, the 15 August projected text will be "more of a General Framework Agreement than a traditional legalistic constitution" (2005; see Khalilzad 2005b). In the words of BBC correspondent Paul Reynolds, it is a "milestone along the way, not the destination itself" (2005).

Bush welcomed the news of the final text as a welcome distraction from the problems of Hurricane Katrina.

> Today Iraqi political leaders completed the process for drafting a permanent constitution. Their example is an inspiration to all who share the universal values of freedom, democracy, and the rule of law. The negotiators and drafters of this document braved the intimidation of terrorists and they mourn the cowardly assassination of friends and colleagues involved in the process of drafting the constitution. (Bush 2005c)

The Constitution of Iraqi Territory

While on the one hand Iraq's constitution raised issues around the problem of founding, in that the sovereign "we" was both posterior to the legitimacy of the event and prior to it, on the other hand the entity doing the constituting was already decided, predetermined. This is the territorial extent of the constitution's sovereignty, and the people who would be included within it. A key part of Iraq's constitution is thus an extraconstitutional act.[7] In an article looking at the issue of earned sovereignty, and particularly the case of Kosovo, Williams and Pecci suggest that certain elements of "phased sovereignty" are relevant to the case of Iraq. But there are important differences, "most importantly the final status of the territory (i.e., Iraq as a sovereign nation) is not in question" (2004, 39). While Williams and Pecci are clearly suggesting that options available in the case of Kosovo are not possible for Iraq—such as an autonomous region within a larger state or an international protectorate—and that Iraq is obviously destined to be a "sovereign nation," the implicit assumption is revealing. This is that it is a question of the "final status of the territory," and that territory is Iraq. Iraq's territorial settlement is not in question. Despite the well-known issues around the artificial nature of the Iraqi state, comprised of three ex-provinces of the Ottoman Empire, today this territorial settlement is seen as inviolable. As Anderson and Stansfield note, "Iraq has maintained its territorial integrity as a state. What it has never succeeded in becoming is a nation" (2004, 6).

Iraq therefore functions as a revealing instance of the way in which the two senses of the international legal term "territorial integrity" are increasingly in tension in the post–September 11, 2001, world. Territorial preservation is almost an absolute, because of the perceived dangers to stability of secession or fragmentation; yet territorial sovereignty is now held to be contingent, for humanitarian reasons, the harboring of terrorists, or the production of weapons of mass destruction (WMD; see Elden 2005, 2006a). Iraq could not be held to be sovereign within its territory, precisely because of what it was doing or allowing to be done within its boundaries. Therefore no-fly zones were established to limit the extent of its power (Yamashita 2004; Elden 2006b), and arguments were made for the overthrow of the existing regime. And yet the status of that territory was precisely the key thing not to be questioned.

This territorial integrity, in the sense of the preservation of the existing boundaries, was an explicit war aim, underlined in the Azores Summit Statement (Bush, Blair, and Aznar 2003), speeches by Blair (2003) and Bush (2003a), and UNSC Resolution 1441 (8 November 2002). Several of Iraq's neighbors, notably including Turkey (see Brewin 2005), have similarly stressed the importance of this, fearing that an unraveling of this settlement would have far wider implications.[8] Internally, too, there are complications: the oil is largely concentrated in the north and south, the fertile land is between the rivers Tigris and Euphrates—the original meaning of the term Mesopotamia means "between the rivers"—and there is marshland to the south, mountains to the north, and desert to the west. Equally, even the crudest maps of ethnic grouping demonstrate that the borders for a federal solution would be difficult to draw, and more subtle mappings demonstrate the complexities of the distribution of populations.

After the first Gulf War, Colin Powell declared that "it would not contribute to the stability we want in the Middle East to have Iraq fragmented into separate Sunni, Shia, and Kurd political entities" (Powell 1996, 512), and a White House policy paper said that "in no way should we associate ourselves with the 60-year-old rebellion in Iraq or oppose Iraq's legitimate attempts to suppress it" (quoted in Kaplan and Kristol 2003, 41). This was one of the main reasons why the march to Baghdad had been halted in 1991, and why uprisings in the North and South had gone unsupported. For the neocons Lawrence Kaplan and William Kristol, though, in 2003 this was now a risk worth taking.

> We have long ago passed the threshold where the prospect of, say, a fragmented Iraq is a greater evil than the persistence of Saddam Hussein. That things might be worse without him is of course a possibility. But given the status quo in Iraq, it is difficult to imagine how. (2003, 96)

Drawing on some of the predictive work of Marr on political factions in Iraq (2003), they expect that there will be few problems, but suggest that a federal system is the answer (Kaplan and Kristol 2003, 97–98). The problem is, of course, among other things, where would the boundaries of such federal divisions be drawn?

One of the ironies of the territorial settlement desired by the United States is that the 1990 Constitution itself declares that "the sovereignty of Iraq is an indivisible entity" and that "the territory of Iraq is an indivisible entity of which no part can be ceded"(Article 3). But apart from the inappropriateness of carrying that over into the new post-Saddam Iraq, they would also like to diminish central control. Indeed, the TAL makes some progress along this path, seeking to dilute federal power, to "encourage the exercise of local authority" yet still preserve "a united Iraq" (2004, Article 52). Indeed the CPA tasked the new Ministry of Foreign Affairs with "actively working to reverse Iraq's former isolation and pursue the following objectives of our new foreign policy," foremost of which is to "protect Iraq's security, stabilize the country and preserve Iraq's territorial integrity" (CPA 2004, 46).

There are some telling claims in the prelude to the 2005 Constitution which showcase a particular geographical imagination.

> We the sons of Mesopotamia, land of the prophets, resting place of the holy imams, the leaders of civilization and the creators of the alphabet, the cradle of arithmetic: on our land, the first law put in place by mankind was written; in our nation, the most noble era of justice in the politics of nations was laid down; on our soil, the followers of the prophet and the saints prayed, the philosophers and the scientists theorized and the writers and poets created. (Prelude)

A subsequent litany of the travails of the people of Iraq is notable because the people are not taken as a whole, but as discretely persecuted groups. It seeks to constitute them as a people through a reference to the January 2005 elections, where "inspired by the suffering of Iraq's martyrs—Sunni and Shiite, Arab, Kurd and Turkomen, and the remaining brethren in all communities," they supposedly voted to put all this behind them. The final lines of the prelude reassert the bringing together "freely and by choice . . . to write down this permanent constitution," in order to preserve the "free union of people, land and sovereignty."

Importantly, this union of people and land is reinforced in a number of clauses. The president is seen as "the symbol of the nation's unity and represents the sovereignty of the country," and is charged with guaranteeing adherence to the constitution as well as "the preservation of Iraq's independence and unity and the security of its territory, in accordance to the law" (Article 65). Similarly, the central federal authority "will maintain the unity of Iraq, its integrity, independence, sovereignty and its democratic federal system" (Article 107). In addition, in a phrase which bears the bootprint of Bush's War on Terror, "the state will be committing to fighting terrorism in all its forms and will work to prevent its territory from being a base or corridor or an arena for its (terrorism's) activities" (Article 7.2). Aside from the interesting geographical frames used—neither a base of operation, nor a corridor of passage for actions outside, nor an arena in itself—this is a telling sign of the contingent nature of Iraqi sovereignty. It was Iraq's supposed complicity in such actions before that led to U.S. arguments for limitations on the right to noninterference within the territorial boundaries of a state. Where a state was not in control of that territory, and therefore was unable to prevent injurious actions beyond those boundaries, or acted in particular ways within its boundaries—such as persecution of groups or pursuit of WMD—their territorial sovereignty could be overrun (see Elden 2006b).

As a federal republic, it is crucial that the arrangements are carefully constituted for the future polity. And yet in the actual constitution text, these issues are glossed over, masked, or deferred. There are a number of indications, but crucial issues are left undeveloped. The different parts of Iraqi society necessarily have quite different perspectives on this. Gareth Stansfield's work is extremely useful in setting out the positions. In his analysis the Kurds want three main things: to maintain their current autonomy and "augment it with control of Kirkuk"; to "secure control of oil resources in Kurdish territory (including the major oilfield of Kirkuk)"; and to "control a Kurdish military force, and have the power to block the military deployment of Iraqi forces to the north." This last point means that this "would, in effect, make Iraqi Kurdistan an independent state in all but name" (2005, 144), since it would limit the projection of federal power and prevent the effective monopoly of violence. By limiting the spatial extent of their sovereignty, this Kurdish demand necessarily brings opposition from the Sunnis, who "demand that the territorial integrity of Iraq should not be threatened by Kurdish autonomy" (2005, 145). This belief in the maintenance of the territorial integrity is shared with the

Shi'a populations, but in part this is because they are the dominant group and most likely to benefit from a combination of representative democracy and the territorial status quo. As Stansfield notes, "[F]or the Shi'a the issue is about who controls Iraq, for the Kurds it is about whether they should even be 'in' Iraq" (2005, 144). One of the other key issues for Shi'a religious elements is to "reverse the secularising policies of Saddam," and for others to obtain more of the country's wealth in oil (Hardy 2005).

In the constitution itself, article 113 notes that "the federal system in the republic of Iraq is made up of the capital, regions, decentralized provinces, and local administrations." There are several levels of government noted here. The provinces are the eighteen governorates carried forward from the Saddam era, which were preserved in the TAL (Article 53). The TAL had declared that "any group of no more than three governorates outside the Kurdistan region, with the exception of Baghdad and Kirkuk, shall have the right to form regions from amongst themselves" (Article 53), which again is carried forward in the 2005 Constitution. Article 114 of the Revised Constitution notes that "the regions comprise one province or more, and two regions or more have the right to join into one region." This ability to merge as regions is poorly formulated, as late amendments to this article proposed by Kurds and Shi'as as a concession to the Sunnis meant that final procedures were delayed until after the December 2005 elections (see Carroll 2005h; Revised Constitution, Article 114). One thing is clear, which is that a decision must be approved in a referendum of the people of the relevant provinces, but this referendum is notably only of those people within the provinces, rather than the country as a whole. It therefore gives a right to limited secession. Equally new regions can only be formed from existing provinces, thus potentially perpetuating minority problems.

Kurdistan is notably the key region to be formed, and Article 113 of the revised text states that "this constitution shall approbate the region of Kurdistan and its existing regional and federal authorities, at the time this constitution comes into force," and that it shall "approbate new regions established in accordance with its provisions." This is a continuation of the policy of the TAL, which had sought to move the de facto to the de jure with regard to the Kurdistan Regional Government, consolidating the status it had enjoyed under the no-fly zones until March 19 "in the governorates of Dohuk, Arbil, Sulaimaniya, Kirkuk, Diyala and Neneveh," without making a move for full independence (Article 53). For Khalilzad, it was much more straightforward than it was being portrayed:

> With regard to federalism [there is] broad agreement and some disagreement. I know that some of the Sunni participants on the outside have spoken out against federalism. . . . On the day that the constitution is ratified the Kurdish entity will be *de jure* what it is *de facto*, an autono-

mous federal unit, a federal unit of Iraq. Federalism is bringing back the Kurdish region into Iraq. It has been away, separated from Iraq *de facto* for a long time. (2005b).

But what Khalilzad fails to take account of is the irony that it is the least powerful community that most wants to preserve the existing situation. The attitudes of Sunnis have been characterized as thinking of Iraq as a whole and themselves as Arab and Iraqi nationalists (Assyrian International News Agency 2005). That they were both the least powerful and most marginalized from the constitutional process required more concessions from the Shi'as and Kurds, in order to better bind them to the political project (*Guardian* 2005b). There is thus an uneasy set of ad hoc alliances. Both the Kurds and the Shi'a want some degree of autonomy, and certainly an end to Sunni dominance. But the Kurds want much more autonomy, and key elements are pushing for full independence. In opposition to this, the Sunni and Shi'a populations adopt "an Arab position," as they "fear it is the first stage in the Balkanisation of Iraq" (Stansfield 2005, 145). The Sunnis in particular see it as cementing their loss of power and threatening territorial unity (BBC News 2005g), and fear Shi'a regions emerging on similar lines to Kurdistan, which would mean the Sunnis would be left with the "sands of Anbar."

With regard to Kurdistan itself, the constitution fudges a number of issues.[9] Laws initiated since the de facto sovereignty of 1992 remain in effect,

> and decisions made by the government of the Kurdistan region—including contracts and court decisions—are effective unless they are voided or amended according to the laws of the Kurdistan region by the concerned body, as long as they are not against the constitution. (Article 150)

This has been a central concession, in order that the Kurds should not enjoy less decentered power than they did in the last decade of Saddam's rule. But for the Kurds the key was not the retention of some autonomy, but the status of Kirkuk, given the importance of the oilfields and its mix of populations (see Brown 2005a). But this was one of the key issues that the constitution has failed to address, and it may be a cause of civil war. Indeed, Article 152 of the new constitution states that it supersedes and voids the TAL, "except for what appears in paragraph (a) of Article (53) and Article (58)." These two articles deal with Kurdistan and the situation in Kirkuk, particularly in terms of addressing the doctoring of its demographic character, respectively (see Carroll 2005d; Brown 2005a).

As Patrick Cockburn notes, this masks some important political problems, as he suggests that a constitution "assumes a stable balance of power." But this is not the case, because "the Kurds are at the peak of their power. They captured the oil city of Kirkuk and intend to keep it. They want to freeze their gains under the new constitution" (Cockburn 2005, 31). But in terms of population, Saddam was able to engineer the makeup of the community, so this too is unstable. In terms of oil, the constitution similarly leaves much unworked through. While Article 109 notes that "oil and gas is the property of all the Iraqi people in all the regions and provinces," it has been claimed that this is merely for currently known resources. As Paul Reynolds of the BBC notes, "[R]egional governments get exclusive access to future fields" (2005), and foreign oil companies can also be involved (Bennis 2005). On resources more generally, Article 110 tries to ensure "fair distribution" of water as part of an overall deal.

The International Situation

While the assertion of the "sovereignty and territorial integrity" of states is a commonplace of UNSC resolutions—including a reaffirmation of "the commitment of all Member States to the sovereignty and territorial integrity of Iraq, Kuwait, and the neighbouring States" in Resolution 1441 in November 2002—there has been a telling shift in the resolutions pertaining to Iraq since the invasion. In May 2003, the UK and U.S. ambassadors to the UN stated that

> the United States, the United Kingdom and Coalition partners, working through the Coalition Provisional Authority, shall inter alia, provide for security in and for the provisional administration of Iraq, including by: deterring hostilities; maintaining the territorial integrity of Iraq and securing Iraq's borders,

as well as finding and removing the WMDs (Greenstock and Negroponte 2003). In these crucial elements, invoking the law of occupation, theirs was the sovereign position, rather than Iraq's. But their position was endorsed by the UN on 22 May, after the formality of the invocation of the "sovereignty and territorial integrity of Iraq," with the UN "recognizing the specific authorities, responsibilities, and obligations under applicable international law of these states as occupying powers under unified command" (UNSC Resolution 1483; on this in the context of the law of occupation, see Benvenisti 2004, viii–xi). Resolution 1500 again pays lip service through the usual phrasing, even though Iraq had been invaded, it was not sovereign, and its territorial integrity had been violated.

Resolution 1511 (16 October 2003) does the same, but there is a notable shift in the attendant register:

> Underscoring that the sovereignty of Iraq resides in the State of Iraq, reaffirming the right of the Iraqi people freely to determine their own political future and control their own natural resources, reiterating its resolve that the day when Iraqis govern themselves must come quickly, and recognizing the importance of international support, particularly

that of countries in the region, Iraq's neighbours, and regional organizations, in taking forward this process expeditiously. . . .

Reaffirms the sovereignty and territorial integrity of Iraq, and underscores, in that context, the temporary nature of the exercise by the Coalition Provisional Authority (Authority) of the specific responsibilities, authorities, and obligations under applicable international law recognized and set forth in resolution 1483 (2003), which will cease when an internationally recognized, representative government established by the people of Iraq is sworn in and assumes the responsibilities of the Authority.

Thus we have an endorsement of the principle, with recognition of the "temporary nature" of the aberration. The occupation is thus recognized but not retrospectively authorized. By 8 June 2004, the UNSC is welcoming the new arrangements, which will lead to "a fully sovereign and independent Interim Government of Iraq by 30 June 2004," as part of the "transition to a democratically elected government," and anticipating "the end of the occupation and the assumption of full responsibility and authority" by Iraq (UNSC Resolution 1546, 8 June 2004). However, the UNSC underscores that this government must refrain from "taking any actions affecting Iraq's destiny beyond the limited interim period until an elected Transitional Government of Iraq assumes office." In other words, the interim government must simply facilitate the existing system until the election of a government that can begin to change it, through, of course, the constitutional process. But it does this without a recognition of the TAL, which without CPA sovereignty was now presumably mutable. Most naïvely, the resolution goes on to welcome that "by 30 June 2004, the occupation will end and the Coalition Provisional Authority will cease to exist, and that Iraq will reassert its full sovereignty" (UNSC Resolution 1546).

Instead of merely the "sovereignty and territorial integrity" of Iraq, UNSC Resolution 1546 now stresses the "independence, sovereignty, unity, and territorial integrity of Iraq." This phrase, which has reoccurred in Resolutions 1557 (12 August 2004), 1619 (11 August 2005), and 1637 (8 November 2005), underscores the constitutive elements of the political process. Sovereignty now can be stressed as "independence"—although it is clearly a deeply compromised and circumscribed independence of action, both in terms of domestic and foreign policy—and territorial integrity can be reinforced by "unity." But these are more than simply superfluous additions. As well as sovereignty being held effectively in trust for the Iraqi people under the occupation, which it has now had restored with independence, they mark a very real fiction in the international community's acceptance of a deeply problematic political position. The UN has established the United Nations Assistance Mission for Iraq (UNAMI), whose mandate has been extended until 11 August 2006 (UNSC Resolution 1619), because it is facilitating "Iraqi national dialogue," which "is crucial for

Iraq's political stability and unity"; and simultaneously endorsed the "presence of the multinational force in Iraq" until 31 December 2006 because it is "at the request of the Government of Iraq" (UNSC Resolution 1637).

Even though the constitution has been adopted, and elections have since taken place under its terms, the occupation continues. In the words of the UN Security Council, though, this is "at the request of the Government of Iraq," and therefore it has reaffirmed "the authorization for the multinational force as set forth in resolution 1546 (2004) and decides to extend the mandate of the multinational force as set forth in that resolution until 31 December 2006" (UNSC Resolution 1637). What it fails to address, however, is that the continual presence of the U.S. forces deeply compromises the independence, and that de facto sovereignty continues to rest with the military. Until the Iraqi government is able to back up its demands with its own monopoly of legitimate violence, it "exercises sovereignty only in a very limited way" (Feldman 2004, 127).

The Referendum

After the constitution was finally approved, copies were distributed and the referendum campaign begun. The question was the simple "Do you approve of the Draft Constitution of Iraq?" Only those present in Iraq could vote: there was no out-of-country voting. Political citizenship was thus effectively tied to geographical presence. Many of the voters had not seen a copy of the referendum, which was being negotiated until at least 12 October. There were some late suggestions that the voting procedure might be changed. Instead of a two-thirds majority of those who voted to reject in a province, it would need to be a majority of registered voters, with the same true for the country as a whole, where a two-thirds majority is needed. But on 5 October, the Iraq National Assembly voted 119 to 28 to restore the original rules, following interventions from UN lawyers (*Guardian* 2005c). The proposals had been strongly condemned by Sunni leaders because not voting—especially likely in the Sunni provinces most affected by the resistance—would effectively be a "yes" vote. "Forgery in advance" was how it had been described by Saleh Mutlaq (*Times* 2005).

In late September some believed that rejection of the constitution was inevitable, but voting on 15 October delivered an overall 78 percent in favor and 21 percent against in Iraq as a whole. There were some instances of violence, but voting took place largely as planned. Turnout was more than 60 percent of the 15.5 million voters (BBC News 2005f). Endorsements in some provinces were very high, including 96 percent in Basra in the south and 99 percent in the three Kurdish-dominated provinces of Dahuk, Irbil, and Sylaimaniya in the north. More mixed areas such as Baghdad (77.7 percent) and Kirkuk (62.9 percent) showed smaller minorities. But the situation was entirely reversed in the two Sunni-dominated provinces, which voted overwhelmingly against: Salahaddin (81.7 percent) and Anbar (96.9 percent). These provinces include the towns of Falluja, Ramadi, and Tikrit. In Nineveh, which includes a mix of Kurds and Christians, there was a 55 percent vote against, but this was too small to provide the third no-voting province needed to reject the constitution. In Diyala there was also a strong "no" vote, but here it did not even achieve a simply majority, with 49 percent against (full results by province in BBC 2005g). But Jonathan Steele suggests that these headline figures mask some awkward and implausible counts, including suspiciously high turnouts and dramatic changes from exit polls. He suggests that the trial of Saddam Hussein was deliberately timed to coincide with the count, and that the leaks of the result before the counting had finished demonstrate that the process was flawed (Steele 2005a). The UN approval of the result has largely displaced such concerns (Steele 2005b), but questions abound about the process, and the starkly geographically polarized support shows the very real divisions in the country.

The referendum on the constitution was predictably trumpeted as the return of the Sunnis to the political process, after their having boycotted the January 2005 elections. Condoleezza Rice, who stated the result was an endorsement before the results were actually known, suggested that "one way or another, the Iraqis will be in a position to move forward" (reported in Behn 2005). For Khalilzad, "[T]his constitution can be a national compact bringing Sunnis in, isolating extremists and Baathists, hard-liners, and setting the stage over time for defeating them" (2005a). But the return of the Sunnis was double-edged in two ways: they largely voted only to vote "no," and large elements of the "insurgency" continue to pair the bomb and bullet with the ballot. For them, these two tactics can work in parallel: resistance through the political process as well as the violence. Carroll reports a conversation with a former army colonel, suggesting that they see the ballot box as "a complement, not a substitute, for armed revolt." Carroll goes on to suggest this may be modeled on the 1980s strategy of Sinn Fein "'ballot box and Armalite' . . . though in their case an AK-47" (2005i). Nonetheless, the increased participation—whichever way they voted—was seen as progress: "In the January elections I think the turnout was 58 percent, in the referendum almost 64 percent, and we are hopeful that even more want to participate in the December elections" (Blair 2005).

Once again the headline figures mask divisions within the communities, with the Sunni Iraqi Islamic Party initially offering a cautious welcome to the document, on the condition that disputed points were resolved by the end of August (Carroll and al-Bashir 2005a). By the middle of October, just as voting was about to begin, the party endorsed the constitution, partly because of the last-minute inserted clause that allows "articles to be re-examined by a new government if the National Assembly desires" (Beaumont 2005b). Nor are these internal tensions simply within Sunni communities. Within the Shi'as, Abdul-Aziz al-Hakim, who has strong ties to Iran, has called for greater autonomy for the South, with the support of Ayatollah al-Sistani. Other key figures, including Moktada al-Sadr and Ayatollah Muhammed Yacoubi, think this goes against central Islamic rule (Wong 2005), leading to common cause with some elements of the Sunni population (Carroll and al-Bashir 2005a). And disagreements are not merely the democratic disputes that Bush and others have explained them away as. Bush claims,

> Some observers question the durability of democracy in Iraq. They underestimate the power and appeal of freedom. We've heard it suggested that Iraq's democracy must be on shaky ground because Iraqis are arguing with each other. But that's the essence of democracy: making your case, debating with those who you disagree—who disagree, building consensus by persuasion, and answering to the will of the people. . . . It is true that the seeds of freedom have only recently been planted in Iraq—but democracy, when it grows, is not a fragile flower; it is a healthy, sturdy tree. (2005d)

Yet what Bush fails to realize, or to accept, is that the disputes are not merely those that take place within any democratic polity, but go to the root of the very constitution of that polity itself. This is constitution not as a document or process of making, but constitution as composition, the very makeup of land and people. One of the key concerns should be that elements both see themselves as having more in common with neighboring states and communities than with other Iraqi populations, and perceive that of those others as well. Indeed, for many Sunnis the Shi'as are "Islamic fanatics in league with Iran," and the Kurds "traitors working with the Americans" (*Guardian* 2005d).

For some the passing of the constitution may lead to partition (ICG 2005b), while for others it may be the only thing that can forestall it (Jenkins 2005b). Philip Bobbitt has made a similar claim to that of Jenkins, stressing that asking the people was a crucial step, whichever way the vote had gone. He noted that "though Americans rightly venerate the role of our framers, it was the ratification of the US constitution by the people that endowed it with sovereignty" (2005). However, Bobbitt raises another related point about the remit and potential of the constitution, suggesting that endowing the state directly with Iraq's oil wealth, instead of allowing the people a share which is then taxed, may present problems of its own.

> We long ago learned the error of taxation without representation. Now we are learning there is no real representation without taxation. (Bobbitt 2005; see Jabar 2004, 3, 13)

Looking Toward the Future

It would obviously be unwise to try to predict the future for Iraq, and inevitably things will have changed by the time this chapter is in print. Yet some key issues can be outlined. In terms of the British and U.S. positions, a key debate is the question of when the troops are coming home. This is inherently related to the political process, and for Iraqi politicians the support they receive. Successful elections in December 2005 and a new Iraqi government under a new constitution will be claimed as political progress, and used to justify troop withdrawals.

> Our job is to assist in that process under the United Nations mandate that we have, but to do so in a way that makes it clear that the vision of a sovereign Iraq, run by Iraqis, for Iraqis, is a vision shared by the Iraqi people and also the international community. And so whatever the difficulties are, and whatever the challenges, that is why it is important that all of us stay the course and see this thing through, and we intend to do so. (Blair 2005)

But as MacAskill notes, the ambitions of what they had hoped for before leaving have been "drastically scaled down." He quotes a Foreign Office source who suggested that "the goal of the US administration to turn Iraq into a beacon of democracy in the Middle East had long ago been shelved." The source is quoted as saying that "we will settle for leaving behind an Iraqi democracy that is creaking along" (MacAskill 2005).

What is labeled "insurgency" has been made possible through the creation of a "failed" state in place of a "rogue" one, and the United States has therefore created the very thing that it claimed threatened stability in the first place. The one group in Iraq that most wants the existing territorial settlement to be preserved is the one most hostile to the political process, and the United States is in part trying to protect that settlement for them in the face of their opposition. Others have suggested that a new balance of power needs to emerge in Iraq before it can begin to stabilize. For some, the presence of coalition troops is not allowing this, and is probably preventing it. "The coalition can no longer influence this balance, only postpone its resolution" (Jenkins 2005b).

> Neoconservatives might fantasise over Iraq as a democratic Garden of Eden, a land re-engineered to stability and prosperity. Harder noses were content to dump the place in Ahmad Chalabi's lap and let it go to hell. Had that happened, I suspect there would have been a bloody settling of scores but by now a tripartite republic hauling itself back to peace and reconstruction. Iraq is, after all, one of the richest nations on earth. (Jenkins 2005a)

A similar argument has been made by 2004's Democrat presidential candidate, John Kerry (2005). Other writers have suggested that the situation is likely to get worse if premature withdrawal takes place, suggesting that "having brought down Saddam, there is an obligation to try to establish a largely stable Iraq." The use of the phrase "largely stable" is intended to be a recognition of the utopian notion of a problem-free Iraq. But Beaumont goes on to note that "abandoning a failed state in the throes of a violent struggle between

Shia and Sunni has consequences for the whole region, and a civil war risks sucking in Saudi Arabia, Iran, Jordan and Syria" (Beaumont 2005a; Allaf et al. 2004). Similar claims have been made by figures in Iraq, such as President Jalal Talabani (reported in *Guardian* 2005f), and by the then British Defence Secretary John Reid (see Jenkins 2005c).

Those who see a moral case for the occupation and reconstruction, however, suggest that "elections must be understood as the midpoint of the nation-building undertaking, not the end of the nation builder's obligations toward the country in question" (Feldman 2004, 3), and see the potential for much longer scale assistance. Certainly issues will remain. Indeed, as Carroll wrote when it was first delayed, the new constitution "will not settle the question of what is Iraq" (2005d). It may well be that by refusing to even consider that question, rather than the process of reconstituting Iraq building on and securing its territorial integrity, there is a serious possibility that the United States has, instead, hastened its territorial and political decomposition. It is an irony that as this chapter's final lines are written, days before the 15 December 2005 elections, the United States finally publishes its "National Strategy for Victory in Iraq" (National Security Council 2005; see Bush 2005f), two and a half years after "Mission Accomplished."

Acknowledgments

I am grateful to Alison Williams for her comments on an earlier version of this chapter, and Luiza Bialasiewicz and Joe Painter with whom I first worked on the territorial issues of constitution in relation to the European Union.

Appendix: Iraqi Constitutions

1990: Iraqi Interim Constitution, http://www.oefre.unibe.ch/law/icl/iz01000.html.

2004: Law of Administration for the State of Iraq for the Transitional Period (Transitional Administrative Law [TAL]), http://www.cpa-iraq.org/government/TAL.html.

2005: Draft Iraqi Constitution, translated by the Associated Press, http://www.iraqigovernment.org/constitution_en.htm//2005 revised Iraqi constitution. This is a later version, in a different translation, http://www.globalpolicy.org/security/issues/iraq/document/2005/1015textofdraft.htm. I have used this latter text only for amendments.

Appendix: United Nations Security Council Resolutions

Available at http://www.un.org/documents/scres.htm.

1441 (8 November 2002): "The Situation between Iraq and Kuwait"
1483 (22 May 2003): "The Situation between Iraq and Kuwait"
1500 (14 August 2003): "The Situation between Iraq and Kuwait"

1511 (16 October 2003): "The Situation between Iraq and Kuwait"
1546 (8 June 2004): "The Situation concerning Iraq"
1557 (12 August 2004): "The Situation concerning Iraq"
1619 (11 August 2005): "The Situation concerning Iraq"
1637 (8 November 2005):"The Situation concerning Iraq"

Notes

1. White House (2004-a).
2. White House (2004-b).
3. When the CPA was dissolved, the building was "magically transformed into an annex of the U.S. Embassy to the nominally sovereign Iraqi government" (Feldman 2004, 33).
4. For example, see Bush (2005e, 2005f) and National Security Council (2005, 1).
5. The text of the fatwa can be found in Feldman (2004, 140 n. 32).
6. See also Talabani and Bremer (2003), which outlines the main contours of the political process, including the framework for the TAL.
7. See Bialasiewicz, Elden, and Painter (2005), which discusses some of the general territorial issues in constitutions on 339–43.
8. Turkey's position may change if it realizes that "it has more to gain than to lose from the existence of a Kurdish buffer state between its European Unionist aspirations and Iraqi violence" (Feldman 2004, 35; see Allaf et al. 2004, 4, 22–23; Barkey 2005).
9. For general analyses of these issues, see O'Leary, McGarry, and Salih (2005) and O'Shea (2004).

References

Allaf, Rime, Ali Ansari, Rosemary Hollis, Robert Lowe, Yossi Mekelberg, Soli Özel, Gareth Stansfield, and Mai Yamani. 2004. Iraq in transition: Vortex or catalyst? Chatham House Middle East Programme Briefing Paper 04/02, September. London: Chatham House.

Anderson, Liam, and Gareth Stansfield. 2004. *The future of Iraq: Dictatorship, democracy or division?* London: Palgrave Macmillan.

Assyrian International News Agency. 2005. Iraq Assembly faces 18 difficult steps. http://www.aina.org/news/2005089113116.htm.

Barber, Benjamin R. 2004. *Fear's empire: War, terrorism, and democracy.* New York: W. W. Norton.

Barkey, Henri J. 2005. Turkey and Iraq: The perils (and prospects) of proximity. United States Institute of Peace Special Report 141. Washington, DC: United States Institute of Peace.

BBC News. 2003. Bush doll has waiting list. August 27. http://news.bbc.co.uk/1/hi/world/americas/3184709.stm.

———. 2005a. Bush hails Iraqi Constitution bid. August 16. http://newswww.bbc.net.uk/2/hi/middle_east/4155086.stm.

———. 2005b. Iraqis differ on charter progress. August 27. http://news.bbc.co.uk/2/hi/middle_east/4186052.stm.

———. 2005c. Iraq's Sunnis reject constitution. August 28. http://news.bbc.co.uk/1/hi/world/middle_east/4192122.stm.

―――. 2005d. Iraq charter a recipe for chaos. August 29. http://news.bbc.co.uk/2/hi/middle_east/4194214.stm.

―――. 2005e. Q&A: Iraq referendum. 15th October, http://news.bbc.co.uk/1/hi/world/middle_east/4337200.stm.

―――. 2005f. Iraq awaits Constitution result. October 16. http://news.bbc.co.uk/1/hi/world/middle_east/4346322.stm.

―――. 2005g. Iraq voters back new constitution. October 25. http://news.bbc.co.uk/1/hi/world/middle_east/4374822.stm.

―――. 2005h. Life in Iraq: Oil. http://news.bbc.co.uk/1/shared/spl/hi/in_depth/post_saddam_iraq/html/4.stm.

―――. 2005i. US used white phosphorus in Iraq. November 16. http://news.bbc.co.uk/1/hi/world/middle_east/4440664.stm.

―――. 2005j. Iraq suicide attacks kill dozens. November 18. http://news.bbc.co.uk/1/hi/world/middle_east/4448798.stm.

Beaumont, Peter. 2005a. Despair is still not an option. September 25. http://observer.guardian.co.uk/comment/story/0,,1577939,00.html.

―――. 2005b. Sunnis venture down political path. October 16. http://www.politics.guardian.co.uk/Observer/international/story/0,6903,1593254,00.html.

Beck, Sara, and Malcolm Downing, eds. 2003. *The battle for Iraq: BBC News correspondents on the war against Saddam and a new world agenda.* London: BBC.

Beehner, Lionel, and Sharon Otterman. 2005. Iraq: Drafting the constitution. Council on Foreign Relations. http://www.cfr.org/publication.html?id=8044.

Behn, Sharon. 2005. Constitution headed for win in Iraq. October 17. http://www.washingtontimes.com/world/20051016-112542-5903r.htm.

Bennis, Phyllis. 2005. The Iraqi Constitution: A referendum for disaster. October 13. http://www.ips-dc.org/comment/Bennis/tp34constitution.htm.

Benvenisti, Eyal. 2004. *The international law of occupation.* 2nd ed. Princeton, NJ: Princeton University Press.

Bialasiewicz, Luiza, Stuart Elden, and Joe Painter. 2005. The constitution of EU territory. *Comparative European Politics* 3 (3): 333–63.

Blair, Tony. 2003. Prime minister's statement opening Iraq debate, House of Commons. March 18. http://www.number-10.gov.uk/output/Page3294.asp.

―――. 2005. PM says troops will leave Iraq "when job is done." November 14. http://www.number-10.gov.uk/output/Page8521.asp.

Bobbitt, Philip. 2005. How to ruin a milestone constitution. August 25. http://www.guardian.co.uk/comment/story/0,3604,1555759,00.html.

Brewin, Christopher. 2005. Turkey: Democratic legitimacy. In *The Iraq War and democratic politics*, edited by Alex Danchev and John Macmillan, 96–113. London: Routledge.

Bright, Martin. 2005. Iraq envoy's tell-all memoir blocked. October 16. http://observer.guardian.co.uk/politics/story/0,6903,1593370,00.html.

Brown, Nathan J. 2005a. Iraq's constitutional process plunges ahead. Carnegie Endowment for International Peace. http://www.carnegieendowment.org/files/PO19Brown.pdf.

―――. 2005b. Constitution of Iraq—draft bill of rights: Commentary and translation. http://globalpolicy.igc.org/security/issues/iraq/document/2005/0630billofrights.pdf.

Bush, George W. 2003a. President discusses the future of Iraq. February 26. http://www.whitehouse.gov/news/releases/2003/02/20030226-11.html.

————. 2003b. President Bush announces major combat operations in Iraq have ended. May 1. http://www.whitehouse.gov/news/releases/2003/05/ iraq/20030501-15.html.

————. 2003c. President Bush names Randall Tobias to be global AIDS coordinator. July 2. http://www.whitehouse.gov/news/releases/2003/07/20030702-3.html.

————. 2004. President Bush discusses early transfer of Iraqi sovereignty. June 28. http://www.whitehouse.gov/news/releases/2004/06/20040628-9.html.

————. 2005a. President discusses Iraqi constitution with press pool. August 23. http://www.whitehouse.gov/news/releases/2005/08/20050823.html.

————. 2005b. President addresses military families, discusses war on terror. August 24, http://www.whitehouse.gov/news/releases/2005/08/20050824.html.

————. 2005c. President discusses Hurricane Katrina, congratulates Iraqis on draft constitution. August 28. http://www.whitehouse.gov/news/releases/2005/08/20050828-1.html.

————. 2005d. President discusses war on terror at National Endowment for Democracy. October 6. http://www.whitehouse.gov/news/releases/2005/10/20051006-3.html.

————. 2005e. President addresses troops at Osan Air Base in Osan, Korea. November 19. http://www.whitehouse.gov/news/releases/2005/11/20051119-5.html.

————. 2005f. President outlines strategy for victory in Iraq. November 30. http://www.whitehouse.gov/news/releases/2005/11/20051130-2.html.

Bush, George W., Tony Blair, and José Maria Aznar. 2003. Azores Summit statement. March 16. http://news.bbc.co.uk/2/hi/middle_east/2855567.stm.

Carroll, Rory. 2005a. Iraq's Shias in landmark poll victory. February 14. http://www.guardian.co.uk/international/story/0,1412277,00.html.

————. 2005b. US steps in to end Iraq deadlock. August 14. http://observer.guardian.co.uk/international/story/0,6903,1548823,00.html.

————. 2005c. Iraq extends constitution deadline. August 16. http://www.guardian.co.uk/Iraq/Story/0,2763,1549962,00.html.

————. 2005d. Iraq: Arab champion or cauldron of civil war? August 16. http://www.guardian.co.uk/Iraq/Story/0,2763,1549724,00.html.

————. 2005e. Sunnis get last chance for deal. August 23. http://www.guardian.co.uk/Iraq/Story/0,2763,1554619,00.html.

————. 2005f. Hopes fade for deal on Iraqi Constitution. August 26. http://www.guardian.co.uk/Iraq/Story/0,2763,1556803,00.html.

————. 2005g. Iraq gamble as Sunnis left out of constitution deal. August 29. http://www.guardian.co.uk/Iraq/Story/0,2763,1558602,00.html.

————. 2005h. Fragile agreement for Sons of Mesopotamia. August 29. http://www.guardian.co.uk/Iraq/Story/0,2763,1558435,00.html.

————. 2005i. First results show victory for Iraqi Constitution. October 17. http://www.guardian.co.uk/Iraq/Story/0,2763,1593678,00.html.

Carroll, Rory, and Qais al-Bashir. 2005a. Sunnis in crisis over Iraqi Constitution. August 30. http://www.guardian.co.uk/Iraq/Story/0,2763,1558913,00.html.

————. 2005b. Sunni Party backs blueprint. October 13. http://www.guardian.co.uk/Iraq/Story/0,2763,1590994,00.html.

Carroll, Rory, and Julian Borger. 2005. US relents on Islamic law to reach Iraq deal. August 22. http://www.guardian.co.uk/Iraq/Story/0,2763,1553862,00.html.

Cheney, Dick. 2005. Vice president's remarks at the Frontiers of Freedom Institute 2005 Ronald Reagan Gala. November 16. http://www.whitehouse.gov/news/releases/2005/11/20051116-10.html.

Coalition Provisional Authority (CPA). 2004. An historic review of CPA accomplishments. http://cpa-iraq.org/pressreleases/20040628_historic_review_cpa.doc.

Cockburn, Patrick. 2005. Diary. *London Review of Books*, October 20, 30–31.

Cole, Juan. 2004. The new and improved Iraq. June 22. http://www.inthesetimes.com/site/main/article/the_new_and_improved_iraq/.

Corera, Gordon. 2005. Iraqi charter and the insurgency. August 26. http://news.bbc.co.uk/2/hi/middle_east/4186766.stm.

Daalder, Ivo H., and James M. Lindsay. 2003. *America unbound: The Bush revolution in foreign policy*. Washington, DC: Brookings Institution Press.

Diamond, Larry Jay. 2005. *Squandered victory: The American occupation and the bungled effort to bring democracy to Iraq*. New York: Times Books.

Elden, Stuart. 2005. Territorial integrity and the war on terror. *Environment and Planning A* 37 (12): 2083–104.

———. 2006a. Contingent sovereignty, territorial integrity and the sanctity of borders. *SAIS Review of International Affairs* 26 (1): 11–24.

———. 2006b. Spaces of humanitarian exception. *Geografiska Annaler B: Human Geography* 88 (3): 477–85.

———. 2007. Blair, neo-conservatism and the war on territorial integrity. *International Politics* 44 (1): 37–57.

Electronic Iraq. N.d. http://www.electroniciraq.net.

Etherington, Mark. 2005. *Revolt on the Tigris: The Al-Sadr uprising and the governing of Iraq*. London: Hurst & Company.

Feldman, Noah. 2004. *What we owe Iraq: War and the ethics of nation building*. Princeton, NJ: Princeton University Press.

Froomkin, Dan. 2005. Trash talk. November 18. http://www.washingtonpost.com/wp-dyn/content/linkset/2005/04/11/LI2005041100879.html.

Geneva Convention. 1949. Geneva Convention relative to the protection of civilian persons in time of war. http://www.unhchr.ch/html/menu3/b/92.htm.

Glover, Julian, and Ewen MacAskill. 2005. A political war that backfired: Interview with Sir Christopher Meyer. November 5. http://politics.guardian.co.uk/iraq/story/0,12956,1635029,00.html.

Greenstock, Jeremy, and John Negroponte. 2003. Letter from the permanent representatives of the UK and the US to the UN addressed to the president of the Security Council. May 8, Ref. S/2003/538. http://www.globalpolicy.org/security/issues/iraq/document/2003/0608usukletter.htm.

Guardian. 2005a. New deadline on Iraq Constitution. August 22. http://www.guardian.co.uk/Iraq/Story/0,2763,1554267,00.html.

———. 2005b. Beacon of hope fades. August 24. http://www.guardian.co.uk/Iraq/Story/0,2763,1555184,00.html.

———. 2005c. Iraq cedes to UN on referendum. October 5. http://www.guardian.co.uk/Iraq/Story/0,2763,1585451,00.html.

———. 2005d. Ballots against the bombs. October 15. http://www.guardian.co.uk/Iraq/Story/0,2763,1592763,00.html.

———. 2005e. A small and fragile step forward. October 26. http://www.guardian.co.uk/Iraq/Story/0,2763,1600653,00.html.

———. 2005f. Blair: Iraq withdrawal in 2006 possible. November 14. http://politics.guardian.co.uk/iraq/story/0,12956,1642366,00.html.

———. 2005g. UN official calls for inquiry into Iraq torture. November 19. http://www.guardian.co.uk/Iraq/Story/0,2763,1645894,00.html.

Hague Convention. 1907. Convention respecting the laws and customs of war on land. http://lawofwar.org/hague_iv.htm.

Hardy, Roger. 2005. An Islamic Republic of Iraq? August 23. http://news.bbc.co.uk/2/hi/middle_east/4177266.stm.

Harriman, Ed. 2005. Where has all the money gone? *London Review of Books*, July 7, 3–7.

International Crisis Group (ICG). 2004. Reconstructing Iraq. International Crisis Group Middle East Report no. 30. Brussels: International Crisis Group.

———. 2005a. Iraq: Don't rush the Constitution. International Crisis Group Middle East Report no. 42. Brussels: International Crisis Group.

———. 2005b. Unmaking Iraq: A constitutional process gone awry. International Crisis Group Middle East Briefing no. 19. Brussels: International Crisis Group.

Jabar, Faleh A. 2004. Postconflict Iraq: A race for stability, reconstruction, and legitimacy. United States Institute of Peace Special Report 120. Washington, DC: United States Institute of Peace.

Jeffery, Simon. 2005. Iraqis say yes to constitution. October 25. http://www.guardian.co.uk/Iraq/Story/0,2763,1600249,00.html.

Jenkins, Simon. 2005a. To say we must stay in Iraq to save it from chaos is a lie. September 21. http://www.guardian.co.uk/comment/story/0,3604,1574478,00.html.

———. 2005b. Their only redemption is to withdraw in the new year. October 19. http://politics.guardian.co.uk/iraq/story/0,12956,1595536,00.html.

———. 2005c. Blair should stop playing fall guy in Rumsfeld's war games. November 16. http://www.guardian.co.uk/comment/story/0,3604,1643363,00.html.

Kaplan, Lawrence F., and William Kristol. 2003. *The war over Iraq: Saddam's tyranny and America's mission.* San Francisco: Encounter Books.

Keegan, John. 2004. *The Iraq War: The 21-day conflict and its aftermath.* London: Pimlico.

Kerry, John. 2005. Speech at Georgetown University. October 26. http://www.johnkerry.com/pressroom/speeches/spc_2005_10_26.html.

Khalilzad, Zalmay. 2005a. Transcript of interview with Ambassador Khalilzad. *Late Edition*, CNN. August 14. http://iraq.usembassy.gov/iraq/20050814_khalilzad_cnn.html.

———. 2005b. Comments on progress drafting Iraq's Constitution. August 16. http://iraq.usembassy.gov/iraq/20050816_khalilzad_convention_center.html.

Leigh, David. 2004. General sacked by Bush says he wanted early elections. March 18. http://www.guardian.co.uk/Iraq/Story/0,2763,1171880,00.html.

Loughlin, Sean. 2003. Rumsfeld on looting in Iraq: "Stuff happens." April 12. http://www.cnn.com/2003/US/04/11/sprj.irq.pentagon/.

MacAskill, Ewen. 2005. Lofty ambitions reduced to one: Iraq must not be seen as a failure. September 22. http://www.guardian.co.uk/Iraq/Story/0,2763,1575399,00.html.

Marr, Phebe. 2003. Iraq "the day after"s: Internal dynamics in post-Saddam Iraq. *Naval War College Review* 56 (1): 13–29.

Meek, Jamie. 2004. The dawn of a New Iraq—or a return to secrecy and killing? June 29. http://www.guardian.co.uk/Iraq/Story/0,2763,1249695,00.html.

Muir, Jim. 2005. Abuse reports fuel Iraqi tensions. November 16. http://news.bbc. co.uk/1/hi/world/middle_east/4443126.stm.

National Security Council. 2005. National strategy for victory in Iraq. http://www. whitehouse.gov/infocus/iraq/iraq_national_strategy_20051130.pdf.

New York Times. 2005. Q&A: Wrangling over Iraq's Constitution. July 27. http://www. nytimes.com/cfr/international/slot1_072705.html.

O'Leary, Brendan, John McGarry, and Khaled Salih, eds. 2005. The future of Kurdistan in Iraq, Philadelphia: University of Pennsylvania Press.

O'Shea, Maria T. 2004. Trapped between the map and reality: Geography and perceptions of Kurdistan. New York: Routledge.

Parenti, Christian. 2004. The freedom: Shadows and hallucinations in occupied Iraq. London: New Press.

Phillips, David L. 2005. Losing Iraq: Inside the postwar reconstruction fiasco. Boulder, CO: Westview.

Powell, Colin. 1996. My American journey. New York: Random House.

Reynolds, Paul. 2005. Iraq referendum: Milestone not destination. October 25. http:// news.bbc.co.uk/1/hi/world/middle_east/4375160.stm.

Rice, Condoleezza. 2005. Rice congratulates Iraqis on submission of draft constitution. August 22. http://usinfo.state.gov/mena/Archive/2005/Aug/22-151112.html.

Rumsfeld, Donald. 2005. Iraq Constitution major step to new way of life. August 23. http://usinfo.state.gov/mena/Archive/2005/Aug/23-307540.html.

Schuster, Angela, and Milbry Polk, eds. 2005. The looting of the Iraq Museum, Baghdad: The lost legacy of ancient Mesopotamia. New York: Abrams.

Short, Clare. 2003. Resignation statement. May 12. http://news.bbc.co.uk/1/hi/uk_ politics/3022139.stm.

———. 2005. An honourable deception? New Labour, Iraq, and the misuse of power. London: Free Press.

Stansfield, Gareth. 2005. The transition to democracy in Iraq. In The Iraq War and democratic politics, edited by Alex Danchev and John Macmillan, 134–59. London: Routledge.

Steele, Jonathan. 2005a. Saddam's trial is merely a political sideshow. October 21. http://www.guardian.co.uk/Columnists/Column/0,5673,1597319,00.html.

———. 2005b. Iraqi Constitution yes vote approved by UN. October 26. http://www. guardian.co.uk/Iraq/Story/0,2763,1600512,00.html.

Talabani, Jalal, and L. Paul Bremer. 2003. Agreement on political process. November 15. http://www.globalpolicy.org/security/issues/iraq/document/2003/1115nov15agreement.htm.

Times. 2005. UN calls for fair play in constitution vote. October 5. http://www.timesonline.co.uk/article/0,,7374-1811032,00.html.

White House. 2003. Results in Iraq: 100 days toward security and freedom. August 8. http://www.whitehouse.gov/infocus/iraq/100days/100days.pdf.

———. 2005a. Statement on Iraqi leaders submitting draft constitution to National Assembly: Statement by the deputy press secretary. August 22. http://www. whitehouse.gov/news/releases/2005/08/20050822-4.html.

———. 2005b. Renewal in Iraq. http://www.whitehouse.gov/infocus/iraq/.

———. 2004-a. President Bush discusses early transfer of Iraqi sovereignty. http:// www.whitehouse.gov/news/releases/2004/06/images/20040628-9_sovereignty062804-515h.html.

———. N.d.-b. http://www.whitehouse.gov/news/releases/2004/06/images/20040628-9_d0628-1-515h.html.

Williams, Paul R., and Francesca Jannotti Pecci. 2004. Earned sovereignty: Bridging the gap between sovereignty and self-determination. *Stanford Journal of International Law* 40 (1): 1–40.

Williams, Paul R., and William Spencer. 2005. Iraq's political compact. August 13. http://www.boston.com/news/globe/editorial_opinion/oped/articles/2005/08/13/iraqs_political_compact/.

Wong, Edward. 2005. Top Shiite politician joins call for autonomous South Iraq. August 12. http://www.nytimes.com/2005/08/12/international/middleeast/12iraq.html.

Yamashita, Hikaru. 2004. *Humanitarian space and international politics: The creation of safe areas.* Aldershot, UK: Ashgate.

8

War Veterans, Disability, and Postcolonial Citizenship in Angola and Mozambique

MARCUS POWER

Introduction: Postcolonial Transformations

As an imperial power, Portugal encountered numerous difficulties in seeking to integrate its African colonial territories (Angola, Moçambique, Guinea-Bissau, Cape Verde, São Tomé, and Principé) into the empire and the body of metropolitan (geo)politics (Sidaway and Power 2005). The colonial wars fought in Africa by Portugal between 1961 and 1974 were "long, useless, unjust and costly" (Medina 1999, 149), involving nearly one million Portuguese troops (roughly one in five adult men) of which more than thirty thousand were wounded in action (Borges-Coelho 2002). Funding the conflicts cost Portugal close to half of its GNP since it was in Africa that the most substantive and direct challenges arose to Portuguese imperialism with violent uprisings, popular insurrections, and nationalist revolutions rippling out across the continent, involving the peoples of "Portuguese Africa" and Portuguese settlers and conscripts. In Mozambique, for example, the Frente de Libertação de Moçambique (FRELIMO), formed in exile in Tanzania in 1962 from an amalgam of resistance groups, launched a guerrilla war for independence on September 25, 1964. In Angola, a nationalist uprising broke out in Luanda in 1961, and out of a maelstrom of nationalist politics and ideological and ethnonational divisions, three modern nationalist movements emerged: the Movimento Popular de Libertacão de Angola (MPLA), the Frente Nacional de Libertacão de Angola (FNLA), and the União Nacional para a Independência Total de Angola (UNITA).

This chapter explores the emergence of disability movements during and after periods of conflict in Angola and Mozambique, and explores the important roles occupied by war veterans with disabilities in pursuing formal rights of citizenship and new and more comprehensive forms of welfare provision. In so doing, the chapter draws upon postcolonial theory and *African* conceptions of citizenship, particularly those formulated in the work of Mahmood Mamdani (1996). Here the focus is upon institutional arrangements and political culture and the historical conception of citizenship in a postcolonial context, incorporating a challenge to liberal conceptions and "rights-based" discourses. This is partly motivated by the belief that postcolonial studies must (more directly) foreground the state and state-created domains (Werbner and Ranger 1996). In several parts of the Southern African region today, the interests of war veterans have received increasing amounts of attention (particularly in Zimbabwe), raising some important and neglected questions about conflict, citizenship, statehood, and national identity. Further, there are a number of common themes and experiences shared by disability movements within and between Southern African countries, and regional and international cooperation remains an important objective, particularly in the shape of the Southern African Federation of the Disabled (SAFOD).[1] This chapter explores the "commonality of disability" in Angola and Mozambique, where, on almost every indicator of participation in "mainstream life," people with disabilities come out extremely badly (for example, in employment statistics, income levels, access to buildings, and public transport and suitable housing). My research on disability in Southern Africa began in 2000 and sought to understand the ways in which a "private room" of disability is created in the most public spaces and representational discourses of "development"[2] (Power 2001a), aiming to explore how disabled subjectivities are constituted in a struggle with public perceptions and investments in maintaining disability as alterity (Mitchell and Snyder 1999, 30). The term "disability" is used here[3] since it highlights the need for social rather than medical models and conceptions, underlining the ways in which sociopolitical and cultural environments *disable* people. Understanding disability in this way is therefore crucial in avoiding medicalized and disempowering conceptions which foreground medical procedures, prosthetics, and "cures." The term "disability" denotes more than a medical condition or an essentialized "deformity" or difference, and is preferable to the terms "impairment" and "handicapped," which suggest inherent biological limitations and individual abnormalities. In examining debates about war veterans, disability, and citizenship, this chapter seeks to map out some of the social, historical, political, and mythological coordinates that define "disabled people" as excessive to or outside of traditional social circuits of interaction and as the *objects* of institutionalized discourses in the postcolonial period.

Not only did the commencement of conflicts against the anticolonial liberation movements appearing across Lusophone Africa have devastating consequences for Portugal, but it also marked the "last throes of Portugal's imperial dreams" (Medeiros 2002, 93). In both Angola and Mozambique, however, the euphoric optimism engendered by independence quickly evaporated as the nationalist movements that led the anti-colonial struggles became embroiled in wars with externally funded counter-revolutionary movements. In postcolonial society, Angolans were caught between a criminal state that impoverished and battered the people in whose name it claimed to govern and a criminal insurgency that had an equal disregard for the people in whose name it claimed to fight (Malaquias 2001). On one side, the governing MPLA, once guided by Marxist-Leninist ideals, completely abandoned the ideological goals for which it fought against colonialism, undergoing a seismic shift from Afro-Stalinism to "petro-diamond capitalism" (Hodges 2001). Instead, it created an oppressive, intolerant, and corrupt system where a minority became spectacularly rich by embezzling billions of dollars in revenues originating from the exploration of offshore oil while the vast majority of the population lived in absolute poverty. On the other side, the counter-revolutionary movement UNITA (funded by Apartheid South Africa and the CIA) terrorized most of the country by conducting a brutally devastating guerrilla war beginning in 1976. UNITA was once regarded as a legitimate opposition movement fighting to dismantle the MPLA's one-party system and secure democratic representation for other ethnic groups, but quickly degenerated into a powerful private guerrilla force whose primary objective was inflicting unrelenting and indiscriminate suffering upon civilian populations while obliterating all infrastructures and rendering the country ungovernable[4] (Minter 1994; Malaquias 2001). The civil wars claimed more than 500,000 lives, and it wasn't until shortly after the death of UNITA leader Jonas Savimbi in February 2002 that a peace accord was signed (on April 4, 2002).

In Mozambique, a cease-fire was signed with the Portuguese in September 1974, and after having endured Portuguese colonial rule for 470 years, Mozambique became independent on June 25, 1975. The first president, Samora Machel, had led FRELIMO in its anti-colonial struggle, and under his stewardship the new government gave shelter and support to South African (African National Congress) and Zimbabwean (Zimbabwe African National Union) liberation movements, while the governments of first Rhodesia and later Apartheid South Africa fostered and financed an armed rebel movement in central Mozambique called the Resistência Nacional Moçambicana (the Mozambique National Resistance, or RENAMO). Within a short period, the government was embroiled in a paralyzing war with a counterrevolutionary guerrilla movement and was unable to exercise effective territorial control, particularly in rural spaces. An estimated one million Mozambicans died during the civil war, 1.7 million took refuge in neighboring states, and several million more were internally displaced before a cease-fire agreement was signed in October 1992.[5]

Angola: Conflict, Citizenship, and "the Worst Country in the World"

Post-colonial Angola is an important and often neglected example of the complex intersections between war, territory, and citizenship, particularly as they have been played out around disability issues. Many accounts of Angolan post-colonial history often begin by noting the tragedy of how this country, so "fabulously endowed but massively wrecked by conflict" (Cramer 1996, 481), has come to be so impoverished. Hajari and Mabry (2001, 24) describe Angola as the "worst country in the world," for example, and outline the now familiar story of how, despite its enormous mineral wealth, Angola teetered on the "edge of the abyss." Representations abound, then, that this was the "longest and most miserable civil war" (Goldman 1999, 2) that Africa has ever known. There is an important sense, however, in which many discussions rely on a simplistic notion of a singular war with singular causality, leading to considerable misrepresentation. Thus, different periods of conflict in Angola (before and after independence) have often been conflated in many accounts which have tended to ascribe singular explanatory factors or represent the war(s) as universally "anti-imperial," as "revolutionary," as a "Cold War proxy," or (most commonly) as a brutal competition between rival elites for a wealth of natural resources (Goldman 1999; Power 2001b).

Any analysis which reduces the study of extensive conflict (with multiple temporalities) to a single determinant[6] should thus be treated with considerable caution. Angola has at times, for example, occupied the extraordinarily indeterminate position of "no war/no peace" (Messiant 2001, 308). It is important therefore not to obscure the important geographical, historical, sociological, and cultural origins of the war, nor their continued salience (Chabal 2002). Thus, while the geography of international complicity in Angola's war economy was complex and dynamic, the various spatial scales and complex political and economic geographies around which the war proceeded have often been overlooked. Indeed, how is it possible to separate the domestic Angolan political economy from external constituencies such as the global oil and banking industries? As Sogge puts it, Angola's problems of domestic governance "are at the same time problems of global governance" in which the constrained forms of global citizenship "practiced by institutions offshore set limits to citizenship for ordinary Angolans onshore" (Sogge, cited in Kibble 2006, 8). Surprisingly, despite the staggering military expenditures since the 1980s, the fluctuation in oil values, and the widespread corruption of government officials, many commentators and observers continue to have enormous faith in the willingness and capacity of the party-state to oversee the postwar reconstruction and "development" of Angolan society. The Angolan state was, for long periods, unable to carry out vital governance functions of law and order and social service provision (in those areas it periodically occupied). Angola has thus been transformed from a one-party state, not toward multiparty democracy but rather toward a kleptocracy and something of a "phantom state," recognized internationally but not necessarily performing many of the ordinary functions of a state. For much of the last three decades the Angolan state had an extremely limited orientation and concern toward its own citizens, and there have been suggestions that it remained "singularly unprepared to help the Angolan people" (Cilliers 2001, 8). In a sense, then, many Angolan citizens have become "irrelevant" (Kibble 2006, 7) due to the lack of any politico-social contract by which citizens consent to meet demands (such as payment of taxes or compliance with the rule of law) in return for state responsiveness. There thus continues to be a big gulf between the ruling political class (of politician-*rentiers*, technocrats, and military officials) and Angolan "citizens," few of whom have access to basic services, which seem to be allocated not on the basis of right or need but "according to spending power and political connections" (Kibble 2006, 7).

Peace inevitably resulted in a program of demobilization—a poor precedent for which was set by previous UN missions, which had little to offer soldiers and guerrilla fighters for whom war became *mais um dia de vida* (another day of life; Kapuscinski 2001) for many years. This involved plans to demobilize some 500,000 UNITA troops and family members (Parsons 2004). While the process is largely judged a success by the Angolan government and the international community, its implementation reflects the government's military and political advantage and has failed at times to pay sufficient attention to the needs of ex-combatants and to the "reintegration" component in particular (Parsons 2004). The Angolan government has taken full responsibility for the demobilization and disarmament process (which had cost US$187 million by January 2004), but campaigns have enjoyed varying degrees of success and remain poorly conceived and incomplete. Demobilization formally took place on August 2, 2002, by first integrating all former UNITA soldiers into the FAA (the national army) and then demobilizing them. Ex-combatants were to receive five months' back payments of salaries according to military rank, a US$100 reintegration allowance, and a "kit" of basic household items and tools, as well as full identity and demobilization documentation. Demobilization support was made available only to ex-combatants, however, with women eligible to receive only humanitarian support as civilians (Parsons 2004).

Angola states that it has never manufactured anti-personnel mines or exported them to other countries. In all, a total of forty-seven different types of mines from eighteen different countries have been found in Angola, and their varied origins reveal a great deal about the messy geopolitical contextuality of the war(s) (the USSR, the United States, China, North Korea, France, Israel, Italy, Belgium, Austria, South Africa, Sweden, Portugal, Romania, Hungary, East Germany, Vietnam, Yugoslavia, and Czechoslovakia). Landmines (as in Mozambique) were used to defend strategically valuable towns and key infrastructure and were laid along roads to prevent the movement of opposing forces and to depopulate some areas by denying access to water sources and plantations. The continued presence of these mines has caused major problems in the post-war reconstruction process. At a UN-led review conference in Nairobi on anti-personnel mines in late 2004, Angola was identified as one of twenty-four states with significant numbers of mine survivors and the "greatest responsibility to act, but also the greatest needs and expectations for assistance" in providing adequate services for care, rehabilitation, and rein-

tegration of survivors (United Nations 2005, 33). At the Nairobi summit on a
"mine-free world," the Angolan delegation stated that it is

> very much concerned on the situation of mine victims . . . and has
> launched a challenge within the juridical-legal framework in favour
> of mine victims and other disabled people, aiming at ensuring their
> rights . . . to have access to health, education, employment, sports and
> leisure . . . but we will not be able to carry out this task . . . without assis-
> tance. (Angolan delegation statement, quoted in Landmine Monitor
> 2005, 14)

Foreign assistance (on which the country is very dependent)[7] comes from
a variety of sources, including Handicap International (HI), the International
Committee for the Red Cross (ICRC), the Vietnam Veterans of America
Foundation (VVAF), the United States Agency for International Development
(USAID), the Diana Princess of Wales Memorial Fund, the Jesuit Refugee
Service (JRS), and the Jaipur Limb Campaign (JLC), among other international nongovernmental organizations (NGOs), which enable the provision
of rehabilitation services. The true number of mine casualties is undoubtedly
much higher than reported, as many incidents are not recorded due to inaccessibility to casualties and the lack of an organized system for reporting.[8] A
Landmine Impact Survey (LIS) was set up in 2002 to provide a more detailed
picture of the situation nationally, but this was suspended in May 2005 due to
a lack of funds after completing a survey of ten of the eighteen provinces of
Angola. Prior to its suspension, the LIS had identified 1,402 impacted communities with a population of more than 1.6 million people in those ten provinces
(Landmine Monitor 2005).

Angola has three legislative acts, dating back to the 1980s, on protecting
the rights of people with disabilities, including decrees published in 1982 and
1985 that provide for the socio-economic reintegration of people with disabilities. However, the provisions of this legislation are not fully implemented,
and the government has done little to improve the physical or socio-economic
conditions of people with disabilities. There is also Article 48 of the 1992
Angolan Constitution, which states,

> Disabled combatants of the national liberation struggle, the minor chil-
> dren of citizens who died in the war and those physically or mentally
> handicapped as a result of war shall have special protection, to be estab-
> lished by law. (Republic of Angola 1992)

The Ministry of Social Affairs (MINARS) has responsibility for disability
issues along with the National Department of Assistance to People with Disabilities (DNAD), and provides assistance in the form of food aid, housing,
wheelchairs, and socio-economic reintegration. The Ministry of War Veterans
and Former Combatants claims to provide pensions to around one hundred

and twenty thousand beneficiaries, including veterans of the war, former combatants of the liberation struggle, and their widows and orphans. A key distinction is made, however, by the ministry (led by Pedro Van Duném), which has argued that Angolans often talk of former combatants in very general terms and do not seek to differentiate between different periods of conflict and national struggle. The ministry itself, in contrast, distinguishes between former combatants of the struggle for national liberation against the Portuguese (1961–1975) and veterans of the civil war(s) after 1975, suggesting that it is the latter group that requires the most assistance, particularly *os mutilados* ("the mutilated") (Angoflash 2004). The rationale for this preferential treatment is that the civil wars had a longer duration and produced a much larger group of people with disabilities, particularly given the widespread use of landmines and the nature of UNITA's military tactics. In an interview in 2004 with *Journal de Angola*, Van Duném said that the former combatants of the liberation war account for only twenty thousand of the total one hundred and twenty thousand pension recipients and acknowledged the delays in processing pension payments (as if it were simply a problem of claimants lacking the required documentation) (Angoflash 2004). The minister was also asked why, if the state pension provisions were so good, there were so many veterans begging for alms on the streets of Luanda, to which he replied that this was principally a concern for Angolan disability groups and not the state (Angoflash 2004).

Although Disabled People's Organisations (DPOs) have existed in Africa since the 1970s, disability organizations in Angola only started to form in the early 1990s when the government began to allow the formation of private voluntary organizations. One of the Angolan disability movements most closely associated with former combatants is the Associação dos Militares e Mutilados de Guerra de Angola (Association of Angolan Soldiers and War Amputees, or AMMIGA), which is based in Luanda and Malanje. AMMIGA was set up in September 1992, originally as an organization representing former combatants with disabilities from both UNITA and the MPLA. AMMIGA has broadened its approach[9] to reach out to all those with war-related disabilities and had an estimated membership in 1995 of seven thousand people in Luanda Province and fifteen thousand nationally (USAID 1997). Many women representatives now attend meetings outside the community where this would previously have been unheard of. Within Angola, the Federation of Organisations of People with Disabilities (FAPED), which is housed within AMMIGA's head office, has been a crucial vehicle for facilitating debates and exchanges across disability groups and now has nineteen member organizations. Angolan DPOs began attending "capacity-building" workshops funded by foreign donors and involving SAFOD in 2004, representing some of the first attempts to connect with disability movements in the region.

Another important part of the disability movement in Angola with strong connections to ex-combatants is the League for the Reintegration of Disabled People (LARDEF), founded in 1997 by a group of war veterans disabled during the war and who had been frustrated with their desk jobs at the Ministry of War Veterans and Combatants. The veterans were keen to struggle for the rights of all Angolans with disabilities, and LARDEF now has a membership of over five thousand, many of them amputees. Although Angola has a national rehabilitation plan, there is a sense within LARDEF that a strategy for helping amputees and other people with disabilities to survive on a daily basis is missing from the government's agenda. According to Nyathi (2005, 82), given the delicate post-war political situation in Angola, LARDEF "cannot afford to be militant" and so it has had to be strategic in developing a relationship with the government (as well as being mindful of the dangers of co-option). LARDEF came into existence as a cross-disability movement and as a result has had a big impact on government attitudes toward disability in that the government "previously saw disabled people only as ex-combatants or war veterans" (Nyathi 2005, 81)—a perception that the movement has specifically sought to challenge. The majority of LARDEF's leadership are ex-combatants enabling a strong challenge to governmental perceptions, and LARDEF has taken part in drafting Angola's new constitution, insisting on the insertion of a clause of nondiscrimination on the grounds of disability.[10]

Alongside LARDEF in the disability movement of Angola is the National Association of Disabled Angolans (ANDA). The president of ANDA, Silva Etiambulo, has often spoken of the importance of nationalist struggle to Angolan development in the post-colonial period and has emphasized the sacrifices made by many Angolans (military and civilian alike) that have enabled and preserved independence and protected territorial sovereignty and Angolan borders from foreign intruders (Angola Press 2005). For Etiambulo these sorts of sacrifices oblige the state to pay special attention to the needs of people with disabilities, particularly given that many citizens had to postpone or abandon their education altogether in order to "fulfil the sacred duty of the defence of their native land" (Angola Press 2005). This obligation was recently recognized in a speech delivered by Angolan President Eduardo dos Santos on November 11, 2005, celebrating thirty years of independence. In his speech, dos Santos claimed that "assistance will be given in 2006 to thirty-five thousand physically handicapped people. This number will progressively grow over the ensuing years until all are covered" (Dos Santos 2005). In the same presentation, he requested a minute of silence for all "the anonymous heroes who laid down their lives for our Angolan homeland," restating the government's commitment to overseeing the reintegration of former combatants. This level of assistance is extremely limited, however, and there is little sense of how long it will take to reach a level of complete coverage. Thus the state has been quick to nominally recognize the "heroism" of those who fought to protect the

Angolan "homeland" but incredibly slow at recognizing its responsibilities to these citizens (and their rights), preferring to rely on foreign donors and on problematic and undifferentiated notions of "the handicapped."

Mozambique: *Somos os abandanados, os esquecidos* (We Are the Abandoned, the Forgotten)

The importance of former soldiers and new disability movements in the (re)constitution and (re)formulation of post-colonial citizenship, national identity, and statehood in Mozambique should not be underestimated. After a devastating civil war that lasted for nearly sixteen years, destroying much of the country's infrastructure and displacing millions of Mozambicans, FRELIMO and RENAMO signed the General Peace Agreement (GPA) ending the civil war on October 4, 1992. The agreement created a space for the engagement of Mozambicans in post-war reconstruction and also provided an opportunity for the country to take forward the new multiparty constitution agreed on in 1990. As in Angola, the capacity to collect and record data concerning disability in Mozambique is very limited and rarely reflects "on-the-ground" realities. Mozambique (like Angola) is one of the most land-mine-affected countries in the world, with the number of landmines left in the country estimated to be between four-hundred thousand and six-hundred thousand (Mourou and Trouvé 2000, 13). In April 2002, the Director of the National Institute for Mine Clearance (IND) claimed that people were still being injured every day by landmines. According to one media report (Cuambe 2004), there were 615 mine casualties reported between 1996 and 2003, with at least 232 killed and 322 injured (Landmine Monitor 2004). Mozambique's health care infrastructure was severely damaged during the armed conflict, with over 40 percent of health clinics destroyed or forced to close. In 2000 it was estimated that 86 percent of the country's health budget was financed by international aid (Mourou and Trouvé 2000). Responsibility for landmine survivor assistance is shared by the Ministry of Health (MIN-SAU) and the Ministry for Women and the Coordination of Social Action (MMCAS), which assists with transport services and medical and financial support. Unfortunately, many disability organizations in Mozambique regard MMCAS as a "helpless spectator" (Ncube 2005, 5), highlighting the confusion over its role and remit and the lack of resources provided by the government. The only provisions that the government has enacted for accessibility to buildings and transportation for people with disabilities were in the electoral law governing the country's first multiparty elections, which addressed the needs of voters with disabilities in polling booths (Landmine Monitor 2004).

In June 1999, a national disability law was enacted and the Cabinet approved the first national policy on people with disabilities (Resolution no. 20/99) that included principles and strategies to encourage active participation in the country's socio-economic development. However, the policy has not been fully

implemented due to a lack of resources (interview with Farida Gulamo, Associação dos Deficientes Moçambicanos [Association of Disabled Mozambicans,
or ADEMO], June 2000; Ncube 2005). In fact, what unites many Mozambican
disability groups is their desire to decry the lack of government support for
people with disabilities, both politically and financially (Ncube 2005). There is
a significant shortfall between the principles and intent of the legislation and
the reality of the problems faced by people with disabilities in their daily lives.
Article 68 of the Constitution (Republica de Moçambique 1990) states that
"disabled citizens shall enjoy fully the rights" that it provides for; however, the
government provided few resources to implement this provision. Representatives of disability groups and injured veterans have frequently protested that
societal discrimination continues against people with disabilities.

Since the peace accord was signed, there has been a proliferation of social
movements and civil society organizations established with the aim of promoting widespread participation in national debates about the challenges of
the post-war period. In this context, the Mozambique Association of Military
and Paramilitary Disabled (ADEMIMO) came into existence, the objective of
which was to specifically press the citizenship claims of disabled and demobilized military staff. Immediately after the peace accord in 1992, ADEMIMO
took up important roles in promoting reconciliation between Mozambicans,
integrating demobilized troops into a single association struggling for postwar citizenship rights. ADEMIMO is led by Manuel Alberto Chauque, who
began his compulsory military service in 1984, eventually earning the rank of
chief of battalion operations. In May 1987, during an operation against REN-
AMO troops, Chauque lost his left leg when he stepped on an anti-personnel
mine. After his accident, Chauque helped to create ADEMIMO and began
working on anti-landmine activities (interview with Manuel Chauque, June
2000).

ADEMIMO is a nonprofit organization representing approximately 11,525
ex-combatants (from both sides) with disabilities (although not all of these are
members). The grassroots membership is composed of approximately six thousand ex-combatants with disabilities. Manuel Chauque has said that many of
the former soldiers that ADEMIMO represents feel marginalized, "forgotten,"
and "abandoned" because of the lack of a specific law to protect them. This was
highlighted by the fact that nationwide, more than ten thousand former soldiers with disabilities are still not receiving the disability pensions[11] owed to
them. According to Chauque, the Defence Ministry no longer grants medical
schemes for disabled soldiers, and many of ADEMIMO's members feel that
they have been abandoned in accommodation centers, awaiting housing and
other social services that were promised by the government.

To rectify the situation, ADEMIMO has campaigned vigorously on themes
like access to buildings and transportation, access to information and communication, and equal opportunities for employment, as well as providing

prostheses and physical/occupational therapy, providing recreational opportunities, and delivering a community-based rehabilitation program. ADEMIMO is represented in each of the 10 provinces and 90 of the 110 districts throughout Mozambique. The organization has also been keen to push for legislative change and for a refocusing of public policy. Also, as a member of the Forum of Mozambican Associations of Disabled People (FAMOD)—an umbrella organization of disability associations founded in May 1999 to facilitate cooperation and collective action—ADEMIMO works with other disabled associations on various advocacy campaigns. After demobilization, several foreign aid programs dealing with the reintegration of ex-soldiers with disabilities have been organized through ADEMIMO, but the results of these "seem not very satisfactory" (Mourou and Trouvé 2000, 35), whilst some initiatives have failed altogether.

One of the most pressing challenges facing ADEMIMO is that the government continues to rely on foreign donors, aid agencies, and NGOs to assist people with disabilities, almost as an abdication of its own roles and responsibilities. Some members of ADEMIMO feel as if they are treated as "clients or objects" (Ncube 2005, 5) of "capacity building" initiatives led by northern NGOs rather than as genuine *partners*, and are concerned about the overreliance on foreign experts in preference to drawing on local sources. Some of these international organizations have really struggled to traverse the bridge from welfare to development and to move beyond the "charity ethic" (Ncube 2005). Handicap International (HI) is an example of an organization that is trying to make such a transition. HI has operated in Mozambique since 1986, establishing orthopedic centers around the country that are now fully integrated into the Ministry of Health. HI's activities in physical medicine and rehabilitation focus on supporting the quality of national services and improving the skills of staff in the rehabilitation sector. HI also works with the MMCAS and FAMOD to improve access to physical medicine and rehabilitation services, and to promote the rights of all people with disabilities. Another example is the British charity POWER Mozambique (an NGO for landmine victims), which supported the Ministry of Health's prosthetic and orthotic services until the end of May 2002, providing materials for the manufacture of limbs and technical expertise to improve the quality of services. In 2002, POWER changed its focus from prosthetics and orthotics to assisting people with disabilities in Mozambique to participate fully in civil society by "empowering" disability organizations to build capacity and services for their members. The Landmine Survivors Network (LSN) has also been active in Mozambique using community-based outreach workers, who are amputees, to work with individual survivors to assess their needs, offer psychological and social support, and educate families about the effects of limb loss. LSN assists survivors in accessing services that provide mobility devices, health services, or vocational training, and works with local disability associations to increase awareness about disability rights.

When members of ADEMIMO organized a land invasion in the district of Matola in June 2000 to protest the government's neglect of former soldiers, one Mozambican paper referred to the invaders as *os mutilados* (the mutilated), assuming that the protestors constituted a kind of redundant, homogeneous group of disaffected combatants (*Correio da Manhã*, June 30, 2000). War veterans in Matola continued their campaign of illegal land invasions for months, despite the establishment of a commission seeking to find land to distribute among them comprising former soldiers and municipal authorities (Agência de Informação de Moçambique [AIM] 2000a; 2000b). There were then attempts to occupy land belonging to the publicly owned Mozambican Television station (TVM), but these were stopped by local residents. About six hundred plots of land were occupied (where veterans continued in some cases to build houses), but the municipal authorities failed to expel them.

More recently, in 2005 more than 250 members of ADEMIMO in the district of Mocuba complained about the amount of time they had to wait to receive their military pensions, bemoaning the attempts made by the state to ignore and delay the processing of these claims. ADEMIMO's members claimed that the state's commitment to them was rhetorical only. As António Suluvai, president of ADEMIMO in the district of Mocuba, pointed out at the time, the delays in providing pension payments to disabled veterans had severely affected the families involved, preventing them from educating, clothing, and feeding their children (Zambézia Online 2005). Suluvai claimed in a meeting with representatives from POWER Mozambique that ADEMIMO members considered themselves "stepsons of the Mozambican government" (Ncube 2005), in recognition of their contribution to the establishment of FRELIMO as the party-state and their role in protecting national territory. ADEMIMO members thus called for credit schemes to help them promote income-producing activities and urged the provision of extra resources to enable them to promote the reintegration of people with disabilities and to prevent social discrimination. Although the government claims to be aware of the need for pensions for combatants (and to be gradually reaching a solution to the problem), ADEMIMO members have declared their intentions to continue their struggle (Zambézia Online 2005). On December 3, 2001, as part of the celebration of the International day of Disabled People, FAMOD organized a march (involving ADEMIMO members and accompanied by music from a military band) that was well covered by the media and culminated in the placing of a crown of flowers at the Mozambican Heroes monument in Maputo (Tembe 2002).

In addition to ADEMIMO, an important focal point of the disability movement in Mozambique is ADEMO (Associação dos Deficientes Moçambicanos/Association of Disabled Mozambicans), which seeks to address the social and economic needs of people with disabilities. ADEMO's effectiveness has occasionally been hindered by internal conflicts, however, and has been limited by the still embryonic network it has formed in rural areas. In 2000 ADEMO held a landmark conference to address the rights of people with disabilities, highlighting access to socio-economic opportunities and employment, accessibility to buildings and transportation, and a lack of wheelchairs. ADEMO has always maintained an open and inclusive policy of membership, whereas ADEMIMO is an organization established for and on behalf of former military and paramilitary combatants (Power 2001a). The opening paragraph of ADEMO's constitution refers to their desire to contest the legacies of colonial paternalism bequeathed by missionaries and the Portuguese colonial state (ADEMO 1994). Both organizations, despite early conflicts over contrasting notions of membership (and citizenship more generally), have recently begun to work more closely together, and both now belong to FAMOD. The members of FAMOD are well aware that the mere existence of legislation is far from enough and that longer term strategies to guarantee the effective implementation of that legislation will also be necessary (FAMOD 2005). Although there are an estimated 1.6 million people with disabilities in Mozambique (9.9 percent of the population), ADEMO now has approximately seventy thousand members across the country and is growing at a rapid rate, with representations in all ten provinces and even in many districts. ADEMO's work also raises questions about the supposed economic prosperity of postwar Mozambique, campaigning for example against the charges imposed by customs and excise for the importation of "compensation material." By law this ought to be free, but in practice it is for some kinds of material but not the kind required by organizations like ADEMO and its members. In a country where the majority of wheelchairs (not made of local materials) are imported from abroad, these problems have become increasingly acute.

Most importantly, ADEMO publicly represents the "many and rich experiences, capacities and talents of disabled people in implementing small and medium-sized employment generation projects" (ADEMO 1999, 3). ADEMO has also had problems working with aid agencies, however, where NGO support for particular initiatives (e.g., women's sewing projects) has often been inconsistent or withdrawn at short notice. ADEMO is concerned about the lack of effective collaboration between different northern NGOs which promotes unnecessary duplication, waste, and confusion (Ncube 2005), and does not always empower local disability groups to act independently. ADEMO brings together groups of people with disabilities and encourages a common identity, representing a historic leap in defining disability in positive terms. In contrast to the underwhelming reaction by development agencies to the need to further consider disability issues in development planning and practice, organizations like ADEMO in Mozambique are busy confronting these challenges head-on.

At a meeting in Vilankulo of the Mozambican Association of the Blind and Visually Impaired (ACAMO) in March 2006, Mozambican President Armanda Guebuza urged Mozambicans not to marginalize and exclude people with disabilities and restated the government's commitment to social and economic integration (AIM 2006). Guebuza called on Mozambican citizens to value the family as the starting point for success in the struggle against the trauma and feelings of exclusion that affect people with disabilities: "In the effort to overcome these obstacles, we argue that the family is the place where, in the first instance, exclusion should be fought against" (AIM 2006). Critical of the taboos and superstitions surrounding disability in Mozambique, Guebuza seemed to conveniently displace the focus of disability issues away from the state and onto the family. The implications of this are that the state manages to avoid or at least postpone some of its social and political citizenship commitments to people with disabilities by foregrounding the family as the primary source of care and support, whilst disability becomes a private and not a public concern. Thus, no funds are allocated by the government in its general budget, which can be used to subsidize DPO activities—as in Angola, most support continues to come from foreign donors.

Conclusions: anonymous heroes and broken promises

Projects of post-colonial state formation in both Angola and Mozambique were fraught from the very start with tensions and contradictions which conspired against these new and brittle entities. Alas, these post-colonial states were, in some senses, just as artificial as the colonies they had replaced. Following Mamdani (1996), we can raise questions about the nature of colonial power in each country and about the "inherited impediments" bequeathed by colonialism to democratization after independence. Mamdani highlights the institutional segregation between citizen and subject during the colonization of Africa, where "citizen" status was first and foremost the realm of the colonist, who was segregated in numerous ways from the disenfranchised "subject" indigenous majority. Mamdani also highlights the ways in which power was organized differently in rural and urban areas, where the colonial state was Janus-faced and bifurcated in the sense that urban power spoke the language of civil society and civil rights and rural power spoke of community and culture. Mamdani (1996) has argued that many African post-colonial regimes failed to break the distinction between citizen and subject and retained a degree of differentiation while deracializing the colonial state apparatus. This leads Mamdani to a rejection of the liberal notion of the citizen as simply an individual bearer of rights protected by the state and to a conception of citizenship that refers not only to legal status but also to a normative ideal where the governed should be considered full and equal participants in the political process.

In both Angola and Mozambique, there is a sense in which the institutional segregation of "citizens" and "subjects" has not been completely overhauled, and neither have the state machineries inherited from colonialism been fully transformed. There continues to be a sense, therefore, in which post-colonial state power in both countries remains bifurcated and Janus-faced, an inherited impediment, centered upon urban spaces and a notion of citizens as bearers of state-protected rights rather than as a focus of moves to build equality and widen access and participation. In both countries the interactions between the economic and political centers of post-colonial society (Luanda and Maputo) and wider national territories were not the "one-way gaze" of the metropole that the MPLA and FRELIMO sometimes assumed, and both experienced periods of chaos, illegality, disorder, and the collapse of territorial control in ways which affect and alter our use of concepts of citizenship, "state," and nationhood or conventional understandings of state-society and rural-urban interactions and oppositions. What becomes important, then, is the way in which ordinary people negotiated their daily lives as citizens in a context sometimes characterized by chaos, disorder, and illegality, and in the absence of a generalized and overarching (national) civil and political culture.

In 2005 Mozambique and Angola each celebrated thirty years of independence, inviting reflection on the challenges faced and sacrifices made in the defense of national territory. In many ways this was a particularly poignant historical moment in which to reflect on the political narration of national "liberation" and "independence," particularly for war veterans with disabilities who are among the most politically organized citizens in the Southern African region. Each country had highly specific wars and each has its own very specific history, culture, and economy, but both have recently begun to at least debate progressive forms of disability legislation[12] and both have active disability movements that are engaged in a variety of urban and rural communities. Further, in both cases the conception of disabled people's organizations (DPOs) has been widely debated and has been the site of considerable struggle and negotiation, leading to a move away from an initially exclusive focus on former combatants to broader, more inclusive, and ultimately more representative disability movements. What unites many DPOs, then, is a belief that enacting legislative principles is relatively straightforward but actually implementing them is something else, which requires far more commitment from the state in both countries than either currently seems willing to provide.

Mineral wealth in and of itself does not "ruin" a country, but what can is the uneven social distribution of this wealth and its (mis)appropriation by kleptocratic[13] political elites who have exclusionist agendas and have long since lost the right to talk of liberation and development (Hodges 2001). Angola thus clearly requires "a major rethinking of development initiatives" (Cilliers 2000, 345). Progress toward a new constitution has faltered and appears unlikely, whilst key questions concerning the timing of the next multiparty elections remain unanswered. The result of all this is an uncertain and precarious position for the country's poor and particularly for some of its most marginal and neglected citizens—people with disabilities. In Mozambique, the neoliberalization of the post-war economy has taken the country and citizenry a long way from the Marxist-Leninist ideals of the early years of independence, and there is mounting evidence of escalating levels of inequality in Mozambican society, alongside persistent allegations of corrupt practices in FRELIMO's handling of the privatization required by structural adjustment (Hanlon 1996; Pitcher 2002). Thus FRELIMO is keen to recognize the importance of the war with RENAMO to the maintenance and preservation of the country's borders but is seemingly unwilling to do anything about (for example) the customs charges imposed on those importing a wheelchair from across the border with a neighboring country. Both countries claim to provide pensions for their war veterans (dependent on the level of disability and military rank) but these often do not materialize, leading to feelings of abandonment, and anyway they pale in comparison with the generous salaries paid to other (less easily forgotten) representatives of the state.

Important questions need to be asked about the role of foreign aid donors and international NGOs in understanding the interface between disability and development in both countries, particularly about their articulation of "rights-based" discourses on citizenship. In Angola, in particular, for much of the war NGOs "unwittingly propped up the kleptocratic state" (Malaquias 2001, 13). There is a sense in which the explosive growth of foreign aid and development agencies in these two countries enables state institutions to abdicate their responsibilities toward their own citizens. More problematically, perhaps, there is often a total lack of coordination between NGOs, many of whom have very similar thematic priorities, leading to excessive duplication and a lack of willingness to engage with each other, let alone "national" NGOs. Additionally, many of these agencies are really struggling to understand the kind of "partnerships" that African DPOs are seeking and seem unable to make the transition from welfare to development in the ways they theorize and practice disability policy, which are reminiscent of Portuguese colonial paternalism. Many Southern African DPOs prefer to work with northern DPOs (such as Disabled People's International) rather than northern NGOs as they seem to be more transparent and less complicated to understand (Ncube 2005, 15). A key issue here is that many development agencies and charitable organizations tend to emphasize their own agenda and their own particular liberal conceptions of citizenship, which may not necessarily dovetail with those of African people with disabilities. As a result, the anticipated impact of development assistance in the Southern African region for people with disabilities has not been realized (Kabzems and Chimedza 2002). At present, many of these aid and development agencies refuse to accept that they might be a part of the problem and not always a part of the solution.

In regional terms "umbrella" federations like SAFOD can and have attempted to consider the collective nature of experiences of disability and to explore the possibility of collective responses.[14] Thus, perhaps what is needed is more reflection on what distinctively *African* conceptions of citizenship might involve as well as a reconsideration of the notion of "capacity building" in ways which would see northern donors, NGOs, and charities seeking to *enable* deeper and wider exchanges, engagements and conversations *between* DPOs, North and South. Exploring and mapping out the competing cultural understandings of physical disability in Africa is not a simple process (Devlieger 1995, 1999) but a strengthening of links between DPOs within Africa and across the North-South divide can (along with much more participatory research) help to contest some of the increasingly pervasive negative and disabling cultural myths and stereotypes that construct "disabled" subjectivities in African societies.

Acknowledgments

This research was partly made possible by an award from the Economic and Social Research Council (ESRC), award no. R000223079. ADEMO and ADEMIMO offered their time, help, and encouragement. I am particularly grateful to Manuel Chauque at ADEMIMO, to Pedro Francisco and Fatima Gulamo at ADEMO, and to all the staff at the Research Unit of the Instituto da Comunicação Social in Maputo. I also wish to acknowledge the help and support of Emily Gilbert and Deborah Cowen in providing useful comments and suggestions on earlier drafts of this chapter.

APPENDIX: List of Acronyms

Associação dos Deficientes de Moçambique (ADEMO)
Associação dos Deficientes Militares e Paramilitares de Moçambique (ADEMIMO)
Associação dos Militares e Mutilados de Guerra de Angola (AMMIGA)
Associação Nacional dos Deficientes Angolanos (ANDA)
Disabled People's International (DPI)
Disabled People's Organisations (DPOs)
Forum of Mozambican Associations of Disabled People (FAMOD)
Forum of Mine-Affected Countries (FOMAC)
Frente de Libertação de Moçambique (FRELIMO)
Frente Nacional de Libertacão de Angola (FNLA)
International Committee for the Red Cross (ICRC)
Landmine Impact Survey (LIS)
Landmine Survivors Network (LSN)
League for the Reintegration of Disabled People (LARDEF)
Ministry for Women and the Coordination of Social Action (MMCAS)
Ministry of Health (MINSAU)

Ministry of Social Affairs (MINARS)
Movimento Popular de Libertacão de Angola (MPLA)
Mozambican Campaign against Mines (CMCM)
National Department of Assistance to People with Disabilities (DNAD)
Southern African Federation of the Disabled (SAFOD)
União Nacional para a Independência Total de Angola (UNITA)
United States Agency for International Development (USAID)
Vietnam Veterans of America Foundation (VVAF)
World Health Organisation (WHO)
World Veterans Federation (WVF)

Notes

1. SAFOD has been active during the African decade of Persons with Disabilities (1999–2009) and has contributed to debates about the UN Comprehensive and Integral Convention on the Protection and Promotion of the Rights and Dignity of Persons with Disabilities, which has been drafted and revised between 2001 and 2005.

2. For more on the relationship between disability and development, see Coleridge (1993), Ingstad (1995), Jones (1999), Stone (1999), Hirst (2000), and Power (2001a).

3. The term "people with disability" is used here primarily as a consequence of discussions with ADEMO (the major national disability movement in Mozambique), which has recently campaigned for the use of the term *pessoa portadora de deficiência* (person that carries a disability or people with disability) in preference to the term *deficiente* (disabled).

4. Originally, this strategy was aimed at eroding the authority and legitimacy of the post-colonial state to accelerate its expected implosion, but given the state's uncanny ability to survive—through a blend of coercion and corruption—UNITA redirected its efforts to plundering the country's resources; first ivory, timber, and gold, then diamonds.

5. In multiparty elections in 1994, President Joaquim Chissano won and FRELIMO has now been elected three times. In 2002 Chissano announced he would not seek a third term. FRELIMO's candidate, independence hero Armando Guebuza, was elected president and sworn in on February 2, 2005.

6. For a useful review of the origins of the Angolan war, see Marcum (1978), Minter (1994), Guimarães (1998), or Kambwa et al. (1999).

7. Less than 30 percent of Angolans have access to health care, and the public health situation in the country remains critical. The conflict reportedly destroyed an estimated 60 percent of the health care infrastructure, and as such there are few qualified medical personnel, while medicines and equipment are in short supply.

8. In 1997, the ICRC estimated that there were at least 120 new landmine casualties each month, or 1,440 a year, in Angola (ICRC 1997, 1). In 2002, the U.S. State Department estimated that there were 800 new mine casualties each year in Angola (U.S. Department of State 2002, 12). From 1999 to 2002, there were at least 2,686 new casualties reported in Angola from mines and unexploded ordnance (Landmine Monitor 2004). In September 2004, the government

reportedly stated that 700 people had been killed and 2,300 injured in landmine incidents "over the last six years" and estimated that there were 80,000 mine survivors in the country (Landmine Monitor 2004).

9. AMMIGA now works closely with other disability groups in the country and has established international connections with other movements of ex-combatants, primarily through the World Veterans Federation (WVF). AMMIGA originally had no gender perspective but now works with war widows, and in general terms women's groups have been formed within the movement and are participating actively in community affairs.

10. In September 2001, the Jaipur Limb Campaign UK (JLC) started a program, called Dignidade, in conjunction with LARDEF to promote the economic reintegration, empowerment, and employment of people with disabilities. Alongside Jaipur, LARDEF has set up income-generating taxi cooperatives using auto-rickshaws from India. The program operates small cooperatives with three-wheel vehicles that provide a taxi service for people and goods and transport to orthopedic centers in order to improve access to rehabilitation services. Since August 2005, the JLC has been called Disability and Development Partners.

11. The pensions paid by the government amount to about 350,000 to 6 million Meticais per month (US$13–225) depending on the degree of disability and grade in the army. About 70% of the population of ex-soldiers with disabilities does draw a pension (established in law in 1992). According to ADEMIMO, the level of the pensions can potentially support a family of 5–6 members. (Mourou and Trouvé 2000, 35).

12. Mozambique has a National Action Plan for people with disabilities (2005–2010), which represents a further attempt to explore how disability policy can be implemented across the country.

13. The IMF found that between 1997 and 2001 alone, $8.45 billion of public money was unaccounted for (Kibble 2006, 15).

14. Further, at the global level, the Landmine Survivors Network (LSN) has proposed a global network that aims to stimulate demobilized communities toward reflection and self-empowerment. The experience of veteran-organized networks in countries like Angola and Mozambique is being held up by the LSN as reason to believe that such networks can be replicated in other countries in conformity with local traditions and culture (LSN 2006). There is also the Forum of Mine-Affected Countries (FOMAC), a high-level group of representatives from mine-affected countries including Mozambique and Angola that was formed to encourage cooperation between countries, the first meeting of which (in 2004) was chaired by Angola's ambassador to the UN in New York.

References

Agência de Informação de Moçambique (AIM). 2000a. ADEMIMO calls for law to protect disabled soldiers. November 8. Brighton, UK: Agência de Informação de Moçambique.

———. 2000b. Handicapped former soldiers invade land. August 22. Brighton, UK: Agência de Informação de Moçambique.

Angoflash, 'Governo nunca se esqueceu dos antigos combatentes', Edição especial 3 de Maio', http://angoarussia.Ru/press/angoflash/angoflash2004-02-04.doc (May 3, 2004).

————. 2006. Guebuza against exclusion of disabled people. March 8. Brighton, UK: Agência de Informação de Moçambique.

Angola Press. 2005. Trinta anos de independência marcam início do desenvolvimento—presidente da ANDA. http://www.angolapress-angop.ao/noticia.asp?ID=393057/ (accessed November 21, 2005).

Associação dos Deficientes de Moçambique (ADEMO). 1994. *Estatutos da Associação dos Deficientes de Moçambique*. Maputo, Mozambique: ADEMO.

————. 1999. *Deficiente*, Octobre, no. 4. Maputo, Mozambique: ADEMO.

Borges-Coelho, João Paulo. 2002. African troops in the Portuguese Colonial Army, 1961–1974: Angola, Guinea-Bissau and Mozambique. *Portuguese Studies Review* 10 (1): 129–50.

Chabal, Patrick. 2002. *The history of postcolonial Lusophone Africa*. London: C. Hurst.

Cilliers, Jackie. 2001. Business and war in Angola. *Review of African Political Economy* 28 (90): 636–41.

————, ed. 2000. *Angola's war economy: The role of oil and diamonds*. Pretoria, South Africa: Institute for Security Studies (ISS).

Coleridge, Peter. 1993. *Disability, liberation and development*. Oxford: Oxfam.

Cramer, Christopher. 1996. War and peace in Angola and Mozambique. *Journal of Southern African Studies* 22:481–90.

Cuambe, Jaime. 2004. Acidentes com minas fazem 615 victimas no país [Accidents with mines cause 615 victims in the country]. *Notícias*, May 2.

Devlieger, Patrick. 1995. Why disabled? The cultural understanding of physical disability in an African society. In *Disability and culture*, ed. Benedicte Ingstad and Susan Reynolds Whyte, 94–106. Berkeley: University of California Press.

————. 1999. Frames of reference in African proverbs on disability. *International Journal of Disability, Development and Education* 46 (4): 439–51.

Dos Santos, Eduardo 2005. Speech by President José Eduardo dos Santos on the thirtieth anniversary of independence: Luanda, November 11th. http://www.un.int/angola/press_release_11_nov_2005_pr_speech.htm/ (accessed March 29, 2006).

Federation of Mozambican Disability Associations (FAMOD). 2005. *Strategic plan 2005–2009*. Maputo, Mozambique: FAMOD.

Goldman, A. 1999. Angola: The roots of conflict. BBC News: http://www.bloc.co.uk/1/hi/special_report/1999/01/99/angola/263954.stm.

Governo nunca se esqueceu dos antigos combatentes. 2004. *Angoflash*, special issue, May 3. http://angolarussia.ru/press/angoflash/angoflash_2004-02-04.doc (accessed May 3, 2004).

Guimarães, Fernando Andreson. 1998. *The origins of the Angolan Civil War: Foreign intervention and domestic political conflict*. Basingstoke, UK: Macmillan.

Hajari, Nisid, and Marcus Mabry. 2001. The worst countries in the world. *Newsweek*, July 9, 24.

Handicap International. 2005. *Country situation analysis: Angola*. Brussels: Handicap International.

Hanlon, Joe. 1996. *Peace without profit: How the IMF blocks rebuilding in Mozambique*. London: Heinemann.

Hirst, Rachel. 2000. The international disability rights movement. Text of a public lecture, given as part of the New Directions in Disability Studies seminar series, Disability Studies Unit, University of Leeds, UK. http://www.leeds.ac.uk/disability-studies/.

Hodges, Tony. 2001. *Angola from Afro-Stalinism to petro-diamond capitalism.* London: James Currey.

Ingstad, Benedicte. 1995. Public discourses on rehabilitation: From Norway to Botswana. In *Disability and culture,* ed. Benedicte Ingstad and Susan Reynolds Whyte, 174–95. Berkeley: University of California Press.

International Committee for the Red Cross (ICRC). 1997. *Antipersonnel mines: An overview.* Geneva: ICRC.

Jones, H. 1999. Integrating a disability perspective into mainstream development programmes: The experience of Save the Children (UK) in Asia. In *Disability and development,* ed. E. Stone, 54–71. Leeds, UK: University of Leeds, Disability Press.

Kabzems, Venta, and Robert Chimedza. 2002. Development assistance: Disability and education in Southern Africa. *Disability and Society* 17 (2): 147–57.

Kambwa, Augusto Eduardo, Daniel Mingas Casimiro, Ngongo Joao Pedro, and Lucas Bhengui Ngonda. 1999. Angola. In *Comprehending and mastering African conflicts: The search for sustainable peace and good governance,* ed. Adebayo Adedji. London: Zed.

Kapuscinski, Ryszard. 2001. *Another day of life.* London: Vintage.

Kibble, Steve. 2006. Angola: Can the politics of disorder become the politics of democratisation and development? *Review of African Political Economy* 33 (109): 525–42.

Landmine Monitor. 2004. Mozambique. http://www.icbl.org/lm/2004/mozambique#fn4311/ (accessed March 29, 2006).

———. 2005. Angola. http://www.icbl.org/lm/2005/Angola/ (accessed March 27, 2006).

Landmine Survivors Network (LSN). 2006. What we do. http://www.landminesurvivors.org/what.php/ (accessed April 3, 2006).

Malaquias, Assis. 2001. Making war and lots of money: The political economy of protracted conflict in Angola. *Review of African Political Economy* 28 (90): 521–36.

Mamdani, Mahmood. 1996. *Citizenship and subject: Contemporary Africa and the legacy of late colonialism.* Princeton, NJ: Princeton University Press.

Marcum, John. 1978. *The Angolan revolution,* vols. 1 and 2. Cambridge: MA: MIT Press.

Medeiros Paulo, de. 2002. War pics: Photographic representations of the colonial war. *Luso-Brazilian Review* 39 (2): 91–103.

Medina, João. 1999. The old lie: Some Portuguese contemporary novels on the colonial wars in Africa (1961–1974). *Portuguese Studies Review* 15:149–61.

Messiant, Christine. 2001. The Eduardo Dos Santos Foundation: Or, how Angola's regime is taking over civil society. *African Affairs* 100:287–309.

Minter, William. 1994. *Apartheid's contras: An inquiry into the roots of war in Angola and Mozambique.* London: Zed.

Mitchell, David, and Sharon Snyder. 1999. Introduction: Disability studies and the double bind of representation. In *The body and physical difference: Discourses of disability,* ed. David Mitchell and Sharon Snyder, 1–34. Ann Arbor: University of Michigan Press.

Mourou, Berenice, and Bernard Trouvé. 2000. *Response to injury and disability due to antipersonnel landmine accidents.* Handicap International. Paris: Vitton Press.

Mutilados de Guerra justificam occupação de Terras: "Também temos direito á posse da terra." 2000. *Correio de Manhã,* June 30, 6.

Ncube, Jabulani. 2005. *Capacity building of disabled people's organisations in Mozambique,* Disability Knowledge and Research series. Windhoek, Namibia: Phanda.

Nyathi, Isaac. 2005. Advocacy and the disability movement in Angola. In *Filling gaps and making spaces: Strengthening civil society in unstable situations*, ed. J. Twigg. London: Baring Foundation.

Parsons, Imogen. 2004. Beyond the silencing of guns: Demobilization, disarmament and reintegration. *Accord* 15. http://www.c-r.org/accord/ang/accord15/08.shtml/ (accessed March 29, 2006).

Pitcher, Anne. 2002. *Transforming Mozambique: The politics of privatisation 1975–2000.* Cambridge: Cambridge University Press.

Power, Marcus. 2001a. Geographies of disability and development in Southern Africa. *Disability Studies Quarterly* 22 (1): 11–22.

———. 2001b. Patrimonialism and petro-diamond capitalism: Geo-politics and the economics of war in Angola. *Review of African Political Economy* 28 (90): 489–502.

Republica de Moçambique. 1990. Constituição da Republica. http://www.mozambique.mz/pdf/constituicao.pdf/ (accessed April 3, 2006).

Republic of Angola. 1992. Constitution part II: Fundamental rights and duties. http://www.angola.org/referenc/constitution/con3.htm/ (accessed April 2, 2006).

Sidaway, James Derrick, and Marcus Power. 2005. "The tears of Portugal": Empire, identity, "race" and destiny in Portuguese geopolitical narratives. *Environment and Planning D: Society and Space* 23 (4): 527–54.

Stone, Emma. 1999. *Disability and development.* Leeds, UK: University of Leeds, Disability Press.

Tembe, Francisco Manuel. 2002. Mozambique: Using the International Day of Disabled People to lobby. *Disability World* 12 (January–March). http://www.disabilityworld.org/01-03_02/news/mozambique.shtml/ (accessed March 2, 2006).

United Nations. 2005. *Final report: First review conference of the states party to the Convention on the Prohibition of the Use, Stockpiling, Production and Transfer of Anti-Personnel Mines and on their destruction, Nairobi, Kenya, November 29–December 3 2004.* APLC/CONF.2044/5. Nairobi, Kenya: United Nations.

U.S. Agency for International Development (USAID). 1997. *Women's participation in Angola's reconstruction process and in its political processes and institutions.* Washington, DC: USAID.

U.S. Department of State. 2002. *To walk the earth in safety.* Washington, DC: U.S. Department of State.

Werbner, Richard, and Terence Ranger, eds. 1996. *Postcolonial identities in Africa.* London: Zed.

Zambézia Online. 2005. 250 membros da ADEMIMO em Mocuba de costas voltadas com o governo. http://www.zambezia.co.mz/content/view/1663/2/ (accessed November 29, 2005).

9

Who Are the Victims?
Where Is the Violence?
The Spatial Dialectics of Andean Violence as Revealed by the Truth and Reconciliation Commission of Peru

MAUREEN HAYS-MITCHELL

Introduction

Throughout the 1980s and early 1990s, political violence convulsed the Andean country of Peru as the insurgent movement Sendero Luminoso (Shining Path) challenged the legitimacy of the Peruvian state. In the course of the conflict, over twenty-three thousand violent attacks occurred, nearly seventy thousand Peruvians were killed, over six thousand people disappeared, more than half a million persons were displaced from their homes, thousands of innocent Peruvians were imprisoned, material damages exceeded $21 billion, and nearly half the national territory was designated an emergency zone (Truth and Reconciliation Commission 2003, vol. 1). Despite widespread destruction and suffering, the violence is only now being documented officially.

With release of the *Final Report* of the Truth and Reconciliation Commission (TRC) in late 2003, the people of Peru are confronting the immense legacy of their country's recent internal conflict. The *Final Report* makes official what many Peruvians had long suspected; the violence was more extensive, profound, and discriminatory than previously acknowledged. It occurred unevenly across distinct geographical regions and demographic strata. The overwhelming majority of victims were concentrated in the poorest regions of the country, were of rural or campesino (peasant) origin, and spoke indigenous languages. They had long been socially, economically, and politically marginalized within the country to which their homes, lands, and bodies pertained. Their level of education was far below the national average; they had limited access to economic resources, and they received little consideration as citizens of the country (see TRC 2003). In essence, the *Final Report* throws into relief the relationship between (1) geographical isolation, social exclusion, and political marginalization; and (2) the selectivity and intensity of the violence that characterized Peru's internal armed conflict.

Inasmuch as Peru's TRC blames centuries of entrenched racism for the denial of the rights of citizenship to a large segment of the Peruvian population, this study analyzes the particular convergence in Peru of political violence with axes of race, socioeconomic and sociopolitical exclusion, and territory that the *Final Report* implies. In what follows, I examine how these historically embedded processes relating to citizenship and territory unfolded in the course of the conflict. I am especially interested in exploring how the representation of the recent past in the *Final Report* of the Truth and Reconciliation Commission of Peru is related to the contemporary project of overcoming an entrenched history of social exclusion, racial and gender discrimination, and injustice—the guiding principle and hard-hitting admonition of the TRC in Peru. In what follows I ask, if the goal of a truth and reconciliation commission is to educate future generations of their country's violent history to ensure that such acts cannot recur, then to what extent can Peru's TRC (1) open a space for meaningful discussion of the causes of the internal conflict that convulsed this Andean country for nearly two decades, and (2) serve to catalyze genuine action for substantive change? That is, can the TRC of Peru set in motion a new relationship between the Peruvian state and civil society that guarantees the inclusion of all Peruvians?[1]

Conceptualizing the Spatial Injustice of Andean Violence

Insights from Feminist Geopolitics

In this study, I draw on feminist geopolitical theory, as recently theorized by Jennifer Hyndman (2004), to advance understandings of the findings of the Peruvian Truth and Reconciliation Commission. Feminist geopolitics is "an embodied view from which to analyze visceral conceptions of violence, security and mobility" (Hyndman 2004, 315). It argues for a reconceptualizing of geopolitical landscapes apart from the scale of the nation-state, an important theme in this volume. Just as transnationalism calls for deconstructing conventional political borders in order to analyze disparities among transnational subjects and/or relationships that transcend such divides (e.g., Grewal and Kaplan 1994), feminist geopolitics calls for deconstructing conventional political borders in order to understand disparities internal to them (Hyndman 2004). In asking, "Security for whom, and how?" Hyndman's theory of feminist geopolitics specifically calls for a rescaling of geopolitical landscapes to individuals or collectivities who exist within state borders and without state security. Because it "aims to forge more accountable and material conceptions and scales of security" (Hyndman 2004, 308), it can be applied appropriately to the work of the Peruvian Truth and Reconciliation Commission.

Yet how can feminist geopolitics help privileged scholars located in the Global North, such as myself, to understand the work of a truth commission charged to investigate the causes and effects of an armed conflict internal to a society of the Global South, particularly when its work is premised on the experiences of those for whom the axes of poverty, race, and geographical isolation intersect to render them socially, economically, and politically marginalized? Feminist geopolitics is grounded specifically in feminist poststructuralist and postcolonial theory, which are helpful in recovering the agency of marginalized peoples. Chandra Talpade Mohanty suggests that to explore unequal relations of power, we should start with the most marginalized and "read up the ladder of power" (personal communication, May 1, 2002). Location, according to Hyndman's theory of feminist geopolitics, implies dimensions of power and identity that contribute to the very constitution of people and places as subjects. It is appropriate to this case in that location, expressed as geographical isolation and social exclusion, justified the disregard of indigenous and campesino peoples as citizens. Following Haraway (1991), positioning implies responsibility for practices of seeing and doing or, as in this case, *not* seeing and *not* doing. This is relevant to analysis of citizenship within Peru as we consider the commission's findings on (1) human rights abuses committed by state security forces, as well as (2) mainstream Peruvian society that refused to see and to take action until violence reached their lives.

Moreover, feminist thought analyzes the constitution and location of the subject as the bases of knowledge production. Peru's TRC perceived itself as a victim-based commission and explicitly defined itself as a partner in the process to seek justice. Hence, it is involved in the production of knowledge about the civil war and its aftermath. As Kimberly Theidon, an expert in violence-induced trauma and rehabilitation in Peru, reminds us, the deployment of "memory" and the creation of "truth," in reference to an internal armed conflict such as that experienced in Peru "ha[ve] much to do with forging new relations of power, ethnicity, and gender that are integral to the contemporary politics of [a] region." Furthermore, "These new relations impact the construction of democratic practices and the model of citizenship being elaborated in the current context," concerns central to the themes of this volume (Theidon 2003a, 67). Feminist geopolitics builds on critical geopolitics and powerful feminist theorizing in political geography, poststructuralist and postcolonial theory, and international relations. It synthesizes these perspectives/theories into a cogent theory relevant to this case study that makes it possible not simply to "study down" but also, as Mohanty suggests, to "think up."

Spatial Justice and Citizenship

I further draw, in this discussion, on the emergent concept of spatial justice as it refers to the fair and democratic distribution of societal benefits and burdens across spaces of various scales. Spatial justice strengthens concepts of social justice by recognizing that space (1) is socially produced and (2) in turn shapes social relations. The concept of spatial justice assumes an attentiveness to see injustice in its spatial dimension (Dikeç 2001). It is appropriate to apply to struggles for political change in Peru, a country where the rights and duties of democratic citizenship are determined in large extent by discrepancies in geographic, social, and economic location. For those who endeavor to act on the recommendations of the Truth Commission, spatial justice can provide a framework for action.

In Peru, hierarchies of citizenship are related to race, gender, class, and geographical location. They are normalized and form a profound part of what Goldberg (2002) refers to as a historically rooted "racialized common sense." Hierarchies of citizenship are embodied in policies, performances, and popular thought in Peru. By applying the concept of spatial justice to this case study, where particular strata of the Peruvian population have been denied the rights of democratic citizenship on the basis of geographical and social (i.e., racial, ethnic, and class) location, we can critically engage both the spatialization of race and the racialization of space. That is, a focus on the spatiality of economic, cultural, social, and political power relations can advance our understandings of how identity and inequality (premised on race, ethnicity, and class) are constructed across scales and in particular places. The concept of spatial justice further explains the selectivity and intensity of the violence, for these particular communities, that characterized Peru's internal conflict.

In her socially grounded analysis of state development planning in Nepal, Katharine Rankin (2004) invokes Antonio Gramsci and Pierre Bourdieu's practice theory to explore the manner in which neoliberal strategies of development planning perpetuate existing social inequalities in particular places. The case study of this chapter is similarly grounded in a context where neoliberal development strategies (preceding, during, and subsequent to armed conflict) perpetuate inequalities and injustices across space. Neoliberal development policies, imposed by the international financial community, work through historically embedded cultural ideologies to maintain these inequalities and injustices. The concept of spatial justice helps us understand how race, class, geography, and spatial scale (from the international to the local) are implicated in the neoliberal state of Peru; how neoliberal strategies affect everyday practices and subjectivities of citizenship in particular regions; and why more effective political-economic practices must be implemented. In short, it calls attention to the interrelatedness of injustice and spatiality as producing, reproducing, and sustaining each other through specific institutions and practices (Dikeç 2001).

Spatial justice, or in this case injustice, therefore provides a framework for exploring the spatial dialectic between the negation of citizenship rights and the infliction of physical and/or structural violence on specific groups of peoples within Peru. Coupled with feminist geopolitical theory, it specifically enables us to conceptualize (1) the ways in which rights of citizenship within the Peruvian nation have been selectively denied to particular strata of the population depending on the racial, economic, and geographical location of subjects; and (2) the recommendations of the Peruvian Truth and Reconciliation Commission to develop a new practice of citizenship that permits these individuals and collectivities to benefit from the sense of belonging as full members of the national community. And although beyond the scope of this discussion, it reminds us that the spatial injustices of this intrastate conflict are linked to processes operating at broader geographical scales.

Citizenship, Ethnicity, and the Deployment of Violence in Andean Peru[2]

Tiers of Citizenship

Citizenship is generally thought to comprise several elements, including identity, belonging, status, rights, and responsibilities, that produce what T. H. Marshall considers the acceptance of a person as a full member of a given society (Marshall 1973). Yet citizenship is more than a status. According to Turner, it is a "set of practices (juridical, political, economic and cultural) which define a person as a competent member of society and which, as a consequence, shape the flow of resources to persons and social groups" (Turner 1993, 2). These practices entail rights and duties that define a relationship between the state and its citizens which takes place in political society—that is, in the "realm of intermediation between civil society and the state" (Lynch 1997).

These classic definitions of citizenship are telling when applied to a country such as Peru, for they similarly define who is *not* a citizen and, by extension, who is excluded from the protection of the law. Turner suggests, as feminist scholars have long noted, that state institutions and practices treat de jure citizens in differentiated ways according to hegemonic imaginations of, and standards for, proper citizens (i.e., "competent member[s] of society") as civilized and virtuous members of the polis (Turner 1993). The Peruvian state's historical centralization of power and control in the primate capital city Lima (the "polis") reflects a classic divide, as much real as imagined, between the urban modern sector and the rural indigenous population—a schism maintained by historically entrenched notions of racism and endemic poverty.[3] The consequent exclusion, on the basis of race, class, and region, has had devastating effects for the indigenous population. If citizenship is understood as the equivalent of formal belonging within a nation-state, and if the rights

204 • Maureen Hays-Mitchell

and responsibilities associated with citizenship are distributed through the nation-state, then the disproportionate impact of the internal conflict reveals that "citizenship" has failed the rural indigenous and campesino populations of Peru.

Despite de jure status as citizens, these populations have never had access to justice, in the conventional state-sanctioned juridical sense, nor have they ever known the state as the bearer or arbiter of justice. They must fight for the ability to participate and/or be included in political structures that affect their lives as well as for access to their social rights, in the form of distribution of resources, bodily protection, and other basic needs. In writing of ritual displays of citizenship in highland Peru, Stepputat argues that the conditions and practices of citizenship are shaped by political projects that work through specific political, social, economic, racial, and spatial organizations of society. Citizenship, accordingly, can be shaped "from below" as movements react to the "differentiating practices of state institutions and to the lack of recognition of particular identities" (Stepputat 2004, 245). Although Isin and Turner (2002) suggest that the concept of citizenship has been broadened in recent years to include social and political struggles for recognition and redistribution, the editors of this volume accurately note that the "only very recent acquisition of citizenship by indigenous peoples helps to affirm their accusations of persistent state racism" (Cowen and Gilbert, chapter 1 of this volume). In Peru, universal suffrage was only achieved in 1980 when the voting age was lowered to eighteen and illiterate individuals were extended the right to vote. Notwithstanding, a profound gulf—determined by race/ethnicity, class, gender, and regional background—persists between the formal rights and the substantive rights of citizenship experienced by many Peruvians.

Citizenship and Ethnic Identity

In writing of the crisis of representative democracy in Peru, Nicolás Lynch reminds us that citizenship is "a proposal of equality according to which all members of the same political community enjoy the same rights and thus the same citizen status" (Lynch 1997, 126). Yet in this context, the entrenched history of marginalization and exclusion repudiates the egalitarian and integrating nature of citizenship rights in Peru. The Peruvian state and mainstream Peruvian society do not perceive rural indigenous and campesino peoples as their equal. According to Lynch, the exclusive and exclusionary character of political society in Peru lacks organic ties with these communities. It does not see them as individual citizens but rather as a mass to be manipulated for short-term gain (Lynch 1997).

In her recent article about postconflict Peru, Kimberly Theidon invokes the concept of "disjunctive democracy" to highlight the disparate sense of belonging to the nation-state, unequal access to rights, and divergent meanings of citizenship that characterize much of contemporary Peru. The concept speaks to the conflict between social inequalities and citizen equality identified by Lynch. Theidon argues that disjunctions reflect the axes of differentiation that operate within Peruvian society and that "the distribution of democracy varies according to [these disjunctions]" (Theidon 2003a, 68). In short, state duties—the parallel component of citizen rights—are truncated and differentially channeled according to prevailing norms of what constitutes a "proper" or "competent" citizen.[4]

Returning to Stepputat's argument that citizenship can be molded from below in reaction to the differentiating practices of state institutions and to the lack of recognition of particular identities, would this not encourage the formation of a counterhegemonic identity based on ethnic difference? In their analysis of the relationship between inequality, ethnicity, violence, and mobilization in three Latin American countries, Thorp, Caumartin, and Gray-Molina argue that Peru is a "country and a society where the concepts of ethnicity and race have been and continue to be very much suppressed, both in society at large and within the marginalized indigenous populations" (Thorp, Caumartin, and Gray-Molina 2006, 465). Indigenous identity is weak, shaped at the local scale around one's own community. Instead, indigenous identity is focused in a contradictory manner on assimilation and denial and is channeled into nonconfrontational cultural forms (Thorp, Caumartin, and Gray-Molina 2006). Indeed, Stepputat finds that the rituals of citizenship enacted in highland indigenous communities privilege the urban modern "citizen" and denigrate the rural indigenous "peasant"; they do not advance an ethnically empowering counterhegemonic identity.

The relationship between ethnic demands and access to citizenship would seem counterintuitive in indigenous Peru. Ethnic demands, according to Lynch, do not imply confrontation between ethnically different communities. They instead take place in conjunction with demands based on class, region, and gender—the very factors that define social inequality in Peru. It was through struggles for material well-being that indigenous ethnic majorities won de jure recognition as part of the national community with the expansion of suffrage in 1980. Hence in the Andean context, winning citizen rights implies progress in terms of equal status and ethnic integration—that is, assimilation into *criollo* (urban white) society and the loss of ethnic distinctiveness (Lynch 1997).

Although ethnicity in Peru has not been a mobilizing factor against structural violence, Thorp, Caumartin, and Gray-Molina find that ethnicity is highly relevant to the degree of violence that marked Peru's internal conflict. They argue that Peru's conflict was not a "proto-typical ethnic conflict" in that it did not pit clearly defined ethnic groups against each other, nor did mobilization revolve around ethnicity. Instead, discourses were clearly delineated along class lines.[5] They maintain that "[the conflict] was a classic situation of weak identity and a tremendous sense of powerlessness, combined with very weak community institutions and little presence of the state" (Thorp, Caumartin, and Gray-Molina 2006, 469). The resulting violence was widespread, devastating, and "ethnic" in the sense that, as confirmed by the TRC, 75 percent of those killed were of indigenous origin (Thorp, Caumartin, and Gray-Molina 2006). To the extent that the armed conflict only reached some one-third of the national territory, violence was also geographically uneven—illustrating the spatial dialectics of injustice. The disregard, as individual citizens, of indigenous and campesino peoples in the Andean region throws into relief the complex relationship between inequality, ethnicity, territory, and political violence. Tiers of citizenship, forged by structural and armed violence, were deployed to justify the denial of citizen rights and state responsibilities to those considered less than equal citizens residing in inconsequential places.

The Truth and Reconciliation Commission in Peru: Genesis, Mandate, and Logistics

In July 1980, Peruvians elected a democratic government to replace the military regimes that had governed the country since 1968. Shortly thereafter, the Maoist-inspired guerrilla group and official communist party of Peru, Sendero Luminoso, emerged in Ayacucho, a historically impoverished region in the south-central Andean highlands. (See figure 9.1.)

Together, though not in concert, with the Marxist Movimiento Revolucionario Tupac Amarú (MRTA), Sendero began a campaign of violence designed to overthrow the Peruvian government. Violence quickly spread throughout the rural countryside and crowded cities. The state response was inconsistent and disorganized. Its policies and approaches led to progressively more severe human rights abuses, all within the framework of democratically elected governments. Although Sendero Luminoso and the MRTA had been effectively defeated by the mid-1990s, the cost in terms of respect for human rights and democratic norms was especially severe.

Throughout the 1990s, President Alberto Fujimori deployed the specter of violence to legitimize his increasingly authoritarian rule. He implemented a series of amnesty laws designed to maintain the de facto impunity of the military and security forces. Following Fujimori's ouster in late 2000 amid widespread charges of corruption, Interim President Valentín Paniagua took action to restore democracy to Peru. In response to long-standing calls from throughout civil society, Paniagua formed a working group to propose a framework for a truth commission. In June 2001 he issued an executive decree that established a truth commission, claiming that a "state must guarantee society's right to the truth without vengeance and under free and democratic principles" (Executive Decree 065-2001).

Interestingly, the original charge of the Truth Commission (as it was originally called) was to investigate human rights violations limited to the Fujimori regime (1990–2000). That is, the first decade of armed conflict between

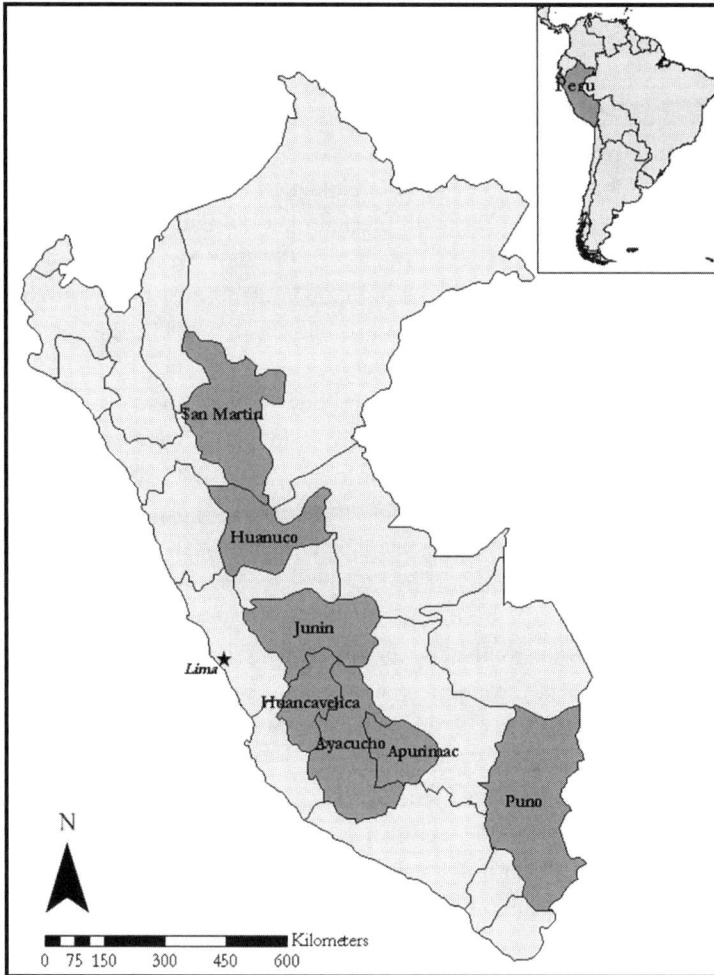

Figure 9.1 Departments Experiencing the Majority of Conflict-related Deaths in Peru.

Sendero Luminoso and state forces was explicitly excluded. Moreover, of the original seven Peruvians named to the Truth Commission, all but one was from Lima, reflecting the historic privileging of urban coastal society. Pressure brought to bear by religious, human rights, and victims' advocacy groups succeeded in extending the commission's charge to violations that occurred throughout the two decades of violence (1980–2000). In September 2001, at the behest of the Catholic Church and diverse associations within civil society, newly elected President Alejandro Toledo signed a supplementary decree expanding the commission to include more diverse perspectives and transforming it into a Truth and Reconciliation Commission (Executive Decree 101-2001-PCM). In January 2002, the commission began its work, documenting "the most intense, extensive and prolonged episode of violence in the entire history of the Republic" (*Final Report*; TRC 2003, vol. 8, 315). It presented its *Final Report* in Spanish on August 28, 2003.

The commission's mandate was threefold: first, to provide an official record of violations of human rights and international humanitarian law alleged to have occurred between May 1980 and November 2000;[6] second, to analyze the causes of these violations; and, third, to recommend measures to strengthen human rights and democracy (Human Rights Watch 2003). The commission was to investigate acts imputed to rebel organizations, state agents, and paramilitary groups, such as torture, kidnappings, killings, and forced disappearances, as well as violations to the collective rights of indigenous communities (Executive Decree 101-2001-PCM). Internally, the TRC conceptualized its mandate in terms of six principal objectives. For our purposes, the most relevant is the first objective: to analyze the political, social, and cultural conditions, as well as societal and state institutional actions, that contributed to two decades of political violence (Crandall 2004). Questions raised in addressing this objective allow us to identify the relationship between the prevalence of violence and the social, economic, political, and geographical marginalization of the majority of the war's victims—that is, the spatial dimensions of power relations in contemporary Peru.

The political climate of change (e.g., transition from authoritarian to democratic rule) in which the TRC was created infused it with a dynamic uncharacteristic of many truth commissions. It opened regional offices throughout the country, taking care to establish a presence in the regions most affected by the conflict. It collected seventeen thousand testimonies from victims, witnesses, and survivors; interviewed political leaders, legislators, military officers, and former leaders of Sendero Luminoso; and identified more than one thousand sites thought to contain victims' bodies (Human Rights Watch 2003). The nationally televised hearings of the TRC were the first time in the Americas that a truth commission had conducted its truth-seeking process so publicly, and is cited as an important step toward disseminating the truth and redignifying the victims (Crandall 2004). The intent was to begin the process of publicly acknowledging the individual and collective trauma associated with the armed violence, a possible first step in the state's duty to restore citizenship. They also called attention to the skepticism of many Peruvians toward the formal legal process. One witness before the TRC expressed his view: "Justice in Peru is not justice. . . . [I]f there is justice, it is for the rich, not for the poor like me" (quoted in Lozada 2002).

TRC Revelations and Recommendations in Relation to Race and Space

Who Were the Victims? Where Was the Violence?

The *Final Report* bears out the contention of Thorp, Caumartin, and Gray-Molina that ethnicity was highly relevant to the degree of violence committed in Peru's internal conflict. It reveals that Sendero Luminoso and Peruvian state forces killed indiscriminately throughout the conflict. The figure of nearly seventy thousand deaths far exceeds previous estimates. Of these, approximately four-fifths could be considered noncombatants. Sendero Luminoso is attributed with killing approximately one-half of the victims, government security forces with killing approximately one-third, and the MRTA and local militias with the rest.[7] That over half of the killings were attributed to nonstate actors contrasts with other Latin American countries that have suffered similar episodes of violence and in which the state has been the principal perpetrator of violent deaths (Márquez Restrepo 2004).[8]

In its *Final Report*, the TRC identifies a "clear relationship between social exclusion and the intensity of the violence" (TRC 2003, vol. 1, 158). "[M]ost of the victims belonged to rural (79%) or peasant (56%) groups, which are those that face the greatest social exclusion and have least access to economic resources" (TRC 2003, vol. 8, 316). The percentage of deaths and "disappearances" among people working in the agricultural sector (e.g., farming/livestock) and living in rural areas reported to the TRC is much greater than the percentage of people who, according to the 1993 national census, were working in that sector and living in those areas. The TRC further revealed that a very high proportion of those who died or "disappeared," over 75 percent, spoke indigenous languages as their mother tongue in a country where, according to the 1993 census, only a fifth of the population spoke those languages (Amnesty International 2004, 15).

Findings in relation to levels of education further highlight the disproportionate and race-specific impact of the violence. Victims' educational levels were far below the national average. Nearly 70 percent of the dead and "disappeared" had failed to attain secondary-level education. Nationally, this rate is just 40 percent. Similarly, over 70 percent of the victims of torture and of the internally displaced were Quechua-speaking people of indigenous and campesino origin who had attained at most only primary-level education (TRC 2003, vol. 8, 316; TRC 2003 vol. 6, 256-57, 656). In the course of investigation, the TRC found that "ethnic and racial differences . . . were often cited by the perpetrators to justify action against their victims" (TRC 2003, vol. 8, 105).

That there is a "clear relationship between social exclusion and the intensity of the violence" (TRC 2003, vol. 1, 158) harbors important spatial implications. Nearly all of the aforementioned cases of egregious abuse of rights of citizenship occurred in seven, nearly all contiguous, rural departments (see figure 9.1).[9] Four of these—Huancavelica, Ayacucho, Apurímac, and Huánuco—are among the country's five poorest departments (figure 9.1). In aggregate, they account for less than 10 percent of the overall income of all Peruvian families. In contrast, less than 10 percent of the people who died or "disappeared" belonged to the wealthier sectors of society (Amnesty International 2004, 15).

In view of the social, economic, and regional profile of the majority of the victims,

> It is not surprising that [the] Peruvian rural, Andean, jungle-dwelling, Quechua and Asháninka, peasant, poor and uneducated [were] left to bleed for years without the rest of the country feeling or assuming as its own the true extent of the tragedy being endured by that 'alien people within Peru'. (TRC 2003, vol. 1, 163)

Only did "[t]he violence and its victims gradually [take] on greater importance for public opinion [when] the conflict began to attack the centers of economic and political power within the country" (TRC 2003, vol. 1, 180–81). The TRC argues that this "demonstrates the veiled racism and scornful attitudes that persist in Peruvian society" (TRC 2003, vol. 8, 316). It concludes that "[d]ue to the racism and the fact that those people of indigenous, rural and poor origin were given little consideration as citizens, the deaths of thousands of Quechua-speakers went unnoticed by national public opinion" (TRC 2003, vol. 8, 101–3).[10] Such findings tragically highlight Turner's point that state practices treat de jure citizens in differentiated ways according to hegemonic imaginations of who is a "proper citizen." Viewed through a spatial lens, these findings throw into stark relief the spatial injustice of the internal conflict.

Recommendations to Redress Violations of the Rights and Duties of Citizenship

Although the *Final Report* is not framed explicitly as a study of citizenship rights and duties, it can be read as such. Dikeç (2001) suggests it is useful to assess under the concept of justice the processes that could be the sources and resources of injustice in their specific contexts. To this end, the *Final Report* identifies the institutions and practices that worked together to produce, reproduce, and sustain injustice for particular individuals and communities within specific places. The TRC places blame across the political and civil spectrum for the violence, destruction, and fear that plagued Peru through the final two decades of the twentieth century. Notwithstanding, the Peruvian state is held particularly responsible for upholding and deploying institutionalized notions and practices of discrimination that allowed the parallel components of citizenship—both (1) the rights of all citizens and (2) the state's responsibilities and duties to these very peoples—to be blatantly violated.

Prominent in the Commission's recommendations to redress injustices is the Programa de Reparaciones Integral (PRI). This is a comprehensive program of reparation, which is intended to help victims of the internal conflict recover a sense of personal security and their rights of citizenship. The PRI calls for not only symbolic reparations but also monetary reparations in the fields of health, education, legal assistance, and financial losses for victims and their families. It seeks to ensure that compensation is provided, where possible, for damages caused to local areas or communities for losses and suffering experienced at that scale. It stipulates that reparations should be both individual and collective (TRC 2003, 147). Reparations such as these further offer moral and political vindication. While most victims' advocates want perpetrators of crimes prosecuted and punished, they believe that monetary compensation is a crucial step in transitional justice toward ending impunity and reconstituting the rights of citizenship. In the words of Gisela Ortíz, whose brother disappeared after arrest by state security forces, reparations amount to a "recognition that these violations occurred, the damage they have caused, the responsibility of the state and the indifference of society" (Human Rights Watch 2003).

Mindful of the economic reality of Peru, a country that foregoes on average 20 percent of export revenue to servicing its foreign debt and where more than half its citizens live in poverty (World Bank 2007), victims' demands—especially monetary demands—are met with indifference, if not outright hostility, by those sectors of society that have never known social exclusion or political marginalization. Regardless, victims are resolute. Implicit in their demands is an understanding of Pateman's parallel components of citizenship—rights of citizens on one hand, and duties and responsibilities of the state on the other (Pateman 1985). Edgar Rivadeneyra, a member of the Association of Peruvians Unjustly Imprisoned for Terrorism, states, "We believe it is a matter of political will. The government has not understood its obligation. Individual reparations are our right. We are not asking for a handout, only that which was robbed from us" (Laplante 2003). Victims and victims' advocates consider implementation of the PRI to be a key stage in Peru's transitional justice. They see it specifically as an important commitment to the reconstitution of citizenship through state acceptance of its responsibility to victims of the internal armed conflict.

Prospects for the Reconstitution of Citizenship

We return now to the original question that guides this discussion. To what extent can the *Final Report* of the TRC set in motion a new relationship between the Peruvian state and civil society that ensures the inclusion in the nation-state and extends the benefits of citizenship to all Peruvians?

Whither the Recommendations of the TRC?

To begin, the Peruvian TRC identifies the underlying historical conditions that led to and resulted in twenty years of armed political violence, and it provides concrete proposals that can create the basis for reconciliation to address (1) the losses and suffering of twenty years of extreme violence, and (2) the underlying historical issues of poverty, racism, and marginalization. Salient recommendations look to address the absence of a constructive state presence in the regions where violence was most concentrated. And, the *Final Report* insists that the rights of indigenous peoples and their communities must be recognized specifically in national legislation in order to guarantee legal protection for them. Many of the reforms that attend to the failure of state authorities to protect the citizenship rights of all Peruvians could be implemented relatively quickly and inexpensively. They are primarily a matter of political will.

However, as Carlos Parodi observes, the creation and unfolding of Peru's TRC, as well as its potential effects, take place within a context of power relations. When the TRC's *Final Report* entered into Peru's struggle for truth, justice, reparation, and reconciliation, it highlighted both possibilities and limitations in terms of its relations with different political and civil actors (Parodi 2004). The Commission has faced a vexing task as the country's traditional political parties and mainstream society have refused to accept its charges of indifference and complicity on their parts (Shifter and Jawahar 2004, 131). There has been little self-reflection and self-criticism about what could have been done to avert or mitigate the violence that fell so disproportionately on socially, economically and politically excluded populations in geographically marginalized regions. Although the themes of social, economic, and political exclusion were deployed to great effect in the recent presidential campaign, the discourse of the newly elected García administration has revolved primarily around international economic relations. Bearing in mind the role of his first administration (1985–1990) in the escalating violence, it is doubtful that García would choose to revisit issues associated with that era.

Faltering Prospects for Reconciliation

The *Final Report* of Peru's Truth and Reconciliation Commission (1) "confirmed acts that violated fundamental human rights (with the possibility of establishing presumed responsibility)," and (2) offered an "explanation of the political, social, and cultural process that made such violations possible" (TRC 2003, vol. 1, 28). Despite the fact that over 80 percent of the national population and the military publicly stated support for the creation of the TRC, military and former officials have distanced themselves from the commission since publication of the *Final Report*. Commission members' credibility has been impugned, and some have received death threats (Amnesty International 2004).

Kimberly Theidon notes that the political and economic elite of Lima are more concerned with retribution for the corruption of the Fujimori regime than for human rights violations. Theidon posits this is because the political and economic corruption touched their class, while the majority of disappearances and deaths during the armed conflict were among the rural poor and urban working classes. She suggests that the urban elite so ardently opposes "reconciliation" because,

> They do not have to confront on a daily basis the legacy of a fratricidal war. They do not have to interact with neighbors who chose differ- ent—often lethal—sides during the war. Nor did soldiers knock on their doors in the middle of the night to haul off men and wait in line to rape women (Theidon 2003b, 2).

Reconciliation between rural communities that were terrorized by state forces and the Peruvian state is an unfinished matter. Victims' advocacy groups argue that the Peruvian state has a responsibility to remember and to address the brutality exacted by many Peruvians against fellow Peruvians, some in the name of the state and others in the name of destroying the state (Hays-Mitchell, field interviews, July 2004). Some of the hardest hit commu- nities have found ways to administer justice and rehabilitate their own mem- bers (see Theidon 2003b). National reconciliation lags well behind processes underway in rural communities; at the national scale, the mere value of rec- onciliation is questionable.

The TRC perceived and promoted itself as a victim-based commission, as giving voice to victims of the internal conflict. Notwithstanding, it remains to be seen whether the TRC can serve as a catalyst for moving discussion beyond the redignification of victims to the reconstitution of citizenship. Because it is involved in the production of knowledge about the civil war and its after- math, the TRC is, logically, a site of struggle over who produces and narrates the "truth" contained in it. Moreover, its voluminous content can be read in varying ways. Mainstream urban society has elected to focus on retribution and legislative reform to redress the excesses of the Fujimori era, while rural highland society focuses on reparation and reconciliation. Read in another light, however, the efforts toward reparation advanced by the TRC in the Plan Integral can be understood as efforts toward inclusion—toward developing a sense of belonging to a reconfigured and evolving political community. Inclu- sion and a sense of belonging are commonly understood to mean "citizen- ship." Yet, the fact that the Peruvian state is not accustomed to fulfilling duties (i.e., the parallel component of citizenship rights) is a potential obstacle to action on the TRC's recommendations.

Prospects for Creating a New Political Culture

Although prosecutions and reparations are widely considered central to the task of constructing durable and high-quality democracies in postconflict set- tings, Shifter and Jawahar (2004) suggest that truth commissions should serve as instruments to achieve wider political objectives. Accordingly, we must ask, in what ways could the Peruvian TRC be used to forge a political culture premised on strong democratic institutions and practices that ensure that the benefits of citizenship extend to all within the national territory?

As the editors to this volume note, the ability to participate and be included in political structures is a formidable concern, and the lack of citizenship participation has been sounded as the death knell of liberal democracy. Although the number of de jure citizens has greatly increased over the past twenty-seven years in Peru, these "citizens" are yet to find representation in existing state institutions and the current political process. Lynch warns that the "difficulty of finding political expression and institutional representation is the fundamental cause of Peruvians' [current] frustration with democracy [and] [t]his frustration, in turn, finds fertile ground for the authoritarian regression" that characterized the final years of the Fujimori regime and the reactionary trends seen in the 2006 presidential election (Lynch 1997, 124).

The TRC is unequivocal in that, if Peru is to become a country in which the rights of all its citizens are respected, the historically embedded legacy of discrimination and exclusion that precludes many from accessing, exercising, and enjoying their rights as citizens must be addressed. Although some of the recommendations of the TRC may involve little more than political goodwill, others involve radical structural reform or require changes in the culture and perceptions of a significant portion of Peruvian society. They will therefore need sustained commitment to a long-term program of social and political reform (Amnesty International 2004). To this end, the *Final Report* of the TRC must be taken seriously. Examples abound of "efforts to promote truth commissions [that] have become a way of avoiding efforts to do justice" (Aryeh Neier, quoted in Crandall 2004, 3). The creation of a new political culture premised on strong democratic institutions and practices in Peru is entwined with the "tasks of uncovering the truth, reconstructing historical memory, implementing justice, and carrying out institutional reforms" (Amnesty International 2004, 31). In short, it means the state will need to accept and act on its duties to citizenship. This will not be easy for a state long thwarted in achieving democratic legitimacy and severely constrained by the strictures of neoliberal economic reform.

Conclusion: Memory, Truth, Citizenship, and Spatial Injustice

According to Kimberly Theidon, "War and its aftermath serve as powerful motivators for the elaboration and transmission of individual, communal, and national histories. These histories both reflect *and* constitute human experience as they contour social memory and produce their truth effects" (Theidon 2003a, 67). "Truth effects" are the undercurrent of new power relations, which in turn shape the contemporary politics, democratic practices, and models of citizenship that will be elaborated. Theidon cautions that the competition over history and memory, for our purposes the creation of "truth," can obscure the disjunctive and contradictory construction of citizenship (Theidon 2003a). In its narration of Peru's internal conflict, the Truth and Reconciliation Commission treads a fine line between advancing the project of national integration, as an outcome of the internal conflict, and establishing a false duality in an "official" and a "popular" version of the internal conflict. As Theidon suggests, a false duality such as this (e.g., bad/repressive versus good/emancipatory) would obscure both "the fluidity within such a dichotomy and the fragmentation that exists on each side of the great divide" (Theidon 2003a, 68). This risk is made more real by the TRC's self-depiction as a victim-based commission, as giving voice to "the victims" of the conflict. While "victim" may be one form of subalternity, its markers of "otherness" are in turn inflected by race, ethnicity, gender, generation, class, and location, among others.

The work of the TRC is to open a space for the internally differentiated and unequal groups of citizens on both sides of the divide to make claims upon the construction of the history, the national imaginary, and ultimately the future of the nation-state of Peru. Drawing on Theidon, I suggest that, if the "truth" inherent in the *Final Report* can transcend the false dichotomy between an "official" (i.e., bad) and a "victims'" (i.e., good) history, then it may be possible to catalyze genuine action for substantive change. That is, change that will permit (1) all Peruvians—regardless of social class, race, ethnicity, gender, or regional background—to claim their rights to citizenship; and (2) a "deeper democracy that permits all members . . . to benefit from a new sense of being full members of the national community" to evolve (Theidon 2003a, 84). However, this cannot come about without taking action to address the historical legacy of discrimination, exclusion, and marginalization that haunts contemporary Peruvian society. If the intended outcome is to educate future generations of their nation's violent past in an attempt to overcome this legacy, then the testimonies archived by Peru's TRC hold immense pedagogical value and potential.

Yet what is the power of probing the relationship among war, citizenship, and territory in this particular case? Read through a geographer's lens, the *Final Report* of the Peruvian TRC is a study in spatial injustice. A spatial perspective throws into relief not only the relationship among geographical isolation, social exclusion, and political marginalization within Peru, but also the convergence of those factors with the spatially selective and intense violence that characterized two decades of internal conflict. As mentioned above, three-quarters of those who died as a consequence of the internal conflict were rural peoples of indigenous or campesino origin concentrated in seven extremely poor Andean departments. In this particular case, applying a spatial lens to the nexus of war, citizenship, and territory produces a "critique of systematic exclusion, domination and oppression; a critique [that should be] aimed at cultivating new sensibilities that animate actions towards injustice embedded in space and spatial dynamics" (Dikeç 2001, 1793). By exposing the spatial dynamics of the injustices inherent in this conflict, it is my hope to foster sensitivity to the spatial dimensions of: (1) the armed violence that characterizes most conflicts as well as (2) the structural violence embedded in those same societies. This may be the broader purpose that this truth commission will serve.

It would seem that Peru is at a critical juncture where there is sufficient will to resist a return to violence, but insufficient will "to manage effective change to right injustice, given the incoherence of local and national [political] institutional structures" (Thorp, Caumartin, and Gray-Molina 2006, 471). If Peru is to pass successfully from an authoritarian to a democratic society, it must address the discrepancies between the formal and substantive rights of citizenship that characterize its society. The distribution of political, economic, and social resources continues to be uneven across space. Social divisions along the lines of race, class, and regional background reinforce these inequities. Peruvian novelist and statesman Mario Vargas Llosa wrote in 1983, after leading a commission to investigate the deaths of eight journalists in a poor Andean community, "Democracy will not be strong in our country while it remains the privilege of one sector and an incomprehensible abstraction for everyone else" (Vargas Llosa 1983, 22). If unaddressed, the racial-geographical rift that emerges from a critical read of the *Final Report* of the Truth and Reconciliation Commission not only undercuts prospects for democratic reform, but also may well portend the return of violence and tragedy.[11]

Notes

1. This study is an outgrowth of my ongoing research into postconflict reconstruction in Peru. That research represents one stage of a larger project on postconflict landscapes in Latin America that will address the reconciliation process in several countries (e.g., Peru, Chile, Argentina, Guatemala, and El Salvador).

2. In using the term "Andean Peru," I refer to both the mountain highlands and the high-altitude jungle that is located on the eastern flank of the Peruvian Andes. The indigenous peoples of both these regions, though ethnically distinct, experienced intense violence during the internal conflict.

3. Despite massive rural-urban migration, Lima is a socially and spatially "divided city."

4. Carole Pateman (1985) argues that citizenship entails duties in addition to rights. This conceptualization of citizenship is especially important in Peru, where the development of rights has not been accompanied by the development of duties (Lynch 1997).

5. Sendero Luminoso adopted a class-based Maoist philosophy that rejected the primacy of politics in favor of the primacy of violence. Its goal was the destruction of authority. It was originally formed by university professors at the University of Huamanga in Ayacucho, a departmental capital in the south-central Andean highlands. Initially, students in the university were mobilized and in turn sent out to mobilize their home communities. Official documents of Sendero Luminoso reject Andean cultural reevaluation as folklore or bourgeois manipulation (DeGregori 1992).

6. This time frame encompassed the three presidential administrations of Fernando Belaúnde (1980–1985), Alan García (1985–1990), and Alberto Fujimori (1990–2000). It is worth noting that in June 2006, former President Alan García was again elected president in a hotly contested election.

7. Some killings remain unattributed due to insufficient or inconclusive evidence.

8. For example, Argentina, Chile, Guatemala, and El Salvador. The Peruvian experience further distinguishes itself in that the overwhelming majority of deaths occurred under democratically elected governments.

9. A "department" is an administrative unit in Peru similar to a "state" in the United States or Mexico. The seven departments referenced here are Ayacucho, Junín, Huánuco, Huancavelica, Apurimac, Puno, and San Martín.

10. Although beyond the scope of this study, it is important to note that the TRC pays special attention in its *Final Report* to gender abuses and violations, including hundreds of cases of sexual violence against Peruvian women and girls. The racial, economic, and regional profiles of the majority of female victims fit that described in the text. In the eyes of human rights organizations, such discriminatory attitudes toward women and girls, coupled with discriminatory attitudes toward those who have limited financial resources and/or are of peasant or ethnic origin, exacerbated the atmosphere of violence in the country for the two decades of armed conflict. Moreover, it continues to affect the ability of thousands of women in Peru to exercise their civil, political, economic, and cultural rights as citizens (Amnesty International 2004, 31). For a discussion of the varying impact of the conflict on some indigenous women, see Hays-Mitchell (2004).

11. Since 2004, numerous protests and demonstrations by various sectors of civil society have taken place in both Lima and the Andean highlands. Some have been violent.

References

Amnesty International. 2004. Peru: The Truth and Reconciliation Commission—first step towards a country free from injustice. http://news.amnesty.org/index/ENGAMR460102004 (accessed March 12, 2007).

Crandall, Joanna. 2004. Truth commissions in Guatemala and Peru: Perpetual impunity and transitional justice compared. *Peace, Conflict and Development* 4:1–19.

DeGregori, Carlos I. 1992. The origins and logic of Shining Path: Two views. In *The Shining Path of Peru*, edited by D. S. Palmer, 413–39. London: Hurst and Company.

Dikeç, Mustafa. 2001. Justice and the spatial imagination. *Environment and Planning A* 33:1785–805.

Goldberg, David T. 2002. *The racial state*. Malden, MA: Blackwell Publishing.

Grewal, Inderpal, and Caren Kaplan. 1994. Introduction: Transnational feminist practices and questions of post-modernity. In *Scattered hegemonies: Postmodernity and transnational feminist practices,* edited by I. Grewal and C. Kaplan. Minneapolis: University of Minnesota Press.

Haraway, Donna. 1991. *Simians, cyborgs, and women: The reinvention of nature*. New York: Routledge.

Hays-Mitchell, Maureen. 2004. Women's struggles for sustainable peace in post-conflict Peru: A feminist analysis of violence and change. In *A companion to feminist geography*, edited by L. Nelson and J. Seager, 590–606. Malden, MA: Blackwell.

Human Rights Watch. 2003. Peru. Human Rights Watch press release, August 12. http://www.hrw.org (accessed March 12, 2007).

Hyndman, Jennifer. 2004. Mind the gap: Bridging feminist and political geography through geopolitics. *Political Geography* 23:307–22.

Isin, Engin F., and Bryan S. Turner, eds. 2002. *Handbook of citizenship studies*. London: Sage.

Laplante, Lisa. 2003. Reparations for justice. *Latinamerica Press*, December 18. http://www.latinamericapress.org (accessed March 12, 2007).

Lozada, Carlos A. 2002. Peru casts light on a dark chapter from its past. *Christian Science Monitor*, October. http://www.ictj.org/en/news/coverage/article/436.html (accessed March 12, 2007).

Lynch, Nicolás. 1997. New citizens and old politics in Peru. *Constellations* 4 (1): 124–40.

Márquez Restrepo, Martha Lucia. 2004. Memoria y consolidación democrática. *Revista Javeriana* (January–February): 16–22.

Marshall, Thomas H. 1973. Citizenship and social class. In *Class, citizenship, and social development*, ed. T. H. Marshall. Westport, CT: Greenwood Press.

Parodi, Carlos A. 2004. Readings of the Final Report of Peru's Truth and Reconciliation Commission. Paper presented to 2004 meeting of the Latin American Studies Association, 1–17. http://www.cholonautas.edu.pe/modulo/upload/lasa-parodi.pdf (accessed March 12, 2007).

Pateman, Carol. 1985. *The problem of political obligation*. Berkeley: University of California Press.

Rankin, Katharine. 2004. *The cultural politics of markets: Economic liberalization and social change in Nepal*. London and Toronto: Pluto and University of Toronto Press.

Shifter, Michael, and Vinay Jawahar. 2004. Reconciliation in Latin America: A fine balance. *Brown Journal of World Affairs* 11 (1): 127–35.

Stepputat, Finn. 2004. Marching for progress: Rituals of citizenship, state, and belonging in a High Andes district. *Bulletin of Latin American Research* 23 (2): 244–59.

Theidon, Kimberly. 2003a. Disarming the subject: Remembering war and imagining in Peru. *Cultural Critique* 54:67–87.

———. 2003b. La micropolítica de la reconcilación: Practicando la justicia en comunidades rurales Ayacuchanas. *Revista Allpanchis*, número especial sobre *Justicia Comunitaria en los Andes* 60:113–42.

Thorp, Rosemary, Caumartin, Corinne, and George Gray-Molina. 2006. Inequality, ethnicity, political mobilisation and political violence in Latin America: The cases of Bolivia, Guatemala and Peru. *Bulletin of Latin America Research* 25 (4): 453–80.

Truth and Reconciliation Commission (TRC). 2003. *Final Report*. Lima: La Comisión de la Verdad y Reconciliación.

Turner, Bryan S., ed. 1993. *Citizenship and social theory*. London: Sage.

Vargas Llosa, Mario. 1983. Inquest in the Andes. *New York Times Magazine*, July 31, 18–23.

World Bank. 2007. Peru at a glance. http://devdata.worldbank.org/AAG/per_aag.pdf (accessed January 22, 2007).

10

Unreliable Chinese
Internal Security and the Devaluation and Expansion of Citizenship in Postwar Hong Kong

ALAN SMART

Introduction

Warfare has often resulted in increases in social welfare programs (Castells 1983; Cowen 2005b; Turner 2004; chapter 1 of this volume). The sacrifices of the working class, whether serving in the armed forces or on the home front, seemed to deserve greater rewards, both in the eyes of the elite and of themselves. But what are the effects on social entitlements when international tension translates into state worries about the dangers of "fifth columns" and subversion from within, as in the Cold War or the contemporary post-9/11 period? Is social welfare likely to be expanded, in order to solidify loyalty among the population? Or are services more likely to be restricted, redirected, or targeted to particular groups in order to expand governmental control over suspected disloyal elements (Cowen 2005a; Rose 2000)? What are the conditions under which different strategies are more likely to be adopted? A full answer to these questions would require a broad comparative study, and is beyond the scope of this chapter. Instead, a case study of Hong Kong in the 1950s will explore how deep suspicions about the reliability of the indigenous population produced conflicting tendencies but ultimately resulted in a dramatic expansion of social welfare programs. The precarious nature of Hong Kong's continued existence as a British colony due to the geopolitics of the early Cold War era had a strong conditioning effect on outcomes, mediated by local responses such as illegal encroachment on unguarded space that generated problems, which challenged the colonial state at its very core: government revenues from land.

Hong Kong was dramatically transformed by the victory of the Chinese Communist Party and the emerging Cold War. Among other reactions, the border with China was closed in 1950 for the first time ever in peace. These conditions resulted in the reconfiguration of citizenship in this British colony. In this chapter, I will concentrate on two linked but inverted processes. First, the citizenship of Chinese residents in Hong Kong was devalued through concerns by the governor and other senior colonial officials about their unreliability. The government was concerned about the internal security situation, and feared that their ultimate loyalty was to China rather than to Hong Kong. Among other things, this resulted in efforts to keep Chinese in the Hong Kong Regiment at less than half the force, and the establishment of an Essential Services Corps composed of "reliable" non-Chinese employees in facilities such as light and power. Paradoxically, this distrust of the Chinese and concern about internal security ultimately resulted in the establishment of a massive Squatter Resettlement Programme that in the 1970s was transformed into a broad-ranging public housing program. By the end of the twentieth century it housed half of Hong Kong's population. The chapter will trace the complex cultural and geopolitical processes that transformed distrust into a dramatic escalation of elements of social citizenship. By the 1970s, public housing was a crucial arena for efforts to enhance Hong Kong residents' attachment and commitment to the colony. Most dimensions of political citizenship followed on these elements of social citizenship only later, and have yet to be achieved, given the continued denial of full democracy (Ho 2004). Ip (2004, 37) suggests that this can be seen as "a 'premature' achievement of socio-economic citizenship, while, in contrast civil rights and political rights in the city were under-developed."

Peter Nyers (2006) has recently discussed the "accidental citizen." Noting that the invention of any technology entails accidents caused by it, Nyers shows how bureaucratic and legal definitions of citizenship create accidents of people who fit the rules but are considered problematic. Concern about such "problematic" citizens has increased since 9/11. For Nyers (2006, 25), the term "accidental" is applied to citizens as a "discursive means to unmake citizenship" and does so by "conferring an unqualified enmity and danger to that which is identified as being accidental." The cases of accidental citizens that he concentrates on, interned Japanese Americans during World War II and American-born "enemy combatants" after 9/11, both pose comparable issues of populations seen as being potentially disloyal or unreliable. As a *Los Angeles Times* editorial expressed this viewpoint,

> A viper is nonetheless a viper wherever the egg is hatched. . . . So, a Japanese American born of Japanese parents . . . notwithstanding his nominal brand of *accidental citizenship* almost inevitably . . . grows up to be a Japanese, and not an American. (Quoted in Nyers 2006, 24)

Chinese in Hong Kong in the early 1950s, particularly those living in squatter settlements, were seen as having a similarly unbreakable link to China. Hong Kong was seen as a place of convenience for them, not a place of commitment, and repressive policies resulted from this colonial worldview. Many officials would have been happy to drive all squatters across the border to China, if it had been remotely "practicable."

I next discuss the nature of citizenship in a colonial state, and how it affects the political and social dimensions in different ways. In the third section, I sketch Hong Kong society and governance in 1950, and the impact of the Cold War on its fragile geopolitical situation. The fourth section describes the distrust of the Hong Kong government for the Chinese subject population, and several programs in which it was expressed. The next section explains how a colonial state subscribing to a laissez-faire ideology ended up resettling squatters and eventually providing housing for half of the population. The consequences of this intervention, particularly the need for the state to become more actively involved in the daily life of the ordinary populace, will be discussed in the fifth section. I will conclude with some consideration of the broader implications of this case study for our knowledge of the relationship between conflict, internal security, and citizenship.

Citizenship and Colonial Urbanism

Citizenship concerns rights and responsibilities of membership in a common national community (Barbalet 1988, 67), although in some contexts such as early reform China local membership is more important for most (Smart and Smart 2001). Distinctions are usefully made between civil, political, and social citizenship. Civil citizenship emphasizes freedoms of expression, association, and belief. Political citizenship emphasizes electoral franchise and participation. Social citizenship refers to entitlements such as universal public education, and other aspects of public welfare which may vary according to individual circumstances such as means-tested health insurance or social assistance. Most broadly, social citizenship concerns the provision of those resources necessary for people to fully partake in the political and economic institutions of the nation. In the influential views of T. H. Marshall (1950), citizenship is a status that is attached to full membership in a community, and the provision of social services may be necessary to facilitate full participation. It is widely assumed that civil citizenship and political citizenship precede social citizenship. While this may reflect the historical experience of Western European nations, the patterns seen in colonies and other authoritarian states diverge considerably. The People's Republic of China, for example, criticizes Western conceptions of human rights as overemphasizing formal rights of freedom of expression and association at the expense of substantive rights to the amelioration of poverty and access to food, shelter, and health care. As a result, citizenship in China has been concentrated more on substantive issues of welfare entitlements than on civil and political citizenship (Smart and Smart 2001).

The situation in colonies varies quite substantially from the Western teleological account. For Ku and Pun (2004, 4), citizenship formation under colonial governance is distinguished by three features:

First, the dependent status of political membership attached to the colonial sovereign rather than to the nation; second, the making of a new urban-civic subject as a civilizing (modernizing), depoliticizing, and denationalizing project; and, third, the limited development of rights and the prioritizing of economic development, with a residual conception of social welfare, over political participation within the colonial state.

While useful, this account neglects the extent to which the treatment and experience of colonized peoples vary over time and space between different kinds of colonies, and internally within specific colonies (Ahluwalia 2001, 69). To a large extent, it was only the European settlers who were seen as having any citizenship rights, at least until quite late in most transitions to independence. Settler colonies were "forged out of the very idea of the elimination of the indigenous population" (Ahluwalia 2001, 65). Moves toward home rule and eventual independence were assumed to apply only to those with the right civilizational backgrounds. Even this changed over time. Engin Isin (1992, 99) has described how practices of citizenship such as town meetings were not allowed to develop in colonial Canada since such practices were "considered to have caused the rebellion of the thirteen colonies."

In colonies without large European settler populations, the indigenous population did not necessarily have any greater rights of citizenship or even residency. British conceptions of indirect rule legitimated a form of governance in which control was achieved without responsibility in areas without substantial European populations. Far from having citizenship rights, they were often not even permitted to reside in areas of strategic importance to the Europeans. The demographic weakness of the Europeans often fostered efforts to keep the native populations in the countryside and in villages or plantations, and to discourage migration to the cities. This was particularly true of the African colonies, where "the towns were for Europeans and the rural areas were for Africans. It followed that no African should be in town except to provide labour as and when required by a European employer" (Collins, quoted in King 1990, 51). The South African system of apartheid was a particularly strict variant of a more common tendency. The rationales for such antiurban policies varied over time and space, but common ideas included the fear of loss of productive labor for mines and plantations, the need for government provision of expensive infrastructure in cities, the idea that cities were places of consumption more than production, and fear that urban living would corrupt migrants (Ross and Telkamp 1985). Another set of worries that legitimated restrictions on urban migration focused on the ways in which non-Europeans would transform the cities, in deleterious and undesirable ways, through dangers to public health, public order, and public safety. In a colonial context, cities brought proximity with many potentially dangerous non-Europeans. Just as in nineteenth-century Europe, cities brought risks that could spread from the disadvantaged to the privileged: epidemic, riot, and fire (de Barros 2003; Der Derian 2003). Fear of such threats has long been a structuring principle for urban planning and interventions (Wekerle and Jackson 2005, 34). Government intervention to ameliorate problems that were not seen as likely to spread to the elite, such as malnutrition, poverty, and unemployment, occurred at a substantially later date. In Hong Kong, for example, before the 1960s, most government services were targeted at the European minority of the population, particularly those who were employed by the colonial government itself. Managing risks that could expand outwards from the nonwhite quarters while maintaining access to necessary labor (domestic servants, laborers, shopkeepers, and clerks) were key challenges for the administrators of the colonial city. Migration restriction was only one way in which administrations attempted to reduce these risks. Whether or not city growth was discouraged, a common way of controlling the dangers posed by non-European residence was through the construction of what Janet Abu-Lughod described as "dual cities," one of the most distinctive features of colonial urbanism.

The largest city in almost all colonies and former colonies was not "a single unified city, but, in fact, two quite different cities, physically juxtaposed but architecturally and socially distinct." These "dual cities have usually been a legacy from the colonial past" (Abu-Lughod 1965, 429). This morphological duality resulted from cultural pluralism combined with concentration of power in the hands of a nonindigenous minority (King 1990, 19). Government services, often state of the art and monumental, were restricted to the European city, while intervention in the "native city" was generally restricted to efforts to control public health and security threats. In Bombay, for example, the ground around the white town was "leveled and cleared of buildings and trees, to create a free field of fire," which became an area for horse riding and other recreation (Home 1996, 66). Although hygiene and sanitation tended to be emphasized in accounts of colonial city planning, internal security was also a common concern. The result was that in many colonial cities, more so than in the nonurban parts of European colonies, some government services, such as public health interventions and fire services, were often provided in advance of any movement toward political rights, although this was done primarily to protect the minority European population.

Hong Kong in 1950

Hong Kong's very survival as a British colony had been in question since the Japanese invasion in 1941. The restoration of British rule was the subject of negotiation at the highest levels among the Allies. Andrew Whitfield (2001, 1) has stated that the most basic "threat to British sovereignty came not from Japan but from her own allies, China and particularly, America." In addition to strong opposition from the Americans to the idea of assisting Britain in the restoration of its empire, President Franklin Roosevelt also found it useful to elevate Chiang Kai-shek's China to one of the "four policemen" of the postwar era. He could count on Chiang's support, preventing Britain and the Soviet Union from outvoting him. Britain's difficult situation in 1942, combined with the United States' anti-imperialist pressure, led to serious consideration within the British government about whether ceding the colony to China "might not be more effective sooner rather than later." The Foreign Office suggested that Hong Kong could be considered to be already a lost cause so that a "gesture of cession would demonstrate to the Americans that the British were not fighting the war for the reactionary purposes of preserving the British Empire" (Louis 1997, 1062). The Colonial Office, with Churchill's support, managed to sidestep these proposals. By 1944 the ineffectiveness of Chiang's military efforts and rising American concern about the Soviet Union resulted in acceptance of the return of Hong Kong to Britain.

Hong Kong had almost no electoral democracy except for the Urban Council, with its carefully restricted franchise and functions. Governance relied on the "administrative absorption of politics" through the appointment of prominent businesspeople, primarily Anglicized Eurasian and Chinese merchants, to various advisory boards including the Legislative and Executive Councils (King 1975). Mark Young, interned in Hong Kong during the war and reinstalled as governor from 1946 to 1947, was concerned to increase identification with Hong Kong after the restoration of colonial rule through limited expansion of political representation. Rather than considering elections to the Legislative Council, he proposed the establishment of a municipal council that would control only the urban area. Two-thirds of its members would be elected in equal numbers by Chinese and non-Chinese literate voters (with longer residency requirements for Chinese). It was intended to take over all urban services, education, social welfare, town planning, and other functions, while leaving critical issues of finance and security in official and appointed hands (Endacott 1964, 185, Miners 1981, 137). His successor, Alexander Grantham, was skeptical about the merit of such reforms. Various studies and discussion continued without conclusion until the Communist victory and the Korean War raised other concerns, or at least provided Grantham with an excuse to shelve any reform, as Steve Tsang (1988) argues. In 1952, Grantham reported to London that the Executive Council had become apprehensive about reforms. The prewar structure was to stay in place with only minimal modifications in the 1970s, such as the establishment of elected District Boards, until the 1990s.

The victory of the Chinese Communist Party and the economic blockade imposed after the beginning of the Korean War also threatened Hong Kong's dominant prewar industry: serving as an entrepôt in trade between China and the West. On July 2, 1955, Governor Grantham wrote to the Secretary of State for the Colonies Alan Lennox-Boyd that since 1950, Hong Kong had been called upon to "cut off, at its own expense, a major part of its own livelihood," and asked how anyone could expect "this dying city" to survive with its "swollen population and with a great part of its normal trade sacrificed for the greater good, should the China embargo continue to handicap Hong Kong's much needed trade expansion in the region?" (quoted in Zhang 2001, 133). The China trade's importance declined steadily until 1979, as manufacturing grew to new strengths. Manufacturing not only grew in relative importance after 1945, but also began to be encouraged by a government that had previously hardly recognized it (Choi 1999, 147). Tak-wing Ngo (1999, 134) argues that the laissez-faire policy was only retrospectively constructed as a framework that supported industrial expansion: previously, it had reflected a policy bias against manufacturing for the benefit of primarily British merchant firms. Goodstadt (2005, 120) emphasizes instead that noninterventionism provided excuses "to intervene as little as possible in economic and social affairs," and this in turn resulted from a "siege mentality" where even the best expatriates were distant from Chinese society, and were beset by "fear of an unruly populace" (126). While financial constraints were often cited by senior officials restricting expenditures on housing and other badly needed infrastructures and social services, the statistics do not support them. By 1950, surplus funds of HK$178 million had been accumulated, while public debt had risen to only HK$65 million with an estimated HK$200 million having been spent on rehabilitation of the colony. Revenue rose from HK$82 million in the first year after the restoration of civil government to HK$274.25 million, with anticipated expenditures of HK$233.5 million in 1950–1951.[1]

In 1950, the Hong Kong government did not believe that most Hong Kong residents felt themselves to be "Hong Kong people" in any significant way. Instead, they saw them as "sojourners" residing temporarily in the colony for reasons of economic advancement or for safety from the frequently dangerous conditions in China. Governor Grantham's 1956 description of the border is illustrative of this perspective:

> The frontier with China runs for about 20 miles across a neck of land dividing the Colony from the mainland. There is no marked geographical feature to form a natural frontier and the country and people on either side come from the same stock and lead the same sort of lives. It has, until some five years ago, been customary ever since the Colony's foundation for persons from the adjoining Chinese Province of Kwangtung to have free access to the Colony without immigration or other restrictions and likewise for Chinese from Hong Kong to have free access to Kwangtung. There was accordingly a constant flow in both directions. When times were bad in South China people would cross into Hong Kong to seek temporary shelter in the Colony, where most would have relatives or connections. When conditions in Kwangtung improved, they would return.[2]

It was initially hoped that this pattern would resume after the Chinese Communist Party moderated its policies, so that provision for the huge influx of refugees would not be necessary. In fact, one argument frequently made against "generous" social expenditures was that it might encourage people to stay or more to enter illegally.

In 1950, then, the British colony of Hong Kong was very reluctant to provide any significant elements of either political or social citizenship. Although certain civil freedoms were needed for the benefit of the economy, there were serious restrictions even on these in the name of security, such as the Societies Ordinance which banned many apparently innocuous groups. Yet by March 1963, there were 462,582 people living in government-constructed Resettlement Estates, plus 73,377 in 14 Cottage Resettlement Areas, with total building costs amounting to HK$177,745,000.[3] This paradox is amplified by officials' deep distrust for the resettled squatters, who were seen as even less deserving and trustworthy than the general Chinese population of Hong Kong. The next section will examine the nature of this distrust and how it interacted with the fragile geopolitical situation of Hong Kong to prompt a variety of government interventions related to fears about the internal security position.

Internal Security and Unreliability

The governor of Hong Kong responded on March 22, 1952, to a query from the secretary of state for the colonies about the defensibility of Hong Kong. Governor Grantham stated,

Any evaluation of Hong Kong's ability to survive made purely on a basis of the premise stated (namely, blockade and air attacks) would be unrealistic for two reasons. (A) In addition to blockade and air bombing, it is clear that a third and most potent weapon would be used against us. I refer to the capacity of the C.P.G. [Communist People's Government] for fomenting internal disturbances whether by strikes, riots or extensive sabotage and terrorism. Ability to survive blockade and air bombing is of no significance if the internal security position cannot be held. (B) Freedom from attack by Chinese ground forces is postulated. This also is of little practical significance since, whether or not the attack actually developed, the threat of attack would remain, and our present resources of manpower are frankly insufficient to cover that threat and the threat to internal security simultaneously. An examination of the position on 1st March when the disturbances occurred in Kowloon leaves no room for doubt on this point. . . . By withdrawal of labour, and the internal disturbances that would certainly ensue, Hong Kong . . . could be made untenable quickly and without much effort on the part of the enemy. This unpalatable fact is, therefore, an essential background to our ability to resist any specialized form of attack . . . and my answers to the questions asked in your second paragraph must be understood to rest on one basic assumption, namely that the internal security position can be held.[4]

What happened on March 1, 1952? According to the *Hong Kong Standard*,

> Thousands of Communist-led students and workers marching along Nathan Road yesterday afternoon attacked police, servicemen and Europeans, overturned and burned vehicles, and smashed property in a roaring riot.... The crowd had gathered at the Kowloon Railway Station at Tsimshatshui around noon in order to await the expected arrival of the Canton 'comfort' mission to the Tung Tau Village fire victims. When the mission failed to arrive, having been denied entry into the Colony, the crowd started its parade, waving banners and shouting slogans. The mood of the paraders grew uglier as they marched, and disturbances broke out.[5]

This riot clearly worried Governor Grantham because of the connection between local resistance and resentments and the ways in which this prompted intervention from Beijing. Such "comfort missions" emerged repeatedly in the following decade. Grantham's concerns about the internal security situation produced a set of initiatives to deal with the threat to internal security.

The riot reinforced broader concerns that Governor Grantham had about both internal security and the risk that Beijing or Guangzhou would use disturbances as an excuse to intervene in Hong Kong affairs. This concern for internal security had been apparent since much earlier. For example, Steve Tsang says that in 1949 Grantham rejected the idea of a municipal council "because it could be infiltrated by the Communists." Drawing on Department of Defence documents, Tsang notes that the Chiefs of Staff Committee in early 1949 assessed the most serious threat to Hong Kong to be an influx of refugees, while an additional threat was

> thought to be Communist-inspired strikes. The Committee was not of the opinion that the Chinese Communists would invade the colony, but it considered that the local security forces would need to be reinforced by a brigade group if they were to be capable of coping with both an influx of refugees and a Communist guerilla attack from across the border. (Tsang 1988, 101, 103)

Mark (2000, 838) found from his study of Foreign Office records that the "likelihood of a direct Communist military attack on Hong Kong worried the British less ... than the internal unrest caused by the influx of refugees and Communist-inspired strikes." David Clayton (1997, 102) claims that the "Colonial Office and the authorities in Hong Kong recognised, and were extremely concerned by, the colony's vulnerability to communist insurrection." Whether or not the fears and distrust were justified, they had their effects on colonial governance, and Leo Goodstadt (2005, 26) concludes that "fear of an unruly populace was prominent in the colonial service culture."

Defense was one of the largest areas of spending in the early 1950s, with total cost of the Hong Kong Regiment (the Reserves), the Home Guard, and the Royal Hong Kong Defence Force in January 1954 totaling HK$2,418,286. It is symptomatic of the concerns about reliability that

> [t]he overall agreed role for the Hong Kong Regiment is two fold: — (a) to support the civil power in maintaining intact the security of the Colony against internal unrest; (b) to support the military in the event of external aggression against the Colony.[6]

In subsequent discussion it was confirmed that the internal security role was primary. In order to serve this role, it was considered essential that the Chinese did not predominate in the regiment, as reflected in the following decisions during the Defence Review:

> That the racial proportions between Europeans (including Portuguese) and Asians (including Indians) be confirmed at a 50:50 ratio until the Royal Hong Kong Defence Force reaches its approved establishment . . . [and] Asians should in future be directed to the Royal Hong Kong Defence Force only as required by the Commandant . . . [and t]hat a review of European manpower at present enrolled in the Essential Services Corps should be undertaken with the aim of ensuring that the strictest economy in holdings of European manpower is observed by that Corps, and of making available to the Special Constabulary and the Royal Hong Kong Defence Force any European manpower that can be released by the Essential Services Corps without endangering services.[7]

The corps was composed of "reliable" non-Chinese employees in facilities such as light and power. They received substantial supplements to their salary and were to be issued pistols to defend their plants in the case of civil disturbances. The Assistant Defence Secretary minuted that the "managers of the two electricity companies count only on the services of their non-Chinese staff in an emergency, and one can only agree with this desire to play safe in two very essential undertakings."[8] In another minute, an official responsible for the program reports that he asked the general manager of one of the power companies how he would view a suggestion that some of his Chinese staff should be

> encouraged to join the Essential Services Wing with a view to trying to secure their loyalty in this manner. Both he and Mr. Duckworth re-acted very strongly against this. They felt that it was likely to have little success in compelling loyalty, and they pointed out in addition that their workers

were foremost in the Union movement in the Colony and they were always looked to for a lead by other unions contemplating a strike. They felt that it would be exceedingly dangerous in these circumstances to try to enlist members of their Chinese staff into the Essential Services Wing.[9]

As late as April 1960, the commissioner of the Emergency Services Corps wrote to the colonial secretary, "It is the policy of the Unit Controller to build his Unit as far as possible into one comprising non-Chinese members hoping thereby to establish a more reliable 'production team.'"[10]

Another key institution established in preparation for internal emergencies was the Chinese (Emergency) Advisory Committee. The decision to establish it was made in late 1949, and its role would be "(a) to keep the Government in the closest possible touch with current Chinese opinion, before and during an emergency, (b) censorship, and (c) propaganda." In addition to government officials, several Chinese members of the Executive Council and other prominent Chinese were appointed to this secret committee.[11]

Other policies that reflect the widespread distrust of the loyalties of the Hong Kong Chinese include the shutting down of schools that had been "infiltrated" by communists[12] and the promulgation of the Societies Ordinance in 1949 to prevent subversion by either CCP or Kuomintang (KMT, the Chinese Nationalist Party) sympathizers.[13] Steve Tsang demonstrates how the ordinance was related to Hong Kong's strategy for survival in the 1950s: while finding itself "vulnerably placed amidst the conflict of the superpowers and unable to afford becoming a flash point, Hong Kong tried to minimize such risks by ignoring the Cold War." It was able to do so because all of the Great Powers preferred to avoid a showdown there. In this context, the "basic threat to the colony's security" arose from the contest between the Communists and the Kuomintang, which could undermine its balancing act. As a result, only a policy of neutrality and suppression of political activity from both sides would preserve Hong Kong's security (Tsang 1997, 317). Thus, the considerable political repression in place (at a time when Hong Kong was seen as a place of freedom on the frontier of communism) could be justified as a necessity for survival.

Squatter settlements were seen as a particular threat to internal security. The McDouall report emphasized that "from a military point of view," the principal objection to the squatter colonies was no longer their harboring of brothels but

> on account of defence problems. Dense new squatter colonies are now astride or uncomfortably close to all the main approaches to Kowloon, and are being forced more and more towards Lyemun. It is of course dangerous to think that squatter colonies in Hong Kong are virtually the same as, or present identical problems to, the scattered and inaccessible hotbeds in Malaya. Nevertheless, even in the unlikely event of its happening in an emergency that 90% of Hong Kong's squatters proved not

only to be peaceable but also to be co-operative with the authorities, the remaining 30,000 could constitute a very real potential threat.[14]

One document provided a long list of ways in which the squatter colonies were a menace to public order. It was asserted that

no single factor in the Colony has so much bearing on the crime situation as the squatter problem. Because of the geographical nature of squatter settlements, the complete lack of planning and the absence of lighting of any kind, no proper police supervision can be exercised and patrol work is almost impossible at night in these areas.

In addition to common crime, "[T]hese areas provide shelter and meeting places for political agents of all kinds."[15]

A meeting took place on June 4, 1951, between military representatives Brigadier Neilson and Wing Commander Marwood-Elton and a variety of government representatives to discuss the Wakefield Report on the squatter problem. One issue of particular concern was its recommendations of sites for approved and tolerated resettlement areas. This appears to have been the key meeting in which decisions were made on which parts of the Wakefield Report would be recommended to the Executive Council and which would be modified. Objections and suggestions offered by the military representatives included that the gridiron system of streets should be avoided in new areas since it "presents serious problems when an area has to be combed by security forces." The commander-in-chief and the commissioner of police stressed the "importance from the security angle of having a record of every family which is moved into 'tolerated' and 'approved' areas." In order to move into an approved area, each squatter would have to establish that he not only has the necessary financial resources but also "is accepted as a law-abiding and useful citizen."[16] The strategy at the time of gradually forcing squatters out of unregulated areas and into regulated areas would be insufficient for these security interests if they did not have adequate control over who would be moved into the new approved areas.

Squatter Resettlement and the Beginnings of Social Citizenship

In a recent book (Smart 2006), I have tried to demonstrate the inadequacy of alternative explanations for the beginnings of the Squatter Resettlement Programme. The first important program to provide any kind of subsidized services for ordinary Chinese residents of Hong Kong, it set the path for public housing provision that expanded continually until recent years. It involves the commitment of substantial resources to what can be considered an important element of social citizenship: basic shelter. In *The Shek Kip Mei Myth* (Smart 2006), I try to reconstruct the Hong Kong colonial mentality and context that made such decisions possible. How were certain choices made while others were dismissed as "impractical," and still others not even considered? I argue that previous explanations of the Hong Kong government's decision to build seven-story Resettlement Estates to resettle squatters fail to answer some basic questions. While they identify sound reasons for the government's desire to eradicate squatter settlements, such desires fail to explain why squatters were *resettled* rather than simply *cleared* from the spaces they were illegally occupying. Resistance is usually underplayed, even if mentioned in passing, and some prominent publications saw squatter apathy as a key element of Hong Kong's housing success.

Vociferous and sometimes violent resistance to clearance without acceptable resettlement arrangements emerges again and again in the files. Concern about the possibility of resistance or violence seems to have had an impact on official thinking about what courses of action were practical. In 2004, I interviewed Denis Bray, a retired Hong Kong government official who was a young assistant secretary in the early 1950s and whose name appears a number of times in files related to the squatter problem. When I asked him why squatters were not simply cleared without worrying about providing resettlement, Mr. Bray replied, "We were frightened. Doing that would be unacceptable. To go into a big area and tell them they would have to go tomorrow, there would be murder." He made it very clear that they were worried about the possibility of riots: "no one in their senses" would try to evict large numbers of squatters without anywhere to go.

While there were concerns about the possibility for violence resulting from widespread clearance without adequate resettlement, it seems to me to be unlikely that this consideration alone could have compelled the Hong Kong government to commit substantial resources to Resettlement Estates. The vulnerable diplomatic situation gave potential violence much more leverage. A statement by Mao Zedong to a British journalist in 1946 is suggestive (although given the context, one cannot place too much weight on it):

> I am not interested in Hong Kong; the Communist Party is not interested in Hong Kong. . . . Perhaps ten, twenty or thirty years hence we may ask for a discussion regarding its return, but my attitude is that so long as your [British] officials do not maltreat Chinese subjects in Hong Kong, and so long as Chinese are not treated as inferiors to others in the matter of taxation and a voice in the Government, I am not interested in Hong Kong, and will certainly not allow it to be a bone of contention between your country and mine. (Louis 1997, 1055)

Although regularly cited as reassurance that Hong Kong would be left alone by a victorious Chinese Communist Party, the caveats about mistreatment of Chinese subjects are usually not accorded much consideration. Given the long history of popular mobilization within China against the evildoing of Western imperialists, this could be simply a rhetorical device. It could also, however, have been a genuine signal that maltreatment of Chinese subjects could provoke intervention in the interests of justice. When I asked Mr. Bray about whether China influenced considerations about the squatter problem, he agreed that deliberately provoking thousands of people would have invited intervention from China. He explained that there was

> a mutual understanding that the communists wouldn't cause too much trouble for us, and we wouldn't cause too much trouble for them. . . . China was prepared to accept the colonial situation. If you were to interfere with any of the tripartite legs [Hong Kong, China, and Britain], it could cause problems. This situation continued right up to 1997.

In support of this view, a memo dated February 18, 1950, from Ernest Bevin, Britain's foreign minister, to the Far Eastern Department argued that "we must do everything we can in Hong Kong to prevent [and] avoid incidents which give additional ammunition to the Chinese communists" (Clayton 1997, 101–2).

The geopolitical situation significantly constrained government efforts to resolve the squatter problem (Smart 2006). Domestic politics in Britain limited the degree of repression that could be endured without embarrassing questions, and did encourage some efforts to deal with the abysmal housing situation in Hong Kong (Faure 2003). But, given the inability of Britain to provide adequate financial support for housing provision on the scale that would be necessary to generate appreciable improvements, moral arguments in the British legislature and press, mediated through the Colonial Office, could not compel heavy expenditure on the part of the Hong Kong government. If clearances of Crown land required heavy repression against protesting squatters, though, British domestic politics could have restrained or punished such actions. A greater limit on the repressive squatter clearance option was the fragile international situation of Hong Kong during the early Cold War period. Hong Kong was held only at the forbearance of China. The United States was prepared to mute its disapproval of British imperialism for the "greater good" of solidarity against the Communist bloc and maintaining "stability" within the British Empire. But Washington was not prepared to give London carte blanche, particularly should the colony provoke intervention in Hong Kong by Beijing. While diplomatic and media criticism and comfort missions were largely posturing rather than precursors to more radical interventions against Hong Kong, violence on the streets resulting from attempts to deal with the squatter problem posed serious diplomatic problems. In addition, Governor Grantham and other colonial authorities, particularly the commissioners of police and commanding officers of the defense forces, saw squatter settlements as serious security concerns. If an invasion, or even a blockade, were to be launched by Beijing, civil disturbances might render Hong Kong ungovernable.

These constraints on clearance without resettlement derive in turn from the possibility that squatters would not accept eviction quietly. In fact, they often did go relatively quietly, particularly when clearances were kept small enough that the power of a crowd to create a confrontation did not come into play. The more basic problem, though, was that even when squatter settlements were cleared without disruption, many or most of the dispossessed attempted to resquat in the same location, unless the site were vigilantly guarded. As long as there was no other viable housing alternative for the displaced squatters, or the attractions of squatting compared to available legal options compensated for the risk of eviction, the squatter problem was like squeezing a balloon: what was displaced would reappear elsewhere. If an adequate supply of affordable housing was not produced, profit opportunities in the squatter housing market invariably undermined squatter control unless considerable resources were devoted to patrolling. This limitation on ending the squatter problem altogether did not necessarily prevent land development for the government's needs; clearance would simply be another cost whenever land was needed for development. Comments from government officials suggest that clearance without adequate resettlement arrangements became particularly problematic as small squatter settlements grew together into vast agglomerations, particularly in New Kowloon. Here another kind of politics comes in, the constitution of legitimacy and illegitimacy. If squatters believed that the colonial government was acting unjustly and illegitimately depriving them of the only homes that they could find, organized protest and violence became more likely. Although the extent of public legitimacy of the colonial government was very low at least until the 1970s, routine injustices were widely accepted. It was when government actions went beyond certain expectations, or when groups were left with no alternatives, that grievances could spark social unrest.

The main limits on the ability of the Hong Kong government to resolve the squatter problem were the sheer scale of the problem, the potential political and diplomatic consequences of clearance without resettlement, and the tendency for squatters to rebuild on-site or elsewhere after demolition of particular settlements. Underlying everything was the government's failure to ensure the provision of adequate quantities of affordable housing. That is where the innovation of the multistory Resettlement Estates was of the utmost importance. Previous resettlement schemes required more land than was made available by clearance. By maximizing the density of residential accommodation on a site, the estates could "get ahead" of the problem, accommodating cleared squatters while eventually making surplus land available for other public purposes or for auction to the private sector. This could be done without excessive public subsidies while keeping the rents much lower than in private tenements or even in squatter settlements.

The desire to eradicate squatter settlements without causing political problems conflicted with the desire to avoid rewarding lawbreakers, or at least to minimize the cost of any resettlement arrangements that might be offered to some of those who were displaced. Development clearances, while frequently contentious, did not challenge the government as fundamentally as did the large squatter fires that broke out every few months in the early 1950s.

Most narratives of the beginnings of public housing accept to some degree what I have described as the "Shek Kip Mei myth" (Smart 2006). The official version, as summarized by Secretary for Housing, Planning and Lands Michael Suen Ming-yueng (2003), is that "we built simple, low-cost shelters to a minimum standard to meet emergency needs resulting from a tragic Christmas night fire in 1953 in Shek Kip Mei." Academic versions differ on the motivations underlying the resettlement of the fire victims and its social and economic consequences, but don't question the basic features of the narrative: squatter resettlement began in response to this massive fire, and the genealogy of the contemporary public housing programs can be traced back to this founding moment. I describe this story as a "myth," not simply because I think that in many important ways it is inadequate or wrong, but also because it has a mythical quality in the more positive sense: a "narrative that effects identification within the community that takes it seriously, endorsing shared interests and confirming the given notion of order" (Coupe 2005, 6). Given the low level of development of public participation and social welfare in colonial Hong Kong, public housing came to be both a key strategy for building a sense of citizenship and commitment by Hong Kong residents, and a symbol for the positive dimensions of the colonial legacy. Both became extremely important after the 1966 and 1967 riots and in the long transition to the return to Chinese sovereignty in 1997, and can be seen clearly in the housing reforms of the 1970s initiated by Governor Murray MacLehose. The Shek Kip Mei story simplifies and intensifies a much more complicated history. It expresses an important truth, but the antagonist that had to be responded to by the colonial culture hero was not a single fire, but a whole series of large squatter fires that plagued Hong Kong throughout the 1950s. The enemy was a hydra rather than a single great serpent.

While certain innovations, particularly direct governmental construction of multistory buildings, are undoubtedly present in the responses to the loss of homes by 58,000 squatters, there had previously been other massive squatter fires, such as the 1950 Kowloon City and 1951 Tung Tau fires that left tens of thousands without shelter. The minimum number of people who lost their homes during the decade to squatter fires totals 190,047. While Shek Kip Mei was larger than any of the other fires, the difference of scale by itself doesn't account for a dramatic shift in government policy.

Government documents indicate that at least the initial response to the Shek Kip Mei disaster was not a sharp break from earlier policies. Previous fires had also prompted significant shifts in government legislation, policies, and practices. Furthermore, it is only subsequent fires, such as the one in Li Cheng Uk in November 1954, that turned a provisional experiment into a permanent program.

Whether academics conclude that the Resettlement Programme that started in response to the great fire on Christmas Eve 1953 should be explained by concern for the welfare of the fire victims or the badly housed population generally, or how it cleared the ground for profitable private development, or because it subsidized labor costs for the manufacturing boom that ensued, the core narrative of immediate response to a great disaster is generally not questioned. Nor is the inevitability of public housing as the only viable solution to the unmet demand for affordable housing doubted: the only issue was when and how the colonial government would step in, and more recently whether or not they should step back out. One result of this is that another foundational myth of Hong Kong, firm adherence to laissez-faire or "positive non-interventionism," is preserved. If there were no viable alternatives to public provision of low-cost housing, then these principles were not compromised by this response to "market failure." As a consequence, the nature of Hong Kong's political economy need not be seriously reconsidered. One powerful myth has helped to preserve another.

The adoption of multistory resettlement is better understood as the eventual result of a learning process punctuated by a continuing series of crises. The 1950 Kowloon City fire showed the potential catastrophes that lurked behind the rapid growth of illegal settlements, but the lessons taken by the chief officer of the fire brigade on the need for greatly enhanced precautions against future fires were not adopted due to considerations of cost and the risk of giving the appearance of legality to squatter structures, resulting in casual neglect of the possible fates of thousands of people. The Tung Tau fire in 1951 made clear the political and diplomatic costs of inadequate arrangements for resettlement for fire victims. Important legal innovations for more effective squatter clearance followed, but the types of resettlement provided could not resolve the fundamental problems due to their inefficient use of scarce land. Even if early resettlement failed to "break the logjam," its techniques continued to be utilized as a component of squatter resettlement for decades afterwards. The Shek Kip Mei fire did not immediately result in the beginning of an ongoing multistory Resettlement Programme, despite its common presentation as having done so. Instead, commitments undertaken by the Executive Council to rehouse all the fire victims and to set the rent at HK$10 a month produced a context in which new architectural models were needed if these commitments were not to demand the provision of housing off the fire site to tens of thousands of victims. How and why they were convinced to make these commitments remain uncertain. There is insufficient evidence to decide whether the text of the commitments was a shrewd device to guarantee the acceptance of innovative programs, or a miscalculation in the heat of the moment. I believe, however, that even before the fire, the old resettlement approach had been recognized as unworkable and that a policy shift in the direction of something like the multistory approach was already underway. Shek Kip Mei provided the perfect excuse and opportunity to change directions. In a context of recurrent crises, diplomatic instability, and ineffective early strategies, a great fire that evoked a heroic response would have probably happened eventually, even if it had been a wet winter in 1953.

Public housing required that the government involve itself in how the tenants lived there, which was the immediate source of many efforts to foster civic duty among estate residents. As Ip Iam-chong emphasizes, the Resettlement Estates "brought about a special kind of citizenship expansion as well as a form of cultural cultivation" (2004, 48). This was the first time that the Hong Kong government became involved so intimately in "regulating the masses directly." The Resettlement Programme "could be seen as a laboratory experiment for running a miniature of a sanitary city. And the 'citizens' were imagined as people following sanitary rules and living under the colonial enlightenment project" (Ip 2004, 48). Again, however, they may have learned as much from their failures as from their successes. Since the October 10, 1956, riots that began in an estate to the 1966 and 1967 disturbances that ushered in a greater governmental emphasis on citizen involvement and communication, the crowded, substandard estates were seen as potential breeding grounds for social disorder, even though still a major improvement from the many problems of the squatter areas. Each intervention spawned expanded government actions in the future, as they struggled with the problems caused by the past efforts.

The invention of the Resettlement Estates created a whole range of new governmental problems that gradually involved the colonial territory of Hong Kong in the everyday life of people in order to fix the problems that the prior interventions had engendered. The causal entrainment of these governance accidents are still unfolding in contemporary Hong Kong, causing many new challenges (Smart and Lee 2003; Smart and Lin 2004).

Conclusions

The case of Hong Kong offers insights into the questions raised in the introduction about the impact of government suspicions about the loyalty and reliability of its own population during periods of international tensions such as the Cold War. The results of Governor Grantham's convictions about the unreliability of Hong Kong Chinese were initially a series of repressive interventions. Civil freedoms were even more restricted than they had been in the prewar period, and the diplomatic vulnerability of Hong Kong to invasion and internal unrest was given as a reason for sidelining the modest political reforms proposed by former Governor Mark Young. The idea that Hong Kong must maintain a careful balancing act between Beijing and Taipei, as well as Washington and London, justified an expansion of surveillance and control measures again both pro-Beijing and pro-Taipei groups and individuals.

Repression had its limits in this context. One crucial challenge facing the colonial government in the early 1950s was illegal occupation of Crown land, a crisis in a land-scarce and densely populated city. The centrality of revenues based on real estate in the government's finances made the situation even more problematic. While the colonial government would have preferred simply displacing these squatters, if possible back across the border to China, this was not seen as a practical solution, due to the likelihood of violence and the possibility of provoking intervention by Beijing on behalf of "oppressed victims of British imperialism." "Comfort missions" repeatedly put the welfare needs of squatter fire victims on the agenda. The repressive option was not capable of resolving the squatter problem.

Clearing squatters required certain kinds of expenditures on rehousing or at least site formation and services for self-built housing. These expenditures did not begin with the response to the destruction of the homes of fifty-eight thousand squatters in the Shek Kip Mei fire on Christmas Eve 1953. Previous resettlement schemes, however, were structured primarily by a desire to minimize expenditures and government involvement. They might have reduced expenditures, but they were less efficient in the use of space than the squatter areas that they replaced. The importance of the response to the Shek Kip Mei fire was that it produced an innovation that delivered high densities without requiring much government spending per household due to the minimal space allocation and amenity provision, below what was legal in the private sector. An expansion of government spending on the Resettlement Estates ultimately was a cost-effective solution to a developmental logjam that the repressive option could not resolve due to the geopolitics of the early Cold War.

This new direction for Hong Kong's government was not primarily intended to provide services for a population that had suffered during World War II and the Chinese Civil War, or for its contributions to the Hong Kong economy. Indeed, the government generally saw squatters as among the least deserving recipients of colonial largesse. It was only the situation that produced this considerable expansion of government activity, which ultimately became the most important element of social service provision. It also led to a chain of events in which the colonial government became ever more heavily involved in the daily life of its subjects.

What are the broader implications of this case study for our knowledge of the relationship between citizenship and internal suspicion in contexts of international conflict? Perhaps the most important point is that when the scope of citizenship expands during these contexts, we cannot assume that this was the preferred strategy for the government. Instead, at least in this case, the first important beginnings of social citizenship resulted from constraints more than from intentions. The repressive strategy used in other contexts, such as control over associations and political activity, was incapable of resolving the squatter problem, so other approaches had to be taken instead. The second point is that a decision to engage in a provisional, experimental response to a particular crisis set in motion a continuing process of expansion that is only now beginning to be reversed. Accidents and contingency create responses, which in turn create new accidents and unintended consequences, requiring further intervention.

Notes

1. Address by Governor Alexander Grantham, *Hong Kong Hansard*, March 7, 1951.
2. Governor Alexander Grantham to Secretary for State Alan Lennox-Boyd, June 25, 1956 CO/030/292. (Public Records Office, London)
3. Memorandum for the Working Party on Housing, 1963, prepared by Resettlement Department, Paper no. WPH 3/63 HKRS 163-3-87, "Grading of Departments and Superscale Salaries: Resettlement Department."
4. "Inward Telegram to the Secretary of State for the Colonies," March 22, 1952, COS37-17669.
5. "Huge Kowloon Parade Turns into Violent Riot; Police Attacked; Tear Gas Used to Disperse Mob," *Hong Kong Standard*, March 2, 1952.
6. Memorandum from Commander, Hong Kong Regiment, April 9, 1951, HKRS 369-1-15, "Defence Force Review."
7. HKRS 369-1-15, "Defence Force Review."
8. Assistant Defence Secretary to Defence Secretary, "Civil Measures for Defence Scheme: Light and Power Emergency Plans," November 24, 1956, HKRS 369-11-5.
9. "Discussion with Hong Kong Electric, II ACS (D) to A5," March 8, 1949, HKRS 369-11-5, "Civil Measures for Defence Scheme: Light and Power Emergency Plans."
10. Commissioner, Essential Services Corps to Colonial Secretary, April 30, 1960, HKRS 369-11-5, "Civil Measures for Defence Scheme: Light and Power Emergency Plans."
11. "Minutes of a Meeting Held in the Secretariat for Chinese Affairs," September 23, 1949, HKRS 42-5-3, "CMDS: Chinese (Emergency) Advisory Committee."
12. "I am getting extremely tired of the phrase 'schools for workers' children'. Those we have had so far have been more than a thorn in the flesh and I cannot see the schools suggested ... being any better. ... Sufficient damage has already been done by the Bishop's committee trying to run five schools for workers' children." Director of Education to Colonial Secretary John Nicoll, June 24, 1950, HKRS 163-1-1153, "Low Cost Housing Scheme—Labour House—Proposal of Trade Union Council For."
13. HKRS 920-1-2, Societies Ordinance. This file includes a compilation of societies denied registration, and it is a fascinating list ranging from a drivers' instructors association to the Hong Kong Chinese Basket-ball Society.
14. J. C. McDouall, "Report on Squatters," November 8, 1950, HKRS 163-1-779, "Squatter Problem in Hong Kong."

15. DCI Johnston, appendix to McDouall "Report," HKRS 163-1-779, "Squatter Problem in Hong Kong."
16. "Minutes of a Meeting Held at the Colonial Secretariat," June 4, 1951, HKRS 163-1-779, "Squatter Problem in Hong Kong."

References

Abu-Lughod, J. 1965. Tale of two cities: The origins of modern Cairo. *Comparative Studies in Society and History* 7 (4): 429–57.

Ahluwalia, P. 2001. When does a settler become a native? Citizenship and identity in a settler society. *Pretexts: literary and cultural studies* 10 (1): 63–73.

Barbalet, J. M. 1988. *Citizenship: Rights, struggle and class inequality.* Minneapolis: University of Minnesota Press.

Castells, M. 1983. *The city and the grassroots.* Berkeley: University of California Press.

Choi, A. H. 1999. State-business relations and industrial restructuring. In *Hong Kong's history*, edited by T. Ngo, 141–61. London: Routledge.

Clayton, D. 1997. *Imperialism revisited: Political and economic relations between Britain and China, 1950–54.* Houndmills, UK: Macmillan.

Coupe, L. 2005. *Kenneth Burke on Myth: An Introduction.* New York: Routledge.

Cowen, D. 2005a. Suburban citizenship? The rise of targeting and the eclipse of social rights in Toronto. *Social and Cultural Geography* 6 (3): 335–56.

———. 2005b. Welfare warriors: Towards a genealogy of the soldier citizen in Canada. *Antipode* 37 (4): 654–78.

de Barros, J. 2003. *Order and place in a colonial city: Patterns of struggle and resistance in Georgetown, British Guiana, 1889–1924.* Montreal: McGill-Queens University Press.

Der Derian, R. L. 2003. Urban space in the French imperial past and the postcolonial present. *Asia Europe Journal* 1 (1): 75–90.

Endacott, G. B. 1964. *Government and people in Hong Kong 1841–1962: A constitutional history.* Hong Kong: Hong Kong University Press.

Faure, D. 2003. *Colonialism and the Hong Kong mentality.* Hong Kong: Hong Kong University Press.

Goodstadt, L. F. 2005. *Uneasy partners: The conflict between public interest and private profit in Hong Kong.* Hong Kong: Hong Kong University Press.

Ho, D. K. 2004. Citizenship as a form of governance: A historical overview. In *Remaking citizenship in Hong Kong: Community, nation and the global city*, edited by A. S. Ku and N. Pun, 19–36. London: Routledge Curzon.

Home, R. K. 1996. *Of planting and planning: The making of British colonial cities.* London: Spon.

Ip, I. 2004. Welfare good or colonial citizenship? A case study of early resettlement housing. In *Remaking citizenship in Hong Kong: Community, nation and the global city*, edited by A. S. Ku and N. Pun, 37–53. London: Routledge Curzon.

Isin, E. 1992. *Cities without citizens: Modernity of the city as a corporation.* Montreal: Black Rose Books.

King, A. D. 1990. *Urbanism, colonialism end the world economy.* London: Routledge.

King, A. Y. C. 1975. Administrative absorption of politics in Hong Kong. *Asian Survey* 15:422–39.

Ku, A. S., and N. Pun. 2004. Introduction: Remaking citizenship in Hong Kong. In *Remaking citizenship in Hong Kong: Community, nation and the global city*, edited by A. S. Ku and N. Pun, 1–15. London: Routledge Curzon.

Louis, R. W. 1997. Hong Kong: The critical phase, 1945–1949. *American Historical Review* 102:1052–84.

Mark, C. 2000. A reward for good behaviour in the cold war: Bargaining over the defence of Hong Kong, 1949–1957. *International History Review* 22 (4): 7837–61.

Marshall, T. H. 1950. *Citizenship and social class and other essays*. Cambridge: Cambridge University Press.

Miners, N. 1981. *The government and politics of Hong Kong*. Hong Kong: Oxford University Press.

Ngo, T. 1999. Industrial history and the artifice of laissez-faire colonialism: Hong Kong's history state and society under colonial rule. In *Hong Kong's history: State and society under colonial rule*, edited by T. Ngo, 119–40. London: Routledge.

Nyers, P. 2006. The accidental citizen: Acts of sovereignty and (un)making citizenship. *Economy and Society* 35 (1): 22–41.

Rose, N. 2000. The death of the social? Re-figuring the territory of government. *Economy and Society* 25:327–56.

Ross, R., and G. J. Telkamp. 1985. Introduction. In *Colonial cities: Essays on urbanism in a colonial context*, edited by R. F. Betts, R. Ross, and G. J. Telkamp, 1–6. Dordrecht: Nijhoff.

Smart, A. 2006. *The Shek Kip Mei myth: Squatters, fires and colonial rule in Hong Kong, 1950–63*. Hong Kong: Hong Kong University Press.

Smart, A., and J. Lee. 2003. Financialization and the role of real estate in Hong Kong's regime of accumulation. *Economic Geography* 79 (2): 153–71.

Smart, A., and G. C. S. Lin. 2004. Border management and growth coalitions in the Hong Kong transborder region. *Identities: Global Studies in Culture and Power* 11 (03): 377–96.

Smart, A., and J. Smart. 2001. Local citizenship: Welfare reform, urban/rural status, and exclusion in China. *Environment and Planning A* 33:1853–69.

Suen, M. M. 2003. Foreword. In *Fifty years of public housing in Hong Kong: A Golden Jubilee review and appraisal*, edited by Y. M. Yeung and Timothy K. Y. Wong, xvii–xviii. Hong Kong: Hong Kong Housing Authority.

Tsang, S. Y. S. 1997. Strategy for survival: The Cold War and Hong Kong's policy towards Kuomintang and Chinese Communist activities in the 1950s. *Journal of Imperial and Commonwealth History* 25 (2): 294–317.

———. 1988. *Democracy shelved: Great Britain, China, and attempts at constitutional reform in Hong Kong 1945–1952*. Hong Kong: Oxford University Press.

Turner, B. S. 2004. Foreword: Making and unmaking citizenship in neo-liberal times. In *Remaking citizenship in Hong Kong: Community, nation and the global city*, edited by A. S. Ku and N. Pun, xiv–xxiii. London: Routledge Curzon.

Wekerle, G. R., and P. S. B. Jackson. 2005. Urbanizing the security agenda: Anti-terrorism, urban sprawl and social movements. *City* 9 (1): 33–49.

Whitfield, A. J. 2001. *Hong Kong, empire and the Anglo-American alliance at war, 1941–45*. Houndmills, UK: Palgrave.

Zhang, S. G. 2001. *Economic Cold War: America's embargo against China and the Sino-Soviet alliance 1949–1963*. Washington, DC: Woodrow Wilson Centre Press.

11

Conflict, Citizenship, and Human Security

Geographies of Protection

JENNIFER HYNDMAN

Can human security be an effective safety net for civilians whose lives are imperiled in places like Kosovo or Darfur? Is it a thinly veiled imperial strategy on the part of industrialized countries that wish to prevent significant human displacement from war zones into their own territory or protect access to valuable resources like oil? Does human security theoretically recalibrate the state-centrism of geopolitical conceptions of security and legal understandings of citizenship? This chapter attempts to outline the architecture of human security, some conditions of its possibility in a state-centric political system, and alternative ways of thinking within and beyond the state. Following a discussion of human security and humanitarian intervention, I introduce the main tenets of "The Responsibility to Protect," a contradictory document recently adopted by the United Nations Security Council. "Responsibility to Protect" aims to reinstantiate the responsibility of states to protect their own in return for sovereignty respected, but also outlines principles for international emergency intervention in the event that states fail to protect their populations. I argue that human security is theoretically an expression of global citizenship based on human rights, but is a conditional strategy of "imperial benevolence" exercised by groupings of industrialized countries on an ad hoc basis. As such, it is more politically fraught than it appears at face value.

"Human security," in the first instance, emerged from a 1994 United Nations Development Program (UNDP) *Human Development Report* in which a broad notion of human well-being was advocated, encompassing economic security, food security, health, and environmental security. As foreign policy, analysts have adopted more restrictive definitions of human security that focus on civilian safety and basic survival (Global Development Research Center 2007). Discussions of human security have thus encompassed two main themes: "freedom from fear" and "freedom from want." In both cases, however, human security outlines basic entitlements that *should* be provided by a national's own government, through citizenship. This chapter is less concerned with the technical content of human security than with its tacit assumptions of scale and state-centrism.

In theory, human security disaggregates the conventional notion of state security to scales finer and coarser than the state. In so doing, human security renders vulnerable groups visible and focuses on smaller political constituencies. Ideally, it reconstitutes the territorial foundation upon which security is based, and identifies ways to assist those who are effaced by dominant geopolitical discourse or harmed by policies in the name of state or global security. Human security aims to create a supranational form of citizenship, applicable to all but especially those whose protection and well-being have been forsaken by their respective governments. It is about transforming the legal discourse of human rights into that of international relations or security discourse.

War is increasingly waged on the bodies of unarmed civilians, and human security has been mounted as one response to civilian suffering. Human security aims to foreground the security of vulnerable groups of people, especially when states cannot or will not protect them. As a global safety net, at least in theory, it points to what might be considered an expression of global citizenship: protection and possible provision to civilians at risk by international or multilateral bodies.

However, the selective application of security provisions aimed at saving civilian lives in the recent past is troubling. For example, the U.S.-led mission into Somalia in December 1992 was a fascinating humanitarian and geopolitical act. Certain Somali clans were experiencing devastating famine, despite plentiful food supplies in other parts of the country. For the first time in its history, the UN Security Council passed a resolution authorizing intervention in a state that was not a threat to another state, but to itself. As a government, what remnants of the Somali state that remained were unable to protect many of its people from starvation, a phenomenon transmitted to televisions everywhere by CNN and others. Before long, however, this "rescue mission" turned sour (Hyndman 2000). Political factions responsible for the famine did not support foreign intervention and refused the script of "grateful beneficiary" tacitly expected by intervening governments and their troops. The abduction and murder of fourteen UN peacekeepers by one Somali faction led to a UN Security Council resolution to bring the perpetrators to justice, and UN forces essentially found themselves fighting a war in a country they were mandated to help. While humanitarian intervention in Somalia ended in failure, it began as a humanitarian mission with largely high hopes, a huge budget, and few obvious ulterior motives (such as securing oil reserves).

Just months after the United States and its allies pulled out of Somalia, one of the greatest mass murders of the twentieth century occurred, with no intervention, in Rwanda during the spring of 1994. A full-scale genocide against the country's Tutsi minority killed between eight-hundred thousand and one million people within one hundred days (Gourevitch 1998). Even with evidence in hand that signaled the killings months before they began, the UN retreated after the killing of Belgian peacekeepers. The preservation of human life and protection of human rights did not register on the radar of the "international community" in Rwanda, just next door to Somalia, despite knowledge of the killings. These highly uneven geographies of humanitarian intervention and protection, the pillars of human security, are the basis of my concern about its potential uses and abuses.

At the time of writing, human security in Darfur, Sudan, is precarious. More than three-hundred thousand people have died and two million have been forced into refugee camps. The Arab-dominated government of Sudan is stoking the violence, letting rebel groups known as the *janjaweed* wage war against a predominantly poor, black population in Western Sudan since 2003. Diplomacy has been tried and has failed. The United States has declared Darfur a genocide, while other states are more reluctant to make the claim (Patrick 2005). Whose responsibility is it to protect these citizen-civilians if the Sudanese state is unwilling to do so? What do human rights mean if they are not enforceable?

In September 2005, the UN Security Council adopted a resolution endorsing the principles of "Responsibility to Protect." In May 2006, a peace agreement on Darfur was signed by the Sudan Liberation Movement and the Government of Sudan, requiring the government to disarm and demobilize the *janjaweed* militia by mid-October 2006. Despite the peace agreement and the presence of African Union peacekeepers to oversee its implementation, civilian deaths continued to mount. This led to UN Resolution 1706 in August, authorizing deployment of UN peacekeepers to Darfur to stop the bloodletting. The Sudanese government refused, arguing,

> In the absence of Sudan's consent to the deployment of UN troops, any volunteering to provide peacekeeping troops to Darfur will be considered as a hostile act, a prelude to an invasion of a member country of the UN. (United Nations 2006)

By November 2006, there was a tentative agreement to allow a hybrid force of African Union soldiers and UN peacekeeping troops to patrol the Darfur region, but no actual measures had been taken by the end of the year. Sacrosanct sovereignty and the protection of human rights battled to a stand-off. After the Rwandan genocide world leaders tried to claim, "We didn't know," but in Darfur, world leaders are witnesses to the blood shed but seem to be arguing, "They won't let us in" (Dallaire 2006).

A parallel phenomenon to the emergence of human security in the mid-1990s was the respatialization of humanitarian protection. Both phenomena correspond to the end of bipolar Cold War politics. The practice of accepting refugees and providing them with material support on the part of competing superpowers fell away during the 1990s, giving way to assistance that helps refugees in their "region of origin," in camps or adjacent states that would accept them. Taken to an extreme, the respatialization of asylum has advocated helping would-be refugees at home, before they leave their countries of origin. Complementary asylum adjudication practices aim to process refugee claims and keep refugees "offshore" until their cases are accepted.

The rise of safe spaces "at home" for civilians-at-risk has ranged from "safe havens" in Northern Iraq (1991) to "preventive zones" in Somalia (1993) to "safe corridors" to Muslim enclaves in Bosnia (1993–1995). The massacre of more than seven thousand Muslim men and boys at Srebrenica in July 1995, however, led to political reflection among donors and those participating in this humanitarian mission in Bosnia. Preventing and containing forced migration by confining it to the war zone do not always work (Hyndman 2003a). International interventions to employ force to protect civilian populations against genocide, war crimes, ethnic cleansing, and crimes against humanity, however, remain a critical political tool of last resort in the absence of other options.

Human security discourse emerged after the Cold War, as did experimentation with safe spaces and new forms of humanitarian intervention and asylum processes. All are expressions of the respatialization of forced migration by states. One can read these moves as efforts on the part of advanced liberal nations to galvanize their now uncontested position as watchdogs of the world's woes and interveners where civilians were at risk. However, the selectivity of interventions in Somalia but not Rwanda, in Bosnia but not Burma, and in Kosovo but not Chechnya attests to a disturbingly disparate geopolitical reality and dangerously uneven geography: the principles of human security are constantly undermined by claims of state sovereignty.[1]

Human Security, Human Rights, and Humanitarianism

> To govern, it is necessary to render visible the space over which government is to be exercised.

Rose (1999, 36)

"Human security" is a foreign policy concept that renders "governable" all world territory. It defines security in terms of human safety and well-being, but necessarily safety delivered through or by states. Human security is part of a discourse of crisis on two counts: first, it is invoked only when states fail to protect their citizens, resulting in some kind of humanitarian emergency; and, second, such emergencies are not confined to the countries or regions in which they occur. They have migration and security implications for neighboring states and those that are the major asylum-seeking destinations for potential refugees. Human security, then, is part of international relations discourse, if a variant on the major theme of state sovereignty, security, and prosperity.

Human security implies a kind of global citizen or subcitizen, who becomes visible only in times of acute crisis when her human rights have been so grossly violated that other states are outraged, not simply when her life is endangered.

The conditions that constitute a threshold for asylum and refugee status, a legal regime that has lost credibility since the Cold War, are no longer enough. Because human security is predicated on the willingness of multilateral organizations or coalitions of advanced liberal states to intervene in less powerful ones, human security is not underwritten by law but by the vagaries of "political will," raising the question of whether "global citizenship" may not have imperial tinges. The distinct concepts of human security, human rights, and humanitarian intervention thus require elaboration.

How does human security differ from human rights? As noted above, human security is part of international relations and geopolitical discourse. Human rights are, by contrast, encoded in United Nations documents, like the Universal Declaration of Human Rights, and in international law. A brief tracing of the antecedents of what I call "UN humanism" is relevant to understanding the emergence of the modern subject of human rights (Hyndman 2000).

UN Humanism

Humanism has a long history as a project that gives human agency and awareness theoretical salience, and serves as a general critique of positivist, structuralist, and Marxist perspectives. Most geographers, among others, eschew the "vulgar" strand of UN humanism broached here, for

> it is now widely accepted that autonomous, neutered and sovereign subject at its core was a fiction, implicated in an ideology of humanism which suppressed the multiple ways in which subjects were constructed in order to promote a white, masculine, bourgeois subject as the norm, from which others were to be seen as departures or deviants. (Gregory 1994, 265)

"UN humanism" might be past its prime as a normative project that seeks to provide human rights to all, but selectively tracing its genealogy elucidates meanings and political weaknesses of human rights discourse in a contemporary context.

In 1948, the Universal Declaration of Human Rights was proclaimed, a declaration in which "universal man" replaced "international man" in a final amendment. René Cassin, who lobbied for this change, argued that "'universal' man is more easily extracted from the complications of history" (Haraway 1989, 198). Cassin did not consider the ramifications of these "complications," namely, the importance of political geographies among nation-states for the subject "universal man." The abstract, "race"-neutral, gender-blind concept of humanity soon encountered its own limitations. In 1950 and 1951, the United Nations Educational, Scientific, and Cultural Organization (UNESCO) published statements on the (scientific) nature of "race" and racial differences. Donna Haraway (1989, 199) spells out the connections between these statements and the construction of "universal man" after the Second World

War: "the authority of the architects of the modern evolutionary syntheses was crucial to the birth of post-W.W.II universal man, biologically certified for equality and rights to full citizenship." Authorized by science, the "birth" of a universal subject was timely. Poised between the victory over fascism and the horror of the Holocaust, the politically significant emergence of the "united family of man" was legitimized by evolutionary biology and physical anthropology. Although differences among ethnic and cultural groups could not be denied, they were considered minor gradations among *populations*, whereas human beings shared a single species status, that of *Homo sapiens*. The rallying point for humanists was that the scientific differences among individuals of the same so-called race were greater than those among different "races," the corollary of which was the birth of UN humanism and a universal rights-bearing subject to whom international law and UN declarations of human rights could apply. Science was used as a key legitimation device in creating "UN humanism" (Hyndman 2000). However flawed this emerging discourse of humanism and the universal rights-bearing subject was, everyone in the world was theoretically a subject of human rights. Human security relies upon UN humanism and its equal, rights-bearing global citizens to authorize its humanitarian interventions when necessary.

Yet, human security is conditional. While it continues to gain ground within the UN Security Council and draws on existing human rights law to gain legitimacy, efforts to protect human security are only mobilized *if* states fail to protect their nationals and *if* the international community, specifically the UN Security Council, decides to intervene. There is nothing inalienable about human security; it is part of geopolitical, not legal, discourse. Human security and human rights are conceptually linked by their *reference* to codified legal minimum standards, but human security is mobilized only selectively, in some humanitarian emergencies where insecurity is rampant but not others.

Without launching into an entire genealogy of human security, one can correlate its emergence with the rise of neoliberal state formation. Human security represents a strategic move to repackage human rights, a post–World War II discourse which, like many welfare-based institutions of that period, have been largely replaced by more market-oriented, "risk" societies (Isin 2004; Sparke 2006). Human security is, in effect, a political practice that aims to reconstitute human rights as part of international relations discourse. The security of civilians is invoked not by law but through ad hoc decisions of international bodies such as the UN Security Council.

The scales at which security is invoked also vary between human rights and human security. Human rights take the individual liberal subject as a rights-bearing being by virtue of being human. Many legal frameworks, such as the International Covenant on Civil and Political Rights (1966), encode human rights as borne by individuals, whereas human security tends to apply to groups of people, notably those denied basic human rights in emergency contexts. Scale is critical in structuring political action (Staeheli 1994), yet it is historically produced and contested (Swyngedouw 2000). Human security aims to trump, if not deconstruct, dominant geopolitical narratives of state sovereignty when a human crisis emerges, so that foreign intervention can be read off as (1) upholding human rights; and (2) a legitimate intervention where the state hosting the crisis cannot or will not protect its nationals.

Humanitarian intervention and humanitarian emergency are also notoriously ill-defined terms. Both refer to circumstances where human life is imperiled. Humanitarian principles, as outlined by the SPHERE Project (n.d.), clearly state that no (civilian) human beings, regardless of which side of the conflict they fall under, or their religion, ethnicity, nationality, gender, or other socioeconomic status, should be denied food, water, shelter, and basic medical treatment. In short, humanitarian principles uphold the right to life. SPHERE attempts to ensure that organizations providing services to civilians in warzones meet these standards, so that food does not become a weapon of war, for example, as it did in Afghanistan under the Taliban. At that time, foreign governments made humanitarian aid to the Taliban to prevent widespread starvation among civilians contingent upon improving its human rights record. Such contingency is not condoned by SPHERE, despite the Taliban's atrocious human rights record. Humanitarian aid to prevent starvation of civilians should not be conditional upon a state's behaviors, however heinous that state's practices may be.

Humanitarian law, on the other hand, is something quite different. Made up of the four Geneva Conventions and two additional protocols, it legally encodes the legal basis of armed conflict. Humanitarian law aims to protect noncombatants from being used or attacked in war, outlines provisions for the humane treatment of prisoners of war, and is highly geographical in that it declares safe spaces that should not be targeted by warring parties (i.e., medical facilities for injured combatants).[2] Humanitarian law makes some provisions for conflicts within nations, but for the most part, it applies to wars between countries, not within a single state. One could argue that human security for civilians affected by violent conflict within the borders of a country fills the void left by humanitarian law within the same territorial jurisdiction.

My point in drawing out these dramatically different definitions of "humanitarian," and with them security, is to underscore the lack of clarity around its use and the potential paradox and territorial lacuna these definitions pose. Humanitarian intervention in Somalia led to an outright conflict between a de facto governing authority and the United Nations, one in which elements of humanitarian law became relevant. The lines between humanitarian intervention and law are fine. The lawless borderlands in which humanitarian intervention operates are much more blurred than the provisions of humanitarian law.

Furthermore, the conditions of possibility for humanitarian intervention can be traced to the gaps and slippage of humanitarian legal discourse in the current context. The ways in which war is waged today are vastly different now than during the early and mid-twentieth century when international humanitarian law was drafted. Most contemporary wars occur *within* the borders of sovereign states, not between countries as they did during the Second World War, after which numerous human rights instruments and humanitarian laws were written. Notions of what constitutes a conflict zone are similarly outdated. The idea that feminized civilians and masculinized military spaces are distinct and separate no longer holds. Civilian homes may be technically out of bounds according to the rules of war, but in practice, they are often targets. Noncombatants are also supposed to be safeguarded from war, and yet civilians comprise the vast majority of casualties in current conflicts. Whereas most casualties at the turn of the nineteenth century occurred among soldiers at the battlefront, civilian deaths and injuries constituted 60 to 80 percent of casualties at the end of the twentieth century (Boutwell and Klare 2000, 52). Other estimates are as high as 90 percent (Weiss 1999). Humanitarian law and intervention sit in uneasy relation to one another.[3]

This idea of human security is not particularly new. It is an alternative articulation of human rights, in one sense, upholding the basic minimum standards that all human beings should expect. Its formulation as human security, however, locates it in a geopolitical discourse rather than a legalistic one. Hannah Arendt (1976) argued in the aftermath of World War II that human rights were largely ineffectual and undesirable because they lacked a guarantor to provide them in meaningful, concrete form. Stateless persons were particularly at risk for having their rights violated precisely because they had no government to safeguard their rights. In a more contemporary context, Geraldine Pratt (2004, 85) explores the limits and possibilities of human rights discourse, noting that any form of the universal is "necessarily exclusionary but paradoxically holds within it the means to be challenged by those who are excluded by it." This paradox is evident in many political struggles, among them those of Filipina caregivers who live in their employers' homes and trade their freedom and mobility for paid work. Pratt maps the ways rights are mobilized in different spaces: at the scale of the body, between the (private) home and (public) Canadian society, in the context of the Canadian state, and on the global commons. Filipina caregivers in Canada have yet to mobilize the language of human security, though they have employed human rights. Could human security be the purview of states despite its claim to safety at other scales? I return to this question when I examine "Responsibility to Protect," a study of if, when, and how human security should be enacted by international actors.

Human security creates the basis for a supranational form of citizenship, applicable to all in theory, especially people whose protection and well-being have been forsaken by their respective governments. Human security is arguably an act of citizenship (Isin 1999), an active effort to protect rights-bearing subjects but only *if* there is political will by other governments to ensure safety. Shifting from the scale of the nation-state to both coarser and finer scales of security, however, human security can in principle offer greater accountability to individuals and/or groups that might be ignored by or at odds with their government, assuming that parties outside the state take an interest in the plight of such citizens. Critics maintain that the notion of human security has been used to justify breaches of state sovereignty by more powerful nations, under the rubric of the "international community," especially in the context of international intervention. Where it provides an alibi for foreign intervention that serves to prevent migration flows, contain instability, or secure access to vital resources, it is simply state security and state-centric geopolitics under another guise.

Security and Scale

Security is as much about people, households, and livelihoods as about state sovereignty or global economy. Feminist geopolitics, for example, illustrates an epistemologically embodied approach from which to analyze visceral conceptions of violence, security, and mobility (Hyndman 2001, 2004). While the state remains a vital subject of interrogation in relation to security, it obscures fear and violence at other scales, beyond its purview. Christine Sylvester (1994) argues that security is a process of contentious struggle by people, not states. Likewise, citizenship is not merely a legacy of the liberal model of rights derived from seventeenth-century political thought that focuses on the rights accorded to individuals as well as the obligations individuals owe society and the state (Kofman 2003). Critics of liberalism question the scale at which rights are borne, that is, that of the individual, and highlight group or communal rights (Isin and Wood 1999) or deconstruct political community as pregiven (Mouffe 1992).

A dramatic illustration of slippage between geographical scale, specifically between state security and the security of persons, can be traced to the potentially contradictory terms enshrined in the 1945 UN Charter (for member states) and the 1948 UN Declaration of Human Rights. While the

> General Assembly shall initiate studies and make recommendations for the purpose of . . . promoting international co-operation in the economic, social, cultural, educational, and health fields, and assisting in the realization of human rights and fundamental freedoms for all without distinction as to race, sex, language, or religion (Article 13 (1b))

its constituent members are states whose sovereignty and security prevail. The UN Charter has mechanisms to ensure the protection and enforcement of peace and international security, but there are few duties or obligations in the charter for the protection of human rights. Instead, these are outlined in the legally nonbinding UN Declaration of Human Rights. UN Secretary-General Kofi Annan has made several statements denigrating state sovereignty when it is used as a veil for committing human rights atrocities.

Interestingly, the former chairman of the Organization for African Unity, Abdelaziz Bouteflika of Algeria, has a different take on the use and abuse of sovereignty:

> we do not deny that the United Nations has the right and the duty to help suffering humanity. But we remain extremely sensitive to any undermining of our sovereignty, not only because sovereignty is our last defense against the rules of an unequal world, but because we are not taking part in the decision-making processes of the Security Council. (Cited in Crossette 1999)

Bouteflika sees sovereignty as a last line of defense for weaker, postcolonial states against the will and ways of the more powerful industrialized states that fly above sovereignty under the rubric of a quasi-imperial "international community." While states remain major actors and members of the UN, the balance between the legitimate power of states and individual human rights appears to be shifting. The shift, however, also marks the will of the influential industrialized nations within the UN that largely support and fund its activities.

Since the early 1990s, the UN Security Council has extended the meaning of what constitutes a threat to international peace and security in the UN Charter, and increased the conditionality of sovereignty. Developing countries have expressed concern about this interpretation as potentially interfering in internal affairs. As mentioned above, sovereignty is seen as a last line of defense against the will of the (largely Western) international community. While the UN remains an organization comprised of member states within a framework of liberal rights and freedoms, it has challenged the abuse of sovereignty in places like Northern Iraq, Bosnia-Herzegovina, Somalia, and East Timor. Sovereignty is qualified, and the abrogation of people's human rights within a given state is no longer a domestic, sovereign matter, at least within a UN context.

Reinterpretation of the charter by the UN Security Council over the past decade has extended the meaning of what constitutes a threat to international peace and security, and in so doing, the UN Security Council has reorganized the geographical scope of what counts as "its business," that is, what should be of concern to UN member states. Where threats to international peace and security were once predicated on attacks by states against other states, they now include threats made by a state against segments of its own population, though UN interventions in this regard have been geographically uneven at best. As discussed above, the UN intervention into Somalia in 1992 was the first in UN history where a country was thought to be a danger to *itself* and no neighboring country was threatened; this unusual intervention made even more noticeable the absence of international intervention during the Rwandan genocide of 1994.

In more recent crises from Kosovo to Darfur, refugees and internally displaced persons have become the fodder of militarized conflict. They are the casualties in struggles over land, resources, national identity, and territory. The issue of state sovereignty versus international responsibility is at the core of "human security" and a recent proposal to formalize supranational protection adopted by the United Nations, called "Responsibility to Protect" (International Commission on Intervention and State Sovereignty [ICISS] 2001; Foreign Affairs Canada 2006).

"The Responsibility to Protect"
[R]uling becomes a 'reflexive' activity: those who would rule must ask themselves who should govern, what is the justification for government, what or who should be governed and how. Hence, 'modern' governmental rationalities, modern ways of exercising rule, inescapably entail a certain investment of thought, however attenuated, and a certain form of reason, however much it may be obscured.

Rose (1999, 7)

"The Responsibility to Protect" is a policy experiment in "exercising rule"; specifically, it outlines the conditions and principles for international intervention where human security is at risk. Initiated by the Government of Canada in 2000 with the support of major foundations, it was endorsed at the UN World Summit in 2005. "Responsibility to Protect" codifies UN members' willingness to take timely and decisive action when national governments fail to take action and more peaceful means of resolving conflict fail. It promises political intervention in relation to humanitarian crises: no more Rwandas, no more Srebrenicas, no more fear.

Yet, "[m]ilitary protection for human protection purposes is an exceptional and extraordinary measure" (ICISS 2001, xii). The Library of Congress headings that follow the ISBN in the front matter of the document denote a distinct *continuation* of modern governmentality:

1. Intervention (international law).
2. Sovereignty.
3. National Security.
4. United Nations. Security Council.
5. Pacific settlement of international disputes. (ICISS 2001, iv)

It foreshadows what follows: that states are the main, if not sole, actors in providing security, and that sovereignty should be respected except in acute crises when all other avenues have been exhausted. States should *prevent* humanitarian crises where possible, and *react and rebuild* where necessary.

The report identifies a "just cause threshold" as large-scale loss of life or ethnic cleansing, actual or apprehended, as the basis for intervention. It underscores the authority of the UN Security Council to authorize such interventions, and subscribes to a diplomatic, perhaps watery political sensibility; one operational principle reads,

> Acceptance of limitations, incrementalism and gradualism in the application of force, the objective being protection of a population, not defeat of a state. (ICISS 2001, viii)

Yet, in Kosovo the UN could not agree on an intervention; in the end, NATO attacked Serbian military installations (and civilian ones), but long after many ethnic Albanian Kosovars had been ethnically cleansed and run out of their homes. The report discusses NATO interventions into nonmember countries as "controversial" (ICISS 2001, 54). The acceptance of half measures in Rwanda, including the posting of but one UN military officer and his assistant to stave off genocide, was part of the problem, not a solution (Dallaire 2003). Wariness about safe cities, like Srebrenica in Bosnia-Herzegovina, is founded. In Srebrenica, the UN Security Council resolution to create safe cities with military presence inside the country rather than nonmilitarized refugee camps outside was flawed when the military presence of Dutch peacekeepers was insufficient to protect people.

The events of 9/11 profoundly transformed the geopolitical context into which the report's findings were released, generating extraordinary anxiety about security at home and less interest in crises elsewhere. Matters of state security (particularly that of the United States), not human security, prevailed at the UN Security Council. It would be four more years before the UN Security Council revisited the proposal and adopted its principles. Following the attacks of September 11, 2001, the UN Security Council reverted to its conventional mandate, one of supporting individual or collective self-defense (Article 51) to protect member countries against threats to their security. Evidence that the Taliban was harboring Osama bin Laden, the mastermind of the attacks, led to two UN Security Council resolutions that instigated military intervention in Afghanistan. The extant human suffering created by the Taliban in that country *before* 9/11 did not constitute an official humanitarian crisis. The invasion of Afghanistan that followed it, however, was scripted as a rescue mission to liberate Afghans, especially women, from conditions of oppression, yet tens of thousands of Afghan civilians were killed (Hyndman 2003b).

The political aftermath of 9/11 produced all kinds of other casualties too. The United States refused most refugee admissions processed abroad and restricted access for asylum seekers at its borders, even though no refugees were responsible for the attacks. Canada and the United States concluded a thirty-point "Smart Border" accord with the goal of increasing cooperation and hence the effectiveness of border security and control measures. The irony that bona fide refugees also flee conflict, terror, and insecurity seemed lost. States have become particularly creative in their interdiction practices abroad and have enhanced these measures in times of crisis (Mountz 2003).

This chapter has come full circle, then, from the quest to provide freedom from fear for civilians in conflict zones *outside* advanced liberal states, also known as "human security," to the quest to provide freedom from fear for civilians *inside* advanced liberal states, namely, the "War on Terror." Yet "government practices of border control do not simply defend the 'inside' from the threats 'outside', but continually produce our sense of the insiders and outsiders in the global political economy" (Amoore and de Goede 2005, 168). Working on this chapter in 2006, five years after the attacks of 9/11, not to mention those in Bali, Madrid, Saudi Arabia, and elsewhere, fear of terrorism has led to the *securitization of fear* (Hyndman forthcoming). Terrorism is another ill-defined term (Denike 2006), but its primary purpose is to instill fear among civilians. Political action, whether humanitarian or antiterrorist, remains the purview of states. Protecting civilians in other countries remains discretionary and ad hoc, rendering global citizenship based on human security elusive. Protecting citizens of advanced liberal states against terrorist threats is, on the other hand, a full-time job. This geographic alterity creates at least two classes of global citizens.

Concluding Thoughts

Can human security be an effective safety net for vulnerable civilians in places like Rwanda, Kosovo, Bosnia, or Somalia in the absence of state protection? Is it a thinly veiled imperial strategy on the part of industrialized countries that wish to prevent significant human displacement from warzones into their own territory or to secure access to oil? Does human security recalibrate the state-centrism of security and citizenship, even if it does not deconstruct them? Can it be and do all of these things?

This chapter has analyzed the antecedents and investments of human security, its utopian theoretical possibilities, and, more cynically, its political probabilities. Human security embodies a set of standards, outlined in "Responsibility to Protect," that ensures basic civilian safety and freedom from fear. To date, it has largely failed for two reasons. First, as part of international relations and geopolitical discourse, it lacks the neutrality of humanitarian principles and the legal accountability—however weak—of international law. To the extent that human security repackages human rights for the liberal subject and provides better security based on this approach, human security retains political potential, especially since 2005 when the UN Security Council adopted a resolution based on its principles. Second, the capricious behaviour of international players in, for example, Afghanistan illustrates how humanitarian efforts to protect the right to life were largely forgotten after 9/11 and rapidly replaced with the imperatives of U.S. state security. Human security is largely a question of state will and geopolitical context.

In his genealogy of freedom, Nikolas Rose is interested in "what authorities of various sorts wanted to happen, in relation to problems defined how, in pursuit of what objectives, through what strategies and techniques" (1999, 20). Rose alludes to the "various international adventures of advanced liberal nations" (1999, 10), of which "human security" might be one and the "War on Terror" another. The political question of when, if at all, such nations should intervene in the affairs of states that abdicate the responsibility to protect is not really answered in "The Responsibility to Protect." Since the UN World Summit in 2005, the question of when and how intervention will proceed can be decided at the UN Security Council, but its structure does not necessarily promise consensus on action to be taken. State sovereignty is reinscribed, and the aberrations and casualties that occur in the absence of state protection are not systematically addressed. The modern state system and its offspring, the modern subject of these anxiety-ridden societies, are not queried (Walters 2004). Conventional understandings of sovereignty and scale are reiterated in "Responsibility to Protect."

In theory, human security provides protection through a more global form of citizenship, which is granted only in the absence of state protection. In practice, the provision of such security, including the right to life, is geographically uneven. Human security is tinged with an imperial benevolence because only those people deigned to be in danger by the world's most powerful states at the UN Security Council will be worthy of discussion. With the demise and restriction of asylum as a political option for those fleeing persecution and violence, human security has become a post–Cold War, post-9/11 rationale for international intervention. What remains to be done, following Foucault's famous dictum, is careful analysis of the "conduct of conduct" of humanitarian intervention. What conditions, atrocities, political stakes, and resources contribute to the naming of a "crisis" and to crisis response?

Giorgio Agamben (1998) argues that conditions of crisis, or states of exception, ultimately become the rule by the extension of their power over the entire population. Following Agamben, Alison Mountz (forthcoming) analyzes the respatialization of sovereign power in which states of exception and geographies of exclusion figure centrally, especially in relation to migrants. The respatialization of humanitarian intervention also corresponds with the state of exception: "a society is portrayed in which various groups mobilize their concerns about risks that are already agreed upon and governments attempt to respond to them by enacting policies that are designed to manage or reduce these risks" (Isin 2004, 218–19). What precipitates the declaration of a crisis remains less clear, though the securitization of fear by states is an obvious starting point.

Notes

1. The political economy of conflict has never been more vivid than in wars that are dependent on the extraction and trade of resources located in or near a region of conflict. The diamond trade in Angola and Sierra Leone, for example, fuels conflict and pays for arms that deepen militarization among warring parties. These economies of conflict are no less vivid in struggles over oil and pipelines in Sudan, Chechnya, and Burma.

2. The Geneva Conventions (GC) are the most widely accepted international law, signed and ratified by 189 countries. The first GC addresses amelioration of the condition of wounded and sick combatants in the field; the second, with the amelioration of wounded and sick shipwrecked at sea; the third GC relates to treatment of prisoners of war; and the fourth relates to the protection of civilians in time of war. Article 3 is common to all four Geneva Conventions, outlining minimum standards in the case of a noninternational armed conflict: persons taking no active part in the hostilities including members of armed forces, who have laid down their arms and those placed *hors de combat*, shall in all circumstances be treated humanely without any discrimination.

   The Geneva Conventions of 1949 and their two additional protocols of 1977 cover two kinds of conflicts, international—between warring states—and internal armed conflict, specifically the situation in which people rise up against colonialism to exercise self-determination. Self-determination in a noncolonial context, however, is not recognized, an important consideration given that most armed conflict today is internal and noncolonial. International law is binding only on entities that are subject to it, that is, chiefly states.

3. An expert consultation organized by the Office for the Coordination of Humanitarian Affairs (OCHA) and the Harvard Center for Population and Development Studies in February 1999 highlighted this uneasy relationship. A familiar debate between advocates of humanitarian law versus those of humanitarian operations authorized by the UN Security Council resolutions ensued. This tension *between* legal and political approaches to complex emergencies had the effect of foreclosing debate around these seemingly mutually exclusive options. From the outset, the experts agreed upon the geographical and historical contingency of protection: "The concept of protection was recognized to be sensitive to elements of place (*i.e.*, terrain, climate, geographic location) size (*i.e.*, population, spatial area), time (*i.e.*, duration, stage of conflict) and overlapping regulatory regimes" (OCHA 1999, 5). Yet little if any genuine analysis of the local political context was discussed.

   Margaret Denike (2006) has illustrated the connections between war and law, arguing that conflict is often an exercise of sovereignty that reproduces state legitimacy. Denike builds on the idea that "war is the father of law" (Douzinas 2002, 24) and that the two are co-constituted in political discourse. Similarly, Denike probes the meaning of military humanitarianism, challenging the idea that militarized interventions to protect civilians are oxymoronic.

References

Agamben, Giorgio. 1998. *Homo sacer: Sovereign power and bare life*, trans. D. Heller-Roazen Stanford, CA: Stanford University Press.

Amoore, Louise, and Marieke De Goede. 2005. Governance, risk and dataveillance in the war on terror. *Crime, Law and Social Change* 43:149–73.

Arendt, Hannah. 1976. Decline of the nation-state: End of the rights of man. In her *The origins of totalitarianism*, 267–302. San Diego, CA: Harcourt.

Barthes, Roland. 1973. *Mythologies*. London: Paladin.

Boutwell, James, and Michael T. Klare. 2000. A scourge of small arms. *Scientific American*, June, 47–55.

Crossette, B. 1999. "Dictators face the Pinochet Syndrome," *New York Times*, August 22.

Crossette, Barbara. 1999. "U.N. chief issues a call to speed interventions and halt civil wars," *New York Times*, September 21.

Dallaire, Romeo. 2003. *Shake hands with the devil: The failure of humanity in Rwanda*. Toronto: Random House Canada.

———. 2006. History will judge Canada, not Sudan, on the fate of Darfur. *Globe and Mail*, September 14.

Denike, Margaret. 2006. Sovereignty's vengeance: Victims, villains and saviours in the "War on Terror." Presentation to the Feminism and War Conference, Syracuse University, NY, October 19–21.

Douzinas, Costas. 2002. Postmodern just wars: Kosovo, Afghanistan and the New World Order. In *Law after Ground Zero*, edited by John Strawson, 20–36. London: Glasshouse Press.

Foreign Affairs Canada. 2006. The responsibility to protect. http://www.dfait-maeci.gc.ca/foreign_policy/un_reform_en.asp (accessed April 29, 2006).

Global Development Research Center. 2007. Comparison of human security definitions. http://gdrc.org/sustdev/husec/comparisons.pdf (accessed April 14, 2007).

Gourevitch, Philip. 1998. *We wish to inform you that tomorrow we will be killed with our families: Stories from Rwanda*. New York: Farrar, Straus & Giroux.

Gregory, Derek. 1994. Humanistic geography. In *The dictionary of human geography*, 3rd. ed., edited by R. J. Johnston, D. Gregory, and D. M. Smith, 263–66. Oxford: Blackwell.

Haraway, Donna. 1989. Remodeling the human way of life. In her *Primate visions*, 186–206. New York: Routledge.

Hyndman, Jennifer. 2000. *Managing displacement: Refugees and the politics of humanitarianism*. Minneapolis: Minnesota University Press.

———. 2001. Towards a feminist geopolitics. *The Canadian Geographer* 45:210–22.

———. 2003a. Preventive, palliative, or punitive? Safe spaces in Bosnia-Herzegovina, Somalia, and Sri Lanka. *Journal of Refugee Studies* 14:167–85.

———. 2003b. Beyond either/or: A feminist analysis of September 11th. *ACME: An international e-journal of critical geographies* 2:1–13.

———. 2004. Mind the gap: Bridging feminist and political geography through geopolitics. *Political Geography* 23:307–22.

———. Forthcoming. The securitization of fear in post-tsunami Sri Lanka. *Annals of the Association of American Geographers* 97 (2): 361–72.

International Commission on Intervention and State Sovereignty (ICISS). 2001. *The responsibility to protect*. Ottawa: International Development Research Centre.

Isin, Engin F. 1999. *Being political*. Minneapolis: University of Minnesota Press.

———. 2004. The neurotic citizen. *Citizenship Studies* 8 (3): 217–35.

Isin, E. F., and Patricia K. Wood. 1999. *Citizenship and identity*. London: Sage.

Kofman, Eleonore. 2003. Rights and citizenship. In *A companion to political geography*, edited by J. Agnew, K. Mitchell, and G. Toal, 393–407. Oxford: Blackwell.

Mouffe, Chantal. 1992. Feminism, citizenship, and radical democratic politics. In *Feminists theorize the political*, edited by Judith Butler and Joan Scott, 369–84. New York: Routledge.

Mountz, Alison. 2003. Human smuggling, the transnational imaginary and everyday geographies of the nation-state. *Antipode* 35:622–44.

———. Forthcoming. *Encountering the state: Transnational sovereignties of migration.* Ithaca, NY: Cornell University Press.

Office for the Coordination of Humanitarian Affairs (OCHA). 1992. Report on the Inter-agency Expert Consultation on Protected Areas, rapporteur F. Johns, April 7. Cambridge, MA: Harvard University.

Patrick, Erin. 2005. Intent to destroy: The genocidal impact of forced migration in Darfur, Sudan. *Journal of Refugee Studies* 18:410–29.

Pratt, Geraldine. 2004. *Working feminism*. Philadelphia: Temple University Press.

Rose, Nikolas. 1999. *Powers of freedom: Reframing political thought.* Cambridge: Cambridge University Press.

Sparke, Matthew. 2006. A neoliberal nexus: Economy, security and the biopolitics of citizenship on the border. *Political Geography* 25:151–80.

SPHERE Project. N.d. Humanitarian Charter and minimum standards in disaster response. http://www.sphereproject.org (accessed February 26, 2006).

Staeheli, Lynn. 1994. Empowering political struggle: spaces and scales of resistance. *Political Geography* 13:387–91.

Swyngedouw, Erik. 2000. Authoritarian governance, power, and the politics of rescaling. *Environment and Planning D: Society and Space* 18:63–76.

Sylvester, Christine. 1994. *Feminist theory and international relations in a postmodern era.* Cambridge: Cambridge University Press.

United Nations. 2006. UN slams warning from Sudan: Khartoum says any contribution of troops to Darfur force will be seen as "hostile act." *Globe and Mail*, October 6.

Walters, William. 2004. Secure borders, safe haven, domopolitics. *Citizenship Studies* 8 (3): 237–60.

Weiss, Thomas. 1999. *Military civilian interaction: Intervening in humanitarian crises.* Lanham, MD: Rowman & Littlefield.

Part III
Citizens and the Body Politic

12
Citizenship in the "Homeland"
Families at War

DEBORAH COWEN AND EMILY GILBERT

INTRODUCTION

On September 20, 2001, George W. Bush announced the creation of the Office of Homeland Security, invoking intimate longings for a secure and familial polity in response to the trauma of 9/11. When criticized for not thanking Canada for crisis support in this speech, Bush responded, "I didn't necessarily think it was important to praise a brother; after all, we're talking about family." Colin Powell, writing about U.S. foreign policy and multilateral relations, affirmed that the world need not become multipolar "because there need be no poles among a family of nations that shares basic values" (Powell 2004). Familial metaphors of nationhood have a long history, and the United States is certainly not the first to invoke the image of homeland. But historically, a familial imaginary has not been a prominent feature of U.S. nationalist discourse. Yet this framing has found meaning in the crisis of the contemporary War on Terror. Moreover, just as metaphors of family are more frequently being deployed in U.S. political discourse, public policy is also increasingly geared toward "marriage promotion" and "safe and stable families" and away from any form of social and sexual alternative. Since the initiation of the "War on Terror," the private family stands at the center of U.S. domestic and foreign policy, with the "failure" of the family understood as a cause of suffering, misery, disease, and even terrorism, particularly in racialized communities across the nation and around the world.

It is this wartime "familialization" of political discourse and policy, and the shifting contours of citizenship and national political space, that is the focus of this chapter. We begin by outlining how a normative nuclear family has become a central focus of U.S. politics in recent decades, with increasing intensity since the War on Terror. We then examine the familial metaphor of "homeland" that has gained currency in the context of this war. We consider how "homeland" provides a provocative counterpoint to the "monstrous" construction of the nation-state more typical of neoliberal antagonism toward central government in the early 1990s (Rose and Miller 1992). We investigate how a familial imaginary has helped constitute an expanded "paternal" U.S. state, while also serving to naturalize hierarchal relations between states. We ask how metaphors of families and homelands may fix particular spaces and spatial relations (cf. Kaplan 2003). How does this familial discourse render some people familiar and intimate, while others are made foreign, perverse, and even disposable? We suggest that the family is emerging (again?) as an increasingly important sovereign political "body." Contemporary U.S. politics, we argue, demonstrates not simply an inclination to govern *through* the family, but also a reinstatement of the family as a *model for* government. The spatial fixing of the familial makes possible the management of pain for globally privileged forms of injury but fuels the infliction of tremendous violence and suffering at "home" and abroad.

Fighting for Family

The catastrophic events of September 11, 2001, have been interpreted and commemorated largely through the lens of emotional trauma. The scale of feeling—of shock, pain, and loss associated with these events—constituted a stark rupture to everyday life in New York City and across the nation. "Fortress America" (MacNamara 1968) no longer seemed secure. Trauma has lingered and become normalized in political culture. The repeated commemoration of trauma and loss through "9/11 anniversaries" has encouraged *emotional* political response.[1] Self-help support groups dedicated to healing the traumatized American spirit, and self-help books with the same mission, are now plentiful. Health and medical researchers have studied "post-9/11 traumatic stress disorder" and have detailed its social and medical contours. Post-9/11 trauma, the experts assert, affects some social subjects more than others. Epidemiologists now argue that women were most severely impacted by "feelings of powerlessness and victimization on a massive scale in this one apocalyptic moment" that compounded their "daily experiences of interpersonal victimization" (Richman et al. 2004). In other words, the acute trauma of 9/11 combines with everyday sexual and social harassment to make women extra-traumatized subjects. Public health researchers have also identified children as particularly subject to lasting trauma, with large numbers in New York City experiencing anxiety about leaving their homes a year after the attacks (Citizens Committee for Children 2002). Studies have also indicated that babies born to women who were pregnant and present in New York at the time of crisis evince physiological traits of post-traumatic stress, hence directly inscribing trauma onto the bodies of future Americans (Yehuda et al. 2005).

If the trauma suffered by the United States since 9/11 has been read onto the bodies of women, children, and the unborn, it is also the family that has been mobilized to cope with that trauma, and to strengthen the domestic response to the War on Terror. In particular, the terrorist attacks have been interpreted as a loss to families, with the grief of the nation and of families conflated at official commemorative events. For example, the National Day of Mourning on September 14, 2001, saw the president assemble multicultural and multi-faith nuclear families to commemorate the national loss, and it was family members who were asked to read the names of the dead. Trauma has been "rescaled" as a national event (Smith 2001), but is made interchangeable with familial grief.

A familialization of politics has been underway for some time and is not simply a feature of the contemporary War on Terror. For three decades, neo-liberal political projects have worked to reconfigure the relationship between state and market. Proponents of neoliberalism have described the postwar state in terms of "too much" government, and argue that public provision is inefficient and responsible for cultivating a "culture of dependency" (cf. Friedman 1962). The market, understood as the space of individual freedom, has been consistently expanded, as has the responsibility of individuals and families (Rose 2002). The family has assumed more and more of the responsibilities formerly assigned to the welfare state. Indeed, Brenda Cossman (2002a, 484) argues that neoliberalism introduces forms of citizenship that recode "the sphere of the familial" and naturalize the family as a site for social reproduction. In a context where poverty is understood as dependency and dependency is conceptualized as a moral failing, drawing "excluded" citizens into the "virtuous community" through moral reformation of the family furthermore becomes a central neoliberal strategy (Rose 1999, 266).

In the United States, efforts to put the "traditional" family at the center of political life received a tremendous boost three decades ago with the merging of the political right and the evangelical Christian movement (Somerville 1992, 97). The family became a touchstone issue in the election of Ronald Reagan, who implemented dramatic changes to social welfare and public policy. Cuts to public expenditures were severe and sustained, with the very notable exception of defense spending, which skyrocketed. The restructuring of U.S. welfare was fundamentally racialized as well as gendered. Reagan's "welfare queen," the poor African American single mother who he accused of "defrauding the system" with her "80 names, 30 addresses, 12 Social Security cards," became the central trope of the failure of state welfare (Hill Collins 1990). Policy restructuring would aim to put these supposedly lazy, single mothers back into the nuclear family, as well as "back" to work. The pro-family 1988 Family Support Act also served as the first federal mandatory workfare policy.[2] At a public inauguration of the legislation, Ronald Reagan asserted that the act would "lead to lasting emancipation from welfare dependency" by returning responsibilities appropriated by the state to parents. He continued,

> The Family Support Act says to welfare parents, "we expect of you what we expect of ourselves and our own loved ones: that you will do your

share in taking responsibility for your life and for the lives of the children you bring into this world." (Reagan 1988)

This familialization of policy continued right through Bill Clinton's presidency with the passing of the Federal Defense of Marriage Act, which reinforced the federal legal definition of marriage as the union of a man and a woman. The deeply racialized Personal Responsibility and Work Opportunity Act also became law. This brought an end to six decades of federally guaranteed Aid to Families with Dependent Children (AFDC), commonly known as welfare. In its place, Temporary Assistance for Needy Families (TANF) was enacted. With this legislation, Congress asserted that the nuclear family is the foundation of a successful society and, as such, should be actively promoted by the federal government. Explosive debates continued among mostly white politicians on the figure of the African American "welfare queen," who was accused of deliberate dependency and of using welfare to fund drug addiction and promiscuity. These racist and misogynist accounts of poverty have a long history in the United States. They were most powerfully accounted for in Daniel Patrick Moynihan's 1965 report "The Negro Family," which argued that the failure of the black family caused welfare rates to rise. Moynihan, a sociologist, politician, and assistant secretary of the U.S. Department of Labor under Lyndon Johnson, blamed African American men, who he understood to be scarred from a legacy of emasculating slavery, for failing to assert patriarchal power over African American women. The burden of rising dependency was thus a failure of the family and, more precisely, a classed and racialized "failure" to perform patriarchal gender roles.

The promotion of the family in public policy has been particularly intense since the election of George W. Bush, and especially following 9/11. In this time, an earlier program entitled Safe and Stable Families was elevated to the status of an act, Marriage Protection Week was declared in 2003, and in 2004 administration officials announced plans to introduce a $240 million initiative to promote healthy marriages through "research" and the dubious sounding "demonstration projects, and technical assistance" (Pear and Kirkpatrick 2004). Marriage promotion has also become a key poverty alleviation strategy. As an extension of TANF, the Administration for Children and Families (ACF) Healthy Marriage Initiative was created, with targeted initiatives like the African American Healthy Marriage Initiative. Echoing Moynihan's report, ACF has declared a crisis of the black family. Boosting the rate of marriage among African Americans, the ACF promises, will decrease poverty, crime, child and sexual abuse, and unemployment, while also raising the education levels of children, thereby raising their prospects for success and indeed improving communities and the nation as a whole (U.S. Department of Health and Human Services n.d.).

Bush has furthermore made aid to groups that support "traditional" family values a federal priority. As one of his first acts as president, Bush instituted policy that prohibits U.S. family planning assistance to foreign NGOs that "use money from any other source to perform abortion counseling or lobby to make abortion legal" (Fritz 2006). In the fights against AIDS, nearly one-quarter of Bush's $15 billion investment has been funneled into religious groups, including one run by the son of evangelist Billy Graham, and another by a Christian hunger relief agency (Beamish 2006). Dr. Abeja Apunyo, the Ugandan representative of Pathfinder International, a reproductive health NGO, has been quoted as saying that Bush's "abstinence before marriage" strategy is "putting a lot of pressure on girls to get married earlier" (Beamish 2006). In fact, Bush created legislation that mandates that a third of U.S. funds for sexually transmitted disease prevention be reserved for abstinence programs (Fritz 2006).

Family form is increasingly the explicit subject of domestic policy debate. Debates over same-sex marriage have been explosive in recent years, not only polarizing the electorate but also giving rise to creative forms of political activism. It would not be an exaggeration to suggest that same-sex marriage has become one of the most divisive issues in U.S. politics. A recent move by the Bush administration to support a motion introduced by Iran that would ban gay and lesbian rights groups from observer status at the UN raises pressing questions about the changing status of "enemies" at home and abroad.

In fact, the problem of the family and the problem of terrorism have been understood as deeply entwined, with U.S. experts increasingly arguing that terrorism can be understood through the lens of the "failed family." "Terrorist psychology," with its concern for the childhood development and familial relations in fundamentalist Muslim communities, has become a flourishing field of study. As Jasbir Puar (2006, 73) has recently argued, proponents of "terrorist psychology" argue that "terrorists are created by 'inadequate or absent mothering' that has resulted in depression, hypochondria, dysphoria, and destructiveness." But more insidious, according to Puar, is the fact that social researchers, including some leading feminist scholars, are producing gendered analyses of terrorism that support an Orientalist, middle-class, and nuclear conception of normative familial and gender relations (Puar 2006, 75).

Notwithstanding this important critique, feminist scholarship offers a long-standing and powerful analysis of the family as a political institution that is directly helpful to the question of the wartime familialization of citizenship. While deeply heterogeneous, common to much feminist work on the family is a critique of the constitution of "separate spheres." In advanced capitalist Western nations, the family operates as something of a "supplement"—a necessary but excluded element of the public sphere that is *made* private and governed differently. In this literature the family is alternately a key site of women's subordination, where social reproduction is organized as private and women's work is unpaid (Dalla Costa and James 1972; Luxton 1980; Armstrong and Armstrong 1994); the central institution of the private sphere where (feminized) qualities of intimacy and emotion are located and "enclosed" in contrast to the (masculine) rational and objective public sphere (Gordon 1990; Fraser 1993; Pateman 1992; Bock 1992; Lister 1997); and a heteronormative institution that serves to reproduce the population biologically, and normative sexualities ideologically (Yuval-Davis and Anthias 1989; Valentine 1993; Cooper 1995; Ross 1998; Berlant 1997).

However, in the context of our analysis of the current familialization of politics, two key questions remain unanswered. Cossman (2002b) writes of a privatization of citizenship with the family as a central social institution that facilitates the expansion of the private realm. In particular, the growing "space" of the family in citizenship facilitates the privatization of responsibility for social reproduction. This insight, astute as it is, does not question what it means that the family is increasingly becoming a *model and metaphor* for political relations. The familialization of politics is indeed a constitutive element of the privatization of citizenship over the past few decades, as several scholars suggest. However, when the question shifts from the refigured role of the *family within politics and policy*, to one of the *family as a model for political relations* (which includes the prior question but extends beyond it), then historical questions of a different order emerge. For example, what can be said about the history of the family as a metaphor for political geographic relations? Out of what kinds of material worlds has the familial imaginary emerged, and what kinds of relations has it helped constitute? What kinds of geographies does the emergent familial imaginary produce with its "homelands" and "families of nations"?

War, Homeland, Family

The trope of "homeland" has worked to reformulate a familial imaginary since its official deployment in 2001. The Office of Homeland Security (OHS), created as part of the largest restructuring of U.S. federal government agencies in fifty years, is the institutional hub through which the mass security investment of the War on Terror has been channeled. The term evokes, as Amy Kaplan (2003, 84) observes, strong nationalist sentiments that root place and national identity "deeply" in a past that extends back through immemorial time (see also Pease 2003). Homeland "conveys a sense of native origins, of birthplace and birthright. It appeals to common bloodlines, ancient ancestry, and notions of racial and ethnic homogeneity" (Kaplan 2003, 86). But it is also understood through a sense of "loss, longing, and nostalgia," in that the homeland is an elusive "home" to which a people or ethnic group aspires and desires (Kaplan 2003, 89). The sense of loss and longing was made explicit in President Bush's influential speech of September 20, 2001, when he referred to the terrorist attacks as a "wound to our country." It was a description that appealed to an idea of the United States as Virgin Land, previously unviolated by foreign powers, laced through with an expectation of the recovery of innocence (Pease 2003, 3).[3]

"Homeland" thus evokes a strong nationalist narrative that speaks to a particular and powerful reproduction and reinvention of the nation (Gellner 1983; Hobsbawm and Ranger 1983; Anderson 1991). This singular narrative, however, belies the many heterotopic discourses of and relationships to nation that abound and the ideological and material struggles at work (cf. Chatterjee 1993; Bhabha 1990). Nonetheless, the idea of homeland reinscribes the nation-state as the apotheosis and most legitimate form of political organization, and affirms affective attachments to the nation-state through its familial reference. The appeal to heightened forms of nationalism with ethnonationalist dimensions in the context of war is not unusual. These appeals frequently cast the nation as a family unit—a bloodline—and posit religious, linguistic, ethnic, or "race" differences as a threat to the purity and so to the survival of the national family (Yuval-Davis 1997; Yuval-Davis and Anthias 1989; Mayer 2000; Elden 2002). However, this kind of national imaginary is striking in the United States, where there is little precedent for this mythology (but see Bartlett 2001). At his inaugural address on January 20, 2001, President George W. Bush pronounced a quite different nationalist narrative:

> America has never been united by blood or birth or soil. We are bound by ideals that move us beyond our backgrounds, lift us above our interests and teach us what it means to be citizens. Every child must be taught these principles. Every citizen must uphold them. And every immigrant, by embracing these ideals, makes our country more, not less, American.[4]

This speech resonates with Kaplan's assertion that most common U.S. national myths have revolved around ideas of progress, pluralism, tolerance, and freedom, all woven through with a notion of futurity (Kaplan 2003, 86). It is against this context of "metaphors of spatial mobility" that the recidivist and nativist associations of homeland, and its "spatial fixedness and rootedness," must be understood (Kaplan 2003, 86).

Familial metaphors have been deployed not only to define domestic institutions, but also to make international relations understandable in new ways. The Canada-U.S. relationship has been especially scripted as familial, particularly in response to crisis. When President Bush visited Canada in December 2004, his first official visit since becoming president, he asserted that "our two peoples are one family, and always will be." Canada's then Prime Minister Jean Chrétien evoked similar sentiments. At a memorial service on Parliament Hill on September 14, 2001, Chrétien remarked that Americans are "a people who, as a result of the atrocity committed against the United States on September 11, 2001, feel not only like neighbours but like family" (cited in

Roach 2003, 5). These comments were explicitly picked up in a speech by Paul Cellucci, American ambassador to Canada, some two years later. Responding to the tensions that had escalated when Canada decided not to participate in the War on Iraq, Cellucci remarked,

> There is no security threat to Canada that the United States would not be ready, willing and able to help with. There would be no debate. There would be no hesitation. We would be there for Canada, part of our family. That is why so many in the United States are disappointed and upset that Canada is not fully supporting us now. (Cellucci 2003)

What stands out in these examples are not simply the ways that the Canada-U.S. relationship take on connotations of familial relations, but also that in each instance the allusions were uttered in response to a perceived crisis, whether specifically that of 9/11, or the border crises such as those around beef and softwood lumber, or the disagreements over invading Iraq. The references to family have served as an appeal to affinities outside the arena of formal politics to achieve U.S. and Canadian goals. At the same time, familial metaphors serve to circumvent political debate by naturalizing unequal relations. For example, when Bush backpedaled for not thanking his Canadian "brother," he also suggested that "those who try to play politics with my words and drive wedges between Canada and me [should] understand, at this time, when nations are under attack, now is not the time for politics" (Diebel, cited in Cohen 2002, 36).

Allegories of the family have thus been deployed to manage the Canada-U.S. relationship and to appease the criticism, hurt feelings, and sting of disagreement, as well as the sorrow and grief in the wake of 9/11. It is in light of all the affective dimensions to these geopolitical relations that the appeals to family and the familial make sense, just as they do with respect to the events of 9/11 and the evocation of homeland. Here too homeland is not simply a recidivist nationalist rhetoric, but also speaks to a renegotiation of the constitution and rationalization of state power. And the manifestation of these tropes works to "map, blur, and reconstruct the conceptual, affective, and symbolic borders between spheres once thought of as distinctly separate—as either national or international, domestic or foreign, 'at home' or 'abroad'" (Kaplan 2003, 82).

Thus what concerns us is the specific work that metaphors of homeland and geopolitical allusions to family accomplish in the context of the War on Terror. Tim Cresswell observes that metaphors are "constitutive moments in the spatiality of everyday life" (Cresswell 1997, 334). They help to frame our understanding of political matters, to shape the interpretive frame through which events are understood, and the responses that can be effected. Moreover, metaphors work to fix borders and identities in particular spatial formations. A number of critical geographers have noted that a proliferation of spatial metaphors in current political discourse has paradoxically taken place while material political geographies are increasingly neglected (Smith and Katz 1993; Sparke 2005). However, as these scholars and others have argued, to neglect a geographical analysis is to neglect a sophisticated political analysis. As Claire Rasmussen and Michael Brown argue, "[A] more self-conscious examination of the metaphor can not only reveal the politics inherent in the apparently innocent rhetorical move but may also open up a space for contestation" (Rasmussen and Brown 2005, 477). Metaphors like "homeland" and "family" are not benign gestures, but central to the production of political space. We are suggesting that "homeland" is not simply a new kind of national metaphor, but, rather, that the family is becoming a model of political relations with familial spaces like the home commanding our political geographic imaginaries. The domestic and international reformulations of nations as families described above signal a new way of conceiving the family not only as an institution through which neoliberal states can govern, but also as the model of political relations that underpin the new, "soft paternalism" of the U.S. "avuncular state" (*Economist* 2006).

The scholarship on governmentality is helpful to this analysis, not only because it is centrally concerned with the role of models and metaphors in the constitution of our perception and practice. This literature insists on the intimacy of rule and questions the genealogy of its forms. It furthermore offers highly pertinent insights to the question of the family as a model of political relations. In fact, one of Michel Foucault's central arguments in his writing on governmentality relates directly to this question of the family as a model of government. However, in contrast to aspects of our analysis, Foucault (1991) claims the family was a crucial *historical* model of government that became *less important* with the rise of the modern nation-state system.

Foucault contends that in the Middle Ages, government was understood and practiced according to a model of sovereignty which was both embodied in an actual sovereign (the king or prince) and organized through the image of family and the household. With the rise of the administrative state, the image of the sovereign continued to define government. In the Classical age, Mitchell Dean writes,

> [T]he art of government is still enmeshed in a particular image of the household or family as a sphere of patriarchialist relations of service and obligation between sovereign and subjects, heads of households and wives, parents and children, masters and servants, and so on. (Dean 1999, 94)

The emergence of the sovereign state form was achieved through a scalar configuration whereby the management of the household by a benevolent patriarch was projected at the scale of the state. The household became a microcosm of the polis, and the sovereign state was understood as both a household and a set of relations between households. Until the seventeenth century, the conception of "Oeconomy" practiced was understood as the "wise government of the family for the common welfare of all" (Foucault 1991, 92).

The rise of the modern state saw the emergence of a different logic of government that was no longer conceptualized around the metaphor of the sovereign, the family, or the judicious management of the household. By the eighteenth century, older forms of power were increasingly articulated into what Foucault would come to call "biopower." Government was no longer centrally concerned with the body of the sovereign but instead the "species-body," which was now composed of "populations" of individual bodies. Population itself became the object of government. The family did not in any sense disappear with the rise of population. A relationship persists between state and family, just as between state and economy: both are juridically constituted as versions of the public-private dichotomy, in that they are separate from the state (Dean 1999, 127). However, while scholars working within this tradition see the family as an important element of contemporary governmentality, they understand the family's role as a *model* of political relations to be a historical artifact.

Our investigation of the emergence of the family as a model of government in the current period thus questions the finality of these historical shifts. We can question, as others have, the discreteness of these periodizations and the "cleanness" of their breaks. For example, Collier and Lakoff (2006; and this volume) suggest that various forms of collective security—"state sovereign," "population," and what they term "vital systems"—coexist today, although in different projects and institutions and with varying degrees of centrality to the government of citizens. However, in the following section, we raise a different set of questions about this narrative of populations and families that takes aim at the conception of subjectivity and citizenship that scholarship in this area often assumes.

Familial Politics and Neurotic Citizens

Engin Isin (2004) argues that scholarship that informs contemporary debates about citizenship often assumes a "phantastic" model of government and subjectivity. This "phantastic" model produces insights that conform more to the desires of theorists than to the empirical configurations and assemblages of contemporary political problems. Reflecting on governmentality scholarship and work on the "risk society," Isin suggests that their rational and calculating model of the citizen leaves little room for the affective dimensions of the government of the self. He quotes Slavoj Žižek, who argues that risk society theories "leave intact the subject's fundamental mode of subjectivity: their subject remains the modern subject, able to reason and reflect freely, to decide on and select his/her set of norms" (Žižek, 1999, 342, cited in Isin 2004, 219).

Isin suggests that this calculating and impervious subject is in no way given in the work of Foucault, but rather has come to characterize some of the work of those who follow in his tradition. Nevertheless, the persistence of this problem, and the fact that core concepts in this lexicon can encourage such a reading, demands a new vocabulary. The metaphor of "biopolitics," for example, "does not adequately capture or account for the subject who is governed through its affects," and hence presumes a "bionic citizen, a subject whose rational and calculating capacities enabled it to calibrate his conduct" (Isin 2004, 222). Instead, Isin introduces a compelling new figure, the "neurotic citizen," who is governed through both calculation and affect. The neurotic citizen, Isin explains, "governs itself through responses to anxieties and uncertainties." Isin suggests "a new concept, neuroliberalism—a rationality of government that takes its subject as the neurotic citizen—as an object of analysis." Isin argues,

> Governing through neurosis means that the neurotic subject is incited to make two adjustments in its conduct to render itself a citizen. While on the one hand the neurotic citizen is incited to make social and cultural investments to eliminate various dangers by calibrating its conduct on the basis of its anxieties and insecurities rather than rationalities, it is also invited to consider itself as part of a neurological species and understand itself as an affect structure. (Isin 2004, 223)

The neurotic citizen is thus a feeling and desiring being who can be governed through affect. She or he oscillates between an unlimited sense of entitlement to impossible rights of all kinds—for example, tranquility, serenity, and security—and an intense anger when these demands are not met. In a related vein, the neurotic citizen seeks out conditions that will alleviate this pervasive anxiety, but instead of the success implied in narratives of bionic citizenship, the quest for security tends to have the paradoxical effect of creating *new and greater forms of anxiety*. Moreover, because "neurotic rights" are not realizable, anger, angst, hostility, and discontent are chronic for the neurotic citizen. Thus importantly, "the neurotic subject is one whose anxieties and insecurities are objects of government not in order to *cure* or *eliminate* such states but to *manage* them" (Isin 2004, 225, emphasis in the original).

This idea of managing anxieties and insecurities resonates clearly with the discussion of homeland and familial metaphors described above. While Isin's remarks do not speak directly to the family in the context of "neuropolitics," he does discuss the ways that the home has been cast as a space of salvation in the management of neurosis: "Being continuously neuroticized in other domains, the home perhaps becomes the last remaining domain in which the subject can manage and stabilize anxieties and insecurities cultivated in them" (Isin 2004, 231). With respect to the War on Terror, we see a similar phenomenon with the very public nature of the terrorism and security threats (to work, transit, and monuments) countered with the private, familial dimensions of the home. And yet, as Isin points out, homes, while cast as sites of salvation, are not outside of the phenomenon of securitization. From domestic security services to gated communities, the desire for safe and secure homes that are impermeable to intruders has radically intensified in recent years. And in fact, Isin remarks that the idea of "homeland security" might be drawing more upon the idea of "home" security rather than nationalist ideas of homeland.

Kaplan makes a parallel observation with the term "homeland" and the very affective connotations of familial belonging, attachment, and rootedness that it embodies. As she asks, "Does the word homeland itself do some of the cultural work of securing national borders? Might it also produce a kind of radical insecurity?" (Kaplan 2003, 85). In the War on Terror, "the home itself serves as the battleground," and hence homes must be "protected and mobilized" against threats as much as the public sphere (Kaplan 2003, 90). This provides further justification for the intrusion and surveillance of lives in the home to ensure its security, alongside intensified roles for government, military, and intelligence.

It is in this context that *securing* the family and familial space is able to mobilize massive government intervention. The "traditional" Western family form becomes the mechanism to understand and to manage the threats of the foreign at home and abroad. When Bush proclaimed the first National Day of Prayer and Remembrance on September 13, 2001, he rallied his "one nation under God" with the following words: "I call on every American family and the family of America to observe a National Day of Prayer and Remembrance, honoring the memory of the thousands of victims of these brutal attacks and comforting those who lost loved ones" (White House n.d.-a). A day later, at the remembrance ceremony, this very concept of kinship was used to help differentiate between those "with" and "against" the United States. Surrounded by families of all colors and religions but only one nuclear shape and size, Bush remarked, "Our unity is a kinship of grief, and a steadfast resolve to prevail against our enemies and this unity against terror is now extending across the world" (White House n.d.-c). Bush again defined the family as the glue of American society at a 2004 Iftaar Dinner, when he identified the parallels between Muslims and Americans of other faiths as being rooted in family values. "In recent years," Bush asserted,

> Americans of many faiths have come to learn more about our Muslim brothers and sisters. And the more we learn, the more we find that our commitments are broadly shared. As Americans, we all share a commitment to family—to protect and to love our children. (Bush 2004)

These examples typify the ways that the normative family form is used to articulate modes of belonging that elide the domestic and national sphere.

This positive vision of the American family is contrasted with depictions of the failed and violent families of "the enemy." In the lead-up to the invasion of Iraq, Bush made repeated references to Saddam Hussein's cruelty to families. Violence toward his own family and other peoples served as indication and explanation for his general monstrosity. "The dictator of Iraq is a student of Stalin, using murder as a tool of terror and control, within his own cabinet, within his own army, and even within his own family," Bush (2002) explained. He continued, "On Saddam Hussein's orders, opponents have been decapitated, wives and mothers of political opponents have been systematically raped as a method of intimidation, and political prisoners have been forced to watch their own children being tortured." More recently, a powerful body of work has explained the acts and agents of terrorism by outlining the failed family structure of al Qaeda networks and fundamentalist Islam more broadly, as Jasbir Puar (2006) has recently outlined.

The normative family helps to naturalize inequalities and allay insecurities that are mapped onto the struggles within and against the United States. Offering helpful insights into this case, Anne McClintock explores the cult of domesticity of the British imperial project. She describes how prevalent Narratives of Family of Man ordered national differences. "The family as a *metaphor* offered a single genesis narrative for global history," McClintock explains,

> while the family as an *institution* became void of history. As the nineteenth century drew on, the family as an institution was figured as existing, naturally, beyond the commodity market, beyond politics and beyond history proper. The family thus became both the antithesis of history and history's organizing figure. (McClintock 1995, 44, emphasis in the original; see also Larner and Walters 2002, 398)

The family hence naturalizes differences within the national body, while projecting a particular decontextualized and timeless model of the normative Western family that helps to legitimize particular forms of exclusion and hierarchy. To put it more strongly, "Projecting the family image onto national and imperial progress enabled what was often murderously violent change to be legitimized as the progressive unfolding of natural decree" (McClintock 1995, 45).

Ann Laura Stoler's attention to the micropolitics of state rule, with a particular eye to the colonial state's concern with attachment and family, suggests that colonial regimes were justified in terms of reason and reasonableness, but that this was not quite their sole guiding force. Rather, such projects were organized around "'private feelings,' 'public moods,' and their political consequences, around the racial distribution of sensibilities, around assessments of affective dispositions, and their beneficent and dangerous political affects" (Stoler 2004, 5). That there are parallels between the deployment of family and intimacy in older imperial contexts is perhaps not coincidental, for the United States has been associated with a new imperialism, a new empire, even before the advent of the War on Terror (e.g., Hardt and Negri 2000; Mann 2003; Sparke 2005). And certainly, like the contemporary discourses described above, the colonial projects sought to secure and mobilize resources and funds, and to produce mythologies that would draw together the domestic population and at the same time could be used to subdue and suppress those who were being colonized.

As Isin identifies, there is a double movement at play whereby "the home and the nation become both the same and different—the same because they provide models for each other and different because each provides an evasion or sanctuary from the other" (Isin 2004, 231). This brings us back to one of our central arguments: that there is evidence to suggest a significant shift in governmentality. That is, the family is not simply a social entity through which states govern, but is also (re-)emerging as a model for political relations. The Office of Homeland Security, with its mandate for and legislative authority over domestic security, perhaps typifies this mode of governmentality. The national and private family and their respective homes are presented as a response to and means for managing the anxieties and insecurities generated in and through the War on Terror, even as they too are increasingly securitized. Subjects are encouraged to produce stable homes to help protect the stability of the homeland, as domestic family and domestic politics are intertwined: not quite conflated but interdependent. Hence the home also becomes a site of anxiety as the home and the family must be secured—not just for the tranquility, serenity, and calm of individuals, but also for the good of the nation.

The Family at War: A New Sovereign?

American neoliberalism has been transformed since the initiation of the War on Terror. In contrast to the fiscal austerity and attacks on central government that characterized neoliberalism in the 1990s, a rapid expansion of federal power and spending defines the era of the Office of Homeland Security. In place of the overgrown, bureaucratic, "monstrous state" of early neoliberal critiques, we are seeing the return and growth of the "paternal" state (*Economist* 2006). The choice of the term "paternal" is evocative, for as we have argued, the familial imaginary of "homeland" has helped to engineer new practices that inculcate the state as a patriarchal institution. While feminist scholars have argued that neoliberalism has been centrally concerned with reworking gendered and familial norms, and, in a sense, downloading the responsibility for social reproduction from the state to the family unit, we'd like to suggest an additional shift. The trauma of 9/11 has helped to vault the family into a central place not only as a mechanism of governance but also as a model for government. The family is positioned in contrast to politics even as it is mobilized politically. It has become a model for unequal but "natural" relations—one that promises security in place of democracy or equity.

Contemporary familial politics are also centrally implicated in the complex form of nationalism particular to the United States at war that is simultaneously multicultural *and* racialized. This nationalism is defined, first and foremost, by its explicit casting of citizenship in antiracist terms, even as it is centrally organized around a racialized imaginary and perpetuates racialized and racist economic, police, and military violence. Contemporary American nationalism denies an ethnonationalist foundation, and instead promotes values and institutions. But a highly normative model of the family that is white, Western, middle class, and heteronormative has been elevated to universal status as the core institution and values of American life. The nuclear family, not "race" or religion, becomes the unifying principle of citizenship. It is through promotion of the family that government reproduces and responds to the racialized "challenges" of black families at home, of fundamentalist terrorists abroad, and also of the global AIDS epidemic. The "traditional" (white, Western, and heteronormative) family form will normalize these "problem" citizens.

If the family is emerging not simply as the material form and social institution making possible the privatization of public life, but also, even more profoundly, as a very model and metaphor of government, then attempts to radicalize its form should be treated as highly significant political projects. While the feminist, queer, and socialist left has been broadly critical of the familialization of politics and so too of gay, lesbian, bisexual, and transgender (GLBT) movements adopting family-based rights struggles, progressives rarely ask what kind of family is invoked. Is the family of the fundamentalist Christian right the same family that is celebrated in Sister Sledge's lyrics to "We Are Family"—a staple of women's "take back the night" rallies and GLBT political marches for decades? Does the word "family" actually or potentially signify a radically diverse range of material social practices and relations? The demand that we explore the form of the family being invoked and not simply whether the familial imaginary is present echoes the arguments of feminist scholar Meg Luxton (1997), who suggests that abandoning the family to the right has had devastating consequences for progressive politics.

None of this is to suggest that family politics should necessarily be embraced. Rather we argue that progressives could adopt a more nuanced lens on the form it takes. We furthermore argue that challenges to the enclosure of politics into a firmly guarded model of the nuclear family assume tremendous importance in this context. By asking, "What kind of family?" we can better understand the explosive nature of struggles for same-sex partnership rights across the United States and internationally. These struggles are not simply a conservatizing move on the part of gay and lesbian activists (which they certainly *can* be), but also offer a serious challenge to a singular model of social relations and to the ideological powers of naturalized hierarchy, particularly gendered and racialized hierarchies of the kind which the nuclear family imaginary has historically made real, and which citizens of the United States and the world are threatened with today. While war has made the security of the national family a popular obsession and a salient and powerful project, practicing politics as a defense of homelands and families threatens to augment violence in its most brutal and organized forms.

Notes

1. As the National Association of Social Workers advised at the six-month anniversary, official commemorations can stir "a host of unexpected emotions" (2002).
2. An earlier act—the 1981 Omnibus Budget Reconciliation Act—allowed states to experiment with making workfare mandatory for Aid to Families with Dependent Children recipients.
3. Donald Pease reminds us, however, that the appellation "Ground Zero" perpetuates a "fantasy of radical innocence" that conceals earlier U.S. histories of violence against indigenous peoples and their displacement (Pease 2003, 3).
4. See White House (n.d.-b). And thanks to Elizabeth Gagen for prompting us to return to this inaugural address. See also Flint (this volume) for a historical account of U.S. nationalism as evinced in ideals and institutions.

References

Anderson, Benedict. 1991. *Imagined communities: Reflections on the origin and spread of nationalism*. London: Verso.

Armstrong, Pat, and Hugh Armstrong. 1994. *The double ghetto: Canadian women and their segregated work*. 3rd ed. Toronto: McClelland & Stewart.

Bartlett, James A. 2001. Homeland: Behind the buzzword. *Ethical Spectacle*, December, http://www.spectacle.org (accessed February 20, 2006).

Beamish, Rita. 2006. Religious groups get nearly one-quarter of Bush administration's AIDS money. *Associated Press*, online ed., January 29. http://www.findarticles.com/p/articles/mi_qn4155/is_20060130/ai_n16031892 (accessed March 13, 2007).

Berlant, Lauren. 1997. *The queen of America goes to Washington City: Essays on sex and citizenship*. Durham, NC: Duke University Press.

Bhabha, Homi K. 1990. DissemiNation: Time, narrative and the margins of the modern nation. In *Nation and narration*, edited by Homi K. Bhabha, 319–42. New York: Routledge.

Bock, Gisela. 1992. Equality and difference in national socialist racism. In *Beyond equality and difference: Citizenship, feminist politics, female subjectivity*, edited by Gisela Bock and Susan James, 89–109. London: Routledge.

Bush, George W. 2004. President hosts Iftaar Dinner. November 10. http://www.whitehouse.gov/news/releases/2004/11/20041110-9.html (accessed March 12, 2007).

Cellucci, A. Paul. 2003. Speech by U.S. Ambassador to Canada A. Paul Cellucci to the Economic Club of Toronto. March 25. http://canada.usembassy.gov/content/textonly.asp?section=embconsul&document=cellucci_030325 (accessed March 12, 2007).

Chatterjee, Partha. 1993. *The nation and its fragments: Colonial and postcolonial histories*. Princeton, NJ: Princeton University Press.

Citizens Committee for Children. 2002. Burden of 9/11 trauma remains with children, delivery of health and human services uneven, says citizens' committee for children citywide poll. http://www.kfny.org/publications/FinalRelease_ChildrenandCrisis.pdf (accessed January 1, 2006).

Cohen, Andrew. 2002. Canadian-American relations: Does Canada matter in Washington? Does it matter if Canada doesn't matter? In *Canada among nations 2002: A fading power*, edited by Norman Hillmer and Maureen Appel Molot, 34–48. Toronto: Oxford University Press.

Collier, Stephen, and Andrew Lakoff. 2006. Vital systems security. Berkeley, CA: Anthropology of the Contemporary Research Collaboratory. http://www.anthropos-lab.net (accessed March 12, 2007).

Cooper, Davina. 1995. *Power in struggle: Feminism, sexuality and the state*. New York: New York University Press.

Cossman, Brenda. 2002a. Sexing citizenship, privatizing sex. *Citizenship Studies* 6 (4) 483–506.

———. 2002b. "Family feuds": Neo-liberal and neo-conservative visions of the reprivatization project. In *Privatization, law and the challenge of feminism*, edited by B. Cossman and J. Fudge, 169–217. Toronto: University of Toronto Press.

Cresswell, Tim. 1997. Weeds, plagues, and bodily secretions: A geographical interpretation of metaphors of displacement. *Annals of the Association of American Geographers* 87 (2): 330–45.

Dean, Mitchell. 1999. *Governmentality: Power and rule in modern society*. London: Sage.

Diebel, Linda. 2001. "Not important to promise 'brother,'" *Toronto Star, September 25.*

Economist. 2006. The avuncular state. April 8, 67– 69.

Elden, Stuart. 2002. The war of races and the constitution of the state: Foucault's "Il faut defendre la société" and the politics of calculation. *boundary 2* 29:125–51.

Foucault, Michel. 1991. Governmentality. In *The Foucault effect: Studies in governmentality*, edited by C. Gordon, G. Burchell, and P. Miller, 87–104. Chicago: University of Chicago Press.

Fraser, Nancy. 1993. Rethinking the public sphere: A contribution to the critique of actually existing democracy. In *Habermas and the Public Sphere*, edited by Craig Calhoun, 109–42. Cambridge, MA: MIT Press.

Friedman, M. 1962. *Capitalism and freedom*. Chicago: University of Chicago Press.

Fritz, Nicole. 2006. Cash for abstinence with Bush's no-sex diplomacy. *Business Day*, online ed. http://www.businessday.co.za/articles/topstories.aspx?ID=BD4A136774 (accessed February 8, 2006).

Gellner, Ernest. 1983. *Nations and nationalism*. Ithaca, NY: Cornell University Press.

Gordon, Linda. 1990. The new feminist scholarship on the welfare state. In *Women, the state, and welfare*, edited by Linda Gordon, 9–35. Madison: University of Wisconsin Press.

Hardt, Michael, and Antonio Negri. 2000. *Empire*. Cambridge, MA: Harvard University Press.

Hill Collins, Patricia. 1990. *Black feminist thought: Knowledge, consciousness, and the politics of empowerment*. Boston: Unwin Hyman.

Hobsbawm, Eric J., and Terence Ranger, eds. 1983. *The invention of tradition*. Cambridge: Cambridge University Press.

Isin, Engin. 2004. The neurotic citizen. *Citizenship Studies* 8 (3): 217–35.

Kaplan, Amy. 2003. Homeland insecurities: Reflections on language and space. *Radical History Review* 85 (Winter): 82–93.

Larner, Wendy, and William Walters. 2002. The political rationality of "new regionalism": Towards a genealogy of the region. *Theory and Society* 31:391–432.

Lister, Ruth. 1997. *Citizenship: Feminist perspectives*. New York: New York University Press.

Luxton, Meg. 1980. *More than a labour of love: Three generations of women's work in the home*. Toronto: University of Toronto Press.

———, ed. 1997. *Feminism and families: Critical policies and changing practices*. Halifax, NS: Fernwood Publishing.

MacNamara, Robert S. 1968. *The essence of security: Reflection in office*. New York: Harper & Row.

Mann, Michael. 2003. *Incoherent empire*. London: Verso.

Mayer, Tamar, ed. 2000. *Gender ironies of nationalism: Sexing the nation*. London: Routledge.

McClintock, Anne. 1995. *Imperial leather: Race, gender and sexuality in the colonial conquest*. New York: Routledge.

National Association of Social Workers. 2002. Six month anniversary of 9-11 brings a host of unexpected emotions. Press release, March 11. https://www.socialworkers.org/pressroom/2002/031102.asp (accessed March 12, 2007).

Pateman, Carole. 1992. Equality, difference, subordination: The politics of motherhood and women's citizenship. In *Beyond equality and difference: Citizenship, feminist politics, female subjectivity*, edited by Gisela Bock and Susan James, 17–31. London: Routledge.

Pear, R., and D. Kirkpatrick. 2004. Bush plans $1.5 billion for promotion of marriage. *New York Times*, online ed., January 14. http://www.nytimes.com (accessed January 2, 2006).

Pease, Donald E. 2003. The global homeland state: Bush's biopolitical settlement. *boundary 2* 30 (3): 1–18.

Powell, Colin. 2004. A strategy of partnerships. *Foreign Affairs* January–February. http://www.foreignaffairs.org/20040101faessay83104/colin-l-powell/a-strategy-of-partnerships.html (accessed March 13, 2007).

Puar, Jasbir K. 2006. Mapping US homonormativities. *Gender, Place and Culture* 13 (1): 67–88.

Rasmussen, Claire, and Michael Brown. 2005. The body politic as spatial metaphor. *Citizenship Studies* (9) 5: 469–84.

Reagan, Ronald. 1988. Remarks on signing the Family Support Act of 1988. October 13. http://www.reagan.utexas.edu/archives/speeches/1988/101388a.htm (accessed March 12, 2007).

Richman, J. A., J. Wislar, J. A. Flaherty, M. Fendrich, and K. M. Rospenda. 2004. Effects on alcohol use and anxiety of the September 11, 2001 attacks and chronic work stressors: A longitudinal cohort study. *American Journal of Public Health* 94:2010–5.

Roach, Kent. 2003. *September 11: The consequences for Canada*. Montreal: McGill-Queens University Press.

Rose, Nikolas. 1999. *Governing the soul: The shaping of the private self*. London: Free Association of Books.

———. 2002. *Powers of freedom: Reframing political thought*. Cambridge: Cambridge University Press.

Rose, Nikolas, and Peter Miller. 1992. Political power beyond the state: the problematics of government. *British Journal of Sociology* 43 (2): 173–205.

Rosenkrantz, Holly. 2004. Same-sex marriage ban is pro-family, Bush says. *Chicago Sun-Times*, online ed., July 11. http://www.findarticles.com/p/articles/mi_qn4155/is_20040711/ai_n12551454 (accessed February 8, 2006).

Ross, B. 1998. A lesbian politics of erotic decolonization. In *Painting the maple: Essays on race, gender and the construction of Canada*, edited by V. Strong-Boak, S. Grace, A. Eisenberg, and J. Anderson. Vancouver: University of British Columbia Press.

Smith, Anna Marie. 2001. The politicization of marriage in contemporary American public policy: The Defense of Marriage Act and the Personal Responsibility Act. *Citizenship Studies* (5) 3: 303–20.

Smith, Neil, and Cindi Katz. 1993. Grounding metaphor. In *Place and the politics of identity*, edited by Michael Keith and Steve Pile, 67–83. London: Routledge.

Somerville, Jennifer. 1992. The new right and family politics. *Economy and Society* 21 (2): 93–128.

Sparke, Matthew. 2005. *In the space of theory: Postfoundational geographies of the nation-state*. Minneapolis: University of Minnesota Press.

Stoler, Ann Laura. 2004. Affective states. In *A companion to the anthropology of politics*, edited by David Nugent, 1–20. London: Blackwell.

U.S. Department of Health and Human Services, Administration for Children & Families. N.d. Healthy Marriage Initiative. http://www.acf.hhs.gov/healthymarriage/index.html (accessed March 12, 2007).

Valentine, Gill. 1993. (Hetero)sexing space: Lesbian perceptions and experiences of everyday spaces. In *Environment and Planning D: Society and Space* 11 (4): 396–413.

White House. N.d.-a. National Day of Prayer and Remembrance for the victims of the terrorist attacks on September 11, 2001. http://www.whitehouse.gov/news/releases/2001/09/20010913-7.html (accessed February 23, 2006).

———. N.d.-b. President George W. Bush's inaugural address. January 20. http://www.whitehouse.gov/news/inaugural-address.html (accessed March 12, 2007).

———. N.d.-c. President's remarks at National Day of Prayer and Remembrance. http://www.whitehouse.gov/news/releases/2001/09/20010914-2.html (accessed February 23, 2006).

Yehuda, R., S. M. Engel, S. Brand, J. Seckl, S. Marcus, and G. Berkowitz. 2005. Transgenerational effects of posttraumatic stress disorder in babies of mothers exposed to the World Trade Center attacks during pregnancy. *Journal of Clinical Endocrinology & Metabolism* 90 (7): 4115–8.

Yuval-Davis, N. 1997. *Gender and nation*. London: Sage.

Yuval-Davis, N., and F. Anthias, eds. 1989. *Woman-nation-state*. New York: St. Martin's.

Žižek, S. 1999. *The Ticklish Subject: The Absent Centre Of Political Ontology*. London; New York: Verso.

13

Resistance, Detainment, Asylum
The Onto-Political Limits of Border Crossing in North America

DAVINA BHANDAR

Inadmissible, deportable, undesirable, terrorist, no-fly list: all of these categories exist on a continuum that marks the border crosser. Crossing borders, even the borders that are understood to be "friendly," often reveals the production of differentiated racial ontologies of immigrant/migrant communities situated within nation-states. The experience of border crossing is an ontological one whereby both the technologies used in border security and the mode of securitization are understood to have a profound effect on the immigrant and migrant communities within nation-states. In North America, as well as other "securitized" regions, the coupling of racial profiling strategies and the renewed politics of nationalizing identity as a response to the "War on Terror" has revealed the extent of the racial ontological formation of border crossing.

With the manifestation of the "War on Terror," scholarship has focused on questions regarding the limitations of civil liberties, the limits to human rights, and changes in legal and extrajudicial processes. While it is important to note the particular shifts and changes that have been brought about through national security policies, domestic policing, and border control agendas, it is also necessary to question the relation of the present to the past. In the context of border control in North America, and specifically the border shared between Canada and the United States, the public image of this "friendly" border has radically altered through the "War on Terror" discourse. What was once regarded as a "friendly" border has become a "leaky border" and a suspect border. Canadian media have reported on the resistance of Canadians to the compulsory use of passports or national identity cards to travel to the United States (*Globe and Mail* 2006). This national representation of the border is somewhat disturbing to me, and I think it reveals the historical vestige of this border crossing. For many migrants and nonwhite immigrants, the experience of crossing this border is not necessarily so "friendly." In the first half of the twentieth century in both Canada and the United States, Asian and South Asian migrants faced insidious forms of surveillance and management through rigid forms of border controls including the introduction of identification certificates predating the instantiation of passports (Torpey 2000). In this context, it is important to examine how contemporary regressive border control mechanisms, such as racial profiling, have indeed shaped and informed the development of the shared border between Canada and the United States. In turn, these processes have shaped a racial ontological condition in both Canada and the United States.

Formal and informal practices of border controls regulate the mobility of citizens, nationals, and noncitizens in distinct ways. In the case of crossing borders, identity and the condition of being human comprise a highly categorized experience. Various technologies of border crossing, such as picture identification, retina eye scans, human thermal recognition, and the constitution of detailed personal data, determine the state of being human in numerous public contexts. Border technologies permit the state to substantiate the ontological status of a person who is subjected to modes of categorization, such as inadmissible, deportable, detainee, or terrorist suspect. Through the acts of detainment, deportation, and imprisonment, the condition of being human is rearticulated, as the act of crossing borders is taking on greater significance in the intensive securitization of borders. By viewing border crossings as a racial ontological practice, I am not only investigating how borders act as a technology of self, identification, and subjection, but also showing how the border is present in the day-to-day lives of border crossers. Is it possible that by examining border crossings as a racialized ontological practice, the extension of the border into the day-to-day lives of border crossers is made evident? By viewing the crossing of borders as a racial ontological practice, in which ways has national identity been rearticulated through the management of borders? In the present context of the securitization and militarization of North American borders, what significance do racial profiling and racial targeting play, and how does this affect the ideological and policy manifestation of multiculturalism and cultural plurality? I examine the racial ontology of border crossing to highlight the multiple ways in which the human condition is reorganized by border control mechanism[1] and by nation-state processes in this present period of militarized imperialism otherwise known as the "War on Terror."

The border separating the United States of America from Canada is popularly imagined as the "world's greatest undefended border" or as a "friendly border dividing two great neighbors" (Drache 2004; Laxer). Until recently, crossing this border was paid little attention in the public political and cultural sensibilities in either the Canadian or American perspectives. The border, which is the conduit of something in the realm of $1.3 (U.S. dollars) billion of two-way daily trading (Andreas 2006, 10), has—somewhat remarkably—been understood in the public discourse as something unremarkable and uneventful.[2] After the attacks of September 11, 2001 in New York and Washington and the ensuing proclamation of an endless "War on Terror," which has come to define American and Canadian foreign policy, this border has been produced somewhat differently in the public imagination. Rather than a friendly border, Canada has come under suspicion from the United States regarding its domestic immigration and refugee policies. Canada's national character as a multicultural, tolerant, and plural nation is questioned. This suspicion has resulted in a newly emergent sense of risk regarding Canada's shared border with the United States of America. The internalization of fear produces an experience or ontology of race in a very particular way in the subject who is surveyed. This does not simply help produce the Islamic fundamentalist, the inadmissible, or the deportee, but, rather, security and surveillance borrowed from the border and deployed in the subject produce ontological "effects." The effects may range from the feeling of not belonging or of being external to the nation-project, to being forcibly made external, policed, and detained. Such effects can be demonstrated in the case of Maher Arar, in his self-restricted movement, state-produced immobility, and general paralysis of identity (discussed below). Securitization is also dependent on a circulation of fear that externally manifests itself as new border regulations and forms of detainment and control. Fear of this kind is "ontologized" in the form of border guards and border detainees. But this border and detention are forms of ontology that have also been exported to the internal limits of citizenship and the immigrants, police, and newcomers who practice that limit on a day-to-day basis. This is the onto-connection to the "war on terror."

Borders Defining National Identity

Citizenship as a form of governing populations carries with it an established set of demarcations, as those who can act, who are restricted or are included within political community, and those who do not belong and are excluded. In other orders of political belonging or political activity, citizenship has also been a regime not of regulation or restriction, but one which has provided resistance, forms of acquisition, the forging for rights, and so on. On the question of how human beings are made external to a system of rights, or abject to the value of human rights, the limit point of the political ontology of the migrant bodies needs to be evaluated. How do particular migrants become abject (see Nyers 2003)? How do the practice and logic of racialization act to create, legitimate, and produce hierarchal modalities of being human? Are these systems codependent?

The claim of the "greatest undefended border" myth is dependent on an embedded relationship between race and nation. In other words, for these two nations to be the greatest of friends, they must not only identify similar enemies but also share a mutual recognition of values, identity, and subjectivity. This historical relationship of mutual recognition has undergone various stresses and strains. The border has not been a friendly point of entry and exit for those who fit uncomfortably within the boundaries of a national sense of belongingness on either side of the border. I question the changing nature of racialized subjects through this border crossing in order to highlight how racial profiling and targeting have systematically been a part of the border management agenda of both nations.

In Canada, since the introduction of official state multiculturalism policy, which coincided with an apparent deracialization of immigration policies (Arat-Koc 1999; Abu-Laban and Gabriel 2002), the challenge to how Canada determined its national subjectivity as an officially bilingual multiculturalism entered into a new racialized national narrative. This complicated and incomplete racial grammar, which occurs through the shift in the national narrative, has come to play a significant part in the ensuing "War on Terror" rhetoric that Canada and the United States are currently negotiating regarding Canadian-U.S. border security, Canadian immigration and refugee policies, and the suspicion of Canadian citizens (Philipose 2006; Puar and Rai 2002). There is a complicated set of reversals that have taken place in Canada's reaction to the American suspicions of particular Canadian immigrant communities. This is particularly evident in the complicity of Canadian multiculturalism in this border security agenda. In the context of the "War on Terror" and increasing militarization of its borders, the United States has questioned Canada's national self-image. Indeed, it is Canada's position as a pluralist, multicultural nation that has become the focus of the contemporary border debates on security and increasing surveillance. As such, it is becoming increasingly important to view the racialized construction of border crossing and border security along the euphemistically identified "49th parallel."

The shift in the characterization of the 49th parallel signals the changing perception of national identity and narratives of national belonging in both Canada and the United States of America in a context of security. What is revealed through this shift is the importance of how each nation relied on a narrow construction of national identity. For this border to have been understood as the "greatest undefended border" between two friends, there was a privileged subject understood as the border crosser. As the border discourse has shifted to reveal a less friendly border, I provide a historical comparison which situates the similarity of the policies and practices regarding inadmissibles and undesirable migrant subjects.

Crossing the Canada-U.S. border is understood as a shared sense of entitlement, and it has remained relatively unprotected because those the nation-state deemed to pose a threat or deemed to be undesirable or inadmissible are held in common. This chapter examines the production of this border through a comparative lens. In particular, I pay attention to the significance of the shifting representations of national identity and belongingness as a way to highlight the changing discourse of race and racialization that has occurred in a post–September 11, 2001, era. I examine two cases. An examination of the border in the early twentieth century reveals how the border was constituted through a mutual understanding of similar undesirables and inadmissibles. This is the case if we view border crossers through the selective economy of national subjects. However, if we view the border crosser in a broader spectrum of migrant classes who move through and between these borders, a different picture emerges. I have chosen to reflect on the crisis that arose during the Anti-Asiatic riots in the early 1900s as a case in point to illustrate the contentious formation of the western border. For instance, a shared sense of enmity regarding Asian migration in both Canada and the United States of America resulted in similar anti-Asian migration policies. The border between Canada and the United States was viewed as a "suspect" site as a possible point of entry for these "undesirable subjects."

The second case reflects on the introduction of official multiculturalism policy in Canada, and how national narratives attempt to shift the racialized economy of the Canadian national subject. I question whether the border management strategies reflect this changing view. This case has become particularly relevant post September 11, 2001, where racial profiling and targeting have become central components in border management, and increasing surveillance and security measures have extended the border control agenda into the cities and towns of Canada. The spatiality of the border has indeed extended itself beyond the border itself. In brief I discuss the case of Maher Arar, a Syrian-born Canadian citizen whose experience as a border crosser has manifestly altered his sense of self and self-recognition. The imagined production of this friendly border seeks to reassure and comfort those who cross frequently as it enables an unencumbered flow of traffic, goods, holiday tourists, and day-to-day shoppers. However, this notion of the friendly border crossing also serves to mask what John Torpey has suggested is the expropriation of the means of mobility by the state and the freedom of movement (Torpey 2000).

Contemporary debates regarding migration and immigration are established through a discourse of fear and anxiety which in turn is supported by and supports the military securitization of the border in North America (Tirman 2006). These debates are easily overlain in the public's imagination with images of laboring undocumented migrant bodies, war, and detainment and displacement.[3] Are we not witnessing an emergent racialized ontology? Is the practice of border crossing and migration a practice that has come to have daily lived effects in the understanding of self and being in the context of these foreign-founded democracies? Is sovereign power revealed in this understanding of the production of the border? The racial ontological status of the person crossing the border is hence the question that is currently being managed, organized, and categorized through the new technologies of border control. How is it that suspect classes are being organized? Who is suspect, and how will they be managed? It is simplistic to understand the suspect class as someone who neatly fits into a racial profiled category, as the Arab Other, or the Asian economic migrant, or the Chicano identity. Rather we must closely examine the sets of practices and technologies that enable the production of these highly differentiated relationships to the state and day-to-day living within and outside of the borders of the nation-state.

Racial Ontologies: "Risky Subjects"

In 1907 on the west coast of Canada, a palpable state of fear and anxiety was growing with the seeming increase in migration of South Asians and Asians. During this time, anti-Asiatic riots occurred on both sides of the Canada-U.S. border, which precipitated border crossings of people attempting to escape from the rioters. In this instance, through the act of violence and increasing antagonism of Asian migrants in both Canada and the United States, border crossing between these regions became both more persistent and also considerably more risky. The border itself became constituted as this "leaky" border, through which these "unacceptable" migrants were seeking refuge. Through the act of crossing the border, these migrants were therefore organized and characterized through particular categories. Alongside the ontological condition of being from unassimilable races, the Chinese, Japanese, and Indian subjects were often referred to as "hordes" and "menaces" in the media.

Both the destruction to personal property during the anti-Asian riot and the delicate balance of foreign relations affected by this violence in Vancouver were significant enough to warrant an investigation and response by the Canadian government. William Lyon McKenzie King, deputy minister of labor, headed two Royal Commissions that each produced a report: "Losses Sustained by the Chinese Population of Vancouver, BC: On the Occasion of the Riots in That City, September 7, 1907," and a report on the losses sustained by the Japanese population of British Columbia, by way of compensating and assessing damages incurred through the riots (referred to as the Royal Commissions of Losses; Canada n.d.-b, n.d.-c). The writing of these reports positioned the victims of the riots, not as citizens, but as residents of the city, and was also careful to point out that the cause of the riots was not "personally" based on the peoples of Japan (in particular), but rather was a result of the "feeling against the sudden influx in large numbers of people from *other* parts of the world" (emphasis added). In both reports, McKenzie King was mindful of foreign representatives, consular officials from both Japan and China who represented the interests of these residents of Vancouver. In the case of the Chinese officials, this included an intricate transnational set of communications between Chinese consular officials in London, Washington, and Canada. Although the intended effect of this report was to establish some form of compensation to the damaged property of Chinese and Japanese merchants and business owners in Vancouver, the report also acted in a way to further entrench the status of these migrants as the foreigners living within the national borders of Canada (Canada n.d.-b, n.d.-c).

The border between Canada and the United States played a significant role in the riots that occurred in both Washington State and Vancouver. The movement of Asians and South Asians across this border spurned the anti-Asiatic feelings and the construction of the border as being a source of this unmitigated influx. In this context, the border was viewed, less as a friendly border, but rather as a potential source for the uncontrolled border crossing of nonwhite bodies. The racialized nature of the border was, therefore, evident and understood. It was not being produced as a "friendly" border, but rather a potentially hazardous one. The American border was characterized in British Columbia at the time as a "leaky border" where "impecunious persons" and other "undesirables" were likely to enter. It was noted in several places through the immigration and refugee branch records that the immigration officers at this time were tirelessly working to protect the interests and the moral virtues of places like Victoria and Vancouver, British Columbia. In this newspaper clip from 1906 found in the *Colonist*, it was reported,

> It is not only from the Orient that this danger threatens the municipal rates for it is an almost everyday occurrence that from the American side and elsewhere attempts are made to foist upon this community aged, infirm and impecunious persons, and it is only the perpetual watchfulness of the inspector of immigration that this is invariably prevented. It is only by ocular demonstration at Dr. Milne's office that one grasps the amount of clerical and documentary work that has to be transacted there, and the public generally has little or no idea of the dangers to both health and pocket from which they are preserved by the energetic conduct of an important department. (Canada n.d.-a)

The viewpoint expressed in this report was further echoed by Lord Grey, as historian Mary Hallett argues in "A Governor-General's Views on Oriental Immigration" (1972). In this article Hallett investigates the opinions and views expressed by the 4th Earl Grey, governor-general of Canada from 1904 to 1911, on the Anti-Asiatic riots in Vancouver and the general politics of Oriental immigration to British Columbia. At the outset of his tenure as governor-general, Hallett argues that he was in favor of Canada and British Columbia accepting Oriental immigration for the purposes of domestic and hard labor as a way to entice and secure the immigration of preferred British immigrant classes to British Columbia. In part as a way to stem the flow of what was perceived as "radical" American immigration to Canada at the time by labor union organizers and miners, Grey argued for the need for the indentured servitude of Asian labor. The events of the September 7, 1907, anti-Asiatic riots in Vancouver were preceded by a similar riot in Bellingham, Washington, two days earlier. The anti-Hindu riots in Bellingham had led to a migration of Hindus across the border on September 6. This period of migration was closely monitored by the dominion government and the imperial interests expressed by Lord Grey. This migration coincided with reports of another boatload of "Hindus" that were reported to be entering British Columbia in the following days, possibly in the number of the thousands. The reporting on the Anti-Asiatic riots and the perceived rampant rise in Asian migration was viewed as hazardous to the peaceable relations in British Columbia (Hallett 1972).

The debate regarding British Indians entering the Dominion of Canada informed the ontological status of being for the racialized migrant class. Various indications of how the "undesirable" class of migrant was produced speaks to how the border was managed, imagined, and organized spatially and temporally. The municipal committee dealing with the issues of "Hindoo" migrancy in 1906 wrote on October 15 that "the Hindoos by reason of caste prejudices, peculiar religious conventions, loathsome habits and obnoxious manner of living, can never assimilate with white people or perform the duties of desirable citizens of the country" (Canada n.d.-a). This letter further communicates that the government should put to an end any continued immigration from Asiatic countries, and argues,

> If the positions in British Columbia now filled by Asiatics were filled by white workers at living wages, then from amongst the families of these workers there would soon grow up a sufficient supply of youthful labour for farmers, fruitgrowers, canneries and for domestic service and if the progress of the country in the future demands the introduction of labour from outside sources, we are of the opinion that the government should look to the crowded centers of population in Great Britain for the additional labour to assist in building up the country in preference to allowing the admission of a race of people who can never be of any use to Canada as citizens and whose very existence amongst our people would be a menace to the wellbeing of the community. (Canada n.d.-a)

Comparatively, the United States also began to question the undefended borders shared between Mexico and Canada. Although border controls were heavily developed along coastlines to determine European and Asian migration, there was very little emphasis placed on their land borders. As Daniel Tichenor in his study of American immigration and border control policy comments,

> This contrast was not lost on the nation's first commissioner general of Immigration. In the Immigration Bureau of 1903 annual report, he warned that the Canadian and Mexican borders were largely unmonitored. Only a handful of inspection stations were scattered along national land borders. . . . Significantly, Congress authorized a modest Border Patrol force largely in response to Immigration Bureau reports

that inadmissible Asians and Europeans were being smuggled across the Canadian and Mexican borders. That is[,] the problem with illegal immigration was initially associated in the American mind not with Latin American migrants but unwanted Asian and European ones. (Tichenor 2002, 168)

The problematic border crossing demonstrates the combined needs of Canada and the United States to determine exclusion and management strategies of Asian migration. Both countries at this time pass exclusion acts of Chinese migration, enter into agreements with Japanese governments, and attempt to manage the flow of Indian migrants from the subcontinent of British India. Through this process, both countries assert a similar management strategy that ultimately aims to aid the management of the shared border. Both countries, regardless of their distinct national identities, assert similar desires regarding the development and racial categorization of national bodies. This process of definition and categorization also results in the onto-specific positioning of various migrant and immigrant communities within the national landscape. These categorical specificities, although based in particular historical moments, do not necessarily become easily undone through the renegotiation of border control policies and the elimination of racist formations of state control. Rather, the recognition of how border controls are in fact maintained through a racial language is revealed in these historical examples. In this sense, there is a temporality of the border, which is written through the racial experience of border crossing.

Borders: Temporal Spaces

Border crossing between Canada and the United States of America is often contextualized in time. The time-consuming activity of waiting at the crossing, traffic piling up, and the experience of agitation, inconvenience, and encumbrance to the day's purpose of cross-border shopping, visiting, or business. This temporal relation to the border speaks to the ways in which time is used in the logic of border management under the security regime: the use of detainment[4] as a technology can be seen as an effective weapon in the arsenal of the militarized border controls. This is a significant factor or weapon that can be used as a point in border-crossing management. The wait time is increased for the day-to-day shoppers when there is a potential suspect amongst the crowd. The quality of time management at border crossings speaks to the absolute mechanism of control over the practices of the everyday that is organized by the state. Because the nature of time under capitalist technologies is effectively challenged and subordinated by the economic function of time, the nature of time extends to the further economic regulation of the border. In this sense border management and time regulation effectively challenge the freedom of people. By viewing the border as a tool for the state to manage both sovereign space and time, the connection between those who are able to pass through the border and those who pass with difficulty takes on a greater significance. John Torpey argues, "A critical aspect of this process has been that people have also become dependent on states for a possession of an 'identity' from which they cannot escape and which may significantly shape their access to various spaces" (Torpey 1998, 250). In this sense, the production of identities that occur through the management of border processes should not be understood to simply be relegated to the moment and space through which passing through the border occurs. As Torpey and others have pointed out, borders exist and are instrumental to the shaping and production of identities within and without the state. Nandita Sharma has also argued that the border is less an instrument of restricting access to a national territory, and more importantly acts in multiple ways to create and produce *differential* inclusions (Sharma 2006, 145). The subject of the border, not simply the privilege of citizenship, is held to a greater mode of control and significance when moving between two nations has become increasingly important to understand, particularly when viewing the impact that acts of detainment, detention, interdiction, and possible imprisonment have on border crossers. The case of Maher Arar instructs us on how border crossing needs to be read as a temporal zone. The extremity of this case is only used here as an illustration of the ontological limit point that is arrived at through border crossing. In the instance of border crossing, Arar, a Syrian-born Canadian telecommunications engineer, was detained by U.S. customs officials, questioned, interrogated, and then sent to Syria, where he was imprisoned and tortured for thirteen months (Arar 2005). His status radically altered through the securitization of the border. In the context of the War on Terror, his status and rights as a citizen were redefined. The state appropriated the means by which his identity was established, and it was reshaped through the ideological means of border control mechanisms.

Nandita Sharma argues,

> National borders do not now, or in some mythical past, correlate with classifications of national membership. It is the nationalization of identity, and of society itself through juridical legal state practices and the everyday social practices[,] that produce certain people as national-subjects and others as foreign objects within the same territorial and legal landscape. (Sharma 2006, 141)

In the case of Arar and many other cases of border crossers, the ideological operation of the border as manifesting the "Other" or the foreigner forms a part of the practice of border crossing. It is through the asking of intimate details during an interview with an immigration officer, or being asked populist nationalist questions, that the practice and discipline of nationalizing identity occur (Bannerji 2000). Through these means in the name of border management, the effects of a nationalized identity are experienced, often in spite of the juridical-legal status of the passport or green-card holder.

Racializing the 49th parallel

The increased militarization of borders within North America has given rise to a fortress mentality and the implementation of new border controls. This militarization, which has typically secured the southern American border shared with Mexico, is ideologically being reproduced along its northern border shared with Canada. The contemporary politics of border controls and formation in North America is shifting between a strongly protected American border, militarized on both the southern and northern borders, and a "Fortress North America" approach that establishes a perimeter surrounding the continent (Andreas 2006, 14). Both approaches will greatly affect the claims to sovereign control over border management and immigration for Canada and Mexico. The ideological nature of security and border control is evident by the nature of so-called illegal migrants becoming legitimate, by virtue of the fact that the economy in the United States, and increasingly in Canada, is heavily dependent on "illegal" work. As Sharma (2006) has argued, this is a management strategy that compels migrant subjects to remain on the outside of society. The public media discourse regarding the controls and maintaining the border has led to significant concerns regarding sovereignty; however, these practices were put into effect far before the crisis that arose in response to the "War on Terror."

In this sense, the national imaginary shared between Canada and the United States of its "great undefended border" is starkly contrasted to the other North American border between the United States and Mexico. Here the border has been constituted through a racialized and colonial project of administration. The study of borders in a North American context has overwhelmingly been focused on the cultures and formation of the "Spanish borderlands" between Mexico and the United States of America. The study of border cultures, the political economy of borders, security, and transmigration have been overlain with postcolonial critiques, the development of the discourse of Chicana/Chicano and mestizo cultures. The border communities and the transborder crossings have been understood through a racial and ontological lens that has been grounded in an absolute difference between the Mexican body and that of the American (writ throughout as the middle-class, white body). The creation and manifestation of Otherness inscribed in the border cultures explore the production of racial difference that easily collapses national identity with the racialized body. In very particular and in stark contrast, the study of the northern North American border, the 49th parallel, has been racialized as the "white" border crossing.

Border crossings in North America have supported a variety of nationalist myths and ideologies that contribute to a formation of racist thinking or racial discourse. In the context of the Mexican American border, the racialized economy of migrant workers, transgressive acts of border crossing, and the highlighting of the erotic zone of the border have been the topics of much debate and analysis.[5] And yet, the northern North American border, which resituates the "whiteness" of the national identities of both Canada and the United States, has remained unremarkable. The border crossing between Canada and the United States has historically been produced through an unspoken racial economy that further cements a normative assumption of the construction of citizenship in both Canada and the United States. Due to increasing pressures to create a securitized border, the American government, post September 11, 2001, has in a way exposed this mythic northern border.

In the case of Canadians moving across to the United States, the presumption in this great unprotected border has been that the Canadian citizen/national is presumed the white national subject.[6] This particular racial economy is highlighted in the Canadian response to increasing border harmonization with the United States in the post–September 11 era.[7] The contemporary North American security agenda has come to challenge modern nation-state territorialization of borders. Indeed, histories such as Bruno Ramirez's *Crossing the 49th Parallel* (2001) relay a somewhat incomplete historical picture of the movements over the border in the early twentieth century. This reading of Canadian mass migrations across the borders compares the experience of migrants from Anglo-Canadian groups and French Canadian groups, and mentions other European groups such as Polish, Italian, and Jewish immigrants moving from Canada to the United States. Even though the racial grammar at the time would have distinguished between these various races, and indeed the U.S. immigration control from the late nineteenth century was very concerned with the class of European immigration entering from Canada, this historical viewpoint acts to situate the "whiteness" of this border crossing. This history does not include the movement of Asians, indigenous peoples, or black people who also constituted important border-crossing subjects. Indeed, such an inclusion would necessarily trouble the nationalizing framework that this history unwittingly produces. To include these "other" raced bodies would mean to question the discourse of national identity production, even as this identity was not based exclusively on the juridical-legal formation of citizenship.

The border is constituted differentially depending on the racialized, classed, and gendered bodies that pass through its mechanisms. The use of border control technologies such as passports works in consort with the ideological formation of national identity. Isabel Kaprielian-Churchill argues, "The impetus for the requirement that travelers to Canada carry passports appears to have come initially from a wish to use such documents as a means of exclusion" (Kaprielian-Churchill 1994, 293). The introduction of the passport in Canada for this purpose illustrates the degree to which border control technologies effectively produce and extend beyond the territorial boundaries of a nation-state. With the introduction of the passport, travelers to Canada (with the exception of those from the British Isles or the United States of America) were required to provide passport documents at the point of departure to Canadian consular officials (Kaprielian-Churchill 1994).

The border undergoes new management policies in times of perceived national crisis, or in particularly risky events. The value of examining the current context of border management and security in relation to the Anti-Asiatic riots in 1907 exists as a historical remainder of how border practices are constituted and aim to constitute national identity. During the time of the 1907 riots, both nations were engaged in raging debates regarding the inadmissibility of "Asiatics," specifically targeting Chinese, Japanese, and Indian migrants. In this context it is also important to note that both Canada and the United States of America set out to establish immigration policies that curtailed or managed the in-migration from these populations. New technologies of management such as in the form of identification documents, and in the Canadian instance, the issuance of "Head Tax certificates," act in multiple ways, by both curtailing immigration from China and also legitimizing and managing populations as border crossers. John Torpey points out how the introduction of the Chinese Exclusion Act in the United States was central to the imposition of documents restricting the movement of particular bodies (Torpey 2000, 96). My rationale for examining the practices of border controls and viewing the processes through which migrant bodies move across the border is to understand the connection or unearth the racialized border practices existent in North America. This example needs to be juxtaposed to contemporary discussions of security and border debates that produce the racialized border through a somewhat distinct racial language. Contemporary debates of security, immigration, and border control in Canada are produced through the ideological lens of multiculturalism. In the following sections, I examine the relationship between the government's support of racial profiling and the language of official multiculturalism as a central feature of contemporary Canadian national identity.

"Securing an Open Society"

Our commitment to include all Canadians in the ongoing building of this country must be extended to our approach to protecting it. We reject the stigmatization of any community and we do not accept the notion that our diversity or our openness to newcomers needs to be limited to ensure our security. No one better appreciates the need to protect our society than those who chose this country as a place to build a better life or who fled the consequences of instability and intolerance in other parts of the world.... A deep commitment of Canadians to mutual respect and inclusion helps to mitigate extremism in our society.

"Securing an Open Society: Canada's National Security Policy" (Canada Privy Council Office 2004)

In April 2004, the Canadian government produced a strategic action plan designed to assert Canada's security goals for the future. This plan, titled "Securing an Open Society: Canada's National Security Policy" (Canada Privy Council Office 2004), lays claim to being the first comprehensive statement of national security policy in Canada's history.[8] The double-speak of an "open" security approach to the consolidation of border control and tighter scrutiny and surveillance of immigrant/migrant communities in the name of pluralism and multicultural values is directly in response to increasing pressures from the American government to coordinate efforts regarding the shared border in a post–September 11, 2001 society. This analysis is made necessary because of the myriad and often contradictory ways in which the rhetoric of the "War on Terror" is embedded and contributes to a historical practice of the racialization of immigrant/migrant subjects.

The rhetorical power in this document operates by simultaneously placing the relationship of the "other" or the subject of multiculturalism as that which needs to be both protected *and* feared through a national policy of security. It is because Canada has opened its doors to the world that Canadians must not only value difference and diversity, but also discover methods of creating a system of self-actualizing surveillance amongst those who represent this diversity. Indeed, the relationship of security and borders is juxtaposed to the openness of Canadian society and the reliance on a notion of plurality. However, unlike past national representations of multiculturalism and Canadian tolerance, there is a noted shift in the discourse of the limit of tolerance that is found in this document.

In a reading of "Securing an Open Society," the lineage of the shared racialized border between Canada and the United States of America is revealed. In the aftermath of the September 11 attacks on the World Trade Center and the Pentagon, the "greatest undefended border" shared between Canada and the United States of America became a suspect site. Indeed, through the increasing discourse of security and militarization that has ensued, the practice and technologies of border crossing have appeared to take on a new significance. In the face of being portrayed as a suspect nation in the crime scene, Canadian government officials were placed in a precarious position, on the one hand having to face the label of a suspect, and on the other hand having to defend Canadian nationalist mythologies of being a proud pluralistic and ethnically diverse nation-state. This is an insecure position for Canada, because the government had to speak the unspeakable: to acknowledge the racialization and potential crisis of race politics that it attempts to question or sidestep at any given moment. Through the revelation of the stark contrast of the racial politics that ensued in this new security regime, Canada was asked either to support outward racial profiling of immigrant and "newcomer" communities from Asian, South Asian, and Arab countries, or to attempt to make the case for a liberal multicultural tolerance that would make the distinction between Canada and the United States more prevalent (Mackey 2002). With predictable Canadian nationalist rhetoric, this movement around racialized security agendas once again uses the discourse of diversity and multiculturalism to assert a nationalist ideological distinction from the warring, racist practices of the United States while simultaneously organizing the management of difference and diversity in the Canadian context (Mackey 2002). Through this double movement, Canada is complicit in the production of the suspect within or the "fear of the foreigner."

The relationship of security and borders is juxtaposed to the openness of Canadian society and the reliance on the notion of plurality. The agenda that is set by the national policy on security is important to note for one particular reason, the response of the Canadian government in examining the position of newcomers and immigrants within Canadian society, and the national imagination of itself committed to a multicultural policy or an imagination of pluralism. The ideological nature of the use of multiculturalism in this document is relevant to understanding how the state is instilling a sense of managing the very diversity and plurality of its citizenship that it seeks to celebrate.[9] In the outline of the Canadian government's strategic framework, what is revealed is the response by the government to place multiculturalism, or the management of the nation's differences, at the center of the policy of security and indeed of policing. Through a sleight of hand revealed through the development of a cross-cultural roundtable or consultation, which is meant to establish a process to discuss national security and possible threats placed on immigrant communities in Canada, it is left to wonder how security and multiculturalism are linked when examining the politics of security within a North American context and increasing border controls. In the aftermath of the attacks in New York and the Pentagon on September 11, 2001, the reaction of Canada was interesting to note. On the one hand, they issued travel advisories for all Canadian citizens and landed immigrants who were considered at "risk." Of course the question raised asks what the context of the "risk" is, and who is the "risky" subject of the border crossing. How does border crossing enable a set of racialized practices that constitute ontological negotiations of human subjectivity?

The production of the "fear of the foreigner" in this document is presented in the context of Canada's own experience with terrorism. The act of terrorism that is referred to is the Air India bombing. Canadian Prime Minister Paul Martin states in his preamble to the document:

The horrific events of September 11, 2001, demonstrated how individuals could exploit such openness to commit acts of terrorism that attempt to undermine the core values of democratic societies. Those events were a stark reminder to Canadians of the tragic loss of 329 lives aboard Air India flight 182 in 1985.

At the time of the Air India bombing, one of the most revealing sentiments of how Canadians experienced the tragic loss of life occurred when Prime Minister Brian Mulroney phoned Indian Prime Minister Rajiv Gandhi and expressed his deepest sympathy for the loss of Indian citizens. At the time, there was an absolute disavowal of the victims as being Canadian citizens. Now twenty years later, the idiom of the "War on Terror" requires the memorializing of this event to have been a national tragedy. By signifying the need for the Canadian public to remember the act of terror when the Air India flight was targeted, the immigrant community cast out of national citizen belonging is actively resituated. It is also significant that the act of terror committed has yet to be punished and the "known-unknowns" of Canadian nation-space is also resituated within the South Asian community. It is the imperative of this security framework for the various immigrant communities, both targeted by antiterrorism law enforcement strategies and modes of surveillance, to be included in the very act of surveillance and security. Through a resituating of this act of terror, the state reasserts its sovereign control through the renarration of the nation's traumatic loss.[10]

Onto-Political Limit

Canada's position as outlined in the policy statement above highlights its reliance on the ideological project of multiculturalism, which insists that its basic tolerance of cultural diversity and pluralism will help to abate terrorism, and to aid in the protection and security of Canadian society. Often the idea of multiculturalism and Canada's respect for cultural diversity is starkly contrasted with that of states, such as France and the United States, that more readily promote a singular vision of nationalist secular democratic states.

Is an official state policy of multiculturalism inherently at odds with racial profiling? Or does multiculturalism in its promotion and production of distinct *authentic* cultural traditions and heritage actually provide a rationale for racial profiling?

In the "Securing an Open Society" policy statement, the respect and tolerance of cultural pluralism have been shifted by subjecting culture to modes and practices of surveillance and policing. The logic of multiculturalism has indeed become an effective tool in contemporary Canadian policing and security initiatives. The ideology of multiculturalism relies on the understanding that, for instance, Muslims practice a distinct and wholly different set of cultural traditions and differences, which while tolerable in the Canadian landscape, nonetheless produces and fuels the discourse of Islamophobia within the monolithic West. The racialized immigrant figure, in both Canada and the United States, illustrates the instability of the categories of citizenship and nationality altogether. The overarching historical typology, such as the Asiatics or the "hordes" arriving to the shores from the Orient, has similarly given way to the contemporary suspicions of Muslims, Arabs, and others who do not "value the traditions and customs" of their new land (even if in fact this new land is not so new to them). Previous to the official multiculturalism policy, inadmissibility to Canada was articulated on the basis of cultural values of the "other" as being inassimilable in Canadian society. The language of the time viewed culture and race as coterminous. With the linking of racial profiling and the official policy of multiculturalism in security and policing strategies, it appears as if this is once again the case.

Detainment Indefinite Time

The border crossing for some has become a treacherous place. At the moment of crossing borders, one's status of being is evaluated. In the event that you are considered a threat, to be detained, deported, or sent to another country for the purpose of interrogation and subjected to torture would be considered some sort of Kafkaesque fantasy along the 49th parallel. And yet, this act is becoming normalized in the current political agenda of security. The public inquiry into the imprisonment and deportation of Maher Arar has revealed that he was not the only Canadian citizen to be sent to the Syrian prisons. In the fact-finding report written by Stephen J. Toope, "Commission of Inquiry into the Actions of Canadian Officials in Relation to Maher Arar" (2005), Toope identifies four other Canadian citizens who were rendered to Syrian prisons. In each of these instances, Canadian citizens were crossing borders when they were detained and deported to Syria. The border crossing, which was once a routine and normalized aspect of their working lives, has become an act that is filled with fear and distrust.

In the course of being interviewed by Stephen Toope, Arar revealed the continued sense of fear that he has of traveling:

> The distrust is based on continuing fear. Mr. Arar cannot yet contemplate travel by air, even within Canada. He is afraid that the plane might be diverted to the United States, that he might be seized and that the ordeal could begin again. He is afraid that he will not be able to resume any "normal" life. He is afraid that his story will not be believed. (Toope 2005)

In the case of Arar, the temporal extension of the border has greatly altered his sense of being. In the context of being detained at the border, imprisoned, tortured, and released, and now the interminable wait for a sense of closure to what had happened to him in the course of a public Commission of Inquiry, the act of crossing the border has radically altered his sense of self and his identity. The power of the border technology through the act of detainment illustrates how the everyday is shaped through the state's power to "expropriate" the means of freedom (Torpey 1998).

Judith Butler points to the problem of naming or racial-profiling populations as potential risky subjects or "dangerous persons." She points out that in the process of detaining and imprisoning people who are "deemed" suspicious or dangerous, it has become the state's prerogative to do so and leads to the "potential license of prejudicial perception and a virtual mandate to heighten racialized ways of looking and judging in the name of national security" (Butler 2004, 77). This increasingly acceptable norm in the racialization of perceived threats permits an act of dehumanization. In the case of Arar and the other Canadian citizens of Syrian origin, the act of being rendered to Syrian prisons is an act that stands outside of the juridical-legal and political culture of Canadian society and yet is completely complicit with it. Although the report on the public inquiry on Maher Arar's case is not released at the time of writing this article, we are able to clearly view the profound effects that border crossing has had on Arar's ability to function in his daily life. The technology of border crossing in this instance operated in such a way as to reveal the ontological limit point that has been reorganized and recalibrated in this contemporary militarization of the border.

In this chapter, I examined how the function of the myth of the 49th parallel has been formed through the racialization of that border. Border crossers who have been categorized and viewed as dangerous, risky, or suspect have not been able to recognize this as a "friendly border." The manifestation of the border myths is intimately tied to the nationalization of identity on both sides of the border. In the period during the liberalization of immigration policies in Canada, the introduction of official multiculturalism coincided with the attempt to deracialize the immigration procedures. However, border crossing between Canada and the United States has undergone a replacement of a different kind of cultural racism. In this instance, the introduction of this new cultural racism is coterminous with official multiculturalism in Canada. Immigrant communities, particularly Muslim faith-based communities, are culled into place by increasing surveillance and policing on the one hand, and exhaustive community consultations on the other. In this increasingly Islamophobic society, it is in the name of cultural diversity and pluralism that these communities are continually asked to respond to and defend themselves against allegations of being held outside of Canadian society and values.

Notes

1. In a different context, Judith Butler raises the following questions regarding the practice of indefinite detention with relation to the detainees in Guantánamo Bay: It is crucial to ask under what conditions some human lives cease to become eligible for basic, if not universal, human rights. And to what extent is there a

racial and ethnic frame through which these imprisoned lives are viewed and judged such that they are deemed less than human, or as having departed from the recognizable human community? (2004, 57) Butler is not the first to comment or raise the question of the construct of humanity or the question of the human that is shifting in this particular period of intense imperialism. What is remarkable is how ubiquitous the question over the meaning of the category "human" has become in the past five years. This remark, I think, also shows the necessity of viewing shifts and changes arising to border control mechanisms, in the name of security, as instances of this reshaping of the question of the "human category."

2. Although the public discourse regarding the Canada-U.S. border before September 11, 2001, was not one of great interest, there were various sets of negotiations between the two countries throughout the 1990s that attempted to streamline and harmonize border policies. See Pratt (2005) for an analysis and discussion of these agreements.

3. It is important to note the convergence between security discourses of the "War on Terror" and the increasing political urgency that has taken place in both the United States of America and Canada regarding undocumented workers and people living without documented status. The securitizing of the borders has meant an increasing role of border control agents in the day-to-day lives of the undocumented. This attention and politicization have also led to an increasing awareness of the economic dependency of both Canada and the United States on the "black market" labor of the undocumented.

4. Look at Rachel Meeropol, "The post-9/11 Terrorism Investigation and Immigration Detention," in which she states that on any given day over 20,000 men, women, and children languish in indefinite detention in the United States . . . these thousands of people are "immigrant detainees" and they comprise the fastest-growing population of incarcerated people in the country and the highest incarceration rate in the world. Immigration detainees serve indeterminate sentences in federally run detention facilities, state prisons and county jails, as well as private facilities licensed by the federal government, under conditions that are often deplorable and inhuman (Meeropol 2005).

5. See Andreas (2000, 2006) and Gutierrez (1997).

6. John Torpey points out, "In the United States, for example which has been more or less open to free movement for the white population, the development of passports and identification documents grew dramatically toward the end of the 19th century" (2000, 93).

7. It is interesting to note the mythic production of the 49th parallel in relation to current public discourses of how increased security at the shared border will somehow establish a different feeling or nature of relations between the two countries. Ibbitson (2006) discusses the inconveniences that both Americans and Canadians will face when having to cross the border if they have to take the time and make the expense of getting a passport.

8. See the preamble to "Securing an Open Society: Canada's National Security Policy" (Canada Privy Council Office 2004).

9. Both Himani Bannerji (2000) and Eva Mackey (2002) have contributed to the understanding of how the federal policy of multiculturalism in Canada is a useful ideological tool in the management of diversity and cultural difference at times of national crisis in Canada.

10. It is interesting to note that Canada's greatest act of terror was not the October crisis of 1970 in which we witnessed the state's swift response in an unprecedented act of repression through the enactment of the War Measures Act. Even though the loss of life was not comparable to the loss of life in the Air India bombing, there is at least an understanding of how the nation experienced that act as a collective sense of terror. The use of this event as the national site of memorialization is interesting to note when examining who is chosen to be both victim and perpetrator of this act of crime. Not the "homegrown" terror of the FLQ (Front de liberation du Quabec), a political organization fighting for the independence of Quebec from the rest of English Canada (named a "terrorist" organization in 1963), but the externalized immigrant community, who remain both within and outside of this national space.

References

Abu-Laban, Yasmeen, and Christina Gabriel. 2002. *Selling diversity: Immigration multiculturalism, employment equity and globalization*. Peterborough, ON: Broadview Press.

Agamben, Giorgio. 1998. *Homo sacer: Sovereign power and bare life*, trans. Daniel Heller-Roazen. Stanford, CA: Stanford University Press.

Andreas, Peter. 2000. *Border games: Policing the US-Mexico divide*. Ithaca, NY: Cornell University Press.

———. 2006. Politics on the edge: Managing the US—Mexico border. *Current History* 105 (688): 64–68.

Andreas, Peter, and Thomas Biresteke, eds. 2003 *The rebordering of North America: Integration and exclusion in a new security context*. New York: Routledge.

Arar, Maher. 2005. Statement. In *America's disappeared: Detainees, secret imprisonment and the "War on Terror,"* edited by Rachel Meeropol, 60–71. Toronto: Seven Stories Press.

Arat-Koc, Sedef. 1999. Neoliberalism, state restructuring and immigration: Changes in Canadian policies in the 1990's. *Journal of Canadian Studies* 26:31–57.

Bannerji, Himani. 2000. *Dark side of the nation: Essays on multiculturalism, nationalism and gender*. Toronto: Canadian Scholar's Press.

Butler, Judith. 2004. *Precarious life: The power of mourning and violence*. London: Verso.

Canada. N.d.-a. Immigration Branch RG 76, vol. 34 5036999.

Canada. N.d.-b. Royal Commission to investigate the losses by the Chinese population of Vancouver, British Columbia on the occasion of the riots in that city in September 1907. http://www.canadiana.org (accessed June 2006).

Canada. N.d.-c. Royal Commission to investigate the losses by the Japanese population of Vancouver, British Columbia on the occasion of the riots in that city in September 1907. http://www.canadiana.org (accessed June 2006).

Canada Privy Council Office. 2004. Securing an open society: Canada's National Security Policy. http://www.pco-bcp.gc.ca. (accessed March 2006).

Cunningham, Hilary. 2001. Transnational politics at the edges of sovereignty: Social movements, crossing and the state at the US-Mexico border. *Global Networks* 1 (4): 369–87.

Daniels, Ronald, Patrick Macklem, and Kent Roach, eds. 2001. *The security of freedom: Essays on Canada's anti-terrorism bill.* Toronto: University of Toronto Press.

Drache, Daniel. 2004. *Borders matter: Homeland security and the search for North America.* Halifax, NS: Fernwood Publisher.

Gutierrez, Raymond. 1997. The erotic zone: Sexual transgression on the US-Mexican border. In *Mapping multiculturalism,* edited by Avery Gordon and Christopher Newfield. Minneapolis: University of Minnesota Press.

Hallett, Mary E. 1972. A governor general's views on oriental immigration to British Columbia, 1904–1911. *B.C. Studies* (15): 53–67.

Ibbitson, John. 2006. New rules will make us strangers at the Canada-US border. *Globe and Mail,* March 23.

Kaprielian-Churchill, Isabel. 1994. Rejecting "misfits": Canada and the Nansen passport. *International Migration Review* 28 (2): 281–306.

Lai Cheun-Yan. 1972. The Chinese Consolidated Benevolent Association in Victoria: Its origins and functions. *BC Studies* (15): 53–67.

Landon, Fred. 1920. The Negro migration to Canada after the passing of the Fugitive Slave Act. *Journal of Negro History* 5 (1): 22–36. http://www.jstor.org (accessed February 6, 2006).

Lefebvre, Henri. 1998. *The production of space,* trans. Donald Nicholson-Smith. London: Blackwell.

Mackey, Eva. 2002. *House of difference: Cultural politics and national identity in Canada.* Toronto: University of Toronto Press.

Meeropol, Rachel, ed. 2005. *America's disappeared: Secret imprisonment, detainees, and the "War on Terror."* Toronto: Seven Stories Press.

Mountz, Alison. 2003. Human smuggling, The transnational imaginary, and everyday geographies of the nation-state. *Antipode* 35 (3): 622–44.

———. 2004. Embodying the nation state: Canada's response to human smuggling. *Political Geography* 23:323–45.

Mountz, Alison, Richard Wright, Ines Miyares, and Adrian Bailey. 2002. Lives in limbo: Temporary protected status and immigrant identities. *Global Networks* 2 (4): 335–56.

Neyers, Peter. 2003. The politics of protection in the anti-deportation movement. *Third World Quarterly* 24 (6): 1069–93.

Philipose, Elizabeth. 2006. The politics of pain and uses of torture. Paper presented in Syracuse, New York.

Pratt, Anna. 2005. *Securing borders: Detention and deportation in Canada.* Vancouver: University of British Columbia Press.

Puar, Jasbir K., and Amit S. Rai. 2002. Monster, terrorist, fag: The war on terrorism and the production of docile patriots. *Social Text* 72 (20): 117–48.

Ramirez, Bruno. 2001. *Crossing the 49th Parallel: Migration from Canada to the US 1900–1930.* Ithaca, NY: Cornell University Press.

Roach, Kent. 2003. September 11: Consequences for Canada. Montreal: McGill Queen's University Press.

Sharma, Nandita. 2006. *Home economics: Nationalism and the making of 'migrant workers' in Canada.* Toronto: University of Toronto Press.

Slowe, Peter M. 1991. The geography of borderlands: The case of the Quebec-US borderlands. *Geographical Journal* 157 (2): 191–98.

Tichenor, Daniel. 2002. *Dividing lines: The politics of immigration control in America.* Princeton, NJ: Princeton University Press

Tirman, John. 2006. Immigration and insecurity: Post 9/11 fear in the United States. In *The audit of conventional wisdom*, MIT Center for International Studies. http://web.mit.edu/CIS/acw.html (accessed July 2006).

Toope, Stephen. J. 2005. A commission of inquiry into the actions of Canadian officials in relation to Maher Arar. http://www.ararcommission.ca/eng/TooperReport_final.pdf (accessed June 2006).

Torpey, John. 1998. Coming and going: On the state monopolization of the legitimate "means of movement." *Sociological Theory* 16 (3): 239–59.

———. 2000. *The invention of the passport: Surveillance, citizenship and the state.* Cambridge: Cambridge University Press.

Wright, Richard. 2004. Operations on the boundary: The state, the border and marginalized identities. *Antipode* 36 (1): 138–41.

14

IDs and Territory

Population Control for Resource Expropriation

NADIA ABU-ZAHRA

The occupation of land is concrete while the control of computer databases and their documents appear to be virtual.

Amira Hass (2005a)

We become the colonists and they become the owners of the land.[1]

M. Shinneh (interview, June 27, 2004)

The thesis of this paper is that territory can be acquired by depopulating areas and using population registries, identity cards, and permit systems to zone population movement. In other words, the manipulation of forms of (non-) citizenship, to displace and dispossess some people, thereby gains territory for others.

Zureik (2001, 227) was one of the few to predict that "population management, in addition to the now familiar spatial control," would gain precedence in future geopolitics. Most writers on similar "administrative" tools—maps and censuses in particular—concentrate on issues of representation (Anderson 1991; Appadurai 1993; Cohn 1987; Mitchell 1988). They ask, How is nationhood imagined or ideologized? Some take this further and ask, How is nationhood institutionalized? (through identity documentation, for instance; Torpey 2000, 14). This paper is based on a third question: How is nationhood territorialized?

Yet while the above studies concentrate on the system from within, this chapter is intended to provide a complementary perspective. Thus, it does not cover the system's contradictions, dysfunctions, improvisations, a posteriori rationalizations, indeterminacy, and counterproductiveness, as described by others (Parizot 2006a, 2006b; Hass 2002). Instead, it approaches the question from the perspective of those dispossessed in the process. It therefore looks not so much at territorialization as it does at *de*territorialization. The chapter is based on participant observation in intervals over a seven-year period, and on in-depth interviews during the latter intervals. Interview excerpts are also drawn from testimonies documented and published by human rights groups.

Internal passports: past and present

You know when you get married, you change your ID from single to married. Imagine, I just went to the Ministry of Interior—I had to give birth—two more [months until the birth]. If I give birth, and I'm not married [it will create a legal] problem [for registering the child, etc.] The crowd, you can't imagine, except those who go there.

I have diabetes (from pregnancy) and I take insulin. The time came for insulin and food. I knew that I would faint, but said, "I'll be up there soon and upstairs I'll relax." . . . In these moments, I was very close to the door. . . . In the end, I fainted. People threw on me water, gave me sweets, water . . . and requested from the guards downstairs just to let me in. . . . They didn't agree—even to look at me. . . . They also let me in from the electric door [which the doctor had warned against due to the pregnancy]. They said, "Enough, enough," in a severely cruel way as if they dealt with animals, not people.

But I'm sure my complaints, for *sure*, these are the least of problems (others have much more). All my complaints are about the checkpoints. I am living a blessed life for sure; there are people who really are in sad situations.

Majda (interview, June 27, 2004)

And she is probably right. The difficulty of her situation is not that it is extreme, but rather that it is everyday; marriage registration is unlikely to catch headlines, and the situation is unlikely to change. One of the key difficulties she faces is the link between identity documentation and movement restrictions: her "complaints are about the checkpoints," where a kind of internal passport is needed. In many parts of the world, internal passports are an artefact of history, with few remnants in the present: feudal Europe (Torpey 2000), the Nazi regime (Torpey 2000; Aly and Roth 2004), China (Torpey 1997, 2000), post-Revolution France (Torpey 1997, 2000), the former Soviet Union (Torpey 1997, 2000; Matthews 1993; Smith 1989), Apartheid South Africa (Giliomee and Schlemmer 1985), colonial Egypt (Mitchell 1988), and the former Yugoslavia (Hayden 1996). The decline in the use of internal passports has been so marked that Torpey's (2000) history of the passport argues that borders have effectively shifted outward and states have monopolized—from previous smaller entities—the right to control movement.

Centralizing control, however, has not necessarily eliminated internal checks on documentation, as demonstrated in Torpey's (1997) discussions on China, for instance. Internal checks are on the rise in the United States, where for fifteen years municipalities have shouldered the responsibility of checking individuals' identity documents (Mathew Coleman, personal communication,

March 24, 2006). Today in the United States, a driver's license renewal can trigger a check on immigration status, police can search vehicles at internal checkpoints, and employers can be punished for employing individuals without the required documents. Looking outside North America and Europe, checkpoints can be found in the Congo, Somalia, the Sudan, Egypt, India, Indonesia, and Sri Lanka, and across the former Soviet Union. In Uzbekistan, for example, internal checkpoints simply changed hands; the old Soviet style of governing continued, just with a new government (Nick Megoran, personal communication, May 26, 2006). If anything, the external borders of Uzbekistan hardened, and internal checkpoints became stricter. Although the literature on internal passports outside Europe and North America is sparse, cursory observation suggests that identity documentation is related to internal mobility restrictions. This is not solely an issue of migration; citizens are restricted in their own states, as well as others.

Identity documentation can be composed of numerous components, including a "code" and "card," terms developed by Noiriel (1996) and described by Torpey (2000).[2] In Palestine, the code and card correspond to the Population Registry and identity cards, respectively. All Palestinians living in the West Bank, for instance, are assigned an identity number by the Israeli Ministry of Interior. This began following Israel's military occupation of the West Bank in 1967, pursuant to Article 2 of Military Order no. 297 (Order concerning Identity Cards and Population Registration) of 1969 (Al-Haq 1989, 336). The Population Registry today contains ID numbers, place of residence, and any history of political activism (Cook, Hanieh, and Kay 2004, 55). It also contains a host of other information, including names, parents' names, sex, religion, births, deaths, marriages, and many other details. While the information is kept from the Palestinians it describes, much or all of it "can be seen on a screen by the lowest-ranking soldier at the most remote checkpoint in the West Bank or on the computers at the Erez [Gaza] crossing point" (Hass 2005a).

In addition to being coded into a Population Registry through identity numbers, Palestinians also carry identity cards. The same military order as the Population Registry (no. 297) compelled all males to apply for an identity card at the age of sixteen (Al Haq 1989). In 1988, Military Order no. 1232 extended this to females (Al-Haq 1989). The key to mobility restrictions lies in these military orders: IDs must be presented "upon the request of any soldier on duty or to any other soldier so authorised" (Al-Haq 1989, 323). Failure to do so is punishable with up to one year's imprisonment. Creating the obligation to display identification gives police, soldiers, and other authorities the power to limit mobility. Random identity checks are far more difficult to avoid than physical barriers.

Following a system of identification, the next steps toward mobility restriction involve zoning areas and then matching those zones to categories of identity numbers and identity cards. In 1967, Military Order no. 5 declared the West Bank a closed military area; anyone who wished to leave was required to obtain a permit from the military to do so (Al-Haq 1989). In 1971, General Exit Permit no. 5 was issued, allowing most Palestinians living in the Occupied Territories to enter Israel subject to certain restrictions: for example, remaining in Israel between 1:00 and 5:00 a.m. was prohibited without a special permit (Al-Haq 1989).

To travel anywhere other than Israel entailed obtaining a "certificate of exoneration" and then a permit[3] from the military authorities (Al-Haq 1989).[4] The certificate required clearance from a number of departments in the "Civil Administration," the Israeli military authorities ruling the West Bank and Gaza Strip, including the Income Tax Department, the Customs and Excise Department, the police, the Village Leagues (the puppet regime of the time), the municipality, and the village leader (Al-Haq 1989). Then and now, decisions concerning travel restrictions are often arbitrary, or guided by considerations such as payment of taxes and health insurance. No formal appeal procedure is in place; if a lawyer seeks a review, the case is simply resubmitted to the General Security Service for another security check (Al-Haq 1989). The end result is that instead of internal mobility being the rule with restrictions being the exception, restrictions are the rule, and mobility—through permits—is the exception.

Tools in policing hierarchy: Registry, IDs, license plates, and checkpoints

Thus, the cumulative effect—of a registry, identity cards, and corresponding zones—is that areas can be depopulated and repopulated. Figure 14.1 illustrates where a Palestinian living in the West Bank could go prior to 1948, after 1948, and today. These cutoff points mark key moments in the area's history, but they hide the intermediary shifts involved, such as the selective dispensation of permits, gradually decreasing over time. Nevertheless, the maps are useful as a starting point to illustrate two main transitions. The first transition, less than sixty years ago, cut villages in half along the 1949 Armistice Line, today called the Green Line. The second transition, when Israel occupied several areas including the West Bank, made interactions within these villages somewhat easier. But it also made thousands of people refugees, and marked the expansion of Israeli colonization into the West Bank.

Mitchell (1988), writing about colonialism in general, suggests that imposed state boundaries are policed not only at the border but also internally. This continues to be true in the case of Palestine. In 1967, as in 1948, internal borders were again created—this time in the West Bank. Areas were zoned off, such that Palestinians were forbidden on their own land except by special permission—usually as construction or domestic workers.[5] The Oslo Agreements, beginning in 1993, were some of the first explicit admissions of the demographic engineering processes taking place. They zoned areas into A, B, and C, where C represented areas of Israeli colonies, forbidden to Palestinians. Most B areas have since been annexed to these colonies, while Pales-

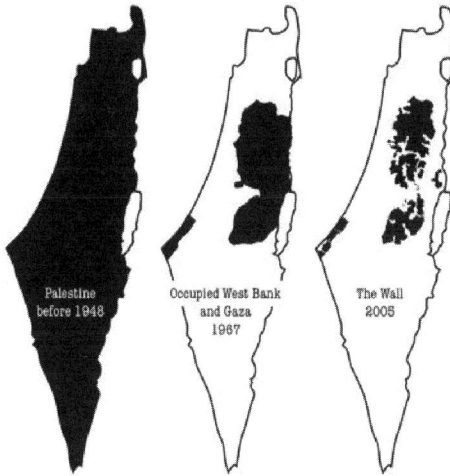

Figure 14.1 The Two Main Transitions in Mobility Restrictions: The 1949 Rhodes Armistice Line, and the Apartheid Wall, (Anti-Apartheid Wall Campaign 2004).

tinians have been enclosed into A areas (roughly corresponding to the areas shown in black in the third map) with what has come to be known as the Apartheid Wall (the word "Apartheid" has entered daily speech, and some Arabic-speaking villagers simply refer to the Wall *in English* as "the Apartheid"; Chris Harker, personal communication, June 7, 2006).

Years before both Oslo and the Wall, Mitchell (1988, 166–67) described

a state whose existence is contingent upon maintaining a radical difference between itself and the identity of those outside it . . . the outside must be represented as negative and threatening, as the method of maintaining meaning and order within.[6]

In this state, however, the supposed internal-external boundary is false, and is instead composed of "internal boundaries of hierarchical separation which must constantly be policed" (1988, 167). Although Mitchell was referring to Israel, this is very similar to the situation of "highland peoples" in Thailand, where Toyota (2005) argues for their incorporation as citizens in the Thai state.[7] Her key argument is that any formal separation, such that the highland peoples obtain statehood, would lead to a worsening of discrimination against them inside Thailand. As in Palestine, movement is fluid and geographic areas have been created relatively recently and arbitrarily. Intermarriage and socioeconomic interactions are typical, such that no clear line can be drawn—either geographically or demographically—to definitively separate some people from others. Her description of the situation fits well with Mitchell's analysis: no colonial border is ever external and is instead a blunt policing of hierarchy that can descend to the scale of the individual.

In the Population Registry, Palestinians are coded into geographic zones—something they resist with varying degrees of success. Correspondingly, Israeli-issued ID cards are color-coded, signifying instantly the geographic zone to which each person is confined. Initially, Palestinians in the West Bank were obliged to carry their IDs in orange "jackets" (plastic wallets); Palestinians in the Gaza Strip had red ones, and Palestinians in Jerusalem had blue (Al-Haq 1989). As is the case internationally, there are also "church-related" IDs (Van Teeffelen 2001, 2), diplomatic IDs, and United Nations refugee IDs.[8] Nongovernmental organizations, as well as international organizations like the UN, issue cards to their employees with the aim of easing passage through Israeli checkpoints.

From 1987 to 1991, movement restrictions were applied to villages and regions, and blanket curfews imprisoned people in their homes on a regular basis and for extended periods. In 1989, Military Order no. 1269 introduced green jackets for the IDs of former detainees—including those who were detained and released without charge (Al Haq 1969). In a green ID, the ID number remains unchanged, but the card expires after six months and requires renewal. Green IDs prohibit travel to areas occupied by Israel in 1948, as well as East Jerusalem—thereby also making travel difficult between the southern and northern West Bank, and impossible beyond the boundaries of either the West Bank or Gaza Strip, whichever area is ascribed to the ID holder. Green IDs annul chances to study, to seek medical treatment, to see or live with family, and to enjoy all other daily life experiences barred by the geographic "divides" of IDs.

Identity and mobility restrictions are bound together by checkpoints. An international aid volunteer describes the links:

> To be a Palestinian is to be categorized. You are yellow-plated or blue-plated; a holder of a Jerusalem, Israeli or West Bank/Gaza ID or, the lucky ones, a foreign passport or a church-related ID. When you live in the West Bank or Gaza, you are an inhabitant of area 1, 2 or 3 (in Hebron H1 or H2). You are a Christian or Moslem (the religion is obligatory mentioned in the passport) [sic]. Or a refugee with a United Nations pass, or an "indigenous" Palestinian. In this country, categorization is a mechanism to control people, with the checkpoint the big categorizer. (Van Teeffelen 2001, 2)

Notable is the comment "You are yellow-plated or blue-plated." License plates follow the same pattern as ID cards (Parry 1995). License plates are coded according to the vehicle's owner and permits acquired for the vehicle's travel. Different colored plates include white or green for the West Bank and Gaza Strip, blue for West Bank or Gaza taxis, white and red for Palestinian VIPs, yellow for Israelis or Jerusalemites—with a special sticker for some: red for the Israeli police, black for the Israeli military, and white and black for

United Nations and diplomats. Interestingly, license plates have not been a major point for discussion in literature on colonial technologies. Observing a recent census in India, Sharma and Gupta (2006, 15) note that, "jeeps with official license plates and development workers with census forms and a particular tone of voice are markers of status and power." In Palestine, license plates are far more commanding than a simple tone of voice. They define who can go where. Without the correct license plate and identity card to travel on the colonist-only highways, the sick and elderly must pass through full-height swiveling metal gates (see figure 14.2), their walking sticks of no use, and their walkers impossible. No burden too heavy to carry can be transported, because without the correct license plate, no vehicle can pass. Color-coded license plates are an oppression unknown in most parts of the world, an undocumented technology of hierarchy in today's "administrative" armory.

In 1993, following the first Oslo Agreement, all Palestinians in the West Bank and Gaza Strip were given the "prisoners'" green IDs, and for the first time since 1967, passage between the Gaza Strip and the West Bank was formally forbidden. From that point onward, all movements outside the West Bank or Gaza Strip required permits. In effect, the West Bank and Gaza Strip became enclosure zones, and to their inhabitants, Israel and by extension the rest of the world became closed zones. Furthermore, the West Bank became a closed zone to residents of the Gaza Strip, and the Gaza Strip a closed zone to residents of the West Bank. This was made possible through the Population Registry. Journalist Amira Hass (2005a) explains that prior to the year 2000, "Israel did not automatically approve moves from Gaza to the West Bank, or vice versa," and since then, no change of address has ever been approved. This is contrary to the Oslo Accords, which state (in Hass's words again), "Palestin-

Figure 14.2 Women Passing through Part of the Checkpoint at Huwwara in the Northern West Bank, (Machsom Watch 2006).

ians merely need to notify Israeli authorities of a change of address, and Israel must record it." The result of Israeli refusals is that "thousands of Gazans currently living in the West Bank are considered illegal residents and, if caught at a roadblock, could be deported back to Gaza" (Hass 2005a). In sum, passage out of an enclosure zone or into a closed zone is possible only through application to the Israeli military authorities for a series of certificates and permits.

An open-air prison for "voluntary expulsion"

With this system of identity documentation and mobility restrictions, all movement can be obstructed at any given time. A typical United Nations report illustrates this:

> [In 2003] As in previous years, with the onset of the Jewish holidays, the IDF completely sealed the entire West Bank, prohibiting all entry and exit and movement on most roads, for over one and a half million Palestinian civilians.

> During the Jewish holiday of Sukkoth on 8 October 2003, the IDF issued an order prohibiting movement for four days of all Palestinian cars in C area of the entire northern area of the West Bank. Area C contains the only open roads without roadblocks for vehicular travel between the major Palestinian urban centers. (OCHA 2003)

Of course, attempts to circumvent checkpoints are commonplace. Anthropologist Tobias Kelly, based on his experiences in the West Bank, describes how people use international passports, detours around checkpoints, and modifications of appearance and behavior to pass checkpoints. He cautions, however, that while everyday efforts at resistance are often successful, their failure can spell disaster on personal and intimate levels. While going around checkpoints is common, it opens "the greater risk of being shot by the Israeli military" (Kelly 2006, 102). His neighbor was shot in the stomach.

To the villages and cities along the Green Line, including Jerusalem, the enforcement of zones A, B, and C solidified the 1949 split that fell in the middle of roads, fields, and even houses. Villagers describe their homes as having a head inside the West Bank and feet outside (Galili 2003). Beyond jokes, the reality now is that the boundaries within which Palestinians may live and move are rapidly tightening. As of August 2005, according to the conservative estimates of the U.S. Central Intelligence Agency (CIA), 242 Israeli "settlements and civilian land use sites" were in the West Bank, 42 in the Israeli-occupied Golan Heights, and 29 in East Jerusalem (CIA 2006). A plan announced in October 2004 would construct over 500 kilometers of roads, 16 tunnels, and underground passages in order to extend the dual-road system: one for Israeli colonists and one for Palestinians, whereby any intersection between the two would result in a tunnel for the Palestinians (Applied Research Institute of

Jerusalem 2006). Given that Palestinian passage is only allowed through gated tunnels beneath these roads, a complete curfew on Palestinians in the West Bank will require sixteen military cars only: one for each tunnel (Juma 2005).

Few parallels of this kind of open-air imprisonment exist in the literature on mobility restrictions. In 1830 in colonial Egypt, a government ordinance restricted Egyptian villagers from traveling across district boundaries, making them "inmates of their own villages" (Mitchell 1988, 34). An 1852 text records that "it was scarcely possible for a *fellah* [farmer] to pass from one village to another without a written passport" (Mitchell 1988, 34). The apparent goal was conscription, and to prevent soldiers from deserting the army (Mitchell 1988, 34–62). The affected, however, were not only military-aged men. All Egyptians were confined, regulated, and supervised; all were inspected (*taftish*) or instructed by officials (34). As Egyptians were cramped into ever more crowded quarters, the cities of colonists are described as spacious and open (164). Territory in colonial Egypt was as much a factor in draconian prohibitions on movement as it is today—nearly two hundred years later—in Palestine.

Looking back even earlier, the French once passed a measure issuing "passports specific to cantons" and threatening "up to a year of detention" for no passport (Torpey 2000, 51). In retrospect, John Torpey writes that "if the government had had the teeth to make this measure bite, it would have turned France into a gigantic prison in which the cantons constituted the individual cells" (2000, 51). The unfortunate situation for Palestinians is that today's "teeth," and the prison accomplished by their bite, are internationally accepted as administrative measures for security (although ruled illegal in 2004 by the International Court of Justice). The Apartheid Wall's "new" route is a minimum of 670 kilometers,[9] twice the length of the Green Line (Human Rights Watch [HRW] 2006a). Only about one-fifth of the route follows the Green Line itself (HRW 2006a). Completion of the Wall's four phases will annex to Israel 47 percent of the West Bank, including 90 percent of the Jerusalem district (Anti-Apartheid Wall Campaign 2005). It will bring over 300,000 West Bank and East Jerusalem colonists and a minimum of 135,000 acres of West Bank territory over to the Israeli side (HRW 2006a). The West Bank will be cut into three, with at least twenty-two encircled enclaves, directly affecting 780,000 Palestinians (Barghouthi 2004).

Construction sites for the Apartheid Wall are the focus of popular resistance. In many areas, like Imneizil, villagers managed physically to climb onto and block army bulldozers (Anti-Apartheid Wall Campaign 2006b).[10] In June 2006, farmers from Imneizel, Tuwani, and Susia[11] mounted a series of protests against a road reserved solely for colonists, guarded by sniper towers.

> As demonstrators entered the road they blocked it with rocks in order to prevent settler traffic from moving. The road connects the settlements

in the Hebron area with those in the Naqab (Negev) district. A size-able contingent of Occupation Forces were stationed in the area and attempted to stop the people. Clashes ensued as soldiers used sticks and gun backs to beat back the villagers. The crowd resisted and succeeded in maintaining the roadblock. (Anti-Apartheid Wall Campaign 2006b)

This was the second time in a short period that villagers succeeded in block-ing the colonist-only road despite attacks and beatings by Israeli soldiers. A few days earlier, the villagers had blocked the road and forced the soldiers to dismantle parts of the concrete foundation (Anti-Apartheid Wall Campaign 2006c). This is an area where the route of the Wall has ostensibly been modified and shifted closer to the Green Line. The protests are against not only the Wall but also a new, second wall along Road 80, mentioned above. This second wall will separate them from the remaining West Bank and sandwich them against the "official" Wall. The 1,500 villagers in the area risk losing access to urban facilities and services nearby, upon which they are dependent and without which they will be forced to leave (Anti-Apartheid Wall Campaign 2006d).

A paradox of such a situation is that the prohibition on movement is com-bined with the creation of conditions generating the compulsion to move (Zolberg 1978, cited in Torpey 2000). Describing the emergence of the inter-national refugee regime between the two world wars, Torpey (2000) explains that where people most required mobility for survival, they were forbidden from moving. In 1922 in Russia, following a three-year period of mass emi-gration during civil war and famine, the Soviet government banned further departure (Torpey 2000, 124–25). Postrevolutionary Russia was the "textbook combination of restrictions on departure and the production of a desire to leave" (Torpey 2000). Today, "producing a desire to leave" could be termed "voluntary expulsion"—this is the term common in Palestine, where everyday resistance is met with suppression until only one option remains—to leave. As is probably the case elsewhere, the desire to leave is not immediate—it is the result of failure in all attempts at earning an income and meeting one's needs, which occurs quietly, internally, and without international attention.[12]

Labor is not the issue: A biopolitics of the unwanted

Literature on biopolitics (defined as power over the body; Foucault 1978) and identity documentation often looks at the body as a source of resources to be expropriated, and as a source of labor in particular. The attempts described in this paper by Israeli institutions that imply control of the body (and its move-ment especially) treat the body as something extraneous, not something valu-able. Palestinians in this system are valued more for their absence than their presence (Rosenhek 2006, 3). While this attitude toward their expendability is most evident in aspects of force (extrajudicial assassinations, daily injuries and killings, demolitions, and economic strangulation; see United Nations

2006, HRW 2006 2, and Cook, Hanich and Kay 2004), it is institutionalized in the system of identification and mobility restrictions. The following paragraphs explore three aspects of this. First, they consider the literature on Palestine that *does* emphasize the issue of labor. Then, they weigh the possibility that permits are a "safety-valve." Finally, they return to the issue of geography in determining identity status.

Numerous authors have written of the situation of Palestinian workers in Israel, with the latest publications referring to the Wall and its concomitant "cross-border industrial zones" (CBIZ) (for early works, see Democracy and Workers' Rights Center 1996; Elzein et al. 1997; Bornstein 2002; for a focus on the Wall and the CBIZ, see Juma 2005; Rapoport 2004). Anthropologist Cédric Parizot (2006b) predicts that any end to the use of Palestinian labor would raise protest from the "middlemen" (the gendered use of this word is appropriate here), usually Palestinians with Israeli citizenship. The cheap labor keeps property prices low, and is therefore demanded by relatively impoverished but expanding Palestinian communities inside Israel. Due to a combination of need for labor and profitability, Parizot argues, labor may continue to be brought in from the West Bank and Gaza Strip. Notwithstanding these arguments, the importance of discussing the labor situation rests more on Palestinian workers' reliance on this source of income than on any Israeli dependence. Israel is relatively free to choose from labor pools around the world, and has illustrated its ability to do so, by ejecting Palestinian workers and replacing them with workers from the Thailand, Romania, Turkey, China, the Phillippines. sub-Saharan Africa and Latin America (Rosenhek 2006, 2). While the CBIZ are undoubtedly a central component in an architecture of oppression, and while they will very likely become a key source of income for Israelis and Palestinian middlemen, at the expense of Palestinian exploitation, nevertheless the CBIZ are—as with Palestinian labor elsewhere—expendable.

Lack of dependence on labor does, however, raise the question of why such a complex and burdensome system of permits is in place. Smith (1989, 337), using the example of Soviet internal passports, suggests that under stringent mobility control, permits create a "docile class" and act as a "safety valve" on pressure to redistribute unequal resources. This may be the case in Palestine (Hass 2002, 14–15). Arguably, however, the valve's released steam is equally useful to screen military activities from international attention (Hass 2002, 13). Were permits not issued, international organizations would take issue with expropriation and illegal bans on movement. As it is, they take issue with permits. For instance, concerning an order confiscating 18,000 acres of Palestinian land for the Apartheid Wall in October 2003, the UN writes that "the orders prohibit any person from entering or exiting those areas without a special or general permit," (OCHA 2003). This takes promises of permits at face value.[13] Palestinians do not.[14] While permits may indeed be issued at first, they are ephemeral. A Beit Surik villager explains that she is told by soldiers that permits will be issued, then when the area has been sealed, no permits are issued (personal communication, June 27, 2004). Such reports are found throughout the West Bank. In the village of Masha, 80 percent of village lands have been taken by the Wall, and villagers' sole access to these lands is through a gate in the north (Anti-Apartheid Wall Campaign 2006a). Over a six-month period in 2006, farmers were allowed to pass through this gate for only five days, and even then, only those with permits; 150 farmers were denied permits (Anti-Apartheid Wall Campaign 2006a).

In October 2003—just as permits were being promised with respect to the Apartheid Wall—permits for employment were suspended indefinitely (OCHA 2003). The complete suspension of all permits ends any doubts as to Israeli dependence on Palestinian labor. While the benefits of exploitation are high, and the mobility situation has been manipulated so as to maximize these benefits, they remain unessential to the Israeli economy. Ultimately, the system of identification and mobility restrictions has ends other than simply human labor.

The presence of Palestinians, even as captive laborers, is not the goal of this system. Indeed, this lack of economic interdependence is often cited as a key differentiating factor between Israel and Apartheid South Africa (Adam and Moodley 2005). Yet even in South Africa the purpose of influx control was not to exploit labor but to uphold a racist distribution of land and wealth. Anthony Lemon (2004, 60) describes how "geographical separation" was a useful euphemism for a system of exclusion that relied on race. Given that Jewish colonists—but not Palestinians—in the West Bank are treated as Israelis, heavily subsidized, and given access to a complex system of colonist-only roads and land blocs, the term "geographical separation" seems also rather euphemistic in this case. Thus, in neither situation are identity documentation and mobility restrictions solely about labor. Why, therefore, maintain a system so costly, in all senses of the word?

Bringing it all together: Maps, codes, cards, and land

In response to the question of why the system was in place, a former member of the Israeli army (IDF) gave the following response:

> You're probably aware that Israel, in the 38 years of occupation did run only one census of the Palestinian population (in 1967). The explanation for this, and for the lack of use/interest in geodemographics, I would argue, is the Israeli worldview that Israel "is not interested in control" of the Palestinian people. This is a very deep belief (in my view) and it means that the mission of the IDF and other bodies in Israel that are involved in the occupation is to "contain" of the Palestinians, which is very different from "control" [sic]. (Personal communication, June 18, 2005)

He also felt quite strongly that mapping was only used for familiarizing the army with terrain, unrelated to its inhabitants. This response reflects two problems with the literature on the colonial census. First, the reiterated pairing of census with population, and maps with territory, precludes thinking of these tools in other terms. Second, the census has become the symbol of population control to the point that, without a census, control is presumed absent. The response also suggests that lack of interest in a population translates into a less interventionist kind of governing: "containment" rather than "control." The following paragraphs explore these three elements—(1) tools for controlling population and territory, (2) population and the census, and (3) containment versus control—and close with some reflections on why the system is in place.

The colonial link between maps and territory has been explored in the literature on critical cartography, and repeated throughout literature on the census and population (see Craib 2000 for a review of critical studies on colonial cartography from 1989 to 2000; numerous major studies have also been published since, e.g. Harris 2004, Smith 2003, Harley 2001 and Driver 2001). Despite their common perspectives on issues of representation and power, analysts of map and census rarely shuffle the pairs: maps are said to correspond to territorial control, and censuses to population control. Military surveyors are seen "to put space under the same surveillance which the census-makers were trying to impose on persons" (Anderson 1991, 173). Meanwhile, "statistics are to bodies and social types what maps are to territories: they flatten and enclose" (Appadurai 1993, 334, cited in Kertzer and Arel 2002, 6). In comparison to maps, colonial censuses are not seen as a primary method of obtaining land; rather, they expropriate resources without land, like taxes, labor, military service, and so on. Anderson (1991, 174) does mention an intersection of map and census, whereby the map marks cutoff points to groups of people, while the census lends names to places. Yet such an intersection serves more to fulfill the categorization purposes associated with the census than the expropriation purposes associated with maps.

Yet the counterparts of the census—the population registry and identity documentation—can be powerful tools in expropriation. Even more explicitly connected to expropriation are the tools of zoning and permits. As mentioned earlier, people living in upland Thailand are issued seventeen kinds of color-coded identity cards, only some of which may eventually lead to citizenship (Toyota 2005). Their vulnerable status has made easy the incremental expropriation of their territory since 1896 when the Royal Forestry Department declared large areas to be "protected"—closed zones from which any inhabitants could be deported (Toyota 2005). Such "fortress conservation"—declaring large tracts of land as closed zones in the name of environmental conservation—is practiced around the world (Brockington 2002). In Tanzania, permits were issued to some inhabitants of the created Mkomazi

Game Reserve (Brockington 2002). In a pattern like those described in this chapter, the exclusion of the inhabitants was then gradually enforced: first those without permits, then those with forged permits, and, finally, permit holders (Brockington 2002, 45). To relate permit systems solely to population and not territory is to overlook one of their key functions. Reexamining the dichotomy of census-population and map-territory could lead to substantial findings on how people are dispossessed, and perhaps reshape our impressions of censuses, registries, identity cards, and mobility restrictions.

Too often these numerous colonial tools—from census to mobility restrictions—are viewed in isolation from one another. The census, for example, has received a disproportionate amount of attention. Meanwhile, the synergistic links between "code" and "card"—the Population Registry and identity documentation—have been examined in only some cases. As a result, the census has come to emblemize colonial aspirations to control population, so much so that a lack of census can now be seen as a lack of interest in control. The argument quoted above, that no census means no control, would be plausible if not for the Population Registry. In effect, Palestinians since 1967 have "voluntarily" provided all material normally collected by census. This sounds counterintuitive—why would people volunteer their intimate information, and under the kind of harsh conditions described at the beginning of this chapter? The answer goes back to the code and the card. In the West Bank, if children reach the age of sixteen without their birth being registered in the Israeli Population Registry, they will not be granted an ID card (Hass 2005b). An ID is required for school matriculation examinations, as well as applications for a driver's license, marriage contract, or birth certificate (Al-Haq 1989, 323).[15] It proves residency in the Occupied Territories, and is required to request permission to travel within or outside those territories, including for "family reunification" (discussed below). Quite simply, without an ID, "life is impossible" (Cook, Hanieh, and Kay 2004, 32). The Israeli state has monopolized not only the "legitimate means of movement" (Torpey 2000) for Palestinians, but many other aspects of life also. As a result, Palestinians have no choice but to undergo whatever is necessary to register and obtain an ID. This adds an important point to the existing literature on the colonial census: with a code and a card, no census is needed.

With or without a census, in the case of Palestine, some may argue that control is not the objective. This is the underlying message promoted by those who emphasize Israel's lack of dependence on Palestinian labor and who play down parallels with other authoritarian regimes: no need for labor means no need for control (e.g., Steinberg 2004). Is the purpose to "control" rather than "contain," as asserted above? A close examination of a sample piece of legislation suggests this is the case, and illustrates that Israeli bureaucratic and military control extends to rather personal levels. The following section discusses

Israel's latest amendments to its Citizenship Law, amendments recently reaffirmed by the Israeli court system (HRW 2006b).

"They limit who we can marry"

In Jerusalem, Palestinians are neither eligible for Palestinian passports (which in any case are only travel documents, not passports), nor are they Israeli citizens. The majority are permanent residents of Jerusalem and possess identification cards. Since Israel annexed East Jerusalem, they have been subject to Israeli laws and regulations except those regarding residency, entry, and exit to the remaining West Bank and Gaza Strip. These issues are governed by military orders. For Palestinians in the West Bank and Gaza Strip (WBGS) to be allowed to live with their spouse and/or children in Jerusalem, other cities outside the WBGS, or the other half of villages lying along the Green Line, they must submit applications for "family reunification" and "visa permits" to the Israeli authorities.

The situation leaves thousands of families in a predicament. Majda, the woman who described her marriage registration above, explains her situation:

> They limit who we can love and who we can marry—really—imagine—
> the town my husband is from—I'm forbidden to enter the area of his
> family, and he's forbidden to enter the area of my family. Because he
> is West Bank—he is forbidden to enter Jerusalem. And I, because I'm
> Jerusalem—I am forbidden to enter West Bank.

Application for family reunification is the same as for other permits, and like other permits, was frozen in practice in the year 2000 (Hass 2005a), formally frozen in 2002, and legislatively barred in 2005 (except in certain age categories) (HRW 2006a). In 2003, then Prime Minister Ariel Sharon appointed himself chair of a ministerial committee dealing with the non-Jewish population (Benziman 2003). He then rushed through the Knesset (Israeli parliament) an amendment to the Citizenship Law.

The amendment prohibits Palestinian spouses of Israeli citizens from becoming citizens or even residents of Israel. Meanwhile, holders of Israeli passports are prohibited from even entering Areas A (i.e., most Palestinian urban areas; Amnesty International 2005). The amendment effectively forces all such future couples to leave their homeland—if they can (Amnesty International 2005). Its full ramifications extend further: children of such couples will be unable to apply for residency in Jerusalem (or the other side of any of the villages split along the Green Line). Couples who live apart will be unable to prove they are couples, given the stringent yet arbitrary regulations, and couples who live together, contravening these Israeli regulations, live in fear of being caught. Men and women in this situation speak of being imprisoned in their own homes, to avoid the possibility of being found "illegally" and deported from their spouses and children.

In addition, new measures have now been introduced that radically segregate movement of individuals with differing identity cards—they must take different vehicles and different routes when traveling. New measures have also been introduced to enforce the ban on entry of "internationals" into the West Bank—including all foreign passport holders married to Palestinians, and of course, Palestinians who have no ID but have foreign passports (as always, Jewish colonists are excluded from these restrictions). Rima Saba, one such Palestinian, spent a month to no avail begging the border guards to allow her to return to her young daughter in Ramallah. Another woman was separated from her two children when she was told by an official at the airport, "You have spent eight years here with your husband—that's enough—now go back to your country" (e-mail personal communication, 2006). Yet another man, who I will pseudo-name Raed, writes,

> This also applies to my wife who is European and holds a European passport. She was due to travel on Friday to see her children abroad and her 91-year old mother, and to renew her visa, but she is very much afraid not to be allowed back. . . . I do not cherish the idea of being separated from my wife, after 27 years of marriage, by a soldier in Beit El.

Beit El is "up the road" from his house, an Israeli colony overlooking Ramallah. This dissonance between geography and identity is a metaphor for Mitchell's concept of policing hierarchy. Raed's wife of twenty-seven years, a resident and home owner in Ramallah, as well as being the spouse of a Palestinian, is considered an international. The soldier and the residents in Beit El, in a military base and colony established under military occupation, are considered citizens.

The geographical inconsistency of categories created in mobility restrictions illustrates the internal policing of hierarchy Mitchell observes in colonial Egypt. It also parallels aspects of the situation in Thailand, where some highland peoples are considered citizens, while others are not, based mainly on ethnicity or income (Toyota forthcoming). Post-Revolution France also, at times, referred to and treated its peasantry or its opposition as "foreigners" (Torpey 2000, 24, 28, 51). The unwanted are termed foreigners, irrespective of where they live. Meanwhile, colonists, irrespective of their recentness, are termed residents, entitled to citizenship, freedom of movement, and all other standard rights and freedoms. The key difference between Palestinians and colonists in the West Bank is that the former are earmarked for concentration into shrinking geographic areas, while the latter are earmarked to replace them. Here, finally, is a possible reason for the vast apparatus of identity documentation and mobility restrictions facing Palestinians in their own lands, fields, and homes.

Territory

> We are not fighting for bigger ghettos or for more colorful walls, but for
> liberation and justice in our land.

The Grassroots Palestinian Anti-Apartheid Wall Campaign
(Juma 2005)

A typical military order for a closed zone in the West Bank reads,

> According to my authorities as a Military Chief Commander in the
> Region of Judea and Samaria, and as I believe that it is imperative for
> military reasons due to the special security situation in the region, I
> order the following:
>
> 1- The "Map" signed in scale 1:20000 and attached to the order is an
> essential part of this order. The "Lands": An area of land which is 430.9
> dunums, marked in red in the map . . . [this text is followed by a list of
> villages and land blocks and parcels to be expropriated].
>
> 2- I announce that the above-mentioned lands are seized for military
> reasons.
>
> 3- The IDF seize the lands and have an absolute control over it that is
> given to the Officer of the Central Command, Officer of Lands who is
> responsible in the Ministry of Defense
>
> [. . . the order continues to explain locations for copies of maps].
>
> 7- The owners of land have the right to go to the DCO (District Coordi-
> nation Office) in Jerusalem in order to get more information about their
> right of land use expenses and compensation
>
> [. . . mentions that the order takes effect immediately . . . signed by the
> Chief Commander of the Israel Defence Forces in Judea & Samaria].
> (Israel 2006)

Palestinian analysis of the expropriation maps, in this and two other military orders, concluded that the proposed road to "facilitate Palestinian move
ment" would confiscate over fifteen square kilometers of prime agricultural
land—including 30,000 olive trees, on which most of the 24,000 villagers
relied (Israel 2006). The road would also annex large agricultural and open
space areas from several Palestinian villages (Beit 'Anan, Beit Leqia, Beit Sira,
Khirbet Misbah, Beit Ur al-Fouqa, Beit Ur al-Tihta, Saffa, Deir Ibzid, Kufr
Ni'ma, and 'Ein 'Arik).

These annexed lands would be used to expand the Giv'at Ze'ev bloc of colonies, already spanning nearly 2,000 acres of Palestinian land in the West Bank
and housing nearly 15,000 colonists (Assad 2005; Jewish Virtual Library 2005).
The largest of the five colonies in the bloc, founded in 1982, hopes to more

than double its population to 25,000 plus (Tehilla 2006). Yet Giv'at Ze'ev is one of the smaller blocs. Nearly half a million colonists live in fortified, exclusivist colonies in the West Bank, a number set to increase with the significant colony expansions underway (Anti-Apartheid Wall Campaign 2006e).[16]

The Apartheid Wall will solidify the presence of about 200 colonies, integrating them into colonist-only road networks, which—as mentioned earlier—will be expanded to run another 500 kilometers through the West Bank (Juma 2005). The Wall has taken or destroyed hundreds of wells;[17] Israel uses 73 percent of the water available from West Bank aquifers, Palestinians in the West Bank use 17 percent, and colonists use 10 percent (United Nations 2006). Although the amount of land to be annexed by the Apartheid Wall is said to be 6.1 percent, this—added to 11.8 percent occupied by colonies and 29.1 percent annexed in the Jordan Valley—totals 47 percent of the West Bank and excludes the colonist-only roads (Juma 2005).

Through innumerable military orders like the one above, vast tracts of land are being depopulated and repopulated. Their inhabitants are being forcibly displaced, with identity cards being the key to power over individuals. Vested with certain forms of knowledge about the individual—and with countless aspects of life contingent on the nature of the ID—IDs have become a principal tool of coercion at the individual level, resulting in mass dispossession at the collective level.

Closing thoughts

In spite of this fact, the role of "administrative" measures has been relatively ignored. This could perhaps be considered the slipping of war into everyday life, in the ways described in this book. Robert Hayden (1996)—referring specifically to denaturalization—calls it "bureaucratic ethnic cleansing," a term that perhaps captures some of the violence intrinsic to systems of population control. Yet proponents of such systems describe them as an "administrative" alternative to force, and as a "defense" against war. According to this line of thinking, a "nonviolent" way of waging war (on "terror," for example) is through legislation on citizenship issues like identity documentation, movement restrictions, and other constraints on civil rights.

Such systems are implemented gradually and thus cause maximum effect—in spite of their failings—with minimum attention. Even Palestinians see "administrative measures" as relative: "I'm sure my complaints . . . these are the least of problems." Using manipulations of (non-)citizenship to attain goals typically associated with war thus causes them to fall under the line of vision of international media, governments, and the public. But the effects are there, when we choose to see them. Majda said to me, as we sat on the shaded balcony in an office later made obsolete because of its isolation behind the Wall:

Everything inside you is wilting; your taste for life; can you imagine wishing to die, wishing the night would come so you can sleep—you forget. I'm sure many people feel this way, tired, fed up. I now think it would be better outside [the country]. Maybe I'm bad. [To hope] not to stay walking on the garbage, on the stones, under the sun—[to hope to lead] "lives"—I'd like to live normally—not [especially] nice—normally. So if any chance came to go outside—work, raise a family—in a clean and [natural] normal world. . . . They work on our moods, [in order] so we don't want this home, our homeland. You reach a stage—where—if you're given a choice—you take it. This is what they do—they make everything difficult so if they give the slightest release—you think it's something great. I don't understand why they forget that we must live together—we'd be stupid to leave—they should think ahead. (Majda, interview, June 27, 2004)

Notes

1. Shinneh, who lost all his land in 1948 from the Jerusalem village of Kolonia, now living in the Jerusalem village of Beit Surik, where he is about to lose all his land to the Wall.

2. Caplan (2000) and Caplan and Torpey (2001) describe additional forms of marking identity.

3. Exit visas are present in other states also, such as Syria and Sudan (Embassy of the Republic of Sudan 2006; Syrian Ministry of Tourism 2006).

4. Palestinians in the West Bank (including Jerusalem) and Gaza Strip are not given passports. The Palestinian Authority "passport" is in fact a travel document, acting in much the same way as the Israeli-issued identity cards. Indeed, the Israeli "identity number" for each person is printed on his or her Palestinian "passport." Prior to 1994, Palestinians traveled only on their identity cards and additional Israeli-issued permits (described above). If they owned an additional passport (from Jordan, the United States, etc.), they may use this—they would still, however, be subject to the Israeli permit system, based on their identity cards.

5. An example of this is given later in this chapter (the section entitled "Territory"). Although this example is one of the more recent expropriations, military orders requisitioning land for "military needs" began in 1968, following a halt in land registration in 1967 and a survey of the West Bank to determine the extent of land available for expropriation (Badil 2004). Although a 1979 Israeli court ruling forbade the use of expropriated land for colonization, expropriation continued, and a separate planning system for Jewish colonies was established through Military Order no. 418 (Badil 2004). Palestinian homes are demolished if built outside planning scheme borders retained from the 1940s; meanwhile, new planning schemes continue to be drafted and implemented for Jewish colonies (Badil 2004).

6. Cf. the "Othering" of Said (1978).

7. Other examples that come to mind are predominantly those with visual impressions: Hadrian's Wall, the Great Wall of China, the wall in Namibia, the walls at the U.S.-Mexico border, and others. What is important about the Thai parallel is its reliance on less visible forms of boundaries, through documents.

8. Members of the Christian clergy are given "special identification ... by the Department of the Interior and the Ministry of Religious Affairs" (Abu El-Assal 2006). This does not necessarily ease passage, as demonstrated by the recent refusal of the Israeli authorities to allow an Anglican bishop of Jerusalem to travel abroad (Abu El-Assal 2006).

9. Certain areas of the Wall are ostensibly short in length, but in fact conceal large dips into the West Bank by a so-called colony Wall (which is in fact the original Apartheid Wall, east of the colony). It is predicted that in moments when international attention is diverted, these short lengths will be removed, opening the U-shape, and in effect annexing the colony westward, and retaining the colony Wall on the eastern side.

10. The dynamics of grassroots resistance against armed military forces are difficult to generalize. Each particular moment, event, and site operates under differing dynamics. Sometimes soldiers are disorganized and at a loss as to how to respond—such as during one protest in Imneizil that took place at a different location than usual (Tim, personal communication, August 29, 2006). Other times they watch as protestors temporarily block construction—then they move in and force people back. Sometimes even before protestors can approach, soldiers have shot live ammunition, rubber-coated steel bullets, tear gas, and sound bombs. At least seven Palestinians have been shot dead at protests. Others have been shot simply for walking too close to the Wall. Hundreds of Palestinians have been injured—often repeatedly—by bullets, gas, and sound bombs. In the village of Bil'in alone, over 100 villagers have been injured, including a twenty-five year old shot in 2002 and now paralyzed from the chest down, with only the use of his left hand (and other difficulties resulting from brain damage sustained from his injuries).

11. Susia is one example of depopulating and repopulating areas. Susia was a village of permanent cave homes, one among numerous such villages in the area of al-Khalil (Hebron). "Twenty years ago, the cave dwellers of Susia were evacuated from their original village on the pretext of archaeological digs in the area. Some of the evacuees went to live on their lands close to the Israeli settlement, which was founded a short time before. Five years ago the Israeli army destroyed the caves of these families, and since then they continued to live there in impermanent and improvised housing." (Krinis and Dunayevsky 2006)

12. Already entire communities have been forced to relocate inside the West Bank, due to the land loss, mobility restrictions, and isolation imposed by the Wall. Given that many Palestinians are already refugees, they are strongly resistant to resettlement, making traditional "transfer" methods unviable. With "voluntary transfer," however, those with the means and ability may be forced to migrate internationally.

13. It must be noted, however, that numerous UN reports have repeatedly emphasized the inaccessibility of permits (e.g., UNRWA 2004). Notwithstanding these reports, Israeli military officials still use the issue of gates and permits as evidence of their "allowances" for humanitarian concerns.

14. Palestinians refused to accept permits initially, because they represented a military tactic to force Palestinian acknowledgment of military orders (Anti-Apartheid Wall Campaign 2003). The permits do not recognize Palestinian ownership of the land and instead must be renewed frequently. Furthermore, permits are selectively dispensed, excluding, for instance, land owners born outside the village or land owners born in the village yet living in another village (Anti-Apartheid Wall Campaign 2003).

15. IDs are terminated at death, although the entry remains in the Population Registry. As elsewhere, failure to report a death can have various consequences: accusations can later be leveled of murder; all transactions (taxes, permits, etc.) will be considered fraudulent and risk penalty; and no inheritance can take place. Since 1994, deaths are reported to the Palestinian Authority, which is obliged to transfer all its records to the Israeli authorities, who maintain up-to-date copies of the Palestinian registry for the West Bank and Gaza Strip (Zureik 2001).

16. The Israeli "conversion" plan proposes to evacuate not more than 8–14 percent (Anti-Apartheid Wall Campaign 2006e).

17. Including 70 wells in the area of Qalqilya alone, and 162 in the Jordan Valley (United Nations 2006).

References

Abu El-Assal, Riah. 2006. You will not fly today! Bishop Riah denied his human rights at Tel Aviv airport. http://www.j-diocese.com/DiocesanNews/view.asp?selected=236#slbl236 (accessed August 28, 2006).

Adam, Heribert, and Kogila Moodley. 2005. *Seeking Mandela: Peacemaking between Israelis and Palestinians*. Philadelphia: Temple University Press.

Al-Haq. 1989. *Nation under siege*. Ramallah: Al-Haq.

Aly, Götz, and Karl Heinz Roth. 2004. *The Nazi census*, trans. Assenka Oksiloff. Philadelphia: Temple University Press.

Amnesty International. 2005. Joint letter to Israeli Knesset members: Discriminatory family reunification law must not be extended. http://web.amnesty.org/library/Index/ENGMDE150322005?open&of=ENG-ISR (accessed July 4, 20).

Anderson, Benedict. 1991. *Imagined communities*. London: Verso.

Anti-Apartheid Wall Campaign. 2003. "This is our land!" Jubara's residents reject Israeli permit system. http://stopthewall.org/latestnews/70.shtml (accessed September 3, 2006).

———. 2004. "No to Bantustans": Three maps of Israel's ongoing colonization of Palestine. http://stopthewall.org/activistresources/793.shtml (accessed June 20, 2006).

———. 2005. The new Israeli "Disengagement Plan" map. http://www.stopthewall.org/news/maps.shtml (accessed June 20, 2006).

———. 2006a. Settlement expansion on Masha lands: A Zionist tool to consolidate land theft. http://stopthewall.org/latestnews/1200.shtml (accessed June 29, 2006).

———. 2006b. Apartheid Wall construction sites the target of popular protests as Palestinians unite. http://stopthewall.org/latestnews/1204.shtml (accessed June 29, 2006).

———. 2006c. South Yatta villagers continue to block racist settler highway. http://stopthewall.org/latestnews/1180.shtml (accessed June 29, 2006).

———. 2006d. Resistance against ghettoization and home demolitions in South and East Yatta. http://stopthewall.org/latestnews/1178.shtml (accessed June 29, 2006).

———. 2006e. The "Convergence Plan" map: Reframing the Palestinian ghettos. http://stopthewall.org/maps/1159.shtml (accessed August 28, 2006).

Appadurai, Arjun. 1993. Number in the colonial imagination. In *Orientalism and the postcolonial predicament*, edited by C. Breckenridge and P. Van der Veer, 314–39. Pennsylvania: University of Pennsylvania Press.

Applied Research Institute of Jerusalem (ARIJ). 2006. New colonial road to be constructed on lands of western Ramallah villages. http://www.poica.org/editor/case_studies/view.php?recordID=749 (accessed May 20, 2006).

Assad, Samar. 2005. Settlements, outposts, and the law. Information Brief no. 117. http://www.thejerusalemfund.org (accessed August 28, 2006).

Badil. 2004. *The continuing catastrophe: 1967 and beyond.* Occasional Bulletin no. 19. http://www.badil.org/Publications/Bulletins/Bulletin-19.htm.

Barghouthi, Mustafa. 2004. A new vision for Palestine. Public lecture presented at St. Anthony's College. Oxford.

Beit Surik villager. 2004. Personal communication, June 27.

Benziman, Uzi. 2003. Nationalist tendencies running rampant. *Ha'aretz*, August 4.

Bornstein, Avram. 2002. *Crossing the Green Line between the West Bank and Israel.* Pennsylvania: University of Pennsylvania Press.

Brockington, Dan. 2002. *Fortress conservation: The preservation of the Mkomazi Game Reserve, Tanzania.* Oxford: International African Institute.

Caplan, Jane, ed. 2000. *Written on the body: The tattoo in European and American history.* London: Reaktion Books.

Caplan, Jane, and John Torpey, eds. 2001. *Documenting individual identity: The development of state practices in the modern world.* Princeton, NJ: Princeton University Press.

Central Intelligence Agency (CIA). 2006. Israel. *The world factbook.* https://www.cia.gov/cia/publications/factbook/geos/is.html (accessed June 26, 2006).

Cohn, Bernard. 1987. The census, social structure and objectification in South Asia. In his *An anthropologist among the historians and other essays*, 224–54. Oxford: Oxford University Press.

Coleman, Mathew. 2006. Personal communication, March 24.

Cook, Catherine, Adam Hanieh, and Adah Kay. 2004. *Stolen youth.* London: Pluto Press.

Craib, Raymond B. 2000. Cartography and power in the conquest and creation of New Spain. *Latin American Research Review* 35 (1): 7–36.

Democracy and Workers' Rights Center. 1996. *The Israeli closure.* Ramallah: DWRC.

Driver, Felix. 2001. *Geography militant: Cultures of exploration and empire.* Oxford: Blackwell Publishers.

Elzein, Sa'ed, et al. 1997. *The effects of Israeli closure on Palestinian workers since 30/7/1997.* Ramallah: DWRC.

Embassy of the Republic of Sudan. 2006. Entry procedures to Sudan. http://www.sudan-embassy.co.uk/infobook/entry.php (accessed August 28, 2006).

Former IDF member. 2005. Personal communication, June 18.

Foucault, Michel. 1978. *The history of sexuality.* New York: Random House.

Galili, Lily. 2003. Every prison has a door. *Ha'aretz*, August 29.

Giliomee, Hermann, and Lawrence Schlemmer, eds. 1985. *Against the fences: Poverty, passes and privilege in South Africa.* Cape Town: David Philip.

Harker, Chris. 2006. Personal communication, June 7.

Harley, John Brain. 2001. *The new nature of maps: Essays in the history of cartography.* London: Johns Hopkins University Press.

Harris, Cole. 2004. How did colonialism dispossess? Comments from an edge of empire. *Annals of the Association of American Geographers* 94 (1): 165–182.

Hass, Amira. 2002. Israel's closure policy: An ineffective strategy of containment and repression. *Journal of Palestine Studies* 31 (3): 5–20.

———. 2005a. Go study in Australia? *Ha'aretz*, December 14.

———. 2005b. You exist if the Israeli computer says so. *Ha'aretz*, September 28.

Hayden, Robert M. 1996. Imagined communities and real victims: Self-determination and ethnic cleansing in Yugoslavia. *American Ethnologist* 23 (4): 783–801.

Human Rights Watch (HRW). 2006a. Israel/Occupied Palestinian Territories (OPT). *World report 2006.* http://hrw.org/english/docs/2006/01/18/isrlpa12224.htm (accessed June 26, 2006).

———. 2006b. Israel: Family reunification ruling is discriminatory. http://hrw.org/english/docs/2006/05/18/isrlpa13403.htm (accessed June 26, 2006).

Israel. 2006. Military order no. 66/05/T. Trans. Applied Research Institute of Jerusalem.

Juma, Jamal. 2005. Trapped like mice. *Al-Ahram*, 726, January 20–26.

Jewish Virtual Library. 2005. "Consensus" settlements. Fact sheet no. 40. http://www.jewishvirtuallibrary.org (accessed August 28, 2006).

Kelly, Tobias. 2006. Documented lives: Fear and the uncertainties of law during the second Palestinian intifada. *Journal of the Royal Anthropological Institute* 12:89–107.

Kertzer, David, and Dominique Arel, eds. 2002. *Census and identity: The politics of race, ethnicity, and language in national censuses.* Cambridge: Cambridge University Press.

Krinis, Ehud, and Erella Dunayevsky. 2006. Transportation of school children from Susia to Tweni. http://masha-camp.livejournal.com/27002.html (accessed September 10, 2006).

Lemon, Anthony. 2004. Apartheid and capitalism revisited. *South African Geographical Journal* 86 (2): 58–67.

Machsom Watch. 2006. Pictures. http://www.machsomwatch.org/eng/pictures.asp?link=pix&lang=eng (accessed June 26, 2006).

Majda. 2004. Interview, June 27 (name changed).

Matthews, Mervyn. 1993. *The passport society: Controlling movement in Russia and the USSR.* Boulder. CO: Westview.

Megoran, Nick. 2006. Personal communication, May 26.

Mitchell, Timothy. 1988. *Colonising Egypt.* Cambridge: Cambridge University Press

Noiriel, Gérard. 1996. *The French melting pot: Immigration, citizenship and national identity.* Minneapolis: University of Minnesota Press.

Parizot, Cédric. 2006a. En attendant le Mur. *Migrations Société* 18:15–39.

———.2006b. Entrepreneurs without borders: Policies of closure and border economy between the southern West Bank and the northern Negev, 2000–2005. Working Paper Series. Oxford: RAMSES Workpackage on Borders and Conflict. http://www.sant.ox.ac.uk/esc/ramses/parizot.pdf (accessed March 14, 2007).

Parry, Nigel. 1995. Car license plates: The road to apartheid. http://nigelparry.com/diary/ramallah/plates.html (accessed August 14, 2006).

Rapoport, Meron. 2004. Israel: industrial estates along the wall. *Le Monde Diplomatique*, June.

Rosenhek, Zeev. 2006. Incorporating migrant workers into the Israeli labour market? http://www.carim.org/index.php?areaid=8?contentid=10 (accessed April 15, 2007).

Said, Edward W. 1978. *Orientalism*. New York: Vintage.

Sharma, Aradhana, and Akhil Gupta, eds. 2006. *The anthropology of the state: A reader*. Oxford: Blackwell.

Shinneh, Mohammed. 2004. Interview, June 27.

Smith, Graham E. 1989. Privilege and place in Soviet society. In *Horizons in human geography*, edited by D. Gregory and R. Walford, 320–40. London: Macmillan.

Smith, Neal. 2003. *American empire: Roosevelt's geographer and the prelude to globalization*. Berkeley: University of California Press.

Steinberg, Gerald M. 2004. Abusing 'Apartheid' for the Palestinian cause. *Jerusalem Post*, August 24.

Syrian Ministry of Tourism. 2006. Entry visas and customs facilities. http://www.syriatourism.org (accessed August 28, 2006).

Tehilla: The movement for religious Aliya. 2006. Givat Zeev: A place of Torah and Judaism. http://www.tehilla.com (accessed August 28, 2006).

Tim. 2006. Personal communication, August 29 (name changed).

Torpey, John. 1997. Revolutions and freedom of movement: An analysis of passport controls in the French, Russian, and Chinese Revolutions. *Theory and Society* 26 (6): 837–68.

———. 2000. *The invention of the passport: Surveillance, citizenship and the state*. Cambridge: Cambridge University Press.

Toyota, Mika. 2005. Subjects of the state without citizenship: The case of "hill tribes" in Thailand. In *Multiculturalism in Asia: Theoretical perspectives*, edited by W. Kymlicka and H. Baogang, 110–35. Oxford: Oxford University Press.

———. Forthcoming. Ambivalent categories: 'Hill tribes' and 'irregular migrants' in Thailand. In *Borderscapes: Hidden geographies and insurrectionary politics at territory's edge*, edited by P. K. Rajaram and C. Grundy-Warr. Minnesota: University of Minnesota.

United Nations, General Assembly Economic and Social Council. 2006. Economic and social repercussions of the Israeli occupation on the living conditions of the Palestinian people in the occupied Palestinian territory, including Jerusalem, and the Arab population in the occupied Syrian Golan. May 3. New York: United Nations.

United Nations Office for the Coordination of Humanitarian Affairs (OCHA). 2003. *Occupied Palestinian territory humanitarian update, 01 September—15 October 2003*. http://www.humanitarianinfo.org/opt/docs/UN/OCHA/OCHAHU-01September-15October03.pdf (accessed April 20, 2006).

United Nations Relief and Works Agency (UNRWA). 2004. The permit system: The case of Jayyous and Falamyeh, Qalqilya Governorate. http://www.un.org/unrwa/emergency/barrier/case_studies/permits.pdf (accessed June 20, 2006).

Van Teeffelen, Toine. 2001. Bethlehem diary (19). http://www.lpj.org/Nonviolence/Toine/Diary19.html (accessed June 26, 2006).

Zolberg, Aristide. 1978. International migration policies in a changing world system. In *human migration patterns and policies*, edited by W.H. McNeil and R.S. Adams, 241–86. Bloomington, IN: Indiana University Press.

Zureik, Elia. 2001. Constructing Palestine through surveillance practices. *British Journal of Middle Eastern Studies* 8 (2): 205–27.

15

Nation and Gender in Jewish Israel

TAMAR MAYER

The connections between war, territorial homeland, national sentiments, statehood, and masculinity are well established, especially for frontier societies.[1] Each nation[2] believes that it has a clear idea where its territorial homeland lies, will often strive for autonomy or sovereignty there, and will go to war when another nation or state controls it, or when unsatisfied with the resolution of a territorial dispute. The sons of the nation fight, and sometimes die, to free or defend the homeland, and as their blood is shed the connection to the territorial homeland becomes sacralized. Under the continued challenging of national boundaries, societies become militarized, affecting the priorities set by political institutions. As long as there continues to be a real or imagined threat to the national homeland, and as long as defense and security remain the highest priority, the national narrative of survival is regularly updated and helps justify high military spending in place of social investments in health, education, and economic growth. In these militarized societies, moreover, the connection between the nation and its men is clearly defined.

These connections are best exemplified in the case of Israel, whose size and shape have changed over time as a result of wars, cease-fire agreements, and unilateral withdrawals, and whose final map is yet to be drawn. The fact that Israel's boundaries have been neither clearly defined nor internationally recognized has resulted in a continuous military commitment that has, in turn, shaped Israeli society, culture, politics, and economics and has marked its national identity as inseparable from the struggle to define and defend its territorial homeland. Thus the lack of clear boundaries has shaped the discourse of citizenship in Israel, which became militarized long before statehood and has continued to be—with some variation—to date. Since its establishment, Israel has required military service from all its Jewish citizens, both male and female,[3] reinforcing the inseparability of military and civilian life. In this chapter I will examine the relationship between nation, territorial homeland, war, and gender in Jewish Israel and suggest that changes in the shape of its territory are linked not just to wars but also to ideological changes in Jewish nationalism in Israel and therefore to changes in the articulation of Jewish masculinity. The ambiguity about the exact parameters of the Jewish national homeland, on the one hand, and the process of globalization, on the other, have enabled the conflict among the different factions of Jewish nationalism, which were dormant until 1977, to surface. These multiple ideological voices can also be heard in the shifting articulations of masculinity that reflect the evolving role of the military in Israel's life.

The Study of Nationalism

Scholars from the social sciences and the humanities have made immense contributions to the literature on nation and nationalism over the last two decades. While social scientists have studied the nation as an objective phenomenon, scholars from the humanities have developed and refined the tools we use to analyze the nation as a social and cultural construction. By focusing on the cultural dimensions of nationalism, scholars such as Chatterjee (1993) and Bhabha (1990) have argued that the nation can be viewed as a narrative with a specific, even unique, language, cultural representation, and symbolism.

More important to the present discussion, however, is the fact that the *construction* of the nation as unique can lead scholars (as well as members of the nation itself) to treat it as homogeneous and united. Not only are members of the nation positioned differently vis-à-vis economic resources and political power, but they may also be members of different ethnic and language groups, which may be either disadvantaged by or favored over other national groups.

Moreover, feminist scholars have shown that the nation is also the arena where gender inequalities are played out and that nationhood is almost always a sexist project. Enloe (2000, 1989), Yuval-Davis (1997), Radcliffe and Westwood (1996), McClintock (1995), and others have shown that national ideology is often used to favor one gender and that in the national project women occupy a secondary position. Nationalism thus becomes the language through which gender and sexuality (specifically, women and homosexuals) are controlled and repressed (Mayer 2000a), and the national project is where masculine prowess is expressed.

As theories of deconstruction and poststructuralism gained ascendance in the academy, scholars deconstructed power relations in many different settings, demonstrating gender, nation, and sexuality to be socially constructed categories. Much of the literature on gender and the nation has focused on the centrality of women to the national project, primarily as its biological and cultural reproducers and as the producers and maintainers of ethnic and national boundaries (Mayer 2004; Bracewell 1996; Karakasidou 1996; Yuval-Davis 1996; Yuval-Davis and Anthias 1989). Here, however, I will focus on the nation and its men.

Territoriality and the Jewish Nation

The Jewish nation, like all nations, has an intimate connection to the territory where it believes it was born. That territory, its religious significance, and the events that took place in it have defined the Jewish people. With the birth of Jewish nationalism, Zionism, in the late nineteenth century, the territorial homeland gained further importance, becoming the place where the modern nation sought to establish its own state, regardless of the fact that another people inhabited it. But unlike most other nationalisms, which were conceived in, or in very close proximity to, the territorial homeland, where its national subjects already resided in large numbers, Jewish nationalism was conceived away from the homeland. In order for the national project to materialize and succeed, European Jews were to immigrate to the homeland and appropriate it; thus, Gershon Shafir sees the Jewish national movement as a colonial one (1989).[4]

Over the course of the twentieth century, the Jewish national project and its narrative of nation-building and gender articulations, specifically masculinity, have moved from being hegemonic and monolithic to a more fragmented nationalism that gives voice to once marginal groups. This process can be roughly divided into four periods: the design period in Europe (until World War I); the execution of the Zionist model during the prestate and early state years (until the early 1950s), when both nationalism and masculinity were still presented as hegemonic; the early transitional period (mid-1950s to late 1960s); and finally the period from the 1970s to the present, when these hegemonies have been giving way to multiple articulations of both nationalism and masculinity.[5]

Much of the discourse about nationalism and masculinity is tied to wars and to the nation's attempt to define and defend its borders. It should be noted, however, that masculinity in Jewish Israel was constructed vis-à-vis the effeminate Diaspora Jew and women, rather than the Arab. Moreover, the map of the Jewish homeland, certainly until 1948, was drawn by outside forces, first by Britain and later, in 1947, by the UN. Only after Israel's independence in 1948 did defining its boundaries become an internal Middle Eastern affair.

Period I: The construction of Jewish Nationalism

A distinct and separate Jewish nationalism was born out of necessity. Jews, citizens of European states, were excluded from the nations they inhabited, and often suffered violent manifestations of anti-Semitism such as pogroms. As a means of ensuring their survival, and in the spirit of nationalism that swept Europe in the late nineteenth and early twentieth centuries, Jews of Central and Eastern Europe constructed a national liberation movement that offered them an alternative to life in the Diaspora. Although Zionist writings appeared as early as the mid-nineteenth century, Zionism became an organized movement only after the first Zionist Congress was convened in Basel, Switzerland, in 1897.

Like all other nationalisms, Zionism was a revolutionary movement with a utopian future, but it was perhaps the most ambitious of all national projects. It sought more than just a political change: it called for a total transformation of its subjects in the social, economic, political, psychological, and geographical arenas. It sought to solve the existential problems of Eastern European Jews[6] by bringing them together from their varied places of residence, languages, occupations, and traditional ways of life and to transform the old *Diaspora* Jew, meek and weak, into a *New Jew*, a *Muscle Jew* (Mayer 2000b).

European Jews, the founders of Zionism and its early ideologues and leaders, invented and adopted symbols that would accompany the Jewish nation throughout the twentieth century and beyond (Mayer 2005) and also invented its national subject. The nationalism they constructed was secular and hegemonic, or at least was presented as such, and provided little opportunity for alternative voices to be heard (Ram 1999).

Zionism promised newness and secularism, but was forced to rely on notions of renewal and redemption derived from the traditional religious Jewish past. And although the articulations of Jewish nationalism appeared to have been hegemonic, primarily because of the role of Labor Zionism, the Jewish nation was hardly monolithic. It encompassed religious, economic, and political extremes—socialists and capitalists, liberals and conservatives, religious and secular—which would mark the Jewish nation with internal struggles and tensions.

Jewish Nationalism and the New Jew

For Theodor Herzl and other leaders of the movement, the national project was supposed to create a national subject who would lead the Zionist revolution. Herzl's design for his revolution was gendered from the outset, as can be seen in his diaries;[7] his New Jew, the archetype of the Jewish national subject, was similar to the New Man, the subject of other nationalisms. In his program, manliness was to be achieved through a larger program known as Muscle Jewry (*Muskeljudentum*; Mayer 2000b; Mosse 1985). Much of this construction was accomplished while still in Europe, through sports and youth movements, and once in Palestine also through military and paramilitary training. The New Jew was constructed in the image of the heroic, even mythical figures of the Jewish past, who were revived by design in order to serve the new nation, its goals, and its narrative—not in the Diaspora, but in the Jewish homeland. He was to settle and defend the homeland, which was already occupied by others; overcome its harsh physical, economic, and political conditions; and create a new culture in Palestine. He was a pioneer-soldier whose new Hebrew culture was based on an ideology of land and labor conquests, leaving no room for cultural exchange with the indigenous Arab population.

The Zionist project could not be executed smoothly, and in order to succeed it had to be highly selective.[8] This ensured that only the New Jew—the young and fit who were ready for the hardships in the homeland—would immigrate to Palestine. Indeed, less than 3 percent of the more than 2 million Jews who left Eastern Europe between 1882 and 1914 joined the national project and immigrated to Palestine (Peled and Shafir 2005, 60). Many were simply not interested, while others were not fit for the Zionist design (Penslar 2000). This selection process—of choosing the masculine, strong, and secular Jew—therefore reinforced time and again the monolithic image of the New Jew, the young pioneer fighter who was ready to build the land, defend it, and if necessary sacrifice his life for the nation.

Period II: Putting the New Jew to the test—the implementation stage (1920s to the late 1940s)

1920s–1948

Once in Palestine, both men and women opened up the frontier, built *kibbutzim*, and created a new Hebrew culture, but it was primarily men who were involved in fighting the indigenous population of Palestine and who took the more publicly visible agricultural jobs, which called for greater physical endurance. The emerging priority of security contributed in crucial ways to the masculine image of the Zionist success story. Once European Jews began arriving in Palestine in large numbers and transforming the land they saw as unclaimed, they were met with growing resistance by the indigenous Arab population, which became marginalized from their lands as well as their places of work. Arab attacks on Jewish settlements and farms became progressively more violent, necessitating a stronger Jewish defense force. The training and molding of the pioneer-fighter, integral to both the formal and informal education systems in the prestate years, were clearly legitimized by the governing bodies of Labor Zionism, and the seeds of a militarized Jewish community, which would continue until the mid-1970s, were sown early on.

Because Jewish men carried out most of the duties of defense, they became favored members of the nation. The pioneer-farmer fighter had become the quintessential emblem of Jewish nationalism and masculinity; his acts of bravery continuously refined the blueprint of the Jewish male "hero." In the national imagination, these young men entered what George Mosse (1990) has called "the cult of the fallen soldier." They were perceived as the "silver platter" that enabled the creation of the Jewish State, and they were transformed (in Boyarin's words) "into mimics of gentile heroes" (1997, 273) and remembered in ways that echoed classical Hellenic standards of masculine beauty. They were depicted in poetry, novels, and memorial books as the tall, wide-shouldered, beautiful, and brave heroes that the forefathers of Zionism had imagined (Hirshfield 1994). The retelling of their tales of heroism led to their secular canonization and to their elevation to the mythic realm. This connection between the male "hero" and the nation that was established in the first fifty years of Zionism continued after statehood and was reserved for an elite group of young Israeli men, mostly from agricultural settlements, who tended to volunteer for the most demanding units and daring missions.

But it is hardly a secret that the New Jew was a tiny minority among the Jews who came to Palestine and later to Israel. The New Jew was an ideal, rather than a real figure, and it did not much matter that the majority of world Jewry lived in the Diaspora, not in Palestine, and did not participate in the Zionist project at all. Despite the relatively small number of young men who were "drafted" into Zionist ideology and who actually embodied the New Jew, the ideal was so pervasive (because it fit the colonial project so well) that it soon became hegemonic and marginalized the rest of world Jewry. We should note too that many of the European Jews who came to Palestine in the 1930s left their homes reluctantly, and did so only when it became clear that their physical safety was in danger. Once in Palestine, many of them did not join the nationalist project of settling the frontier and chose instead (whether voluntarily or not) to retain their European culture and language. This was true specifically for German, Austrian, and Czechoslovakian Jews who came to Palestine in the 1930s or Holocaust survivors who came in the 1940s. They simply did not fit the Muscle Jew mold but were offered no viable alternative. Nevertheless, they did fight for Israel's independence, and many died in battle (about 10 percent of the Jewish population of Palestine perished in that war). Yet despite their contributions, they were assigned a lower place in the Zionist-constructed hierarchy that would mark Israeli society for the first few decades after statehood.

Jewish immigrants from the Arab world were marginalized as well. Although they (in particular the Yemeni Jews) came to Palestine in the early part of the twentieth century and were no less idealistic than their European counterparts, they were seen merely as a cheap substitute for Arab labor (Smooha 1978). Like the indigenous Arab population of Palestine, they were Orientalized by the New Jew and his Labor Zionist handlers, and were similarly relegated to an inferior position in the developing socioeconomic and ideological hierarchies.

The third marginalized group consisted of Orthodox Jews[9] for whom Zionism was nothing more than a youth movement for assimilated Jews. In the Zionist narrative, all of these marginalized Jewish groups were associated with the old, the weak, and even the effeminate—in other words, with the Diaspora, as opposed to the newness, secularism, and excitement that Zionism offered.

That Jews marginalized Jews and that the Zionist project was not, after all, about equality may be surprising, but the marginalization of the Arab population of Palestine is not. Zionist ideologues believed it necessary to create a Hebrew culture in Palestine. The Arab was made almost invisible (both in the farms and in the cities), and if it were not for the Arab revolt of 1936–1939, the UN Resolution 181 of November 1947 (which divided Palestine between Jews and Arabs), and its ensuing aftermath culminating in the war of 1948, the Palestinian Arab might have remained invisible to the Jewish Project for much longer. Ironically, his newly acquired visibility, especially after Israel's establishment in 1948, legitimized much of the ideology that was designed and implemented earlier in the twentieth century. I refer here particularly to the emphasis on settlement and defense which was the outcome of the new borders. Now the territory was far larger than either the extent of Jewish settlements prior to 1948 or the land designated for the Jewish homeland by the UN.

The militarization of the civil Jewish society which began in the 1920s and 1930s thus continued for years to come (see Kimmerling 1983). Many of the goals set by the Zionist leadership in the prestate years were implemented after statehood in part because those who defined the goals and helped implement them in the 1930s and 1940s were in positions of power and leadership in the new independent state—indeed, the Labor Party remained in power until 1977.

After Statehood: 1948 to the Late 1950s

The first years after statehood were fraught with serious challenges and conflicts that legitimized what appeared to be the hegemony of Zionist ideology and its monolithic national subject. Although the direction of these struggles (between Israel and the Arab world, Israel and the Palestinians, and internal Jewish factions) had changed over time, they are still present, to some extent, today. The national struggle had to be managed at the same time that the newly established state was working to build its political, economic, and social institutions; absorb hundreds of thousands of new immigrants, especially from the Arab world; and conquer the new frontier.

Israel's new borders, as defined by the 1949 armistice agreement, were rather porous, and activity along them was hectic. Palestinians who now resided in refugee camps in Gaza and the Jordanian West Bank infiltrated the border and attacked individual Jewish communities, some of which stood on the ruins of abandoned Arab villages. When it was clear that the regular military units, despite their experience, could not stop these incursions, Israel created special units whose mission was to attack Arab communities behind the border. These young men became legendary; their clandestine missions, and the myths that surrounded them, raised the bar of heroic masculinity in Israel.[10] They perfected the model of the warrior New Jew to an extent undreamed of during the design period, and they were perceived as the ultimate fighters—men whose actions made possible the settling of hundreds of thousands of Jews from the Arab world in the frontier. Thus the very existence of a new frontier encouraged a hypermasculinity among Israeli Jews.

Even before they came to Israel, and certainly after their arrival, these Arab immigrants were relegated to an inferior position in the national narrative. Israel's Prime Minister David Ben Gurion had voiced his opinion about the newcomers on several occasions: "Those from Morocco had no education. Their customs are those of Arabs. . . . The culture of Morocco I would not like to have here. And I don't see what contribution present Persians have to make" (Moskin 1965, quoted in Smooha 1978, 88). His view that "[w]e do not want Israelis to become Arabs (and) we are in duty bound to fight against the spirit of the Levant, which corrupts individuals and societies" (Rouleau 1966, quoted in Smooha 1978, 88) further reinforced the inferior position of the Arab Jew in Israel and thus justified, in the mind of the hegemon, their relegation to settling the frontier.

Spatially segregated in the periphery, the newcomers' communities lacked physical, social, and economic infrastructure; they were in close proximity to the new borders and were regularly attacked. The New Jew in Israel did what he always did best: he defended the immigrants' communities and aided somewhat in the absorption process,[11] but kept them in inferior social, political, and economic positions. No attempt was made to socialize them into equal citizens, although legally they certainly were equal. Even though they, like all Jewish citizens of Israel, were required to serve in the Israel Defense Forces (IDF), many were not fully accepted and thus missed the traditional rite of passage into Israeli society and into masculinity. The IDF replicated the Israeli social structure: those of European descent held positions of high command and volunteered for the most daring units, while those of Arab descent (*Mizrachi* Jews) were relegated to the lowest position possible for Israeli Jews. IDF service was a national commitment whose primary beneficiaries were the nation's favored subjects. For them, it could open doors in civilian life and lead to entry into the middle class, but the newcomers seldom reaped these advantages. Although some of the technical skills they learned in the IDF could be transferred into civilian life, their training marked them as blue-collar workers. It would take years before the first Mizrachi Jews would enter the officers' ranks or be accepted into the pantheon of Jewish heroes. The frontier, which could have been, as Adriana Kemp suggested, the laboratory for constructing a new New Jew (2000, 19), in fact further entrenched their peripheral position in Israeli society.

Even though by the 1950s Jews from Arab countries constituted more than 50 percent of the Jewish citizenry in Israel, they could not muster the strength to challenge the power structure of Israeli society and the hegemony of the Labor movement (now Labor Party) and its legendary New Jew, whose institutions they continued to be dependent on. As the attacks across the borders, and Israel's retaliation, became more violent, the militarization of Israeli society intensified, further marginalizing the Arab Jew.

The border skirmishes of the early 1950s and Israel's attack of Gaza in 1955, which followed a long escalation in the Israeli-Arab, particularly Israeli-Egyptian relations, and the 1956 Sinai Campaign, which was initiated by Israel in cooperation with France and Britain (Levy 2003, 43; Morris 1995), further legitimized a discourse of security in Israel, and the IDF became increasingly important. The economy was influenced as well: large portions of the national budget were devoted to defense rather than to programs that might narrow the socioeconomic gap and empower Mizrachi Jews. It was during this period that Israel began to develop its own weapons industry, which would become one of the most important export industries in the next few decades, especially after 1967 (Peled and Shafir 2005).

Nevertheless, the hegemony started to show some cracks in the early part of the 1960s, with the Adolf Eichmann trial and the attention given to the Holocaust, which up to that point had not found a prominent spot in the New Jew's psyche. Eichmann's trial began a long process of tearing apart the monolithic identities (masculine and national) that had been perfected through war and hegemony. But because the entire education system was designed to serve the national goals, youth continued to be molded in the image of their predecessors, which resulted in the victory of the Six-Day War of 1967.

Period III: From Monolithic to Fragmented Identities (late 1960s and early 1970s)

As the size of the Israeli territory and its boundaries more than quadrupled, the cracks in the hegemony became more visible. The debate about these borders intensified after the 1967 war. The swift expansions into the West Bank, the Gaza Strip, the Syrian Golan Heights, and the Sinai Peninsula would soon enable a large segment of the Jewish population in Israel to identify the West Bank with the biblical lands of Judea and Samaria, and thus give a voice to a different national element in Israeli society. A new discourse of the desirability of a correspondence between the biblical homeland and the modern Jewish state was initiated by the right (both religious and secular). The discussions about whether the occupied territories lay within the biblical homeland of the Jews, and whether that fact is relevant for defining the boundaries of the Jewish national territory, divided the Jewish nation and ultimately led to the assassination of Prime Minister Yitzhak Rabin in 1995.

This connection between the expanded territory and perceived national strength became even more evident in 1967. Although Jewish presence in the occupied areas remained sparse for the first few years after the war, the newly acquired territories kept the Arab states (which Israelis saw as the real danger to the Jewish nation) at bay, offering the Jewish nation a newfound sense of security that was seen as the fruit of masculine prowess. This strong association of territoriality and masculinity helps to explain why, many years later, those on the right would feel that Jewish national pride would be emasculated if any of the occupied territories were to be returned to the Palestinians or to any of the Arab states.[12]

The boundaries that resulted from the 1967 war were the largest within which a sovereign Israel has ever existed. Ironically, it was during this period of military buildup in defense of the new borders, and perhaps because of the expanded size of Israel, that we started to see different articulations of both masculinity and nationalism. The military discourse about the occupied territories and the increased importance of national security now involved a religious element, giving voice to one of the previously marginalized groups.

Following the 1967 war, and certainly after 1970 (when the attrition war with Syria, Jordan, and Egypt had ended), the border (as a concept), which had been so important in defining Jewish national consciousness from 1948 to 1967, had lost some of its importance (Kemp 2000). No longer was the border so close to home; no longer were Israelis forced to live on the frontier. The frontier became, at least geographically—if not socially, economically, and symbolically—part of the center (Kemp 2000). This new expanse of occupied territories, which allowed Israel breathing room and opened new social, economic, and political opportunities for Israeli Jews, would become an important marker through which national identity would be constructed in the last part of the twentieth century.

Israel experienced at least three more wars, two of which resulted in territorial shifts further challenging both nationalism and masculinity in Jewish Israel: the 1973 Yom Kippur War, the 1982 War in Lebanon, and the two Palestinian intifadas (which were the direct result of the 1967 war and the occupation which followed). These wars, especially the 1973 war, were important not only because of territorial shifts but also because they signaled a crisis in the hegemonic power of the New Jew. In 1973, he was caught unprepared and refused to take responsibility for this failure. All that was historically unique to the successful military operations of the New Jew—meticulous intelligence, ingenuity, and the element of surprise—were in short supply in this one. The culture of elitism and arrogance, at whose center the New Jew was located, was now heavily criticized. Nevertheless the connection between military and civil society in Israel became more, not less, inseparable.

After 1967, as more higher ranking officers entered Israeli politics (a trend that continues to the present), the discourse about the future of the occupied territories and the occupied Palestinians was increasingly influenced by military thinking. Foreign policy as well as national priorities were now designed by soldiers-turned-civilians whose entire modus operandi was based on tactical thinking learned in the IDF. We might have expected that now, after the size of the territory has so expanded and the border was pushed farther away from centers of Jewish population, the obsession with defense and security would lessen. But it did not; in fact, the military industry under the control of the government expanded tremendously during this period and became, as Levy (2003) and Peled and Shafir (2005) argue, the growth engine of the budding high-tech industry—the stimulus for economic modernization and one of the most important export industries of Israel. These are not signs of civil society seeking to become less militarized.

Period IV: Multiple voices

The 1967 war and its territorial expansion posed a major problem for the hege-mon: should he, or should he not, settle these newly acquired territories? This dilemma brought to the surface the ideological differences within the Labor movement, since some of its younger members settled the occupied territories immediately after the war, even before they received government support. Ini-tially, they did what they knew best from the early national experience: they settled the frontier, created facts on the ground, and were now committed to militarily defend these new communities—an indication that the territorial question would not be solved through diplomacy but rather through mili-tancy and violence.

Starting in the mid-1970s, however, the massive settlement program was carried out primarily by Orthodox Jewish youth, members of Gush Emunim. This activity was perhaps the first marker of change in Israeli society; the hegemony of Labor Zionism was broken and the once marginal groups—reli-gious Orthodox Jews and Jewish immigrants from the Arab world who came to Israel in the 1950s, and their children—voted collectively to shift politi-cal power to the Right. This moved them from a marginal position in Israeli politics to its center; they had shifted the national discourse and reprioritized national goals. Just as in the 1910s and 1920s, settling the homeland had become a major national priority for these religious settlers, who saw them-selves as the successors of the old New Jew, as the *real* Zionists (Weisbrod 1985) and as the *new pioneers* (Ben Eliezer 1996). As the religious-national influence on Israeli politics was strengthening during this period, the central-ity of Arab Jewish culture was undisputed as well, and their voices of protest were heard clearly (Ram 1999).

Years of systematic marginalization, accompanied by a steady increase in the relative size of this population, finally produced an effective resistance to the dominant ideology, as substantiated in the 1977 election results. It cracked the illusion of social cohesion in Jewish Israel and challenged the national narrative, helping to redefine and refocus Jewish nationalism. The religious nationalist youth movement Bnei Akiva and, more specifically, the settlers' movement Gush Emunim have stepped into the ideological vacuum left by Labor Zionism. They have adapted to their own ideology the rhetoric of set-tling and defending the historical homeland, including the Palestinian West Bank, Gaza, and the Syrian Golan Heights, justifying their activities in reli-gious texts and in Rabbinical messages which they believe commanded them to redeem all biblical lands with Jewish settlements. They soon became the religious answer to secular Zionism, and their leaders—all male—became role models for Orthodox youth, who mimicked in their dress, body language, and even dialect the farmer-fighter of the first half of the twentieth century.

No longer was the New Jew a secular pioneer; now he was religiously Orthodox and territorially uncompromising. His rationalization for holding on to the occupied territories had far less to do with real security issues than with a religious mission that called for the redemption of the biblical homeland through settlement. This is how he etched himself, as the new pioneer, into the Israeli consciousness and brought to the forefront a different expression of masculinity: the religious zealot, who carried a gun and was highly motivated, filled with nationalist enthusiasm, and willing to dispossess the Palestinians from their lands. The new New Jew could construct this image because at about the same time that the Settlement Project began, more and more young Orthodox men had joined the IDF. In the last decade, in fact, they have tended to enlist in combat units, where they now assume the role previously occupied by members of Labor Zionism (*Kibbutzniks*; Cohen 1997, 96). As the percentage of the old New Jew in these units declined, that of the new New Jew increased. They volunteer for the most selective units—and their ratio there, as well as in junior officer ranks, now exceeds their ratio in the conscript population (3:1; Cohen 1997, 97). And just as for their secular predecessors, enlisting in the most demanding units has been both a sign of manliness and a way to express their nationalism.

As Israel continued to cement its connection to the West Bank, building new settlements and expanding existing ones, and as it intensified its military export, it entered (in 1982) a twenty-year war in Lebanon. But instead of a swift victory, which the ultimate Jewish man had offered his nation in years past, Israel now counted its dead for almost two decades, and unlike any other war in Israel's history it triggered, literally from the first day of the war, a fierce resistance on the part of some soldiers, their commanders, and the citizens at home. Israeli society could no longer be mobilized by war unless the fight was for survival, even if it was justified in formulaic propaganda (as it has been since the 1950s). For the first time, secular Israeli Jews demonstrated against a war while it was in progress, and it became clear that many secular soldiers were not willing to fight a war that was perceived as primarily political. For the first time a high commander publicly resigned his post in wartime. Years of protest against Israel's stay in Lebanon marked a growing division within the Jewish nation, one that is paralleled only by Israel's settlement policies in the West Bank and Gaza and the signing of the Oslo Accords (of 1993). But the protest also came from within the IDF and the civilian population, as more and more soldiers refused to serve in Lebanon and more and more mothers put pressure on the government to withdraw. The only soldiers who were eager to stay in Lebanon and fight, if necessary, and who believed that a withdrawal was a sign of weakness were the new warriors—Orthodox Jews and soldiers who were located on the right in the political map (many of whom were Mizrachi Jews).

Out of the call for withdrawal came a grassroots movement, Four Mothers, which was formed in February 1997 by mothers of soldiers in Lebanon (who were later joined by fathers and other citizens) whose goal was to bring their sons home alive. They succeeded in their mission; Israel withdrew from Lebanon in April 2000. Four Mothers played an important role in showing that the young warriors were really only children in uniform, and that every soldier had a mother who protected him and defended him according to her own visions and maternal instincts (Pinchas-Cohen 2001, 45).

Four Mothers' influence on military decisions has shifted the debate about nation, boundaries, and masculinity. When national subjects care first about themselves and their safety, and only second about the nation and military orders; when an individual's needs come before those of the nation; and when mothers' worries influence policies, the commitment to the nation and to its territories has to be questioned. The Israeli secular Jewish male of the twenty-first century looks and behaves very differently than his counterpart at the turn of the previous century, and if he embodies some of the features of the old New Jew it is for his sake, not the nation's.

Since the latter part of the twentieth century, as the real or imagined threat to Israel's survival abated (with the signing of peace agreements with Egypt, in 1979, and Jordan, in 1994) the discourse and centrality of security in Israel's life has changed. These regional political changes, along with globalization, a twenty-year war with no marked achievements in Lebanon, an aggressive fight against Palestinians in the West Bank and Gaza (in response to the two intifadas), and the absorption of hundreds of thousands of new immigrants from the former Soviet Union, some of whom were not even Jewish, helped lessen the dominance of the IDF. Further, as the goals of defense and security became less clearly defined and politicians (especially, but not exclusively, from the Right) attempted to refocus the security debate, investments previously made in the militarization of Israeli society and in strengthening its military industry were now redirected toward social and economic purposes. And no longer does participation in the labor force, especially in government positions, depend on one's military record.[13]

With the growing political power and cultural visibility of the religious nationalist community (Sheleg 2000), the discussion about territory and the character of the nation have taken center stage. In the last quarter century, as their aggressive settlement activities (in the West Bank, Gaza, and the Golan) and their militant opposition to politicians who were willing to give up the territories in exchange for peace have redefined and refocused Jewish nationalism, the religious nationalist groups have illuminated, once again, that the tie between the nation and its homeland is inseparable. The pictures we saw on television in August 2005 of the intense resistance to the Israeli pullout of Gaza are an excellent illustration of this point. But they also showed that at the turn of the twenty-first century, religious women have become central to the project of defining the boundaries of the homeland. Her home, the community, and the synagogue were supposed to mark that territory, but politics had become more important than religious convictions.

Conclusion

The connection of the Jewish nation in the last one hundred years to its territory, to war, and to masculinity is clear. Jewish nationalism was constructed in response to the Diaspora experiences of European Jews and aimed at solving their problems by establishing a sovereign Jewish state in what the nation believed was its homeland. In order to implement this ideology and carry out the mission of Zionism, a new national subject, the New Jew, was constructed. But because both nationalism and gender are culturally constructed and thus respond to social, political, and economic challenges, the articulations of both have changed over time. Jewish nationalism, like all others, may have appeared to be monolithic, but in reality this was never the case.

The emphasis on settlement and defense which began at the turn of the twentieth century and continued intensively through the nation-building process constructed a very specific national narrative, prioritized national goals, and defined the social structure of the society, first in the Jewish community in the prestate years and later in Israel. Those who implemented the ideology of Labor Zionism and who participated in building the land and defending it were therefore favored, further reinforcing the monolithic image of Labor Zionism and its New Jew.

The boundaries of the Jewish homeland have never been clearly defined, and the Jewish nation's experience in its territory has been marked by wars with Arab States and with the Palestinians. This, of course, had helped reproduce the defensive and offensive ethos of Zionism and rewrite the Jewish national narrative, with its heavy emphasis on security and the survival of the nation. In turn, it justified the militarization of Israeli society and high spending on the military and on the weapons industry, and it enabled further marginalization of Orthodox and Mizrachi Jews, who did not participate in the Zionist project. Hiding behind the veil of security enabled the New Jew to maintain his hegemony, keeping the elite units and the officers' ranks in the IDF almost exclusively for the New Jew, who could use his military service to enter the middle class as well as the political establishment.

The end of more than sixty years of Labor hegemony was the result of the voting power of marginalized groups, especially of the Mizrachi Jews. And even though there was a major political change in Israeli politics in 1977 and the right-wing Likud Party came to power, the discourse of security did not much change. This was the time when these marginalized groups entered the IDF in large numbers, fought in the 1982 Lebanon war, which lasted almost twenty years, fought the Palestinians during their uprising, and actively implemented the settlement policies of the new government. Because neither the war in Lebanon nor the intifadas were wars for Israel's survival, the halo around the IDF and its soldiers decreased quite dramatically. Into the vacuum left by the old New Jew entered the settler who in his militant enthusiasm emulated his dress and speech and thus presented a new and much more nationalistic voice.

As the threat to Israel's survival abates and security can no longer be used to hijack Israel's social and economic agendas two related things must happen. Israel needs to define its permanent borders and involve its Palestinian Arab minority in the discussion of nationalism and citizenship in Israel. It is not enough to bring the Orthodox Jews and the Jews from the Arab world from the sidelines to the political, economic, and social center. Without the involvement of the Palestinian Israelis, the national discourse in Israel remains incomplete, and the intimate relationship among territory, nationalism, and gender will remain the major marker of Jewish nationalism.

Acknowledgments

I thank Orna Blumen of Haifa University, Maureen Mitchell-Hays of Colgate University, and Heidi Nast of De Paul University for helpful comments on early drafts of this chapter.

Notes

1. I recognize that the state of Israel consists of two nations, Jewish and Palestinian (who have been referred to as Israeli Arabs), and that their stories on the land intertwine. I also recognize that gender identity is relational and that there can be no masculinity without femininity. But I chose to discuss here only one nation, the Jewish nation, and only one gender, men, because their construction is so intimately tied. Moreover, as we will see, the construction of the Jewish man was in opposition to the Diaspora Jew and his experiences, and not to the Arab.

2. I distinguish here, as everywhere, between nations and states. Although both derive much of their identity from their territorial homeland, states are political units with internationally recognized boundaries, while nations are glorified ethnic groups whose members believe that they share a common past and aspire to a common destiny and who believe that their nation was born in a particular place, the homeland. The members of a nation believe they share objective characteristics such as language, religion, or DNA, as well as subjective characteristics such as the belief in common origins, in the uniqueness of the nation's history, and hopes for a shared destiny (Smith 1986)

3. Men's IDF service, however, is far longer, and they subsequently become reservists who are often called for active duty until they reach their forties. Women's compulsory service is much shorter and they are relieved from reserve duties shortly after its conclusion.

4. Peled and Shafir (2005) argue that a new society can be labeled colonial if in the process of its construction it uses military, settles new lands, takes advantage of the indigenous population and attempts to remove it from their lands, and if the settlers claim cultural superiority as a justification for their actions (2005, 27).

5. Of course, this last period can be further divided to include the impact of the Ethiopians' and Russians' immigrants on both articulations.

6. Jews in Asia, the Middle East, and North Africa experienced no discrimination at this time. It was only with the Zionist reclamation of lands in Palestine and Israel's independence in 1948 that Jews had to flee their homes in the Arab countries and turned to Zionism. Zionism, then, was not only the cause of the discrimination against Arab Jews but also their salvation.

7. For a detailed discussion of Herzl's vision see Mayer (2000b).

8. Aviva Halamish (2000) explains that from its inception the Zionist movement was selective. Herzl saw it as a temporary necessity, Achad Ha-Am as an inseparable principle of Zionism. Even Zionist leaders such as Arthur Rupin endorsed this principle of selectivity and openly publicized it (in *Der Jude* in 1919).

9. Almost since the beginning of Zionism there existed a small religious faction (*ha-Mizrachi*) that was associated with the movement but rejected the secularism of Zionism and hoped to form a new religious community in Palestine. To that end they were even willing to rethink some of the rudimentary ingredients of the faith (Schwartz 1999). These Religious Zionists also came to Palestine (despite the teachings of their rabbis) and also contributed greatly to the Zionist project. But because they were a small group and because the secular ideas of the Zionist project were so pervasive, they were unable to redirect the debate, and their impact on the movement, at least until the 1950s, was relatively small.

10. I refer here specifically to the 101 Brigade and its legendary fighters, such as Meir Ha-Zion and Ariel Sharon, whose reputation for bravery and military ingenuity had become well-known.

11. The IDF was actively involved in educating the new immigrants as it set up special units of women soldier-teachers, and provided technical, infrastructural, and medical assistance. Drori (2000) suggests that the IDF and its then chief of staff understood that the social and infrastructural problems the newcomers faced had a major impact on Israel's security and thus agreed to use the IDF in this arguably humanitarian effort.

12. For example, the headline "Barak [had] Managed to Emasculate the National Pride of the Jewish People" appeared on Channel 7 on December 27, 1999; such sentiments were not uncommon when Prime Minister Ehud Barak planned to withdraw from the Golan.

13. In 1994 the Israeli government suspended using military records as a prerequisite for government, increasing the job opportunities for women, Palestinian Israelis, and the ultra-Orthodox Jews who never contributed to the IDF the way men have. This move actually disadvantaged young men who for years used their military service and record as a stepping-stone to the middle class (Levy 2003).

References

Ben Eliezer, Uri. 1996. The elusive distinction between state and society: The genealogy of the Israeli pioneer [in Hebrew]. *Megamot* 37 (3): 207–28.

Bhabha, Homi. 1990. *Nation and narration.* New York: Routledge.

Boyarin, Daniel. 1997. *Unheroic conduct: The rise of heterosexuality and the invention of the Jewish man.* Berkeley: University of California Press.

Bracewell, Wendy. 1996. Women, motherhood, and contemporary Serbian nationalism. *Women's Studies International Journal* 19:25–33.

Chatterjee, Partha. 1993. *The nation and its fragments: Colonial and postcolonial histories.* Princeton, NJ: Princeton University Press.

Cohen, Stuart. 1997. Towards a new portrait of a (new) Israeli soldier. *Israel Affairs* 3 (Spring–Summer): 77–117.

Drori, Zeev. 2000. *Utopia in uniform: The Israeli Defense Forces' contribution to settlement, Aliya and education, in the early days of the state* [in Hebrew]. Beer Sheva: Ben-Gurion University of the Negev Press.

Enloe, Cynthia. 1989. *Bananas, beaches, & bases: Making feminist sense of international politics.* Berkeley: University of California Press.

———. 2000. *Maneuvers: The international politics of militarizing women's lives.* Berkeley: University of California Press.

Halamish, Aviva. 2000. A critical analysis of the term 'selective immigration" in Zionist theory, practice and historiography. In *The Age of Zionism* [in Hebrew], edited by A. Shapira, J. Reinharz, and J. Harris, 167–85. Cambridge, MA: Zalman Shazar Center for Jewish History in cooperation with Center for Jewish Studies at Harvard University.

Hirshfield, Ilan. 1994. Men of men: The hero, the man, and heroism. *Mishkafaim* 22:9–15.

Karakasidou, Anastasia. 1996. Women of the family, women of the nation. *Women's Studies International Journal* 19:99–109.

Kemp, Adriana. 2000. Borders, space and national identity in Israel. *Theory and Criticism* 16:13–44.

Kimmerling, Baruch. 1983. *Zionism and territory: The socioterritorial dimension of Zionist politics.* Berkeley: University of California Press.

Levy, Yagil. 2003. *The other army in Israel: Materialist militarism in Israel* [in Hebrew]. Tel Aviv: Yediot Achronot Press.

Mayer, Tamar. 2000a. Gender ironies of nationalism: Setting the stage. In *Gender ironies of nationalism: Sexing the nation*, edited by Tamar Mayer, 1–22. London: Routledge.

———. 2000b. From zero to hero: Masculinity and Jewish nationalism. In *Gender ironies of nationalism: Sexing the nation*, edited by Tamar Mayer, 283–307. London: Routledge.

———. 2004. Embodied nationalism. In *Mapping gender, making politics: Feminist perspectives on political geography*, edited by L. Staeheli, E. Kofman, and L. Peake, 153–67. London: Routledge.

———. 2005. National symbols in Jewish Israel: Representation and collective memory. In *Contested ground: National symbols and national narratives*, edited by M. Geisler, 3–34. Hanover, NH: University Press of New England.

McClintock, Anne. 1995. *Imperial leather: Race, gender, and sexuality in the colonial conquest.* New York: Routledge.

Morris, B. 1995. *Israel's border wars, 1949-1956: Arab infiltration, Israeli retaliation and the countdown to the Suez War* [in Hebrew]. Tel Aviv: Am Oved.

Moskin, Robert. 1965. Prejudice in Israel. *Look*, October 5: 67–72.

Mosse, George. 1985. *Nationalism and sexuality: Respectability and abnormal sexuality in Modern Europe.* New York: Howard Fetig.

———. 1990. *Fallen soldiers: Reshaping memory of the world wars.* Oxford: Oxford University Press.

Peled, Yoav, and Gershon Shafir. 2005. *Being Israeli: The dynamics of multiple citizenships*. Tel Aviv: Tel Aviv University Press.

Penslar, Derek. 2000. Zionism and Jewish social policy. In *The Age of Zionism* [in Hebrew], edited by A. Shapira, J. Reinharz, and J. Harris, 65–90. Cambridge, MA: Zalman Shazar Center for Jewish History in cooperation with Center for Jewish Studies at Harvard University

Pinchas-Cohen, Hava. 2001. Mother Shalom [peace, the fifth mother; in Hebrew]. *Panim* 17:44–50.

Radcliffe, Sarah, and Sallie Westwood. 1996. *Remaking the nation: Place, identity, and politics in Latin America*. London: Routledge.

Ram, Uri. 1999. The state of the nation: Contemporary challenges to Zionism in Israel. *Constellations* 6 (3): 325–39.

Roulleau, Eric. 1967. Interview with Gen Gurion. *Le Monde*, March 9.

Schwartz, Dov. 1999. *Religious Zionism between logic and Messianism* [in Hebrew]. Tel Aviv: Am Oved.

Shafir, Gershon. 1989. *Land, labor and the origins of the Israeli-Palestinian conflict, 1882–1914*. Cambridge: Cambridge University Press.

Sheleg, Yair. 2000. *The new religious Jews: Recent developments among observant Jews in Israel* [in Hebrew]. Jerusalem: Keter Publishing House.

Smith, Anthony. 1986. *The ethnic origins of nations*. Oxford: Basil Blackwell.

Smooha, Sammy. 1978. *Israel: Pluralism and conflict*. London: Routledge and Kegan Paul.

Weisbrod, Lilly. 1985. Core values and revolutionary change. In *The impact of Gush Emunim: Politics and settlement in the West Bank*, edited by D. Newman, 70–90. London: Croom Helm.

Yuval-Davis, Nira. 1996. "Women and the biological reproduction of 'the nation.'" *Women's Studies International Journal* 19:17–24.

———. 1997. *Gender & nation*. London: Sage.

Yuval-Davis, Nira, and F. Anthias, eds. 1989. *Woman-nation-gender*. London: MacMillan.

16

Mobilizing Civil Society for the Hegemonic State

The Korean War and the Construction of Soldiercitizens in the United States

COLIN FLINT

The Korean War was one of the most significant geopolitical events of the twentieth century. It was the first significant military engagement of the Cold War,[1] and had profound social implications. In this essay I focus upon the important role the war played in the formation of a particular type of citizen-soldier: the hegemonic soldiercitizen, and the related necessary construction of a militarized society. The Korean War was used as a rhetorical device to put the United States on a war footing that rallied schoolteachers, the clergy, and other elements of civil society to arms. The language of the call to arms sowed the seeds of neoliberal ideology that was so important in creating the All Volunteer Force in the wake of the Vietnam War (Cowen 2005, 2006).

The empirical focus of this chapter is U.S. prisoners of war (POWs), and the narrative of their "failure" in collaborating with their captors on an unprecedented scale. The degree and nature of the collaboration were fiction (Carlson 2002). However, the myth of the "failure" of American POWs was used by conservatives in a "blame the victims" approach to put civil society at the service of the military.

The narratives of U.S. POWs and the subsequent political commentary are used to exemplify the new concept of the soldiercitizen, or a citizen whose identity and duty are defined by the types of war fought by hegemonic powers. The imperative for constructing the soldiercitizen and mobilizing civil society to fight the Cold War was geographic. Hegemonic powers act extraterritorially by projecting their power into other sovereign spaces. In so doing, soldiers of the hegemonic state have to fight wars that are easily cast as unjust (Flint and Falah 2004). They are unjust because they breach the dominant political geographic imagination of territorial defense. To make the soldiers and society feel they are fighting a just war, defense of the homeland comes to the fore. However, the homeland is seen not in the territorial sense, but in the aterritorial terms of institutions and values. The soldiercitizen is constructed as a political subject simultaneously defending national institutions and disseminating the values of the hegemonic state across the globe.

The chapter begins with a brief and selective history of the war, focusing upon the plight of U.S. POWs. The geopolitical significance of the Korean War is explored through Buck-Morss's (2000) discussion of the role of warfare in defining the nature of sovereign power: the Korean War required the United States, as hegemonic power, to face a new enemy displaying a new political geography of aterritorial class warfare. The Korean War pitted one notion of geopolitics, nation-states, against another, class warfare. The following empirical sections explore how Chinese captors utilized the abnormality of the geopolitics of extraterritorial hegemonic action in a propaganda campaign. The final empirical section discusses how conservatives in the United States manipulated an overreaction to the POW's susceptibility to Chinese propaganda to build a neoliberal agenda whose foil was a new soldiercitizen required to fight the extraterritorial conflicts of the new hegemonic power.

The Korean War

The United States was not prepared for the Korean War,[2] materially or psychologically. After World War II, the U.S. military was being reduced in size, and ground troops were viewed as increasingly irrelevant as the U.S. Air Force proclaimed its ability to project power after the atomic bombing attacks on Japan. Popular attitude was focused upon demobilization, bringing the troops home rather than committing them to a conflict on the other side of the globe. However, the Korean War played a key role in changing military strategy, foreign policy, and public attitudes.

The Korean War consisted of distinct phases. The initial North Korean invasion and dramatic retreat of South Korean and U.S. forces was followed by a bold counterattack that resulted in U.S. forces, and other nations all fighting under the flag of the United Nations, crossing the 38th parallel that marked the border between North and South Korea. U.S. forces pushed toward the Yalu River, the Chinese–North Korean border, but were repulsed by the entrance of Chinese fighters into the conflict. The war then bogged down around the current cease-fire line.

The decision to fight north of the 38th parallel changed the political geographic nature of the conflict. Prior to that moment, U.S. military actions could be conceived as the just defense of sovereign territory from invasion. By crossing the 38th parallel, the United States was itself open to allegations of territorial aggression. The military action, under the auspices of the United Nations, changed from a defensive action repelling invasion from the South into a projection of power into another sovereign space. The key point for the sake of the argument below is that U.S. soldiers fought an extraterritorial war by fighting to control sovereign spaces rather than fighting to evict unjust invasions. This was a key moment in the process of American hegemony:

extraterritorial military action was established as part of world politics. This was a new phenomenon for the American psyche (though not in historical practice), and the Korean War provoked a national movement to explain and embed the authority of such action into soldiers and citizens.

Prisoners of war played an essential role in the conflict itself and the subsequent construction of attitudes and policies within the United States. The retreat from the initial North Korean invasion was chaotic, and atrocities were widespread. Prisoners were commonly shot in cold blood. Later, troops captured by the Chinese, once they had entered the war, were, generally speaking, treated differently. It was in the Chinese camps that the processes of "indoctrination" that so disturbed U.S. politicians, military officers, and commentators occurred.

Official figures state that 7,140 Americans were taken prisoner during the war, and 2,701 died in captivity (Carlson 2002, 2). However, others claim these figures underestimate the numbers who were killed immediately after capture, which some put in the thousands (Wubben 1970). Esensten (1997) estimates that 75 percent of those captured between June 1950 and September 1951 died in captivity. The official statistics, let alone the unofficial estimates, are horrifying. However, opprobrium greeted the prisoners rather than accolades. Why?

In Every War but One, claimed journalist Eugene Kinkead (1959), U.S. prisoners of war sought to escape capture and resist cooperation with their captors. In the Korean War, no successful escape was made, though there were attempts that Kinkead ignored. Kinkead coined the term "give-up-itis" to describe the demeanor of Korean War U.S. POWs—and proclaimed that discipline and officer leadership crumbled. The result, Kinkead argued, was unprecedented collaboration. He claimed up to 30 percent of U.S. prisoners collaborated with their captors—from informing on comrades, to writing letters home advocating a peace settlement favorable to the North Koreans and Chinese, to making radio broadcasts berating American imperialism. Famously, twenty-one captives elected to remain behind Communist lines at the end of the war (Pasley 1955).

Recent scholarship provides a more sober analysis of the behavior of U.S. POWs. The degree of collaboration was no different than in previous wars (Carlson 2002). Of importance is the way the Chinese portrayed the U.S. soldiers and the United States, and how this portrayal sparked a new construction of the U.S. soldier, citizen, and civil society in light of the extraterritorial military actions that were now part of the Cold War. Kinkead's *In Every War but One* and Pasley's *21 Stayed* were complemented by newspaper and magazine articles. Furthermore, Richard Condon's novel (1959) and the subsequent movie *The Manchurian Candidate* offered a combination of "evil" Communist scientists, "brainwashed" Korean War veterans, and Communist conspiracies to destroy the American way of life and made compelling viewing, putting the idea of an "army" of brainwashed veterans into American popular sensibility. Something had to be done, and that something was the construction of a new soldiercitizen and a U.S. civil society primed to fight the Cold War.

In summary, three elements of the Korean War frame my argument. The war marked the beginning of U.S. military action in the name of the Cold War; U.S. soldiers were ordered to act extraterritorially, invading and controlling sovereign spaces rather than freeing them from external aggression; and the behavior of U.S. POWs in Chinese camps was grossly exaggerated in terms of the degree and extent of collaboration.

Clash of Political Geographies

War dominates politics. Napoleon's war against *ancien regimes*, the expansionist tendency and Godless Evil Empire of Communism, the evil and inhumanity of terrorists—all of these definitions of enemies have been crucial in mobilizing political projects within countries as a component of a war against an external enemy. It is the construction of wars and enemies needing to be fought that defines the nature of the collective sovereign, or who we are in order to fight them (Buck-Morss 2000). Violence, in the form of fighting wars and preparing for them, is used to create particular forms of the democratic subject, and hence the sovereign power (Buck-Morss 2000). Who we are is constructed in relation to the constructed image of the enemy. The social construction of the enemy and the collective self is not a denial of actual threats that could result in real harm. Rather, it emphasizes the nature of the enemy as a political construction defining the extent of "our" political collective and the nature of citizenship. The construction of the subject goes beyond the Orientalism of dehumanizing some to humanize others (Said 1979; Gregory 2004). The project is more political, in the sense that it defines citizenship rights and duties.

The idea of political imaginations complements Hardt and Negri's (2004) discussions of contemporary warfare. War is a form of biopower,

> a form of rule aimed not only at controlling the population but producing and reproducing all aspects of social life. This war brings death but also, paradoxically, must produce life . . . daily life and the normal functioning of power has been permeated with the threat and violence of warfare. (Hardt and Negri 2004, 13)

The Cold War also required a construction of society, a form of social life equipped to fight the wars of hegemony.

The response of conservatives to the Korean War was an exercise of biopower. The goal was the construction of a political subject attuned to the Cold War fight against Communism. The result was what I will call the hegemonic soldiercitizen. The term "soldiercitizen" is to be understood in relation to the hyphenated "citizen-soldier," the belief that citizens have a duty to fight to defend their rights that are defined by being members of a sovereign state. The term "soldiercitizen" problematizes the concept of citizen-soldier in two ways. First, it puts the state of emergency or the act of conflict to the fore and makes it the primary role or duty defining the citizen as political subject. Second, the primacy of conflict destabilizes the taken for granted territorial understanding, in that the conflict is within the borders of the state despite the absence of imminent or actual physical invasion. Instead, the soldiercitizen was mobilized in a fight to defend values and institutions, or, more vaguely, a "way of life." The mobilization was both offensive and defensive. It was offensive in the sense that society needed to cultivate young men willing and able to fight the extraterritorial battles of the hegemonic power. It was defensive in the sense that the institutions necessary to produce such young men were deemed under attack from insidious Communist influence. The internal/external and offensive/defensive duties were so intertwined that the hyphen misleads. To be a model U.S. citizen was to be a soldier defending civil society. Further, there was no distinction between the home front and overseas military action. A constant state of vigilance against Communist influence was necessary to maintain the institutions that would generate manpower to fight overseas.

A geographic approach is necessary to understand the manner in which the soldiercitizen political subject was constructed. For Buck-Morss (2000), the Cold War was a conflict between two very different political imaginations. One political imagination centered upon liberal nation-states in conflict with hostile nation-states. The nation needed to be defended by granting authority to the state as the sovereign agency. The other political imagination was one of class warfare. The antagonists of the working class were the owners of capital. To face this threat, the party was granted sovereign agency. The key here is that these were not just political imaginations, but also political *geographic* imaginations; they rested upon different assumptions of the territorial organization of politics. The first rested upon assumptions of the natural or proper compartmentalization of the political collective into territorially discreet nation-states (Murphy 1996; Dijkink 2005), while the other envisioned an international (or even aterritorial) conflict between classes.

In the Western world, the political imagination of territorial nation-states predominated. The Second World War was fought against enemies declared to be "expansionist" or hostile to the existence of the political collective of nation-states and violating sovereign territory. The Second World War was deemed the "good war" because it was portrayed as the defense of the accepted political geographic imagination. Furthermore, the nation-state political imagination of enemy and collective sovereign pervades our understanding of all societal processes (Agnew 2005).

One such example is the discussion of just war, in which the dominant moral imperative for war is defense of the collective sovereign of the nation-state when its territory has been violated by invasion, or the threat of invasion is imminent (Walzer 2000). The predominance of the nation-state political imagination and the sense that it is vital to our lives allow one nation-state to claim it is acting morally when it aids a country facing an invasion. Borders and territory, the political imagination of the nation-state, are the essential components in our evaluation of whether pursuit of a particular war is moral (Flint and Falah 2004).

The implicit acceptance of territorial sovereignty as the basis of fighting just wars is crucial when considering the impact upon the individuals fighting a war. How does their understanding of just war effect their interpretation of their actions, and how does society view itself? The construction of the democratic subject, a liberal citizen whose rights and duties are territorially bound, is not only constructed by viewing a world of hostile nation-states, but also by participating in military actions that are seen as the moral defense of the principles of the nation-state political imagination.

In the Korean War, the U.S. soldiers faced propaganda aimed at shattering their established political imagination. U.S. soldiers were told that the imagined community of their nation was fiction, and they were instead the victims of class warfare. Also, their actions were portrayed as imperialist and violated the assumptions of just war held within the nation-state political imagination. The Korean War was a clash of political geographic imaginations. Chinese propaganda portrayed the U.S. soldiers as immoral, violating the territorial sovereignty of another country in the name of imperialism and also attacking the mythology of the U.S. nation-state. Subsequent scholarly research has disproved the myth that U.S. soldiers fighting in Korea were especially susceptible to enemy propaganda. But the myth was used to provoke a construction of the political subject and the sovereign agent deemed necessary to fight the new enemy of the Cold War (Buck-Morss 2000). The collaboration of POWs with the Chinese was exaggerated to support an argument for conservative projects in American schools, families, and churches.

But what was the nature of the conservatives' concern? It can be understood in two ways. Following Buck-Morss (2000), the role of the enemy in defining the sovereign and the subject means that the soldier (facing the external enemy) must be created at the same time as the citizen (the internal subject). In fact, the two are inseparable. The hyphen in citizen-soldier is misleading. The role of the enemy in creating the subject means that the subject is a soldiercitizen. The focus is simultaneously offensive to allow for the construction of soldiers to fight the wars of the hegemonic state and defensive in creating particular ideas of the citizen and civil society.

The internal/external imperative is especially important for the hegemonic state. From a world-systems perspective, the hegemonic state is the one dominant state in terms of economic, political, cultural, and military power (Taylor and Flint 2000, 62–74). The interstate system in the twentieth century witnessed the decline of Great Britain as hegemonic power and the emergence, through the two world wars, of the United States as the new hegemonic power. Here I focus upon one aspect of hegemony, extraterritoriality. The hegemonic state uses its power to establish economic and political practices providing the greatest benefit to its own economy. Part of this management process is the desire to keep as much of the world-economy "open" to practices of free trade as possible to provide markets for the hegemonic power's economic prowess (Agnew 2005; Taylor and Flint 2000, 72–74). Mostly, this can be achieved through political means. However, the United States faced challenges to its global role from the outset of its reign. Communism offered an alternative ideology, as well as the geopolitical challenge of excluding a large part of the globe from the United States' economic reach. It was these twin challenges that required the United States to take military action in the Korean peninsula.

There is a close and important theoretical connection between the construction of the hegemonic soldiercitizen and extraterritoriality. Most extraterritorial military actions by the hegemonic power are easily categorized as falling outside the common understanding of a just war. Our notions of a just war are embedded within the territorial political imagination. Traveling across the globe to fight in a foreign country in a situation where there is no discernible threat to the "homeland" does not fit into common understandings of just war (Flint and Falah 2004). In the propaganda campaign faced by U.S. POWs in Korea, we see evidence of how the Chinese portrayed such a hegemonic "police action" as immoral. The implication goes beyond the actions of individual POWs, but is a matter of how the political sovereign and its subjects are created by practicing a form of warfare that can readily be portrayed as unjust. The extraterritoriality of hegemonic military action within a territorial political imagination requires a particular form of subject construction. Moreover, conservative and neoliberal ideologies are most readily employed in the construction of the hegemonic soldiercitizen. Why?

A justification for military action resting on the imminent invasion of territory is unsustainable. So, the "homeland" must take on a nonterritorial form. Values, institutions, and traditions are deemed under threat and must be protected. Protection of institutions and values, usually viewed as a return to a mythical past when everything was rosy, is the essence of conservative ideology. It becomes the duty of the hegemonic soldiercitizen to create particular institutions and behaviors into a mythical historical form to face an external enemy. The soldiercitizen at home and the citizen-soldier abroad fight the nonterritorial political imagination of class warfare by protecting values and institutions that the hegemonic power deems universal and final, in the sense that none better have existed or will exist (Taylor 1999). The extraterritorial military actions of the hegemonic state require the twin offensive and defensive foci of the creation of the political subject.

Chinese Propaganda and the Fragility of Political Geography Imaginations

It is now clear that the effectiveness of Chinese propaganda campaigns within the prisoner of war camps was exaggerated (Carlson 2002). However, the content of the propaganda is still of interest in the way it illuminates how Cold War antagonists were aware of the political imagination of their enemies, and how they used the fragility of these mental maps in the ideological weaponry of the Cold War. Furthermore, the specific targets of the nation-state political imagination chosen by the Chinese were the exact same political arenas promoted by conservative commentators in the United States after the war. In other words, Chinese propaganda destabilized the citizenship beliefs within the nation-state political imagination, and conservatives tried to secure the institutional foundations of territorial citizenship while promoting their political agenda.

The Chinese were adept at identifying and co-opting "collaborators" from the American POWs who then partook in a variety of propaganda activities. These included written statements, in the form of letters home that encouraged a peace settlement and intimated that the prisoners agreed with the Chinese and Korean terms, and also essays published across the world as part of the Cold War propaganda campaign. One such publication was *Thinking Soldiers: By Men Who Fought in Korea*, edited, purportedly, by one ex-British Royal Marine and two ex-members of the U.S. Army (Condron, Corden, and Sullivan 1955). This is an alleged series of essays and poems written by British and American servicemen while in captivity, published in Peking in 1955. The book was disseminated into Cold War "hotspots" as a form of propaganda portraying the United States as an imperialist power, rather than a benevolent hegemonic power. Though published after the cease-fire, it still provides insights into the way the Chinese attacked the sensibilities of soldiers fighting within and for a nation-state political imagination.

The book was organized in a strategic and linear progression. The essays first destroyed the sense of imagined community essential for the territorial imagination (Anderson 1991). Next, the essays interjected racial discrimination to promote a new scale of political identity: individual dignity and the politics of mankind or humanity. The conclusion the book attempts to draw is that only a new politics of class will bring justice to the world.

The first essay, entitled "A British Regular; by a Corporal," is a sorry but believable tale of growing up in poverty. The essay describes the writer's mother working in a laundry:

> [W]hile the owner, a big fat man, sat in an office in the corner to ensure that everyone did their share. . . . In the yard where I lived, I was accustomed to seeing the men doing all the heavy work, but here was a man sitting down while the women worked. (Condron, Corden, and Sullivan 1955, 10)

This quote introduces social class injustice as a cancer within the nation-state. Moreover, it corrupts the gendered notion of the nation-state, simultaneously promoting male chivalry and identifying gender inequities.

The next series of quotes from this essay highlights the notion of atomization that, so the story goes, is an obvious response to the class injustices within a nation and demands the rejection of the imagined community myth. The author left home at age fourteen looking for work, "determined that from then on only one person existed—that was myself, to hell with anybody else" (Condron, Corden, and Sullivan 1955, 11). The author's political introspection at that moment was unsophisticated, simultaneously indicating how "obvious" class warfare was, while also laying the groundwork for the necessity of Communist Party leadership.

Next, the essay introduced the territorial basis for just war, which ultimately led to the implication that the nation-state imagination was not only inconsistent domestically, because of class injustice, but also in its extraterritoriality. The corporal fought World War II because he was told Hitler intended to "overrun Britain and that we must defend it" (Condron, Corden, and Sullivan 1955, 19). However, his assignment was to Africa: "Now here was something I just couldn't understand, sending men overseas when the German Army was threatening to attack our country at any time" (22).

The territorial political imagination, the basis for common understandings of just war, was undermined in this essay by identifying World War II as an imperialist war. The extraterritoriality of the Allied campaign was expressed as an act of imperialism and not the just defense of the homeland. The essay concluded with the author rallying against the racial discrimination he witnessed in Cape Town:

> It was forbidden for us soldiers to talk to the coloured people. To hell with that, was my idea; these people are human beings irrespective of what colour they were and like myself they were trying to make a living. (Condron, Corden, and Sullivan 1955, 23)

Race was used to maneuver from the dominant nation-state imagination to one that speaks of humanity, which segued into the identification of the Korean War as an unjust colonial war. The essay ended with an overt discussion of international class awareness and international class struggle. This first essay was a microcosm of the book as it addressed all of the key themes in a linear argument: the myth of the imagined national community, the unjust nature of the Korean War as colonial war, racial discrimination as a violation of human rights and class solidarity, and the solutions offered by international class identity and struggle.

The following essay was entitled "We Thought We'd Get to the Yalu by an American Corporal." Its themes were similar to the previous essay but placed greater emphasis upon the extraterritorial nature of the America "police action" in Korea, comparing it unfavorably with World War II, commonly identified as a just war against territorial invasion. The corporal, just after arriving in Pusan,

> went into a warehouse and saw a group standing over in a corner. They stared out at me and I couldn't figure out whether their gaze was pitiful or angry. There had been many stories about the Second World War and how people would praise the GI's where they occupied a town. But here no one acted that way. All had an unfriendly appearance. (Condron, Corden, and Sullivan 1955, 61)

The essay highlighted the immorality of the extraterritoriality of the U.S. presence even further. On being ordered to cross the 38th parallel,

> Our morale dropped very low on hearing this news. The GI's started to get barbarous, mistreating civilians, wronging women, plundering, stealing and doing other disgraceful things. (Condron, Corden, and Sullivan 1955, 69)

Rape was used as a metaphor, and as an actual shocking fact, to impress upon the reader the violation of the political imagination of territorial nation-states and the related notions of just war.

The point was emphasized in an essay entitled "Bataan to Korea, by Corporal John L. Dixon, U.S. Army" (identified as an American Indian). In a statement that perhaps got at the heart of the United States' concerns of creating soldiercitizens to fight the Cold War, he wrote,

> That war [World War II] was a just war, and because it was just it seemed entirely reasonable to ordinary Americans that we should fight it. That was the spirit that prevailed in Bataan where American troops displayed such heroism against the Japanese. This war is an unjust war and the American troops haven't got their hearts in it. They have no cause to fight for and no just reason for being in Korea. As a consequence, their morale is low. (Condron, Corden, and Sullivan 1955, 108)

The essays by U.S. racial minorities were put together in a section entitled "The Double Burden." Here, the question of citizens' rights, and their violation, was addressed most explicitly. After lamenting a lifetime of racial discrimination, a Negro sergeant proclaimed, "And now the government sends me to Korea to defend my RIGHTS as an American citizen!" (Condron, Corden, and Sullivan 1955, 185). Significantly, the essay emphasized subject status and not membership in a nation.

In "José, Mexican-American, an Autobiography in the Third Person by a U.S. Corporal," the discrimination experienced by a citizen was highlighted:

He was informed that Class E allotments had all been cut off, but Class Q was being put into effect. As usual, all applications had to go through proper channels. José began to hate every minute of the army. (Condron, Corden, and Sullivan 1955, 198)

A segue was made from the theme of discrimination in citizen rights to a new type of political subject: "As he recalls his experiences with bitterness, he knows that peace, brotherhood and mutual love must exist if mankind is to progress" (Condron, Corden, and Sullivan 1955, 199). Discrimination of U.S. racial minority citizens was used to negate the nation-state political imagination and replace it with an aterritorial political imagination that is readily related to class struggle and a new political subject.

The four essays by U.S. racial minorities played an important role in the book. These propaganda essays were meant to put a final nail in the coffin of the reader's belief in the unity and justice of the U.S. and British nation-states and introduce a new political imagination, international class brotherhood. The concluding essays emphasized the commonalities of workingmen (gender specific) across the globe, both in terms of the burden they faced in fighting wars and their contribution to the economy.

The last essay was entitled "Parting Letter by a British Lad, Repatriated in the First Exchange of Sick and Wounded POWs Writes Back to His Mates." Note that the writer and recipients were demilitarized as "lads" and "mates" as the writer had apparently been fully converted into a humanitarian internationalist, or perhaps anationalist. Upon seeing bombed Pyongyang, the writer forcefully stated, "[I]f you have any humanitarian feelings in you at all then you'll see it as I saw it" (Condron, Corden, and Sullivan 1955, 245), for Koreans "want just what we all want, a little happiness—and there's only one way to be sure of that, that's by having peace" (Condron, Corden, and Sullivan 1955, 246).

These were propaganda essays. If they were written by Britons and Americans at all, then it was under varying degrees of duress. Prisoners were encouraged to write about their life experiences over and over again (Carlson 2002). It is probable that most did because they were told to, were bored, and believed that they would lever better living conditions. The degree of ghostwriting and editorial intervention was high. For the sake of the argument being made here, the authenticity of the letters is not what matters. It is of no concern whether the essays were actually written by POWs. Of interest is the content of the essays and the particular themes that the Chinese Communists wanted to disseminate. Why? Because the themes illustrate the perceived weak points of the liberal nation-state political imagination (Buck-Morss 2000). Whether real or not, Communism as the new enemy was defined as the threat to the very foundations of the liberal nation-state political imagination, and part of the response was a political battle over the nature of citizenship and related institutions.

How to Meet an ExtraTerritorial Enemy: Rearming Civil Society

The dominance of political imaginations identified from Buck-Morss (2000) leads to the definition of two forms of geopolitics: normal and abnormal. Normal geopolitics occurs when the enemy is in their place. Or in other words, one territorial entity fights another. In such an event it is easy to frame the conflict, and the actions of citizen-soldiers, as moral. The Korean War, and the remainder of the Cold War, was an example of abnormal geopolitics: different political geographic imaginations were in conflict. The Cold War, the engagement with a new and aterritorial political imagination, required a new understanding of the war to allow for the actions of citizen-soldiers to be framed as just. The result was a blend of the political imaginations. The threat was aterritorial, and the defined response was the defense of institutions that were the foundation of the nation-state: family, schools, and churches. Civil society was defined as a battleground. Citizen-soldiers would not suffice in this conflict. Instead, soldiercitizens were called to arms.

Two separate but related approaches were made. One approach was to emphasize the history, institutions, and values of the United States to assert the territorial basis of conflict in defense of the United States. The second approach was to reterritorialize the conflict at different scales by connecting universal hegemonic values with a particular view of the family with Christianity as the glue. The result was the promotion of militarization, the subordination of all aspects of society to military imperatives (Enloe 2004, 219–20; Woodward 2004, 2005). The student, the family, the church, and so on were oriented to serve the violence of the sovereign.

Eugene Kinkead's (1959) journalism focused upon the response of the military. The prevailing attitude was that the experience of the Korean POWs introduced a new form of conflict and required new training. The outcome was a new Army Code of Conduct defining the duties of the soldier if captured. However, the training was not just a matter for the military. As Hugh M. Milton II, assistant secretary of the army for manpower and reserve forces, interviewed by Kinkead, said,

> Overcoming Communism is not simply an Army problem. . . . It's a truly national program. And don't forget—the battle against Communism is waged largely at the level of the individual, and the earlier he is prepared, the better. The Army would like to see every American parent, every American teacher, and every American clergyman work to instill in every one of our children a specific understanding of the difference between our way of life and the Communist way of life. . . . The Army's period of training is too brief to make changes in the habits of a lifetime. By the time a young man enters the Army, he should possess a set of sound moral values and the strength of character to live with them.

Then, with Army training, he may become something very close to military perfection—the ideal citizen soldier. (Kinkead 1959, 210–11)

Milton gives official gravity to the core of Kinkead's argument. It was not just individual soldiers who faced the Communist antagonist in the Korean War, "but more importantly the entire cultural pattern which produced these young soldiers" (Kinkead 1959, 9–10). The perceived lack of discipline in the prisoner of war camps was "because they had come into battle straight from soft, peacetime lives" (Kinkead 1959, 154). Failure in the military contact with Communism was "the result of some new failure in the childhood and adolescent training of our young men—a new softness" (Kinkead 1959, 156).

The theme of individual responsibility was echoed in the more scholarly prognoses that followed the Korean War. In his *A Guide to Anti-Communist Action*, Anthony Bouscaren stated that "Communism offers a retreat to those who cannot face facts or bear the responsibility of individual action" (Bouscaren 1958, 153). Individual action is a political-spiritual imperative as Bouscaren conflates the "just plain American" all-can-do spirit with the Christian Christopher Movement of Father James Keller. The essence of the Christopher Movement was "active citizenship" to "highlight the importance of 'doing'" (Armstrong 1984). Individual citizen action coupled with Christian spiritual guidance was identified as a bulwark against a "slave state" (Bouscaren 1958, 212).

The moral failures of the individual and society that Kinkead (1959) identified as being the essence of the United States' geopolitical vulnerability in the Cold War required the construction of a spiritually-based individualistic citizenship. Action was "something constructive in behalf of God and America and against Communism" (Bouscaren 1958, 206). The linkage to what we now identify as neoliberalism, justified and given authority by fundamentalist Christianity, is quite clear:

> The basic truths in which the Christopher movement is rooted are exactly the same truths which the Communists everywhere are working to undermine, ridicule, and eliminate. They are: (1) the existence of a personal triune God Who has spoken to the world; (2) Jesus Christ, true God and true man; (3) the foundation by Jesus Christ of a Church to teach all men and bring them to eternal salvation; (4) the Ten Commandments; (5) the sacred character of the individual; (6) the sanctity of the lifelong marriage bond; (7) the sanctity of the home as the basic unit of the whole human family; (8) the human rights of every person as coming from God, not the state; (9) the right, based on human nature, to possess private property, with its consequent obligation to society; (10) due respect for domestic, civil, and religious authority; and (11) judgment after death. (Bouscaren 1958, 208)

Education played a key strategic role in the construction of social life and citizenship post Korean War. Conservatives voiced displeasure at the "New Education" developed in the 1930s and 1940s, and connected it to the geopolitical failure of Korean POWs and a domestic agenda of antistatism. The role of Dr. Harold Rugg in creating an educational agenda for the public schools "supporting statism, and upholding collectivist doctrines as superior to sound American principles," was denounced (Rudd 1957, 4). Augustin G. Rudd (chairman of the Educational Committee of the New York Chapter of the Sons of the American Revolution) berated the New Education for demeaning the "glorious history" of the United States. "Most of us hold the belief that our country is superior to dictatorships of other countries. But apparently we are wrong" (Rudd 1957, 76).

Rudd juxtaposed the two political imaginations later identified by Buck-Morss (2000), though not on the same terms. On the one hand, for Rudd there was the new educationalist emphasis on "social change," an illumination of the social injustices within U.S. history and the discussion of progressive alternatives in the classroom. This emphasis reflected the political imagination of class warfare, or so Rudd and others vigorously asserted. On the other hand, conservatives emphasized a noncritical reading of the U.S. Constitution reflecting the nation-state political imagination. Such an educational approach was seen as building individual character or the "roots of the nation" (Rudd 1957, 186). Moreover, the trope of discipline was evident. Rudd argued that lack of discipline in schools resulted in the promotion of self-interest that undermined patriotism. Lack of discipline was tied to the emphasis on relativism rather than absolutes in the New Education (Rafferty 1968).

Rudd's talk of discipline, individualism, and morality and their juxtaposition against a "slave state" predated the language of contemporary neoliberalism. The motivation for such ideology was based on the new type of foe facing the nation—Communism. Specifically, the experience of the Korean POW collaborators was invoked. The relativism promoted by the New Education was seen as providing no defense against the alternative class-based ideology offered by the Chinese—absolutes were needed (Smith 1949, 24, paraphrased in Rudd 1957, 172; see also Rafferty 1968). Susceptibility to Communist ideology was enhanced by a lack of knowledge of "American political philosophy" (Dorothy Thompson 1948, quoted by Rudd 1957, 221; Rafferty 1968).

Thompson's experience of being susceptible to Communist ideology while in college was linked to the Korean War. Rudd (1957) quoted extensively from an interview with Major William E. Meyer, an army psychiatrist who interviewed prisoners returning from Korea. Meyer argued that "the American educational system, fine as it is, is failing miserably in getting across the absolute fundamentals of survival in a tense and troubled international society" (*U.S. News & World Report* 1956, quoted in Rudd 1957, 223). The *U.S. News & World Report* interviewer prompted Meyer to agree that the POWs were unable to counter Communist views with a historical knowledge of their own: "these Americans' faith in their own country and its principles was so weak that it could be shaken by these Red Chinese in prison-cell interrogations" (quoted in Rudd 1957, 223). Education was not serving the sovereign power's war with Communism. "If our schools do not teach our youth the basic principles of our American way of life, then other ideas of life will dominate their thinking, for nature abhors a vacuum" (Rudd 1957, 231).

Christianity provided the necessary moral scaffold to build American values appropriate for the geopolitics of the Cold War. Patriotism, or more specifically Americanism, was connected to strong Christian religious convictions (Rudd 1957, 168; Rafferty 1968). American individualism and Christian values were blended into the morality necessary to fight the Cold War. Americanism was a tool to reinforce the nation-state political imagination against the new political imagination of class warfare. In addition, the imperative was not just to support the idea of a world political map of nation-states in general, but also to construct a sense of American ideals that could be placed in the service of hegemony. Hence, they had to be universal values. The promotion of Christian values was an effective tool for equating American ideals with a commitment to the whole globe or, in other words, to justify extraterritorial hegemonic actions. Furthermore, the identified foe of Communism promoted a particular conception of United States citizenship and civil society, one that can be viewed as the basis for contemporary neoliberalism: discipline, individual responsibility, and lack of state intervention. A disciplining sense of national community was brought to bear in the call for a new soldiercitizen, able to be moral, and independent and serve in the fight against socialism at home and Communism abroad.

Conclusion

At the conclusion of *The Manchurian Candidate*, hero Major Bennett Marco (played by Frank Sinatra) lamented the death of the brainwashed assassin: "Friendless, friendless Raymond." Raymond's failure was also a failure of society to encompass and delimit Raymond's actions. The weakness was not Raymond's individual morality, but a society that was not geared to socializing men with the right moral fiber to resist Communist conspiracy.

Morality was a key theme because of the unfamiliar geopolitical terrain faced by the United States at the beginning of the Cold War. It was fighting extraterritorial military actions that were deemed unjust in the standard lexicon of just war. The United States was able to find a means of legitimating its actions by the new type of enemy it was facing. Seemingly Communism and its methods of class warfare were operating outside the accepted norms of territorial politics. "Homeland" remained the focus of defense, but it was seen in aterritorial terms of values and institutions. Such a strategy armed conservatives to call for the defense of traditional bastions of authority and ideals in the opening skirmishes of the dissemination of a neoliberal agenda. The necessary citizen was a soldiercitizen who was active in protecting the institutions that were the basis for justifying the hegemonic diffusion of values while also perceiving that these institutions and values were so vulnerable that they required the slaughter of Americans and many more foreigners in the killing fields of Korea, and subsequently Vietnam, Grenada, Panama, Afghanistan, Iraq . . .

Notes

1. The "start" of the Cold War is debatable; perhaps beginning with U.S. support of the White Russians after the Bolshevik revolution? The Korean War marked the beginning of a popular perception that Communism was an enemy that required military engagement and the related rise in military expenditure (Johnson 2004, 56).
2. For a brief history of the Korean War, see the entry in Holmes (2001). See also Hastings (1987).

References

Agnew, J. 2005. *Hegemony: The new shape of global power.* Philadelphia: Temple University Press.

Anderson, B. 1991. *Imagined communities*, rev. ed. New York: Verso.

Armstrong, R. 1984. *Out to change the world.* New York: Crossroad Publishing.

Bouscaren, A. T. 1958. *A guide to anti-Communist action.* Chicago: Henry Regnery.

Buck-Morss, S. 2000. *Dreamworld and catastrophe: The passing of mass utopia in East and West.* Cambridge, MA: MIT Press.

Carlson, L. H. 2002. *Remembered prisoners of a forgotten war: An oral history of Korean War POWs.* New York: St. Martin's.

Condon, R. 1959. *The Manchurian candidate.* New York: New American Library.

Condron, A. M., R. G. Corden, and L. V. Sullivan, eds. 1955. *Thinking soldiers: By men who fought in Korea.* Peking: New World Press.

Cowen, D. 2005. Welfare warriors: Towards a genealogy of the soldier citizen in Canada. *Antipode* 37 (4): 654–78.

———. 2006. Fighting for 'freedom': The end of conscription in the United States and the neoliberal project of citizenship. *Citizenship Studies* 10 (2): 167–83.

Dijkink, G. 2005. Soldiers and nationalism: The glory and transience of a hard-won territorial identity. In *The geography of war and peace*, edited by C. Flint, 113–32. Oxford: Oxford University Press.

Enloe, C. 2004. *The curious feminist: Searching for women in a new age of empire.* Berkeley: University of California Press.

Esensten, S. 1997. Memories of life as a POW 35 years later. *The Graybeards*, July–August.

Flint, C., and G-W. Falah. 2004. How the United States justified its war on terrorism: Prime morality and the construction of a 'just war.' *Third World Quarterly* 25 (8): 1379-99.

Gregory, D. 2004. *The colonial present: Afghanistan, Palestine, Iraq.* Malden, MA: Blackwell.

Hardt, M., and A. Negri. 2004. *Multitude: War and democracy in the age of empire.* New York: Penguin.

Hastings, M. 1987. *The Korean War.* London: Michael Joseph.

Holmes, R., ed. 2001. *The Oxford companion to military history.* Oxford: Oxford University Press.

Johnson, C. 2004. *The sorrows of empire.* New York: Owl Books.

Kinkead, E. 1959. *In every war but one.* New York: W.W. Norton.

Murphy, A. B. 1996. The sovereign state system as political-territorial ideal: Historical and contemporary considerations. In *State Sovereignty as Social Construct*, edited by T. J. Biersteker and C. Weber, 81–120. Cambridge: Cambridge University Press.

Pasley, V. 1955. *21 stayed: The story of the American GI's who chose Communist China—who they were and why they stayed.* New York: Farrar, Straus and Cudahy.

Rafferty, M. 1968. *Max Rafferty on education.* New York: Devin-Adair.

Rudd, A. G. 1957. *Bending the twig: The revolution in education and its effect on our children.* New York: New York Chapter, Sons of the American Revolution.

Said, E. W. 1979. *Orientalism.* New York: Vintage.

Smith, M. 1949. *And madly teach.* Chicago: Henry Regnery.

Taylor, P. J. 1999. *Modernities: A geohistorical interpretation.* Minneapolis: University of Minnesota Press.

Taylor, P. J., and C. Flint. 2000. *Political geography: World-economy, nation-state and locality.* Harlow, UK: Pearson Education.

Thompson, D. 1968. I never became acquainted with American Government. *Ladies Home Journal*, October, 11–12.

U.S. News & World Report. 1956. Why did many GI captives cave in? Interview with Major William E. Mayer, U.S. Army expert. February 24: 56–72.

Walzer, M. 2000. *Just and unjust wars: A moral argument with historical illustrations,* 3rd ed. New York: Basic Books.

Woodward, R. 2004. *Military geographies.* Malden, MA: Blackwell.

———. 2005. From military geography to militarism's geographies: Disciplinary engagements with the geographies of militarism and military activities. *Progress in Human Geography* 29 (6): 718–40.

Wubben, H. H. 1970. American prisoners of war in Korea: A second look at the 'something new in history' theme. *American Quarterly* 22 (1): 3–19.

17

"Not for Queen and Country or Any of That Shit . . ."

Reflections on Citizenship and Military Participation in Contemporary British Soldier Narratives

RACHEL WOODWARD

Soldiers, citizenship, and denial

In his narrative *For Queen and Country*, Nigel "Spud" Ely tells a gripping tale of a military career with the Parachute Regiment and Special Forces, of active engagement as a soldier in the Falklands and Northern Ireland. The narrative is framed by reflection on the disjuncture between Ely's own understanding of his motivations for participation in the British Army, and what he sees as wider cultural myths which rationalize that participation in terms of citizenship as service to Crown and nation. Looking back on his Falklands experiences, he quotes Dick, a friend and fellow soldier, who is adamant in his denial that their actions in the Falklands constituted some sort of personal sacrifice for wider national objectives:

> People have asked me if I'm OK after the war, after killing people and all that shite. Well, I'm fine, thanks. It was my job, not for Queen and Country or any of that shit. Not for the people we liberated and not for the politicians who told the Argentines we were going to attack them the day before we actually did. . . . It was for the men who fought along side of me. (Dick, quoted in Ely 2003, 243–44)

Dick's denial is startling in the degree to which it clearly and explicitly counters a political, cultural, and sociological orthodoxy that equates the practice of military participation with the expression of citizenship through service to the nation. Dick's denial is not unique, however. It is representative of a feature of contemporary British soldier narratives, namely, their engagement with these orthodoxies—more correctly, discourses—through which the meaning of being a soldier is articulated and debated. The ways in which these narratives engage discursively is the focus of this chapter. These narratives, I will argue, are strategic interventions in long-standing and ongoing cultural

363

negotiations over the meaning of military participation, which include arguments about its citizenship effects.

Contemporary British soldier narratives, because of their strategic intent, are a rich resource for the issues around which this edited volume is framed. They are useful because they tell us what their authors—soldiers—think is important that we know. They engage directly with the practice of war, the articulation of citizenship and the construction and control of territory, and they do so in myriad ways. As Dick's denial illustrates, they frequently unsettle the easy conflation of military participation, national gain, and service to the state. They do so in ways that destabilize and disturb comfortable myths about duty and sacrifice, community and nation, nationhood and territory. Sometimes, alternatively, they reinforce prevailing notions of solidarity, cohesion, and bravery. Reading these narratives for what they say about military participation and citizenship means moving beyond the conceptualization of the soldier as the passive recipient of rights and the bearer of obligations, and toward an understanding of the soldier as an active participant and protagonist in uneasy arguments about where, exactly, the contemporary British soldier sits in relation to the wider civilian society that he or she purportedly serves.

In this chapter, I start by outlining some key features of contemporary academic debates with regard to the idea of the soldier as citizen, in order to place my reading of contemporary British soldier narratives in a wider conceptual context. I go on to introduce soldier narratives and argue for their utility as an empirical textual resource in unpacking ideas about military participation and citizenship. I consider narratives' descriptions and reflections on the act of enlistment for what they say—and do not say—about the idea of soldiering as the performance of citizenship, and see the limited reflection on this within these narratives as an outcome not just of the conventions of the genre, but also of the conventions through which the figure of the soldier is understood within British culture. I then go on to look at how a specific discourse of citizenship, as "mateship," is articulated in these narratives, both in lieu of statements about national service, and as a strategy to engage with, counter, and destabilize both state-military and popular discourses about the meaning of the soldier. I conclude that studies of the citizen-soldier need to pay due heed to these statements about what soldiers think, not because of any naïve desire to reclaim lost voices, but rather because of the significance of the genre of the contemporary British soldier narrative in shaping what we, collectively, think of the contemporary British soldier.

The British soldier-citizen

The quotation above, refuting the idea of military action as an act of explicit citizenship in service to the nation, jars when considered in the context of more conceptually abstract writing on citizenship and military participation. This body of work understands military participation as inextricably bound to the expression of and negotiations over citizenship. An orthodoxy in military sociology, drawing on the observations of Weber and expressed most clearly by Janowitz and later Moskos in North American postwar military sociology, rests on the idea of the citizen-soldier. For the citizen-soldier, military participation is understood as service to a wider community beyond the military unit, undertaken in exchange for the (variously defined) benefits of citizen-membership. Whether conceptualized in terms of a liberal discourse of citizenship, where military service is provided by the individual in exchange for political, social, and civic rights (following the work of Janowitz), or a republican discourse where military participation is symbolic of the willingness of the individual to make personal sacrifice for the wider good of the nation, contemporary military sociology is clear on the connections that military participation consolidates between the individual and the nation-state (Barbalet 1988; Heater 1999; Sasson-Levy 2003a, 2003b; Cowen 2005). This connection has been understood as fluid and contingent, varying with the modes of enlistment (conscription or voluntary) and military organizational structure (Burk 1995; van der Meulen and Manigart 1997; Soeters, Winslow, and Wiebull 2003) and with shifts in the moral values of the wider society (Abrams and Bacevich 2001; Morgan 2003). More recent analyses have drawn on the insights of, for example, political economy (see, for example, Cowen 2005), identity politics and nationhood (see, for example, Sasson-Levy 2003a, 2003b; Kanaaneh 2005), and gender (Feinman 2000; Gullace 2002) in promoting greater understanding of the soldier-citizen nexus in both contemporary and historical contexts. Specifically, much contemporary and critical sociological and historical inquiry has opened up academic explorations of the citizen-soldier by examining this nexus in discursive terms, and with a view to the agency of soldiers themselves.

The narratives under discussion here have been written by former members of the British armed forces, self-identified as British nationals, producing books written for a predominantly British readership. In view of this, and in view of my use of these texts to discuss citizenship issues, it is pertinent to consider whether contemporary studies of the sociology of the British military have anything to say about citizenship. In fact, there is a paucity of research explicitly on the citizen soldier issue. Much of the literature outlining the concept of the citizen-soldier is based on empirical materials from the United States, where long traditions stretching back to the Civil War (and indeed to the War of Independence; see Kestnbaum 2000) have been examined to show how ideas of military service as national service are fundamental to the foundation myths of the U.S. nation-state. Similarly, we can identify a rich body of work from Israel, where the citizenship-military service nexus is so visible because of the status of the military in Israeli political, economic, and cultural life (Sasson-Levy 2002, 2003a, 2003b). Studies of the sociology of the military in Britain have concentrated primarily on its institutional and organizational aspects (for an overview, see Dandeker 2000). This literature follows the dominant concerns of the British Armed Forces in the post–Second World War period, a time when military engagements involving British forces have not been about nation building. The discursive framing of British military activities internationally has certainly touched upon issues of nationhood with, for example, state representations of the 1982 Falklands/Malvinas conflict as a British territorial issue, or peacekeeping and conflict resolution operations in, for example, Bosnia or Sierra Leone, portrayed as the gifting of British notions of order and stability to chaotic places. However, nation building has not been a cause of armed conflict for the British armed forces from the mid-twentieth century onwards. Reflecting this, issues of citizenship and nationhood have figured less prominently within British sociological studies of the military than in, for example, the North American or Israeli literature.

This is not to say that these issues have been entirely ignored. Recent work on veterans, for example, explores current policy debates in order to ascertain how veterans of the British armed forces are treated and rewarded for past service (Dandeker et al. 2006). Research on the high levels of homelessness amongst former armed forces personnel has exposed the gulf between ideas of social rewards in return for military service, and the reality of this for many people (Higate 1997, 2000). Research into the attitudes toward and experiences of the British armed forces amongst minority ethnic communities touches on questions of citizenship and belonging for first-, second-, and third-generation minority ethnic citizens, many of whom have their origins in families and communities with long histories of service in the British forces (Hussain and Ishaq 2002a, 2002b, 2002c, 2002d). Research on military personnel and gender identity shows how ideas about masculinity and place intertwine for the soldier (Woodward 1998, 2003, 2006). Yet, as Gibson and Abell (2004) point out, there is little social scientific research in the British context about questions of military participation and identity in terms of national identification. For example, John Hockey's *Squaddies* (1986) and his subsequent reworking of this material (Hockey 2002, 2003), one of the very few sociological studies of contemporary British Army life, are largely silent on questions about soldiers' perceptions of the wider meanings of military service. As a consequence, and in the absence of a coherent body of work on this,

> national consciousness and 'patriotic' motivation are often projected into the mind of the soldier by both politicians and social scientists. (Gibson and Abell 2004, 873)

Gibson and Abell's work, which entailed interviewing a small sample of serving soldiers about their understanding of the meaning of military participation, argues that ideas about identity, nationhood, and service are not absent, but rather that they are qualified and sometimes silenced by competing discourses. For example, the soldiers interviewed for their study are reticent about explaining military participation in terms of national pride and national service because of the connotations within British cultural life between explicit statements on national identity and racism, particularly as articulated by far-right political groups. This observation is interesting when set alongside Dick's denial quoted above; it indicates that the absence of an articulated idea need not be taken at face value, but rather needs to be unpacked in the context of the discourses in which ideas are expressed. We need to look at the details, nuances, and caveats.

With this in mind, my intention here is not to propose a broad agenda for the pursuit of citizenship studies in contemporary British military social science. My aims are more modest, and focused more explicitly on the discursive representation of the figure of the British soldier in contemporary culture. Representations of the British soldier abound;[1] here, my intention is to interrogate one particular resource—contemporary British soldiers' narratives, memoirs, and autobiographical accounts—and to ask what consideration of these texts can bring to our understanding of the citizen-soldier nexus. As Dick's denial illustrates, and as I will argue in this chapter, soldier narratives engage continually with discourses surrounding the figure of the soldier. Indeed, for many of these narratives, this is their point. Furthermore, these discourses speak to a huge variety of issues affecting the representation of the soldier; the citizenship issue is but a small part of the bigger story that these narratives tell. The question that therefore follows is what these narratives, when conceptualized as strategic interventions, bring to our understanding of the soldier as citizen. We can start answering that by turning to the narratives themselves.

On the use of soldier narratives

Soldier narratives are endlessly fascinating. They are many things to many people, offering over time a huge diversity of post-hoc explanations, rationalizations and justifications for actions and activities that are variously and simultaneously unpopular and celebrated, unknown and famous, mundane and extraordinary (for an overview, see Vernon 2005a; Hynes 1997). They continue to fascinate us—as evidenced by sales volumes and their continued presence in the "military" section of bookshops—not only for the stories that they tell about the impact of organized violence on those caught up in its prosecution and effects, but also for what they tell us about our collective cultural responses to the practice of organized violence.

There is, of course, a range of opinion on how these soldier narratives can and should be read, reflecting debates within literary studies over the use and critique of autobiography and memoir in the reconstruction of events and renegotiation of their meanings (and for an introduction to these debates, see King 2000; Anderson 2001). One view of these soldiers' narratives is that they constitute one metanarrative—in Hynes's view, "the soldiers' tale"—that is celebratory of the authenticity of the combat soldier's experience, and the consequences of such activities for the individual (Hynes 1997). Others are more cautious, alert to the partiality of memory, the motivation and intentionality in their writing, and the politics of their production and consumption (for a good overview of these issues, see Vernon 2005b).

Bearing in mind these debates about the universality and partiality of soldier narratives, I want to make two points about their utility for exploring debates about citizenship. First, as I have already suggested, these narratives can be read as strategic interventions in broader social debates about what it means to be a soldier, carrying with them vigorous assertions about their veracity. Alert to their readership and market, these narratives ground themselves on assertions about their "truth" (however fantastical this might appear to the reader) and do so through their presentation of the self, the narrator, as ordinary (however extraordinary that person might be) and thus believable. These assertions about their "truth" are important for marketing purposes; the stamp of authenticity guarantees sales to a readership intrigued by questions about what military violence is actually like. This is significant if we consider how tenuous connections are for most contemporary British citizens with the armed forces. Given the small size of the contemporary British armed forces, these narratives are a significant source of information for a readership which, more likely than not, will have little or no direct or relational experience of the armed forces. In using these narratives as a textual source, we have to be alert to the claims about "truth" that are inherent in a genre that is aware of its role in speaking to a wider readership, whilst remembering that, like all memoirs, they are inherently partial and selective. They tell us what their writers consider important that we should know. This tension in the act of reading does not necessarily close off these narratives as a source of information and reflection about military issues; indeed, there is a significant body of historical and contemporary cultural analysis that has looked explicitly at soldier narratives and their role in shaping social responses and collective myths about specific conflicts. For example, it is a truism that our contemporary understanding of the First World War has been developed by successive generations' readings and interpretations of the memoirs and narratives produced by those participating directly in that conflict (Fussell 1975; Leed 1979; Lunn 2005; Watson 2004; Winter and Prost 2005). For John Newsinger, who has written about military memoirs about the British armed forces' Malayan campaign (1948–1960), and about Special Forces activities in the 1980s and 1990s, these memoirs are a central component of British national culture and identity, promoting ideas about what it means to be British to a wider public hungry for heroic ideas (Newsinger 1994, 1997). Foster (1997, 1999) similarly draws an explicit connection between military memoirs of the Falklands war and their function in articulating ideas about national identity. So these narratives not only are about "telling it like it is" (a common assertion in the genre) but also are strategic engagements with dominant discourses shaping widely shared beliefs about the national significance of specific military actions.

The second point is about who writes, and does not write, narratives about their soldiering experience. Harari (2005), following Leed (1979), argues that the writing of the soldier narrative is an act of self-preservation, a way of getting to grips with and understanding the aberrance of war. They are "the means by which the dreadful events of war were recast into an acceptable story of a 'normal' life" (71). Furthermore, those who actually get down to it and write about their experiences are distinct in that they are those for whom war doesn't entirely contradict their prewar expectations. They see connections between the lived experience of armed conflict and a life beyond and outside that. This is a significant point for soldier narratives because that connection with a life beyond almost inevitably includes within it ideas about the wider meaning and logic of the act of military participation. Soldier narratives are written by those who wish to "tell it like it was," because these truths are often identified as absent in wider social debates about soldiers.

We should approach soldier narratives, then, alert to their purpose and function both as things written and things read. Being aware of this emphasizes the point that they should be read not as innocent tales of reality, but as strategic interventions. This makes them very interesting as commentaries on the issue at the heart of this chapter, about how ideas about citizenship are articulated by soldiers themselves. We should be alert, though, to how the conventions of the genre shape, enable, and restrict the articulation of those ideas; there are epistemological and methodological limits to the use of narratives as a data source for the interrogation of ideas of citizenship, as there are with any empirical resource.[2]

The genre used here is a sizeable one. I focus on published narratives by British soldiers writing about their experiences of military participation from the 1970s onwards in conflicts and situations such as Northern Ireland and the Falklands, Bosnia and the first Gulf War, and Sierra Leone and the Iraq War. This genre is targeted at a specific segment of the British book-buying public, an elusive group of primarily adult male readers, traditionally in publishing terms a segment of the market not much given to buying and reading books. Broadly speaking, two types of narrative dominate this market. First, there are tales of elite combat adventure, a prime example of which would be Andy McNab's *Bravo Two Zero*, an account of Special Forces action behind enemy lines in the 1991 Gulf War. Having sold over 1.5 million copies, McNab has gone on to a successful career as an author of fictional stories about elite forces action, but the fiction is not considered here. McNab is one of many giving contemporary manifestation to a much older tradition in soldier memoirs, noted by Newsinger (1994, following Green 1980), both constituting and feeding into the "energising myths of English imperialism," where action-adventure is celebrated in stories of soldierly skill, technical competence, and masculine virtues. In these we see the simultaneous refutation of easy ideas about military participation as national service, and their replacement with much more equivocal or ambiguous arguments about what military participation may or may not imply in terms of service or commitment to another, wider soldier group, beyond the soldier himself (the author is almost inevitably male). Examples include: Cameron Spence's *Sabre Squadron* and *All Necessary Measures*, Chris Ryan's *The One That Got Away*, Andy McNab's *Bravo Two Zero*, Phil Ashby's *Unscathed*, Michael Asher's *Shoot to Kill*, Nigel Ely's *For Queen and Country*, Vince Bramley's *Forward into Hell*, Sarah Ford's (a female author, which is rare in this genre) *One Up*, Peter Ratcliffe's *Eye of the Storm*, and Hugh McManners's *Falklands Commando*. The second type identifiable in this market constitutes a much smaller body of vindication narratives, where the personal story is set out as a means of writing through trauma and justifying courses of action explained in terms of that trauma. The traumatic impetus may be anything from posttraumatic stress disorder (PTSD) to a disciplinary issue. These narratives are less concerned with consolidating a representation of the soldier, and more with the analysis of the effects of soldierly acts on the individual. Examples include Barry Donnan's *Fighting Back*, Tony McNally's *Cloudpuncher*, and Milos Stankovic's *Trusted Mole*. Although I have drawn a distinction between these two types here, some narratives will inevitably straddle both categories; see for example Kevin Mervin's *Weekend Warrior* and Ken Lukowiak's *A Soldier's Song*.

In this chapter, I have chosen to focus on two ideas common to these narratives—explanations for the act of enlistment, and explanations of the wider social group identified as the beneficiary of military action. I have chosen these, from amongst the huge range of ideas about soldiering that these narratives collectively propose, because they illustrate so clearly both the ideas about citizenship circulating in these narratives, and the wider strategic purpose that these narratives serve.

Enlisting to serve one's fellow citizens

Let us start with the act of swearing allegiance. The process of enlistment into the Army and Royal Air Force[3] is marked by the recruit swearing the "loyal oath," an oath of allegiance to the Crown:

> I [name] swear by almighty God[4] that I will be faithful and bear true allegiance to Her Majesty Queen Elizabeth the Second, her heirs and successors and that I will, as in duty bound, honestly and faithfully defend Her Majesty, her heirs and successors, in person, crown and dignity against all enemies, and will observe and obey all orders of Her Majesty, her heirs and successors and of the generals/air officers [depending on service] and other officers set over me.

The transformation process turning civilian into soldier is set in motion by the act of swearing the loyal oath as a public statement of purpose and intent, binding the would-be soldier to the defense of the state. "Then I held my hand up and swore an oath to protect the Queen" (Asher 1990, 15). This point of entry is useful too for an exploration of military citizenship and participation.

Some narratives omit entirely any discussion of the decision to enlist and the transition process from civilian to soldier. Cameron Spence, for example, writing as a former Special Forces operative with experience in Iraq and the former Yugoslavia, has no need to introduce to the reader any information about a civilian persona he might once have had. This information, by its absence, is rendered irrelevant in a narrative contained entirely within a military life (Spence 1998, 1999). His silence is indicative in a genre that celebrates action rather than reflection. Many narratives, however, break this silence and explore to varying degrees the decision to commit, and the meanings attached to that decision for these young men.

For some writers, the decision to enlist is presented as almost inevitable. Milos Stankovic summarizes the event briskly, telling a tale of enlistment as an almost inevitable progression from leadership and proto-military success at school (head boy, head of the school's Combined Cadet Force)[5] to leadership and success (later thwarted) in the Army. "The day after my last A Level . . . I walked into the Army recruiting office on Mayflower Street in Plymouth and enlisted in the Parachute regiment" (Stankovic 2000, 43). His fall from grace, an investigation into his activities as an interpreter for British forces in Bosnia instigated by a suspicious U.S. government, is all the more shocking given the seeming inevitability of his chosen career. Similarly, Phil Ashby's account of capture and escape in Sierra Leone is introduced with a self-portrait of a sporting, physically resilient, brave (but not reckless) adventurous type (just the sort of man to escape capture in Sierra Leone). He is ready to leave school and is destined for Cambridge University (an elite educational establishment). He is deterred from enlisting by his age and the persona of a recruiting officer. Then a careers officer from the Royal Marines visits his school, takes a group off for a run, a swim in a river, and a trip to the pub. "This was much more my kind of thing. Plus you only had to be seventeen and a half to join the Marines. So, at seventeen and a half and three days, I joined" (Ashby 2003, 7). The idea of military participation as an act of national service is absent in these narratives, which instead recount the decision to enlist as so obvious and seamless that any great introspection is unwarranted.

For many narratives, a fuller explanation of the act of enlistment is more necessary because an explanation of the rationale for joining up establishes at the outset of the narrative a starting point and context for the actions and motivations that follow. In this way, Chris Ryan, in his account of escape and evasion in Iraq following the compromise of his Special Air Service Bravo Two Zero patrol during the 1991 Gulf War, introduces himself as a man who grew up on the rural fringes of industrial north-east England. His involvement with the SAS, he says, "could be traced back to my love of being in open country" (Ryan, 1995, 80). His enlistment was almost inevitable, following a logic established by his semirural background: "By the time I was 16, all I wanted was to join the army" (Ryan 1995, 85). The soldier who walked alone through the Iraqi desert to reach safety in Syria is seen at the outset as the boy who liked to adventure outdoors. A very different explanation, given through the same structural conventions of the narrative form, comes from Ken Lukowiak in his account of a life soldiering and smoking (later smuggling) marijuana. This narrative, shot through with ironic wit, constructs a persona able to rationalize being stoned whilst still in charge of a weapon. Lukowiak's decision to enlist is linked explicitly with a search for male identity: "my reason for joining up was that I wanted to become a 'real man'" (Lukowiak 2000, 9). Michael Asher, with a background in the Parachute Regiment and Special Forces, notes likewise: "As a teenager, the men on those posters seemed to represent everything I wanted to be" (Asher 1990, 10). So he recounts how he becomes just that, and underscores the contrast between the life chosen and the life left behind when he recalls his feelings as he lay in his bunk at the end of his first day of training:

> I was gripped by the same mixture of fear and excitement which had come and gone all day. I had become the hero of one of the adventure books I read so avidly. I was afraid, yet I had no wish to return to my dull town and its dull grammar school. I had finally broken out of the prison of my humdrum childhood. For better or for worse, I had taken my destiny in my own hands. What the army represented most to me at that moment was escape. (Asher 1990, 10)

The idea of enlistment as escape dominates these action-adventure narratives. Sarah Ford joins the Navy (and goes on to serve with an elite intelligence unit in Northern Ireland) precisely, she tells us, to escape from the limitations of a working-class, postindustrial city where for a woman like her money is tight and options limited (Ford 1997). Andy McNab portrays a self that survived a failed Special Forces mission as the same lad that escaped a civilian life of dead-end labor and petty crime that led to a spell on remand:

> I hated being locked up and swore that if I got away with it I'd never let it happen again. I knew deep down that I'd have to do something pretty decisive or I'd end up spending my entire life in Peckham, fucked about and getting fucked up. The army seemed a good way out. (McNab 1993, 20)

For action-adventure narratives, this idea of self-initiated escape is significant in setting up the narrator as an adventurer; subsequent actions stand on foundations established by the transcendent acts of their protagonists. For those less fortunate, those harmed or damaged by military trauma, the act of enlistment similarly serves as a foundation for understanding subsequent acts, although the purpose of setting out an explanation for enlistment is rather different. These narratives are stories of what went wrong, and for those who enlisted looking for adventure, or affirmation of an identity, there is so much further to fall. For Tony McNally, for example, in a memoir of posttraumatic stress disorder that he attributes to things seen and done during the 1982 Falklands campaign, the gulf between expectation as a potential recruit and reality as a soldier is unbearably wide:

> I can always remember wanting to be a soldier from a very early age. I had a fascination for toy guns, tanks, planes, anything military, and spent hours staging my own wars in the back yard destroying whole divisions in one fell swoop with a large mud-ball. (McNally 2000, 1)

He goes into the Cadets at school, presents himself as a keen recruit, yet ends up handing back his medals as a protest at what the Army has done to him.

In all these narratives, then, the connections are made between a civilian life, the features of which prompted a decision to enlist, and the escape offered by a military career. Military participation as service to Queen, country, and the nation is a remote idea, noteworthy by its absence. None of these narratives describes the decision to become a soldier and to enlist in terms of either citizenship rights (where enlistment will bring social benefits) or citizenship obligations (where enlistment entails serving one's country or nation). Furthermore, although we see hints in these accounts of the decision to enlist as an economically rational one—McNab and Ford both talk about the absence of other options open to people of their class and background—the idea of enlistment as primarily economically motivated (see Cowen 2005; Bellany 2003) is played down.

The relative silence about motivations for enlistment is significant in terms of what the narratives tell us about citizenship. One could explain this with reference to the conventions and expectations of the genre. Soldier narratives of the action-adventure type are marketed as stories of action, heroism, and bravery, where an individual's actions are driven through his or her response to events unfolding (often very rapidly) around them. These action narratives are not sold as introspective meditations on the meanings of military action (even though I am of course reading them as this!). Although we find passing comments on either personal or wider meanings, these are incidental. The genre demands that these stories are told using specific conventions, and personal insight into motivations for big questions, such as: "Why am I doing this? Why am I in the Army?" is not one of them. Furthermore, British popular cultural ideas about the figure of the soldier, into which these narratives speak, are traditionally emphatic about the stoicism of the soldier (we talk of "soldiering on" and of being a "real trooper"), the capacity of the enlisted member of the ranks (the grunts, the squaddies) for sustained physical enterprise, and the dangers of too much intellectual introspection when faced with a task in hand. To ponder extensively on the reasons for joining up is simply unsoldierly.

The absence of detail about enlistment, then, is understandable given the conventions of the soldier narrative genre and the wider discourses about the soldier with which these narratives engage. The act of enlistment, culminating in swearing a public oath of allegiance of service to the Crown, a declaration of service and citizenship, merits little introspection.

"Mateship": expressing a different sort of citizenship

I have suggested that statements such as Dick's denial, rejecting notions of military participation as citizenship, are unusual in their vehemence but not in substance. But reading these narratives, it is impossible to ignore how although the idea of "national service" is rejected, an alternative notion of citizenship—in the sense of an individual's service to a wider group, for the benefits of that group—is both articulated and enacted. This alternative notion could be termed "mateship."[6]

That "mateship" as a bond within a group is a feature of military participation is not an original observation. For example, in his examination of the experience of National Service, David Morgan draws out how the mass conscription of young men for National Service after the Second World War relied heavily on the inculcation amongst conscripts of ideas about collective gender identities (Morgan 1987). A current (spring of 2006) advertising campaign for the Army continues this idea through a poster campaign advertising the benefits of Army enlistment as constituting membership of a bonded group: "Stand shoulder to shoulder," says one; "Do it for each other," says another. The idea of a bonded unit or group is a persistent feature of military historical accounts and military fiction; the band of brothers makes for a good war story, as Steven Spielberg recognized. Contemporary soldier narratives share this; the articulation of this idea is common to these narratives and constitutes a key structural feature of the stories within the story. Just as we have the enlistment story, the close combat story, and the drinking story, so we also have stories about mateship. These cluster around two main themes, regimental identification and unit or group cohesion, and it is to these that I now turn.

Stories within these narratives about regimental identification are significant in British soldier narratives, reflecting the fact that the regimental system is a distinctive feature of the British Army, organizationally and culturally (French 2006). Within the infantry, where the majority of soldier narratives are located, regimental affiliation reflects and signifies all sorts of things, from regional identification (many regiments are historically identified with specific parts of Britain, and many still recruit primarily from these areas) to battle roles, and from class connotations to elite aspirations. Love for and loyalty to the regiment are worn visibly through cap-badge, enacted through regimental rituals, and embodied in tattoos. It is learnt: although many soldiers will join a specific regiment because of family connections, many others will not, and regimental loyalty is inculcated, encouraged, enforced, and trained. The regiment becomes many things: a marker of collective identity within the Army, a source of pride, a surrogate family, and a source of wider support for the soldier's own family.

Given the significance of the regimental system to the British Army, it is not surprising that regimental affiliation and identification are discussed throughout these soldier narratives. Asher, Ely, and Lukowiak, all former members of the Parachute Regiment (or Paras), celebrate explicitly in their memoirs the idea of this particular grouping as a warrior elite of resilient men and the glory and traditions of what Lukowiak calls "the maroon machine" (after the claret berets the Paras wear). McNally, whose narrative is one of trauma and recovery written out of betrayal and vindication, still speaks of his inculcation into the regimental culture of the Royal Artillery with pride. He is aware of the intentionality behind practices that promote regimental identification, so talks, for example, of small things like being tormented into buying sips of pop and bites of chocolate bars by his superiors in the ranks: "Eventually, when we became Senior Gunners, we would continue this profitable tradition" (McNally 2000, 4). He talks of his pride in wearing white lanyards, a symbol of regimental identification. Years later, while being treated for PTSD he appears on television to talk about his case, and although he has handed back his campaign medals as a mark of protest against his treatment, he still wears his regimental blazer and campaign ribbons on television. In soldier narratives, to fight, and to fight well and bravely, is an action undertaken not for the good of the wider nation, but for the glory of the regiment. McNab talks repeatedly and proudly of patterns of organization and behavior in "the Regiment," the SAS. Ely reflects on this when he is taken on a tour of the regimental museum of the Scots Guards, and he finds himself moved by the displays of medals and paintings of past conflicts:

> From Waterloo and the Somme through to Tumbledown in the Falklands, men had laid down their lives for their mates and their Regiment and, quite possibly, for Queen and Country as well. That visit reminded me of the feeling I get when I hear the bagpipes play on Armistice Day and I give a thought to all those mates I have lost too. (Ely 2003, 346)

Although national service is invoked, regimental loyalty wins out. Soldier narratives may not express citizenship with reference to a wider civilian social group, but they certainly do with reference to their regiment.

Similarly, at the subregimental level, citizenship as "mateship" is expressed with reference to group or unit cohesion. "Mateship" runs as a distinct thread through soldier narratives, which tell of group solidarity, of teamwork, of reliance on others, and of mutual dependence. In these narratives, there is an overriding sense that this is where citizenship resides; not in the idea of service to an abstract notion of nation or a collective of faceless individuals, but with the immediate unit. This bonded, cohesive unit is celebrated in these narratives, for its existence as well as for its actions, from McNab and Spence's tales of elite infantry performance, to Lukowiak and Mervin's hard slog in the ranks. Ely and his patrol, as they advance toward Goose Green on the Falkland Islands, come under sustained small arms fire and are separated from the rest of their platoon, caught between friendly and enemy fire:

> None of us was in a position to put rounds down on the enemy. So we had to move. It was our job. The passion and the aggression which we all had for getting on and finishing the job did not come from a loyalty to Queen and country or to the politicians who had sent us here, or from the thought of another power taking over a part of the United Kingdom. The officers might have thought about this Queen and country bollocks, but we blokes didn't. We were doing this for ourselves and for the Regiment. (Ely 2003, 187)

Advancing toward Teal Inlet during the same campaign, Bramley, also a Para, explains his motivation for continued endurance in terms of what it would mean for the bonded group if he gave up:

> We set off very slowly, spaced out in one long line. We hobbled over the hill in front of us only to see more hills and marshes. I began to become conscious of my toe, and the more I thought about it, the worse it felt. However, the thought of dropping out at that stage seemed a fate worse than death and so I fought the pain. It *is* funny, looking back, but the further we went into the campaign, the less I thought of my home or family. I wasn't thinking of Queen and Country either. I thought of myself and the lads around me. Letting the side down was my biggest fear. That fear kept me walking. (Bramley 2006, 73-74)

But for two reasons, there is more to this notion of "mateship"—and its function in soldier narratives—than merely romantic notions of a bonded fraternal group, willing to sacrifice the self for the benefit of immediate others.

First, group cohesion, under the label "unit cohesion," is a deliberately inculcated outcome of military training. Seeing it as such is not to dispute the existence of genuine emotion about group loyalty in these narratives. We should be alert, however, to its existence as an intentional product of the military training process. Military training establishments, from the elite Royal Military Academy Sandhurst for officer training down to the Army Training Regiments for infantry, establish through instruction, example, and manipulation the idea in the soldier that unit cohesion is inextricably linked to the successful achievement of military objectives. But the development of the capacity in the soldier to cohere and bond with his or her unit[7] is not only understood as a tactical military necessity. As Rodgers argues, with reference to the use of extensive training for U.S. Army recruits during the Second World War, such training was used as a deliberate compensatory mechanism to substitute for missing organic social bonds that in other times and places might have provided sufficient impetus on their own for soldiers' motivations to fight (Rodgers 2005). There is a wider, strategic purpose to the inculcation of unit cohesion. The inculcation of motivation with reference to the nation and one's fellow citizens is a diffuse, abstract idea; loyalty to the unit (from the regiment down to the platoon) is not. Identifiable individuals—the members of the group—stand in lieu of the nation, and loyalty to this group provides something that rationalizes participation. I would argue that soldiers, in their narratives, "do" citizenship, but through service to the unit, rather than to the nation. Furthermore, this is a practice in which soldiers are trained, a deliberate outcome of Army policy, as much as it is a "natural" response of a group of people under pressure. Whilst dominant state-military discourses might emphasize in public statements the idea of military participation as national service (and I return to this below), at a more practical level the more attainable objective of group motivation is inculcated with reference to the immediate social group, rather than civilian society or the nation.

There is a second observation to make here. The celebration of group cohesion, of mateship, is also a strategy of self-affirmation, used in these narratives as a counter to popular public discourses ambivalent or outright critical of the pursuit of military violence for political ends. In a post-1945 context where the conduct of military operations involving armed, organized violence has frequently been subjected to widespread public condemnation, representing the meaning of military activities in terms of the immediate group with whom those actions are performed is, perhaps, a logical response. The wider nation or civilian society may be perceived by the soldier-writer as uninterested or resistant to the offer of service and sacrifice by the enlisted soldier; many of these narratives, in effect "Other" civilian society, talk in derogatory tones about civvy street. The soldier-writers who perceive themselves to be marginalized by civilian society, despite the possibility of the supreme sacrifice, identify instead the mates, the unit, and the group as the recipient of their citizen-soldier service. Kevin Mervin's narrative about his experiences as a Territorial Army soldier in Iraq is a good example of this. The narrative is framed with what reads as hurt and anger that his actions in what he sees as the liberation of an unfree society might be dismissed by the British public as irresponsible and inexcusable violence. He quotes from a diary entry, written as he waits to enter Iraq on March 20, 2003,

> It'll be our turn soon to go across the border and into a war, and for what? Freedom, fucking freedom? This better be worth it, that's all I can say. They better appreciate it, the Iraqis, and the people back home, moaning

about the war. Do they actually realise what we're going through? Have they been told?

Nah, they won't listen anyway; they couldn't give a shit. (Mervin 2005, 13)

His narrative is shot through with the contrasts he draws between what he and his fellow vehicle recovery drivers think they are doing—the logic of military action—and what he perceives to be the ignorance and rejection of this action by the nation he purportedly serves—he frequently refers to "tree-huggers," an amorphous cluster identified as anyone back in Britain remotely critical of the military actions of Operation Telic. He rationalizes his actions as a soldier, and his participation in the war, in terms of what he and his fellow soldiers can achieve, and celebrates this as a rejection of and in opposition to a civilian discourse, which he perceives marginalizes him as a soldier. This is a familiar story, of course; accounts by soldiers written post 1918 vent this anger too at the misunderstanding of civilian society of the reality of military participation. In its late twentieth- and early twenty-first-century expression, the celebration of the bonded, cohesive unit in these soldier narratives could be read as a celebration of citizenship, when the nation (the potential object of citizenly actions) is uninterested. In Mervin's narrative, as in Ely's and Lukowiak's, the civil-military divide is a yawning chasm.

Conclusions about narratives and citizenship debates

State-military discourses around the meaning of the figure of the soldier, and the meaning of the participation of that soldier in military activities, are adamant and persuasive that military participation constitutes national service. The idea of individual military sacrifice for shared national benefit is quite fundamental to this dominant discursive representation of the meaning of war and militarized violence. The two major mass mobilizations of conscripted British personnel, during the First (1914–1918) and Second (1939–1945) World Wars, relied on explanations of enlistment as a patriotic duty and national service by the individual for the nation. The United Kingdom's sole experiment with peacetime mass conscription, following the end of the Second World War, was named precisely to reflect the idea of military participation as national service. The continued dominance of this idea was evident in the deliberate statement of British Secretary of State for Defence John Reid at the outset of an appearance before the British House of Commons Defence Committee in November 2005. He chose to preface his remarks and answers to a range of defense questions with a statement explicitly linking military participation with national, public service:

I cannot think of any group of people for whom public service is more serious, more dangerous and more comprehensive than the men and women who serve our country. To have a contract that says "I will serve my country even until death" is a very exceptional and rare thing and I am honoured to be able to play some part with them in defence. (House of Commons Defence Committee 2005)

Honored he might be, but the ideas that these contemporary soldier narratives express take issue with this notion. More specifically, they engage with this discourse over the meaning of military participation, as they do with other popular and public discourses around this issue, as part of ongoing and perpetual negotiations over what it means to be a soldier. Soldier narratives, whether talking into arguments about citizenship, or talking to other concerns about meaning (such as, for example, the presence of women in the armed forces), take issue with the simple equation between military partication and national service; they are strategic interventions. I want to conclude with a couple of observations about what these narratives indicate for our understandings of the soldier-citizenship debate and about the utility of narratives for understanding citizenship.

These narratives underscore just how contested and negotiated the idea of military service as citizenship is. These narratives express citizenship in that they talk about the idea that military participation is undertaken for the benefits of a wider group, but they do so in ways that make that service make sense to the soldier. I have suggested here that "mateship" might be a better term for what soldiers do when they are performing and practicing citizenship. Military participation is understood as service, but for the small unit, the identifiable group of fellow-soldiers, and the regiment, rather than for more abstract notions of the Crown, the nation, or the state. The expression of mateship still, however, engages with dominant ideas (what I have termed a "state-military discourse"), even if to contest it.

These narratives also emphasize the significance of cultural context for understanding how soldiers perform and practice citizenship. The narratives discussed here, as I have emphasized, have been written by British soldiers, writing about British army experiences. Although undoubtedly some of what these authors write would resonate with the experiences of other soldiers, in other places, at other times, they remain as powerful engagements with the discourses, cultural constructs, and political contexts that frame their production and distribution, and their origins with the armed forces and military engagements in which their narrators are bound up. As I have already suggested, the military actions with which the contemporary British Army have been engaged in the postwar period have not been about nation building as their primary intention (whatever the discursive framing of those conflicts for domestic and international political ends). For this reason, I suggest, these narratives are largely silent on issues of citizenship and territory, and citizenship and nation. For example, there is little in these narratives that deals with the figure of the enemy soldier as foreign, Other, and non-British, relative to the narrator. The enemy is described—see, for example, Lukowiak, Ely, or McManners's descriptions of Argentine soldiers on the Falklands Islands—but he is invariably explained as just a soldier too, with the same fears, loyalties, and bonds as the narrator. Similarly, soldierly identity, when read from these narratives, seems to have little to do with country of origin. Foreign-born soldiers, primarily from the Commonwealth, have always served in the British armed forces, and there are hints and suggestions from these narratives that many of those soldiers are present in the contexts that the narrators describe. Yet they rarely discuss differences of national origin as an issue, and are largely silent on questions of national identity and citizenship. We can only speculate about this, and about the consideration of this in future narratives—of the Iraq invasion, for example—given that at the time of writing, 10 percent of soldiers serving in the British Army are foreign nationals.[8]

My final observations concern the utility of soldier narratives as a textual source. Like any source of data, they have benefits and drawbacks. They have been useful for this investigation not only for the degree to which they articulate ideas about citizenship and national service, but also because of their status as communicative and strategic documents. They tell us what their writers, soldiers, think is important that we know, and they do so according to the prescriptions of the soldier narrative. We can read them for what they say, how they say it, and why they present the ideas that they do. What we cannot do is probe their silences for detail, and investigate in further detail their explanations. They have utility as cultural texts, talking primarily into wider contemporary cultural and political debates. However, they stand as a proxy for access to the thoughts and understandings of a wider group of soldiers. In stating this, the intention is not to undermine their utility for understanding military participation, but to reinforce the point that the complexities of intention and comprehension in any large social group require a range of approaches and methodologies. Narratives may not provide the empirical context for detailed probing of individual intent, nor do they provide any ideas about representativeness and pattern. What they do give us, though, are points of engagement with a wider cultural context, and the nuances, subtleties, and detail that illuminate that context just a little more. And they also give us, of course, some cracking good stories.

Acknowledgments

I would like to thank Deborah Cowen, Emily Gilbert, K. Neil Jenkings, and Trish Winter for their helpful comments on a previous version of this chapter.

Notes

1. A research project, currently in progress, by me, Trish Winter, and K. Neil Jenkings, investigating representations of the British soldier more widely in both print media and in soldiers' own photography collections. See "Negotiating Identity and Representation in the Mediated Armed Forces" (Jenkings, Winter, and Woodward n.d.).

2. Narratives are a cultural product, read for the ideas and meanings that they convey, and for the ways in which they engage or counter wider discourses about the meaning of the soldier. They are valuable for the exploration of the construction of meaning, in that they are self-conscious about their readership and reception. They are valuable for an examination of the discourses around military participation and citizenship in the public realm. To restate, they tell us what their authors think is important that we know, and they do so unprompted. Their limitation, of course, is that (unlike interviews), we cannot ask questions back to their authors or prompt for a greater degree of explanation.

3. Recruits to the Royal Navy do not swear the loyal oath, for historical reasons relating to the sovereign's prerogative.

4. Those who do not believe in God may "solemnly, sincerely and truly declare and affirm."

5. The Combined Cadet Force (CCF) provides proto-military, adventurous activities for senior school pupils within the school. The implicit intention of the CCF is to encourage officer recruitment; CCF units are primarily associated with public (i.e., private, fee-paying) schools in Britain.

6. What I shorthand as "mateship" has specific connotations in other national contexts, most obviously in the Australian-New Zealand Army Corps (ANZAC) tradition and in the myths about the military and nationhood of Australia and New Zealand. What I identify here, for want of an alternative term, as "mateship" has both continuities and differences between the ANZAC idea—and comparison between the two would be a story in itself.

7. There's an irony here, of course: women's participation in infantry and armored units is currently justified on the grounds that the presence of women within the fighting unit would undermine unit cohesion (Ministry of Defence 2002; Woodward and Winter 2007).

8. Figures from *Daily Telegraph*, April 13, 2006.

References

Abrams, Elliot, and Andrew J. Bacevich. 2001. A symposium on citizenship and military service. *Parameters* 31:18–22.

Anderson, Linda. 2001. *Autobiography*. New York: Routledge.

Ashby, Phil. 2003, *Unscathed: Escape from Sierra Leone*. London: Pan.

Asher, Michael. 1990. *Shoot to kill: A soldier's journey through violence*. London: Cassell.

Barbalet, J. M. 1988. *Citizenship*. Milton Keynes: Open University Press.

Bellany, Ian. 2003. Accounting for army recruitment: White and non-white soldiers and the British Army. *Defence and Peace Economics* 14:281–92.

Bramley, Vince. 2006. *Forward into hell*. London: Blake.

Burk, James. 1995. Citizenship status and military service: The quest for inclusion by minorities and conscientious objectors. *Armed Forces & Society* 21:503–29.

Cowen, Deborah. 2005. Welfare warriors: Towards a genealogy of the soldier citizen in Canada. *Antipode* 37:654–78.

Dandeker, Christopher. 2000. Armed forces and society research in the United Kingdom: A review of British military sociology. In *Military sociology: The richness of a discipline*, edited by Gerhard Kümmel, Andreas D. Prüfert, and Astrid Albrecht-Heide, 68–90. Baden-Baden: Nomos Verlagsgesellschaft.

Dandeker, Christopher, Simon Wessely, Amy Iversen, and John Ross. 2006. What's in a name? Defining and caring for "veterans." *Armed Forces and Society* 32:161–77.

Donnan, Barry. 1999. *Fighting back: One man's struggle for justice against the British Army*. Edinburgh: Mainstream.

Ely, Nigel "Spud." 2003. *For queen and country*. London: Blake.

Feinman, Ilene Rose. 2000. *Citizenship rites: Feminist soldiers and feminist antimilitarists*. New York: New York University Press.

Ford, Sarah. 1997. *One up: A woman in action with the S.A.S.* London: HarperCollins.

Foster, Kevin. 1997. To serve and protect: Textualizing the Falklands conflict. *Cultural Studies* 11:235–52.

———. 1999. *Fighting fictions: War, narrative and national identity*. London: Pluto.

French, David. 2006. *Military identities: The regimental system, the British Army and the British people, 1870–2000*. Oxford: Oxford University Press.

Fussell, Paul. 1975. *The Great War and modern memory*. Oxford: Oxford University Press.

Gibson, Stephen, and Jackie Abell. 2004. For queen and country? National frames of reference in the talk of soldiers in England. *Human Relations* 57:871–91.

Green, Martin. 1980. *Dreams of adventure, deeds of empire*. London: Routledge and Kegan Paul.

Gullace, Nicoletta. 2002. *The blood of our sons: Men, women and the renegotiation of British citizenship during the First World War*. London: Palgrave Macmillan.

Harari, Yuval Noah. 2005. Martial illusions: War and disillusionment in twentieth-century and Renaissance military memoirs. *Journal of Military History* 69:43–72.

Heater, D. 1999. *What is citizenship?* Cambridge: Polity Press.

Higate, Paul. 1997. Soldiering on? Theorising homelessness amongst ex-servicemen. In *Homelessness and Social Policy*, edited by Roger Burrows, Nicholas Please, and Deborah Quilgars, 109–22. London: Routledge.

———. 2000. Ex-servicemen on the road: Travel and homelessness. *Sociological Review* 48:331–48.

Hockey, John. 1986. *Squaddies: Portrait of a subculture*. Exeter: University of Exeter Press.

———. 2002. "Head down, bergen on, mind in neutral": The infantry body. *Journal of Political and Military Sociology* 30:148–71.

———. 2003. No more heroes: Masculinity in the infantry. In *Military masculinities: Identity and the state*, edited by Paul Higate, 15–26. Westport, CT: Praeger.

House of Commons Defence Committee. 2005. Oral Evidence 1 November. http://www.publications.parliament.uk/pa/cm200506/cmselect/cmdefence/556/5110102.htm (accessed April 18, 2007).

Hussain, Asifa, and Mohammed Ishaq. 2002a. British Pakistani Muslims' perceptions of the armed forces. *Armed Forces & Society* 28:601–18.

———. 2002b. Scottish Pakistani Muslims and the armed forces. *Scottish Affairs* 38 (Winter): 27–51.

———. 2002c. The British Armed Forces and the Hindu perspective. *Journal of Political and Military Sociology* 30 (1): 197–212.

———. 2002d. British Sikhs' identification with the armed forces. *Defence and Security Analysis* 18:2.

Hynes, Samuel. 1997. *The soldiers' tale: Bearing witness to modern war.* London: Pimlico.

Jenkings, K. N., T. Winter, and R. Woodward. N.d. Negotiating identity and representation in the mediated armed forces. Economic and Social Research Council ref. no. RES-000-23-0992. http://photoarmy.ncl.ac.uk/ (accessed March 16, 2007).

Kanaaneh, Rhoda. 2005. Boys or men? Duped or "made"? Palestinian soldiers in the Israeli military. *American Ethnologist* 32:260–75.

Kestnbaum, Meyer. 2000. Citizenship and compulsory military service: The revolutionary origins of conscription in the United States. *Armed Forces & Society* 27:7–36.

King, Nicola. 2000. *Memory, narrative, identity: Remembering the self.* Edinburgh: Edinburgh University Press.

Leed, Eric. 1979. *No man's land: Combat and identity in World War 1.* Cambridge: Cambridge University Press.

Lukowiak, Ken. 1993. *A soldier's song: True stories from the Falklands.* London: Phoenix.

———. 2000. *Marijuana time: Join the army, see the world, meet interesting people and smoke all their dope.* London: Orion.

Lunn, Joe. 2005. Male identity and martial codes of honor: a comparison of the war memoirs of Robert Graves, Ernst Jünger, and Kande Kamara. *Journal of Military History* 69:713–36.

McManners, Hugh. [1984] 2002. *Falklands Commando: A soldier's eye view of the land war.* London: HarperCollins.

McNab, Andy. 1993. *Bravo Two Zero.* London: Corgi.

McNally, Tony. 2000. *Cloudpuncher.* Wirral, UK: Classfern.

Mervin, Kevin. 2005. *Weekend warrior: A Territorial soldier's war in Iraq.* Edinburgh: Mainstream Publishing.

Ministry of Defence. 2002. *Women in the armed forces: A report by the Employment of Women in the Armed Forces Steering Group.* London: Ministry of Defence.

Morgan, David H. J. 1987. It will make a man of you: Notes on national service, masculinity and autobiography. Studies in Sexual Politics no. 17. Manchester, UK: University of Manchester, Department of Sociology.

Morgan, Matthew J. 2003. The reconstruction of culture, citizenship and military service. *Armed Forces and Society* 29:373–91.

Newsinger, John. 1994. The military memoir in British imperial culture: the case of Malaya. *Race and Class* 35:47–62.

———. 1997. *Dangerous men: the SAS and popular culture.* London: Pluto Press.

Ratcliffe, Peter. 2000. *Eye of the storm: Twenty-five years in action with the SAS.* London: Michael O'Mara.

Ryan, Chris. 1995. *The one that got away.* London: Ted Smart.

Sasson-Levy, Orna. 2002. Constructing identities at the margins: masculinities and citizenship in the Israeli army. *Sociological Quarterly* 43:357–83.

———. 2003a. Feminism and military gender practices: Israeli women soldiers in "masculine" roles. *Sociological Inquiry* 73:440–65.

―――. 2003b. Military, masculinity and citizenship: Tensions and contradictions in the experience of blue-collar soldiers. *Identities: Global Studies in Culture and Power* 10:319–45.

Soeters, Joseph, Donna Winslow, and Alise Wiebull. 2003. Military culture. In *Handbook of the Sociology of the military*, edited by Giuseppe Caforio. New York: Kluwer.

Spence, Cameron. 1998. *Sabre squadron*. Harmondsworth, UK: Penguin.

―――. 1999. *All necessary measures*. Harmondsworth, UK: Penguin.

Stankovic, Milos. 2000. *Trusted mole*. London: HarperCollins.

Van der Meulen, Jan, and Philippe Manigart. 1997. Zero draft in the Low Countries: The final shift to the all-volunteer force. *Armed Forces and Society* 24:315–32.

Vernon, Alex. 2005a. Introduction: No genre's land: The problem of genre in war memoirs and military autobiographies. In *Arms and the self: War, the military and autobiographical writing*, edited by Alex Vernon, 1–40. Kent, Ohio: Kent State University Press.

―――, ed. 2005b. *Arms and the self: War, the military and autobiographical writing*. Kent, Ohio: Kent State University Press.

Watson, Janet. 2004. *Fighting different wars: Experience, memory and the First World War in Britain*. Cambridge: Cambridge University Press.

Winter, Jay, and Antoine Prost. 2005. *The Great War in history: Debates and controversies, 1914 to the present*. Cambridge: Cambridge University Press.

Woodward, Rachel. 1998. "It's a man's life!": Soldiers, masculinity and the countryside. *Gender Place & Culture* 5: 277–300.

―――. 2003. Locating military masculinities: Space, place and the formation of gender identity and the British Army. In *Military masculinities: Identity and the state*. ed. Paul Higate. Westport, Conncticut: Praeger.

―――. 2006. Warrior heroes and little green men: Soldiers, military training and the construction of rural masculinities. In *Country boys: Masculinity and rural life*. ed. Hugh Campbell, Michael Mayerfeld Bell and Margaret Finnery. Philadelphia: Penn State University Press.

Woodward, Rachel and Winter, Trish. 2007. *Sexing the soldier: The politics of gender and the contemporary British Army*. London: Routledge.

Afterword

NEIL SMITH

War, citizenship, and territory are each in their separate ways quite familiar to us. We live in a period of extended war in Central Africa and Southwest Asia, an ideologically inspired "war against terrorism" emanating from Washington and London (but taken up with greater or lesser enthusiasm in capitals around the world), and numerous smaller wars across the globe. (Indeed, insofar as Hobsbawm's [1988] "short twentieth century" was an especially bloody epoch in human history, the continuation of such conflicts suggests that it may have been a *long* twentieth century and that we are still in the midst of it.) The assumption of nationally based citizenship, to take the second term of the title, is sufficiently reflexive that it is increasingly perceived as natural—what other kind of "citizenship" could there be?—yet as global flows of people, capital, and information corrode national borders and identities (while many states anxiously if selectively plug those leaks), and as more progressive political movements press for alternative definitions of political and cultural belonging, the question of a redefined citizenship has become paramount. Territory, in turn, and the related questions of space and environment, has been the focus of a several-decades-long intellectual rebirth, centered in the academic discipline of geography but expressed throughout the social sciences and humanities, even the arts, and spreading into public discourse. Taken together as in this book's title, therefore, these three themes may not be immediately startling.

Yet the originality of this book lies precisely in the fact that no matter how familiar they are individually, these themes of war, citizenship, and territory are rarely made to converse with each other. Citizenship as definition of domestic belonging is taken to be the antithesis of war "over there," the territorial dimensions of passport-defined citizenship are largely given on the world map, and the nexus of war and territorial nationalism is widely associated either with the historical process of modern state making stretching back several centuries or with the arcane study of military geography. That these presumptions are all now under challenge is testimony to their enduring power. As a group, therefore, the chapters of this book stand as a stark and original demonstration of the fact that, in practice, war, citizenship, and territory are being reground and reformulated together in the single crucible of contemporary social and political change.

Historically, as the editors suggest, "the territorial form of the modern state was assembled at the nexus of citizenship and war," while geographically, as this volume also insists, such a development was always incomplete and uneven, and the form it took highly differentiated. It is vital to bear in mind that no such coming together of national institutions and effective citizenship graced colonial societies, nor indeed has it made an appearance in many post-colonial worlds, whereas war, by contrast, has been widespread and locally enduring in many places without establishing territorially stable definitions of identity or citizenship. Yet regardless of how partial and idealized the European-based models of nation building may be, it is still of great significance that this nexus of war, citizenship, and territory is again being brought into the glare of public scrutiny as it is reworked. It is being reworked globally in and from precisely those places where it was most established, or at least revered, and in places too where this nexus never pupated into any recognizable reality. The implications of this reworking can be seen not just in Europe and North America; rather, as Iraqis, Palestinians and Israelis, Congolese, and Colombians will surely attest, they are global in scope.

The modern nexus of war, citizenship, and territory was infused with an economic dimension as well. The remaking, amalgamation, and invention of local administrations, city-states, and other domains into the form of national states provided a political framework for regulating the contradictory impulses of an emerging capitalist mode of production. The emerging capitalist world was premised as never before on competition between the owners of the means of production, and yet the emerging capitalist order was equally in need of finding means of cooperation concerning a complex of vital social and economic conditions: regulation of labor, definition of property rights, defense of private property, policing public space, minting and circulating money, a legal system, military defense, and so forth. How were economic competition and political cooperation amongst the new ruling-class configurations to be rationalized? Wars not only determined the extent of national state territory but also, in the same aggressive sweep, created and nurtured legal, geographical, and cultural definitions of citizenship, bound up with reframed patriotism and loyalties forged anew at the national scale. However unpredictable in many of its details, uneven geographical development was the increasingly systemic solution to this fundamental dilemma of competition and cooperation (Smith 1990).

It should hardly be surprising, therefore, that the reworking of war, citizenship, and territory today is also accompanied by and imbued with a significant shift in the global political economy. Without getting into the mire of debate about globalization and neoliberalism, it is nonetheless true that states around the world, whether they did or did not have the luxury of adopting some version of Keynesian social liberalism in the twentieth century, are currently recalibrating their relationship to capital—global, national, and local. A transformation in the meaning of citizenship, whether wedged into the social fabric by state institutions (including the military) or advanced on behalf of more progressive "postnational" agendas, is integral to this shift. European territorial ambition, of which colonialism was most emblematic, has been eclipsed by efforts at an American empire that seeks to rule less through direct territorial control than via overwhelming leverage in the global market and the exercise of its unprecedented military power, and which consequently frames citizenship more flexibly. Trade embargoes notwithstanding, the implosion of state socialism in the Soviet Union and Eastern Europe and the consequent end of the Cold War (1989–1991) were in the first instance socio-political more than economic events, but the divergent fates of these erstwhile Soviet and sovereign republics very quickly became entwined with the trajectory of global economic change, even as the region reterritorialized itself and in the process rewrote its own meanings and maps of citizenship.

Historically, war has involved the acquisition of territory, but it has also revolved around access to women and labor, and citizenship evolved as one means of codifying, locating, and guaranteeing that access. Slavery in its many forms was the antithesis of citizenship, the anticitizenship that maximized the more or less coercive work of social production and reproduction performed by slaves (including sexual slavery) while shrinking their social rights close to zero. Feudal "citizenship" tied minimal social rights not to the territory and authority of some national state but to the local "land-lord," chief, duke, warlord, or other ruler who owned a portion of the social labor power (domestic, agricultural, or military) by dint of territorial patrimony if not outright ownership. It was the potential to perform labor (labor power), not the laborer per se, that was owned in feudal societies, therefore distinguishing feudalism from slavery. The particular nexus of war, national territory, and citizenship which formed with the advent of capitalist social relations was equally tied to a restructuring of the relationship connecting labor and citizenship, and while dispensing certain social rights and entitlements with one hand, the new bourgeois state circumscribed some rights on the other.

Following T. H. Marshall, many scholars have traditionally distinguished between civic, political, and social forms of citizenship, but as Nancy Fraser and Linda Gordon (1992, 49–50) point out, while Marshall was well aware of social differences and intended his analysis of social citizenship as a solvent of class disparities, he "slights other key axes of inequality" such as race and gender. Even concerning labor and class, however, the political and cultural understanding of citizenship bequeathed to subsequent theorists by Marshall was underlain by a largely uncritical conception of labor power in a capitalist society, allowing the role of labor to be airbrushed out of many later treatments of citizenship. Capitalist social relations are founded on two deeply ironic "freedoms," as Marx ([1867] 1967, 168) put it: the freedom *from* any ownership of the means of production, as these are dispossessed through theft and enclosures into the private property of a few; and the freedom to sell one's own labor power in the market for a wage. The latter of course was not much of a freedom, but was more a powerful social compulsion, given the former "freedom" from any alternative means of providing a living; and, for all but the independently wealthy, this compulsion becomes a quintessentially social pillar of capitalist citizenship long before the social citizenship of the postwar world that Marshall lionized. The enforcement of wage labor in practice actually eroded certain civic freedoms, such as the freedom to glean a living from an increasingly enclosed and privatized nature. The modern worker-citizens are increasingly leashed to capital through the resulting "wage slavery," and through national legislation—outlawing or circumscribing vagabondage, poaching, worker organization, and prostitution, while legislating the length of the working day and working conditions—it also leashed workers to the emerging national state. Viewed this way, the duality of so-called rights and responsibilities that marks contemporary ideologies of citizenship is revealed as a much more contradictory affair. Just as the "freedom" to work is in fact a social necessity—to this day in the United States, the "right to work" is associated with draconian workplace legislation and state rejection of union rights—the rights of citizenship associated with this freedom actually institutionalize social protocols of exploitation and oppression.

While the notion of citizenship is explicitly intended to create a sense of undifferentiated belonging and inclusion in a given territorially defined polity, national or otherwise, in practice different types of labor are quite differently integrated into citizenship. The social, cultural, territorial, and political racism encased in early modern definitions of citizenship may today have been ameliorated on some fronts in some places for some people, but it nonetheless endures, not least in the racial segmentation of labor markets, which differentiates access to a living wage, medical care, pension rights, workplace organization, education, and so forth. The distinction between, on the one hand, work deemed worthy of a wage, whether in the private or public economic spheres, and, on the other, the multifaceted labor of social reproduction in the household and the community further fissures any purported homogeneity of citizenship, largely along gender lines. Transnational migrant labor increasingly undergirds the global economy, not least the economy's military component, and its multiplicity of territorial commitments, belongings, and legalities directly challenges inherited assumptions of citizenship. Military labor is different again. Organized for the purpose of attacking or defending the territory, institutions, wealth, and populace of a state, military war work is integral to the functioning of a "permanent war economy" (Melman 1974). Hardly as invisible as domestic labor, for example, it is much more opaque, and is integrated into ideologies of citizenship more in terms of obligation and responsibility than as labor. Whether mandatory or voluntary, military labor actually involves the drastic suspension of the very same rights of citizenship that a military supposedly secures and defends, in return for significant social entitlements. The treatment of military labor as exceptional, however, obscures the powerful role of the military whose norms of social entitlement were, in many advanced capitalist states, institutionalized in the postwar "breadwinner welfare state"; today, by contrast, in the wake of neoliberal dismantlement of many state welfare provisions, military labor increasingly stands out as the locus of whatever social entitlements are left (Cowen 2007).

As regards state power in which the right to declare modern war is supposedly invested, Giorgio Agamben (2005), building on Carl Schmitt, identifies a certain "state of exception" according to which state rulers summarily suspend the operation of their own laws. The state of exception for Agamben is not separate from legal power but written into its very constitution. The suspension of Geneva Conventions for Guantánamo (Smith 2005) is an obvious case in point. But what Agamben so sharply detects is not so much an ur-characteristic of power per se or of its legal constitution, as he seems to suggest insofar as his argument spans the gamut from Roman law to the present; rather, he is rediscovering, relocating, and ultimately obscuring the specific contradictoriness of the modern state. Gerry Pratt (2005) has pointed to and explored the racialized and gendered social geographies that are simultaneously the condition for and result of this state of exception, and, as Pratt's analysis of migrant Filipina domestic workers hints at, a collinear argument. The parallel with the discussion of Marshall here is appropriate: just because labor plays little or no explicit role in expositions of the "state of exception" should not blind us to the ways in which it nonetheless stalks the text. The contradictoriness of the state of exception—law circumscribes the power of the state, but the very establishment of that law by the state demonstrates the ability of state rulers to except themselves from that law—does not reside within power itself, and even less does it reside in a generic state or legal system disembodied from that context. Schmitt and Agamben would presumably agree that power per se is barely contradictory at all, ubiquitous rather than exceptional: whatever the opposition, regardless of any constraints on success, no matter how reckless, and whatever the calculation of outcomes (predictable or otherwise), where social power exists those wielding it can use it as they wish.

But power does not sit isolated beneath, above, or beyond the historical geography of social relations that constitute it. Rather, the state of exception today presupposes a particular panoply of capitalist social relations which help constitute the contours of state power even as the state defends and regulates these same social relations. The political economic origins of the modern capitalist state lie in the specific struggles and interests of a rising bourgeois power. On the one hand, they struggled to advance their own interests over the absolutism that oppressed them, and the language of freedom and democracy, justice, and equality was generalized for that purpose; on the other hand, they sought hegemony over subordinate populations that did not share the socioeconomic interests of the property-owning, male, European bourgeoisie, most notably the emerging working class. This involved naked force at times, but it also involved striking (and continually restriking) a social bargain with that class which, after all, produced the social wealth. "Citizenship" was and is a crucial pillar of that bargain, embodying as much as it papers over the structured social differences constituting modern capitalist society: the difference between exploiter and exploited or between oppressor and oppressed is barely visible in undifferentiated declarations of citizenship but is forcefully expressed in the "state of exception" precisely at those moments when the "socially excluded" threaten to cash in on the promise of freedom and democracy, justice, and equality.

The social acid to dissolve the absolute power threatened by the state of exception therefore already always exists in the social opposition that provoked the need for law in the first place. More simply, from a political economic slant, "the accumulation of capital" *is* "increase of the proletariat" (Marx [1867] 1967, 576). The state of exception only exists insofar as the state fears, anticipates, or moves against an opposition internal to it; the social acid always exists in the constitution of state power, and thereby the state of exception, itself. This may not alleviate the need to fight "crude wars" against state power—quite the opposite (Brennan and Ganguly 2006; Brennan 2006)—but it does invert the political focus from the seeming unchallengability of that power and recenter attention on a crucial target of any ambition for political change, namely, the modern capitalist state formed precisely at the nexus of war, territory, citizenship, and the control of work.

If nothing else, this argument illuminates the need to explore the connections between the Iraq War, Guantánamo, and the "war at home." The end of the Cold War, paradoxically, left the rising hegemonic state—the United States—in crisis, with no major war through which to press its claims of dominance and stretch its global disciplinary muscle, no palpable threat to global security against which it could lead a worldwide crusade. Quickly, however, against a backdrop of sustained, ignominious failure by successive U.S. administrations to establish an operable hegemony in the Middle East, an already suspect Islam became the new communism, and Arabs the new communists. Reds under the bed morphed all too easily into suicide bombers in the basement. The event now entombed in global history as "9/11" by a menacing U.S. state that feigns global victimhood did *not* change the world, but the belligerent reactions to it most certainly did. It provided the perfect opportunity for a particularly pugilistic neoconservative sector of that country's ruling class to blackmail the world into acquiescence before its "full-spectrum dominance."

In the resulting insecurity state, war is justified as necessary for the guarantee of domestic security, but this security, conversely, needs to be guaranteed only insofar as the here and now is already characterized as dangerously *insecure*. That this insecurity is energetically manufactured detracts in no way from its reality; rather, it helps to account for the Arendtian banality with which many British and a majority of U.S. citizens supported the Bush and Blair governments in their early pursuit of the Iraq War. Ontological insecurity is pervasive in a turbulent, restructuring capitalism: economic restructuring threatens jobs and livelihoods; the hard-won victories of women, people of color, immigrants, gays, and lesbians—for all that their "complaints" can be mulched back into the bourgeois mainstream—are experienced as impingements on the privilege of those whose grasp on such privilege is most tenuous; and global multiculturalism, which actually colludes with the self-interestedness of laissez-faire neoliberalism, nonetheless also threatens deep-seated identities. The dismantling of the welfare state and the privatization and/or underfunding of social security, broadly conceived, all exacerbate such insecurities, while war works to externalize the threat, expelling the sources of insecurity into an abstract geography beyond the pale of comprehensibility. The banality of support for war in the face of ontological insecurity is rewarded and strengthened by the refusal of gory images of mangled bodies and the gruesome parade of returning flag-draped coffins, while the threat is pumped up even further. Perceived in terms of absolute national, cultural, and biological difference, rather than in the tangible threats that make up everyday life, ontological insecurity is positively affirmed as it refracts itself back from the pale of incomprehensibility as racism.

And yet the borders of the mind, like those of the nation, are never so hermetically sealed. Insofar as the sources of insecurity actually invade the sanctum of national territory, citizenship, and ontological surety, the resulting contradiction throws up a panic about insidious betrayal by "homegrown terrorists." The ontologically unknowable are not just beyond the pale but also among us, and the insecurity is heightened amidst intensified inexplicability: if they are us, we could be them.... If Britons or Americans can be terrorists, the war on terrorism must be fought as aggressively "at home," and the incomprehensibility of ontological threat attaches more and more to the state itself. As much as "homegrown terrorists" are explained away as exceptions, the state itself risks appearing more and more exceptional.

The opportunistically named War on Terror that engulfs the beginning of the twenty-first century simultaneously territorializes and globalizes war, and it reframes citizenship as geographically rhizomatic, a Swiss cheese of dense and hollow definitional pockets of belonging and identity that looks very different for very different social groups. Far from diminishing the importance of geographical space, the limited dismantling of spatial absolutism associated with nationally defined practices of citizenship gives way to a far more complicated relational conception of territory and place. Such a shift presents political opportunities. New processes and ensembles of uneven development can already be glimpsed, and the essays in this book take us a significant way toward understanding the revamped nexus of war, citizenship, territory, and social difference being fashioned today. In laying out such terrain, these essays, taken together, also suggest an urgency in our inquiries insofar as the uneven-ness of capitalist development results from social practices which, while repet-itive of and attendant to powerful social structures, are also radically unfixed and open to invention. As with past social inventions, a collective translation from idea into practice, and from analysis into oppositional politics, and an organization of collective social interests into political power will require its own kind of work.

References

Agamben, Giorgio. 2005. *State of exception*. Chicago: University of Chicago Press.

Brennan, Timothy. 2006. *Wars of position: The cultural politics of left and right*. New York: Columbia University Press.

Brennan, Timothy, and Keya Ganguly. 2006. Crude wars. *South Atlantic Quarterly* 105 (1): 19–35.

Cowen, Deborah. 2008. *Military workfare : The soldier and social citizenship in Canada*. Toronto: University of Toronto Press.

Fraser, Nancy, and Linda Gordon. 1992. Contract versus charity: Why is there no social citizenship in the United States? *Socialist Review* 22 (3): 45–67.

Hobsbawm, Eric. 1994. *The age of extremes*. New York: Vintage.

Marx, K. [1867] 1967. *Capital*, vol. 1. Moscow: International Publishers.

Melman, S. 1974. *The permanent war economy: American capitalism in decline*. New York: Simon & Schuster.

Pratt, Geraldine. 2005. Abandoned women and spaces of exception. *Antipode* 37 (5): 1052–78.

Smith, N. 1990. *Uneven development: Nature, capital and the production of space*. Oxford: Basil Blackwell.

———. 2005. *The endgame of globalization*. New York: Routledge.

About the Contributors

Nadia Abu-Zahra is a D.Phil. student in geography at St. Antony's College and the Oxford University Centre for the Environment. She has guest-edited the journal *Practicing Anthropology*, contributed to an anthology against the war in Iraq by Clergy against Nuclear Arms, and written on development, education, environmental issues, and human rights in the *Arab World Geographer*, *Borderlands e-Journal*, the *Attaché Journal of International Affairs*, the *Encyclopedia of Women in Islamic Cultures*, and the UNHCR publication, the *State of the World's Refugees*. Forthcoming chapters are planned in *Fear: Critical Geopolitics and Everyday Life* (edited by Rachel Pain and Susan J. Smith), and in an edited book on state terrorism. She can be contacted by e-mail at nadia.abu-zahra@sant.ox.ac.uk.

Davina Bhandar teaches in the Canadian Studies Program at Trent University. Her research engages in contemporary critiques of the concept of citizenship that have emerged through notions of transnationalism and politics of diaspora, particularly focused on examining the notion of the migrant concept of citizenship. Her teaching and research intersect in the fields of contemporary political and social theory, critical race studies, postcolonial theory, and feminist theory. Her work focuses on the examination of citizenship practices from "below" or rather through acts of governance, freedom, migration, and immigration.

Stephen J. Collier is an assistant professor in the Program in International Affairs at the New School. He works on neoliberalism, postsocialist transformation, social modernity, and political rationalities of contemporary security. His past and present projects include a book on post-Soviet transformation in Russia entitled *Post Soviet Social*; a coedited volume, *Global Assemblages: Technology, Politics, and Ethics as Anthropological Problems* (Blackwell, 2005); a comparative project on welfare state transformation in Russia and Georgia; and a project on vital systems security.

Deborah Cowen is an assistant professor in the Department of Geography at the University of Toronto. She is the author of *Military Workfare: The Soldier and Social Citizenship in Canada*, (2008. Toronto: University of Toronto Press), and has published her work on war, citizenship, and cities in edited collections and journals including *Antipode*, *Citizenship Studies*, *Social & Cultural Geography*, and *Theory & Event*.

Stuart Elden is a reader in political geography at the University of Durham, and the academic director of the International Boundaries Research Unit. He is the author of *Mapping the Present: Heidegger, Foucault and the Project of a Spatial History* (2001); *Understanding Henri Lefebvre: Theory and the Possible* (2004); and *Speaking against Number: Heidegger, Language and the Politics of Calculation* (2006). He is currently working on a history of the concept of territory.

Matthew Farish is an assistant professor in the Department of Geography, University of Toronto. His research interests include the historical geographies of militarism, geopolitics, and urban culture. He has published articles in the *Annals of the Association of American Geographers*, the *Canadian Geographer*, *Cultural Geographies*, *Society and Space*, and the *Transactions of the Institute of British Geographers*. He is currently completing a book manuscript on geographical thought in the United States during the early Cold War, and beginning a project on the Distant Early Warning Line.

Melissa L. Finn is a Ph.D candidate in the Department of Political Science, York University in Toronto. Her current research employs Sufism, phenomenology, political theory, and critical epistemologies and methodologies to grapple with political violence, the neuroses of social bodies, and identity abeyances/aporias.

Colin Flint is associate professor of geography at the University of Illinois at Urbana-Champaign. He has published on the topics of hate crime, terrorism, American hegemony, and war and peace. He is editor of *Spaces of Hate* (Routledge) and *The Geography of War and Peace* (Oxford University Press). He is author of *Introduction to Geopolitics* (Routledge) and coauthor, with Peter Taylor, of *Political Geography: World-Economy, Nation-State and Locality*.

Emily Gilbert is associate professor in the Program in Canadian Studies and the Department of Geography at the University of Toronto. Her current research deals with questions relating to monetary organization, governance, citizenship, borders, nation-states, and globalization, particularly in the heightened risk and security context in North America. She is coeditor (with Eric Helleiner, Trent University) of *Nation-States and Money: The Past, Present and Future of National Currencies* (Routledge, 1999), and has published papers in several books and numerous articles in journals such as the *Annals of the Association of American Geographers*, *Economy and Society*, *Environment and Planning D: Society and Space*, and *Antipode*.

Stephen Graham is professor of human geography at Durham University in the United Kingdom. He has a background in urbanism, planning, and the sociology of technology. His research addresses the intersections of urban places, mobilities, technology, war, surveillance, and geopolitics. His books include *Telecommunications and the City, Splintering Urbanism* (both with Simon Marvin), *the Cybercities Reader and Cities, War and Terrorism.*

Matthew G. Hannah is associate professor of geography at the University of Vermont in Burlington, Vermont. His research on the interrelationships between space, power, and knowledge have led to published work on the administrative control of the Lakota ("Sioux") by the U.S. government during the 1870s, and on the governmentalization of the state in the late nineteenth-century United States, more generally. His current research focuses on the meaning of citizenship in the information age, approached via a study of census boycott movements in West Germany during the 1980s. He is author of *Governmentality and the Mastery of Territory in Nineteenth-Century America* (Cambridge University Press, 2000).

Maureen Hays-Mitchell is associate professor and chair of the Department of Geography at Colgate University in Hamilton, New York, where she serves on the advisory boards of the Peace and Conflict Studies, Women's Studies, and Latin American Studies programs. Her scholarly interests lie in the gendered dimensions of economic development in Latin America. She has conducted grassroots research in Peru, Chile, and Mexico. These projects reflect her ongoing interest in the urban informal economy, grassroots social movements, human rights, conflict resolution, and postconflict reconstruction. She has published numerous book chapters and articles in journals such as the *Geographical Review, Environment and Planning A*, and *Society and Space.*

Jennifer Hyndman is professor of geography at Syracuse University, New York. Her research spans the continuum of forced migration, from conflict zones to refugee resettlement in North America, and embodies a feminist approach that attends to issues of displacement and subjectivity, broadly speaking. She is the author of *Managing Displacement: Refugees and the Politics of Humanitarianism* (University of Minnesota Press, 2000) and coeditor of *Sites of Violence: Gender and Conflict Zones* (University of California Press, 2004).

Engin F. Isin is professor of citizenship in politics and international studies (POLIS), Faculty of Social Sciences, the Open University in the United Kingdom. He is the founder of the Citizenship Studies Media Lab (CSML) at York University and now directs the Centre on Citizenship, Identities and Governance at the Open University. He is author of *Cities without Citizens* (Montreal, 1992), *Being Political* (Minnesota, 2002), and (with Patricia Wood) *Citizenship & Identity* (London, 1999). He edited *Democracy, Citizenship & the Global City* (London, 2000); (with Bryan Turner) *Handbook of Citizenship*

Studies (London, 2002); and (with Gerard Delanty) *Handbook of Historical Sociology* (London, 2003).

Andrew Lakoff is assistant professor of sociology and science studies at the University of California, San Diego. He is the author of *Pharmaceutical Reason: Knowledge and Value in Global Psychiatry* (Cambridge, 2005) and coeditor of *Global Pharmaceuticals: Ethics, Knowledge, Practices* (Duke, 2006). His current research concerns the intersection of public health, national defense, and emergency management around problems of collective security.

Tamar Mayer is a professor of geography at Middlebury College in Middlebury, Vermont and the editor of *Women and the Israeli Occupation: The Politics of Change* (Routledge 1994) and *Gender Ironies of Nationalism: Sexing the Nation* (Routledge 2000). She is also the coeditor of *Jerusalem: Idea and Reality* (Routledge 2008). Her research interests focus on the interplay among nationalism, gender, and sexuality, particularly in the Middle East, and on the relationships among nationalism, landscape, and memory.

Marcus Power is lecturer in the Department of Geography at Durham University in the United Kingsom. He has conducted research on geopolitics and development, with particular reference to the Lusophone world and Southern Africa. His research interests also include geographies of disability and development, postsocialist transformations in the periphery, and film and popular geopolitics. He is author of *Rethinking Development Geographies* (Routledge, 2003).

Alan Smart is professor at the Department of Anthropology, University of Calgary in Alberta, Canada, and has been conducting field research in Hong Kong and China since 1982. In 1986, he completed his Ph.D. in social anthropology at the University of Toronto, on the topic of the political economy of squatter clearance in Hong Kong. His research has focused on urban issues, housing, foreign investment, and social change. He is the coeditor (with Josephine Smart) of *Petty Capitalists and Globalization*, and he is the author of *Making Room: Squatter Clearance in Hong Kong*; *The Shek Kip Mei Myth: Squatters, Fires and Colonial Rule in Hong Kong, 1950–1963*; and articles in journals such as *Urban Anthropology, International Journal of Sociology of Law, Cultural Anthropology, Critique of Anthropology, International Journal of Urban and Regional Research, Society and Space, City & Society, American Anthropologist*, and a variety of edited volumes.

Neil Smith is distinguished professor of anthropology and geography at the Graduate Center of the City University of New York, where he also directs the Center for Place, Culture and Politics. He recently won the *LA Times* Book

Prize for Biography for his book, *American Empire: Roosevelt's Geographer and the Prelude to Globalization* (2003). He works on the broad connections between space, nature, social theory, and history, and is author of numerous other books, including *Uneven Development: Nature, Capital and the Production of Space* (1991), and *The Endgame of Globalization* (2005). He is an organizer of the International Critical Geography group.

Rachel Woodward is a reader in critical geography in the School of Geography, Politics and Sociology, Newcastle University, United Kingdom. Her research interests include military geographies and land-use issues, the politics of gender in contemporary armed forces, and representation and identity issues amongst serving military personnel. She is the author of *Military Geographies* (Blackwell, 2004) and (with Trish Winter) of *Sexing the Soldier: The Politics of Gender in the Contemporary British Army* (Routledge, 2007).

Index